W9-DDR-318

Understanding Politics

Ideas, Institutions, and Issues

9e

THOMAS M. MAGSTADT, Ph.D.

European Studies Program
University of Kansas

WADSWORTH
CENGAGE Learning

Australia • Brazil • Japan • Korea • Mexico • Singapore • Spain • United Kingdom • United States

WADSWORTH
CENGAGE Learning™

Understanding Politics: Ideas, Institutions, and Issues, **Ninth Edition**
Thomas M. Magstadt

Senior Publisher: Suzanne Jeans

Acquisitions Editor: Edwin Hill

Development Editor: Elisa Adams

Assistant Editor: Kate MacLean

Editorial Assistant: Matthew DiGangi

Senior Marketing Manager: Amy Whitaker

Marketing Coordinator: Josh Hendrick

Marketing Communications Manager: Heather Baxley

Content Project Manager: Jessica Rasile

Associate Media Editor: Caitlin Holroyd

Art Director: Linda Helcher

Print Buyer: Paula Vang

Text Permissions Manager: Katie Huha

Production Service/Compositor: Elm Street Publishing Services/Integra Software Services Pvt.Ltd.

Text Designer: Stratton Design

Photo Manager: Jennifer Meyer Dare

Cover Designer: Stratton Design

Cover Image: © Mark Stay

© 2011, 2009, 2006 Wadsworth, Cengage Learning

ALL RIGHTS RESERVED. No part of this work covered by the copyright herein may be reproduced, transmitted, stored or used in any form or by any means graphic, electronic, or mechanical, including but not limited to photocopying, recording, scanning, digitizing, taping, Web distribution, information networks, or information storage and retrieval systems, except as permitted under Section 107 or 108 of the 1976 United States Copyright Act, without the prior written permission of the publisher.

For product information and technology assistance, contact us at
Cengage Learning Academic Resource Center, 1-800-423-0563

For permission to use material from this text or product,
submit all requests online at **www.cengage.com/permissions**
Further permissions questions can be emailed to
permissionrequest@cengage.com

Library of Congress Control Number: 2009934653

ISBN-13: 978-0-495-79776-0
ISBN-10: 0-495-79776-6

Wadsworth
20 Channel Center Street
Boston, MA 02210
USA

Cengage Learning products are represented in Canada by Nelson Education, Ltd.

For your course and learning solutions, visit **www.cengage.com.**

Purchase any of our products at your local college store or at our preferred online store **www.CengageBrain.com.**

Printed in the United States of America
1 2 3 4 5 6 7 14 13 12 11 10

BRIEF CONTENTS

Contents

We live in a global village. The concepts of space and time are not the same for us as they were for our grandparents. We are all connected and we can carry on face-to-face conversations with friends and loved ones who are thousands of miles a away. Without leaving Kansas, we can look down from the heavens and see where somebody lives in Kenya.

Today, events anywhere in the world can affect people everywhere. Terrorist acts, wars, natural disasters, economic downturns, banking crises, and volatile stock markets can destabilize countries and disrupt international relations. So, too, can a national election that changes the power balance in Washington or London—like the one in the United States that swept the Republicans out of power in November 2008 or the one likely to bring the Conservatives back to power in the United Kingdom no later than the spring of 2010.

Things change with blinding speed in this age of globalization, but the basic nature of politics remains unchanged. The struggle for power continues; so, too, does the search for order and justice all over the world. The limits of power, even in its most concentrated forms, are glaringly apparent—from ancient places such as Palestine and Iraq in the Middle East and Afghanistan in Central Asia to the United States of America, with its relatively short history and even shorter memory.

The cost of failed policies and corrupt, cynical, or simply incompetent leadership is clearly apparent not only in dictatorships abroad but also in democracies, including our own. Leadership is vital to achieving good government, but so is citizenship, and the quality of citizenship in the modern world is no cause for celebration. This double deficiency—both at the top and the bottom of political society—is a crisis rarely mentioned in public, one that gives ample evidence of its existence but continues to go largely unnoticed. Meanwhile, there is no absence of injustice, intolerance, misguided idealism, zealotry, and human suffering—proof enough that the increasingly polluted and crowded planet we inhabit has not changed for the better, even though the fortunate few are far more secure and comfortable than the less fortunate many.

Since *Understanding Politics* made its debut in 1984, nothing has shaken my conviction that politics matter. As young citizens with a voice and vote, college students need to acquire at least a rudimentary knowledge of the political and economic forces that shape our world. Ironically, as news and information have become more and more accessible, thanks in no small part to the Internet, voters in the United States remain largely ignorant of the issues, interests, and arguments that occupy the attention of elected officials and policy makers. Indeed, the vast majority of citizens are not engaged in the political process at all except perhaps to vote. This fact is all the more discouraging because a heightened political awareness is only the first step in the educational preparation—and empowerment—of the next generation of citizens who will be called upon not only to vote and pay taxes, but also to lead the nation in the difficult decades that lie ahead. Global warming, the shifting global power balance, and the precarious global economy—these are but three of the challenges that will define world politics and determine who gets what, when, and how in the brave, new world order of the twenty-first century.

The study of politics is a gateway to a broader and better understanding of human nature, society, and the world. There can be no better reason to write a book, or to continue rewriting one. The first edition of this book appeared more than a quarter of a century ago and is now in its ninth edition. Like the murky political world it seeks to unmask, it is and always will be a work in progress.

The science and philosophy of politics fall squarely within the liberal arts tradition. The phrase "science and philosophy of politics" points to one of the deepest cleavages within the discipline: Analysts who approach politics from the standpoint of science often stress the importance of power, whereas those who view it through the wide-angle lens of philosophy often emphasize the importance of justice. But the distinction between power and justice—like that between science and philosophy—is too often exaggerated.

Moral and political questions are ultimately inseparable in the real world. What makes the exercise of power—as distinct from the use of brute force—*political* is public debate, free speech, criticism, dissent, and the certainty that elections will occur at regular intervals. Whenever moral issues arise in the realm of public policy (for example, questions concerning abortion, capital punishment, or the use of force by police or the military), the essential ingredients of politics are present. A single-minded emphasis on power or morality—on either at the expense of the other—is likely to confound our efforts to make sense of politics or, for that matter, to find lasting solutions to problems that afflict and divide us. Thus, it is always necessary to balance the equation, tempering political realism with a penchant for justice.

Similarly, the dichotomy so often drawn between facts and values is misleading. Rational judgments, in the sense of reasoned opinions about what is good and just, are sometimes more definitive (or less elusive) than facts. For example, the proposition that "genocide is evil" is true. (Its opposite—genocide is good—is morally indefensible.) It is a well-known fact that Adolf Hitler and the Nazis committed genocide. We can therefore say that Hitler was evil as a matter of fact and not "simply" because mass murder is abhorrent to our personal values.

Other value-laden propositions can be stated with a high degree of probability but not absolute certainty. For example, "If you want to reduce violent crime, first reduce poverty." Still other questions of this kind may be too difficult or too close to call—in the abortion controversy, for example, does the right of a woman to biological self-determination outweigh the right to life of the unborn? It makes no sense to ignore the most important questions in life simply because the answers are not easy. Even when the right answers are unclear, it is often possible to recognize wrong answers—a moderating force in itself.

Understanding Politics employs a foundation-building approach to the study of politics and government. It begins by identifying political phenomena (such as war and terrorism) that students find interesting and then seeks to describe and explain them. In an effort to build on students' natural curiosity, I try to avoid much of the jargon and many of the technical or arcane disputes that too often characterize the more advanced literature in the field of political science.

Inevitably, some themes and events are discussed in more than one chapter: The world of politics is more like a seamless web than a chest of drawers. In politics as in nature, a given event or phenomenon often has many meanings and is connected to other events and phenomena in ways that are not immediately apparent. Emphasizing the common threads among major political ideas, institutions, and issues helps beginning students make sense of seemingly unrelated bits and pieces of the political puzzle. Seeing how the various parts fit together is a necessary step toward understanding politics.

Rather than retreating into the dark recesses of a single discipline, the book unapologetically borrows insights from various disciplines, including history, economics, psychology, and sociology, as well as philosophy. It is intended to be a true liberal arts approach to the study of government and politics. The goal is ambitious: to challenge students to begin a lifelong learning process that alone can lead to a generation of citizens who are well informed, actively engaged, self-confident, and thoughtful, and who have a capacity for indignation in the face of public hypocrisy, dishonesty, stupidity, or gross ineptitude.

In the ninth edition, I have retained the pedagogical features that characterized the previous editions of the book. Thus, each chapter begins with an outline and ends with a summary, highlights key terminology, poses review questions for measuring comprehension, and provides an annotated list of recommended readings. In addition, the text contains a wide variety of photos, figures, maps, tables, and boxed features, many of which have been revised or replaced with updated materials. Most chapters also include a "Spotlight" feature that highlights events in a particular region or state and draws together relevant and interdisciplinary themes that converge on that time and place.

New in the Ninth Edition

Like the previous edition, the ninth contains new features while remaining true to its original design and scope. Its preparation included a thorough updating of every chapter to reflect the sweeping changes that have occurred since the publication of the eighth edition. These include a recession-induced global economic crisis; the 2008 election to the presidency of Barack Obama who ran on a platform calling for major change; a U.S. Congress with a solid Democratic majority in both houses; a reduction in the level of violence in Iraq; an escalation of the war in Afghanistan; a continuing shift in the global distribution of economic power from the United States to Europe and Asia; a push to develop clean energy driven by warnings that Planet Earth is a reaching a climate-change tipping point; and a renewed sense of urgency surrounding the dangers of nuclear proliferation, blackmail, and terrorism prompted by North Korea's bomb and missile tests in the spring of 2009.

Part 1, "Comparative Political Systems: Models and Theories," analyzes utopian, democratic, and authoritarian forms of government, as well as political systems caught in the difficult transition from authoritarian to democratic institutions. The first four chapters are theoretical (basic concepts, ideologies, utopia, and liberal democracy); these chapter are updated and pared down but otherwise essentially unchanged. Chapter 1, "Introduction: The Study of Politics," defines the basic concepts of politics and centers on how and why we study it. This chapter lays the groundwork for the remainder of the text. Chapter 2, "The Idea of the Public Good: Ideologies and Isms," deals with the belief systems that have shaped our world, including ideologies of the Right and Left, such as communism and fascism, and "isms" of the Right and Left such as liberalism and conservatism. Chapter 3 explores ideal states, identifies elements common to many utopias, and considers both the allure and perils of utopianism, closing with a look at dystopias. Chapter 4 is devoted to the theory of liberal democracy and examines the classical Aristotelian view that the best regime imaginable is not possible, and that what Aristotle called a "mixed regime" (combining elements of monarchy, aristocracy, and democracy) is the best possible. Chapter 5, "The Authoritarian Model," expands and updates material on Zimbabwe to reflect developments surrounding the 2008 election and Robert Mugabe's refusal to step down despite losing the popular vote to Morgan Tsvangirai. It also includes a brand new "Spotlight" on the March 2009 coup in Madagascar. Chapter 6 features new material on Iran and Afghanistan.

Part 2, "Established and Emerging Democracies," consists of three chapters and examines parliamentary democracies (Chapter 7), transitional states (Chapter 8), and developing countries (Chapter 9). Virtually all governments in today's world either aspire to some form of democracy or claim to be "democratic." This startling fact is itself irrefutable evidence of the power of an idea. Though often abused, the idea of democracy has fired the imaginations of people everywhere for more than two centuries, as the popular protests and mass street demonstrations against the outcome of Iran's rigged presidential election in June 2009 served to remind us. The crushing defeat of Japan's long-ruling Liberal Democratic Party (LDP) a few months later was another reminder that politicians can ignore the power of the people only so long—eventually there will be a day of reckoning. In an age when bad news is written in blood, and body counts are more likely to refer to innocent civilians than armed combatants, it is well to remember that democratic ideals have never before been so warmly embraced or so widely (if imperfectly) institutionalized.

Chapter 8 now treats China as an example of "police-state capitalism"—a model in a class by itself. The case for this approach was reinforced by two late developments: (1) the official ban on any public mention or commemoration of the Tiananmen Square massacre on its twentieth anniversary (June 4, 2009); and (2) press reports that Beijing was blocking dozens of Websites, including Bing.com, Live.com, Hotmail.com, Twitter, YouTube, Bing, Flickr, Opera, Live, Wordpress, and Blogger. Developing countries continue to be the focus of Chapter 9. This edition expands the treatment of Nigeria, Sri Lanka, and Sudan and features Somalia, Afghanistan, and Zimbabwe as contemporary examples of failed states, as well as Sierra Leone as a failed state struggling to overcome its past.

In Part 3, "Politics by Civil Means: Citizens, Leaders, and Policies," four chapters (10 through 13) focus on the political process and public policy. The United States continues to be featured in this section, which, as before, examines citizenship and political socialization, political participation (including opinion polling and voting behavior), political organization (parties and interest groups), political leadership, political ideologies (or divergent "approaches to the public good"), and contemporary public policy issues. Chapter 10 contains new features on the FCC and restricted speech, on the gender gap in the 2008 elections, on campaign spending in 2008, and updates throughout. Chapter 11 on elections covers the 2008 national elections and features a "Focus" box on the problem of civic literacy, as well as a new subsection ("The Obama Factor") on the changing role of technology in the political process.

Chapter 12 on leadership—a topic greatly undervalued in a troubled world where political spin is all too often a substitute for policy wisdom—includes important new material on the corrupting influence of money in national politics and the so-called revolving door of Big Government and Big Business. Chapter 13 on public policy retains its earlier structure but by its very nature requires considerable revision with each new edition; the ninth is no exception. This edition, for example, looks at the crisis in the Social Security system in greater depth than previous editions and also expands the treatment of health care reform, the environment, and fiscal policy (budget deficit and taxation). In addition, it incorporates new Supreme Court decisions on affirmative action and reverse discrimination, freedom of speech and the Patriot Act, and freedom of religion and public education. There is also new material on civil liberties and ID cards focusing on the Real ID Act of 2005.

Part 4 ("Politics by Violent Means: Revolution, War, and Terrorism") examines conflict as a special and universal problem in politics. It divides the problem into three categories: revolution, terrorism, and war (Chapters 14, 15, and 16, respectively). The Bush administration's curious response to the problem posed by the existence of a malevolent terrorist network (Al Qaeda) harbored by a fundamentalist regime (the Taliban) in a land virtually impossible to subdue by conquest (Afghanistan) still affords ample opportunity for contemplation about the motives, causes and consequences of war at the beginning of a new millennium in the post-Bush era—not least because that war shows no signs of winding down any time soon. In an effort to deal with this escalating conflict, President Obama ordered a troop surge in Afghanistan shortly after taking office. He also revisited US anti-terrorism policies, changing some things but, to the consternation of left-leaning critics, leaving the substance and strategy largely intact. These three chapters reflect the changing international scene and the efforts of the Obama administration to adjust pre-existing policies to meet the new circumstances. Chapter 16 ("War"), for example, closes with a new section entitled "Weapons of Mass Disruption: Cyber War," dealing with the threat posed by cyber terrorists not only to the Internet and but also to the whole gamut of computer-based data storage and communications systems from banking and finance to intelligence and defense networks.

Finally, Part 5, "Politics without Government," introduces students to key concepts in the study of international relations, describes key patterns, and discusses perennial problems. Chapter 17 examines the basic principles and concepts in international relations and the evolving structure and context of world politics; it also gives special attention to high-priority global issues, such as the global economic recession, the danger of nuclear proliferation, global warming, and the impact of the revolution in information technology. As in the previous edition, Chapter 18 looks at international law and organizations and the search for world order; the ninth edition, however, contains a brand-new section on the European Union—a unique combination of international and supranational organization encompassing 27 member-states that has quietly grown into the largest single economy in the world. A fitting note on which to end the course.

Note to Instructors

A PowerLecture CD-ROM with ExamView®, ISBN: 0-495-90153-9, is available to instructors who adopt the text. The PowerLecture CD-Rom includes interactive **PowerPoint® lectures**, a one-stop lecture and class preparation tool, to make it easy for you to assemble, edit, publish, and present custom lectures for your course. The interactive PowerPoint® lectures bring together outlines specific to every chapter of Understanding Politics; tables, statistical charts, and graphs; and photos from the book. In addition, you can add your own materials—culminating in a powerful, personalized presentation. A **Test Bank** in Microsoft® Word and ExamView® computerized testing offers a large array of well-crafted multiple-choice and essay questions, along with their answers and page references. An **Instructor's Manual** includes learning objectives, chapter outlines, discussion questions, suggestions for stimulating class activities and projects, suggested readings, and Web resources. The Instructor's Manual and PowerPoint Lecture Outlines are also available on the Instructor's section of the book's companion website at www.cengage.com/politicalscience/magstadt/understandingpolitics9e. For more information, contact your local sales representative. I also encourage readers to visit my WorldViewWest Website at http://www.worldviewwest.com and to direct any comments or questions to tom@worldviewwest.com.

Acknowledgments

Through nine editions and more than two decades, many individuals associated with several different publishing houses and universities have helped make this book a success. Among the scholars and teachers who reviewed the work for previous editions in manuscript, offering helpful criticisms and suggestions, were Donald G. Baker, Southampton College, Long Island University; Peter Longo, University of Nebraska at Kearney; Iraj Paydar, Bellevue Community College; Henry Steck, the State University of New York at Cortland; Ruth Ann Strickland, Appalachian State University; Sean K. Anderson, Idaho State University; Daniel Aseltine, Chaffey College; Thomas A. Kolsky, Montgomery County Community College; and Linda Valenty, California Polytechnic State University–San Luis Obispo.

For the current edition, that vital role fell to reviewers Chris Farnung, Wake Technical Community College; Himanee Gupta-Carlson, Tacoma Community College; Henry Patterson, Lorain County Community College; John Payne, College of DuPage; and Stephen Robertson, Middle Tennessee State University .

I also wish to express my appreciation to Edwin Hill, Political Science Editor at Wadsworth, who has kept this project on track and on schedule from day one. A very special thanks to Elisa Adams, my development editor, who once again made this book so much better in so many ways. As always, I owe a large debt of gratitude to my family, especially Mary Jo (who died in 1990) and Becky, but also David, Michael and Alexa. It takes time to write a book and time is the most precious thing we give—and give up. Once lost, it can never be regained. Finally, to the "Coffee Boys" of Westwood Hills—Hugh Brown, Glion Curtis, Grant Mallet, Howard Martin, Stan Nelson, Norm Olson, Harris Rayl, Gary Ripple, and G. Ross Stephens—what can I say? Some guys will do anything to have the last word.

Thomas M. Magstadt earned his doctorate at the Johns Hopkins School of Advanced International Studies (SAIS). He has taught at the Thunderbird School of Global Management, Augustana College (Sioux Falls), the University of Nebraska at Kearney, the Air War College (Maxwell Air Force Base), the University of Missouri—Kansas City, and the University of Kansas. He has worked as an intelligence analyst at the Central Intelligence Agency, served as director of the Midwest Conference on World Affairs, and lectured as a Fulbright scholar in the Czech Republic. Dr. Magstadt is the author of *An Empire If You Can Keep It* (Washington, DC: Congressional Quarterly Press, 2004); *Nations and Governments: Comparative Politics in Regional Perspective,* 5th edition (Belmont, CA: Wadsworth, 2005); Contemporary European Politics (Belmont, CA: Wadsworth, 2007); and *The European Union on the World Stage: Sovereignty, Soft Power, and the Search for Consensus* (BookSurge, 2009). He has a Website devoted to world affairs at **www.worldviewwest.com.** He currently lectures in the European Studies Program at the University of Kansas.

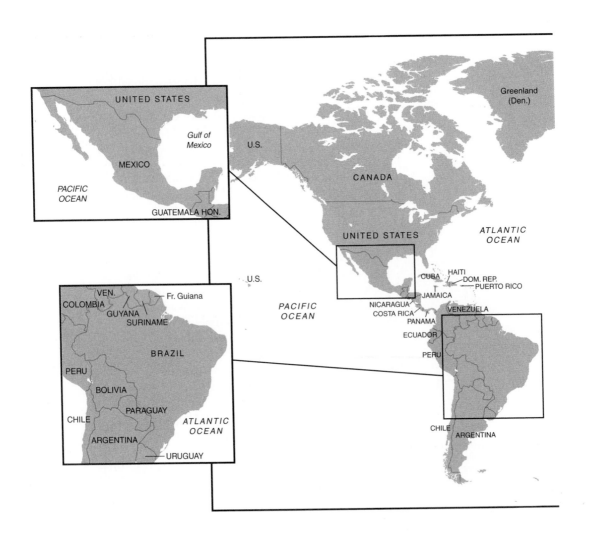

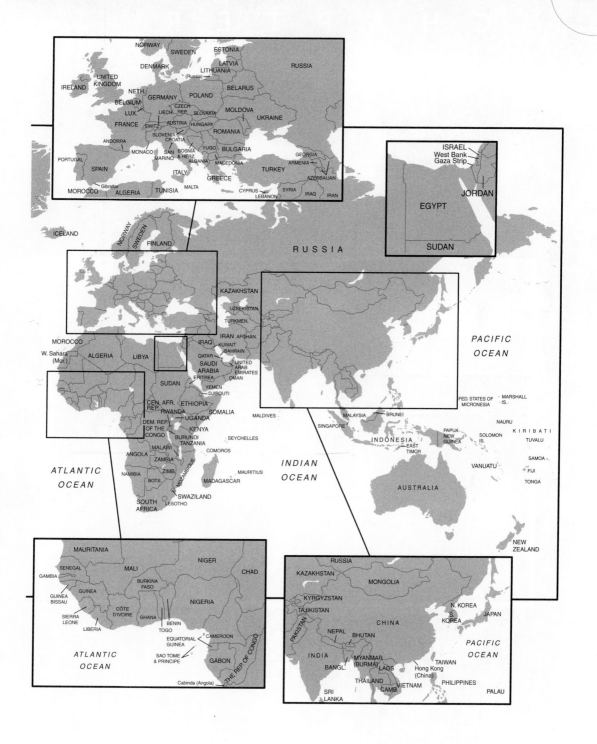

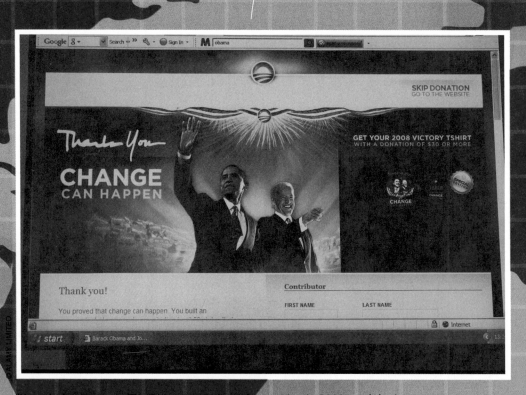

© ALAMY LIMITED

"Knowledge is power. The Obama presidential campaign in 2008 used the Internet to generate popular support, raise unprecedented sums of money in small donations, and communicate with its rapidly expanding base. As a result, experts say, the 2008 election was a transformational event that will forever change the way political campaigns in the United States are run."

Introduction
The Study of Politics

When the previous edition of this book was released in 2007, polls showed that many in the United States were disenchanted with politics and dismayed at the decline in U.S. prestige in the eyes of the world. How things have changed! Two events in the second half of 2008 largely account for the sea change in public opinion. First, a financial meltdown and plummeting stock market wiped out fortunes and rocked the global economy to its very foundations. Second, in the midst of this maelstrom, Barack Obama became the first African-American elected to the nation's highest office. Obama had energized millions, many of whom were first-time voters. Nearly eight million more Democrats voted in 2008 than in 2004, whereas almost four million fewer Republicans bothered to go to the polls. Even so, it was the largest turnout for a presidential election in history (though the percentage was about the same as in 2004). In spite of the deepening recession, there was a new sense of hope, if not optimism. There was also a new sense of urgency about dealing with the nation's troubled economy and a host of other problems that President Obama inherited from his predecessor.

Such dramatic events as a stock market crash or a pivotal presidential election have one thing in common: they are intensely political. Politics is everywhere, even when it's less obvious. To see it we often have to read between the lines or go behind the scenes. That is not always easy to do, but in a democratic republic where citizens have the right and duty to vote, it is a vital check on the arbitrary exercise of power and often the only non-violent way for "we, the people" to limit the temptations—and prevent or punish the excesses—of elected officials. The other way, the way of revolution or rebellion (see Chapter 14), is a drastic measure and a last resort—one the American colonists chose in 1776 and the Confederate South chose in 1860.

In a real sense, war and revolution represent the failure of politics. As citizens in a civil society, we too often take the value of civility and "politics as usual" for granted. At a minimum, responsible citizenship requires us to have a basic understanding of the ideas, institutions, and issues that constitute the stuff of politics.

BASIC CONCEPTS OF POLITICS

politics
The process by which a community selects rulers and empowers them to make decisions, takes action to attain common goals, and reconciles conflicts within the community.

Politics has been variously defined as "the art of the possible," as the study of "who gets what, when, and how," as the "authoritative allocation of values," and in countless other ways. A simple definition of politics is surprisingly elusive, but most of us know it when we see it. Like any other branch of human knowledge, political science—the systematic study of politics—has a lexicon and language all its own. We start our language lesson with three little words that carry a great deal of political freight: *power, order,* and *justice.*

Power

The ability of governments and their leaders to make and enforce rules, and to influence the behavior of individuals or groups by rewarding or punishing certain behaviors, constitutes one important form of **power**. Governments cannot maintain peace, guarantee security, promote economic growth, or pursue effective policies without power. The effective exercise of political authority includes much more, however, than the ability to use physical force. Indeed, the sources of power are many and varied. A large and well-educated population, an overwhelming election mandate, an inspiring leader, vast oil reserves, a booming economy, a strong work ethic, a well-trained and well-equipped military, an arsenal of nuclear weapons, a large foreign trade surplus, a stable currency, international good will, defensible borders, a cohesive society, a ruthless and efficient secret police, a surge of national patriotism, a grave external threat—all are examples of quite different power sources.

We often define power in material terms—population size, armies, and national wealth. We call a country with a large population, well-equipped military forces, and a flourishing economy a "great power" or even, in the case of the United States, a "superpower." Power defined in this way is tangible and we can readily measure it. Critics argue, however, that although this definition has obvious merit, it is too narrow. They make a useful distinction between "hard power" and "soft power." Hard power refers to the means and instruments of brute force or coercion, primarily military and economic clout. Soft power is "attractive" rather than coercive: the essence of soft power is "the important ability to get others to want what you want."[1]

Power is never equally distributed in any society or state. Yet the need to concentrate power in the hands of a few inevitably raises big questions in the minds of the many. Who wields power, in whose interests, to what ends? The most basic question of all in any political order is "Who rules?" Sometimes the answer is simple; we have only to look at a nation's constitution and observe the workings of its government. But it may be difficult to determine who really rules when the government is cloaked in secrecy or when, as is often the case, informal patterns of power are very different from the formal structures outlined in the nation's basic law. The number of people holding political office and exercising power is always minuscule compared with the population at large.

The terms *power* and *authority* are often confused and even used interchangeably. In reality, they denote two distinct dimensions of politics. Mao Zedong, the late Chinese Communist leader, famously quipped that "Political power flows from the barrel of a gun," which is true but grossly oversimplified. Political power is clearly associated with the means of coercion (the police, the secret police, the militia, the military), but power can also flow from wealth, personal charisma, ideology, religion, and many other sources, including the moral standing of a particular individual or group in society.

Authority, by definition, flows not only (or even mainly) from the barrel of a gun but also from *norms* the vast majority of a society's members recognize and embrace. These norms are moral, spiritual, and legal codes of behavior or good conduct. Therefore, authority as we use it in this text implies legitimacy—a condition in which power is exercised through established institutions and according to rules the people freely accept as right and proper. Note this definition does not mean, nor is it meant to imply, that democracy is the only legitimate form of government possible. A monarchy or other form of dictatorship could qualify as legitimate, as long as the ruled recognize the ruler's right to rule.

power
The capacity to influence or control the behavior of persons and institutions, whether by persuasion or coercion.

authority
Command of the obedience of society's members by a government.

legitimacy
The exercise of political power in a community in a way that is voluntarily accepted by the members of that community.

legitimate authority
The legal and moral right of a government to rule over a specific population and control a specific territory; the term *legitimacy* usually implies a widely recognized claim of governmental authority and voluntary acceptance on the part of the population(s) directly affected.

The acid test of **legitimate authority** is not whether people have the right to vote or to strike or dissent openly, but how much *value* people attach to these rights. If a majority of the people are content with the existing political order just as it is (with or without voting rights), the legitimacy of the ruler(s) is simply not in question. Power in this case is suffused with legitimacy as well as authority. Political stability follows as a natural consequence. As history amply demonstrates, it is possible to seize power and to rule without a popular mandate or public approval, without moral, spiritual, or legal justification—in other words, without true (legitimate) authority. Power seizures occurred in Mauritania and Guinea in 2008; more than a dozen contemporary rulers, mostly in Africa, came to power in this manner. Adolf Hitler's failed "Beer Hall Putsch" in 1923 is a famous example of an attempted power seizure. Such attempts often fail, but they are evidence of political instability—as Hitler's eventual rise to power amply illustrates.

However, a ruler cannot seize authority; he or she can only assert or claim it. Claiming authority, however, is useless without the means to enforce it. The unchallenged right to rule that makes mass coercion unnecessary hinges in large part on legitimacy. If the people refuse to accept a government's authority, illegitimate rulers are faced with a choice: relinquish power or repress opposition. Whether repression works depends, in turn, on the answer to three questions. First, how widespread and determined is the opposition? Second, does the government have adequate financial resources and coercive capabilities to defeat its opponents and deter future challenges? Third, does the government have the will to use all means necessary to crush the rebellion?

If the opposition is broadly based and the government waivers for whatever reason, repression is likely to fail. Regimes changed in Russia in 1917 and 1992 following failed attempts to crush the opposition. Two other examples include Cuba in 1958, where Fidel Castro led a successful revolution, and Iran in 1978, where a mass uprising led to the overthrow of the Shah. A similar pattern was evident in many East European states in 1989, when repressive communist regimes collapsed like so many falling dominoes.

Even dictatorships are better off having public approval than not having it, if for no other reason than the relatively high cost of repression over a long period of time. Obviously, if people respect the ruler(s) and play by the rules without being forced to do so (or threatened with the consequences), the task of maintaining order and stability in society is going to be much easier. It stands to reason that people who feel exploited and oppressed make poorly motivated workers. The perverse work ethic of Soviet-style dictatorships, where it was frequently said, "We pretend to work and they pretend to pay us," helps explain the decline and fall of communism in the Soviet Union and Eastern Europe, dramatized by the spontaneous tearing down of the Berlin Wall in 1989.

order
In a political context, refers to an existing or desired arrangement of institutions based on certain principles, such as liberty, equality, prosperity, and security. Also often associated with the rule of law (as in the phrase "law and order") and with conservative values such as stability, obedience, and respect for legitimate authority.

Order

Order, the second basic concept of politics, exists on several levels. First, it denotes the structures, rules, rituals, procedures, and practices that make up the political system, which is built upon the foundations of society. What exactly is society? Closely related to **community**, society is an association of individuals who share a common identity. Usually that identity is at least partially defined by geography, because people who live in close proximity often know each other, enjoy shared experiences, speak the same language, and have similar values and interests. The process of instilling a sense of common purpose or creating a single political allegiance among diverse groups of people is complex and works better from the bottom up than from the top down. The breakup of the Soviet Union and Yugoslavia in the early 1990s, after more than seven decades as multinational states, suggests new communities are often fragile and tend to fall apart quickly if there are not strong cultural and psychological bonds under the political structures.

The idea that individuals become a true community through an unwritten *social contract* has been fundamental to Western political thought since the seventeenth century. Basic to social contract theory is the notion that the right to rule is based on the consent of the governed. Civil liberties in this type of community are a matter of natural law and natural rights—that is, they do not depend on written laws but rather are inherent in Nature. Nature with a capital N is a kind of ultimate truth that, in the eyes of social contract theorists, can be known through a combination of reason and observation. A corollary of this theory is that whenever government turns oppressive, when it arbitrarily takes away such natural rights as life, liberty, and (perhaps) property, the people have a right to revolt (see Chapter 14).

Government is a human invention by which societies are ruled and binding rules are made. Given the rich variety of governments in the world, how might we categorize them all? Traditionally we've distinguished between **republics**, in which sovereignty ultimately resides in the people, and governments such as monarchies or tyrannies, in which sovereignty rests with the rulers. Today, almost all republics are democratic (or representative) republics, meaning elected representatives responsible to the people exercise sovereign power.[2]

Some political scientists draw a simple distinction between democracies, which hold free elections, and dictatorships, which do not. Others emphasize political economy, distinguishing between governments enmeshed in capitalist or market-based systems and governments based on socialist or state-regulated systems. Finally, governments in developing countries face different kinds of challenges than do governments in developed countries. Not surprisingly, more economically developed countries often have markedly more well-established political institutions—including political parties, regular elections, civil and criminal courts—than most less developed countries, and more stable political systems.

In the modern world, the **state** is the sole repository of **sovereignty**. A sovereign state is a community with well-defined territorial boundaries administered by a single government. It typically claims a monopoly on the legitimate use of force or coercion; makes and enforces the rules (laws) that govern society; raises armies for the defense of its territory and population; levies and collects taxes; regulates trade and commerce; establishes courts, judges,

community
Any association of individuals who share a common identity based on geography, ethical values, religious beliefs, or ethnic origins.

government
The persons and institutions that make and enforce rules or laws for the larger community.

republic
A form of government in which sovereignty resides in the people of that country, rather than with the rulers. The vast majority of republics today are democratic or representative republics, meaning that the sovereign power is exercised by elected representatives who are responsible to the citizenry.

state
In its sovereign form, an independent political-administrative unit that successfully claims the allegiance of a given population, exercises a monopoly on the legitimate use of coercive force, and controls the territory inhabited by its citizens or subjects; in its other common form, a state is the major political-administrative subdivision of a federal system and, as such, is not sovereign but rather depends on the central authority (sometimes called the "national government") for resource allocations (tax transfers and grants), defense (military protection and emergency relief), and regulation of economic relations with other federal subdivisions (non-sovereign states) and external entities (sovereign states).

sovereignty
A government's capacity to assert supreme power successfully in a political state.

and magistrates to settle disputes and punish lawbreakers; and sends envoys (ambassadors) to represent its interests abroad, negotiate treaties, and gather useful information. Entities that share *some* but not all of the characteristics of states include fiefdoms and chiefdoms, bands and tribes, universal international organizations (such as the United Nations), regional supranational organizations (such as the European Union), and military alliances (such as NATO).

In the language of politics, state usually means country. France, for instance, may be called either a state or a country. (In certain federal systems of government, a state is an administrative subdivision, such as New York, Florida, Texas, or California in the United States; however, such states within a state are not sovereign.)

The term *nation* is also a synonym for *state* or *country*. Thus, the only way to know for certain whether *state* means part of a country (for example, the United States) or a whole country (say, France or China) is to consider the context. By the same token, context is the key to understanding what we mean by the word *nation*.

A **nation** is made up of a distinct group of people who share a common background, including their geographic location, history, racial or ethnic characteristics, religion, language, culture, or belief in common political ideas. Geography heads this list because members of a nation typically exhibit a strong collective sense of belonging associated with a particular territory for which they are willing to fight and die if necessary.

Countries with relatively homogeneous populations (with great similarity among members) are most common in Europe. Poland, for example, is a very homogeneous nation, as are the Scandinavian countries (Denmark, Sweden, and Norway), Finland, Austria, Portugal, and Greece. The United Kingdom, France, Germany, the Netherlands, Spain, and Italy are somewhat more diverse, but each speaks a national language (with different dialects in different areas). Belgium is one of the few countries in Europe clearly divided culturally and linguistically (French-speaking Walloons and Dutch-speaking Flemish).

India, Russia, and Nigeria are three highly diverse states. India's constitution officially recognizes no fewer than eighteen native tongues! The actual number spoken is far larger. As a nation of immigrants, the United States is also very diverse, but the process of assimilation eventually brings the children of newcomers, if not the newcomers themselves, into the mainstream.[3]

The **nation-state** is a state encompassing a single nation in which the overwhelming majority of the people form a dominant in-group who share common cultural, ethnic, and linguistic characteristics and all others are part of a distinct out-group or minority. This concept is rooted in a specific time and place—that is, in modern Western Europe. (See Box 1.1 for the story of the first nation-state.) The concept of the nation-state fits less comfortably in other regions of the world, where the political boundaries of sovereign states—many of which were European colonies before World War II—often do not coincide with ethnic or cultural geography. In some instances, ethnic, religious, or tribal groups that were bitter traditional enemies were thrown together in new "states," resulting in societies prone to great instability or even civil war.

BOX 1.1 SPOTLIGHT ON The Peace of Westphalia (1648): The Origins of the Modern Nation-State System

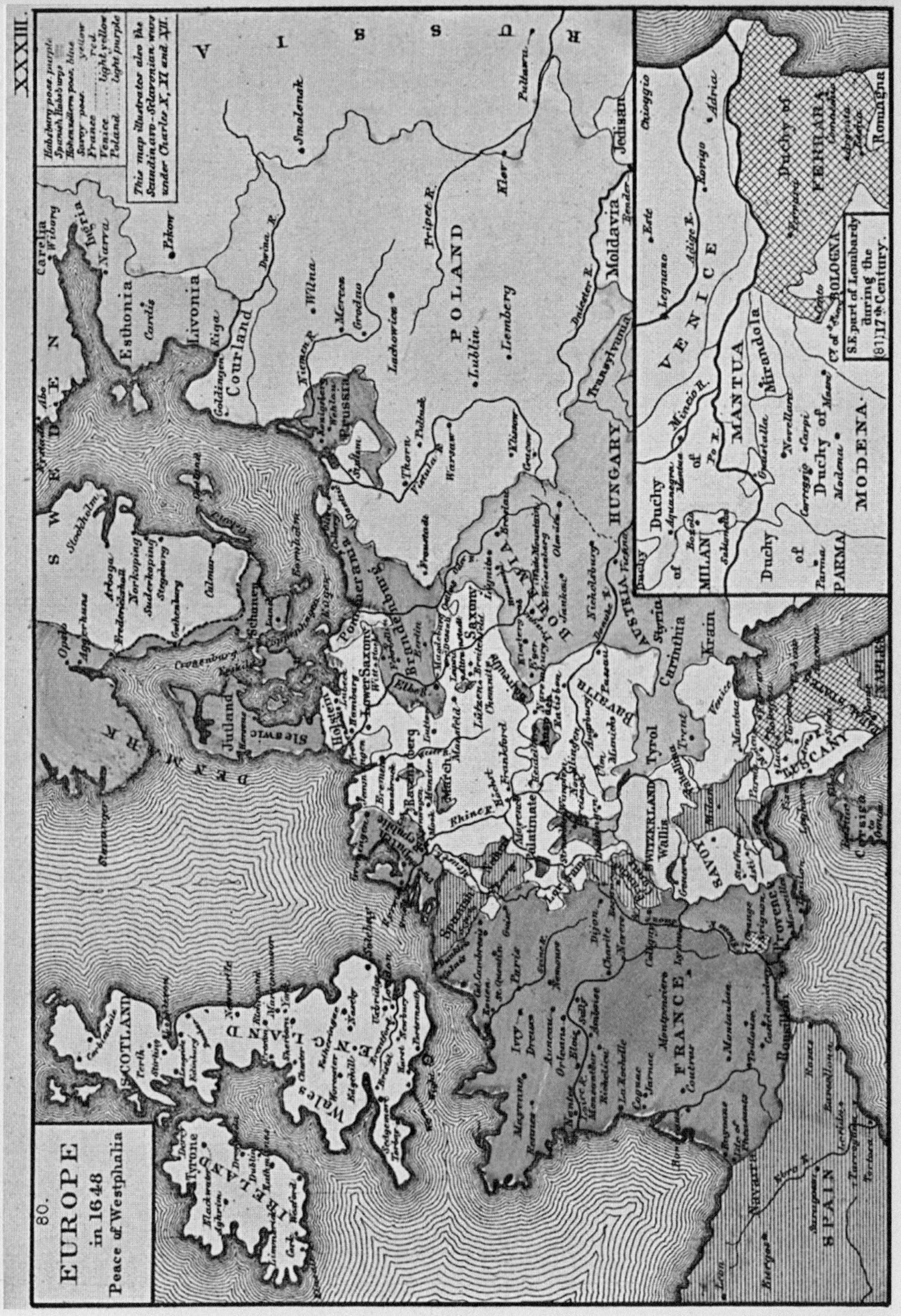

MAP 1.1 Dawn of the Nation-State System: Europe in 1648.

(Continued)

BOX 1.1 SPOTLIGHT ON   *(Continued)*

Most historians believe the Peace of Westphalia marks the beginning of the modern European state system. The main actors in forging the peace, which ended the Thirty Years War in 1648, were Sweden and France as the challengers, Spain and the dying Holy Roman Empire as the defenders of the status quo, and the newly independent Netherlands.

At first glance, the map of Europe in the mid-seventeenth century does not look much like it does today. However, on closer inspection we see the outlines of modern Europe emerge (see Map 1.1)—visual proof that the treaty laid the foundations of the nation-state as we see it in Europe today.

The emergence of the nation-state system transformed Europe from a continent of territorial empires to one based on relatively compact geographic units that share a single dominant language and culture. This pattern was unprecedented and it would shape both European and world history in the centuries to come.

France under Napoleon attempted to establish a new continental empire at the beginning of the nineteenth century but ultimately failed. Two other empires—Austria-Hungary and Russia—remained, but they were eclipsed by a rising new nation-state at the end of the nineteenth century and perished in World War I. After World War I, only the newly constituted Soviet empire existed in Europe. After World War II, what remained of Europe's overseas colonial empires also disintegrated. Today, the entire world, with few exceptions, is carved up into nation-states—the legacy of a treaty that, for better or worse, set the stage for a new world order.

country
As a political term, it refers loosely to a sovereign state and is roughly equivalent to "nation" or "nation-state"; *country* is often used as a term of endearment—for example, in the phrase "my country 'tis of thee, sweet land of liberty" in the patriotic song every U.S. child learns in elementary school; *country* has an emotional dimension not present in the word *state.*

Decolonization after World War II gave rise to many instant **multinational states** in which various ethnic or tribal groups were not assimilated into the new social order. Many decades later, the task of nation-building in these new states is still far from finished. A few examples will underscore this point. In 1967, Nigeria plunged into a vicious civil war when one large ethnic group, the Igbo, tried unsuccessfully to secede and form an independent state called Biafra. In 1994, Rwanda witnessed one of the bloodiest massacres in modern times when the numerically superior Hutus slaughtered hundreds of thousands of Tutsis, including women and children. In early 2008, tribal violence in Kenya's Rift Valley and beyond claimed the lives of hundreds of innocent people following the outcome of a presidential election that many believed was rigged.

In India, where Hindus and Muslims frequently clash and sporadic violence breaks out among militant Sikhs in Punjab and where hundreds of languages and dialects are spoken, characterizing the country as a nation-state misses the point altogether. In Sri Lanka (formerly Ceylon), Hindu Tamils have long waged a terrorist guerrilla war against the majority Singhalese, who are Buddhist.

Even in the Slavic-speaking parts of Europe, age-old ethnic rivalries have caused the breakup of preexisting states. The Soviet Union, Yugoslavia, and Czechoslovakia are all multinational states that self-destructed in the 1990s.

Finally, there are **stateless nations,** such as the Palestinians and Kurds, who share a sense of common identity (or community) but have no homeland. The existence of these nations without states has created highly volatile situations, most notably in the Middle East.

Justice

The fact that the governed always vastly outnumber the governors gives rise to competing—and sometimes conflicting—claims about the fairness of a government's policies and programs. We accept the rule of some citizens over others only if the public interest—or common good—is significantly advanced in the process. Thus, the exercise of power must be tempered by **justice,** the third of our basic political concepts: Is power exercised fairly, in the interest of the ruled, or merely for the sake of the rulers? For more than 2,000 years, political observers have maintained the distinction between the public-spirited exercise of political power on the one hand and self-interested rule on the other. This distinction attests to the importance of justice in political life.

Not all states and regimes allow questions of justice to be raised; in fact, throughout history, most have not. Even today, some governments brutally and systematically repress political discussion and debate, because they fear that if public attention focuses on basic issues of justice and the common good, then the legitimacy of the existing political order might come under attack. All too

Citizens unhappy about government policies at home or abroad can express themselves in any number of ways, including demonstrations and marches. In 2009, economic recession and an influx of foreign workers led to widespread labor strikes in the United Kingdom.

© GETTY IMAGES

nation
Often interchangeable with *state* or *country*; in common usage, this term actually denotes a specific people with a distinct language and culture or a major ethnic group—for example, the French, Dutch, Chinese, and Japanese people each constitute a nation as well as a state, hence the term nation-state; not all nations are fortunate enough to have a state of their own—modern examples include the Kurds (Turkey, Iraq, and Iran), Palestinians (West Bank and Gaza, Lebanon, Jordan), Pashtuns (Afghanistan), and Uighurs and Tibetans (China).

nation-state
A geographically defined community administered by a government.

multinational state
Sovereign state that contains two or more (sometimes many more) major ethno-linguistic groups (or nations) in the territories it controls; notable examples include India, Nigeria, Russia, and China as well as the former Yugoslavia.

stateless nation
People (or nations) who are scattered over the territory of several states or dispersed widely and who have no autonomous, independent, or sovereign governing body of their own; examples of stateless nations include the Kurds, Palestinians, and Tibetans (see also *nation*).

justice
Fairness; the distribution of rewards and burdens in society in accordance with what is deserved.

often, criticism of *how* a government rules may call into question its moral or legal *right* to rule. This is one reason political liberty is so important. We often define justice today as the extent to which government respects natural, human, or civil rights. Among the most important of these is the right to question whether the government is acting justly.

Questions about whether this ruler is legitimate or that policy is desirable naturally invade our thoughts and engage our interest. They stem from human nature itself. The famed Greek philosopher Aristotle (384–322 BCE) observed that although animals can only make sounds signifying pleasure and pain, human beings use reason and language "to declare what is advantageous and what is just and unjust." Therefore, "it is the peculiarity of man, in comparison with the rest of the animal world, that he alone possess a perception of good and evil, of the just and unjust."[4]

The same human faculties that make moral judgment possible also make political literacy—or the ability to think and speak intelligently about politics—necessary. In other words, moral judgment and political literacy are two sides of the same coin.

HOW WE STUDY POLITICS

The Greek philosopher Aristotle is the father of political science.[5] He not only wrote about politics and ethics, but he also described different political systems and suggested a scheme for classifying and evaluating them. For Aristotle, political science simply meant political investigation; thus, a political scientist was one who sought, through systematic inquiry, to understand the truth about politics. In this sense, Aristotle's approach to studying politics more than two thousand years ago has much in common with what political scientists do today. Yet the discipline has changed a great deal since Aristotle's time.

Today, there is no consensus on how to best study politics. Thus we have a multifaceted discipline with different political scientists choosing different approaches, asking different kinds of questions, and addressing different audiences.

The resulting ferment is not necessarily bad. It means the discipline is vital and diverse, and it reflects the vast universe of human activity with which political science must deal. Let us explore why and how contemporary political scientists study politics.

For What Purposes?

Just as students in other disciplines seek answers to basic questions about, say, photosynthesis in plant biology or the causes of depression in psychology, historians and political scientists seek answers to perennial questions about politics and government. Some lend themselves to rigorous investigation as in the natural sciences, whereas others do not. Often, the most important questions in politics are "should" and "ought" questions that we cannot answer without resorting to moral philosophy, reason, and logic. These are the great *normative* political questions that resonate throughout human history: When is war justified? Do people have a right to revolt? Is the right to life absolute? Does anyone have a right to die? Does everyone have a right to liberty?

In addition to a better understanding of political ideas and issues, we reap other rewards from the disciplined study of political institutions. For example, not only does studying interest groups in the United States reveal a great deal about their number, composition, and influence, but it can also shed light on how they can become more effective. Studying elections can reveal flaws in the voting process or voting districts or the system of voter registration and lead to appropriate changes or reforms, such as redistricting or switching from written ballots to voting machines. Public opinion surveys tell voters how elections are likely to turn out, and candidates use them to tailor campaign strategy and fine-tune tactics in different regions and states (see Chapter 11). Experts in foreign policy and international relations can analyze and explain the implications of entering into new alliances or making new commitments around the world (see Part V).

Yet experts and specialists frequently disagree. In political science, this disagreement can even include such basic questions as whether it is possible to have a "true" science of politics. Should political science strive to predict or forecast events to the degree chemists and physicists can? Should political scientists be held to the same standards as, say, meteorologists? To appreciate the diversity among political scientists, we will look first at what is commonly called **methodology**.

By What Methods?

There are many ways to classify political scientists. We will focus on one basic division—between *positivism* and the *normative approach*. **Positivism** emphasizes empirical research (which relies on observation) and couches problems in terms of variables we can measure. **Behaviorism** is an offshoot of positivism that focuses mainly on the study of political behavior. Behaviorists typically subject common notions about politics—for example, what motivates voters or why a given election turned out the way it did—to rigorous empirical tests, often casting long-standing "truths" into serious doubt or exposing "facts" as fallacies.

The Normative Approach Sticking to the facts, a trademark of positivism, raises a problem for political scientists who favor a **normative approach**. Although facts are important, normative political scientists give equal emphasis to values. They want to assess not merely *how* a particular policy, process, or institution works, but also *how well* it works according to certain moral or legal standards. They study politics from the perspective of the values and interests at work in social, political, and economic arrangements. In considering Congress, for example, normative political scientists might ask: Do special

---

methodology
The way scientists and scholars set about exploring, explaining, proving, or disproving propositions in different academic disciplines. The precise methods vary according to the discipline and the object, event, process, or phenomenon under investigation.

positivism
A philosophy of science, originated by Auguste Comte, that stresses observable, scientific facts as the sole basis of proof and truth; a skeptical view of ideas or beliefs based on religion or metaphysics..

behaviorism
An approach to the study of politics that emphasizes fact-based evaluations of action.

normative approach
An approach to the study of politics that is based on examining fundamental and enduring questions.

interests unduly influence tax legislation? Or with respect to U.S. foreign policy: Was the invasion of Iraq in 2003 necessary?

The criteria for answering such questions include philosophy and formal logic, constitutions, treaties, the texts of official documents, court cases, and expert opinions. Individual investigators choose the research topics and methods they consider most important. For example, in a study of the separation of powers into executive, legislative, and judicial branches of government they might begin with a review of the Constitution that included *The Federalist Papers* (1787–1788)—a famous series of commentaries written by James Madison, Alexander Hamilton, and John Jay. Or they might focus on the economic interests the Founding Fathers represented or the social class to which they all belonged. Obviously, these questions touch on values as well as facts. They cannot be answered without reference to both.

After comparing positivist and normative political science, you might ask, Are facts and values total opposites? Do values influence how even the most rigorous of scientists see the facts? In truth, it is not always easy to distinguish between a fact and a value. Moreover, in politics, values *are* facts. We all bring certain values to everything we do. At the same time, however, we can never get at the truth if we don't place a high value on facts.

The Study of Human Behavior Behavioral scientists shy away from studying values and avoid making subjective moral and philosophical judgments about politics, preferring instead to concentrate on facts. They employ the scientific method familiar to investigators in such fields as biology, physics, and chemistry, asking the sort of questions that can only be answered by carefully putting together a research design, gathering observational data, using the tools of statistical analysis, and constructing experiments to test hypotheses. Some behaviorists develop elaborate mathematical models to explain the behavior of voters, political parties, decision makers, coalition members, and the like. For more than half a century, they have undertaken elaborate statistical and mathematical studies to identify the causes and products of war.

In December 1996, a study titled "Partisan Effects of Voter Turnout in Senatorial and Gubernatorial Elections" was published in a prominent scholarly journal.[6] The authors of the study asked the following precise question: Is it really true, as is widely believed, that high voter turnout favors Democrats? The prevailing belief that Democrats benefit from high voter turnout assumes that: (1) people with lower socioeconomic status (SES) vote less often than people with higher SES; (2) as voter turnout rose, more people on the lower end of the SES ladder voted; and (3) these lower-end voters were likely to vote for the party they thought would most effectively advance working-class interests—namely, the Democratic Party. Many political observers treat this belief, which is reinforced whenever low voter turnout coincides with Republican victories, as an established fact. This belief also explains why most Democrats favored (and Republicans opposed) the 1993 National Voter Registration Act. (Popularly known as the Motor Voter Bill, this law eased voter registration procedures.)

The researchers used statistics that started in 1928, examining 1,842 state elections: 983 for senator and 859 for governor. The study omitted two kinds of elections: (1) elections in the Deep South between 1928 and 1965, in which there was effectively only one party with any chance of winning (the Democratic Party), and (2) elections in which third-party candidates received more than 5 percent of the vote. Applying a mathematical test, the researchers concluded that from 1928 to 1964, high voter turnout aided the Democratic Party, as was generally believed. However, after 1964 the results were markedly different. In senatorial races, there was no relationship between turnout and votes for Democrats; in gubernatorial elections, Republicans, rather than Democrats, fared slightly better, but the difference was not statistically significant.

Why was the conventional theory of voter turnout invalidated after 1964? Although this question was beyond the scope of the study, its findings were consistent with another complex theory of voting behavior. The rise in the number of independents since 1964 (and the resulting decline in party identification and partisan voting) made it difficult to calculate which party would benefit from a large voter turnout in any given race. By the mid-1990s, nearly one-third of all voters identified themselves as independents, while ticket splitting (not voting for *only* Republicans or *only* Democrats—a so-called straight ticket) became common.

This sophisticated research project epitomizes the kind of methodology employed by behavioral political scientists. Behaviorists, like other research scientists, are typically content to take small steps on the road to knowledge. Each step points the way to future studies.

Political scientists analyze patterns and trends in voting behavior to learn more about who votes, how different segments of the population vote, and why people vote the way they do. Political strategists use this information to help candidates for office get elected.

© DILIP VISHWANAT/GETTY IMAGES

Studying human behavior can be as frustrating as it is fascinating. There are almost always multiple explanations for human behavior, and it is extremely difficult to sort out and isolate a single cause, and distinguish it from a mere statistical correlation. For instance, several studies indicate that criminals tend to be less intelligent than law-abiding citizens. If so, is low intelligence a cause of crime (perhaps because many criminals cannot understand the consequences of violating the law or the value of deferred gratification in civil society)? How does low intelligence connect to other correlates (and perhaps causes) of crime, including age, gender, personality type, a history of being abused or neglected as a child, and drug or alcohol addiction? What about free will? Are we to believe that society—rather than an individual who commits a wrong act—is somehow responsible for crime?

Political scientists often disagree not only about how to study politics but also about which questions to ask. Behaviorists typically prefer to examine specific and narrowly defined questions, answering them by applying quantitative techniques—sophisticated statistical methods such as regression analysis and analysis of variance. Many broader questions of politics, especially those raising issues of justice, lie beyond the scope of this sort of investigation. Questions such as "What is justice?" or "What is the best political system?" require us to have subjective policy preferences or make mere value judgments. Normative analysts counter by arguing that even if we cannot resolve such questions scientifically, they are worth asking because not all value judgments are arbitrary or based on mere prejudice. Confining the study of politics only to questions with answers we can measure, they argue, risks turning political science into an academic game of Trivial Pursuit.

Which Methodology Is Best? Given the complexity of human behavior, it is not surprising that experts argue over methodology, or how to do science. Positivism and the normative approach have each made notable contributions to the study of politics and government. Although the debate between them has cooled, it has divided the discipline for several decades and is likely to continue to do so for a long time to come.

The Political (Science) Puzzle

Thus, political science, like politics, means different things to different people. Not only is the subject matter of politics difficult to define to everyone's satisfaction, but it also is wide ranging and difficult to study without being broken down into more manageable pieces. Those pieces can take various shapes and forms. There is no perfect way to dismantle a discipline as all-encompassing as political science, but one useful way is to look at specialties and subfields that have emerged over time. Thus, some political scientists specialize in *political theory*, whereas others focus on *U.S. government, comparative politics, international relations, political economy,* or *public administration*.

More specialized areas within these include *constitutional law*, a traditional specialty that focuses on a specific aspect of U.S. government, *public policy*, which stresses modern management techniques such as zero-based budgeting and cost accounting in both U.S. government and public administration, and *political parties* and *interest groups,* which falls within either U.S. government or comparative politics. Let's look more closely at the five subfields into which political science programs are often divided.

Political Theory Normative political theory, or political philosophy, dates back to Plato (circa 400 BCE). Plato's method in searching for the truth was to ask important questions: What is the good life? What is good government? Are people basically good or bad? When is revolution justified?

Political theory tries to answer these questions through reason and logic supported by the writings of political thinkers, such as Aristotle, Jean-Jacques Rousseau, John Locke, and John Stuart Mill, among others. The aim of this type of inquiry is to make judgments as to right and wrong or good and bad. Because people who advocate change and those who oppose it both do so in the belief that they are morally right, understanding politics requires us to be familiar with the criteria by which policies and programs are judged good and bad.[7] Normative theorists contend that without knowledge of the moral costs and consequences in politics, citizens and leaders alike will lack direction and a clear sense of purpose.

There is a long-running debate in political science between "rational choice" theorists and "political culture" theorists. Advocates of **rational choice** theory emphasize the role of reason over emotion in human behavior. Political behavior, in this view, follows logical and even predictable patterns so long as we understand the key role of self-interest. This approach, which forms the basis for a theory of international relations known as **political realism** (see Chapter 17), holds that individuals and states alike act according to the logic of self-interest.

Other political scientists argue that rational choice theory is an oversimplification because states and groups are composed of human beings with disparate interests, perceptions, and beliefs. We cannot explain their behavior by reference to logic and rationality alone. Instead, the behavior of individuals and of groups is a product of specific influences that vary from place to place. We call such influences "culture"—if the behavior under investigation is political, it grows out of a process rooted in political culture.

Rational choice and political culture theory are not mutually exclusive, and most political scientists do not adhere dogmatically to one or the other. Both contain important insights and we can best see them as complementary rather than conflicting.

U.S. Government Understanding our own political institutions is important. We can best achieve it by careful study of public opinion, voting behavior, party alignment, campaign financing, elections, race relations, and foreign policy. When we speak of U.S. government, our frame of reference changes depending on whether we mean national, state, or local politics. Similarly, when we study political behavior in the United States, it makes a big difference whether we are focusing on individual behavior or the behavior of groups such as

rational choice
The role of reason over emotion in human behavior. Political behavior, in this view, follows logical and even predictable patterns so long as we understand the key role of self-interest.

political realism
The philosophy that power is the key variable in all political relationships and should be used pragmatically and prudently to advance the national interest; policies are judged good or bad on the basis of their effect on national interests, not on their level of morality.

interest groups, ethnic groups, age cohorts, and the like. Political scientists who teach courses on U.S. government and politics are, in effect, engaging in civic education.

Citizens in a democracy must understand how the government works, what rights they are guaranteed by the Constitution, and so on. U.S. politics also merits study because the United States is home to the oldest written constitution, the most powerful military establishment, and an economy second in size only to that of the European Union—none of which means the U.S. "model" of democracy is necessarily the best one.

Comparative Politics Comparative politics seeks to contrast and evaluate governments and political systems. Comparing forms of government, stages of economic development, domestic and foreign policies, and political traditions allows political scientists to formulate meaningful generalizations. Some comparative political scientists specialize in a particular region of the world or a particular nation. Others focus on a particular issue or political phenomenon, such as terrorism, political instability, or voting behavior.

All political systems share certain characteristics. Figure 1.1 depicts one famous model, first formulated by political scientist David Easton in 1965. This model suggests that all political systems function within the context of political cultures, which consist of traditions, values, and common knowledge. It assumes citizens have expectations of and place demands on the political system. But they also support the system in various ways: They may participate in government, vote, or simply obey the laws of the state. The demands they make and supports they provide in turn influence the government's decisions, edicts, laws, and orders.

FIGURE 1.1   A simplified model of the political system

SOURCE: Copyright© 1965, 1979 by David Easton. All rights reserved. Reprinted by permission of the author.

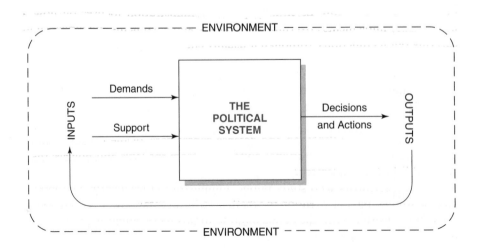

Countries, of course, differ in countless ways. Some political scientists see the differences among countries as being more significant than the similarities, and they differentiate among political systems in various ways. This text, for example, distinguishes among democratic, authoritarian, and totalitarian states. Some political scientists contrast only democratic and nondemocratic states. Others stress the economic context of politics in different places: in the postindustrial world (the United States, Canada, Western Europe, Australia, and Japan) and in the prospering states of east Asia (China, South Korea, Taiwan, and Singapore); in the remnant of the communist world (Vietnam, North Korea, and Cuba); and in the developing countries. After the fall of Communism, the distinction between established liberal democracies and "transitional states" gained currency (see Chapter 8). Finally, some observers distinguish between viable states and so-called failed states (see Chapter 9).

International Relations Specialists in international relations analyze how nations interact. Why do nations sometimes live in peace and harmony but go to war at other times? The advent of the nuclear age, of course, brought new urgency to the study of international relations, but the threat of an all-out nuclear war now appears far less menacing than other threats, including international terrorism, global warming, energy security, and, most recently, the economic meltdown. Thus, although war and peace are ever-present problems in international relations, they are by no means the only ones. The role of morality in foreign policy continues to be a matter of lively debate. Some political scientists, called *realists*, argue that considerations of national interest have always been paramount in international politics and always will be.[8] In contrast, some *idealists* contend that morality-driven policies will lead to world peace and an end to the cycle of war that the realists accept fatalistically. Still others say the distinction between the national interest and international morality is exaggerated; that democracies, for example, derive mutual benefit from protecting each other and that in so doing they also promote world peace.[9]

Public Administration Essentially, public administration focuses on how a bureaucracy implements governmental policies, and what helps and hinders it in carrying out its functions. Although it usually emphasizes national government, public administration also looks at state and local government and intergovernmental relations. It examines bureaucratic structures, procedures, and processes in an attempt to improve efficiency and reduce waste and duplication. The field of public administration also studies bureaucratic behavior: How and why, for example, do bureaucracies develop vested interests and special relationships (such as between the Pentagon and defense contractors, or the Department of Commerce and trade associations) quite apart from the laws and policies they are established to implement?

Political scientists who study public administration frequently concentrate on case studies, paying attention to whether governmental power is exercised in a manner consistent with the public interest. In this sense, public administration shares the concerns of political science as a whole.

WHY STUDY POLITICS?

A basic understanding of politics is a vital part of any undergraduate's education. To realize the full benefits, make a sincere effort to learn and, above all, keep an open mind.

Self-Interest

Because personal happiness depends in no small degree on what government does or does not do, we all have a considerable stake in understanding how government works (or why it is not working). To college students, for example, federal work-study programs, state subsidies to public education, low-interest loans, federal grants, and court decisions designed to protect (or not protect) students' rights are political matters of great significance. Through the study of politics, we become more aware of our dependence on the political system and better equipped to determine when to favor and when to oppose change. At the same time, such study helps to reveal the limits of politics and of our ability to bring about positive change. It is sobering to consider that each of us is only one person in a nation of millions (and a world of billions), most of whom have opinions and prejudices no less firmly held than are our own.

The Public Interest

What could be more vital to the public interest than the moral character and conduct of the citizenry? Civil society is defined by and reflected in the kinds of everyday decisions and choices made by ordinary people leading ordinary lives. At the same time, people are greatly influenced by civil society and the prevailing culture and climate of politics. People with very similar capabilities and desires can develop quite different moral standards, depending on the circumstances. Politics plays a vital role in shaping these circumstances, and it is fair to say the public interest hangs in the balance.

An Infamous Example The rise and fall of Nazi Germany (1933–1945) under Adolf Hitler illustrates the tremendous impact a political regime can have on the moral character of citizens. The political doctrine of Nazism was explicitly grounded in a doctrine of virulent racial supremacy. Hitler ranted about the superiority of the so-called Aryan race. The purity of the German nation was supposedly threatened with adulteration by inferior races, or *untermenschen*. Policies based on this *weltanschauung* ("worldview") resulted in the systematic murder of millions of innocent men, women, and children. Approximately six million Jews and millions of others, including Poles, Gypsies, homosexuals, and people with disabilities, were killed in cold blood.

During the Nazi era, the German nation appears, at first glance, to have become little more than an extension of Hitler's will—in other words, the awesome moral responsibility for the Holocaust somehow rested on the shoulders of one man, Adolf Hitler. But some dispute this interpretation. For example, according to Irving Kristol,

> When one studies the case of The Nazi there comes a sickening emptiness of the stomach and a sense of bafflement. Can this be all? The disparity between the crime and the criminal is too monstrous.
>
> We expect to find evil men, paragons of wickedness, slobbering, maniacal brutes; we are prepared to trace the lineaments of The Nazi on the face of every individual Nazi in order to define triumphantly the essential features of his character. But the Nazi leaders were not diabolists, they did not worship evil. For—greatest of ironies—the Nazis, like Adam and Eve before the fall, knew not of good and evil, and it is this cast of moral indifference that makes them appear so petty and colorless and superficial.[10]

One such person, according to political theorist Hannah Arendt, was Adolf Eichmann, a Nazi functionary who administered much of the extermination program. In Arendt's view, Eichmann was not a particularly unusual man.[11] He had a strong desire to get ahead, to be a success in life. He took special pride in his ability to do a job efficiently. Although not particularly thoughtful or reflective, he was intelligent. Arendt also describes Eichmann as somewhat insecure, but not noticeably more so than many "normal" people.

Eichmann claimed to have no obsessive hatred toward Jews (although, obviously, he was not sufficiently skeptical or mentally independent to resist the widespread anti-Semitism that existed in Germany at that time). In short, Eichmann was morally indifferent; in Kristol's words, he "knew not of good and evil."

Nazi mass murderer Adolf Eichmann: An ordinary man?

© STR/AP PHOTO

If it is true that Adolf Eichmann was an ordinary man, why are there so few Eichmanns? In large measure, the answer can be found in the fortunate fact that the political regimes under which most people live are nothing like Nazi Germany. The Nazi experience was a crucial factor in shaping the personality and character of all the Eichmanns in Germany between the two world wars. Eichmann knew that his success would be measured largely in terms of a single criterion: efficiency. What mattered to Eichmann was not what he was doing but how well he did it. Very likely he would have discharged his responsibilities with equal zeal had he been in charge of park planning or flower planting rather than mass extermination. The banality of this evildoer and the magnitude of his evil are both appalling and instructive, for they accurately reflected Germany's prevailing policies.[12]

The German leadership equated mass extermination with patriotism and the public interest. It would have required a rare combination of intellectual independence and moral courage not to go along with this prevailing view. Tragically, those were precisely the qualities countless people like Eichmann so sorely lacked. The lesson that the public interest can never be served by blind obedience to authority illustrates the importance of understanding politics.

GATEWAYS TO THE WORLD: EXPLORING CYBERSPACE

On a recent afternoon, a Google search found 480 million sites for the keyword *politics*. Obviously, that is way too many for anyone to check out. Fortunately, there are gateways to politics on the World Wide Web. You just have to know where (or how) to look. One good place to start is at http://www.politicalinformation.com/. This site contains over 5,000 "carefully selected political and policy websites" in the following major categories: Campaigns and Elections, Commentary and News, Federal and State Government, Grassroots, Issues, Parties and Organizations, Portals and General Political Sites, and Research Tools. Each of these categories, in turn, is broken down into subcategories, which in turn are subdivided into more specific categories. As the size of this list indicates, you are not alone in your interest in this subject.

Throughout the rest of this book, you will find more of these Gateways to the World, leading to a vast array of resources related to the material in a given chapter. You will find everything from suggested search terms to the uniform resource locators (URLs) of specific websites. These gateways will prove useful as you seek to learn about a concept in more depth or as you research and write papers.

The URLs in this section will provide you with hints for getting involved in organizations that deal with issues relevant to the chapter. You should keep in mind that the Internet is constantly changing, so some of the sites to which this text refers may no longer be available.

http://cqpolitics.com/

Website for Congressional Quarterly, Inc., a subscription-based publisher of all things political

Governing.com at http://www.governing.com/politics.htm

Website for *Governing*, a monthly magazine from Congressional Quarterly, Inc., for state and local government officials

http://www.politics1.com/

Claims to be "the most comprehensive guide to U.S. politics"

http://www.politicalwire.com/

Offers up-to-date coverage of news and commentary about politics

http://www.politicsnationwide.com/

Allows viewers to search a variety of categories, from voting to state executives

SUMMARY

A good way for us to begin the study of politics is to focus on three fundamental concepts: power, order, and justice. If we understand the inter-relationships between power and order, order and justice, and justice and power, we will be well on our way to a deeper understanding of politics.

Political power, which has many sources, can be defined as the capacity to act in the public arena. We see political power in action when the government promulgates a new law or when sovereign states sign treaties or go to war. In fact, we see the power of government in all sorts of ways: when we are assessed taxes, or fined for a traffic violation, or made to remove our shoes prior to boarding an airplane. When governments exercise power they often do it in the name of order. Power and authority are closely related: authority is the official exercise of authority. If we accept the rules and the rulers who make and enforce them, then government also enjoys legitimacy. Questions of justice arise if the public interest is not advanced by the exercise of governmental power or if society no longer accepts the authority of the government as legitimate.

Political scientists seek to discover the truth about political institutions, forces, movements, and processes. Whereas traditional political scientists are interested in assessing the workings of government and shy away from normative questions, behaviorists use scientific methods to describe and predict political outcomes but generally try to avoid making value judgments. Almost all political scientists specialize in some topic, with the broadest subfields being political theory (or philosophy), U.S. government, comparative politics, international relations, and public administration.

Among the many valid reasons for studying politics, two are worthy of special emphasis: (1) understanding politics is a matter of self-interest, and (2) by exploring politics, we gain a better appreciation of what is, and what is not, in the public interest. The critical importance of this awareness among ordinary citizens was tragically illustrated by the rise of Nazism in Germany.

KEY TERMS

politics
power
authority
legitimacy
legitimate authority
order
community
government

republic
state
sovereignty
country
nation
nation-state
multinational state
stateless nation

justice
methodology
positivism
normative approach
behaviorism
political realism
rational choice

REVIEW QUESTIONS

1. On what three fundamental concepts is the study of politics based?
2. How does one identify a political problem? Are some conflicts more political than others? Explain.
3. How do political scientists differ from one another?
4. In what ways can individuals benefit from the study of politics and government?

RECOMMENDED READING

Anderson, Benedict. *Imagined Communities: Reflections on the Origin and Spread of Nationalism*, 3rd ed. New York: Verso, 2006. Explores the question: What makes people live, die, and kill in the name of nations?

Aristotle. *The Politics*. Edited and translated by Ernest Barker. New York: Oxford University Press, 1962. An account of the necessity and value of politics.

Bettelheim, Bruno. "Remarks on the Psychological Appeal of Totalitarianism." *Surviving and Other Essays*. New York: Random House, 1980. Bettelheim provides an excellent account of the less obvious ways the Nazi regime imposed conformity and obedience on its citizens.

Crick, Bernard. *In Defense of Politics*. Magnolia, MA: Peter Smith, 1994. An argument that politics is an important and worthy human endeavor.

Drucker, Peter. "The Monster and the Lamb." *Atlantic* (December 1978): 82–87. A short but moving account of the effects of the Nazi government on several individuals.

Easton, David. *The Political System: An Inquiry into the State of Political Science*, 2nd ed. Chicago: University of Chicago Press, 1981. A pioneering book that laid the foundation for a systems theory approach to political analysis.

Gellner, Ernst. *Nations and Nationalism*. Ithaca, NY: Cornell University Press, 1983. Argues that nationalism is an inescapable consequence of modernity.

Lewis, C. S. *The Abolition of Man.* New York: Simon & Schuster, 1996. An elegant discussion of the necessity of moral judgments.

Manent, Pierre, translated by Marc LePain. *A World Beyond Politics? A Defense of the Nation-State.* Princeton, NJ: Princeton University Press, 2006. Asserts that both democracy and the nation-state are under threat today and argues that the notion we would be better off without nations or politics or national politics is an illusion.

Milgram, Stanley. *Obedience to Authority.* New York: HarperCollins, 1983. A report on a series of social science experiments that demonstrated the degree to which many individuals obey authority.

Mueller, Dennis C. *Public Choice III.* New York: Cambridge University Press, 2003. An elegant survey of public choice theory, which emphasizes the rational side of political behavior and the logic in political institutions, policies, and actions.

Pollock III, Phillip H. *The Essentials of Political Analysis.* Washington, D.C.: CQ Press, 2009. The author discusses facts and values in the introduction; the rest of the book elucidates how political scientists engage in empirical research using the tools of statistical analysis.

Schmitt, Carl, Tracy B. Strong, Leo Strauss, and George Schwab. *The Concept of the Political: Expanded Edition.* Chicago: University of Chicago Press, 2007. The title says it all.

Strauss, Leo. "What Is Political Philosophy?" *What Is Political Philosophy? and Other Studies.* Chicago: University of Chicago Press, 1988. A cogent introduction to the value and necessity of political philosophy.

Tinder, Glenn. *Political Thinking: The Perennial Questions*, 6th ed. Reading, MA: Addison-Wesley, 1995. A topical consideration of great and lasting controversies in politics.

© SCOTT MORGAN/GETTY IMAGES

Campaigning for the presidency in 2007, Barack Obama declared that the war in Iraq "was based on a flawed ideology" and called on the United States to "lead the world, by deed and example"; in early 2009 newly elected President Obama announced a timetable for withdrawal of U.S. forces from Iraq, promised to close the Guantanamo detention center, and ordered an end to harsh interrogation methods (such as waterboarding) widely denounced as torture.

The Idea of the Public Good
Ideologies and Isms

In Lewis Carroll's classic tale, popularly known as *Alice in Wonderland*, Alice, who has lost her way in a dense forest, encounters the Cheshire Cat who is sitting on a tree branch. "Would you tell me, please, which way I ought to go from here?" asks Alice. "That depends a good deal on where you want to get to," replies the Cat. "I don't much care where," says Alice. "Then it doesn't matter which way you go," muses the Cat.

Like Alice lost in the forest, we too occasionally find ourselves adrift. Governments and societies are no different. Political leadership can be woefully deficient or hopelessly divided as to what course of action is best in a crisis or what to do about the economy or the environment or health care or a new threat to national security. Intelligent decisions, as Alice's encounter with the Cheshire Cat illustrates, can take place only after we have set clear aims and goals. Before politics can effectively convert mass energy (society) into collective effort (government), which is the essence of public policy, we need a consensus on where we want to go or what we want to be as a society a year from now or perhaps ten years up the road. Otherwise, our leaders, like the rest of us, cannot possibly know how to get there. This is why it is so essential for citizens in a democracy to be politically literate. There are always plenty of people eager to tell us *what* to think, but in this book we will learn *how* to think about politics.

POLITICAL ENDS AND MEANS

public good

The shared beliefs of a political community as to what goals government ought to attain (for example, to achieve the fullest possible measure of security, prosperity, equality, liberty, or justice for all citizens).

In politics, ends and means are inextricably intertwined. Implicit in debates over public policy is a belief in the idea of the **public good**, and that it is the government's role to identify and pursue aims of benefit to society as a whole rather than to favored individuals. But the focus of policy debates is often explicitly about means rather than ends. For example, politicians may disagree over whether a tax cut at a particular time will help promote the common good (prosperity) by encouraging saving and investment, balancing the national budget, reducing the rate of inflation, and so on. Although they disagree about the best monetary and fiscal strategies, both sides would agree that economic growth and stability is a proper aim of government.

In political systems with no curbs on executive authority, where the leader has unlimited power, government may have little to do with the public interest.[1] In constitutional democracies, by contrast, the public good is associated with core values such as security, prosperity, equality, liberty, and justice (see Chapter 13). These goals are the navigational guides for keeping the ship of state on course. Arguments about whether to tack this way or that, given the prevailing political currents and crosswinds, are the essence of public policy debates.

IDEOLOGIES AND THE PUBLIC GOOD

The concept of Left and Right originated in the European parliamentary practice of seating parties that favor social and political change to the left of the presiding officer, and those opposing change (or favoring a return to a previous form of government) to the right. "You are where you sit," in other words.

Today people may have only vague ideas about government or how it works or what it is actually doing at any given time.[2] Even so, many lean one way or another, toward conservative or liberal views. When people go beyond merely leaning and adopt a rigid, closed system of political ideas, however, they cross a line and enter the realm of **ideology**. Ideologies act as filters that true believers (or adherents) use to interpret events, explain human behavior, and justify political action.

The use of labels—or "isms" as they are often called—is a kind of shorthand that, ideally, facilitates political thought and debate rather than becoming a way to discredit one's political opponents. One note of caution: these labels do not have precisely the same meaning everywhere. Thus, what is considered "liberal" in the United Kingdom might be considered "conservative" in the United States (see Figure 2.1).

Conservatives in the United States typically favor a strong national defense, deregulation of business and industry, and tax cuts on capital gains (income from stocks, real estate, and other investments) and inheritances. They often staunchly oppose welfare on the grounds that "giveaway" programs reward the lazy. Until the Reagan Revolution of the 1980s, conservatives often led the fight for balanced budgets. By contrast, liberals tend to favor public assistance programs, cuts in military spending, a progressive tax system (one that levies higher taxes on higher incomes), and governmental regulation in such areas as the food and drug industry, occupational safety and health, housing, transportation, and energy.

ideology
Any set of fixed, predictable ideas held by politicians and citizens on how to serve the public good.

FIGURE 2.1   FOCUS Conservative or Liberal?

	U.S. Conservatives*	British Liberals§
Constitutionalism	Yes	Yes
Religious tolerance	Yes	Yes
Market economy	Yes	Yes
Protectionism	No	No
Pacifism	No	No

* Values historically associated with the Republican Party in the United States, though not necessarily with the policies of any given administration or president
§ Values historically associated the Whig Party in the United Kingdom, often called classical liberalism

The entire political spectrum is shifted toward the right in the United States, which is why liberals in the United States look a lot like conservatives in most European countries. Leftists in Europe often belong to Socialist parties, but there is no viable Socialist party in the United States. Prior to British Prime Minister Margaret Thatcher's makeover of the Conservative Party after 1979, many British Conservatives resembled Democrats ("liberals") in the United States as much or more than Republicans ("conservatives").

In this chapter, we group ideologies under three headings: antigovernment ideologies, right-wing ideologies, and left-wing ideologies. Left and Right are very broad categories, however, and there are many shades of gray on both sides of the political spectrum. Only when the political system becomes severely polarized, as it did in Germany between the two world wars, are people forced to choose between black and white. In the two-party system of the United States, the choice is limited to red (Republican) and blue (Democrat). Up until September 11, 2001, both parties were typically closer to the center than to either extreme. After 9/11, however, this pattern changed as the political climate became more polarized and partisan, as evidenced by the vicious mud-slinging in the 2008 presidential campaign and the vitriolic rhetoric of right-wing media figures like Rush Limbaugh and Sean Hannity. We turn first to a consideration of ideologies that oppose not only the existing form of government but also the very idea of government.

Antigovernment Ideologies

anarchism
A system that opposes in principle the existence of any form of government, often through violence and lawlessness.

Opposition to government *in principle* is **anarchism.** The Russian revolutionary Mikhail Bakunin (1814–1876), who reveled in the "joy of destruction" and called for violent uprisings by society's beggars and criminals, is often considered the father of modern anarchism. A close relative of anarchism is **nihilism,** which glorifies destruction as an end in itself rather than as a means to overthrow the existing system or rebuild society. Extremely malevolent ideologies of this kind have, fortunately, had relatively little impact outside prerevolutionary Russia (and possibly Spain), although terrorism is perhaps inspired by anarchistic impulses at times.

nihilism
A philosophy that holds that the total destruction of all existing social and political institutions is a desirable end in itself.

libertarianism
A system based on the belief that government is a necessary evil that should interfere with individual freedom and privacy as little as possible; also known as minimalism.

Proponents of **libertarianism** would object to being put in the same category as anarchists. Although they are not opposed to government as such, they do agree with the oft-quoted axiom, "That government is best, which governs least" and they tend to be quite dogmatic about it. (For this reason, they are sometimes called *minimalists*.) Libertarians value individual freedom above all and oppose government regulation—even measures aimed at public safety or income security for the elderly. They interpret the right to privacy in the broadest possible way. Thus, doctrinaire libertarians defend the right of a citizen to print and distribute pornographic materials no matter how obscene or repugnant those materials might be to the majority (including most libertarians), and they oppose a military draft on the ground that joining the armed forces ought to be a matter of personal choice.

Ideologies of the Right

At the opposite end of the political spectrum are ideologies like **monarchism** that stress the paramount importance of a central authority and political order. Until the twentieth century, monarchy was the prevalent form of government throughout the world. Whether they were called kings or emperors, czars or sultans, sheiks or shahs, monarchs once ruled the world. Today, **royalists** or **monarchists** are rare, but it was not always so. Aristotle regarded monarchy— rule by a wise king—as the best form of government (although he recognized that wise kings, as opposed to tyrants, were very rare).

However archaic it may look to modern eyes, monarchism is not dead. Jordan, Kuwait, Morocco, Saudi Arabia, and the oil-rich Persian Gulf mini-states, as well as Bhutan, Brunei, and Swaziland, are still monarchies. Jordan and Morocco are limited monarchies; in both countries, the chief executive rules for life by virtue of royal birth rather than merit, mandate, or popular election. Most other countries that still pay lip service to monarchism are, in fact, *constitutional* monarchies in which the king or queen is a figurehead. The United Kingdom is the example we know best in the United States, but Belgium, the Netherlands, Spain, Denmark, Norway, and Sweden all have monarchs as titular rulers.

After World War I, **fascism** superseded monarchism as the principal ideology of the extreme Right. In Germany, National Socialism—more commonly known as **Nazism**—was a particularly virulent form of this ideology (see Chapter 6). Predicated on the "superiority" of one race or nation and demanding abject obedience to authority, fascism exerted a powerful influence in Europe and South America from the 1920s to the 1940s. The prime examples in history are the Axis powers (Germany, Italy, and Japan) in World War II, but other often-overlooked instances of fascism existed in this period as well—Spain, Hungary, and Argentina to cite but three.

Despite its elitist and exclusionary character, fascism enjoyed genuine mass appeal, in part due to its ultra-nationalism. In addition to this heavy stress on the concept of nation or ethnic group (and, in Hitler's case, race), fascism had varied ideological roots, including romanticism, xenophobia, populism, and even a hierarchical, non-egalitarian form of socialism (see below).

One of the distinguishing features of many extreme right-wing ideologies is a blatant appeal to popular prejudices and hatred.[3] Such an appeal often strikes a responsive chord when large numbers of people, who are part of the racial or ethnic majority, have either not shared fully in the benefits of society or have individually and collectively suffered severe financial reversals. In turbulent times, people are prone to follow a demagogue, to believe in conspiracy theories, and to seek scapegoats, such as a racial, ethnic, or religious minority group; an opposing political party; a foreign country; and the like. Xenophobia and antipathy to foreigners, immigrants, and even tourists, has been on the rise in many European countries (including France, Germany, the Netherlands, and the United Kingdom) and in the United States since the 1990s. Remnants of the American Nazi Party and the Ku Klux Klan (KKK) have lingered, as well.

monarchism
A system based on the belief that political power should be concentrated in one person (for example, a king) who rules by decree.

royalist
One who favors absolutism or rule by an all-powerful monarch.

monarchist
One who supports the idea of absolute rule based on divine right or any other principle of hereditary rule; most often associated with pre-modern times, when kings ruled over feudal systems and land ownership was a matter of aristocratic entitlement.

fascism
A totalitarian political system that is headed by a popular charismatic leader and in which a single political party and carefully controlled violence form the bases of complete social and political control. Fascism differs from communism in that the economic structure, although controlled by the state, is privately owned.

© PAT SULLIVAN/AP PHOTO

Hate groups like the Ku Klux Klan feed on ignorance, prejudice, and fear and often use racial or religious differences to create a scapegoat. As human beings, we want simple answers, quick fixes, and someone to blame when things go wrong.

Nazism
Officially called National Socialism, Nazism is a form of fascism based on extreme nationalism, militarism, and racism; the ideology associated with Adolf Hitler and the Holocaust.

This notion of racial superiority, now confined to a lunatic fringe, nonetheless supplies an underlying rationale for a whole range of radical policies dealing with immigration (foreigners must be kept out), civil rights (African Americans, Jews, and other minorities are genetically inferior and do not deserve the same constitutional protections as whites), and foreign policy (threats to white America must be met with deadly force). At the far-right extreme, these groups are organized along paramilitary lines, engage in various survivalist practices, and preach violence. Although the KKK has largely faded from view, it still has die-hard followers, including some in law enforcement. In February 2009, the Nebraska Supreme Court upheld the firing of State Highway Patrol trooper Robert Henderson for his ties to the KKK. The KKK's long history of violence toward African-Americans—symbolized by the white sheets worn by its members and the crosses set ablaze at rallies—has made it synonymous with bigotry and racial intolerance.

The Religious Right The religious right in the United States emerged as an important nationwide political force in 1980. The election as president of a conservative Republican, Ronald Reagan, both coincided with and accelerated efforts to create a new right-wing political coalition in the United States. The coalition that emerged combined the modern political techniques of mass mailings, extensive political fund raising, and the repeated use of the mass media (especially television) with a call for the restoration of traditional values, including an end to abortion, the reinstatement of prayer in public schools, a campaign against pornography, the recognition of the family as the basis of U.S. life, and a drive to oppose communism relentlessly on every front.

This movement contained a core of fundamentalist or evangelical Christians, called the New Right, who saw politics as an outgrowth of their core religious values. Beginning in the 1980s, television evangelists such as the late Jerry Falwell (who spearheaded a movement called the Moral Majority) and Pat Robertson (who ran unsuccessfully for president in 1988) gained a mass following. The far right suffered a setback in 1992 when Pat Buchanan's presidential bid also fizzled.

Many viewed the election of George W. Bush, who openly courted the fundamentalist Christian vote, as a victory for the religious right. Roman Catholics and Southern Baptists, along with other evangelical groups, joined forces in a new kind of coalition against what many regular churchgoers saw as an alarming upsurge in immorality and sinful behavior, including abortion, gay marriage, and the teaching of evolution in public schools. The last issue, along with stem cell research, pitted religion against science.

The Christian Coalition, another conservative group, has roots in the Pentecostal church. Boasting as many as one million members, the Christian Coalition produces and distributes a kind of morality scorecard, evaluating political candidates' positions on key issues from the perspective of religious dogma. Its members focus on getting elected to local school boards in order to advocate for patriotism (as opposed to multiculturalism), religion, and a return to the basics in education.

The Christian Coalition's success raised two serious questions. First, was the Christian Coalition best understood as a well-meaning effort by decent citizens to participate in the political arena, or as a dangerously divisive blurring by

© SHUTTERSTOCK

Republican vice-presidential candidate Sarah Palin addressing a crowd during the 2008 presidential campaign.

capitalism
An economic system in which individuals own the means of production and can legally amass unlimited personal wealth. Capitalist theory holds that governments should not impose any unnecessary restrictions on economic activity and that the laws of supply and demand can best regulate the economy. In a capitalist system, the private sector (mainly business and consumers), rather than government, makes most of the key decisions about production, employment, savings, investment, and the like. The opposite of a centrally planned economy such as existed in the Soviet Union under Stalin and Stalin's successors.

religious bigots of the separation between church and state? Second, was it an interest group or a political party?

The midterm elections in 2006 and the presidential election in 2008 were both resounding defeats for the policies of George W. Bush and the Republican Party, raising the possibility of a popular backlash against the rising influence of religious fundamentalism in U.S. politics. Presidential candidate John McCain's surprise choice of Sarah Palin, the relatively obscure governor of Alaska and an unabashed religious fundamentalist, as his running mate, turned out to be a serious misstep.

So it is likely that the political potency of the religious right in U.S. politics is declining. Some critics even suggest revoking the tax-exempt status of religious establishments that cross the line and transform themselves into political movements.[4]

Capitalism By far the most prevalent and powerful ideology in the United States, Europe, and Asia today is **capitalism.** Even in Communist China, where Maoism remains the official ideology, capitalism is the engine driving the amazing revitalization of the economy since the death of Mao Zedong in 1976 (Figure 2.2). The collapse of communism and its explicit rejection of private property, the profit motive, and social inequality was a triumphant moment for proponents of free enterprise and the free-market economy. Indeed, the Cold

FIGURE 2.2   Since the 1990s, China's economy has made the "great leap forward" that Mao Zedong had promised in the late 1950s but that communism never delivered. Prior to the global recession in 2008–2009, China's share of global GDP was expected to reach 19 percent by 2015, while U.S. and EU shares were expected to continue on a downward trend.

SOURCE: *Economist*, March 29, 2007, at http://www.economist.com/surveys/displayStory.cfm?story_id=8880918.

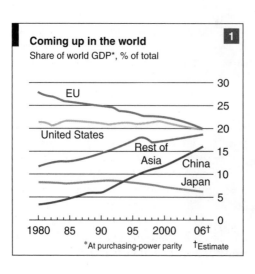

Coming up in the world
Share of world GDP*, % of total

War was in no small measure an ideological contest between the United States and the Soviet Union over this very issue.

In the contemporary world, capitalism is the ideology of mainline conservatives; at the same time, however, it is a basic feature of classical liberalism. In the United States, it is the Republican Party that most enthusiastically embraces capitalism, although few Democrats in Congress ever dare to denounce big business. However disappointing or frustrating this fact may be to some rank-and-file voters, it is not difficult to discern the reasons for it. Capitalism is the ideology of big business, as well as of powerful Washington lobbies, including the U.S. Chamber of Commerce and the National Association of Manufacturers. It also provides the moral and philosophical justification for the often ruthless practices of multinational corporations (MNCs), such as Walmart, Microsoft, McDonald's, and Wall Street financiers, practices that would otherwise appear to be based on nothing more high-minded than the idea that "greed is good." The U.S. actor Michael Douglas won an Academy Award for his performance in *Wall Street*, a 1987 film in which his "Master of the Universe" character spoke those very words.

What is capitalism? It means different things to different people. It can refer to an economic theory based on the principles found in Adam Smith's *Wealth of Nations* (discussed later in this chapter). Or it can mean an ideology that elevates the virtues of freedom and independence, individualism and initiative, invention and innovation, risk-taking and reward for success. We can also view it as an elaborate myth system used to justify the class privileges of a wealthy elite and the exploitation of the workers who produce society's wealth. The latter interpretation, of course, derives most notably from the writings of Karl Marx (see "Communism" section in this chapter).

As an economic theory, capitalism stresses the role of market forces—mainly supply and demand—in regulating economic activity; determining prices, values, and costs; and allocating scarce resources. In theory it opposes government interference, and in practice it opposes government regulation. It applauds the notion that, in the words of President Calvin Coolidge, "the business of America is business." Capitalism's proponents, however, often *assume* we have a free market operating solely on the principles of supply and demand; they seldom consider whether it really exists. In fact, the free market is a myth, useful for public relations or propaganda but not for understanding how modern economies actually work. No modern economy can function without all sorts of rules and regulations. The question is not whether rules are necessary, but rather who makes the rules and in whose interests. The key to the success of a market economy is competition, not de-regulation.

As an ideology, capitalism opposes high taxes (especially on business), social welfare, and government giveaways. Conservatives tend to believe wealth is a sign of success and a reward for virtue. Rich people deserve to be rich. Poverty is the fault of poor people themselves, who are lazy, indolent, and irresponsible. Relieving poverty is the job of charity and the church, not government. Capitalists also tend (or pretend) to believe in the trickle-down theory: if the most enterprising members of society are permitted to succeed and to reinvest wealth rather than handing it all over to the tax collector, the economy will grow, prosperity will trickle down to the lower levels, and everybody will be better off.

Critics of capitalism argue that the free market is a fiction, and that big business only pretends to support deregulation and the increased competition it fosters. Meanwhile it routinely seeks tax favors, subsidies, and regulatory concessions and fights antitrust legislation at every turn. Revelations of large-scale fraud and corruption in recent years, symbolized by such fallen corporate outlaws as Enron and WorldCom, had badly stained the image of U.S. business even before the financial meltdown in the fall of 2008. But then came the failure of major investment firms like Lehman Brothers, Wachovia, and Merrill Lynch in 2008, followed by bailouts of the U.S. automakers and banks teetering on the brink of bankruptcy. The U.S. Justice Department filed criminal charges against prominent financiers such as Bernie Madoff and Robert Allen Stanford for carrying off the biggest financial scams in U.S. history—resulting in massive loss of public trust in business, banks, and Wall Street. One measure of how far the corporate sector had fallen in the public esteem: the insurance giant AIG (American International Group) saw its stock plunge from a 52-week high of $52.25 to a low of 38 cents in February 2009.

Another U.S. company that has given capitalism a bad name in recent years is Halliburton, along with its subsidiary Kellogg, Brown, and Root (KBR). Halliburton was accused of exploiting close ties to former Vice President Dick Cheney to obtain multibillion dollar no-bid government contracts in Iraq, while engaging in unethical or illegal business practices including committing accounting fraud, bribing foreign officials, and operating in Iran despite U.S. government sanctions against doing business there. Cheney, who retired as chair and CEO of Halliburton in 2000 so he could be George W. Bush's running mate, received $34 million in severance pay and another $8 million in stock options from the company.

© CHIP SOMODEVILLA/GETTY IMAGES

Critics of capitalism often allege collusion between big government and big business. In the minds of his critics, former Vice President Dick Cheney, who famously espoused the doctrine that "greed is good," is a notorious case in point. Cheney served as Secretary of Defense from 1989 to 1993. When he left the government he became the chair and CEO of a major defense contractor called Halliburton. Was it a mere coincidence that the U.S. Department of Defense awarded billions of dollars in no-bid contracts to Halliburton to support military operations in Iraq beginning in 2002, and that Cheney, a vociferous war hawk, was then back in the government as the most powerful vice president in U.S. history?

Ideologies of the Left

Left-wing ideologies propose a view of human beings living together coopera-
tively, freed of demeaning and invidious social distinctions. In the realm of economics, these ideologies are often rooted in the principle of **collectivism**, which
holds that the public good is best served by common (as opposed to individual)
ownership and administration of the political community's means of production and distribution.

Collectivism is fundamentally opposed to the theory of capitalism, which
contends that individual ownership of the means of production, in the form of
private wealth (capital), offers the most efficient and equitable way of enriching
the community as a whole. In modern times, the collectivist principle has been
expressed most often in the form of **socialism**, which we can define as "an ideology that rejects individualism, private ownership, and private profits in favor of
a system based on economic collectivism, governmental, societal, or industrial-
group ownership of the means of production and distribution of goods, and
social responsibility."[5]

The French revolutionary François-Noël Babeuf (1760–1797), who advocated economic equality and common ownership of land, is the father of modern
socialism. Babeuf's ideas were adapted and moderated by the so-called **utopian
socialists,** including the Comte de Saint-Simon (1760–1825) and Charles Fourier
(1772–1837), who envisioned an ideal (utopian) society based on collectivism,
cooperation, and benevolence. Louis Blanc (1811–1882), who was active in
worker uprisings in 1848, advocated a more down-to-earth form of socialism,
including the establishment of worker-controlled councils and workshops. Out
of this ferment evolved the theories and methods espoused by most left-wing
ideologies, from revolutionary communism to democratic socialism.

Communism An extreme left-wing ideology, **communism** has also been
named **Marxism** after its founder Karl Marx (1818–1883). Marx and his associate Friedrich Engels (1820–1895) broke with the more benign utopian socialists, asserting that a radical transformation of society could be attained only
by open class conflict. The scientific "laws" of history preordained the conflict's outcome—the overthrow of "monopoly capitalism." Its preference for a
proletarian (working class) revolution distinguishes Marxism, or communism,
from other approaches to socialism.

Marx and Engels opened the famous *Communist Manifesto* (1848) with
the bold assertion, "All history is the history of class struggle." This statement is
based on two premises: (1) economic or material, forces are behind all human
activities, and (2) in history, change and progress are produced by a constant
clash of conflicting economic forces—or, to use the term borrowed from the
German philosopher G. W. F. Hegel (1770–1831), by a process Marxists call
the **dialectic** or **dialectical materialism.** All societies, Marx contended, evolve
through the same historical stages, each of which represents a dominant economic pattern (the thesis) that contains the seeds of a new and conflicting pattern
(the antithesis). Out of the inevitable clash between thesis and antithesis comes
a synthesis, or new economic stage. The Industrial Revolution was, according

collectivism
The belief that the
public good is best
served by common
(as opposed
to individual)
ownership
of a political
community's means
of production and
distribution.

socialism
An ideology
favoring collective
and government
ownership over
individual or private
ownership.

utopian socialist
Individuals who
believed that public
ownership of
property could be
effectively

communism
A political system
based on radical
equality; the
antithesis of
capitalism.

Marxism
The political philosophy of Karl Marx (1818–1883), who theorized that the future belonged to the industrial underclass ("proletariat") and that a "classless society" would eventually replace one based on social distinctions (classes) tied to property ownership. During the Cold War (1947–1991), the term was often mistakenly applied to everyone who embraced the ideology or sympathized with the policies of the Soviet Union or the People's Republic of China against the West.

proletarian
In Marxist theory, a member of the working class.

dialectical materialism
(dialectic) Karl Marx's theory of historical progression, according to which economic classes struggle with one another, producing an evolving series of economic systems that will lead, ultimately, to a classless society.

bourgeoisie
In Marxist ideology, the capitalist class.

law of capitalist accumulation
According to Karl Marx, the invariable rule that stronger capitalists, motivated solely by greed, will gradually eliminate weaker competitors and gain increasing control of the market.

to Marx, the capitalist stage of history, which succeeded the feudal stage when the **bourgeoisie** (urban artisans and merchants) wrested political and economic power from the feudal landlords.

The laws of history (dialectical materialism), which made the rise of capitalism inevitable, also make conflict between capitalists and the proletariat inevitable; the same laws also guarantee the outcome. (We discuss the utopian idea of the classless society in Chapter 3.)

Marxist theory holds that the main feature of modern industrial capitalism is the streamlining of society into two antagonistic classes—the capitalists, who own the means of production, and the proletariat, who have no choice but to work long hours for subsistence wages. The difference between those wages and the value of the products created through the workers' labor is surplus value, or excessive profits, which the capitalists pocket. In this way, capitalists systematically exploit the workers and unwittingly lay the groundwork for a proletarian revolution.

This revolution, according to Marx and his adherents, will come about in the following way. Under the so-called **law of capitalist accumulation**, capitalists must expand at the expense of their competitors or be driven from the marketplace. As the stronger capitalists expand, they eliminate the weaker ones and capture an ever-increasing share of the market. Eventually, the most successful competitors in this dog-eat-dog contest force all the others out, thus ushering in the era of monopoly capitalism, which immediately precedes the downfall of the whole capitalist system. Why should capitalism be overthrown at this stage, when it appears that the monopoly capitalists have taken the reins of power? Because, according to Marx, the gap between rich and poor gets wider and wider. As human labor is replaced by more cost-effective machine labor, unemployment grows, purchasing power dwindles, and domestic markets shrink. This built-in tendency toward business recession and depression, in turn, gives rise to still more unemployment and even lower wages, as the downward spiral continues.

Countless human beings become surplus labor—jobless, penniless, and hopeless. According to the **law of pauperization**, this result is inescapable. For orthodox Marxists, the "crisis of capitalism" and the resulting proletarian revolution are equally inevitable. Because capitalists will not relinquish their power, privilege, or property without a struggle, the overthrow of capitalism can occur only through violent revolution.

The belief that violent mass action is necessary to bring about radical change was central to the theories of Marx's follower Vladimir Lenin (1870–1924), the founder of the Communist Party of the Soviet Union and the foremost leader of the Russian Revolution of 1917. Lenin argued that parliamentary democracy and "bourgeois legality" were mere superstructures designed to mask the underlying reality of capitalist exploitation. As a result, these revolutionaries disdained the kind of representative institutions prevalent in the United States and Western Europe.

With the fall of communism in the Soviet Union and Eastern Europe, **Marxism-Leninism** has lost a great deal of its luster (see Box 2.1). Even so, the doctrine retains some appeal among the poor and downtrodden, primarily due to its crusading spirit and its promise of deliverance from the injustices of "monopoly capitalism."[6] After World War II, communism spearheaded or sponsored "national wars of liberation" aimed at the overthrow of existing

BOX 2.1 FOCUS ON   MARXISM AND DEMOCRACY

FIGURE 2.3   **The leaders of three Latin American democracies (shaded here) have expressed Marxist ideas and adopted anti-capitalist rhetoric and policies. Cuba (also shaded) has been a nondemocratic Marxist state since the late 1950s.**

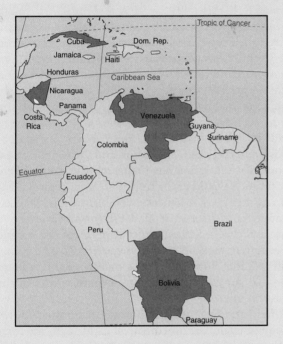

Marxist ideology has never gained a toehold in the United States. Indeed, very few U.S. citizens have any sympathy for socialism or communism to this day. Yet in many other parts of the world, Marxist parties have flourished. In Eastern Europe, China, North Korea, Vietnam, Cuba, and many other Third World countries, Communist or Socialist parties dominated the political scene for most of the second half of the twentieth century. Especially in Africa, Asia, and Latin America, Marxists spearheaded "national wars of liberation" aimed at the overthrow of existing governments.

In many other countries, most notably in Western Europe, non-ruling Communist parties achieved democratic respectability. The Communist parties of France, Italy, and Spain, to cite three examples, were (and still are) legally recognized parties that regularly participated in national elections and, occasionally, in coalition governments, whereas Socialist parties are mainstream political parties throughout Europe.

In the 1970s, Communist Party leaders in Italy and Spain led a movement called Eurocommunism. They sought to change society from within by winning elections, thus downplaying such time-honored tenets of revolutionary Marxism as the advocacy of violent revolution, belief in the dictatorship of the proletariat, and democratic centralism (which demands strict obedience to the party line and forbids dissent).

Although the power and influence of Marxist parties declined after the Berlin Wall was torn down in 1989, it has by no means disappeared. After the "Plural Left" coalition won the French parliamentary elections in May 1997, three Communists were appointed to the cabinet of Socialist Prime Minister Lionel Jospin. In recent years, the elected leaders of Venezuela, Bolivia, and Nicaragua, who are pictured here, have all expressed sympathy with Marxist ideas and have embraced socialist policies.

governments, especially in the Third World. Since the collapse of communism in Europe, however, the revolutionary role played by the Soviet state and Marxist ideology on the world stage has given way to Islamism—not Islam, the religion, but Islamism, an anti-Western ideological offshoot that seeks to restore the moral purity of Islamic societies (see Chapter 15).

law of pauperization
In Karl Marx's view, the rule that capitalism has a built-in tendency toward recession and unemployment, and thus workers inevitably become surplus labor.

Marxism-Leninism
In the history of the Russian Revolution, Lenin's anticapitalist rationale for the overthrow of the czar (absolute monarch) and the establishment of a new political order based on communist principles set forth in the writings of Karl Marx.

democratic socialism
A form of government based on popular elections, public ownership and control of the main sectors of the economy, and broad welfare programs in health and education to benefit citizens.

gradualism
The belief that major changes in society should take place slowly, through reform, rather than suddenly, through revolution.

welfare state
A state whose government is concerned with providing for the social welfare of its citizens and does so usually with specific public policies, such as health insurance, minimum wages, and housing subsidies.

Democratic Socialism As the other main branch of socialist ideology, **democratic socialism** embraces collectivist ends, but it is committed to democratic means. Unlike orthodox Marxists, democratic socialists believe in **gradualism**, or reform, rather than revolution, but they hold to the view that social justice cannot be achieved without substantial economic equality. They also tend to favor a greatly expanded role for government and a tightly regulated economy. Most socialist parties advocate the nationalization of key parts of the economy—transportation, communications, public utilities, banking and finance, insurance, and such basic industries as automobile manufacturing, iron and steel processing, mining, and energy. The modern-day **welfare state**, wherein government assumes broad responsibility for the health, education, and welfare of its citizens, is the brainchild of European social democracy.

The goal of the welfare state is to alleviate poverty and inequality through large-scale income redistribution. Essentially a cradle-to-grave system, the welfare state typically features free or subsidized university education and medical care, generous public assistance (family allowances), pension plans, and a variety of other social services. To finance these programs and services, socialists advocate heavy taxation, including steeply progressive income taxes and stiff inheritance taxes designed to close the gap between rich and poor.

After World War II, democratic socialism had a major impact in Western Europe. Classic examples existed in the United Kingdom and the Scandinavian countries, but the welfare state was (and remains) the norm in Europe, where even the former Communist states are making the transition from central planning and a radically egalitarian society that left little room for a middle class to market economies that mimic the welfare-state model. Ironically, with a few exceptions such as Denmark and Sweden, the political appeal of democratic socialism in Western Europe appeared to be fading in the 1990s. The global recession in the second half of 2008, however, greatly enhanced the popular appeal of social democracy—the flip side of plummeting public trust in the financial markets and business elites.

Until the fall of 2008, democratic socialism as an organized political force had little impact on postwar politics in the United States. In 1932, in the early stages of the Great Depression, Socialist candidate Norman Thomas polled nearly 900,000 votes, but that result amounted to barely more than 2 percent of the total votes cast. Surprisingly, the elections of 1912 and 1920, immediately before and after World War I, rather than the Great Depression era, represent the high-water marks of socialism in the United States.

Why? U.S. adults tend to be individualistic and distrustful of "big government." In addition, they came to identify socialism with communism, communism with Stalinism, and Stalinism with the totalitarian state. After World War II, the Soviet Union became the enemy of the Free World—the "evil empire" as President Ronald Reagan called it. Nonetheless, many public programs that are now firmly entrenched resemble measures associated with the welfare state. Examples include Social Security, Medicare, family assistance, unemployment compensation, and federally subsidized housing. Still, compared with most Europeans, U.S. citizens do pay less in taxes but also get considerably less in social benefits—except for the privileged professional military class, who enjoy cradle-to-grave benefits that would make even the most ardent socialist blush.

IDEOLOGIES AND POLITICS IN THE UNITED STATES

U.S. politics is essentially a tug-of-war between **liberals** and **conservatives**. Because these two terms often generate confusion, and because it is difficult to understand the central issues in U.S. politics apart from the liberal–conservative distinction, let us analyze these two approaches to the public good.

The Uses and Abuses of Labels

U.S.-style liberalism and conservatism evolved from a 300-year-old liberal tradition in Western political thought that sees the safeguarding of individual rights as the central aim and purpose of government. Today, liberals typically stress social and political rights, whereas conservatives highlight economic rights. Liberals and conservatives alike champion freedom and fundamental rights, but they argue about which rights are fundamental. Liberals generally favor narrowing the gap between rich and poor, whereas conservatives tend toward a minimalist definition of equality (for example, equal rights = the right to vote, equal opportunity = the right to basic education, and the like). In general, liberals typically define equality broadly in social, political, and economic terms; conservatives tend to confine equality to the political realm.

Several factors blur the distinction between liberalism and conservatism in the United States. First, although there are always plenty of doctrinaire liberals and conservatives eager to sound off on television talk shows, in practice voters in the United States tend to be more pragmatic than dogmatic. Barack Obama's unsuccessful attempt to reduce partisan bickering and enlist the support of moderate Republicans in dealing with the economic crisis in 2009, however, reminds us that politicians are not always in step with the voters. Second, although politicians often make bold campaign promises, few have been willing to lead the charge for radical reform (for example, campaign finance reform, health care reform, or bank nationalization). Third, liberals and conservatives sometimes come down on the same side of an issue. For example, libertarians oppose restrictions on the sale, display, distribution, or ownership of any kind of reading material, as do most liberals, but there are activists on the left (radical feminists, for example) who favor a ban on "dirty" books, arguing that pornography exploits and degrades women. Of course, many members of the Religious Right also oppose pornography, as do many others who are middle-of-the-road on most other issues.

liberal
A political philosophy that emphasizes individualism, equality, and civil rights above other values (see also conservative).

conservative
A political philosophy that emphasizes prosperity, security, and tradition above other values (see also liberal).

Common Themes

Liberalism and conservatism represent variations on principles found in the political philosophy of John Locke.[7] These principles, enshrined in the Declaration of Independence, hold that all human beings are created equal; that they are endowed with certain unalienable rights, including the rights of life, liberty, and the pursuit of happiness (Jefferson's expansion of Locke's "right to property"); and that government exists to protect these rights. Furthermore, governmental legitimacy derives from consent of the governed rather than royal birth or divine right. When government becomes alienated from the society it exists to serve, the people have the right to alter or abolish it. Indeed, the purposes of government are clearly spelled out in the preamble to the U.S. Constitution: to "…establish Justice, insure domestic Tranquility, provide for the common defence, promote the general Welfare, and secure the Blessings of Liberty." As we are about to discover, however, these stirring words are also an invitation to debate.

Conservatives: The Primacy of Economic Rights

In stressing economic rights and private property, modern-day conservatives echo and expand on arguments first propounded by certain political philosophers in the seventeenth and eighteenth centuries. Early democratic theorists sought the "Blessings of Liberty" in order to break the power monopoly of the monarchy and landed aristocracy. The result was to unleash the economic potential of a nascent middle class and thereby set the stage for the Industrial Revolution.

commercial republic
This concept, found in the Federalist Papers, is most closely identified with Alexander Hamilton, who championed the idea of a democracy based on economic vitality, capitalistic principles, and private enterprise free of undue state regulation.

John Locke (1632–1704) Locke contributed greatly to the idea of the **commercial republic**, an economic concept that forms the core of modern conservatism. Locke declared unequivocally that individuals have a right to property—especially to *earned* income or wealth acquired as a result of hard work and personal merit. For Locke, protecting private property is one of the main purposes of government. Locke thus helped lay the foundations for the commercial state, including such basic concepts as legal liability and contractual obligation.

Many earlier philosophers, from Aristotle to Thomas Aquinas (1224–1274), cautioned against excessive concern for worldly possessions. Locke, in contrast, envisioned a society in which the instinct to acquire goods would be encouraged, the spirit of enterprise and invention would flourish, and money would serve as the universal medium of exchange. Wealth could then be accumulated, reinvested, and expanded. Society would prosper, and a prosperous society, Locke reasoned, would be a happy one.

Baron de Montesquieu (1689–1755) Although Locke developed the general theory of the commercial republic, the French political philosopher Baron de Montesquieu, in his famous *The Spirit of the Laws* (1748), identified a number of specific advantages of business and commerce. In Montesquieu's view, nations that trade extensively with other nations would be predisposed toward peace because war disrupts international commerce. Montesquieu also asserted that commerce would open up new avenues for individual self-advancement; in other words, through hard work and perseverance, even those born into poverty could become wealthy. In addition, an emphasis on commerce would protect society against religious fanaticism, as a preoccupation with creature comforts and "keeping up with the Joneses" would replace the fanatical zeal that leads to religious strife. The final advantage of a commercial order would be its positive effect on individual morality. A commercial democracy, Montesquieu believed, would foster certain modest bourgeois virtues, including "frugality, economy, moderation, labor, prudence, tranquility, order, and rule."[8]

Adam Smith (1723–1790) Following in the footsteps of Locke and Montesquieu, the Scottish "worldly philosopher" Adam Smith set forth the operating principles of the market economy. Smith is the pre-eminent theorist of modern capitalism. He theorized that individual happiness and social harmony are both closely tied to the ways in which goods and services are produced. In his famous treatise, *An Inquiry into the Nature and Causes of the Wealth of Nations* (1776), he explored and explained the dynamics of a commercial society free of regulations or interference from the state. Like Locke, Smith observed that self-interest plays a pivotal role in human relations:

> It is not from the benevolence of the butcher, the brewer, or the baker that we expect our dinner, but from their regard to their own self-interest. We address ourselves, not to their humanity but to their self-love, and never talk to them of our own necessities but of their advantages.[9]

Smith famously theorized about the "invisible hand" of the marketplace, expressed in the *law of supply and demand*. This law, he argued, determines market value. Where supply is large and demand is small, the market value (or price) of the item in question will be driven down until only the most efficient producers remain. Conversely, where demand is great and supply is low, the market value of a given item will be driven up. Eventually, prices will decline as competition intensifies, again leaving only the most efficient producers in a position to retain or expand their share of the market. In this way, the market automatically seeks supply-and-demand equilibrium.

Smith believed self-interest and market forces would combine to sustain economic competition, which in turn would keep prices close to the actual cost of production. If prices did rise too much, producers would be undercut by eager competitors. In this view, self-interest and market conditions make prices self-adjusting: high prices provide an incentive for increased competition, and low prices lead to increased demand and hence increased production.

Finally, Smith's free-enterprise theory holds that individuals voluntarily enter precisely those professions and occupations that society considers most valuable because the monetary rewards are irresistible, even if the work itself is not particularly glamorous.[10] Taken as a whole, these concepts define what has come to be known as ***laissez faire* capitalism**, or the idea that the marketplace, unfettered by central state planning, is the best regulator of the economy. Although the French term *laissez faire*—literally "let do" or "let be"—is often

laissez-faire capitalism
An ideology that views the marketplace, unfettered by state interference, as the best regulator of the economic life of a society.

associated with Adam Smith's philosophy, Smith did not actually use the term. The first known use of this term in an English-language publication appeared in a book entitled the *Principles of Trade* (1774)—written by George Whatley and Benjamin Franklin.

Modern Conservatism Conservatives today champion the right of people to pursue happiness as individuals, emphasizing the right to hold, accumulate, and dispose of property. Conservative political parties and politicians typically represent business interests and corporate industry, arguing along the lines of Smith that the private pursuit of wealth will ultimately lead to public prosperity. Finally, critics fault conservatives for obstructing state regulation even at the cost of consumer safety or environmental protection.

Conservatives argue that the quest for individual affluence brings with it certain collective benefits, including a shared belief in the work ethic, a love of order and stability, and a healthy self-restraint on the part of government. These collective "goods" are most likely to result, they argue, from a political system that ensures the best possible conditions for the pursuit of personal gain.

Two of the most prominent conservative thinkers in the post–World War II period were Friedrich Hayek (1899–1992) and Milton Friedman (1912–2006). Hayek was a leading member of the Austrian School of Economics, who won the Nobel Prize in Economics (with Gunnar Myrdal) in 1974. His book *The Road to Serfdom* (1944) inspired a generation of Western free-market economists, and he became an iconic figure for libertarians in the United States.

It was Friedman, however, who did the most to restore classical liberalism to the pedestal of official economic orthodoxy in the United States (under Ronald Reagan), the United Kingdom (under Margaret Thatcher), and subsequently elsewhere in Europe and beyond. According to *The Economist*, Friedman "was the most influential economist of the second half of the twentieth century . . .

© GEORGE ROSE/GETTY IMAGES

Economist and presidential adviser Milton Friedman embraced Adam Smith's free-market ideas. Friedman advocated low taxes and a minimalist approach to spending and state regulation, while opposing income redistribution schemes, including farm subsidies and welfare programs.

possibly of all of it."[11] In his most famous work, *Capitalism and Freedom* (1962), Friedman argued forcefully that the secret to political and social freedom is to place strict limits on the role of government in the economy. In other words, capitalism is the key to democracy. In this view, it is desirable to minimize government by assigning to the public sector only those few functions that the private sector cannot do on its own—namely, to enforce contracts, spur competition, regulate interest rates and the money supply, and protect "the irresponsible, whether madman or child."

Liberals: The Primacy of Civil Rights

Liberals tend to hold civil rights most dear. They are often vigorous defenders of individuals or groups they see as victims of past discrimination, including racial minorities, women, and the poor. Rightly or wrongly, liberals are often associated with certain social groups and occupations such as blue-collar workers, minorities, gays and lesbians, feminists, intellectuals, and college professors. In general, liberals favor governmental action to promote greater equality in society. At the same time, however, they oppose curbs on freedom of expression, as well as efforts to "legislate morality."

In the classical liberal view, respect for the dignity of the individual is a seminal value. In his treatise *On Liberty* (1859), John Stuart Mill eloquently stated the case for individualism:

> He who lets the world, or his own portion of it, choose his plan of life for him, has no need of any other faculty than the ape-like one of imitation. He who chooses his plan for himself, employs all his faculties. He must use observation to see, reasoning and judgment to foresee, activity to gather materials for decision, discrimination to decide, and when he has decided, firmness and self-control to hold to his deliberate decision . . . Human nature is not a machine to be built after a model, and set to do exactly the work prescribed for it, but a tree, which requires to grow and develop on all sides, according to the tendency of the inward forces which make it a living thing.[12]

Mill was at pains to protect individuality from the stifling conformity of mass opinion. Democracy by its very nature, Mill argued, is ill-equipped to protect individuality, as it is based on the principle of majority rule. Thus, following Mills, liberals point out that defenders of majority rule often confuse quantity (the number of people holding a particular view) with quality (the logic and evidence for or against it) and equate numerical superiority with political truth. In a political culture that idealizes the majority, dissenters are often frowned on or even persecuted.

Liberals value individualism as the wellspring of creativity, dynamism, and invention in society, the source of social progress. Protecting dissent and minority rights allows a broad range of ideas to be disseminated; keeps government honest; and sets up a symbiotic relationship between the individual and society, one that benefits both.

Essential Differences

Liberals and conservatives often hold sharply contrasting views on human nature. Liberals typically accent the goodness in human beings. Even though they do not deny human vices or the presence of crime in society, they tend to view antisocial behavior as society's fault. Thus, liberals believe that to reduce crime, society must alleviate the conditions of poverty, racism, and despair. Human beings are innocent at birth and "go bad" in response to circumstances over which they have no control. If you are raised in a violent, drug-infested, inner-city neighborhood with inadequate police protection, you are far more likely to turn to a life of crime than if you are raised in a comfortable and safe middle-class neighborhood in the suburbs.

Conservatives take a dimmer view of human nature. They argue that human beings are not naturally virtuous; that coercion, deterrence, and punishment are necessary to keep people in line; that individuals differ in motivation, ability, moral character, and luck; and that it is not the role of government to minimize or moderate these differences. Consequently, conservatives are seldom troubled by great disparities in wealth or privilege. By the same token, they are generally less inclined to attribute antisocial behavior to poverty or social injustice. There will always be some "bad apples" in society, conservatives argue, and the only solution to crime is punishment. Liberals, on the other hand, maintain that alleviating poverty and injustice is the best way to reduce crime, and that punishment without rehabilitation is a dead end.

Is change good or bad? Liberals generally take a progressive view of history, believing the average person is better off now than a generation ago or a century or two ago. They adopt a forward-looking optimism about the long-term possibilities for peace and harmony. As they see it, change is often a good thing.

Conservatives, by contrast, look to the past for guidance in meeting the challenges of the present. They are far less inclined than liberals to equate change with progress. They view society as a fragile organism held together by shared beliefs and common values. Custom and convention, established institutions (family, church, and state), and deeply ingrained moral reflexes are the keys to a steady state and stable social order. Like society itself, traditions should never be changed (or exchanged) too rapidly. As Edmund Burke put it, "change in order to conserve."

The "Values Divide" and the War on Terror

The tension between liberals and conservatives escalated into what came to be called a "culture war" or "values divide" in the 1980s.[13] In the 1990s, then Speaker of the House Newt Gingrich launched the "Contract with America"—a conservative agenda aimed at preventing tax increases and balancing the federal budget, as well as a series of congressional reforms. In 2001, a new divide was opened up after the September 11 attacks. The ensuing "war on terror" was framed within a **neoconservative** worldview and carried out by a president bent on making homeland security and the military defeat of international terrorism the twin pillars of U.S. policy.

neoconservative
In the United States, a term associated with the ideology of top advisors and Cabinet members during the presidency of George W. Bush; neoconservatives advocate a strong national defense, decisive military action in the face of threats or provocations, pro-Israeli policy in the Middle East, and a minimum of government interference in the economy. In general, neoconservatives are opposed to federal regulation of business and banking.

war on terror
After 9/11, President George W. Bush declared a worldwide "war on terrorism" aimed at defeating international terrorist organizations, destroying terrorist training camps, and bringing terrorists themselves to justice.

On the economy, President George W. Bush, who pushed through the then-Republican Congress deep tax cuts for corporations and the super-rich, turned a blind eye to escalating budget deficits, to the dismay of many in his own party. Not surprisingly, the tax cuts were opposed by liberal Democrats.

Deep divisions over social issues, such as abortion, gay marriage, and stem cell research, have also contributed to the polarization of the U.S. body politic in the new century. Underlying these issues is a moral disagreement. For conservatives, right and wrong are grounded in a transcendent philosophy or religion, and as such, they are universal and unambiguous. By contrast, the liberal attachment to diversity leads naturally to an attitude of tolerance, reflected in the belief that moral and political decisions are intensely personal matters. For example, most liberals oppose prayer in schools, favor broad legal and social rights for gays and lesbians, and are pro choice on abortion. Most conservatives, on the other hand, argue that banning school prayer, allowing gay marriage, and legalizing abortion are morally wrong. Liberals counter that policies denying individual choice violate what is morally right.[14]

The pivotal role of the religious right in electing George W. Bush president in 2000 and reelecting him in 2004 raised fears in some quarters that "homelanders," or evangelical Protestants, Roman Catholics, and a dwindling but politically overrepresented rural population, were gaining control of government at all levels in the United States. However exaggerated, this fear was not entirely

© KAREN BLEIER/AFP/GETTY IMAGES

During the presidency of George W. Bush, the United States became increasingly polarized over social issues and questions of morality in what pundits called the values divide.

unfounded. In his book *Welcome to the Homeland* (2006), broadcast journalist Brian Mann wrote,

> Let's pause a moment to give due credit . . . Men like George Bush, Tom DeLay, Dennis Hastert, and Roy Blunt translated razor-thin electoral victories—and fragile congressional majorities—into a daringly conservative agenda that conflicts with the urban values of most Americans. In order to pull it off, they manipulated an entrenched political system, and engineered new alliances with groups that had viewed rural evangelicals with deep distrust, like the Roman Catholic Church.[15]

Conservatives have traditionally placed little trust in government, believing that less is more. Where tax-funded public programs are necessary, state and local governments are closer to the people and therefore better suited than the federal government to administer them. This long-standing tenet of U.S. conservatism has recently been called into question, however, as government in the United States became more and more centralized under President Bush.

A somewhat harsh view of human nature predisposes conservatives to be tougher than liberals in dealing with perceived threats to personal safety, public order, and homeland security. Bush's military response to the 9/11 attacks, which at first greatly boosted his popularity ratings, was in keeping with this stance.

Conservatives typically do not share liberals' concern for protecting provocative speech, especially when they perceive the speakers as "radicals." Thus, in the war on terror, liberals have expressed alarm at provisions of the Patriot Act that allow for increased surveillance powers, warrantless searches and seizures, and, in general, invasions of personal privacy long held to be barred by the Fourth Amendment. Section 215 of the act gives FBI agents pursuing an antiterrorism investigation broad power to demand personal information and private records from citizens. The act includes the following paper-thin veneer of judicial review: "Upon an application made pursuant to this section, the judge shall enter" an order. Note the language here: it does not say the judge "shall consider entering an order" but that he or she "shall enter" one. In addition, this law contains a gag rule prohibiting public comment on Section 215 orders. Not surprisingly, libertarians have joined liberals in objecting to what they see as a blatant violation of the Bill of Rights (especially the First and Fourth Amendments). Although Section 215 was set to expire in December 2009, President Obama backed its reauthorization.

Conservatives, Liberals, and Public Policy

Liberals are apt to see opportunities for cooperation, accommodation, and remedial action where conservatives see challenges, threats, and dangers. In foreign affairs, liberals tend to favor reduced defense spending, whereas conservatives tend to follow the adage, "Fear God and keep your powder dry." In domestic affairs, liberals generally believe that government has a responsibility to reduce gross inequalities in wealth and living standards.

Liberals also insist that the rights of the accused be protected even if it means some criminals will escape punishment. The war on terror gave rise to a new controversy over these rights when the Bush administration refused to classify captured alleged terrorists as criminals or prisoners of war, preferring instead to create a new category of detainee—illegal enemy combatants. As such, the government said, these people were entitled to none of the legal protections provided in the U.S. Constitution or under international law.

President Barack Obama has taken a very different (and far more liberal) view in both foreign and domestic policy than his predecessor. Accordingly, he has vowed to close the Guantanamo prison (the notorious "Gitmo") and to stop the practice of extraordinary rendition, whereby suspected terrorists were grabbed anywhere in the world and taken to secret detention centers to be harshly interrogated—or even tortured.

In general, liberals believe democracy can best be served by maintaining a steady vigilance against government encroachment on the constitutional rights of free speech, press, religion, assembly, association, and privacy. Conservatives are equally adamant about the need for limited government to protect individual rights. However, in addition to basic freedoms found in the Bill of Rights, they stress property and corporate rights and oppose government regulation of the economy, except when it is good for business.

Choosing Sides

Politics is often called a game, as in the "game of politics" or the "political game." But the word game implies sport or amusement, whereas politics is serious business. In games, we typically choose sides; we cheer for our team and celebrate when "we" win. In addition, most games have clear winners and losers—they are seldom allowed to end in a tie (hence the extra innings in baseball, overtimes in basketball and football, and the like).

Politics also has winners and losers—for example, in elections. However, many outcomes are not so simple or clear-cut. Winning an election means bearing the burdens of government as well as gaining power. When the winners abuse that power or use it for personal gain or make bad decisions with disastrous consequences, many people can get hurt, and trust in government, a precious thing in itself, is damaged. Thus, choosing sides in politics is, arguably, the most important thing a citizen in a constitutional democracy can do.

But how to choose? Many moderates in the United States do not, in fact, choose. They reject labels altogether, preferring not to be identified as Republicans or Democrats, liberals or conservatives. Moderates often become independents. Roughly 30 percent of the U.S. electorate classify themselves as independent in opinion polls.[16] Independents do not have to choose one political party or the other. They can pick and choose from the "menus" of both parties, deciding where they stand on individual issues rather than choosing a particular ideology.

We can easily fall into the trap of believing there are two (and only two) sides to every argument—one right and the other wrong. But the more adamant or partisan each side becomes, the more likely that the truth will elude both, that it will be found somewhere in the gulf between the two extremes. Why? Because politics, like life itself, is too complicated to be reduced to pat answers, populist slogans, or simple solutions.

GATEWAYS TO THE WORLD: EXPLORING CYBERSPACE

Websites vary greatly in quality and content, and the ethereal realm of cyberspace is constantly changing. The following is a short list of URLs for websites related to various ideologies—just enough to get you started on your very own journey of political self-discovery:

http://flag.blackened.net/revolt/anarchism/

This is a website devoted to Anarchism.

http://www.counterorder.com/

This website offers information about Nihilism.

http://www.libertarian.org/

http://www.libertarianism.com/

These two websites provide information about Libertarianism.

http://www.publiceye.org/eyes/whatfasc.html

This website offers information about Fascism.

http://www.cc.org/

http://www.theocracywatch.org/

These websites offer information about the Religious Right.

http://home.vicnet.net.au/~dmcm/

http://www.lastsuperpower.net/

These websites offer information about Socialism.

http://www.broadleft.org/

http://www.marxists.org/

http://www-formal.stanford.edu/jmc/progress/marxism.html

These websites provide information about Communism.

http://www.dsausa.org/

http://en.wikipedia.org/wiki/Social_democracy

These websites offer information about Democratic Socialism.

http://www.whereistand.com/

This website offers information about Independents.

Note: Wikipedia.org is listed only one time above, but it is a good place to begin any Web search for information on ideologies (as well as many other topics covered in this book). A word of caution is in order, however. Wikipedia.org is not edited like a standard encyclopedia or reference work, and the entries are uneven in quality and reliability.

SUMMARY

Governments seek to attain certain social and economic goals in accordance with some concept of the public good. How vigorously, diligently, or honestly they pursue these goals depends on a number of variables, including the ideology they claim to embrace. An ideology is a logically consistent set of propositions about the public good.

We can classify ideologies as antigovernment (anarchism, libertarianism), right-wing (monarchism, fascism), or left-wing (revolutionary communism, democratic socialism, radical egalitarianism). U.S. politics is dominated by two relatively moderate tendencies that are both offshoots of classical liberalism, which stresses individual rights and limited government. It is surprisingly difficult to differentiate clearly between these two viewpoints, principally because so-called liberals and conservatives in the United States often share fundamental values and assumptions. Conservatives stress economic rights; liberals emphasize civil rights. Conservatives are often associated with money and business on the one hand, and religious fundamentalism on the other; liberals are often associated with labor, minorities, gays and lesbians, feminists, intellectuals, and college professors. However, these stereotypes can be misleading: not everybody in the business world is conservative, and not all college professors are liberal.

Liberals look to the future, believing progress will ensure a better life for all; conservatives look to the past for guidance in dealing with problems. Liberals believe in the essential decency and potential goodness of human beings; conservatives take a less charitable view. These differences are reflected in the divergent public policy aims of the two ideological groups.

KEY TERMS

public good
ideology
anarchism
nihilism
libertarianism
royalist
monarchist
monarchism
fascism
Nazism
capitalism

collectivism
socialism
utopian socialist
communism
Marxism
proletarian
dialectic
dialectical materialism
bourgeoisie
law of capitalist accumulation
law of pauperization

Marxism-Leninism
democratic socialism
gradualism
welfare state
liberal
conservative
neoconservative
commercial republic
laissez-faire capitalism
war on terror

REVIEW QUESTIONS

1. Constitutional governments might define the public good in terms of attaining certain goals. What are these goals?
2. In what sense does the performance of a government depend essentially on its success in promoting the public good?
3. What is ideology? Is it a scientific term that is easily applied to a political analysis? Why or why not?
4. In twentieth-century Europe, communism and democratic socialism vied for popular approval. What are the main points of agreement and disagreement between these two ideological camps?
5. How can we distinguish between a liberal and a conservative in the United States? What fundamental assumptions separate these two ideologies?

RECOMMENDED READING

Bernstein, Edward. *Evolutionary Socialism: A Criticism and Affirmation.* Translated by E. C. Harvey. New York: Schocken Books, 1961.

A classic work espousing the cause of evolutionary socialism.

Friedman, Milton. *Capitalism and Freedom.* Chicago: University of Chicago Press, 1994.

A classic argument in favor of minimal governmental participation in the private sector.

Galbraith, John Kenneth. *The New Industrial State,* 4th ed. Boston: Houghton Mifflin, 1985.

A vigorous argument that concentrated economic power requires a powerful, active government.

Hayek, Friedrich. *The Road to Serfdom.* Chicago: University of Chicago Press, 1956.

A classic attack on the welfare state.

Heywood, Andrew. *Political Ideologies: An Introduction.* New York: St. Martin's Press, 1992.

A comprehensive survey of contemporary ideology.

Hunter, James Davison. *Before the Shooting Begins: The Search for Democracy in America's Culture War*. New York: Free Press, 1994.

Hunter continues (see next entry) his examination of America's culture war, examining the basis of America's political beliefs and contending that this deep split endangers the nation's democratic future.

———. *Culture Wars: The Struggle to Define America*. New York: Basic Books, 1991.

An argument that America is fundamentally split politically according to different moral perspectives.

Mann, Brian. *Welcome to the Homeland*. Hanover, NH: Steerforth Press, 2006.

A searching and introspective explanation for the rise of the religious right in America. The author also explores the political implications of this phenomenon.

Runciman, David. *Political Hypocrisy*. Princeton, NJ: Princeton University Press, 2009.

The author argues that a degree of cunning is necessary to succeed in politics. If the author is correct, it follows that politicians rarely say what they mean or mean what they say—and it's anybody's guess what they actually believe.

Schaeffer, Frank. *Crazy for God: How I Grew Up as One of the Elect, Helped Found the Religious Right, and Lived to Take All (or Almost All) of It Back*. Cambridge, MA: Da Capo Press, 2008.

White, John Kenneth. *The Values Divide*. New York: Chatham House, 2003.

Explores the role values play in U.S. politics.

PART 1

Comparative Political Systems: Models and Theories

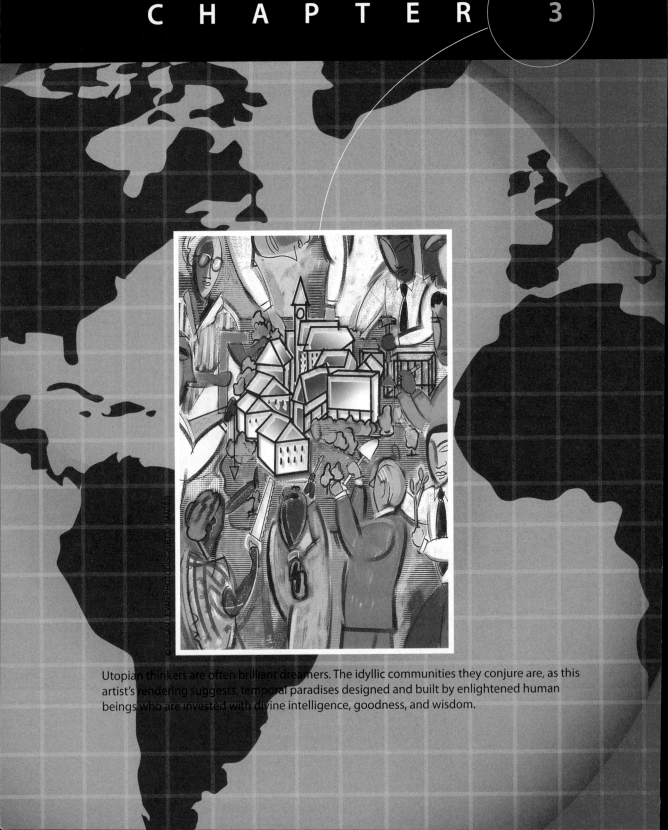

© SUSAN LEVAN/PHOTODISC/GETTY IMAGES

Utopian thinkers are often brilliant dreamers. The idyllic communities they conjure are, as this artist's rendering suggests, temporal paradises designed and built by enlightened human beings who are invested with divine intelligence, goodness, and wisdom.

Utopias
Model States

Plato's Republic: Philosophy Is the Answer
The Just City

The Noble Lie

Francis Bacon's New Atlantis: Science Is the Answer

Karl Marx's Classless Society: Economics Is the Answer
The Centrality of Economics

The Road to Paradise

The Classless Society

B. F. Skinner's Walden Two: Psychology Is the Answer
The Good Life

The Science of Behavioral Engineering

The Behavioral Scientist as God

Utopia Revisited
Utopia and Human Nature

Utopia and the Rejection of Politics

Dystopia: From Dream to Nightmare
Orwell's World

Utopia and Terrorism

As citizens, we often favor (or oppose) policies and leaders because we believe they will (or will not) help make ours a better or more just society. But what constitutes the public good and the good society?[1] If we are to make meaningful comparisons between or among political systems, we need to clarify what the public good is and what it is not. Ideas about utopia found in the writings of philosophers, theologians, and others can help us better understand both the possibilities and the limits of politics. What would the best political order look like? Why is it often said that the best is the enemy of the good? Is it more dangerous in politics to settle for too little or to strive for too much?

The word *utopia* comes from the title of a book written by Sir Thomas More (1478–1535), the lord chancellor of England under King Henry VIII and an influential humanist. More coined the word from the Greek terms *ou topos*, meaning "no place," and *eutopos*, "a place where all is well." Hence, we might say that a **utopia** is a nonexistent place where people dwell in perfect health, harmony, and happiness.

The literature of Western political philosophy contains a number of elaborate utopian blueprints, each of which represents its author's best attempt at formulating the complete and good (or completely good) political order. In the process, utopia inventors have often engaged in implicit and explicit criticism of existing political, social, and economic conditions. Because of this critical function, society can—and does—use utopian constructs as criteria for judging the performance of political systems and as practical guides to political action. Thus, despite its appearance of impracticality, utopian thought serves significant purposes and affects political activities, directly or indirectly.

Our exploration of famous utopias begins with Plato's *Republic*, which we contrast with three later versions of utopia—those found in Sir Francis Bacon's *New Atlantis*, in Karl Marx's "classless society," and in B. F. Skinner's *Walden Two*. Each author finds answers in a different place. For Plato, the answer lies in the realm of philosophy; for Bacon, in science; for Marx, in economics; and for Skinner, in psychology.

There are many other noteworthy examples of utopian literature, including More's *Utopia* (1516) and U.S. writer Edward Bellamy's *Looking Backward, 2000–1887* (1888). There is also a fascinating body of literature on dystopia—well-intended political experiments that went terribly wrong. The purpose of these works, which we review at the end of the chapter, is to demonstrate the danger of trying to build a perfect order in an imperfect world.

utopia
Any visionary system embodying perfect political and social order.

PLATO'S *REPUBLIC*: PHILOSOPHY IS THE ANSWER

Plato's *Republic* takes the form of a long dialogue between Socrates (c. 470–399 BCE) and several imaginary participants. Socrates, considered the first Western political philosopher, held that "the unexamined life is a life not worth living," an idea that has become a cornerstone of Western civilization. As portrayed by Plato (c. 428–348 BCE), Socrates' most brilliant student, Socratic philosophy—the notion that there is no higher purpose than the fearless pursuit of Truth—represents a fundamental alternative to the earlier works of Homer, who praised the virtues of courage and honor, and the later teachings of Jesus, who proclaimed belief in God and moral behavior in accordance with God's word to be the basis of the most exalted life.

Socrates lived for the sake of knowledge unadulterated by power, prejudice, politics, or religion, and in the end he died for it. The rulers of Athens mistrusted Socrates' relentless search for answers to penetrating philosophical questions. Eventually he was accused and convicted of undermining belief in the established gods and corrupting Athenian youth. His execution (by a self-administered drink of hemlock) stands as a poignant reminder of the tension between intellectual freedom and the political order.

In *The Republic*, Plato has Socrates begin with an inquiry into the meaning of justice. He then describes the best political order: a society devoid of all tension between philosophers and rulers.[2] (In such a society, the charges leveled against Socrates would have been groundless. There would be no fear of teachers making youth disloyal, for it would be possible to be both philosophic and patriotic.) The founding and construction of such a city would reflect nothing less than the perfection of political thought.

The Just City

As Plato tells the story, a skeptical listener challenges Socrates to explain why it is better to be just than unjust. Is it not true, he asks, that the successful man who gains power and possessions from unjust actions is much happier than the just man who, like Socrates, has neither power nor possessions? Because justice is easier to identify in a city than in a person, the search for the just city begins.[3]

Socrates first proposes that political life arises from the fact that no individual can be self-sufficient. He then describes a very simple society with no government and no scarcity, whose farmers, shoemakers, and other artisans produce just enough for the perpetuation of a plain and placid way of life. In this society, which seeks to satisfy the basic needs of the body (food, drink, shelter, and so on), each person performs one specialized function.

To avoid monotony, adornments are required. However, the creation of luxury liberates desire and gives rise to restless spirits. The city then becomes "feverish" and needs to expand. Specifically, it must acquire more land, and for that task, soldiers are necessary. The soldiers, who form the second class in the republic, are initially called guardians. They are to protect the *polis* (city or civic society) as sheepdogs protect a flock of lambs.

As described in *The Republic*, the education of the guardians encompasses the entire range of human activities, including the aesthetic, intellectual, moral, and physical aspects of life. Socrates suggests that the purpose of education is to teach the truth. Therefore, it is necessary to censor untrue or dangerous ideas. Strict

BOX 3.1 SPOTLIGHT ON   Ancient Greece: Birthplace of Justice

FIGURE 3.1   The Beginnings of Historic Greece, 700–600 B.C.

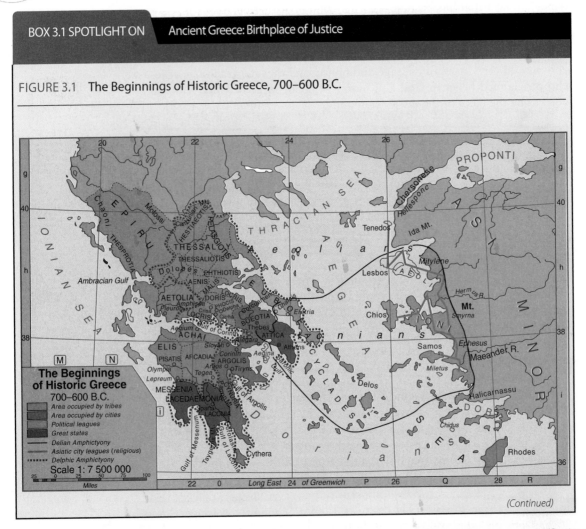

(Continued)

(Continued)

discipline is maintained, and everything is held in common, including personal property and spouses. Love of the community replaces ordinary human love.

At age twenty, some students are designated auxiliaries and assigned the role of defending the city. They will be the republic's soldiers. The others, who retain the name of guardian, continue their education. At the end of a prolonged period of study, a guardian, by understanding the truth of things, may become a philosopher. Supreme in wisdom, philosophers alone are fit to hold the highest offices. Thus, **philosopher-kings** govern the republic.

So Plato's republic is made up of a class of farmers and artisans, a class of warrior-auxiliaries, and a class of philosopher-guardians. Each class embodies one essential virtue. Workers and artisans, who provide for the city's physical necessities, possess moderation. Warrior-auxiliaries possess courage, the

philosopher-king
Wise philosopher who governs Plato's ideal city in *The Republic*.

BOX 3.1 SPOTLIGHT ON *(Continued)*

Ancient Greece was home to Socrates and Plato and the birthplace of political philosophy, thanks in no small part to these two great thinkers. It was the Greeks who invented political philosophy and who placed justice at the very heart of political thought and practice.

Political philosophy is the study of fundamental questions about the state, government, politics, law, and, above all, justice. Indeed, justice is the common thread running through virtually all public policy issues today, but it is often implicit rather than openly acknowledged, despite the fact that we often closely associate justice and liberty. The U.S. Pledge of Allegiance, for example, speaks of "liberty and justice for all."

Of course, justice means different things to different people, depending on the culture and context in which it is used. In the Western tradition, its meaning often depends on whether we use it in a broad or narrow sense. Broadly speaking, justice is essentially a matter of distribution (who gets what, when, and how). In the narrower sense, it is about punishment for breaking the law and about rules of truth and evidence that determine judgments in the law. Today, justice is often couched in the language of political economy (property rights, taxation, contracts, fair trade practices, capital markets, and the like). Although "justice" has

© COMSTOCK/JUPITER IMAGES

been adapted to fit the needs and values of modern society, the concept has been central to Western political thought since at least the time of the ancient Greeks, nearly two and a half millennia ago.

perfection of the spirited part of the soul. Philosophers possess wisdom, or reason. Only philosophers possess a completely excellent soul; every part of their being is perfect, as is the relationship among the parts of their soul. They alone understand justice, the most comprehensive virtue.

Because each component of the republic does its job well (growing food and making things, defending the city, or ruling), and in so doing displays a particular cardinal virtue (moderation, courage, or wisdom), this imaginary city is also considered just.

And what a city it is! One commentator has declared "all of Western man's aspirations to justice and the good life are given expression and fulfillment in

© ROGER-VIOLET/THE IMAGE WORKS

One of the great philosophers of ancient Greece, Plato believed ideal state authority should rest in the hands of the philosopher-king: "Until philosophers are kings, . . . cities will never have rest from their evils."

Socrates' proposals."[4] This is a city where men's and women's faculties are not denied their exercise by poverty, birth, or sex, where the accidental attachments of family and city do not limit a man's understanding and pursuit of the good. It is a regime where wise, public-spirited citizens rule for the common good.[5] All perform the tasks for which they are best equipped and receive recognition and respect in proportion to the value of their contributions.

This utopian city suggests an answer to the original question asked of Socrates: Why is it better to be just? It is the philosophers who are just and who seem the happiest (certainly happier than the unjust), but their happiness does not depend on possessing unjustly obtained power. Because philosophers are just and wise, they can institute otherwise objectionable practices. To ensure that public servants place the public interest above private interests, family relationships are banned among the soldier and guardian classes. A eugenics program provides for state control of human sexual relations and ensures the continued existence of exceptional individuals. The guardian class propagates only through carefully orchestrated "marriage festivals" planned for the sole purpose of collective (and selective) breeding. Nothing is left to chance.

The Noble Lie

To convince the lower class of its proper status, the philosopher-kings are in charge of perpetuating the noble lie on which the just city depends. Thus all citizens (except the philosophers) are told their memories of past experiences are only dreams, and they have actually been beneath the earth, where they were fashioned and trained. When they were ready, their mother, the earth, sent them to the surface. During the formative process, they were given souls fashioned of gold (in the case of philosophers), silver (auxiliaries), or iron and bronze (farmers and artisans). This myth is designed to persuade residents of the republic that they are all brothers and sisters and to ensure popular acceptance of the class system essential to the republic's existence.

In describing his model republic, Socrates uncovers serious difficulties. His model is highly impractical, if not impossible. It comes at a dear price—the abolition of families, the establishment of censorship, the perpetuation of a widespread falsehood regarding the moral basis of the regime, and the rule of philosopher kings who do not desire to rule. For Socrates, rulers who have a lust for power are not fit to rule; he reasoned that philosophers have an unquenchable thirst for knowledge and care not at all for power. Therefore, philosophers were paradoxically best suited to be kings.

Although *The Republic* may not be a blueprint for a future political regime, it is valuable in other respects. Above all, it insightfully explores important political ideas such as justice, tyranny, and education. It also demonstrates a thoughtful model of the best political order, while simultaneously exposing the practical impediments to its implementation. In sum, we should take *The Republic* less as a political prescription than as a philosophical exercise. Socrates' excursion into utopia represents an attempt to perfect human thought, not a formula for the perfection of human deeds.

FRANCIS BACON'S *NEW ATLANTIS*: SCIENCE IS THE ANSWER

The idea that utopias can actually be achieved first gained currency in the seventeenth century. In *The New Atlantis* published in 1627, Francis Bacon describes the imaginary voyage of travelers who discover an island called Bensalem. The travelers have suffered greatly during their long sojourn in the Pacific, and they need food and rest. At first the islanders warn them not to land, but after some negotiations the travelers are allowed to disembark. Their negative first impressions fade as they come to see the island as it really is: a blissfully happy place.

Bacon merely sketched most of the practical details of day-to-day life in Bensalem. Although its envoys have made secret expeditions to Europe to learn about advances in science, the island is otherwise completely cut off from other societies, eliminating the need for self-defense. It is also economically self-sufficient, endowed with abundant natural resources.

Bensalem is a Christian society, but one that emphasizes religious freedom. Members of various religious faiths hold important positions, and toleration is the norm. The foundation of Bensalem society is the family, and marriage and moral behavior are celebrated. An ancient ruler named Solamona, renowned for his benevolence and wisdom, promulgated laws so perfect that some 2,000 years later they still require no revision.

© HULTON ARCHIVE/GETTY IMAGES

Francis Bacon (1561–1626)—English philosopher, scientist, essayist, and statesman—promulgated the idea that science is the key to humanity's comfortable self-preservation: "Nature to be commanded must be obeyed."

Bensalem is also a progressive society. Its best minds are assembled at a great college, appropriately called Solomon's House. There, through experimentation and observation, they apply the rules of science to the discovery of "knowledge of causes, and secret motions of things; and the enlarging of the bounds of human empire, to the effecting of all things possible." In contrast to Plato's Republic, Bensalem pursues knowledge not simply for its own sake but also for the conquest of nature. Greater material comfort, better health, and a more secure and prosperous way of life make up the great legacy of the academy's laboratories, experimental lakes, medicine shops, and observatories. In Bensalem, science can and should be used for "the relief of man's estate."

In many respects, Bacon's seventeenth-century vision seems prophetic. Through science, for example, life expectancy on the island increases dramatically as whole strains of illness are eradicated. New types of fruits and flowers are produced, some with curative powers. Medical treatment undergoes a technological revolution. The Bensalemites' love of learning and science leads to remarkable discoveries that unlock some of nature's darkest secrets—for example, they can predict impending natural disasters.

Scholars disagree about Bacon's true intentions in *The New Atlantis*, but few dismiss him as frivolous or a dreamer. One noted authority sees him as the "first really modern utopian," because Bacon expected his ideal society, based on science rather than on superstition or religious dogma, to come into being.[6] Although his book was not meant to be a precise outline of the future, Bacon envisioned a time and place in which science and social progress, which in his mind go hand in hand, would proceed unimpeded. Bacon's vision of a technological utopia was not a protest against existing society so much as a key to the future, and an invitation to imagine a world where science is set free to bring about the radical improvement of the human condition.

KARL MARX'S CLASSLESS SOCIETY: ECONOMICS IS THE ANSWER

Karl Marx (1818–1883) was also a utopian thinker, but in a different way from Plato or Bacon. Marx's predecessors began with elaborate descriptions of their paradises, and when they engaged in social criticism, it was usually implicit. Marx, by contrast, began with an explicit criticism of existing society and sketched only the broadest outlines of his utopia. Because he considered his worldview to be scientific (that is, the product of empirical observation rather than religious belief or abstract reasoning), Marx would have adamantly objected to any suggestion that his ideas were rooted in visionary thinking.

Nevertheless, the utopian element in Marxism is evident. Unlike earlier utopians, Marx believed his ideal society was not only possible but also inevitable. We can correctly understand the class struggle he envisaged only as the necessary prelude to a utopian life in a promised land of peace and plenty. This prophecy represented to Marx the end product of irresistible forces propelling human history toward its inevitable destiny—the **classless society**.

The Centrality of Economics

The harsh working conditions and widespread suffering associated with capitalism in the mid-nineteenth century provoked Marx's attack on economic inequality. The wealthy commercial and industrial elites—the bourgeois

classless society
In Marxist political theory, the ideal society in which wealth is equally distributed according to the principle "from each according to his ability, to each according to his needs."

© THE GRANGER COLLECTION LTD.

Karl Marx—German philosopher, economist, and revolutionary—believed a just world could be achieved only through the evolution of humanity from a capitalist to a socialist economy and society: "The history of all hitherto existing society is the history of class struggle."

capitalist class—opposed reforms aimed at improving the living conditions of the impoverished working class—the proletariat. Marx's *Das Kapital* is punctuated with vivid descriptions of employment practices that aroused his anger, such as the following:

> Mary Anne Walkley had worked without intermission for 26 1/2 hours, with 60 other girls, 30 in one room that only afforded 1/3 of the cubic feet of air required for them.... Mary Anne Walkley fell ill on the Friday [and] died on Sunday.... The doctor, Mr. Keys, called too late to the death-bed, duly bore witness before the coroner's jury that "Mary Anne Walkley had died from long hours of work in an overcrowded work-room."[7]

To Marx, the death of Mary Anne Walkley was no mere accident. The machinery of capitalism was remorseless: Mary Anne Walkley was just one of many children who would not live to adulthood.

Marx believed economics, or the production and distribution of material necessities, was the ultimate determinant of human life and that human societies rose and fell according to the inexorable interplay of economic forces. He believed Mary Anne Walkley's harsh life and premature death were dictated by the profit-driven economics of the mid-nineteenth century. But the internal progressive logic of capitalism made it equally inevitable, according to Marx, that the superstructures of power built on greed and exploitation would collapse in a great social upheaval led by the impoverished and alienated proletariat.

The Road to Paradise

Marx referred to the first stage in the revolution that would overthrow capitalism as the **dictatorship of the proletariat**. During this time, the guiding principle would be, "From each according to his abilities, to each according to his needs." Private ownership of property would be abolished. Measures would be put into effect that set the stage for a classless society—including a very progressive income tax, abolition of the right of inheritance, state ownership of banks and communications and transportation systems, introduction of universal (and free) education, abolition of child labor, the "extension of factories and instruments of production owned by the State," and, finally, "the bringing into cultivation of waste-lands, and the improvement of the soil generally in accordance with a common plan."[8] Eventually, the state and government as we know it would vanish. In the absence of social classes, class antagonisms would disappear according to Marx's collaborator Friedrich Engels, the role of the state as the arbiter and regulator of social relations would become unnecessary, and "the government of persons [would be] replaced by the administration of things and by the direction of the processes of production." In the end, "The State is not 'abolished,' it withers away."[9]

dictatorship of the proletariat
In Marxist theory, the political stage immediately following the workers' revolution, during which the Communist Party controls the state and defends it against a capitalist resurgence or counterrevolution; the dictatorship of the proletariat leads into pure communism and the classless society

The Classless Society

The natural demise of government, Marx prophesied, would usher in a new and final stage—the classless society. Under capitalism, Marx wrote, "everyone has a definite, circumscribed sphere of activity which is put upon him and from which he cannot escape. He is hunter, fisherman or shepherd, or a 'critical critic,' and must remain so if he does not want to lose his means of subsistence."[10] Under communism, in contrast,

> [when] each one does not have a circumscribed sphere of activity but can train him self in any branch he chooses, society by regulating the common production makes it possible for me to . . . hunt in the morning, to fish in the afternoon, to carry on cattle-breeding in the evening, also to criticize the food—just as I please—without becoming either hunter, fisherman, shepherd or critic.[11]

Marx believed that human beings come into the world with a clean slate, and what is subsequently written on that slate is determined by society rather than by genetic inheritance. Along with individual self-fulfillment, social bliss would blossom in the new order, which would be populated by "loyal, wise, and incorruptible friends, devoted to one another with an absolutely unselfish benevolence."[12] One student of Marxist utopianism observed that its description of communist society shares with most other utopian works a "single ethical core," characterized by "cooperative rather than competitive labor, purposeful achievement for societal ends rather than self-indulgence or private hedonism, and an ethic of social responsibility for each member rather than of struggle for survival of the fittest."[13]

The **withering away of the state** so central to Marxist ideology was thus based on a belief in the natural harmony of interests: Eliminate private property and the division of labor, and you eliminate social inequality. Eliminate social inequality, and you eliminate the cause of armed conflict. Obviously, no class struggle is possible when classes no longer exist. Finally, eliminate armed conflict, and you eliminate the need for the state. After all, past societies were nothing more than human contrivances for the perpetuation of class dominance. With the disappearance of social classes, according to Marx, government as we have known it will simply atrophy as a result of its own obsolescence.

The picture of the future that Marx and Engels presented to the world was indeed captivating—and thoroughly utopian:

> Crime would disappear, the span of life would increase, brotherhood and cooperation would inculcate a new morality, [and] scientific progress would grow by leaps and bounds.

Above all, with socialism spreading throughout the world, the greatest blight of humankind, war, and its twin brother, nationalism, would have no place. International brotherhood would follow.... With the socialist revolution humanity will complete its "prehistoric" stage and enter for the first time into what might be called its own history.... After the revolution a united classless

withering away of the state
A Marxist category of analysis describing what happens after capitalism is overthrown, private property and social classes are abolished, and the need for coercive state power supposedly disappears.

society will be able for the first time to decide which way to go and what to do with its resources and capabilities. For the first time we shall make our own history! It is a "leap from slavery into freedom; from darkness into light."[14]

B. F. SKINNER'S *WALDEN TWO*: PSYCHOLOGY IS THE ANSWER

behavioral psychology
A school of psychological thought that holds that the way people (and animals) act is determined by the stimuli they receive from the environment and from other persons and that human or animal behavior can be manipulated by carefully structuring the environment to provide positive stimuli for desired behavior and negative stimuli for unwanted behavior.

Psychologist B. F. Skinner (1904–1990) was perhaps the most influential contemporary writer on **behavioral psychology**. Skinner believed that all human behavior is environmentally determined, a mere response to external stimuli. His experiments, designed to control animal behavior (including the training of pigeons to play Ping Pong), and his theories about the relationship of human freedom to behavior modification have been the object of both acclaim and alarm. In his fictional work *Walden Two* (1948), Skinner outlined his notion of a modern utopian society. He actually believed it possible to create the society described in *Walden Two* with the tools made available by the new science of human behavior.

The Good Life

As described in *Walden Two*, Skinner's imagined utopia is a world within a world. Its fictional founder, psychologist T. E. Frazier, has managed to obtain "for taxes" a tract of land that previously contained seven or eight rundown farms, conveniently self-enclosed, symbolizing its self-sufficiency.

© CHRISTOPHER S. JOHNSON/STOCK BOSTON

A pioneer in the field of behavioral psychology, U.S. psychologist B. F. Skinner described a utopian society fashioned by the modification of human behavior: "We simply arrange a world in which serious conflicts occur as seldom as possible."

Although concerned about the problem of creating a good society, Frazier disdains philosophy. Difficult questions such as "What constitutes the good life?" he dismisses as irrelevant. "We all know what's good, until we stop to think about it," he declares.[15] For Frazier, the basic ingredients of the good life are obvious: good health, an absolute minimum of unpleasant labor, a chance to exercise your talents and abilities, and true leisure (that is, freedom from the economic and social pressures that, in Frazier's view, render the so-called leisure class the least relaxed of people). These goals are realized in *Walden Two*'s pleasant atmosphere of noncompetitive social harmony.

The Science of Behavioral Engineering

Frazier summed up his view about how to produce individual happiness and group harmony in this way:

> I can't give you a rational justification for any of it. I can't reduce it to any principle of "the greatest good." This is the Good Life. We know it. It's a fact, not a theory. . . . We don't puzzle our little minds over the outcome of Love versus Duty. We simply arrange a world in which serious conflicts occur as seldom as possible or, with a little luck, not at all.[16]

The key word here is "arrange." The *kind* of world to be arranged is of only passing interest to Frazier; what commands his attention is the question of *how to do* the arranging. He is concerned not with ends but with means, not with philosophy but with scientific experimentation. He is the quintessential methodologist.

Because political action has not helped build a better world, "other measures" are required. What other measures? A revolution in the science of behavior modification:

> Considering how long society has been at it, you'd expect a better job. But the campaigns have been badly planned and the victory has never been secure. The behavior of the individual has been shaped according to revelations of "good conduct," never as the result of experimental study. But why not experiment? The questions are simple enough. What's the best behavior for the individual so far as the group is concerned? And how can the individual be induced to behave in that way? Why not explore these questions in a scientific spirit?[17]

The Walden Two experiment represents this kind of scientific exploration. Initially, Frazier develops an experimental code of good behavior. Everyone is expected to adhere to it under the supervision of certain behavioral scientists (such as Frazier) called managers. Positive reinforcement, rather than punishment, helps instill behavioral patterns, and a system of finely tuned frustrations and annoyances eliminates the destructive emotions of anger, fear, and lust. For example, to engender self-restraint Frazier has the schoolteachers hang lollipops around the children's necks which they are not to lick. Such **behavioral engineering** will prove successful, Frazier asserts, not because it

behavioral engineering The carefully programmed use of rewards and punishments to instill desired patterns of behavior in an individual or an animal.

physically controls outward behavior but because the conscious manipulation of stimuli effectively influences "the *inclination* to behave—the motives, the desires, the wishes."[18]

To ensure proper socialization and the elevation of community, children are placed in a scientifically controlled environment from infancy. They are raised in nurseries and never live with their parents. (Nor do their parents live with one another.) Private property is abolished, all eat together in common dining halls, and boys and girls marry and have children at fifteen or sixteen.

The Behavioral Scientist as God

Much that is familiar in the outside world is notably absent at Walden Two. Although its residents feel free, there is no freedom in this community. The idea of freedom is illusory, Frazier argues, because all behavior is conditioned. History is viewed "only as entertainment"; schoolchildren do not even study this "spurious science." Religion is not forbidden, but, like government in Marx's utopia, it has withered away through social obsolescence ("Psychologists are our priests," Frazier asserts). Moral codes of right and wrong have given way to "experimental ethics." Politics has no value: "You can't make progress toward the Good Life by political action! Not under any current form of government! You must operate upon another level entirely."[19]

Life at Walden Two has, in fact, been organized to create the most propitious circumstances for the managers' experiments in behavior modification. Although Frazier justifies this on the basis of increased human happiness, we are left with the gnawing sense that something significant is missing—some sort of check on the power of the behavioral engineers who run the community. Power will not corrupt the managers, we are told, for they "are part of a noncompetitive culture in which a thirst for power is a curiosity."[20] They do not use force (nobody does at Walden Two), and the offices they hold are not permanent. These reassurances have a hollow ring, however. Clearly, the love of power—an obsessive need to control others—is not absent from Frazier's own soul. As the founder of Walden Two, he appears to view himself as a kind of messiah who has discovered the secret to a whole new way of life: "I look upon my work and, behold, it is good."[21] Frazier is the ultimate "control freak"; a mere mortal who would be God.

UTOPIA REVISITED

In every utopia we have examined, conflicts, jealousies, rivalries, rancorous disputes, and individual frustrations have ceased to be. No deep-seated tensions divide individuals; no great antagonisms exist between society and the state. Each of these ideal states, however, is inspired by a different vision and is ordered according to a different plan.

In *The Republic*, Plato explored the limits of human perfection; he sought not only to depict his idea of the best political order but also to make clear the problems in attempting to bring it about. Bacon wrote *The New Atlantis* to show not the limits of human achievement but the possibilities that a society wholly predicated on modern science might achieve. His is a hopeful work that promises tangible improvement in human welfare.

Without the promise of a classless society at the end of the road, the violence and suffering Marx believed were inevitable to accompany the end of capitalism would seem senseless. His utopia, a necessary part of his worldview, provides a beacon of hope in an otherwise dark vision of revolution and struggle. Skinner's *Walden Two*, by contrast, sought to demonstrate how a rational and scientific approach to behavior modification could produce dramatic social improvements.

To create a completely happy and harmonious world, a writer must postulate a breakthrough in the way society is constituted. As we have seen, Plato saw philosophy as the key. His republic could not exist until or unless the wisest philosophers ruled (an unlikely prospect at best). Not so with Bacon, for whom technical mastery of the scientific method, not a quest for human knowledge, would blaze the trail. For Marx, philosophy and science were overshadowed by economics; non-exploitative economic relationships, he believed, would guarantee a peaceful and plentiful world. Finally, Skinner viewed the scientific manipulation of human behavior as the key to social and personal fulfillment.

With the advent of modern science and technology, some political thinkers began to take more seriously the practical possibility of achieving utopia. Armed with increasingly sophisticated tools—a new science, a new economics, and a new behavioral psychology—utopian thinkers such as Bacon, Marx, and Skinner began to view heaven on earth as something more than an implausible pipe dream. In sum, utopias have often assumed the form of blueprints for the future. Underlying them are certain shared assumptions about human beings and what is best for them. Let's examine these assumptions.

Utopia and Human Nature

According to one interpretation of *The Republic*, Plato understood that even if an ideal state could be brought into existence, it could not last indefinitely; it would degenerate. Why? The answer is simple logic. If utopia is the best form of government possible, any change is change for the worse. But no one has figured out how to stop the world from changing.

Then there is the problem of **human nature**. If people are to live together in peace and harmony, all-too-human traits such as lust, greed, malice, and caprice must be eradicated, sublimated, or suppressed. Not surprisingly, utopian thinkers have often sought ways to reengineer the human heart and

human nature
The characteristics that human beings have in common and that influence how they react to their surroundings and fellow humans.

eugenics
The science of
controlling the
hereditary traits in a
species, usually by
selective mating, in an
attempt to improve the
species.

instincts—through **eugenics**, compulsory education, and abolition of private property. Most utopians assume human selfishness is caused by institutions that protect, sanction, and perpetuate inequalities, and that we can eliminate these institutions only by a fundamental reordering of society. In many utopias, therefore, communal activities, common residences, and public meals replace the private ownership of property in the hope that cooperation will triumph over competition.

Utopia and the Rejection of Politics

If utopians are correct that environment can influence individuals so profoundly, then malleable humans are capable not only of moral perfection but also of moral corruption. Any flaw in the construction of a utopia can therefore turn a dream into a nightmare.

In almost every utopia (including Marx's dictatorship of the proletariat stage), political power is centralized, giving utopian governments powerful tools with which to control human behavior. By themselves these tools are neutral; everything depends on how they are used—wisely or foolishly, efficiently or wastefully, morally or immorally. Utopian thinkers tend to assume they will always be used benignly. But given the power of the modern technocratic state and the malleability of human nature, this assumption seems tenuous at best. What troubles many critics of utopian schemes is not only their concentration of power but also the total absence of checks and balances on that power.

Utopian thinkers generally display little interest in politics and government or in reconciling the conflicting claims of power and justice. Given material abundance, public-spirited citizens, and little or no conflict between human desires and well-being (or between socioeconomic equality and individual excellence), achieving social justice becomes a technical, rather than a political, problem. Indeed, the nuts and bolts of actual governments—mechanisms for separation of powers, checks and balances, judicial review, and so forth—hold little or no interest for most utopians.

dystopia
A society whose creators
set out to build the
perfect political order
only to discover that
they cannot remain
in power except
through coercion
and by maintaining
a ruthless monopoly
over the means of
communication.

DYSTOPIA: FROM DREAM TO NIGHTMARE

The dangers of unchecked political power, and the more general theme of utopia-turned-nightmare, are vividly developed in such well-known works as George Orwell's *Nineteen Eighty-Four* (1949) and Aldous Huxley's *Brave New World* (1932). Both books, as well as more recent literary utopias such as Margaret Atwood's *The Handmaid's Tale*, P. D. James's *Children of Men*, Cormac McCarthy's Pulitzer–Prize-winning *The Road*, and Lois Lowry's *The Giver*, provide graphic descriptions of a **dystopia**, or a society whose creators set out to build a perfect political order only to discover that, having promised the impossible, they could remain in power only by maintaining a ruthless monopoly through coercion and communication.

Orwell's World

In *Nineteen Eighty-Four*, the totalitarian rulers (personified by a shadowy figure called Big Brother) retain power by manipulating not only the people's actions and forms of behavior but also their sources and methods of thought. Thus, the Ministry of Truth is established for the sole purpose of systematically lying to the citizenry; a new language ("Newspeak") is invented to purge all words, ideas, and expressions considered dangerous by the government; and a contradictory kind of logic ("double-think") is introduced to make the minds of the citizenry receptive to the opportunistic zigzags of official propaganda.

According to the official ideology, the purpose behind state terror, strict censorship, and constant surveillance is to prevent enemies of the revolution from stopping the march toward full communism—a worker's paradise in which everyone will be happy, secure, prosperous, and equal. In theory, the masses are finally put in control of their own destiny; in practice, they become a new class of slaves whose fate is in the hands of the most ruthless tyrant(s) imaginable.

Utopia and Terrorism

In Chapter 15, we explore the nature of terrorism and its impact on domestic and international politics in the contemporary world. Acts of terror are often associated with religious or ideological zeal, especially when they include the ultimate sacrifice, as in the case of suicide bombers. At least one scholar sees a close connection between the utopian quest for social justice and the Islamist glorification of "martyrs."[22]

We might well wonder what could possibly motivate another human being to carry out a mission that is at once barbaric and self-destructive, like the September 11, 2001, attacks on the World Trade Center and the Pentagon, the horrific commuter train bombings in Madrid in March 2004, or the London subway bombings of July 2005. Indeed, terrorist attacks against civilians continue on a daily basis in Iraq and all too frequently in other parts of the world. Such acts are shocking and difficult to understand. What motivates a group of people to plan, prepare, and finally execute a mass murder based on a joint suicide pact?

There is no simple answer. It is quite likely that some terrorists are motivated by a perverted idea of the possible, a misguided sense of what could be if only the imagined source of all evil were annihilated.[23] The identity of the targeted "evil" is almost incidental. Extremists who imagine a time when, for example, Islamic societies were pure and unadulterated—a time before Western ideas, values, music, money, and military occupation corrupted the faithful—can too easily find a justification for killing innocent people in the name of a higher purpose. It is a disturbing fact that in modern history a longing for utopia, a place on earth where happiness knows no limits, is often associated with violence that knows no limits either.

 GATEWAYS TO THE WORLD: EXPLORING CYBERSPACE

http://users.erols.com/jonwill/utopialist.htm

This site is a virtual gateway to information on utopias. Visitors will find an impressive list of websites broken down into useful categories.

http://utopia.nypl.org/Pt1exhibit.html

Maintained by the New York Public Library, this site contains artwork, information on utopian literature, and related links. The site notes, "In the ongoing search for the ideal society, the Internet has been proposed as a 'place' in which an ideal society could exist." It also affords visitors an opportunity to take a poll that encourages the user to think about and give an opinion on the Internet as a utopia.

http://www.levity.com/alchemy/atlantis.html

Online text of Francis Bacon's *New Atlantis*.

http://classics.mit.edu/Plato/republic.html

Online text of Plato's *Republic*.

http://www.luminarium.org/renlit/tmore.htm

Site devoted to Thomas More. Includes online text of More's *Utopia*.

http://www.constitution.org/jh/oceana.htm

Online text of James Harrington's utopian work, *The Commonwealth of Oceania* (1656).

http://xroads.virginia.edu/~HYPER/BELLAMY/toc.html

Online text of Edward Bellamy's *Looking Backward: 2000-1887*.

To do more research into utopias and dystopias on the Web, use the keywords *utopia* or *dystopia* with two or three different search engines. Also, try combining these key words with other search terms, such as "utopia and ideology" or "utopia and terrorism."

SUMMARY

In the sixteenth century, Sir Thomas More coined the term *utopia* to signify an imaginary society of perfect harmony and happiness. More's *Utopia* was a subtle attack on the ills of English society under Henry VIII. The first important attempt to define the "perfect" political order, however, had been made by Plato in *The Republic*.

Four works stand out as representative of utopian thought in the history of Western political philosophy. In *The Republic*, Plato sought the just society through philosophical inquiry. In the seventeenth century, Francis Bacon's *New Atlantis* demonstrated how the human condition could be elevated through modern science. Karl Marx later propounded the view that only through the radical reorganization of economic relationships within society could true justice and an end to human misery be achieved. The ultimate aim of Marx's theory of social transformation is the creation of a classless society. Finally, in B. F. Skinner's *Walden Two*, a prime example of a contemporary utopian scheme, behavioral psychology holds the key to utopia. The form and content of the just society were of less concern to Skinner than the methods for bringing such a society into existence.

Thoughts of utopia have been inspired by idealism and impatience with social injustices. However, its presumed desirability conflicts with its practical possibility. The principal obstacle to utopian society is the unpredictability and selfishness of human nature, which utopian thinkers commonly have sought to control through eugenics programs, compulsory education, and the abolition of private property.

Utopian visionaries often blame politics for the failure to improve society. As a result, in many utopian blueprints, the role of politics in bringing about desired change is either greatly reduced or eliminated entirely. This leaves most utopian schemes open to criticism, for they could easily become blueprints for totalitarianism. Such blueprints often take shape in writings about dystopias—utopias that turn into nightmares.

KEY TERMS

utopia	classless society	behavioral engineering
philosopher-kings	withering away of the	human nature
dictatorship of the	state	eugenics
proletariat	behavioral psychology	dystopia

REVIEW QUESTIONS

1. What is the origin of the term *utopia*? What does the word mean?
2. How have utopian writers differed about the practicality of utopia?
3. Utopian writers often make certain basic assumptions about human nature and society. What are they? Which if any do you agree with and why?
4. What can the study of utopian thought teach us about politics in the contemporary world?

5. In the twentieth century, totalitarianism has greatly influenced certain novelists who have produced chilling stories that turn utopia upside down. Describe one fictional dystopia about which you have read. What, in the novelist's view, brought it into being?

RECOMMENDED READING

Atwood, Margaret. *The Handmaid's Tale*. New York: Everyman's Library, 2006.

In this grim tale, the state has total control and is out of control; sterility is the norm; and fertile women are treated as cattle, producing children for the upper class, which cannot have any.

Bacon, Francis. *The New Atlantis and the Great Instauration*, 2nd ed. Wheeling, W.V.: Harlan Davidson, 1989.

Bacon's seventeenth-century account of a society blessed by scientific breakthroughs is surprisingly modern.

Berman, Paul. "Terror and Liberalism," *The American Prospect*, vol. 12, no. 18, October 22, 2001.

Gilison, Jerome. *The Soviet Image of Utopia*. Baltimore, MD: Johns Hopkins University Press, 1975.

An insightful discussion of the idealist elements in Marxist–Leninist ideology.

Hertzler, Joyce. *The History of Utopian Thought*. New York: Cooper Square Publishers, 1965. An excellent survey of utopian thinkers and their ideas throughout history.

Huxley, Alduous. (Foreword by Christopher Hitchens). *Brave New World and Brave New World Revisited*. New York: Harper Perennial Modern Classics, 2005.

Originally published in 1932, this book is a literary masterpiece that paints a dark portrait of a future world created by the unchecked progress of modern science and the technocratic state.

James, P. D. *The Children of Men*. New York: Vintage, 2006.

"Early this morning, 1 January 2021, three minutes after midnight, the last human being to be born on earth was killed in a pub brawl …" Thus begins the story of a society in which the human sperm count inexplicably fell to zero in 1995, setting the stage for all sorts of perverse policies and practices. (For example, the infirm are encouraged to commit suicide, criminals are exiled and abandoned, and immigrants are enslaved.)

Kateb, George. *Utopia and Its Enemies*, rev. ed. New York: Schocken Books, 1972.

A sympathetic defense of the value and contributions of utopian thought.

Lowry, Lois. *The Giver*. New York: Laurel Leaf, 2002.

A 12-year-old living in a world where poverty, unemployment, crime, and disease are nowhere to be found, and chosen to be the community's Receiver of Memories, discovers the truth about his utopian society and decides the price of maintaining a perfect peace and order is too high; a story about hypocrisy, tyranny, and human dignity.

McCarthy, Cormac. *The Road*. New York: Vintage (paperback edition), 2008.

Some sort of cataclysmic event involving "light and then a low series of concussions" has left cities burned, the earth denuded, and most life forms on the edge of extinction. In this bleak landscape, an unnamed man and his son walk to the sea. The man tells his son that they are "good guys," but in the ensuing struggle for survival, the man's actions belie his words.

More, Thomas. *Utopia*. Translated by Paul Turner. Baltimore, MD: Penguin, 1965.

More's imaginary society inspired many later utopian writers; the work remains a charming account of one man's paradise.

Orwell, George. *Nineteen Eighty-Four*. New York: New American Library, 1961.

A classic novel that brilliantly describes a dystopia modeled after Stalin's Soviet Union.

Plato. *The Republic*. Translated by Allan Bloom. New York: Basic Books, 1991.

Bloom's literal interpretation and interpretive essay help make this edition of Plato's classic work especially valuable.

Popper, Karl. *The Open Society and Its Enemies*. Princeton, N.J. Princeton University Press, 1966.
This work argues that Plato and Marx (among others) were advocates of totalitarian government and opponents of free, democratic societies.

Skinner, B. F. *Walden Two*. New York: Macmillan, 1976.

A fictionalized account of a small community founded and organized according to the principles of behavioral psychology.

The Declaration of Independence and Philadelphia's Independence Hall—a brief document and a modest building—are two famous symbols of American democracy.

STEEL SPIEGEL/CORBIS

Constitutional Democracy
Models of Representation

Liberal Democracy: Models and Theories

Republics and Constitutions

The Idea of America

Four Models of American Democracy

Alexander Hamilton: Federalism

Thomas Jefferson: Anti-Federalism

James Madison: Balanced Government

John C. Calhoun: Brokered Government

Back to Basics: Federalism and the Separation of Powers

Tocqueville: The Tyranny of the Majority

John Locke: The Rule of Law

Constitutionalism and Due Process

Remodeling Democracy: Have It Your Way

**The Future of Democracy: Nationalism
or Cosmopolitanism?**

Cosmopolitan Democracy

Democracy in a New World Order

Constitutional democracy is "government by the people"—a government that relies, in the words of the American Founders, on a "scheme of representation." In common usage, the term *democracy* is shorthand for **constitutionalism**, denoting a broad allegiance to a set of universally known rules. Most of the time, these rules are written down, like the U.S. Constitution, and enjoy special status as the supreme law of the land—that is, above ordinary statutory law.

Democracies almost invariably rest on constitutional foundations and typically feature elections, representative assemblies (legislatures), an independent judiciary, a free press, and various other institutional constraints on executive power. Successfully cultivating a political culture that enshrines constitutionalism at its core appears to be a major key to the success of democracies.

constitutionalism
The concept that the power and discretion of government and its officials ought to be restrained by a supreme set of neutral rules that prevent arbitrary and unfair action by government; also called constitutionalism.

LIBERAL DEMOCRACY: MODELS AND THEORIES

Democracy means different things to different people. One prominent political scientist has identified no fewer than nine different models of democracy—four "classical" forms and five "contemporary" ones, including a new model he calls "cosmopolitan democracy."[1] One of the oldest, or classical, models is **direct democracy**, which, in ancient Greece, encompassed a small city-state (Athens) in which citizens (all those entitled to vote) participated directly in political deliberations and decision making. Another classical model is the **republic**, a form of limited democracy more suitable to a large state and pioneered by the Romans in ancient times. Governance in the Roman Republic required elections and two representative bodies (a senate and an assembly), but it was not very democratic by today's standards. The modern form of republican government is **constitutional democracy**, which stresses political equality and individual liberties. A modern democracy, by definition, is a competitive marketplace of ideas and interests.

Political scientist Richard Katz has developed a useful "typology of liberal democratic theories."[2] Katz's typology underscores two key questions. First, is a given society by nature stable or volatile? For a variety of historical, cultural, and demographic reasons, some societies are—or appear to be—more governable than others. Second, do the elites or the masses pose the greatest danger to democracy? Figure 4.1 shows how six different observers—including two famous figures in U.S. history, a British philosopher, and three twentieth-century scholars—came up with different theories of democracy corresponding to these two basic questions.

Two of these theorists, Jeremy Bentham and Joseph Schumpeter, tended to view society as a single undifferentiated mass of individuals rather than as a collection of groups, classes, or factions. The other four believed society is divided or segmented (differentiated), although they differed on exactly how, and what this differentiation means. Two—James Madison and Robert Dahl—believed society is pluralistic, containing many groups, but stressed that individuals

direct democracy
A form of government in which political decisions are made directly by citizens rather than by their representatives.

republic
A form of government in which sovereignty resides in the people of that country, rather than with the rulers. The vast majority of republics today are democratic or representative republics, meaning that the sovereign power is exercised by elected representatives who are responsible to the citizenry.

constitutional democracy
A system of limited government, based on majority rule, in which political power is scattered among many factions and interest groups and governmental actions and institutions must conform to rules defined by a constitution.

FIGURE 4.1   Katz's Typology of Liberal Democratic Theories

Source: Richard S. Katz, "Models of Democracy: Elite Attitudes and the Democratic Deficit in the European Union." An unpublished paper presented at a meeting of the European Consortium of Political Research, Copenhagen, April 2000.

	Greatest Danger from the Elite	*Greatest Danger from the Masses*
Homogenous society	Jeremy Bentham (1)	Joseph Schumpeter (2)
Crosscutting cleavages	James Madison (3)	Robert Dahl (4)
Segmented society	John Calhoun (5)	Arendt Lijphart (6)

(1) Jeremy Bentham, *Principles of Civil Code and Constitutional Code*, 2 vols. (New York: Russell & Russell, 1962).

(2) Joseph Schumpeter, *Capitalism, Socialism and Democracy* (New York: Harper & Row, 1962).

(3) James Madison, *The Federalist* (New York: Modern Library, 1964).

(4) Robert Dahl, *Polyarchy* (New Haven, Conn.: Yale University Press, 1971).

(5) John Calhoun, *Disquisition on Government* (New York: Peter Smith, 1943).

(6) Arendt Lijphart, *Politics of Accommodation* (Berkeley: University of California Press, 1968).

belong to more than one group. This overlapping membership creates *crosscutting cleavages*. In other words, individuals identify simultaneously with various groups and organizations, such as town, city, suburb, neighborhood, school, church, or synagogue. The other two—John Calhoun and Arendt Lijphart—viewed society as segmented rather than fragmented. This means crosscutting cleavages, to the extent they exist at all, cannot break down the barriers that divide groups and interests in society.

The political implications of these different conceptions of society become clearer when we ask the second question: What is the greatest danger to democracy? For Bentham, who advocated "the greatest good for the greatest number," the economic and social elites threaten democracy, whereas for Schumpeter, the masses clamoring for socialism or a welfare state are the problem. In Schumpeter's view, democracy cannot endure without capitalism as the vital source of economic growth and development. In effect, in this model, the marketplace is the key to the success of democracy. But because the masses oppose capitalism and ultimately prevail in a democratic system, Schumpeter was pessimistic about democracy's future.

For the other four theorists, *pluralism* in society is more important than class distinctions. As Figure 4.1 indicates, however, they differ in terms of who and what poses the greatest threat to democracy. Madison and Calhoun saw the elites as the main danger, whereas Dahl and Lijphart saw the masses as the greatest threat.

Clearly, democracy is complex and controversial. The type of liberal democracy we choose depends on a larger political theory that takes account of human nature and makes a judgment about the main threat(s) to peace, security, and stability. Next we take a closer look at republics and democratic constitutions.

REPUBLICS AND CONSTITUTIONS

Countries as diverse as France, Poland, India, South Africa, Brazil, and Mexico are all examples of constitutional democracy in action. Official names, such as the German Federal Republic or the Republic of South Korea, reflect the fact that the essence of modern democracy is representation. For this reason, nothing is more vital to the political life of republics than regular elections based on the right to vote and the secret ballot. It is easy to forget that in the past many people in many places fought and died for this right. Today, more people enjoy the right to vote in more places than at any other time in the history of the world.

But even where the people are the ultimate source of political power, they cannot simply do anything they wish. Every existing democracy imposes limitations on majority rule. These limitations often take the form of minority rights—that is, rights guaranteed even to citizens who are totally out of step with the majority. By the same token, those in power cannot do whatever they wish either, thanks to checks and balances written into the constitution. Constitutions lay out the basic organization and operation of governments, assign powers, and set limits to the exercise of those powers. Most contemporary democracies have written constitutions, but they differ greatly in age and length, as well as in content. Some, like those of the United States and France, are models of brevity. Others, including those of India and Kenya, are lengthy and detailed. India's constitution differentiates governmental powers into federal (97), state (66), and concurrent (47). Kenya's constitution is so explicit in allocating authority between the central and regional governments that it covers such subjects as animal disease control, the regulation of barbers and hairdressers, and houses occupied by disorderly residents.

concurrent powers
Joint federal and state control.

The United Kingdom, the mother of all parliamentary systems, does not have a formal, written constitution. Instead, the British constitution is inscribed in the minds and hearts of the British people. It is a deeply ingrained consensual social contract consisting of custom and convention, and certain bedrock principles found in historic documents, royal decrees, acts of Parliament, and judicial precedent.

Constitutional democracies must satisfy three competing, and sometimes conflicting, requirements. First, because such governments are democratic, they must be *responsive* to the people. Second, because they are governed in accordance with established rules and procedures, they are *limited* in the goals they can pursue and the means by which they can pursue them. Finally, like all governments, constitutional democracies cannot succeed or long survive unless they are *effective* in maintaining law and order, managing complex economies, and protecting the civilian population against external threats, such as incursions and invasions by foreign armies, as well as violent crime, natural disasters, and terrorism.

THE IDEA OF AMERICA

The United States is the birthplace of the first modern theory of representative democracy ever put into practice. From its inception, it was not perfect, but it was a daring departure from the past and a bold attempt to reshape the future,

BOX 4.1   Philadelphia: Birthplace of Liberty

FIGURE 4.2   Map of colonial America. Philadelphia, Boston, and New York were the three major cities. Washington, D.C., did not come into being until after the U.S. Constitution was adopted in 1788.

On July 4, 1776, the Continental Congress, which met in Philadelphia, Pennsylvania, adopted the Declaration of Independence—an audacious act of defiance against the king of England that was certain to provoke war with the world's preeminent naval power. The Declaration, which begins with the ringing words, "We hold these truths to be self-evident, that all men are created equal," followed a long struggle between the colonists and the

(Continued)

BOX 4.1:   (Continued)

colonizers over issues such as the power to tax, regulate trade and commerce, and quarter troops. At the root of all these disputes, however, was a thirst for liberty, a burning desire to escape unjust and arbitrary rule. Other grievances included "imposing Taxes on us without our Consent [and] depriving us in many cases, of the benefits of Trial by Jury."

Today, the Declaration sounds like reason dressed in political garb. People, it asserts,

have "unalienable Rights" (derived from the "Creator"). These rights are "Life, Liberty and the pursuit of Happiness." The "just powers" of governments derive "from the consent of the governed."

The Declaration came at a time when absolute monarchies ruled all Europe. It preceded the French Revolution by 13 years. Its creation was the act that led to the modern world's first, and oldest, constitutional democracy.

which it did. The triumph of the idea that a people can form a republic and govern themselves is a defining moment in the history of the modern world. It so happens this triumph occurred in a place known simply, but imprecisely, as America (see Box 4.1).

The idea of America is, in a very real sense, a product of the eighteenth-century Enlightenment, which, in turn, was a product of the intellectual ferment in Europe that originated during the Italian Renaissance of the late fifteenth century. The political theory of the American Founders, including George Washington, Benjamin Franklin, John Adams, Thomas Jefferson, James Madison, and Alexander Hamilton, drew heavily on the contributions of famous thinkers who lived and wrote during that earlier time—Niccolò Machiavelli, Thomas Hobbes, John Locke, and Baron de Montesquieu, among others. All agreed that the purpose of government was not, as Aristotle had claimed, to nurture virtue, but rather to combat vice. This unflattering view of human nature led these thinkers to stress the pursuit of realistic goals—liberty or security, for example, which may be politically attainable, rather than virtue, which is not.

The idea of America has long been synonymous with liberty in the minds of people all over the world. Arguably, it is the idea itself more than the reality that for many decades gave the United States vast reserves of "soft power" (the ability to get others to want what we want). Unfortunately, the unpopular and protracted Vietnam War eroded that soft power, as did the recent costly invasion and occupation of Iraq.

FOUR MODELS OF AMERICAN DEMOCRACY

The principle of majority rule is basic to constitutional democracy. Free elections decide who rules. Citizens play an important role in government—choosing who will hold high office and, therefore, who will make the laws, formulate the policies, and administer the programs on which well-ordered civil societies depend.

© NATIONAL PORTRAIT GALLERY, SMITHSONIAN INSTITUTION/ART RESOURCE

Alexander Hamilton (1757–1804). One of the principal authors of the Federalist Papers, published serially in two prominent newspapers in 1787–88, still the most authoritative source for the interpretation of the U.S. Constitution. An unrelenting advocate of a strong federal government and an assertive executive branch, Hamilton was the first U.S. Secretary of the Treasury and chief architect of the U.S. system of taxation, the plan for funding the national debt, and the first National Bank. Hamilton died at age 49 from a gunshot wound inflicted by his arch-enemy, Aaron Burr, in a duel.

Alexander Hamilton: Federalism

Constitutional democracies cannot ignore the opinions and beliefs of the majority. However, a popular government is not necessarily a viable one. In the words of Alexander Hamilton (1757–1804), "a government ought to contain in itself every power requisite to the full accomplishment of the objects committed to its care, . . . free from every other control, but a regard to the public good and to the sense of the people."[3]

What good is democracy if the government cannot protect its citizens, promote prosperity, and provide essential services such as education, law enforcement, water treatment, and firefighting? In Hamilton's view, checks and balances, however necessary in a democracy, ought not be carried so far as to impede or impair the government's ability to act energetically. Madison noted that one of the "very important" difficulties encountered at the Constitutional Convention was "combining the requisite stability and energy in Government, with the inviolable attention due to liberty, and to the Republican form."[4]

Hamilton, the indomitable Federalist, argued the most passionately—and fought the most fiercely—for a strong central government. With good reason George Washington turned to Hamilton, the United States' first secretary of the treasury, to put the fledgling national government's finances in order and to create a tax system, a federal budget, a central bank, the Customs Service, and the Coast Guard. A brilliant administrator with a penchant for micromanaging everything he touched, Hamilton applied his formidable talents and energies to the task of constructing a strong central government, one that would be financially solvent, stable, and competent to act without constantly having to secure agreement among the separate states or seek the lowest common denominator among them.

In a real sense, the U.S. Constitution stands as a monument to Hamilton's vision. It created a strong executive capable of conducting the nation's foreign affairs, vetoing legislation, and naming judges (with the approval of the Senate). It empowered Congress "to make all Laws which shall be necessary and proper"—a formulation that underscores the Founders' determination to avoid the kind of political paralysis that had thrown the colonies into a crisis under the ill-fated Articles of Confederation. Finally, it entrenched the **Supremacy Clause** (Article VI, Paragraph 2): "This Constitution, and the Laws of the United States which shall be made in Pursuance thereof; and all Treaties made, or which shall be made, under the Authority of the United States, shall be the supreme Law of the Land; and the Judges in every State shall be bound thereby, any Thing in the Constitution or Laws of any State to the contrary notwithstanding."

Stability and continuity are essential to the success of any government. Established procedures for changing leaders by regularized methods (elections and appointments) are vitally important and represent one of the principal advantages of democracy over modern dictatorships.

History and tradition, along with symbolism and ritual, reinforce the sense of continuity in governments. Citing the need for continuity, Madison opposed Thomas Jefferson's proposal for recurring constitutional conventions, on the grounds that because "every appeal to the people would carry an implication of some defect in the government, frequent appeals would, in a great measure, deprive the government of that veneration which time bestows on every thing, and without which perhaps the wisest and freest governments would not possess the requisite stability" and that even "the most rational government will not find it a superfluous advantage to have the prejudices of the community on its side."[5]

Hamilton and other delegates at Philadelphia sought to create a powerful and unified executive branch capable of resisting both the encroachments of Congress and the centrifugal pull of the states. They believed, correctly, that the absence of a hereditary monarch, regular elections, and the possibility of impeachment effectively checked the executive power.[6]

Nonetheless, the U.S. president is not a dictator or a constitutional monarch. For better or worse, Congress is well equipped to resist an unpopular chief executive. Even a popular president can be impeded or even impeached when the opposition party controls Congress. Thus, President Richard Nixon's attempt to use the IRS and the FBI to intimidate his opponents in 1972 backfired and led to his forced resignation. The American Founders deliberately set the stage for a contest. The document they adopted at Philadelphia left plenty of room for interpretation, maneuver, and debate. Its ambiguity is a source of both frustration and strength. Where the line is—or ought to be—drawn between capabilities and constraints depends on such key variables as political culture and circumstances.

Supremacy Clause Article VI, Section 2, of the Constitution, which declares that acts of Congress are "the Supreme law of the Land...binding on the Judges in every State."

Thomas Jefferson: Anti-Federalism

The validity of democracy is far from self-evident. As Socrates pointed out some 25 centuries ago, faced with big decisions on important matters, people turn to experts. Why, then, if we want good government, would we trust ordinary citizens, who tend to be apathetic and ill-informed, to make wise decisions? As a contemporary commentator pointed out, "If you visited a physician and sought advice as to whether to undergo an operation, you would be appalled if he explained that his policy in such cases was to poll a random sampling of passersby and act in accordance with the will of the majority."[7] Yet that is what democracies do all the time, often with dire consequences.

For example, a study comparing the mental agility of six Republican and six Democratic presidents found that George W. Bush ranked last (by a fairly wide margin).[8] Despite abundant evidence that the incumbent president lacked the most basic qualifications for the nation's highest office, however, the voters reelected Bush by a clear majority in 2004, thus giving him the solid mandate he lacked after the disputed 2000 election.

Thomas Jefferson (1743–1826) had more faith in "We the People" than Socrates did or, for that matter, than did many of the other Founders, including Hamilton and John Adams. For Jefferson, the author of the Declaration of Independence, majority rule was the only way to run a democracy. Unlike James Madison and others at Philadelphia, Jefferson did not see the principle of majority rule as a danger to the stability of a future government. Indeed, it was Jefferson who, in 1787, wrote in defense of Shays' Rebellion: "The tree of liberty must be refreshed from time to time with the blood of patriots and tyrants."

Jefferson and Madison embraced rather different views of human nature. Jefferson believed in the basic goodness of the people; presented with clear alternatives, the majority would normally choose the one that was best for the country. The right of free speech, in this view, is essential because it guarantees that minority views—dissent and criticism—will be aired. The right to criticize means yesterday's majority can become tomorrow's minority and vice versa.

The Jeffersonian model implies an important role for political parties. If majorities are the key to governance in a democracy, then political parties are necessary to give the majority a voice. But having only one party is incompatible with competition. Hence the need for at least two. (Most democracies have multiple parties; the United States is a rare exception.)

Jefferson was not the only prominent theorist to embrace the principle of majority rule. A compelling defense of this principle was given by Alexis de Tocqueville (1805–1859) in his brilliant two-volume study, *Democracy in America* (1835): "The moral authority of the majority is partly based upon the notion that there is more intelligence and more wisdom in a great number of men collected together than in a single individual."

Tocqueville believed the approximate equality of human intellect was a basic assumption of democratic government. Moreover, "The moral power of the majority is founded upon yet another principle, which is, that the interests of the many are to be preferred to those of the few."[9] Furthermore, because the majority is always changing and today's minority can become tomorrow's majority, the principle of majority rule is appealing to all. In the United States, according to Tocqueville, "all parties are willing to recognize the rights of the majority, because they all hope to turn those rights to their own advantage at some future time."[10]

majority rule
The principle that any candidate or program that receives at least half of all votes plus one prevails.

The political principle of **majority rule**, therefore, finds support both in the ideal of equality and in self-interest. However, achieving it is not as easy, nor always as highly prized, as we might think. In the United States, where the two-party system is well entrenched, elections typically produce a clear majority in both state and national legislatures. They also produce the *appearance* of a clear majority in most presidential elections. But as we discovered in the 2000 presidential election, the candidate who wins a majority of the popular votes is not automatically assured of getting elected. The **winner-takes-all system** awards all the electoral votes in any given state to the candidate who gets the most votes in that state, even if nobody gets a clear majority.

winner-takes-all system
Electoral system in which the candidate receiving the most votes wins.

Under parliamentary democracy, the problem of majority rule is rather different. Most parliamentary systems have multiple political parties represented in the national legislature. (We will see why later.) Multiparty systems typically do not produce a clear majority of parliamentary seats for any single party. Two or more parties are then forced into a coalition in order to form a government with enough votes to get its programs and policies approved. As a result, the very *possibility* of majority rule is called into question. When the voters divide into, say, five or six sides rather than just two, there is obviously no clear signal as to where the "majority" stands on anything. Nor can any single party in a coalition government hew to its own platform and ignore the wishes of its partners in the coalition. The upshot is a watering down of positions—a government based more on rule by the lowest common denominator than on majority rule. Often, the voters become frustrated and cynical at what they perceive to be ineffective government.

Even in the United Kingdom, the world's foremost *two-party* parliamentary system, majority rule is problematic. British elections nearly always produce a clear majority in Parliament (see Chapter 7), but the winning party seldom garners more than 45 percent of the popular votes (and often significantly less). In other words, British democracy is more accurately characterized as a **plurality vote system**. Much the same can be said of American democracy, because members of the U.S. Congress are elected in single-member districts and the biggest vote-getter in each district wins the seat, no matter how far short of a majority.

plurality vote system
A system in which candidates who get the largest number of votes win, whether or not they garner a majority of the votes cast; in a majority vote system, if no candidate gets more than half the votes cast, a runoff election is held to determine the winner.

The distinction between majority and plurality voting raises a theoretical problem. If a candidate or government is chosen on the basis of a plurality rather than a majority, it means more voters did *not* vote for that candidate or government than did—possibly many more. The logic of this analysis, however, can easily take a wrong turn. The reason the majority does not rule is not that the minority has usurped power, but that *there is no majority*. Thus, to talk about the myth of the majority is not to denigrate majority rule but rather to recognize the difficulty of putting it into practice.

Governing by majority rule is easier said than done for another reason. The fact that the majority is often elusive raises a problem for democratic theory; the fact that it is often tyrannical raises a problem for democratic practice. We turn next to this problem and how another great democratic theorist proposed to solve it.

James Madison: Balanced Government

Students are often surprised to learn that the majority of delegates to the Constitutional Convention at Philadelphia in 1787 did not fully share Jefferson's faith in the people. James Madison's (1751–1836) theory of democracy stressed the natural tendency of society to fragment into special interests or factions based on egoism and emotion rather than altruism and reason. The proponents of Madisonian democracy thus viewed Jeffersonians as too optimistic about the likelihood that the masses will be high minded and public spirited. Indeed, Madisonians could point to ample anecdotal and historical evidence to justify a more pessimistic view of human nature.

Both Madison and Hamilton expected individuals to act selfishly in politics, just as they do in personal matters, unless they are prevented by political arrangements designed for that purpose. The fairly clear distinctions that already existed between economic and social classes during the colonial period underscored Madison's fear of creating politically paralyzing or polarizing factionalism. How could a democratic government be structured to ensure the public interest would not be sacrificed to the selfish interests of factions?

The Madisonian solution was to ensure factions pursuing selfish ends would encounter as many hurdles as possible. It was this idea that won the day in Philadelphia and came to be enshrined in the Constitution as the famous system of **checks and balances**. The **separation of powers**—so familiar to students of U.S. democracy—is one key; the other is **federalism**. For followers of Madison, good government is all about architecture.

checks and balances
Constitutional tools that enable branches of government to resist any illegitimate expansion of power by other branches.

separation of powers
The organization of government into distinct areas of legislative, executive, and judicial functions, each responsible to different constituencies and possessing its own powers and responsibilities; the system of dividing the governmental powers among three branches and giving each branch a unique role to play while making all three interdependent.

federalism
A system of limited government based on the division of authority between the central government and smaller regional governments.

© NATIONAL PORTRAIT GALLERY, SMITHSONIAN INSTITUTION/ ART RESOURCE

James Madison (1751–1836). Fourth President of the United States (1809–1817). Author of many of the most important Federalist Papers, Madison is often called the "Father of the Constitution" in recognition of his leading role in drafting that document. Madison is also credited with authorship of the Bill of Rights. An ally of Jefferson against the Federalists, Madison opposed various centralizing measures favored by Hamilton and John Adams. As president, Madison led the country into the war of 1812 against Britain. Perhaps more adept as a theoretician than as a practitioner of politics, Madison, as chief executive, changed his position on several key issues, favoring creation of a second National Bank (he had opposed the first), a strong military, and a high tariff to protect so-called infant industries.

The Architecture of Liberty If people are not by nature virtuous and rulers are people, how can any system of rule *not* degenerate into tyranny? Here, in a nutshell, is the universal problem of politics. The Founders tried to solve this puzzle by developing what they called the "new science of politics," an ingenious arrangement of political institutions designed to permit a large measure of liberty while guarding against the arbitrary exercise of power by compartmentalizing the functions of government, thus preventing the concentration of power.

In *The Federalist*, Hamilton argued that the new U.S. Constitution would prevent "the extremes of tyranny and anarchy" that had plagued previous republics. He admonished his readers not to dwell on past examples: "The science of politics, like most other sciences, has received great improvement. The efficacy of various principles is now well understood, which were either not known at all, or imperfectly known to the ancients." Hamilton catalogued the structural improvements built into the Constitution by the pioneers of this new science:

> The regular distribution of power into distinct departments; the introduction of legislative balances and checks; the institution of courts composed of judges, holding their offices during good behaviour; the representation of the people in the legislature by deputies of their own election—these are either wholly new discoveries or have made their principal progress toward perfection in modern times. They are means, and powerful means, by which the excellences of republican government may be retained and its imperfections lessened or avoided.[11]

The Founders understood that, in Madison's words, "enlightened statesmen will not always be at the helm."[12] In the absence of exceptional leadership, only the state itself, properly constructed, could check the ambitions of those who claimed to rule in its name. Elections provide one such check, noted Madison, but "experience has taught mankind the necessity of auxiliary precautions."[13] The chief precaution was to set up a permanent rivalry among the main components of government: "The great security against a gradual concentration of the several powers in the same department, consists in giving to those who administer each department the necessary constitutional means and personal motives to resist encroachments of the others." In short, "Ambition must be made to counteract ambition."[14]

Checks and Balances In pursuit of this goal, the Founders attempted to make each branch of government largely independent of the other branches. Thus, the powers of each respective branch derive from specific provisions of the Constitution—Article I for the legislature, Article II for the executive, Article III for the judiciary. Each branch is given constitutional authority to perform certain prescribed tasks, and each is equipped with the tools to resist any illegitimate expansion of power by the other branches. These tools, known as checks and balances, range from the mundane (the president's veto power) to the extraordinary (impeachment proceedings brought by Congress against a president). Together they make up the "necessary constitutional means" available to members of one branch of government for use against the encroachments of another.

As the authors of *The Federalist Papers* put it, "The interest of the [individual] must be connected with the constitutional rights of the place."[15] Institutionalized self-interest, the Founders felt, would infuse officeholders with a sense of the power, importance, and majesty of their particular institution and heighten their desire to maintain its prestige (and thereby advance their own careers). Thus, Congress brought impeachment charges against President Nixon in 1974, alleging he had flouted the Constitution. (Nixon's abuse of power, including his alleged involvement in the Watergate affair, was the general theme of the case against him.) In 1998, President Clinton was impeached, in part, because he resisted efforts by the Republican Congress to investigate his conduct in office. His opponents also charged he lied to a grand jury. On the other hand, a Democratic Congress resisted public calls for impeachment of President Bush in 2006–2008 over the Iraq War, the methods used in capturing and interrogating suspected terrorists, and a penchant for secrecy that greatly impeded legislative oversight and public scrutiny of the executive branch.

In building democratic institutions on the power of self-interest, the Founders demonstrated a limited faith in human goodness and the likelihood of moral improvement. According to Hamilton, "Men are ambitious, vindictive, and rapacious."[16] Madison concurred, although less bluntly:

> It may be a reflection on human nature, that such devices [as checks and balances] should be necessary to control the abuses of government. But what is government itself, but the greatest of all reflections on human nature? If men were angels, no government would be necessary. If angels were to govern men, neither external nor internal controls on government would be necessary.[17]

In a well-ordered republic, enlightened self-interest would work for the good of all. Ideally, politicians would discover they could best achieve their personal interests (getting reelected) by promoting the public interest. If not, however, Madison's system, like Adam Smith's theory of the "invisible hand" in the marketplace, would automatically adjust itself to correct the balance of institutional power. Thus, it was not on the lofty plane of morality or religious sentiment that the new science of politics in the United States found its justification, but instead on the firmer (if lower) ground of institutionalized self-interest.

John C. Calhoun: Brokered Government

John C. Calhoun (1782–1850) was a younger contemporary of the Founders. In the first half of the nineteenth century, he was a leading political figure in the South and served as vice president of the United States from 1825 until 1832, when he resigned over policy differences with President Andrew Jackson.

Contemporary political scientists often refer to Calhoun as the first prominent exponent of a pluralist model of democracy. In the 1820s, Calhoun championed a theory of **brokered democracy** based on the assumption of selfish

brokered democracy
This theory holds that the interests of major groups cannot be steamrolled by the majority without jeopardizing democracy and that legislators and decision makers should act as brokers in writing laws and devising policies that are acceptable to all major groups in society.

concurrent majority
John Calhoun's theory of democracy, which holds that the main function of government is to mediate between and among the different economic, social, and sectional interests in U.S. society.

nullification
According to this controversial idea, a state can nullify acts of the U.S. Congress within its own borders; John Calhoun and other states'-rights advocates put forward this doctrine prior to the Civil War.

dual federalism
Under this system, which prevailed in the United States between 1835 and 1860, the power of the national government was limited to enumerated powers; during this period, the Southern states claimed sovereign powers.

motives in politics and what was, in his view, a universal tendency to interpret reality, and even *morality*, in self-serving ways—to put private interests *ahead* of the public interest. Calhoun sought to tame this tendency through a mechanism he called the **concurrent majority**. In his model of U.S. democracy, there were (and are) many different economic, social, and sectional interests the government must mediate between and among. In a democracy, he reasoned, if one interest prevails over all the others because it has a majority of the votes on a given issue at a given time, neither justice nor the long-term survival of the system can be assured.

In his *Disquisition on Government*, Calhoun made an impassioned argument for protecting the interests of minorities against a steamrolling majority. The way to do so was to abandon the principle of majority rule in favor of government by concurrent majority. Thus, the decision-making model Calhoun advocated was one of *compromise* and *consensus* among all major competing interests on important policy questions of the day. If compromise failed and consensus could not be reached, the status quo would prevail indefinitely. In effect, Calhoun argued the case for protecting pluralism at all costs, granting a kind of veto power to minority groups.

Calhoun is a prime example of his own theory in action. As it turns out, he was not only a champion of concurrent majority decision-making but also the leading voice in the famous **nullification** controversy that divided the nation in the decades preceding the Civil War. Proponents of nullification, mainly Southerners, held that a state could nullify acts of the Congress within its own borders—if Congress attempted to abolish slavery, for example, the Southern states had the right to ignore it. This concept also came to be called "interposition," because it meant a state could interpose its own authority (or sovereignty) to void an act of Congress. Calhoun was, in effect, using the principle of minority rights *against* an oppressed racial minority, slaves.

For Calhoun and his Southern cohort, "minority rights" and states' rights were inseparable. The tension between Federalists (favoring a strong national government) and Anti-Federalists (favoring states' rights) had been one of the major themes of the nation's founding and continued to be up to the Civil War.

In fact, the notion of **dual federalism** (near and dear to Calhoun's heart) prevailed between 1835 and 1860. Under dual federalism, the power of the national government was limited to its enumerated powers, Southern states claimed sovereign powers, and the all-important question of what would happen or who would prevail in a contest of wills between two "sovereign" governments (national versus state) remained unresolved. The upshot was, of course, the Civil War.

Federalism was at the heart of the fight between the North and South. The Union victory over the Confederacy was a triumph for the concept of a single sovereign seat of government located in Washington, D.C., but it did not resolve the tension between federal authority and the states' rights. An attenuated form of dual federalism survived at least until the Depression Era of the 1930s, when President Franklin Delano Roosevelt launched what political scientists often call "cooperative federalism"—a series of federally funded programs that, in time, redefined the relationship between the national government and the states.

BOX 4.2 FOCUS ON   Federalism in Postwar Germany

The link between federalism and liberty is particularly striking in the case of Germany. Democracy in Germany was reborn after World War II, when the nation was exhausted by war, defeated, and occupied by foreign armies. The Allied powers, led by the United States, were determined to prevent a new German state from again launching a campaign of military aggression in Europe. The best way to do that, they reasoned, was to inoculate Germany against the virus of dictatorship. The "vaccine" they decided to use was democratic federalism.

How could federalism possibly prevent the rise of a new Hitler? The key is the decentralized structure of Germany's government. The German states (called *Länder*) play an important role in governance on *both* the state and national levels. Delegates appointed by the sixteen state governments make up the upper house of the German parliament, the Bundesrat. The upper house has veto power over legislation directly affecting the states, including new taxes. In addition, most of the governmental bureaucracy in Germany falls under the control of the *Länder*. Ironically, the Germany federal system, which was created under close U.S. supervision, is a better example of how federalism is supposed to work than the U.S. system, which once functioned as an effective counterweight to the national (or central) government but no longer does.

From that time to the present, the federal government's power has expanded, and the states have taken a back seat. We turn next to a more detailed look at federalism.

Back to Basics: Federalism and the Separation of Powers

Federalism In theory, one way to limit constitutional government is through a division of powers, called federalism. In practice, however, it does not necessarily work that way. Modern examples of federal republics are the United States, Germany, Canada, India, Brazil, Mexico, and Nigeria. After World War II, federalism in Germany, for example, meant the states played a strong role in governing the country and truly did act as a check on central power (see Box 4.2). In the defunct Soviet Union, by contrast, federalism was a façade that allowed a tightly controlled and highly centralized dictatorship to pretend it was democratic.

True federalism features a division of power between the national government and regional subdivisions. These subdivisions are often called *states*, not to be confused with sovereign states or nation-states. The United States has a constitutional division of power between national and state governments. Article I, Section 8 of the Constitution, for instance, delineates many areas in which Congress is empowered to legislate. At the same time, the Tenth Amendment provides that all powers not granted to the national government are reserved for the states. Traditionally, the states have been empowered to maintain internal peace and order, provide for education, and safeguard the people's health, safety, and welfare—through the government's *police powers*. These powers were once exercised almost exclusively by the states. However, the role of national (or federal) government has grown enormously since the 1930s, when FDR launched a massive set of federal programs called the New Deal, to create jobs and stimulate the economy in the midst of the Great Depression.

President Richard Nixon (1968–1973) tried to reverse this process with a policy called the *new federalism,* which was aimed at making government "more effective as well as more efficient." The two main elements of this policy were the use of so-called block grants to the states and general revenue sharing. Thereafter, other presidents—notably Ronald Reagan (1980–1988), a conservative Republican, and Bill Clinton (1992–2000), a Democrat—also paid lip-service to *devolution,* or transferring power back to the states, but did little to match words with deeds. President George W. Bush paradoxically weakened the role of the federal government in the economy through deregulation of business and banking while pushing the power of the executive branch in the political system to new heights.

Upon taking the oath of office, President Obama moved quickly to enforce existing regulations in some areas, including energy and the environment. His early response to the financial and economic crisis, however, emphasized fiscal stimulus (spending) rather than strict regulation of the banking industry—much to the chagrin of his critics. Others noted the Obama administration was moving faster and more decisively than President Franklin Delano Roosevelt did in responding to the Great Depression in the 1930s.

Why Federalism? What is the rationale for a division of power? The basic idea is to keep government as close to the people as possible. Thus, some delegates at the Constitutional Convention in Philadelphia argued that the existence of states would create a first line of defense against a potentially tyrannical central government. In the Constitution, therefore, the separate states were given equal representation in the newly created Senate, and the federal method of electing the president through the Electoral College was adopted. In addition, the states were to play an important role in amending the Constitution. As we noted earlier, the First Congress deferred to the states in proposing the adoption of the Tenth Amendment.

Federalism in the United States today functions significantly differently from the way it did during the nation's early history. Originally, great controversies flared over the question of whether a state (for example, Virginia and Kentucky in 1798–1799 or South Carolina in the 1830s) or a region (the South in 1860) could resort to states' rights federalism to justify dissent from specific policies undertaken by the national government. When questions of interest or principle—the Alien and Sedition Acts of 1798, the tariff in the 1830s, slavery in the 1860s—divided the nation, political wrangling centered on the constitutionality of particular governmental actions, or on the issue of whether state governments or the national government could legitimately exercise final authority.

Issues the Supremacy Clause of the Constitution could not settle, the Civil War did. Although there have been some notable clashes since then, especially in the South over school desegregation in the late 1950s and early 1960s, the federal government is now clearly in the driver's seat, with the states competing for federal dollars in pursuit of policies hammered out at the federal level.[18]

In the 1990s, however, there was renewed competition between these two levels of government. For example, state governments experimented with educational reforms (charter schools, school vouchers, new ways to bring religion into the classroom) and a variety of anticrime measures (mandatory sentencing, three-strikes laws, victims' compensation). Some states also sought to roll back affirmative action. After 2001, as the Bush administration rushed to deregulate business, California and some other states fought with the federal government over the right to enact tougher environmental standards than those mandated by Washington. The new Obama administration pledged to review and revamp federal environmental policies—a rare intergovernmental victory for the states.

The trend toward a more competitive relationship between the national and state governments was derailed by the war on terror, yet the examples above illustrate the sense in which federalism is *competitive* as well as cooperative. Nonetheless, the federal government towers over the states by virtue of its vast powers to tax and borrow and spend, as well as its status under the Supremacy Clause (see above), which declares that acts of Congress are "the Supreme law of the Land . . . binding on the Judges in every State."

Any talk of redressing the balance between the federal government and the states brings to mind the struggles to defend or extend states' rights associated with major historic figures in the United States, including Thomas Jefferson, John Randolph, and John C. Calhoun. But Jefferson Davis, the institution of slavery, and the Civil War are also part of this story. A century later, Southern segregationists like Strom Thurmond, George Wallace, and Lester Maddox unsuccessfully led the fight for states' rights against federal action to bring about desegregation in the South.

The debate over federalism continues up to the present day. Critics argue that the pendulum has swung too far toward centralization of power, while civil rights advocates point to the pivotal role of the federal government in promoting racial and gender equality. (We examine the recent history of civil rights and the push for racial equality in Chapter 13).

Federalism and Liberty By guarding against the dangers of over-centralization, federalism, in theory, protects liberty, ensuring that the powers of the national government remain limited.[19] However, the post-9/11 expansion of federal law-enforcement powers in the name of **homeland security** raised questions about the compatibility of a centralized model of federalism and liberty in the twenty-first century.

At its origins, American federalism was designed to protect individual liberty by limiting the scope of the national government. Thus, in sharp contrast to a **unitary system** of government (see Box 4.3), the aim is political-administrative decentralization. By "multiplying and simplifying the governments accessible" to ordinary citizens, "creating local organized structures capable of resisting centralized authority or mitigating its excesses," and making it possible for "government to be adapted to local needs and circumstances," decentralization

homeland security
A term President George W. Bush popularized after the 9/11 terrorist attacks; it refers to a whole range of counterterrorist policies, including tighter border and immigration controls, stepped-up airport security, expanded FBI surveillance powers, and more invasive police investigations.

unitary system
A system in which the government may choose to delegate affairs to local government.

BOX 4.3 FOCUS ON   THE UNITARY ALTERNATIVE

Most governments in the world today are not federal systems. A far more common form of government is the unitary system, such as that found in the United Kingdom. It is called *unitary* because there is only one primary unit of government, the central government, which often turns over many affairs to local governments but is not required to do so. Notably absent from these systems is an intermediate layer—the equivalent of states in federal systems—between the center and local political-administrative units. Some unitary systems, for example those in France and Italy, have guarded the powers and prerogatives of the national government against encroachment by local magistrates, mayors, and politicians more jealously than have the British. In France, *prefects*—officials appointed by the central government—mediate between the central government in Paris and the local departments. Until the Socialist government of François Mitterrand instituted reforms in the early 1980s, the prefects were charged with the close supervision of local governments within their departments and had the power to veto local decisions. Admirers have long regarded this system, known as *tutelage,* as a model of rational political administration. Tutelage was so centralized and systematized throughout France that anyone could supposedly tell which subject schoolchildren were studying at any given time simply by glancing at a clock. To many in the United States accustomed to a multiplicity of schools, curricula, accreditation requirements, and academic standards, such government-imposed uniformity would no doubt seem curious.

permits "experimentation in the way problems are met." In short, federalism, in this view, "is a vital safeguard to liberty and a way to educate an energetic and competent citizenry."[20]

Do we still have the necessary degree of decentralization—that "vital safeguard to liberty"? For better or worse, the trend since 9/11 has been toward greater centralization of power in Washington and the White House. This point leads naturally back to one of the perennial questions facing democracy—namely, how to reconcile individual rights and majority rule. We revisit that question in the following section.

The Separation of Powers The U.S. Constitution assigns specific tasks to each branch of government. Congress, for example, is given the **power of the purse.** The president proposes a budget and attempts to influence congressional appropriations, but Congress always has the final word on governmental spending. This potent constraint on the executive has not been widely copied by other **presidential democracies,** which typically give the executive branch the upper hand in setting the budget (expenditures), while giving the legislature the primary role on the revenue side (taxation).

In the U.S. model, power and authority are shared in a few areas. Overlapping responsibilities, for instance, characterize the government's **war powers.** Congress is empowered to raise and support armies (although the

power of the purse
Under the U.S. Constitution, the provision that gives the Congress the exclusive right to impose taxes and the final word on government spending.

presidential democracy
A democratic form of government in which the chief executive is chosen by separate election, serves a fixed term, and has powers carefully separated from those of the other branches of government.

BOX 4.4 FOCUS ON　　PRESIDENTIAL DEMOCRACY

The U.S. government is often called a presidential democracy because the chief executive is elected in balloting separate from the vote for members of Congress. A presidential system is characterized by a separation of powers in which the legislative, executive, and judicial branches of the national government are each responsible to different constituencies for the exercise of their respective powers and responsibilities.

The government is formally organized along functional lines. Because all governments need to formulate, execute, and interpret laws, it is logical to create a legislature to perform the first of these functions (rule making), an executive to carry out the second (rule implementation), and a judiciary to oversee the third (rule interpretation).

The logic of this arrangement knows no political or geographic boundaries. Today it is reflected in the composition of many democracies in all regions of the world. Presidential democracies are especially common in Latin America, but in various forms they are also scattered in such far-flung places as Russia, France, Yugoslavia, Nigeria, South Africa, Indonesia, and the Philippines.

The major alternative to presidential democracy is parliamentary democracy, which is especially common in Europe and which we discuss at length in Chapter 7.

Constitution limits appropriations to two years), to provide and maintain a navy, to make the rules regulating the armed forces, and to declare war. However, the Constitution makes the president the commander in chief of the armed forces. Therefore, any significant military undertaking, declared or undeclared, requires the cooperation of both branches. Countries with similar institutions generally replicate this pattern, although the idea of civilian control over the military is nowhere more firmly established in principle or practice than in the United States. Indeed, in many presidential systems, the possibility of a military takeover (a so-called coup d'état) in times of crisis remains the principal danger to democracy.

Members of the three branches in the U.S. government serve different terms of office and different constituencies. Under the Constitution, as amended, the president must stand for election every four years and is limited to two terms of office. The president and the vice president are the only two governmental officials in the United States who can receive a mandate from the entire national electorate (see Box 4.4). In contrast, congressional representatives serve particular districts (subdivisions of states) and are elected for two-year terms. Senators represent states as a whole and serve six-year terms in office. Supreme Court justices (and all other federal judges) are not elected; they are appointed by the president with the advice and consent of the Senate. The Founders stipulated this mode of appointment because they believed that to render impartial opinions, the judiciary must be free of the political pressures of winning and holding elective office.

The precise term of office for president varies from country to country. Presidents in Russia and Brazil, for example, are elected to four-year terms and

war powers
The U.S. Constitution gives the Congress the power to raise and support armies, to provide and maintain a navy, to make rules regulating the armed forces, and to declare war; it makes the president the commander in chief of the armed forces.

can run for a second consecutive term, as in the United States. The president of Mexico is elected to a six-year term but cannot run for reelection. Until recently, France's president was elected to a renewable seven-year term, reduced to five years in 2000.

TOCQUEVILLE: THE TYRANNY OF THE MAJORITY

Imagine this Wild West scenario: A drifter falsely accused of the cold-blooded murder of a local citizen is jailed, pending trial by a judge and jury. An angry mob clamors for instant justice, but against this throng stand two solitary figures—a crotchety old deputy and the brave sheriff. The inevitable show-down takes place in the street in front of the sheriff's office. Led by the mayor and town council members (one of whom is the actual murderer), a lynch mob demands "the killer" be handed over immediately. Clearly, major-ity rule is at war with impartial justice. In the end, only heroic action by the sheriff saves the innocent man from being dragged off and hanged from the nearest tree.

When democratic government turns into mob rule, it becomes what Alexis de Tocqueville called the **tyranny of the majority**.[21] For this reason, political thinkers through the ages have often rejected democracy, fearing a majority based on one dominant class, religion, or political persuasion would trample the rights of minorities. The American Founders were conscious of this danger

tyranny of the majority The political situation in which a dominant group uses its control of the government to abuse the rights of minority groups.

© ROGER-VIOLET/THE IMAGE WORKS

Alexis de Tocqueville (1805–1859). French political thinker and writer best known for his two-volume masterpiece, *Democracy in America*, widely considered the most insightful work on American society and politics in the Jacksonian era. An admirer of Americans' penchant for business and commerce, and genius for money-making innovation, he was nonetheless sharply critical of the still-young republic's tendency toward crass individualism and a "middling" mediocrity in politics and the arts. Many of de Tocqueville's observations, both pro and con, still resonate today.

BOX 4.5 FOCUS ON   CONSTRAINTS ON MAJORITY RULE

The Founders of the U.S. political system were troubled by the possibility that the majority would trample the rights of the minority. To some extent, **bicameralism**, or the division of the legislative branch into two houses, was designed to balance the power of large and small states and to provide a barrier against the majority steamroller. The presidential veto, the independence of the courts, and federalism were also intended as safeguards against the potential excesses inherent in majority rule.

Again, this political-institutional pattern is discernible in other countries as well. The bicameral arrangement of the legislature is the rule nearly everywhere. In most cases, presidents have a veto power over legislation, but a determined and united legislature can override it. Courts are typically set up to be independent, although ensuring judges are politically neutral or jurisprudentially impartial is often problematic.

Many of the world's federal systems are also presidential. As noted earlier, examples include Russia, Mexico, Brazil, and Nigeria. Examples to the contrary include Canada, Germany, and India.

and sought to combat it by structural and procedural prescriptions written into the Constitution (see Box 4.5).

The United States witnessed acts resembling mob rule in the fall of 2001, during the crisis that followed the deadly terrorist attacks in New York and Washington, D.C. When the perpetrators were identified as Muslim extremists, many citizens, horrified by the enormity of the crime, turned against Arab and Muslim minorities living in the United States.

Examples of popular tyranny in democratic countries are surprisingly common. In Germany, for example, a sizable Turkish minority has never been granted equal rights. In the Czech Republic (and elsewhere in Eastern Europe), the Czech majority discriminate against the Roma. In Israel, the Arab minority (that is, Arab-Palestinians who are Israeli citizens rather than residents of the West Bank and Gaza) do not enjoy full political and social equality with the Jewish majority. In Turkey, the rights of the Kurdish minority have often fallen victim to the fears and prejudices of the Turkish majority (see Figure 4.3).

The French Revolution was a precursor of the totalitarian mass movements that played a major role in shaping world history in the first half of the twentieth century. In the period between the two world wars, a left-wing dictatorship in Russia and right-wing dictatorships in Fascist Italy and Nazi Germany came to power with broad popular support. In Adolf Hitler's Germany, the persecution of minorities in the name of an "Aryan" majority turned genocidal with at least the acquiescence, if not the active support, of an overwhelming majority within German society.

bicameralism
Division of the legislature into two houses.

FIGURE 4.3   The Kurds predominate on both sides of Turkey's borders with Syria, Iraq, and Iran.

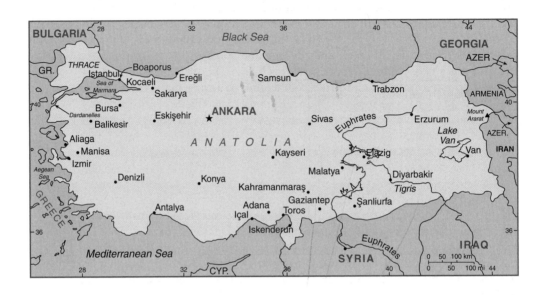

JOHN LOCKE: THE RULE OF LAW

rule of law
The concept that the power and discretion of government and its officials ought to be restrained by a supreme set of neutral rules that prevent arbitrary and unfair action by government; also called constitutionalism.

The idea that nations ought to be governed by impartial, binding laws is not new. Aristotle argued that the **rule of law** is almost always superior to the rule of unrestrained individuals. He based this argument on the concept of fairness, contending that whereas individuals are subject to appetites and passions for physical, material, and psychic satisfaction, the law represents "reason free from all passion."[22] Therefore, a government of laws is superior to one of individuals, even though individuals such as magistrates and ministers of justice must interpret and enforce the laws.

More than 2,000 years later, English philosopher John Locke (1632–1704) defended the rule of law on the basis of its close relationship to individual freedom. Locke believed freedom could not exist without written law and that good government must follow certain precepts (for instance, taxes should not be levied without the consent of the people).

To Locke, these rules constitute "laws" of the highest order because they embody what civil society is all about. They are laws above the law that place limitations on lawmakers. From Locke's concept of a higher law, the idea of constitutionalism evolved. As Locke noted (and as the inscription above the entrance to the Department of Justice building in Washington, D.C., reads), "Wherever Law ends, Tyranny begins."[23]

Locke was part of a proud English tradition that had sought since 1215 to establish limits on government. In that year, rebellious barons forced King John to sign the famous **Magna Carta**. Originally, this document made concessions by the ruler only to the feudal nobility, but its broad clauses were later interpreted more flexibly and expanded to cover increased numbers of people. Ultimately, the Magna Carta became the foundation of British liberties. Containing some sixty-three clauses, it foreshadowed a system that limited the absolute authority of the monarchy. It declared, for instance, that royal vassals must be summoned to councils to give advice and consent, and that they had to approve any extraordinary taxes. Equally important was Clause 39, which guaranteed the accused an impartial trial and protection against arbitrary imprisonment and punishment. To that end it stated, "No free man shall be taken or imprisoned, or disposed, or outlawed, or banished, or in any way destroyed . . . except by the legal judgment of his peers or by the law of the land."

During the seventeenth century, in Locke's time, great advances were made in the limitation of government by law. The Petition of Right (1628) further advanced the idea of due process of law while limiting the monarch's power of taxation. In addition, abolishing the dreaded Star Chamber in 1641 did away with a court that used torture to gain confessions and imposed punishment on subjects at the request of the Crown. Finally, the Habeas Corpus Act (1679) limited government's power to imprison people arbitrarily. It imposed substantial penalties on judges who failed to issue timely writs of *habeas corpus*, which demonstrated the accused had been legally detained and properly charged with a crime.

Also originating in the seventeenth century was a judicial precedent that came to have enormous influence in the United States. Renowned English jurist Sir Edward Coke's (1552–1634) opinion in Dr. Bonham's case (1610) asserted that English common law, including the Magna Carta, should be the standard to which ordinary acts of Parliament, as well as the monarchy, had to conform.[24]

CONSTITUTIONALISM AND DUE PROCESS

Although a higher-law theory was not adopted in England, where parliamentary supremacy became the rule, it eventually found a home in the United States. The U.S. Constitution and Bill of Rights (the latter of which was largely derived from English common law) became the standards against which popularly enacted laws would be judged.

Constitutionalism enshrines proper procedure. For instance, the Constitution as interpreted by the U.S. Supreme Court prohibits the president of the United States, even during wartime, from seizing or nationalizing industries, such as steel mills, without Congressional approval.[25] Similarly, the concept of **due process**— prescribed procedural rules—dictates that a citizen accused of a crime shall be provided with an attorney, allowed to confront witnesses, informed of the charges brought against him or her, and so on. For the same reason, administrative agencies are compelled by law to provide public notice to those who might be adversely affected by a pending decision.

Magna Carta
A list of political concessions granted in 1215 by King John to his barons that became the basis for the rule of law in England.

due process
A guarantee of fair legal procedure; it is found in the Fifth and Fourteenth amendments of the U.S. Constitution.

In each instance, the rationale behind procedural due process is the same: we cannot accept a decision as either fair or final unless we can see that the "rules of the game" have been strictly followed. Hence, in constitutional democracies, if the winner of an election cheated, the results are void. In fact, that is exactly what happened when the so-called Watergate scandal forced President Nixon to resign (or face certain impeachment) in 1974.

Many outside observers, however, think due process of law is taken to extremes in the United States. For example, if the suspect confesses to the crime without being informed that she has a right to remain silent, the confession will be inadmissible in court. In virtually every other liberal democracy in the world, including the United Kingdom, France, Canada, and Australia to cite but a few examples, a confession is a confession as long as it is not extracted by torture or trickery.

It is not enough for a democracy to proclaim the rule of law. Words and deeds must also coincide. Thus, African Americans continued to be victims of discrimination for many years after the Civil War was fought, despite the fact that the Fourteenth Amendment explicitly guaranteed **equal protection** of the laws. Similarly, women did not gain the right to vote until 1920 and enjoyed few opportunities outside the confines of home and family until fairly recently.

Due process is essential to equal justice, but there is no such thing as an iron-clad guarantee against injustice. To prevent the gravest miscarriages of justice (such as lynching), we must place limitations on popular rule. These may take many forms.

In the United States, government is restricted as to how it can make laws or punish citizens accused of breaking laws. For example, under Article I, Sections 9 and 10 of the Constitution, the government cannot pass an **ex post facto law**, which retroactively penalizes acts, or a **bill of attainder**, a legislative act that declares a person guilty.

The Bill of Rights, which consists of the first ten amendments to the Constitution, forbids the government to deny citizens freedom of religion, speech, press, assembly, and privacy, and guarantees the accused a fair trial (see Chapter 13). In practice, however, exactly how or where to draw the line between majority rule (or the state) and minority rights (or society) is often unclear. Citizens are entitled to express themselves, but this right is not absolute—for example, freedom of speech does not give one the right to make obscene phone calls, to send death threats through the mail, or to incite a riot.

equal protection
The doctrine enshrined in the Fourteenth Amendment that holds that the prohibitions placed on the federal government and the protections afforded American citizens under the Bill of Rights also apply to the states.

ex post facto law
A law that retroactively criminalizes acts that were legal at the time they were committed.

bill of attainder
A legislative decree that declares a person guilty and prescribes punishment without any judicial process.

REMODELING DEMOCRACY: HAVE IT YOUR WAY

Political scientists frequently use models to illustrate or clarify a particular theory or to show a range of possibilities. The fact that so many countries became laboratories for democratic experimentation in the 1990s created renewed academic interest in democracy and provided a great variety of "specimens" to study. One upshot was the appearance of a new body of theories and models of democracy.

We give the most attention in this book to three existing models of democracy: the U.S. presidential model, the British parliamentary model, and the French half-and-half, or hybrid, model that combines features of the U.S. and British systems (see Chapter 7). All three are representative democracies and differ primarily in structural and procedural matters—in the way representatives are elected, the relationship between the executive and legislative branches, the role of political parties, and the way the national leader comes to power.

Another way of thinking about democracies is to focus on the role the people play under different models. After all, democracy is, by definition, a form of rule by the people. William Hudson, for example, identified four distinct theories of citizen participation and developed a model of democracy for each (see Figure 4.4).[26]

The main function of government in Hudson's **protective democracy** is to safeguard liberty rather than national security. Citizens may play a passive political role in this model, but they make up for it by playing an extremely active role in economics. The government is the guardian or protector of the free market, but not its master. According to Hudson, this theory holds that "democracy exists so that free competitive individuals may have and enjoy a maximum of freedom to pursue material wealth."[27] The limits on government are ensured through the elements so familiar to students of the U.S. Constitution, including the separation of powers, federalism, bicameralism, and the Bill of Rights.

In Hudson's **developmental democracy**, the government's focus is on the development of virtuous citizens, not modern economies or political systems. This model views democracy as a kind of school for civic education and socialization. It sees indirect or representative democracy as a way to train citizens in those habits and virtues essential to progress, stability, and prosperity. Their

protective democracy
A theory of democracy that places the highest priority on national security

developmental democracy
A model of democracy that stresses the development of virtuous citizens.

FIGURE 4.4 Hudson's Typology of Democracy

Note that although all four models are democratic, the emphasis is different in each one. Does it matter?

Protective democracy = individual liberties + property rights	Pluralist democracy = self-interest + coalescence + oligarchy
Developmental democracy = teaching citizenship through civic activity	Participatory democracy = politically active citizens + multiple opportunities

broad participation through voting and expressing opinions is thus essential to making them *feel* closer to government and help them gain a better understanding of the public good, even if they are not active decision makers in it. The paternalistic element is perhaps what most distinguishes it from Hudson's other models.

pluralist democracy
A model of democracy that stresses vigorous competition among various interests in a free society.

The **pluralist democracy** model is the one most people recognize immediately. It features vigorous competition among various interests in a society where diversity is the norm. Hudson's model of pluralism, however, emphasizes its tendency to evolve into a hierarchical order dominated by economic elites. This tendency occurs naturally in a society where individuals are free to form associations or interest groups, because the success of organizations depends on group cohesion, common purpose, and strong leadership. Thus, pluralistic democracy is inherently oligarchic: In a society that places a high priority on business, entrepreneurship, and the amassing of personal wealth, the natural result is social and economic inequality.

participatory democracy
A model of democracy that seeks to expand citizen participation in government to the maximum possible degree.

The final model—**participatory democracy**—is the most straightforward of the four and the closest to a practicable model of direct democracy. In theory, direct democracy means citizens themselves, not elected representatives, decide all major questions of public life. This model could perhaps work in a community or small city-state of a few hundred or even a few thousand citizens at most. It cannot easily work in a large modern state encompassing much territory, many towns and cities, and millions of inhabitants who may or may not even speak the same language.

Nonetheless, participatory democracy is based on the conviction that apathy is a conditioned response, not a trait inherent in human nature. Deprived of opportunities to participate in meaningful ways, people will naturally tune out or get turned off. The key to a vibrant citizenry—and therefore to a healthy democracy—is active participation on a large scale across a wide spectrum of issues. Participatory democracy goes farther, arguing not only that citizens *would* participate actively in politics given the chance but also that they *should* participate—that is, that they have a right to do so.

Hudson's models of democracy, like all others, are just that—models. They do not represent actual democracies, nor are they necessarily the best way to characterize or categorize different types of democracy. But they do point to basic political questions that confront all contemporary democracies, which was precisely Hudson's intention in developing these models in the first place. The models become the basis for his book analyzing "eight challenges to America's future," namely restoring the separation of powers, restraining the "imperial judiciary," combating "radical individualism," promoting citizen participation, reforming the "trivialized" election process, curbing the "privileged position" of business, addressing problems of inequality, and, finally, making the "national security state" more transparent and less threatening to its own citizens.

Moving from theory to policy, as Hudson does, is, by its very nature, controversial. In matters of politics, scholars disagree on what the problems are as well as how to deal with them. Students may ask, if experts (including college professors) cannot agree on the questions facing democracy, much less on the answers, what is the point of theorizing about democracy? The short answer is

Campaigning for the presidency in 2008, Barack Obama talks to young people during the primary season in Indiana. Nearly 6.5 million voters under the age of 30 participated at the polls, breaking records and helping Obama secure the nomination.

© SHUTTERSTOCK

that even if it does not provide clear-cut solutions, theory helps us think about political problems, identify different policy options, and anticipate their consequences. The study of politics is a *social* science, and there is seldom agreement on the vital issues facing society. The existence of different viewpoints is a trademark of constitutional democracy.

We turn, finally, to the question of democracy's future. Are existing models of democracy still relevant, or is a new one needed that is tailored to fit the needs of a new world order?

THE FUTURE OF DEMOCRACY: NATIONALISM OR COSMOPOLITANISM?

Wherever people have access to computers, they are connected to the outside world. The physical distances that separate us are no longer the great barriers they once were to the spread of popular culture, capital, consumer goods, services, and, yes, even ideas. Given the transforming nature of the new information technologies and an ever-expanding world trade system, is it possible that the state as the vessel of democracy is obsolescent?

Cosmopolitan Democracy

Some scholars do believe we need a new model of democracy suitable to an age of globalization. Political scientist David Held has developed a model he calls **cosmopolitan democracy** that attempts to go beyond existing models.

The word *cosmopolitan* in this context denotes a sense of belonging to the world rather than to a particular nation or state. A cosmopolitan individual is, by definition, a frequent traveler who is comfortable abroad, values cultural

cosmopolitan democracy
A model of democracy that sees the individual as part of a world order, not merely (or even primarily) as a citizen of a particular nation-state.

© AP PHOTOS

Are border controls and immigration restrictions that focus on nationalism justified in an age of globalization? What do you think?

diversity, and respects the rights of others to live and worship as they choose. Cosmopolitans find the nation-state too confining; they blame nationalism and tribalism for the prejudice and patriotic fervor that divides the world into "us" and "them" and instead foresee a strengthening sense of community without borders.

Proponents of cosmopolitan democracy favor the extension of citizenship rights and responsibilities across supranational associations like the European Union (EU). In this way, "people would come . . . to enjoy multiple citizenships—political membership in the diverse political communities which significantly affect them." They would be citizens of a state but also fully empowered members of "the wider regional and global networks" that are shaping the world we all live in.[28]

But it is unclear what it would mean to be governed by the rules and institutions of cosmopolitan democracy or to be a member of the new "polities" that are supposedly coming into existence. In fact, the entire concept remains shrouded in ambiguity. Cosmopolitan theorists have not explained why people should trade exclusive citizenship in a well-established polity (or state) for inclusive membership in unproven associations. As the saying goes, a bird in the hand is worth two in the bush.

But these theorists' challenge to the preeminence and permanence of the nation-state is nevertheless important. It seems unlikely that age-old loyalties, institutions, and ways of thinking will prove highly resistant to change.

Democracy in a New World Order

Nobody knows exactly what globalization and the spread of information, particularly via the Internet, will mean for the future of democracy, but clearly the transformations taking place will change our economic and political institutions.

In Europe, for example, the EU now encompasses 27 member-states and constitutes the largest single economy in the world. Many obstacles still stand in the way of a full-fledged political union, but economic integration, a common currency (the euro), qualified majority voting in the European Council, and a directly elected European Parliament have already brought about significant change in the way Europeans are governed.[29]

Growing economic interdependence among the world's countries is creating an ever-increasing flow of goods, services, labor, and capital across borders and oceans. The most powerful countries in the world, including the United States, exercise less internal control over their fiscal and monetary policies, tariffs, and other trade policies than they once did. Even in the area of immigration and naturalization, long considered a litmus test of state sovereignty, governments are finding it difficult to police international borders and prevent "illegals" from gaining entry.

Democracy, in its many evolving varieties, has been a mainstay of the modern era. The number and variety of democracies multiplied during the course of the twentieth century, a process that greatly accelerated in the 1980s (in Latin America) and 1990s (Eastern Europe). Even so, it is much too soon to declare victory for democracy or defeat for the nation-state.

GATEWAYS TO THE WORLD: EXPLORING CYBERSPACE

kclibrary.nhmccd.edu/constitutions-subject.html

confinder.richmond.edu

www.constitution.org/cons/natlcons.htm

The first URL listed above is an excellent site containing the texts of the constitutional documents for more than seventy-five countries. For many countries, there are also accompanying documents, essays, and historical background. From this site, you will be able to compare and contrast various constitutions from around the world. You may also want to read Alexis de Tocqueville's *Democracy in America* to get a sense of an outsider's perspective on the political culture of a constitutional democracy in its early years. The other URLs listed above are similar sites providing information on constitutions from around the world.

thomas.loc.gov

Thomas is the site for the U.S. Congress on the Internet. This is the definitive resource on the American legislative branch, with categories ranging from information on specific members of Congress, to historical documents relating to Congress, to timely reports from the floor of the House and Senate.

www.whitehouse.gov

This is an excellent starting point for information on the executive branch of the U.S. government. You will find information on the president and vice president, including updates on the presidential agenda; a search function for locating White House documents, photographs, and audio files of speeches; and many other useful features.

www.scaruffi.com/politics/democrat.html

This website features a useful list of democratic regimes around the world).

http://careers.state.gov/students/

This is the section of the official U.S. Department of State website devoted to students.

www.ccd21.org

Council for a Community of Democracies website.

www.abc.net.au/civics/oneworld

One World, Many Democracies website for schools.

http://www.findlaw.com/11stategov/indexconst.html

This site provides the texts for all 50 state constitutions.

SUMMARY

In constitutional democracies, governments derive authority from the consent of the governed. Popular election, in theory, ensures that all viewpoints and interests will be represented. Such representation is the defining principle of a republic. Constitutions are designed to place limitations on what governments can and cannot do.

There is no one universally accepted model or theory of liberal democracy. The type of liberal democracy we choose implies a particular view of the basic nature of human society and the main threat(s) to peace and stability.

The idea of America is synonymous with representative democracy in the minds of people all over the world. For inspiration, the Founders drew upon the writings of political thinkers who lived and wrote from the time of the Renaissance to the Enlightenment and who were themselves inspired by classical political philosophy, particularly the writings of Plato and Aristotle from the time of ancient Greece. "The architecture of liberty" grew out of the new science of politics developed by the Founders. That new science was designed to prevent tyranny by compartmentalizing the functions of government (separation of powers) and ensuring that each of the compartments (branches) would have the means to defend itself against encroachment by the others (checks and balances).

We trace three distinct models of American democracy to the ideas of Thomas Jefferson (majority rule), James Madison (balanced government), and John C. Calhoun (brokered government). A fourth model of strong central government is associated with Alexander Hamilton. These early leaders disagreed about how much democracy was too much. Jefferson, for example, favored broad individual liberties and narrow limits on government, whereas Hamilton and others emphasized the need for an energetic national government. Madison falls somewhere between Jefferson and Hamilton. He recognized the danger of governmental paralysis, as well as the need for "energy," but he argued that the best way to achieve freedom and stability was by encouraging a vigorous pluralism, or competition among rival interests. Calhoun was a proponent of states' rights—his views contrasted most sharply with Hamilton's and were closer to Jefferson's.

The concept of popular control through majority rule is central to the creation of a responsive government and holds that the wisdom and interests of the majority are preferable to those of the minority. However, constitutional democracies also place limits on the powers of the government. Protection of individual rights, the rule of law (constitutionalism), and federalism are the principal strategies used to prevent tyranny of the majority. The chapter closes with a look at four contemporary models of democracy and looks into the future of democracy in the light of globalization. A cosmopolitan model of democracy that has practical appeal is yet to be found, but there is no question that technology and globalizing forces have an impact on governments of all types, including democracies.

KEY TERMS

constitutionalism	nullification	ex post facto law
direct democracy	dual federalism	bill of attainder
republic	Supremacy Clause	protective democracy
constitutional democracy	unitary system	homeland security
concurrent powers	power of the purse	developmental democracy
majority rule	war powers	
plurality vote system	presidential democracy	pluralist democracy
checks and balances	tyranny of the majority	participatory democracy
separation of powers	bicameralism	
federalism	rule of law	cosmopolitan democracy
brokered democracy	Magna Carta	
concurrent majority	due process	
	equal protection	

REVIEW QUESTIONS

1. Describe the model of democracy you prefer, and differentiate it from the others. Why did you choose the one you did?
2. What is a republic? Do you think republics are or are not *real* democracies? Explain.
3. Name at least three classical models of American democracy, and explain how they differ from one another.
4. What is federalism? What advantages does this form of government offer?
5. Why did Alexis de Tocqueville (among others) express certain reservations about majority rule?
6. Discuss John Locke's contribution to democratic theory. Can you locate Locke's influence in the U.S. Constitution? If so, where is it?
7. For the theorists involved in the debate over the U.S. Constitution, what was the philosophy behind the "new science of politics"?
8. Recapitulate William Hudson's typology of democracy, and relate it to the models of democracy discussed at the beginning of the chapter.
9. Define *cosmopolitan democracy*, and explain the political context of theoretical attempts to come up with a new, universal model of democracy.

RECOMMENDED READING

Adair, Douglass. *Fame and the Founding Fathers*. New York: Norton, 1974. The author argues that the key Founders were motivated by a strong sense of history and moral probity, that they desired above all to be remembered for founding a just new political order ("fame"), and that they were not driven by personal political ambition or financial gain, as some revisionist historians have suggested.

Brodie, Fawn. *Thomas Jefferson: An Intimate History*. New York: Norton, 1974. An intriguing study of Jefferson the man rather than the legend. The author interweaves two dimensions of Jefferson's life—the political and the personal. Jefferson comes across as being rather less heroic than the paragon often depicted in conventional histories and far from immune to human frailties.

Chernow, Ron. *Alexander Hamilton*. New York: Penguin Press, 2004. Simply a superb scholarly work on arguably the most important figure to emerge from the American Revolution. This book leaves no doubt that Hamilton was the chief architect of the political system that exists in the United States at present.

Corwin, Edward. *The "Higher Law": Background of American Constitutional Law*. Ithaca, NY: Cornell University Press, 1955. A brief account of the rise of constitutionalism in Great Britain and the United States.

Diamond, Larry. *The Spirit of Democracy: The Struggle to Build Free Societies Throughout the World*. New York: Holt, 2009. A hopeful book by a well-respected scholar who sees a bright future for democracy and makes an intelligent case.

Diamond, Martin. *The Founding of the Democratic Republic*. Itasca, IL: Peacock, 1981. An excellent and readable discussion of the ideas employed by the Founders to create a responsive, limited, and effective political order.

Dunn, John. *Democracy: A History*. New York: Atlantic Monthly Press, 2006. The author traces the history of the word "democracy" through the ages and asks how an idea that was first ridiculed and reviled and then virtually forgotten for centuries has come to symbolize the hopes and dreams of people around the world.

Friedrich, Carl. *Limited Government: A Comparison*. Englewood Cliffs, NJ: Prentice-Hall, 1974. A brief explanation of the relationship between constitutionalism and the idea of democracy.

Greene, Jack, ed. *The Reinterpretation of the American Revolution, 1763 to 1789*. Westport, CT: Greenwood, 1979. An outstanding collection of essays exploring American political ideas at a critical era; the essays by Bailyn, Diamond, and Kenyon are especially noteworthy.

Hamilton, Alexander, John Jay, and James Madison. *The Federalist Papers*. New York: Modern Library, 1964. The foremost exposition of the ideas underlying the American democracy by those responsible for its creation.

Held, David. *Models of Democracy*. 3rd ed. Stanford, CA: Polity and Stanford University Press, 2006.

————. *Democracy and the Global Order: From the Modern State to Cosmopolitan Governance*. Stanford, CA: Polity and Stanford University Press, 1995. These two books from David Held caused a stir in the field of political science when they first appeared. The emergence of fledgling democracies all over the world in the 1980s and 1990s created renewed interest in the theory of democracy.

Hudson, William E. *American Democracy in Peril: Eight Challenges to America's Future*, 4th ed. Chatham, NJ: Chatham House, 2003. This book reflects the continued interest of political scientists in the theories of democracy in general and in the problems and prospects for American democracy.

Irons, Peter. *A People's History of the Supreme Court*. New York: Penguin Books, 2006. This book covers the sweep of U.S. constitutional history from 1787 to the end of the twentieth century. Irons gives the reader a close-up look at the justices (warts and all), as well as the landmark cases they decided. He also writes about the lives and travails of the citizens who brought the cases before the Supreme Court.

Isaacson, Walter. *Benjamin Franklin: An American Life*. New York: Simon and Schuster, 2003. An excellent and entertaining biography of a larger-than-life figure who played a major role in the American Revolution and the founding of the United States. Ben Franklin's literary and scientific achievements are well known and often overshadow his political contributions. Isaacson's well-researched book corrects this deficit.

Mayo, H. B. *An Introduction to Democratic Theory*. New York: Oxford University Press, 1960. This book provides a thorough discussion of the advantages, limitations, and distinctive aspects of democracy.

McCullough, David. *1776*. New York: Simon and Schuster, 2005.

————. *John Adams*. New York: Simon and Schuster, 2001. Like Ben Franklin, John Adams is often overshadowed in history books by such legendary figures as George Washington and Thomas Jefferson or by the intellectual, philosophical, and institution-building contributions of Alexander Hamilton and James Madison. McCullough nicely demonstrates that John Adams's qualities of mind and character more than made up for his lack of charisma, his often dyspeptic temperament, and his occasional lapses in judgment. McCullough also stresses the great behind-the-scenes role of John Adams's wise and devoted wife, Abigail Adams.

Zakaria, Fareed. *The Future of Freedom*. New York: W.W. Norton, 2007. This book argues that democracy is not inherently good; that it works in some situations and not in others; and that it needs strong limitations to function properly.

©REMY DE LA MAUVINIERE/AP PHOTO

Egyptian President Hosni Mubarak.

The Authoritarian Model
Myth and Reality

---

authoritarian state
Government in which all legitimate power rests in one person (dictatorship) or a small group of persons (oligarchy), individual rights are subordinate to the wishes of the state, and all means necessary are used to maintain political power.

Until relatively recently, authoritarian regimes greatly outnumbered democracies in the world. Indeed, prior to the 1980s—when democracies began to spring up in Latin America and, at the end of the decade, in Eastern Europe—democracies, with rare exceptions, existed only in Western Europe and North America. **Authoritarian states** come in a variety of sizes and shapes. They can be traditional (monarchies and theocracies) or modern (personal dictatorships or military juntas). One modern form of authoritarianism is so extreme that it has been given a new name—totalitarianism (see Chapter 6). At the other end of the authoritarian spectrum, a number of traditional monarchies still exist, mainly in the Arab Middle East. Examples include Morocco, Saudi Arabia, Jordan, Kuwait, Oman, Bahrain, Qatar, and the United Arab Emirates, as well as tiny Bhutan, Brunei, and Swaziland.

Whatever precise shape and form they assume, authoritarian states share certain telltale traits. Self-appointed rulers typically run the show, and all political power—in practice and often in principle—resides in one or several persons. Most authoritarian governments spurn utopian goals, although at the totalitarian extremes, the rulers do use a millenarian (or utopian) ideology to justify all state action, no matter how harsh or brutal.

Typically, authoritarian rulers do not try to control every aspect of the society and the economy. Rather, they focus on keeping themselves in power and turning back all challenges to the status quo (the existing structures of state power). Authoritarian regimes continue to be the main alternative to constitutional democracy. As such, they warrant closer examination.

THE VIRTUES OF AUTHORITARIANISM

Virtues? Think about it. Authoritarian regimes have had a great deal more success over a lot longer period than democracies. Outside a few relatively brief historical periods—classical Greece and Rome, medieval and Renaissance Italy, and the contemporary age—monarchy as a political system has had few serious challengers (though many individual monarchs have been less fortunate). Even during the more "enlightened" eras, monarchy was the most prevalent form of government. In the golden age of the Greek city-state system, for example, the principal alternative to monarchy was another form of authoritarianism, oligarchy. Republics were rare.

Why? What are the advantages of authoritarian rule? First, it is relatively simple compared with democracy; there is less need to develop complex structures, procedures, and laws. Second, it is streamlined and thus (in theory) efficient. There is no need to bargain or compromise or cajole. Individuals loyal to the regime typically staff the bureaucracy. Recruitment is based on patronage and nepotism rather than on merit. Third, neither special interest groups nor public opinion can block or blunt state action; a predictably repressive response follows any opposition. Fourth, a strong leader can collect taxes, build infrastructure (canals, roads, bridges), raise armies, and rally the nation for defensive purposes like self-preservation or offensive ones like expansion. Fifth, unlike democracies, dictatorships often remain politically stable for a long time, even in the face of economic failure—witness Fidel Castro's Cuba, where a dictatorship has survived for over half a century despite strenuous U.S. efforts to isolate and overthrow it.

In contrast, democracies depend on economic prosperity and a robust middle class. Countries that can afford the luxury of schools and other social infrastructure essential to an informed citizenry are generally better candidates for democracy than are poor, less-developed countries, where people are caught up in a daily struggle for survival.

THE VICES OF AUTHORITARIAN RULERS

As Lord Acton (1834–1902) famously observed, "Power corrupts; absolute power corrupts absolutely." There is something at once intoxicating and addictive about power—a first taste gives rise to an appetite that cannot be easily satisfied. (As the saying goes, "The appetite grows with the eating.") Thus, the tendency to use power as a means of gaining more power is all too human. In short, whether we like it or not, evidence suggests authoritarian rule is more natural than democracy.

But natural is not necessarily better. In politics, nature—especially *human* nature—is often the problem. The challenge is to find ways to temper the antisocial side of human nature, including greed, lust, jealousy, and desire for vengeance.

In authoritarian states, a single ruler or a ruling elite controls the government. The single-head form of government is called an **autocracy,** whereas the elite-group form is known as an **oligarchy,** sometimes referred to as a **junta**

autocracy
Unchecked political power exercised by a single ruler.

oligarchy
A form of authoritarian government in which a small group of powerful individuals wields absolute power.

junta
A ruling oligarchy, especially one made up of military officers.

© HULTON ARCHIVE/GETTY IMAGES

Lord Acton (1834–1902), known to history simply as Lord Acton, Baron John Emerich Edward Dahlberg-Acton was a distinguished British aristocrat and historian. He greatly admired the American federal structure, which he believed to be the ideal guarantor of individual liberty and as an ardent supporter of states' rights he sympathized with the Confederacy in the American Civil War. Never one to engage in hero worship, Acton admonished that "Great men are almost always bad men."

BOX 5.1 FOCUS ON	Fallen Tyrants of the Postwar Era—A Roll Call		
Ruler	**Country**	**Tenure**	**How Removed**
Rafael Trujillo	Dominican Republic	1930–1961	Assassinated
François "Papa Doc" Duvalier	Haiti	1957–1971	Died in office
Idi Amin	Uganda	1971–1979	Ousted (fled)
Jean-Bedel Bokassa	Central African Republic	1965–1979	Ousted (fled)
Reza Pahlavi	Iran	1941–1979	Ousted (fled)
Augusto Pinochet	Chile	1973–1979	Lost election (fled)
Anastasio Somoza	Nicaragua	1967–1979	Ousted (fled)
Jean-Claude "Baby Doc" Duvalier	Haiti	1971–1986	Ousted (fled)
Ferdinand Marcos	Philippines	1972–1986	Ousted (fled)
Alfredo Stroessner	Paraguay	1954–1989	Ousted (exiled)
Mobutu Sese Seko	The Congo (Zaire)	1965–1997	Ousted (fled)
Slobodan Milosevic	Serbia (former Yugoslavia)	1989–1997	Resigned
Saddam Hussein	Iraq	1979–2003	Ousted (executed)

or ruling clique. Authoritarian rulers are the sole repositories of power and authority within the political system. Their tenure in office depends not on elections, which confer the active consent of the people, but on a combination of myth and might. On the one hand, the people are often told that obedience to authority is a moral, sacred, or patriotic duty; on the other hand, the rulers stand ready to use brute force whenever rebellion rears its head.

Authoritarianism and dictatorship go hand in hand. The dictators who came to power after World War II have nearly all died or been deposed (see Box 5.1). Muammar el-Qaddafi of Libya is one exception; Fidel Castro of Cuba, now old and infirm, handed power to his younger brother Raúl in 2008 but remained First Secretary of the Communist Party. Dictators in Syria and Nigeria died in the late 1990s. Today, Bashar al-Assad, the son of Syria's former dictator, rules as the strongman there; the Congo is in a prolonged state of turmoil after decades of rule by a thieving dictator named Mobutu; and Nigeria's civilian government is plagued by corruption on all levels, threatened by internal ethnic and religious conflicts, and highly dependent on the military for security and stability.

Until its turn toward democracy in the 1980s, Latin America had a long tradition of military rule. Indeed, after World War II, such rule was common in most regions of the world, including Asia, the Middle East and North Africa (the so-called Arab world), and sub-Saharan Africa. Egypt provides a good example

BOX 5.2 FOCUS ON   Egypt's Mubarak: President or Dictator?

Egypt's leader, Hosni Mubarak, came to power following the assassination of President Anwar al-Sadat in 1981. Egypt is a solidly Islamic society, but Mubarak heads a secular state.

President Mubarak was re-elected by plebiscites (direct popular votes) in 1987, 1993, and 1999. These had little or no validity, as Mubarak ran unopposed. In February 2005, in the face of rising domestic and international pressure for reform, Mubarak asked parliament to pass an amendment allowing political parties to contest the presidential election set for later in the year. To no one's surprise, however, he was re-elected a fourth time, as the electoral institutions, security apparatus, and official state media remained firmly under his control. In fact, the election was marred by reports of massive vote rigging and other irregularities. The distant runner-up, Dr. Ayman Nour, contested the result and called for a new election. But he was already awaiting trial on apparently trumped-up charges of fraud, and shortly after the election he was convicted and sentenced to five years in jail. The United States called for his release, but to no avail.

In recent years independent news outlets in Egypt have grown, especially newspapers that occasionally severely criticize the president and his family. However Reporters Without Borders still ranks the Egyptian media 133rd of 168 countries in freedom of the press. According to the Human Development Index, which uses various economic and social standards and measures of comparison, Egypt ranks 111th of 177 countries.

Egypt lacks the oil reserves that have made some other Arab nations rich, and its economy relies heavily on agriculture and on a massive annual foreign aid package from the United States. Many Egyptians blame Mubarak for the extreme social and economic inequality that allows a few wealthy Egyptians to live in luxury while the vast majority remains mired in poverty. Many also resent Mubarak's submissive stance toward the United States and his refusal to confront Israel—policies that contrast sharply with his strong-arm tactics in dealing with domestic opponents.

The Muslim Brotherhood, a militant Islamic group with a large popular following, is the main organized opposition in Egypt, but notorious extremist groups, such as Gamaa Islamiya and al-Jihad (Sadat's assassins), also exist, despite draconian efforts by Egypt's police and security forces to eliminate them. When Mubarak finally steps down, it appears likely his son, Gamal, will succeed him. If history is any guide, Egypt will continue to be a democracy in name only.

of a country in which a military strongman, Hosni Mubarak, exchanged his uniform for a business suit and became a civilian president under the pretext of being "elected" by the people (see Box 5.2). Where the military dominates the political system, it often rules as an *institution* rather than through a single individual. A ruling committee, or junta, consisting of generals headed by a "president" who is also a general, is the usual pattern. The military frequently claims legitimacy on the grounds that civilian leaders are corrupt and venal, or that only the military can maintain order and stability.

Senior military officers continue to play an important governing role even in many of Latin America's emerging democracies, which are headed by popularly elected civilian presidents. In Africa, signs that civilian rule was gaining ground in the 1990s have largely vanished, as many societies in that tragic region have been plagued by violence, disease, and poverty—and official corruption on a scale rarely matched and seemingly impossible to eradicate (see below). Authoritarian rulers generally do not respect individual rights when they interfere with the power or policy goals of the state. The interests of the state stand above the interests of society or the welfare of the rank-and-file citizenry. Arbitrary rules, strictly enforced—that is the essence of authoritarianism.

Yet there are important differences among authoritarian rulers. They vary in the extent to which they impose conformity and suppress intellectual and artistic freedom. The amount of force, repression, and violence they employ also varies greatly. Some rulers use coercion sparingly, whereas others, appropriately labeled tyrants, display an enthusiasm for cracking down on dissenters.

Finally, although all tyrants are dictators, not all dictators are tyrants (see Figure 5.1). Some, like the late Josip Broz Tito of Yugoslavia and Anwar al-Sadat of Egypt, occasionally pursue higher aims even at great personal and political risk. Ambitious national programs undertaken to industrialize, reform, or modernize the economy—as demonstrated by Lee Kuan Yew, the no-nonsense political boss of Singapore for three decades (1959–1990), and Deng Xaioping,

FIGURE 5.1   Types of Authoritarian Governments

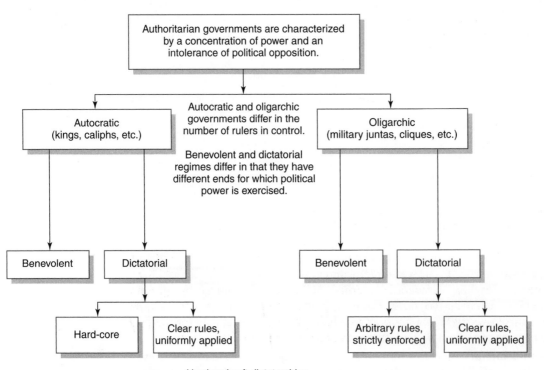

Hard and soft dictatorships
differ in the methods they use to govern.

who engineered China's economic miracle after the death of Mao Zedong in 1976 (see Chapter 8)—point to the possibility of a benevolent dictatorship. Of course, even benevolent dictators generally do not tolerate organized political opposition.

For the people, the dictator's self-restraint is often the only salvation. Iraq under Saddam Hussein was an example of what happens when a dictator recognizes no moral limits to the exercise of power. Self-restrained dictators also use repression at times to maintain law and order (as do democracies), but they typically stage elections, pay lip service to constitutional norms, and show a degree of tolerance toward religious beliefs and cultural differences. Egypt under Mubarak is a good example of a self-restrained dictatorship. The inherent flaw in all dictatorships, however, is that self-restraint never comes with any guarantees.

THE CHARACTERISTICS OF AUTHORITARIAN STATES

Authoritarian rulers frequently come to power by force or violence, using the element of surprise to overthrow the government in a **coup d'etat.** Until quite recently, such power seizures were common in Asia, Latin America, the Middle East, and sub-Saharan Africa.

Maintaining a power monopoly is the main aim of authoritarian states. The army and the police are the principal instruments of coercion, hence the high incidence of military rule. Many civilian rulers of authoritarian states start out as military strongmen. In Egypt, for example, three of the past four leaders—Nasser, Sadat, and Mubarak—were military commanders before becoming president.

To frustrate actual or potential political opposition, authoritarian rulers often impose strict press censorship, outlaw opposition parties, and exert firm control over the legal system, which is manipulated to prosecute (and sometimes persecute) political opponents. Monopoly control of the mass media and the courts gives absolute rulers a potent propaganda tool and the means to suppress dissent in the face of official corruption and often egregious human rights violations, whereas repression is typically justified in the name of order and stability.

Although some authoritarian states have actively promoted social and economic modernization (for example, Turkey, South Korea, and Taiwan have adopted far-reaching democratic reforms), most are characterized by agrarian economies, high unemployment, and mass poverty. Authoritarian rulers tend to seek control over the economy only to a limited extent and chiefly for the purpose of collecting taxes to underwrite military and economic programs as well as lavish personal expenditures.

In sharp contrast to totalitarian regimes (see Chapter 6), most dictatorships are indifferent to the way people live or what they do, as long as they stay

coup d'état
The attempted seizure of governmental power by an alternate power group (often the military) that seeks to gain control of vital government institutions without any fundamental alteration in the form of government or society.

away from politics. To be sure, authoritarian rulers rarely make the lives of the people better—often, exactly the opposite is true. Zimbabwe's President Robert Mugabe is a notorious case in point.

Though authoritarian rulers rarely do what is best for the people, they often do prevent the worst by maintaining law and order, as Robert Kaplan argued in "The Coming Anarchy" (first published in *The Atlantic Monthly* in February 1994).[1] In general, authoritarianism "does not attempt to get rid of or to transform all other groups or classes in the state, it simply reduces them to subservience."[2]

THE POLITICS OF AUTHORITARIANISM

Aristotle argued that all authoritarian forms of rule, despite important differences among them, are a perversion of good government. In his view, "Those constitutions which consider the common interest are *right* constitutions, judged by the standard of absolute justice," whereas "those constitutions which consider only the personal interests of the rulers are all wrong constitutions, or *perversions* of the right forms. Such perverted forms are despotic."[3]

This perversion of ends usually entails a like perversion of means. Despots (cruel dictators) often justify self-serving policies on the grounds that harsh measures are necessary to preserve order or protect the nation from its enemies. Or they may use brute force simply to mask or prevent criticism of their own failed policies. Throughout history, authoritarian rulers and regimes have been notorious for ruthlessly persecuting political opponents. Raising questions regarding who should rule or how is tantamount to treason. In short, where despotism thrives, politics does not.

AUTHORITARIANISM IN PRACTICE: A TALE OF TWO COUNTRIES

Despite a promising trend toward constitutional rule in the 1990s, sub-Saharan Africa continues to be plagued by bad government. In this section we focus on two examples of misrule among many in the region—Zimbabwe and Nigeria. Zimbabwe is a society in crisis due to appalling mismanagement of the nation's finances and agriculture. Nigeria, on the other hand, is sub-Saharan Africa's most populous country (population: circa 150 million) and potentially one of its richest. Until very recently, however, a succession of military rulers squandered its vast oil resources, wasting a golden opportunity to diversify the oil-dependent economy. In the process, corrupt and incompetent generals wrecked Nigeria's public finances and plunged the vast majority of Nigerians into poverty. As recently as 2007, 70 percent of Nigerians earned the equivalent of one dollar a day.

Zimbabwe

Zimbabwe's President Robert Mugabe was born in 1924 in what was then the British colony of Southern Rhodesia. He rose to prominence in the 1960s as the leader of the Zimbabwe African National Union during a long and bitter guerrilla war against white minority rule there. Victorious in 1980, he became the prime minister of the new Black African government of Zimbabwe and gradually gathered dictatorial powers in his own hands. Today, Zimbabwe is a failed state.

At first hailed as a symbol of the new Africa, Mugabe, a lifelong Roman Catholic, has presided over one of the worst and most corrupt governments in the world, while utterly mismanaging Zimbabwe's post-colonial economy. Under his despotic rule, the health and well-being of the people has dropped dramatically, in a natural result of widespread poverty, unemployment, malnutrition, and the absence of medical care—as well as a costly war with the Democratic Republic of the Congo (1998–2002).

The government's chaotic land reform program, which seized white-owned farms with the avowed aim of redistributing the land, effectively destroyed the only functioning sector of the economy and turned Zimbabwe into a net importer of food. Mugabe's response to the economic crisis he created was to print money to cover soaring government deficits while stubbornly refusing to

FIGURE 5.2 Types of Authoritarian Governments

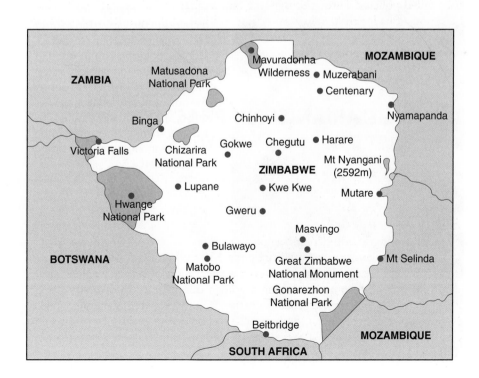

institute economic reforms. The IMF eventually stopped lending to Zimbabwe because of arrears on past loans.

Despite humanitarian food aid from the United States and the EU, according to the World Health Organization, Zimbabwe has the world's shortest life expectancy (37 years for men and 34 for women), the most of orphans (about 25% of the country's children, according to UNICEF), and the highest inflation rate (skyrocketing from over 1,000 percent in 2006 to 11.2 million percent in 2008). An estimated 3,800 Zimbabweans died of cholera in the last half of 2008. Due to mass hunger and disease, the population has shrunk from 12 million to less than 9 million. In January 2009, a newly released $50 billion note was just enough to buy two loaves of bread.

Mugabe "won" re-election in 2002 only after having his leading opponent arrested for treason. In 2008, however, he lost the popular vote to Morgan Tsvangirai, but refused to hand over the reins of power, unleashing a spasm of violence that saw 163 people killed and some 5,000 tortured or brutally beaten.

Under enormous international pressure and facing a re-energized domestic opposition, Mugabe finally agreed to a power sharing deal in September 2008, allowing Tsvangirai to become prime minister in a new dual-executive government. But, true to form, Mugabe broke the agreement, installing his own loyal lieutenants in every ministry. Mugabe, at age 85, remains Zimbabwe's president. In 2009, *PARADE* magazine named Mugabe the world's worst living dictator.

President Robert Mugabe of Nigeria—one of the worst dictators in the world. Too corrupt and venal to allow free elections, Mugabe nonetheless managed to lose a rigged national election for president in 2008, tried to suppress the outcome, refused to step down, and eventually entered into a power sharing agreement with the real winner, whom he quickly marginalized.

© AP PHOTOS

Nigeria

Potentially one of sub-Saharan Africa's great powers, Nigeria endured inept military rule for much of its brief history as an independent state. Although the country accounts for only 3 percent of the African land mass, its 152 million people make up some 20 percent of sub-Saharan Africa's population.

In the 1990s, Nigeria's economy stagnated, growing by less than a half percent per year while corruption reached new heights. A 1996 UN fact-finding mission did not mince words: Nigeria's "problems of human rights are terrible and the political problems are terrifying." A succession of military dictators and ruling cliques enriched themselves shamelessly while utterly neglecting the country's economic and social needs. According to *Transparency International*, a research institute based in Berlin, Germany, Nigeria had the most corrupt government in the world in the mid-1990s.[4]

By this time, bribery and extortion had become a way of life in Nigeria, where the system of "patronage" (with the military rulers bestowing government jobs and other favors on supporters of the regime) produced a bloated, inefficient, irresponsible, and unresponsive bureaucracy that absorbed more than 80 percent of the annual budget. Even today, it is not unusual to find petty civil servants sleeping at their desks or asking visitors for cash. Higher-level officials routinely inflate the contracts for everything the state procures and embezzle untold sums of money.

There is no good reason for Nigeria or Nigerians to be poor. With a gross national product second only to South Africa's, Nigeria is the sixth-biggest oil exporter in the world. But its oil bounty has not been invested in infrastructure, public works projects, or job-creating private business enterprise. In addition to suffering atrocious macroeconomic mismanagement, the country has also been plagued by tribal and ethnic rivalries. Nigeria is not a natural nation-state. Originally a British colony, it was drawn up primarily for the administrative convenience of its colonial rulers (see Chapter 9). Within its borders are peoples divided by region, religion, ethnicity, language, and culture. The fact that some 300 languages and dialects are spoken provides a glimpse of Nigeria's astonishing diversity, which also makes it a breeding ground for social conflict. The country is also divided along religious lines: Muslims dominate in the north, and Christians in the south.

The complexity and diversity of Nigerian society partially explains the failure of two previous experiments with democracy and elected civilian government (in 1960–1966 and 1979–1983). Nigeria's military rulers repeatedly promised free elections, but these promises were not kept. When elections were held in 1993, the results displeased the generals, who nullified the election, imprisoned the winner, and charged him with treason. Thereafter, many other critics of the military regime were also imprisoned and persecuted; some were even executed.

In 1999, a former military leader, Olusegun Obasanjo, became Nigeria's first democratically elected president since 1983. Obasanjo was a rarity in Nigeria—a public figure with a military background and a reputation, justified or not, for personal integrity.

President Obasanjo promised to root out corruption but, despite some eventual arrests and convictions, he had limited success. Here is how one *New York Times* reporter described the situation at the end of 2005:

> Corruption touches virtually every aspect of Nigerian life, from the millions of sham e-mail messages sent each year by people claiming to be Nigerian officials seeking help with transferring large sums of money out of the country, to the police officers who routinely set up roadblocks, sometimes every few hundred yards, to extract bribes of 20 naira, about 15 cents, from drivers.[5]

Nigeria has extensive fossil fuel resources, but crooked officials control the state oil company—the Nigerian National Petroleum Corporation (NNPC)—using it as a cash cow for personal enrichment rather than as a resource for national economic development.

Hopes for a new beginning in Nigeria were dashed in 2007 by widespread reports of fraud in local and parliamentary elections and a sham election for president. What some were calling "gangster politics" eclipsed outgoing President Obasanjo's failed reforms.[6] Despite some signs of recovery in 2008–2009, including an annual growth rate of 5–6 percent, Nigeria's economy remains woefully underdeveloped; its annual per capita gross national product was a mere $1,260 in 2008.

FIGURE 5.3   Map of Nigeria—Note that most of the country's rich oil fields are located in the southern coastal river delta.

BOX 5.3 SPOTLIGHT ON   Madagascar

In March 2009, Andry Rajoelina, who seized power after leading a military coup by junior army officers, was sworn in as Madagascar's president. The South African Development Community (SADC) condemned "in the strongest terms the unconstitutional actions that had led to the illegal ousting of the democratically elected president [Marc Ravalomanana]." The Organization for African Unity (OAU) and larger global community also refused to recognize the Rajoelina government. Rajoelina claimed that "true democracy" had triumphed over dictatorship and promised to abide by "the principles of good government."

Big wrongs call for big lies, like calling what happened in Madagascar "true democracy" or trashing the constitution in the name of "good government." It's enough to make Machiavelli blush.

Andry Rajoelina, the new president of Madagascar

AUTHORITARIANISM IN THEORY: MYTH VERSUS REALITY

The stigma often attached to authoritarianism has given rise to various popular misconceptions. This section focuses on six common assumptions that, on closer examination, are half-truths at best—a blend of fact and myth.

Myth 1: Authoritarianism Is a Sign of the Times

Authoritarianism is neither abnormal nor unique to the modern era. Indeed, at least until the second half of the twentieth century, it was the norm. At the time of the American Revolution, *democracy* was abnormal and widely viewed as a kind of aberration.[7]

In *Politics*, Aristotle provided an impressive catalog of the political tactics designed to render individuals incapable of concerted political action. Persons thought to represent a political threat were eliminated. Autocratic rulers isolated individuals from one another by banning common meals, cultural societies, and other communal activities. Such actions fostered insecurity and distrust and made it difficult for dissidents to create an underground political movement. Secret police and spies increased popular anxiety while obtaining information. Poverty, heavy taxes, and hard work monopolized the subjects' time and attention. (As an example, Aristotle cited the construction of the Egyptian pyramids.) Finally, autocratic rulers viewed warmongering as a useful way of providing a diversion, "with the object of keeping their subjects constantly occupied and continually in need of a leader."[8]

Aristotle's list of autocratic political tactics was expanded and updated by the Italian political thinker Niccoló Machiavelli (1469–1527). We can view his famous book *The Prince* (1532) on one level as a kind of instructor's manual for the successful authoritarian ruler. Those who would rule, Machiavelli contended, must practice "how not to be good." They have no choice but to act immorally in order to survive, but they must take pains to appear honest and upright. It follows that successful rulers must be masters of deception.

Machiavelli also advised would-be rulers not always to keep promises; to dissemble; to inspire both fear and love, but to rely on fear; and to cultivate the appearance of generosity while pursuing self-interest. Generosity for the prince meant giving away what belonged to others.

Punishment should always be severe as well as swift; mild retribution, he observed, is more likely to arouse a spirit of rebellion and makes the ruler look weak and indecisive. By the same token, the sooner the bloodletting was over, the sooner it would be forgotten. Benefits, on the other hand, should be doled out little by little, so as to constantly remind those on the receiving end of the prince's solicitude for the people.

Not surprisingly, the word *Machiavellian* has come to be associated with ruthless, immoral acts. Yet Machiavelli did not invent the methods he prescribed. He simply translated a set of practices prevalent in the dog-eat-dog city-state system of sixteenth-century Italy into a general theory of politics.

MYTH 2: AUTHORITARIAN RULERS ARE ALWAYS TYRANNICAL

Aristotle distinguished between two different forms of authoritarianism. One form, by far the most common of the two, relies on cruelty and repression—crude methods of political control. The purpose of such policies is to intimidate the population, thus inoculating the ruler(s) against a mass revolt.

A second kind of authoritarian ruler displays concern for the common good and avoids ostentation, gives no sign of any impropriety, honors worthy citizens, erects public monuments, and so on. Such a "half-good" autocrat would clearly be preferable to a "no-good" one.

Some autocratic rulers imprison, torture, and even murder real or imagined political enemies; others govern with a minimum of force. Some run the economy into the ground; others give economic development the highest priority. Muhammad Reza Shah Pahlavi (1919–1980) of Iran, for example, was both an

© STAFF/HULTON ARCHIVE/GETTY IMAGES

Niccolò Machiavelli (1469–1527). Renaissance Italy's most famous political philosopher, Machiavelli is also one of its most controversial characters. He approached the study of politics as a scientist determined to record what he observes, not what others want to believe. The political arena was his laboratory. He was a remorseless realist. In *The Prince,* he offered shocking advice to rulers not to let moral inhibitions weaken them in the face of political necessity. But what is often forgotten or overlooked is that he also counseled prudence: " . . . no prince has ever benefited from making himself hated."

unrelenting persecutor of his political enemies and a progressive modernizer in the realm of cultural, economic, and social policy, where some measure of personal freedom existed. Similarly, the present-day governments of Taiwan and Singapore represent a curious mixture of democracy and dictatorship, yet both countries for years have enjoyed relatively high rates of economic growth and standards of living that were the envy of many Third World states.

Myth 3: Authoritarian Rulers Are Never Legitimate

In the United States, we agree with John Locke that legitimacy arises from the consent of the governed. But consent is not the only measure of legitimacy—in fact, for long periods in history popular will was not even recognized as a criterion of legitimacy.

Instead, from the late Middle Ages through the eighteenth century, the prevalent form of government in Europe was monarchy, based on divine right conferred by religious belief or royal birth conferred by heredity. In Imperial China, the dynastic principle was one source of the emperor's legitimacy, but religion also played a major role; the Chinese emperor ruled under the "mandate of Heaven."

Many contemporary dictatorships have relied on a somewhat more informal and personal source of legitimacy—the popular appeal of a **charismatic leader.** Often charismatic rule is grounded in the personal magnetism, oratorical skills, or legendary feats of a national hero who has led the country to victory in war or revolution. Post-World War II examples include Egypt's Nasser (1956–1970), Indonesia's Sukarno (1945–1967), and Libya's Qaddafi (1969–present). Many post-colonial Third World dictators came to power as "liberators" who led the struggle for independence and emerged as objects of hero worship.

charismatic leader
A political leader who gains legitimacy largely through the adoration of the populace. Such adoration may spring from past heroic feats (real or imagined) or from personal oratorical skills and political writings.

Divine sanction, tradition, and charisma, then, are the historical pillars of autocratic rule. More often than not, these wellsprings of legitimacy have effectively sold the idea that the rulers have a *right* to rule without consulting the people. Having the right to rule does not mean the same thing as ruling rightly, of course. And unfortunately, dictators and tyrants have too often used this "right" to commit serious wrongs.

But legitimacy, like beauty, is in the eyes of the beholder. If the people embrace an autocrat or dictator, no matter how brutal, evil, or corrupt he or she might be, that is what counts. What outsiders might think of a ruler like Cuba's Fidel Castro or Venezuela's Hugo Chavez is irrelevant.

Myth 4: Authoritarian Rulers Are Always Unpopular

Given a choice, everyone would choose to live in a democracy rather than a dictatorship, right? If that is so, how do we account for popular dictators? Undeniably, some inspire not only fear but also respect, trust, voluntary obedience, and even love. In the aftermath of war or revolution, for example, dictators sometimes usher in periods of economic development and political stability—changes that improve the lives of the people. One recent example is former President Lee Kuan Yew of Singapore; two historical examples are Catherine the Great of Russia and Frederick the Great of Prussia. Abraham Lincoln, one of our most admired and revered presidents, exercised dictatorial powers during the Civil War.

Personal charisma is another source of popularity. The prototype of the charismatic "man on horseback" was Napoléon Bonaparte (1769–1821). Napoléon seized power in a France convulsed by revolution and led it in a series of spectacularly successful military campaigns, nearly conquering the entire European continent. At the height of his military success, Napoléon enjoyed almost universal popularity in France.

Hitler, too, enjoyed broad support among the German rank and file. As one writer pointed out,

> It is sometimes assumed that one who rules with the support of the majority cannot be a tyrant; yet both Napoléon and Hitler, two of the greatest tyrants of all time, may well have had majority support through a great part of their reigns. Napoléon, in many of his aggressive campaigns, probably had majority support among the French, but his actions . . . were nonetheless tyrannical for that. Hitler, for all we know, might have had at least tacit support of the majority of the German people in his campaign against the Jews; his action was nonetheless tyrannical for that . . . A tyrant . . . may in many of his measures have popular support, but . . . his power will not depend upon it.[9]

Good people will not necessarily stand in the way of bad rulers. As the great Russian writer Fyodor Dostoyevsky (1821–1881) observed, in an age of equality, the masses desire security above all else, and they will gladly accept despotism in order to escape the burdens that accompany the benefits of freedom.[10] The truth is that despotic government is often more popular than we care to believe.

Myth 5: Authoritarianism Has No Redeeming Qualities

Even the worst tyrants can bring order out of political chaos and material progress out of economic stagnation. Hitler jump-started Germany's economy. Apologists for Benito Mussolini (1883–1945), Italy's fascist dictator in World War II, have noted that at least he made the trains run on time. Stalin industrialized Soviet Russia and thus set the stage for its rise to superpower status after World War II. Such public policy successes by no means justify the excesses of these tyrants, but they do help explain their domestic popularity.

Perhaps the most impressive example of an autocratic regime that succeeded in creating sustained social and economic progress comes not from Europe but from China. Baron de Montesquieu, Adam Smith, and Karl Marx were all moved to comment on the classical Chinese system of government.[11] The vast network of dikes, irrigation ditches, and waterways that crisscrossed the immense Chinese realm is particularly noteworthy. This hydraulic system represented a signal achievement, exceeding in scale and scope any public works ever undertaken in the West in pre-modern times. What kind of civilization could build public works on such a stupendous scale?

One modern scholar, Karl Wittfogel, theorized that the Chinese system, which he labeled "oriental despotism," owed its distinctive features to the challenges of sustaining a huge population in a harsh and demanding environment.[12] Rice has long been a staple in China, and rice cultivation requires large amounts of water under controlled conditions. Thus, to solve the perennial food problem, Chinese civilization first had to solve the perennial water problem. This meant building sophisticated flood control, irrigation, and drainage works. The result was a system of *permanent agriculture* that enabled Chinese

ALAN TOWSE; ECOSCENE/CORBIS

Chinese peasant in rice paddy. In his book *Oriental Despotism* (1975), German-American historian Karl Wittfogel called civilizations whose agriculture was dependent upon large-scale waterworks for irrigation and flood control "hydraulic civilizations." In ancient times, massive building projects necessitated centralized control—an absolutist bureaucratic state developed that monopolized political and economic power. Major examples in Wittfogel's study were Egypt, Mesopotamia, India, China, pre-Columbian Mexico, and Peru. Prominent features of this type of civilization included forced labor and a bureaucracy.

peasants to cultivate the same land for centuries without stripping the soil of its nutrients.

Constructing such a system necessitated a strong central government. A project as ambitious as the transformation of the natural environment in the ancient world could not have been attempted without political continuity and stability, social cohesion, scientific planning, resource mobilization, labor conscription, and bureaucratic coordination on a truly extraordinary scale. Thus, the technology and logistics of China's system of permanent agriculture gave rise to a vast bureaucracy and justified a thoroughgoing, imperial dictatorship.

Private property ownership was rare and vast public works projects were designed and implemented by a centralized bureaucracy dedicated to efficient administration. Admission to the bureaucratic class was based on a series of examinations. At the apex of the power pyramid sat the emperor, who ruled under the mandate of Heaven and whose power was absolute.

What about the Chinese people under this highly centralized form of government? The rank-and-file traded labor for food and were treated as subjects, not citizens. The masses had duties in relation to the state but no rights. On the positive side, Imperial China lasted longer than any other system of government the world has ever known (from about 900 to 1800). As the saying goes, nothing succeeds like success.

Imperial China presents us with a paradox. On the one hand, it stands as an example of a ruling order more despotic than most traditional forms of Western authoritarianism.[13] On the other hand, its economic and technical achievements, along with its art, language, and literature, were extremely impressive by any standard. Significant material advances accompanied China's early economic development. Although the emperors and scholar-officials were neither liberal nor politically enlightened, their system of hydraulic despotism resulted in a sufficient supply of food to support a large and growing population for centuries—though not without occasional famines.

Today, China continues to be governed under a centralized, authoritarian system, but despite having the world's largest population (1.3 billion), it boasts one of the world's fastest growing economies (see Chapter 8). On the other hand, China was in continual turmoil and plunged into an economic abyss for a quarter of a century after World War II under Chairman Mao, demonstrating the perils of a dictatorship devoid of checks and balances (see Chapter 6).

Still, we often apply tougher standards to dictatorships than to democracies. No form of government comes with a guarantee, including democracy.

Myth 6: Authoritarianism Is the Worst Possible Government

Totalitarian states (the focus of the next chapter) go well beyond traditional autocracies in trampling on human rights—rounding up enemies, using slave labor, and carrying out acts of mass murder. One of the grim lessons of the last century is that the worst possible government is worse than most of us can imagine.

THE FUTURE OF AUTHORITARIANISM

Between 1974 and 1990, more than 30 countries in Latin America, Asia, and Eastern Europe shifted from a nondemocratic to a democratic form of government.[14] During the 1980s, Ecuador, Bolivia, Peru, Brazil, Uruguay, Argentina, Chile, and Paraguay replaced military rulers, opting for more democratic alternatives. Central American nations followed suit. In 1989, a wave of revolutions swept communist regimes from power across Eastern Europe.

Democracy also made inroads in parts of sub-Saharan Africa. In the early 1990s, many African countries held multiparty elections or adopted reforms designed to lead to such elections.[15] At the same time, South Africa's repressive **apartheid system,** based on a racist ideology of white supremacy, was abolished and replaced by majority rule.

How deep and enduring the trend away from authoritarian governments will be is still an open question. Can we look forward to a future when, for the first time in human history, democracy will be the global norm? Certainly, the contemporary world features many examples of successful democracies and failed dictatorships, and the prosperity common to many democratic states encourages imitators.

But it is premature to proclaim a victory for democracy. Indeed, in the past decade much of Africa has slid back into a chaotic authoritarianism bordering on anarchy.[15] The rise of Islamism, a fanatical, violent, anti-Western form of Islam, is a reminder that Western-style democracy continues to face major challenges in many parts of the world. Another is the return of the centralized authoritarian state in Russia, which is "run largely in the interests of a ruling clique."[16] Democracy has often suffered reversals even in the West, where popular rule has the deepest roots.[17]

In Latin America, democracy is widespread yet in places remains fragile and unstable. Several countries, including Colombia, Peru, and Mexico, face internal threats from guerrilla and terrorist groups. In 2004, a *New York Times* reporter painted this bleak picture:

> In the last few years, six elected heads of state have been ousted in the face of violent unrest, something nearly unheard of in the previous decade. A widely noted United Nations survey of 19,000 Latin Americans in 18 countries in April produced a startling result: a majority would choose a dictator over an elected leader if that provided economic benefits.[18]

He added, "Analysts say that the main source of the discontent is corruption and the widespread feeling that elected governments have done little or nothing to help the 220 million people in the region who still live in poverty, about 43 percent of the population."

Great disparities in wealth and living standards in today's world help explain popular discontent with democracy. There are many countries in Eastern Europe, Asia, Latin America, and sub-Saharan Africa where modern economies have yet to be created. Gross economic and educational inequalities persist and

apartheid system
The South African system designed to perpetuate racial domination by whites prior to the advent of black majority rule there in the early 1990s.

worsen with the passage of time. Stagnant economies and tribal or ethnic divisions destabilize many developing societies.

Even in countries where the military has relinquished power, generals often continue to exert a behind-the-scenes influence over civilian governments. Where the principle of civilian rule is open to question, the government is fragile and the fear of anarchy is real, the abrupt return of military dictatorship remains an ever-present possibility. Dictators come and go, but it is too soon to write the obituary for authoritarian rule.

AUTHORITARIANISM AND U.S. FOREIGN POLICY

Soon after the end of World War II, the United States found itself engaged in a cold war with the Soviet Union. The Cold War was not a natural rivalry between two great powers but rather a struggle to the death between two rival systems of morality, economics, and government. The ideologies of these two rivals were absolutely incompatible. The United States pursued a policy of "containment" based on the theory that communism would eventually collapse of its own dead weight, while the Soviet Union drew upon Marx's prediction that capitalism was headed for the "dustbin of history."

The two principals in this contest divided the world into two halves—East and West, communist and capitalist, good and evil. One thing the implacable foes agreed on, however, was that neutrality was not an option: with few exceptions, the nations of the earth would have to choose between them.

In reality, the world was never so neatly divisible. Many developing countries preferred to remain nonaligned. Egypt, India, and Indonesia attempted to launch a nonaligned movement in the 1950s that, for a time, appeared to be getting off the ground. But the Cold War protagonists cajoled, pressured, and enticed the leaders of these fledgling states with foreign aid, weapons transfers, and cash. By the mid-1960s, most governments in Africa, Asia, and Latin America had chosen sides.

In the rush to recruit Third World leaders who would jump on the anticommunist bandwagon for a price, the United States frequently found itself using "dollar diplomacy" and other inducements to prop up right-wing dictatorships—and looking the other way when friendly regimes committed gross violations of human rights.[19] Although the Cold War is now over, its legacy lives on, as critics of the Bush administration's decision to invade Iraq made clear by pointing out that the United States had secretly supported Saddam Hussein during the bloody Iran-Iraq war in the 1980s (see Box 5.4). That Saddam was a brutal dictator did not matter to Washington; what mattered was that Iraq and Iran were enemies, and, as the saying goes, "the enemy of my enemy is my friend."

Unfortunately, as events in the Balkans, West Africa, and elsewhere in the 1990s showed, when an autocrat dies or is ousted, the result is not always democracy, peace, and prosperity—that is one of the most important lessons of

BOX 5.4 FOCUS ON   The Butcher of Baghdad

In many respects the iron-fisted Saddam Hussein, who was ousted in 2003 after ruling Iraq for 24 years, was the "perfect" tyrant. Saddam's heroes were modern history's most ruthless dictators.

Saddam has been aptly compared with Joseph Stalin, the brutal Soviet dictator who summarily executed countless "enemies" and sent millions more to work and die in slave labor camps. Like Stalin, Saddam ruled through a tightly controlled monolithic political organization, the Ba'ath Party, which was virtually indistinguishable from the state. Like Stalin, he turned the country into a vast prison. And like Stalin, he perpetuated his rule through paralyzing fear, induced by highly publicized mock trials and police-state terror.

No one knows for certain how many Iraqis became victims of the Ba'athist regime during Saddam's 24-year rule. That he routinely imprisoned all whom he suspected of disloyalty, that he used poison gas against whole villages to punish rebellious Kurds in the north, and that he tortured many of his victims without mercy are facts well known to Iraqis. Iraqi "traitors" and "enemies of the state" were not safe even abroad. At Saddam's behest, secret agents murdered scores of dissidents in exile in the 1980s and 1990s.

As Saddam put it, "The hand of the revolution can reach out to its enemies wherever they are found."*

Saddam emulated Stalin's use of ideology and propaganda to justify or legitimize his crimes against humanity by extolling the "historical mission" of the Ba'ath Party. If the regime brutalized and dehumanized anyone who got in its way, it was always for a "higher purpose."

In fact, Saddam's purposes were purely self-serving: to stay in power and live like a king while his people sank ever deeper into poverty. Between 1991 and 1995, he reportedly built fifty new palaces at a cost of $1.5 billion; the largest was bigger than Versailles. Saddam displayed no conscience and no remorse in doing whatever he deemed necessary to control Iraqi society while he plundered the economy.

Following his capture, trial, and conviction for mass murder in the wake of the U.S.-led invasion of Iraq, Saddam was hanged in Baghdad on December 30, 2006. He was defiant and unrepentant to the end—the eternal perfect tyrant.

---

*Quoted in Elaine Sciolino, *The Outlaw State: Saddam Hussein's Quest for Power and the Gulf Crisis* (New York: Wiley, 1991), p. 91.

---

the post–Cold War era. Closer to home, as Robert Kaplan noted, "Look at Haiti, a small country only 90 minutes by air from Miami, where 22,000 American soldiers were dispatched in 1994 to restore 'democracy' Five percent of eligible Haitian voters participated in [the last] election, chronic instability continues, and famine threatens."[20] Kaplan continued,

> Those who think that America can establish democracy the world over should heed the words of the late American theologian and philosopher Reinhold Niebuhr: "The same strength which has extended our power beyond a continent has also . . . brought us into a vast web of history in which other wills, running in oblique or contrasting directions to our own, inevitably hinder or contradict what we most fervently desire. We

cannot simply have our way, not even when we believe our way is to have the "happiness of mankind" as its promise.[21]

These words proved prophetic. In early 2004, exactly a decade after Kaplan's warning about the dangers of anarchy in impoverished, out-of-the-way countries like Haiti was first published in *The Atlantic Monthly*, Haiti's elected president, Jean-Bertrand Aristide, was forced to flee as mob violence threatened to plunge the country into chaos. The crisis ended only after a U.S. Marine Corps contingent was deployed to restore calm.

Autocrats are often brutal and even sadistic. But where the fear and awe they inspire, and the ruthless methods they employ, prevent a descent into anarchy, it is quite possibly the lesser of two great evils. In Kaplan's words:

> The lesson to draw is not that dictatorship is good and democracy bad but that democracy emerges successfully only as a capstone to other social and economic achievements . . . Tocqueville showed how democracy evolved in the West not through the kind of moral fiat we are trying to impose throughout the world but as an organic outgrowth of development.[22]

The U.S.-led invasion of Iraq in 2003 that ousted Saddam Hussein left the U.S. military as the only source of order in the country. After years of misrule and more than a decade under UN.-imposed economic sanctions, Iraq was impoverished and its three major communities—Kurds in the north, Sunni in the center, and Shi'a in the south—were deeply divided. In early 2009, six years after the invasion, Baghdad, despite the heavy presence of U.S. troops, is still an urban battleground, but no longer a house of horrors, with terrorist bombings, kidnappings, torture, and videotaped beheadings.

The immediate danger of Iraq sinking into anarchy has receded but not disappeared. President Obama has set a timetable to withdraw U.S. forces from Iraq that would end the U.S. combat mission on August 31, 2010, although some 35,000 to 50,000 troops would remain (presumably as "trainers"). If all goes according to plan (a big "if" at this point), all U.S. troops will withdraw by the last day of 2011. What will happen next is anybody's guess. In Iraq, as in Afghanistan and other troubled parts of the world, it is possible that the only real choice at this stage in history is between anarchy and authoritarianism.

GATEWAYS TO THE WORLD: EXPLORING CYBERSPACE

Many countries discussed in this chapter have individual Websites devoted to aspects of their political, historical, and social culture. To find a list of these sites, use the name of the specific country of interest as your search term. You should be particularly aware of the group or individual that sponsors or maintains each Website. Shell Oil's Nigeria Website is likely to take a very different stance on the impact of multinational corporations on the Nigerian economy than would the Website of a patriotic Nigerian business leader.

www.gwu.edu/~nsarchiv/special/iraq

This site features information on the fallen Iraqi dictator, Saddam Hussein.

www.amnesty.org

Amnesty International's website is an excellent source of information for further exploration of the impact of Nigerian authoritarianism on human rights.

en.wikipedia.org/wiki/Authoritarianism

A place to start. Click the various terms such as *absolute monarchies, dictatorships, despotisms,* and *theocracies* for definitions and exegesis. Check out *militarchies.* As with all Wikipedia material, the quality is not consistent, so proceed with this caveat in mind.

SUMMARY

When one or more self-appointed rulers exercise unchecked political power, the result is a dictatorship. Benevolent autocrats (who are somewhat concerned with advancing the public good), ordinary dictators (who are concerned solely with advancing their own interests), and tyrants (who exhibit great enthusiasm for violence and bloodletting) all qualify as dictators, but even slight differences can make a significant alteration in the lives of the people who, by definition, have no voice in how they are governed.

Historically, authoritarian rulers have provided the most common form of government. Yet despite their prevalence, authoritarian regimes have been regarded as perversions of good government because they almost always place the ruler's interests ahead of the public good. Nigeria provides a good example of a contemporary authoritarian state.

Misconceptions about authoritarian regimes abound. It is not true that dictatorial rule is a modern phenomenon or that all authoritarian states are identical, illegitimate, or unpopular with their citizens. Further, we can differentiate such governments on moral grounds: Some seek to promote the public interest; others do not. Moreover, authoritarian regimes do not represent the worst possible form of government in all cases.

Finally, despite some evidence that authoritarian government is giving way to democracy, it is too early to draw any definitive conclusions. The record of U.S. relations with authoritarian states is replete with inconsistencies and contradictions. The latter have weakened the U.S. moral position in international politics, complicated its diplomatic efforts, and led to charges of hypocrisy.

KEY TERMS

authoritarian states   junta   apartheid system
autocracy   coup d'etat
oligarchy   charismatic leader

REVIEW QUESTIONS

1. What are the two basic types of nondemocratic government? What are the chief characteristics of authoritarian governments?
2. Are authoritarian governments becoming less prevalent? Where are such governments found today?
3. Are all autocrats tyrannical? Explain.
4. What kind of "advice" did Machiavelli give to rulers bent on maintaining their power?
5. Summarize the six myths that surround authoritarian governments. What fallacies underlie these myths?

RECOMMENDED READING

Boesche, Roger. *Theories of Tyranny, from Plato to Arendt*. University Park: Pennsylvania State Press, 1996. Many authoritarian rulers have been tyrants, and tyranny has been a subject of study for some of the greatest political thinkers. This book examines both.

Brownlee, Jason. *Authoritarianism in an Age of Democratization*. New York and London: Cambridge University Press, 2007. This book is based on fieldwork in Egypt, Iran, Malaysia, and the Philippines and seeks to explain the mixed record of democratic reforms in these countries by comparing how ruling parties originated.

Crick, Bernard. *Basic Forms of Government: A Sketch and a Model*. Magnolia, MA: Peter Smith, 1994. This short, yet comprehensive, outline of types of governments contrasts authoritarian with totalitarian and democratic states.

Kalanthil, Shanthi, and Taylor C. Boas. *Closed Networks, Closed Regimes: The Impact of the Internet on Authoritarian Rule*. Washington, DC: Carnegie Endowment for International Peace, 2003. The title tells the tale.

Kaplan, Robert. *The Coming Anarchy: Shattering the Dreams of the Post Cold War*. New York: Vintage Books, 2000. A nicely arranged collection of insightful pieces on the challenges of the post–Cold War international system, featuring as its centerpiece the author's widely discussed article on the danger of anarchy—most notably in West Africa and the Balkans—originally published in *The Atlantic Monthly* in February 1994.

Karsh, Efraim, and Inari Rautsi. *Saddam Hussein: A Political Biography*. New York: Grove Press, 1991 (revised introduction and epilogue, 2002). Although Saddam Hussein is dead and gone, this book is still worth reading as a study in the personality and practices of a modern tyrant who was apparently quite unencumbered by a moral conscience.

Laber, Jeri. "The Dictatorship Returns." *New York Review of Books*, vol. 40, no. 13, July 15, 1993. This book describes the return of a Soviet-era one-man dictatorship in Turkmenistan. The dictator Saparmurat Niyazov, who died in December 2006, ruled by dint of a personality cult in one of the most authoritarian states in the world.

Latey, Maurice. *Patterns of Tyranny*. New York: Atheneum, 1969. A study that attempts to classify and analyze various tyrannies throughout history.

Machiavelli, Niccolò. *The Prince*, translated by Harvey C. Mansfield Jr. Chicago: University of Chicago Press, 1985. This classic study describes the methods tyrants must use to maintain power.

Moore, Barrington. *Social Origins of Dictatorship and Democracy*. Boston: Beacon Press, 1993. A general discussion of the relationship between social conditions and political systems.

Rubin, Barry. *Modern Dictators: Third World Coup Makers, Strongmen, and Political Tyrants*. New York: New American Library/Dutton, 1989. A good general discussion of various nondemocratic regimes that have held power in the post–World War II era.

Skierka, Volker. *Fidel Castro: A Biography*. Cambridge, UK: Polity Press, 2004. First published in German in 2000, this book is a well-researched narrative of Castro's life.

Szulc, Tad. *Fidel: A Critical Portrait*. New York: Avon Books, 1986. A highly acclaimed biography by a former *New York Times* foreign correspondent based on extensive interviews with Castro, as well as with friends and associates of the Cuban dictator.

North Korea's President Kim Jong Il presides over one of the last Soviet-style totalitarian states still in existence—a country often called the Hermit Kingdom because it is so cut off from the rest of the world, seemingly bent on acquiring nuclear weapons.

©AP PHOTOS

The Totalitarian Model
False Utopias

The Essence of Totalitarianism

The Revolutionary Stage of Totalitarianism

Leadership

Ideology

Organization

Propaganda

Violence

The Consolidation of Power

Eliminating Opposition Parties

Purging Real or Imagined Rivals Within the Party

Creating a Monolithic Society

The Transformation of Society

The Soviet Union under Stalin

Germany under Hitler

China under Mao

The Human Cost of Totalitarianism

Other Faces of Totalitarianism

The Short Lives of the Worst Regimes

totalitarianism
A political system in which every facet of the society, the economy, and the government is tightly controlled by the ruling elite. Secret police terrorism and a radical ideology implemented through mass mobilization and propaganda are hallmarks of the totalitarian state's methods and goals.

A new and more malignant form of tyranny called **totalitarianism** reared its ugly head in the twentieth century. The term itself denotes complete domination of a society and its members by tyrannical rulers and imposed beliefs. The totalitarian obsession with control extends beyond the public realm into the private lives of citizens.

Imagine living in a world in which politics is forbidden and *everything* is political—including work, education, religion, sports, social organizations, and even the family. Neighbors spy on neighbors and children are encouraged to report "disloyal" parents. "Enemies of the people" are exterminated.

Who are these "enemies"? Defined in terms of whole *categories* or groups within society, they typically encompass hundreds of thousands and even millions of people who are "objectively" counterrevolutionary—for example, Jews and Gypsies (Romany) in Nazi Germany, the *bourgeoisie* (middle class) and *kulaks* (rich farmers) in Soviet Russia, and so on. By contrast, authoritarian governments typically seek to maintain political power (rather than to transform society) and more narrowly define political enemies as individuals (not groups) actively engaged in opposing the existing state.

Why study totalitarianism now that the Soviet Union no longer exists? First, communism is not the only possible form of totalitarian state. The examples of Nazi Germany and Fascist Italy are reminders that totalitarianism is not a product of one ideology, regime, or ruler. Second, totalitarianism is an integral part of contemporary history. Many who suffered directly at the hands of totalitarian dictators or lost loved ones in Hitler's Holocaust, Stalin's Reign of Terror, Mao's horrific purges, or other, more recent instances of totalitarian brutality are still living. The physical and emotional scars of the victims remain even after the tyrants are long gone. Third, totalitarian states demonstrate the risks of idealism gone awry. Based on a millenarian vision of social progress and perfection that cannot be pursued without resort to barbaric measures (and cannot be achieved even then), they all have failed miserably as experiments in utopian nation building. Finally, as we will see, totalitarianism remains a possibility wherever there is great poverty, injustice, and therefore the potential for violence and turmoil—recent examples include Iran, North Korea, and Burma.

It is dangerous to assume the world has seen the last of the totalitarian tyrants. Indeed, the 2001 terrorist attacks on the United States raised several poignant questions: Is it possible that future totalitarian threats to peace and freedom will not necessarily be posed by a figure who heads a government or rules a state? Are Osama bin Laden and his al Qaeda network such a threat? After all, the Taliban regime in Afghanistan, which harbored bin Laden and his organization, displayed many of the characteristics of a totalitarian state.

One of the lessons of 9/11 is that extremism remains a fact of political life in the contemporary world. It can take many malignant forms. Terrorism is one; totalitarianism is another. This chapter demonstrates clearly that totalitarianism and terror go hand in hand.

THE ESSENCE OF TOTALITARIANISM

Violence is at the core of every totalitarian state—at its worst, it assumes the form of indiscriminate mass terror and genocide aimed at whole groups, categories, or classes of people who are labeled enemies, counterrevolutionaries, spies, or saboteurs. Mass mobilization is carried out through a highly regimented and centralized one-party system in the name of an official ideology that functions as a kind of state religion. The state employs a propaganda and censorship apparatus far more sophisticated and effective than that typically found in authoritarian states. As the late William Kornhauser, a sociologist, wrote in a highly acclaimed study, "Totalitarianism is limited only by the need to keep large numbers of people in a state of constant activity controlled by the elite."[1]

Totalitarian ideologies promise the advent of a new social order—whether a racially pure "Aryan" society envisioned by Adolf Hitler, or the classless society promised by Lenin and Josef Stalin, or the peasant society in a permanent state of revolution Mao Zedong imagined. All such totalitarian prophets "have exhibited a basic likeness . . . [in seeking] a higher and unprecedented kind of human existence."[2] We can trace the totalitarian leader's claim of political legitimacy directly to this self-proclaimed aim of creating a new utopian society.[3]

Totalitarian societies are "thoroughly egalitarian: no social differences will remain; even authority and expertise, from the scientific to the artistic, cannot be tolerated."[4] Thus, individualism is rejected and even criminalized. The rights of society are paramount, leaving no room at all for the rights of the individual.

At the heart of this harmonious community lies the concept of a reformulated human nature. The impulse to human perfection was reflected in Lenin's repeated references to the creation of a "new Soviet man" and in the Nazi assertion that party workers and leaders represented a new type of human being or a new breed of "racially pure" rulers. Mao Zedong displayed a near obsession with something he called **rectification**—the radical purging of all capitalist tendencies, such as materialism and individualism, at all levels of Chinese society.

The clearest examples of such utopian political orders have been Nazi Germany, the Soviet Union (especially during Stalin's Reign of Terror), and Maoist China. Other examples include Pol Pot's Cambodia (1976–1979) and Mengistu's Ethiopia (1977–1991), and Kim Jong Il's North Korea (still in existence in 2009). In the following section we examine the stages in the evolution of totalitarian regimes.

rectification
In Maoist China, the elimination of all purported capitalist traits, such as materialism and individualism.

THE REVOLUTIONARY STAGE OF TOTALITARIANISM

How do totalitarian movements start? Typically, they emerge from the wreckage of a collapsed or collapsing state. In such turbulent times, a charismatic leader sometimes steps onto the scene. Leadership is crucial to the success of any revolution. In the case of *total* revolution, leadership is one of five key elements. Ideology, organization, propaganda, and violence are the other four.

Leadership

Perhaps the most conspicuous trait of total revolution has been reliance on what we may term the *cult of leadership*. Virtually every such revolution has been identified with—indeed, personified in—the image of a larger-than-life figure. The Russian Revolution had its Lenin, the Third Reich its Hitler, the Chinese Revolution its Mao, Cuba its Castro, and so forth. Each of these leaders became the object of hero worship. Without such a leader, observed Eric Hoffer, "there will be no [mass] movement."

> It was Lenin who forced the flow of events into the channels of the Bolshevik revolution. Had he died in Switzerland or on his way to Russia in 1917, it is almost certain that the other prominent Bolsheviks would have joined a coalition government. The result might have been a more or less liberal republic run chiefly by the bourgeoisie. In the case of Mussolini or Hitler the evidence is even more decisive: without them there would have been neither a Fascist nor a Nazi movement.[5]

Revolutionary leaders instinctively understand that the masses possess the raw power to change the world but lack the will and direction. Without a charismatic leader—one who can read their minds, capture their imagination, and win their hearts—there is nothing to act as a catalyst. A leader such as Lenin or Mao, then, is to a mass movement what a detonator is to a bomb.

Ideology

Whatever the quality of leadership, total revolutions depend in the final analysis on the willingness of converts to engage in extraordinary acts of self-sacrifice in the name of the cause. Such reckless devotion cannot be inspired by rational appeals. It must arise, rather, from the true believer's blind faith in the absolute truth provided by a comprehensive political doctrine.

Consider what an ideology must do for its followers if it is to be successful:

> It must claim scientific authority which gives the believer a conviction of having the exclusive key to all knowledge; it must promise a millennium to be brought about for the chosen race or class by the elect who holds this key; it must identify a host of ogres and demons to be overcome before this happy state is brought about; it must enlist the dynamic of hatred, envy, and fear (whether of class or race) and justify these low passions by the loftiness of its aims.[6]

The Need for a Scapegoat: Reinterpreting the Past As a critique of the past, ideology generally focuses on some form of absolute evil to which it can attribute all national (or worldwide) wrongs and social injustices. To the revolutionary ideologue, the true causes of economic recession, inflation, military defeat, official corruption, national humiliation, moral decadence, and other perceived problems are rooted in the mysteries and plots of a rejected past.

If an enemy does not exist, it is necessary to invent one. Usually it is an individual or a group that was already widely feared, hated, or envied. Lenin blamed the plight of workers on money-grubbing capitalists. Hitler blamed Jews and communists for the German loss in World War I and the economic crises that preceded his assumption of power. Mao found his enemy first in wealthy landlords and later in "capitalist roaders." Clearly, the purpose of these ploys was to focus mass attention on a readily identifiable scapegoat on whose shoulders all the nation's ills could be placed.

According to Hoffer, "Mass movements can rise and spread without a belief in God, but never without a belief in a devil."[7] Hate and prejudice, rather than love and high principle, seem the most effective forces in bringing people together in a common cause.

Revolutionary Struggle: Explaining the Present As a guide to the present, ideology provides the true believer with keys to a "correct" analysis of the underlying forces at work in contemporary society. Concepts such as class struggle for Marxist-Leninists, *Herrenvolk* (master race) for the Nazis, and "contradictions" for Mao's followers were used to explain and predict social reality. Yesterday the enemy was preeminent; today the enemy will be defeated.

Advocates of total revolution believe struggle is the very essence of politics. For Marxist-Leninists, class struggle was the engine of progress in history. For Maoists, struggle was a desirable end in itself; only through the direct experience of revolutionary struggle, they believed, could the masses (and especially the young) learn the true meaning of self-sacrifice. Hitler glorified the struggle for power by proclaiming war to be the supreme test of national greatness. (Revealingly, Hitler outlined his own path to political power in a book titled *Mein Kampf*, "my struggle.") Whether the aim is to overthrow monopoly capitalists or to purify a race, revolutionary struggle is always described in terms of good versus evil. It was common for leading Nazis to depict Jews not simply as enemies of the state but as *untermenschen* ("subhumans") and, frequently, as insects or lice.[8] The repeated use of such degrading characterizations dehumanizes the victims; it is a lot easier to justify the extermination of insects than human beings.

Utopia: Foretelling the Future As a promise of the future, ideology tends to paint a radiant picture of perfect justice and perpetual peace. Marxist-Leninists envisioned this utopia as a classless society, one from which all social and economic inequality would be abolished. Similarly, the Nazi utopia was a society from which all racial "impurities" would be removed through the extermination or enslavement of racial "inferiors."

Whatever its precise character, the vision of the future always included a radical redistribution of wealth and property. Marxism-Leninism promised to take from the rich (the bourgeoisie) and give to the poor (the proletariat). Hitler made a similar promise when he proclaimed his intention to provide *Lebensraum* ("living space") in the east; he would take land from the land-rich but slothful Slavs and give it to the land-poor but industrious Germans.

Marxism is based on a deterministic worldview in which the success of the proletarian revolution is dictated by inflexible "laws" of history. Hitler, too, was an unabashed determinist. In *Mein Kampf*, he wrote, "Man must realize that a fundamental law of necessity reigns throughout the whole realm of Nature."[9] Hitler also frequently ranted about "the iron law of our historical development," the "march of history," and the "inner logic of events." No less than Lenin, Stalin, or Mao, he claimed that he (and the German people or *Volk*) had a world-shattering mission to accomplish, and that success was inevitable. He expressed this notion in what is perhaps his most famous (or infamous) pronouncement: "I go the way that Providence dictates with the assurance of a sleepwalker."[10]

Ideology and Truth   The past, present, and future as described by a given revolutionary ideology may seem far-fetched or even ludicrous to a disinterested observer. The racial theory put forth by the Nazis utterly lacked historical, sociological, genetic, and moral foundations. By the same token, the economic facet of Hitler's ideology—the "socialism" in National Socialism—lacked any meaningful content. So watered down was Hitler's conception of socialism that in the words of one authority, "Anyone genuinely concerned about the people was in Hitler's eyes a socialist."[11]

Why would any sane person embrace such an ideology? First, it appealed to popular prejudices and made them respectable. Second, it was not the message that counted so much as the messenger—the leader's personal magnetism attracted a following, whether the words made sense or not. Third, certitude was far more important than rectitude. Fourth, ideologues can often get away with absurd allegations and gross falsehoods if they also address real problems faced by ordinary people.

© STR/AP PHOTO

The leader of the October Revolution, Vladimir Ilyich Lenin, addressing the masses in Moscow's Red Square following the overthrow of Czar Nicholas II in 1917 and the Bolshevik takeover. Lenin reinvented Marxism. The kind of revolution Marx envisioned did not fit Russia's agrarian economy, which lagged far behind Western Europe in the Industrial Revolution. Nontheless, Lenin seized power in the name of the "proletariat" (industrial working class). In one of history's cruel ironies, the totalitarian state Lenin set in motion denied workers basic rights, including the right to organize or to strike.

Many Germans recognized the extremist nature of the Nazis' racial theories but probably believed Hitler would discard such absurdities once the work of unifying the country, reviving the economy, and restoring the nation's lost honor had been accomplished. By the same token, even if many of Lenin's followers did not truly believe the workers' paradise was just around the corner, the Russian peasants did believe in land reform, an end to Russia's disastrous involvement in World War I, and improvements in nutrition, medical care, and education as promised by Lenin.

Organization

Cohesive structure was one of the missing ingredients in pre-twentieth-century rebellions. Most such outbreaks were spontaneous affairs—they burst into flame, occasionally spread, but almost always burned themselves out. The October Revolution, however, was a different story.

Lenin founded the Bolshevik Party more than 14 years before seizing power in 1917. Admitting only hard-core adherents into the party, Lenin reasoned the czar could be defeated through a long, clandestine struggle led by a small group of disciplined revolutionaries (a "vanguard") rather than by a large, amorphous mass of unruly malcontents.

To ensure secrecy, discipline, and centralized control, Lenin organized the Bolshevik Party into tiny **cells.** As the Bolsheviks grew in number and established cells in cities outside Saint Petersburg (see Box 6.1), however, intermediate layers of authority became necessary, although the principles of strict party discipline and total subordination of lower levels to higher ones were not relaxed. Factionalism was not tolerated; party members were still expected to place party interests above personal interests at all times. This spirit of self-sacrifice and total commitment to the party was called **partiinost.**

Unlike its Russian counterpart, the Chinese Revolution was primarily a rural uprising by a mass of discontented peasants. Mao's most pressing organizational problem was to mold the amorphous peasant mass into an effective military force capable of carrying out a protracted guerrilla war. His success won over many leftists (especially in developing nations), who admired and even imitated Mao's theory and practice of peasant-based revolution in a poor and benighted rural society.

Mao's long march to power contrasts with Hitler's quixotic rise in Germany, which started with a violent, abortive coup in the early 1920s and culminated in a kind of constitutional *coup d'état* in the 1930s. A compliant organization in the form of the Nazi Party was crucial to Hitler's ultimate success. Hitler made extensive use of brute force to intimidate his opposition, but he also created numerous party-controlled clubs and associations. The Hitler Youth, a Nazi women's league, a Nazi workers' organization, a Nazi student league, and various other academic and social organizations gave the Nazis considerable political power even before Hitler took over the reins of government. Later, under an innocuous-sounding policy called **Gleichschaltung** ("coordination"), he destroyed virtually all preexisting social organizations and substituted Nazi associations in their place. Partly for this reason, Hitler's promises and threats carried great weight

cells
Small, tightly knit organizational units at the grassroots level of V. I. Lenin's Bolshevik party.

partiinost
The spirit of sacrifice, enthusiasm, and unquestioning devotion required of Communist Party members.

Gleichschaltung
Hitler's technique of using Nazi-controlled associations, clubs, and organizations to coordinate his revolutionary activities.

BOX 6.1 SPOTLIGHT ON   A Tale of "Two Cities": How Saint Petersburg Became Leningrad

In October 1917, the Russian capital of Saint Petersburg (also called Petrograd) was in turmoil, due to hardships and popular anger caused by the long years of World War I and bitter capitulation to Germany. The October Revolution was led by Nikolai Lenin and the Bolsheviks, with the backing of the Mensheviks, the Left Socialist revolutionaries, and an assortment of anarchists.

There were actually two revolutions in Russia in 1917. The first, the so-called February Revolution, brought about three dramatic results: the ouster of Czar Nicholas II, the end of the Russian monarchy, and the creation of a power vacuum. Following a failed attempt by Aleksandr Kerensky to form a Western-style parliamentary democracy, Lenin masterminded a power seizure in the capital in October. This move had a dual character—half popular uprising and half *coup d'état*. It also became the central myth of Soviet communism: the notion that what happened in Saint Petersburg in October 1917 was a spontaneous proletarian revolution that spread throughout Russia.

In fact, the revolution *did* spread, and it *was* fomented by Lenin's Bolsheviks. However, it was not entirely, or even mainly, a proletarian revolution of the kind Marx had imagined. Instead, it included disaffected soldiers and sailors, as well as land-hungry peasants. Russia did not have an extensive industrial labor force in 1917. It was still primarily a peasant society with an agrarian economy. Moreover, the "revolution" in Saint Petersburg was actually led by Leon Trotsky, not Lenin.

Nonetheless, Lenin was the mastermind behind the October Revolution. His role in creating a conspiratorial organization, orchestrating events between February and October 1917, and inspiring the masses made him the undisputed leader of the revolutionary Soviet state—so much so that Saint Petersburg was renamed Leningrad three days after Lenin's death in 1924. The name was changed back to Saint Petersburg in September 1991, shortly before the Soviet Union was formally dissolved.

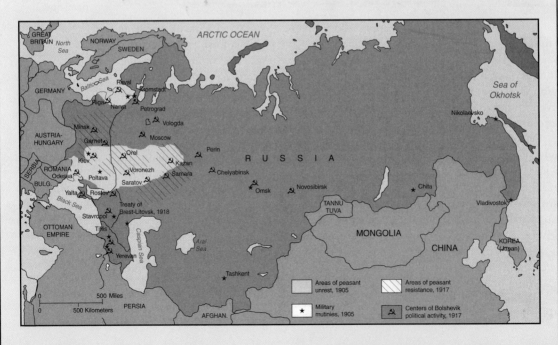

throughout German society. Like all modern revolutionaries, Hitler understood the value of a carefully constructed revolutionary organization.

Propaganda

As more people have become engaged in modern political life, **propaganda**— the dissemination of information based on falsehoods and half-truths designed to advance an ideological cause—has become a potent political weapon.[12] To be successful, as Hitler noted, propaganda must address the masses exclusively; hence, "its effect for the most part must be aimed at the emotions and only to a very limited degree at the so-called intellect."[13]

An avid student of the science of propaganda, Hitler proposed that "all propaganda must be popular and its intellectual level must be adjusted to the most limited intelligence among those to whom it is addressed." Hence, "the greater the mass it is intended to reach, the lower its purely intellectual level will have to be. . . . Effective propaganda must be limited to a very few points and must harp on these in slogans until the last member of the public understands what you want him to understand." Given these premises, it follows that the "very first axiom of all propagandist activity [is] the basically subjective and one-sided attitude it must take toward every question it deals with."[14] And the bigger the lie, the better.

Hitler theorized that the success of any propaganda campaign depends on the propagandist's understanding of the "primitive sentiments" of the popular masses. Propaganda cannot have multiple shadings: Concepts and "facts" must be presented to the public as true or false, right or wrong, black or white. In *Mein Kampf*, Hitler heaped high praise on British propaganda efforts in World War I and expressed contempt for German propaganda, which he faulted for not painting the world in stark black-and-white terms.

© AP Photo

"Man of the Year:" Adolf Hitler on the cover of *TIME* in 1938. Through the implementation of an immense propaganda campaign in combination with the inculcation of the Nazi ideology, Adolf Hitler (1889–1945) was able to persuade the German people of the need to persecute Jews, the necessity of an eventual war, and the radical transformation of German society.

propaganda
The use of mass media to create whatever impression is desired among the general population and to influence thoughts and activities toward desired ends.

Unlike Hitler, who was a highly effective orator, Lenin was a master pamphleteer and polemicist who relied most heavily on the written word. In the infancy of his movement, Lenin's chief weapon was the underground newspaper. Endowed with such names as "The Spark" and "Forward," these propaganda tabloids were printed clandestinely or smuggled into the capital, Saint Petersburg, in false-bottom briefcases.

Violence

The fifth and final characteristic of totalitarian revolution is the use of violence and terror as accepted instruments of political policy. According to the Nazi theorist Eugene Hadamovsky, "Propaganda and violence are never contradictions. Use of violence can be part of the propaganda."[15] Assassinations and kidnappings, indiscriminate bombings and sabotage are all part of the totalitarian tool box. Sabotage is designed to disrupt production, transportation, and communications systems; terror is aimed at a greater, pervasive sense of insecurity (see Chapter 15).

State terror—violence perpetrated by the government—has played a prominent role in mass movements of both the Right and the Left. The notorious "combat groups" (*fasci di combattimento*) Italian Fascist Party leader Benito Mussolini formed shortly after World War I provide a striking example. After attempts to woo the working class away from the Socialist Party failed, Mussolini began to cultivate the middle classes and seek financing from wealthy industrialists and big landowners. One of the more novel forms of terror the fascists devised was the *punitive expedition*, in which armed bands conducted raids against defenseless communities. The local police would often cooperate by looking the other way.

Mussolini's aim was threefold: (1) to create an artificial atmosphere of crisis; (2) to demonstrate that the state was no longer capable of providing law-abiding, taxpaying citizens with protection from unprovoked attacks on their persons and property; and (3) to prod an increasingly fearful, desperate, and fragmented citizenry to turn for refuge and order to the very same political movement that was deliberately exacerbating the problem.

The Nazis in Germany used the same sort of tactics. The similarities between this kind of organized violence and plain gangsterism are obvious—the crucial difference has to do with ends rather than means: Gangsters seek to gain control over lucrative (and often illegal) businesses, not to overthrow the government.

THE CONSOLIDATION OF POWER

Once the old order has been overthrown or fatally discredited, the totalitarian leadership can operate from a solid power base within the government. The next task it faces is to eliminate any competing political parties and factions.

The final step in the consolidation process is the elimination of all those within the party who pose a real or potential danger to the totalitarian leader. At this stage, Machiavelli's advice is especially valuable: "One ought not to say to someone whom one wants to kill, 'Give me your gun, I want to kill you with it,' but merely, 'Give me your gun,' for once you have the gun in your hand, you can satisfy your desire."[16]

Eliminating Opposition Parties

Any opposition group, no matter how small or ineffectual, poses a potential danger to the ruler. By the same token, the mere existence of political opponents inhibits the kind of radical change mandated by the movement's ideology.

In dealing with rival political parties, Lenin famously employed **salami tactics**[17]—the practice of marginalizing or eliminating opposition by slicing it into pieces and playing one group off against the other. Thus, after the new Constituent Assembly (legislature) was elected, Lenin exploited an already existing division in the dominant Socialist Revolutionary Party by forming an alliance with its left wing. This alliance enabled Lenin to move against the party's more moderate wing, as well as against other rightist parties.

Lenin also repressed Russia's huge peasant population. The lack of peasant support for the Bolshevik regime became a particularly acute problem during the civil war (1918–1920), when foodstuffs and other basic necessities were extremely scarce. In response, Lenin "instituted in the villages a 'civil war within a civil war' by setting poor peasants against those who were less poor,"[18] thereby helping to undermine the political opposition.

Hitler employed a different strategy. Bolstered by his Nazi Party's steadily growing popularity in the polls (thanks to a formidable following of true believers), his superb oratorical skills, and a special group of shock troops known as storm troopers, he played a waiting game. Once in office, he gradually expanded his authority, first by gaining passage of new emergency powers and suspending civil liberties. Only then did he move to shut down all opposition parties. Hitler thus used the charade of legality to destroy his opponents politically before using the power of the state to destroy them physically.

Purging Real or Imagined Rivals within the Party

Political **purges** involve removing opponents from the party leadership or from positions of power, or rounding up whole (often fictitious) categories of people ("bourgeois capitalists" or "enemies of the people") but not necessarily killing them. Arresting people you don't trust and either imprisoning or exiling them can be just as effective as killing them—and ostensibly more civilized. In carrying out purges, totalitarian governments almost invariably accuse their victims of subversive activity or treason—a convenient rationale for eliminating individuals who are perceived as threats or political liabilities.[19] Thus, Hitler turned on Ernst Röhm and other party members who had been instrumental in the

salami tactics
The methods used by Vladimir Lenin to divide his opponents into small groups that could be turned against one another and easily overwhelmed.

purges
The elimination of all rivals to power through mass arrests, imprisonment, exile, and murder, often directed at former associates and their followers who have (or are imagined to have) enough influence to be a threat to the ruling elite.

Nazis' rise to power; on the Führer's orders, the Röhm faction was murdered in June 1934. Blaming the whole incident on his political enemies, Hitler used the Röhm purge to solidify his popular support and give credence to his fear-mongering propaganda.

Purges played an even bigger role in the consolidation of power in the Soviet Union. In 1921, thousands of trade unionists and sailors, formerly the backbone of the Bolsheviks' popular support, were murdered by the secret police when they demanded free trade unions and elections. Next, Lenin purged the so-called Workers' Opposition faction of his own Bolshevik party, which demanded worker self-management of industry. Lenin pronounced the group guilty of "factionalism" and accused it of endangering both the party and the revolution. The members of the Workers' Opposition group were expelled from the party but not murdered.

Such relatively mild actions were not characteristic of Lenin's successor, Joseph Stalin, who, as the head of the Soviet Communist Party (1924–1953), did not hesitate to murder those whom he perceived to be his political enemies. How Stalin gathered total power in his hands is a textbook example of cutthroat power politics. He shrewdly adapted Lenin's salami tactics. However, whereas Lenin set rival parties against each other, Stalin set rivals within his own party— virtually all the great Bolshevik heroes of the October Revolution—against each other. Stalin purged and eventually murdered virtually the entire top party leadership after Lenin's death in 1924.

Creating a Monolithic Society

The totalitarian state stops at nothing short of total control over the economy, the arts, the military, the schools, the government—every aspect of society. As Nazi propaganda chief Joseph Goebbels (1897–1945) remarked, "The revolution we have made is a total revolution. . . . It is completely irrelevant what means it uses."[20] Ironically, the golden society at the end of the utopian rainbow is incompatible with intellectual freedom. Thus, one Nazi official asked this rhetorical question: "If the brains of all university professors were put at one end of the scale and the brains of the Führer at the other, which end, do you think, would tip?"[21]

Total control requires total loyalty. During the Nazi era, even in small towns, any magistrates and petty officials who had not publicly supported the Nazis were removed from power. Simultaneously, numerous "enemies of the people" were identified and punished by the brutal **Gestapo** or secret police.[22] The effectiveness of these terror tactics helps explain why there was so little overt resistance to the Nazi takeover, but it does not tell the whole story. Cowardice, apathy, and self-interest played important roles as well. A true story told by a German refugee who had been on the faculty of the prestigious University of Frankfurt speaks directly to this point.[23] Following the appointment of a Nazi commissar at the university, every professor and graduate assistant was summoned for an important faculty meeting:

Gestapo
In Nazi Germany, the secret state police, Hitler's instrument for spreading mass terror among Jews and political opponents.

The new Nazi commissar . . . immediately announced that Jews would be forbidden to enter university premises and would be dismissed without salary on March 15. . . . Then he launched into a tirade of abuse, filth, and four-letter words such as had been heard rarely even in the barracks and never before in academia. He pointed his finger at one department chairman after another and said, "You either do what I tell you or we'll put you into a concentration camp." There was silence when he finished; everybody waited for the distinguished biochemist-physiologist.

   The great liberal got up, cleared his throat, and said, "Very interesting, Mr. Commissar, and in some respects very illuminating; but one point I didn't get too clearly. Will there be more money for research in Physiology?" The meeting broke up shortly thereafter with the commissar assuring the scholars that indeed there would be plenty of money for "racially pure science."[24]

The English philosopher Edmund Burke is reported to have said, "All that is necessary for evil to succeed is for good men to do nothing." Indeed.

THE TRANSFORMATION OF SOCIETY

The transformation stage generally coincides with the regime's assumption of control over the economy and requires active government planning and intervention.[25] In justifying the drive for a new social order, totalitarian regimes typically blame everything that is wrong with the country on counterrevolutionaries, spies, and saboteurs.

   Carl Friedrich and Zbigniew Brzezinski, two respected students of this subject, have identified six characteristics shared by all totalitarian governments—an official ideology; a single, hierarchical party; a secret police; a tightly controlled armed forces; a media monopoly; and central control over the economy.[26] These characteristics derive from the main features and functions of the revolutionary movement we have discussed (leadership, ideology, organization, propaganda, and violence), now redirected to the state's day-to-day administration and transformation.

   The attempted transformation of the state follows a predetermined ideological path, with some concessions to pragmatism where necessary. But practicality is rarely of prime importance for the total tyrant bent on transformation. Examples from the political careers of Stalin, Hitler, and Mao illustrate this point.

The Soviet Union under Stalin

In 1928, having defeated his political rivals, Stalin stood poised to launch his drive to collectivize and industrialize the Soviet economy. His first Five-Year Plan for the Soviet economy (1928–1932) marked the beginning of a cataclysm.

kulaks
A class of well-to-do landowners in Russian society that was purged by Joseph Stalin because it resisted his drive to establish huge collective farms under state control.

collectivism
The belief that the public good is best served by common (as opposed to individual) ownership of a political community's means of production and distribution.

Over the next 10 years, millions of innocent people were killed or sent to labor camps, and a whole class of relatively well-to-do landholders, the **kulaks,** ceased to exist. In addition, the whole pattern of Soviet agricultural production was radically reshaped.

To understand why Stalin would inflict so much suffering on the Soviet farm population, we must first understand the role of ideology in totalitarian systems. Stalin's first Five-Year Plan, which instituted a highly centralized economic system designed to foster rapid development of the Soviet economy, was motivated by a lust for power. However, Stalin was also committed to creating an advanced industrial society based on collective, rather than capitalist, principles. The way to accomplish this remarkable feat in the shortest possible time, Stalin reasoned, was to invest massively in heavy industry while squeezing every last drop of profit from agriculture, the traditional foundation of the Russian economy.

Private ownership of farmland, animals, and implements would have to be eliminated and farming "collectivized." Under Stalin's **collectivization** plan, most agricultural production took place in large cooperative units known as *kolkhozy* (collective farms), whose members shared whatever income was left after making compulsory deliveries to the state, or in *sovkhozy* (state farms), whose laborers received wages.

Soviet agriculture was collectivized to underwrite Soviet industrialization. Through a massive transfer of resources from farms to cities, Stalin believed industrial production could double or even triple during the period of the first Five-Year Plan. But doing so would necessitate crushing all pockets of rural resistance, herding the peasants into collective farms, and imposing a draconian system of "tax" collections, or compulsory deliveries of scarce food supplies to the state in order to feed the growing army of industrial workers and to pay for imported capital goods.

One reason the plan failed was the excessive and indiscriminate brutality Stalin employed. Stories spread through the countryside of how Stalin's agents had machine-gunned whole villages. Many Russian peasants deliberately burned their crops and killed their cattle rather than cooperate with Stalin's requisition squads. Despite an all-out national effort, industrial production grew only slightly, if at all. In the meantime, famine depopulated the countryside.

Stalin made no apologies and no policy adjustments. Instead, he fabricated statistics, which no one dared question, to "prove" that real progress was being made. In the words of one expert, "The Stalin regime was ruthlessly consistent: All facts that did not agree, or were likely to disagree, with the official fiction— data on crop yields, criminality, true incidences of 'counterrevolutionary' activities . . . were treated as nonfacts."[27]

In 1934, as the death toll mounted and the first Five-Year Plan came to an unspectacular end, the Soviet dictator declared he had uncovered a far-reaching conspiracy, orchestrated by foreign agents and counterrevolutionaries, to resurrect capitalism in Soviet Russia. This conspiracy theory gained credibility when Sergei Kirov, the dynamic young leader of the Leningrad party organization, was assassinated in December 1934. Harsh reprisals, numerous arrests, phony trials, summary executions, and large-scale deportations followed. Many of the victims were loosely identified as members of a fabricated conspiracy called the Leningrad Center. The alleged plot furnished Stalin with the pretext for a purge of Lenin's original circle of revolutionary leaders, the so-called Old Bolsheviks.

During the first phase of the Great Terror (January 1934 to April 1936)—also known as the Great Purge—Communist Party membership fell by nearly 800,000, or approximately 25 percent. The Soviet press denounced these ex-communicants as "wreckers, spies, diversionists, and murderers sheltering behind the party card and disguised as Bolsheviks."[28]

The second phase of the Stalin purges (1936–1938) was highlighted by the infamous *show trials*, in which the Old Bolsheviks, along with many other top-ranking party leaders, were placed on public trial and forced to make outrageous "confessions." The trials represented only the tip of the iceberg (see Box 6.2).

Nor were the rank-and-file workers spared. Throughout the mid- to late 1930s, Stalin collectivized the Soviet labor force by means of forced-draft or conscript labor. Work units were structured and regimented along military lines. This policy gave birth to the so-called **gulag archipelago,** a network of draconian slave-labor camps maintained and operated by the Soviet secret police where social and political undesirables were forced to live. Through the gulag system, railroads, canals, and dams were constructed in remote and inaccessible areas where workers would not voluntarily go. Aleksandr Solzhenitsyn, the celebrated dissident writer who chronicled life in the labor camps, estimated

gulag archipelago
Metaphorical name for the network of slave labor camps established in the former Soviet Union by Joseph Stalin and maintained by his secret police to which nonconformists and politically undesirable persons were sent.

© AP PHOTO

One of the most ruthless dictators of the twentieth century, Joseph Stalin (1879–1953) moved away from the Soviet model of an international communist revolution proposed by Marx and Lenin to focus on "socialism in one country." In pursuit of his aims, Stalin committed mass murders on a grand scale and enslaved millions in a vast system of gulags (forced-labor camps). It's amazing, even shocking, given what we now know about Stalin that he was named *Time* magazine's "Man of the Year" in 1942.

BOX 6.2   The Great Purge

Between 1934 and 1938, Stalin ordered most of the Soviet political and military elite executed as enemies of the state, including:

- 1,100 delegates to the 17th Party Congress (more than half)
- 70 percent of the 139-member Party Central Committee
- 3 of 5 Soviet marshals (the highest-ranking generals)

- 14 of 26 army commanders
- All 8 admirals
- 60 of 67 corps commanders
- Half the 397 brigade commanders
- All but 5 of the 81 top-ranking political commissars

---

that they held as many as 12 million prisoners at any given time, perhaps half of them political prisoners. "As some departed beneath the sod," he noted, "the Machine kept bringing in replacements."[29]

At the close of 1938, Stalin stood alone at the top. Industrial development had been spurred, but the Soviet Union was anything but a worker's paradise. Terror had brought about great political changes, with many luminaries from the pages of Soviet Communist Party history uncovered as traitors and placed on public trial. The list of the accused read like an honor roll of the October Revolution. The military high command had been sacked, the party rank and file cleansed of all political impurities, and the "toiling masses" reduced to a new level of industrial serfdom. Although he ruled until his death in 1953, Stalin (and the legacy of Stalinism) would be identified, above all, with the bloody purges of the 1930s.

Germany under Hitler

The overriding theme of National Socialist (Nazi) Party ideology during the Third Reich (1933–1945) was the elimination of the Jews and other "social undesirables" and the ascendency of the "Aryan" race—a fiction that nonetheless obsessed Hitler and his followers. Through Nazi ideology and propaganda, the German people came to accept the persecution of the Jews, the necessity of eventual war, and the radical transformation of society. Every aspect of German life became politicized. Dissident artists, journalists, and academicians were silenced. New state organs, including the Reich chambers for literature, press, broadcasting, theater, music, and fine arts, were created for the primary purpose of censoring or quelling potentially "dangerous" forms of written or artistic expression.

In the realm of music, German folk tunes were exalted over "decadent" modern music and classical music written by composers of Jewish lineage, such as Felix Mendelssohn and Gustav Mahler. Modern art was likewise condemned, and the works of virtually every well-known contemporary artist were banned. Literature under the Nazi regime fared no better. According to one chronicler of the Third Reich, "Blacklists were compiled ceaselessly and literary histories were revised. . . . The 'cleansing' of libraries and bookstores presented some problems, but the destruction and self-destruction of German literature was achieved within a matter of months through the substitution of second- and third-rate scribblers for first-rate writers and by inhibiting contacts with the outside."[30]

The Nazi attack on the arts was indicative of the lengths to which Hitler would go to ensure that Nazi values were propagated. But perhaps no part of German life more vividly demonstrated Hitler's commitment to a new future than the Nazi school system. As Bracher pointed out, "While National Socialism could substitute little more than ideology and second-rate imitators for the literature and art it expelled or destroyed, its main efforts from the very outset were directed toward the most important instruments of totalitarian policy: propaganda and education."[31]

Nazi educational policy was implemented in three principal ways. To begin with, educators and school administrators who were suspected of opposing Hitler, Nazism, or Nazi educational "reform" were promptly removed from their positions. Then all academic subjects were infused with ideological content reflecting Hitler's anti-Semitic racial theories. History became "racial history," biology was transformed into "racial biology," and so on. Finally, the Nazis established special schools to train a future party elite, including military leaders, party officials, and government administrators. Students were assigned to these schools according to age group and career orientation. The Adolf Hitler Schools, to cite one example, taught 12- to 18-year-old students who wished to become high party functionaries. In general, all special schools taught certain basic core courses (such as racial history and biology) and emphasized military drill (for example, the training of the infamous Hitler Youth).

The Nazi educational program turned out to be all too successful. In the judgment of one authority, "Just as teachers and parents capitulated to the pressures of the regime, so on the whole did the indoctrination of the young succeed. The young, who were receptive to heroic legends and black-and-white oversimplifications, were handed over to the stupendous shows of the regime."[32] Education of the young was reinforced by carefully planned pomp and ceremony: "From earliest childhood, they were exposed to flag raisings, parades, nationwide broadcasts in the schools, hikes, and camps."[33] Indoctrination and propaganda, not terror, became the instruments by which the children of the Third Reich were initiated into the new order.

Mass indoctrination combined with a pre-existing anti-Semitism made it possible for Hitler to carry out the murderous racial policies that culminated in the Holocaust. After seizing power, Hitler implemented his anti-Jewish policy in stages, each more radical than the one before.[34] First came the attempt to define who precisely was and was not a Jew. Then the regime launched a systematic campaign to isolate Jews from the mainstream of German life and to expropriate their property. Next all Jews who had not fled the country between

© HULTON ARCHIVE/GETTY IMAGES

The overriding theme of Nazi Party ideology was the elimination of the Jews and other "social undesirables" and the subsequent creation of a "racially pure" Aryan nation. Between 1933 and 1945, at least six million European Jews plus countless others perished in Nazi death camps.

1933 and 1938 were forcibly removed from German society and sent to the infamous concentration camps. This mass deportation presaged the fourth and final step—genocide. Hitler's maniacal obsession was ultimately his undoing. Even on the brink of defeat, Hitler continued to divert resources needed to prosecute the war to the Final Solution (the liquidation of the Jews). In the end, some six million European Jews plus countless others, including the mentally ill, physically disabled, Soviet prisoners of war, gay men, Gypsies, Jehovah's Witness members, and Polish intellectuals, as well as many Polish Roman Catholics, were annihilated.

China under Mao

Mao Zedong's rise to power in China is an epic example of revolutionary struggle—a true mass movement in a poor, peasant-dominated society. For more than 20 years (1927–1949), Mao waged a bitter "war of national liberation" against the **Kuomintang**, headed by Chiang Kai-shek, as well as against the Japanese during World War II. In the mid-1930s, Mao was one of the leaders of the legendary Long March, a 6000-mile trek, during which his ragtag band of guerrillas repeatedly evaded capture or annihilation by the numerically superior and better-equipped forces of Chiang's Nationalist army. By 1949, when Mao finally won the last decisive battle and assumed command of the Chinese nation, Mao had been waging class war in the name of the Chinese masses for more than two decades.

Mao prided himself not only on his revolutionary exploits but also on his political thought. In time, the "thoughts of Chairman Mao," compiled in his pocket-sized little Red Book, of which millions of copies were printed and mass

Kuomintang
The Chinese Nationalist Party, led by Chiang Kai-shek, defeated by Mao Zedong in 1949.

distributed, attained the status of holy scripture in Chinese society. His vision of a new, classless state and of the exemplary communist cadres and comrades who would typify this morally reeducated society inspired the radical policies that have become known collectively as Maoism.

Although Mao's worldview was undoubtedly shaped by the basic tenets of Marxism, 1920s China was a preindustrial society without a true proletarian (industrial-worker) class or a "monopoly capitalist" class of the kind Marx had described in *Das Kapital*. The bane of China's peasant masses was not factory bosses but greedy landlords and bureaucratic officials preoccupied with the preservation of the status quo and of their own power and privilege. If the oppressed majority were to be liberated, those in power would have to be overthrown. To accomplish such a historic mission, Mao believed, violent revolution "from below" was an unavoidable necessity. "Political power," he wrote, "grows out of the barrel of a gun."[35]

As part of his adaptation of Marxism, Mao glorified the Chinese peasants—whom he described as "poor and blank"—as models of communist virtue because they had never been corrupted by "bourgeois materialism" and big-city decadence. Mao thus made the peasantry (not the proletariat) the cornerstone of his visionary utopian society.

Once in power, Mao turned China into a kind of social laboratory. The first step included campaigns to eradicate specific evils such as individualism and bourgeois materialism by "reeducating" the masses or exterminating undesirable social elements (landlords, counterrevolutionaries, and "bandits"). Accompanying mass reeducation was a sweeping land reform program culminating in the wholesale collectivization of Chinese agriculture. This bitter pill was administered with massive doses of propaganda, as well as brute force. In the early 1950s, a major push to industrialize China along Stalinist lines was also launched.

Alternating periods of freedom and repression marked Mao's rule. In 1956, for example, he announced the beginning of the **Hundred Flowers campaign,** which promised a relaxation of strict social discipline. As a high-ranking party official put it at the time, "The Chinese Communist party advocates [that] one hundred flowers bloom for literary works and one hundred schools contend in the scientific field… to promote the freedom of independent thinking, freedom of debate, freedom of creation and criticism, freedom of expressing one's own opinions."[36] What followed probably caught Mao by surprise. Public protests and anti-party demonstrations occurred at Beijing University and other campuses. Strikes and scattered riots, even isolated physical attacks on party officials, occurred in various parts of the country. Instead of a hundred flowers, thousands of "poisonous weeds" had grown in the Chinese garden. The incipient rebellion was rapidly suppressed in a brutal "anti-rightist" crackdown. The official party newspaper, *People's Daily,* announced the whole Hundred Flowers campaign had been a ploy to lure the enemies of the state into the open.

In retrospect, the Hundred Flowers episode was a mere warm-up for Mao's **Great Leap Forward** (1957–1960)—a spectacular but ill-conceived attempt to catapult China onto the stage of "full communism" by means of mass mobilization. Mao set out to prove that anything is possible, and that subjective

Hundred Flowers campaign
A brief period in China (1956) when Mao Zedong directed that freedom of expression and individualism be allowed; it was quashed when violent criticism of the regime erupted.

Great Leap Forward
Mao Zedong's attempt, in the late 1950s and early 1960s, to transform and modernize China's economic structure through mass mobilization of the entire population into self-sufficient communes in which everything was done in groups.

© MAGNUM PHOTOS NEW YORK

Following his successful war of national liberation against Chiang Kai-shek's Kuomintang, Mao's rule between 1949 and 1976 was characterized by periods of vast social experimentation as well as by violent periods of political repression.

factors like human will can triumph over objective conditions such as poverty, illiteracy, and external dependency. Put differently, the idea "was to take advantage of China's rural backwardness and manpower surplus by realizing the Maoist faith that ideological incentives could get economic results, that a new spirit could unlock hitherto untapped sources of human energy without the use of material incentives."[37] Thus did Mao's brand of "Marxism" stand Marx on his head.

The most visible and dramatic symbol of the Great Leap was the establishment of communes—relatively large and self-sufficient residential, social, economic, and political-administrative units. Private plots were absorbed into the communal lands, and private belongings, including pots and pans and other domestic items, were pooled. In addition, as Fairbank noted,

> Many peasants for a time ate in large mess halls. All labor was to be controlled. Everyone was to work twenty-eight days of the month, while children went into day nurseries. This would bring large-scale efficiency to the village and get all its labor, including its womanpower, into full employment.[38]

Why were the unprecedented measures associated with Mao's grandiose concept instituted? According to China scholar John King Fairbank, "The result, it was hoped, would be agricultural cities with the peasants proletarianized and uprooted from their own land"—with an overall view toward giving the state increased control over labor resources and changing the peasants' attitudes.[39]

The Great Leap Forward was a colossal failure with disastrous consequences for the Chinese people, including severe crop failures and food shortages. But Mao was undeterred. After a brief period of retrenchment, he launched a second "revolution from above." From 1966 to 1969, the **Great Proletarian Cultural Revolution** shook Chinese society to its very foundations. In the first stage, designed to wash away all that was "decadent" in Chinese life, Mao closed all schools and urged his youthful followers, called the Red Guards, to storm the bastions of entrenched privilege and bureaucratic authority. Millions of Maoist youths obligingly went on a rampage throughout the country for many weeks. This phase of the revolution accomplished its intended purpose, as the Red Guards "smashed most of the Republic's bureaucratic institutions" and "invalidated [the government's] authority and expertise."[40] Officials were dragged out and put on public display to be ridiculed and humiliated, accompanied by purges and summary executions; temples and historical treasures lay in ruins, as did the party, government, and armed forces.

The second stage of the Cultural Revolution called for positive action to replace the previous order with a new and better one. Unfortunately, the economy and society, especially in urban areas, had been severely disrupted. Factories and schools, shut down by marauding Red Guards, did not reopen for months or even years.

The ultimate cost of the Cultural Revolution is incalculable. One fact, however, is clear: Mao's unrelenting efforts to prove that human nature is infinitely malleable—and society, therefore, infinitely perfectible—foundered on the rocky shores of political reality, not to mention the folly of eliminating a whole generation of educated citizens. His death in 1976 closed a unique chapter in the political history of the modern world.

Great Proletarian Cultural Revolution
A chaotic period beginning in 1966, when the youth of China (the Red Guards), at Mao Zedong's direction, attacked all bureaucratic and military officials on the pretext that a reemergence of capitalist and materialist tendencies was taking place. The offending officials were sent to forced labor camps to be "reeducated."

THE HUMAN COST OF TOTALITARIANISM

Totalitarian regimes present a stark contrast between ends and means—diabolical deeds in pursuit of utopian dreams. The death camps of Nazi Germany and the labor camps of Stalinist Russia stand as the essence of twentieth-century totalitarianism.

By one estimate, about 110 million people have died in the name of the three revolutions—in Nazi Germany, Stalinist Russia, and Maoist China—featured in this chapter.[41] The number defies imagination; but these estimates, which include World War II casualties, are quite plausible and may actually be low.[42] War-related deaths in the European theater during World War II numbered "about six million for Germany and Austria, 20 million for the Soviet Union, and about 10 million for all other European countries, for a total of about 36 million."[43] Hitler's Final Solution was estimated to have resulted in the deaths of an estimated five to six million European Jews, not to mention an indeterminate number of non-Jews whom Hitler considered "social undesirables." All in all, perhaps 42 million people died directly or indirectly as a result of Hitler's policies.

The Russian Revolution of 1917 and its aftermath were hardly less costly in terms of human life. Between 1918 and 1923, approximately 3 million Soviet citizens died of typhus, typhoid, dysentery, and cholera, and about 9 million more disappeared, probably victims of the terrible famine that scourged the country in the early 1920s. Many perished in a severe drought in 1920–1921, but others died of direct or indirect political causes.

In the late 1920s, during Stalin's titanic industrialization drive, the kulaks were annihilated as a class. In addition, another killer famine—at least partially self-inflicted—occurred in the early 1930s. When deaths associated with the early stages of collectivization are combined with deaths brought on by famine, the mortality figures range in the millions for the period from 1929 to 1934.

But the worst was yet to come. After 1934, Stalin's purges directly claimed hundreds of thousands of lives and led to the premature deaths of some two million "class enemies" in Siberian forced-labor camps. Nor did the end of the great purges in 1938 stop the political hemorrhaging that, together with World War II, drained Soviet society of so much of its vitality. Millions of labor camp inmates died between 1938 and 1950 due to the inhumane treatment and harsh conditions they had to endure on a daily basis.

The human cost of the revolution in Maoist China exceeds that of Stalinist Russia. Between the time of the communist takeover in 1949 and the Great Leap Forward in 1957, several mass campaigns were launched to combat allegedly counterrevolutionary forces. After the Chinese Communist takeover, the land reform program cost the lives of several million "landlords" and rich peasants between 1949 and 1952. Other campaigns against counterrevolutionaries in the early 1950s cost another million and a half lives. Periodic anti-rightist campaigns and collectivization of agriculture after 1953 also took a toll.[44] According to scholar C. W. Cassinelli,

> Accurate information is not available—and often even informed guesses are lacking—on the cost of the *first decade* [emphasis supplied] of the People's Republic. An estimate of twelve million lives is modest but reasonable.[45]

These figures do not include deaths caused by hardship and privation, most notably those traceable to the dislocations that accompanied the Great Leap Forward in the late 1950s.

The Cultural Revolution (1966–1969) was another bloody episode in Chinese history, although firm estimates of the number of casualties are impossible to make. A much heavier toll was probably taken by the Chinese gulag system. As many as 15 million may have perished as a direct result of inhumanly harsh labor camp conditions. When Cassinelli tallied the total number of politically related deaths, including "another million from miscellaneous causes," he arrived at the astonishing figure of "about 33.5 million."[46] Though unverifiable, this number is consistent with the available evidence. The mere fact that it is not implausible speaks volumes.

Totalitarian regimes typically refuse to concede that any goal, no matter how visionary or perverse, is beyond political reach. The compulsion to validate this gross misconception may help explain the pathological violence that marks totalitarian rule.

OTHER FACES OF TOTALITARIANISM

In addition to Stalin's Russia, Hitler's Germany, and Mao's China, other totalitarian states deserve mention and study. Although these lesser totalitarian states have mostly disappeared or mellowed, the abuses they perpetrated in every case left deep scars in their nation's history, as well as a bitter legacy.

Pol Pot governed Cambodia (renamed Kampuchea) from 1975 to 1979.[47] He and his followers sought to create a radically new society, based on the rustic and Spartan life of peasant cadres. All vestiges of the old order—everything from the calendar to the family—were eradicated. Pol Pot proclaimed 1978 "Year Zero," which turned out to be grotesquely appropriate, for at the end of his brief rule, some 2 million Cambodians (of a population of 7.5 million) would be dead—the victims of purges, starvation, or persecution.

Another example of totalitarian rulers is Ethiopia's Colonel Mengistu, who ruled from the mid-1970s until 1991.[48] Mengistu attempted to reorganize the nation by physically relocating its people into regimented population and refugee centers for the purposes of permitting intensive governmental surveillance as well as encouraging systematic propaganda and indoctrination. His efforts destroyed the nation's agriculture, and a killer famine resulted. Although the West made efforts to feed the starving children of Ethiopia, their government appeared curiously detached. While his people went hungry, Mengistu staged lavish military parades, sold wheat to neighboring nations, and used the money he received to buy weapons. In May 1991, with his regime under siege by a coalition of rebel forces, Mengistu fled the country.

North Korea is the last Soviet-style totalitarian state still in existence. Kim Il Sung ruled over the so-called Hermit Kingdom until his death in July 1994. Today his son, Kim Jong Il, rules in the same autocratic fashion.

North Korea is widely known as the Hermit Kingdom because of its largely self-imposed isolation from the outside world. The country's leader, Kim Jong Il, heads one of the most rigidly autocratic regimes in the contemporary world. His claim to rule is hereditary—Kim's dead father, Kim Il Sung, the founder of the Kim family dynasty, established a totalitarian dictatorship after World War II.

Kim Jong Il rules North Korea the same way his father did—by perpetuating a personality cult similar to those once perpetrated in Russia by Joseph Stalin or in China by Mao Zedong. In a bizarre twist, when his father died, Kim Jong Il made him president for eternity. North Korean propagandists ascribe to Kim (the son) the authorship of 1,000 books while he was a college student.

North Korea maintains a huge army, entrenched along the 38th parallel that divides Korea, and poses a standing threat to South Korea, a close ally of the United States since the Korean War (1950–1953). That major war was started when northern Korea invaded the south, a fact that continues to shape Western perceptions of North Korea today. The war ended in a draw and without a peace treaty.

In stark contrast to the prosperous south, North Korea remains one of the poorest countries on earth. Malnutrition and even starvation threaten the population—children in North Korea are, on average, considerably shorter and weigh less than children of the same age in South Korea. North Koreans are not allowed to have contact with South Koreans, including family members.

After 9/11, President Bush declared North Korea to be part of an "axis of evil" along with Iraq and Iran. North Korea again found itself in the international spotlight when Kim Jong Il defied the Bush administration's demand for a "complete, verifiable, and irreversible" halt to its nuclear weapons program. U.S. relations with North Korea did not greatly improve in the ensuing years. A pre-occupation with the wars in Iraq and Afghanistan, as well as a deepening recession in the wake of the U.S. financial crisis in 2008–2009, led President Obama, like his predecessor, to seek an accommodation with Pyongyang (the capital).

North Korea conducted a nuclear test in 2006 and in April 2009 attempted to launch a long-range missile, but the test failed. North Korea is also thought to have stockpiles of chemical and biological weapons. Although its extreme self-isolation and secrecy ensure nobody knows for certain what is going on inside North Korea today, if the Hermit Kingdom does have a nuclear gun, there is no doubt whose finger is on the trigger.

Khomeini's Iran displayed most of the elements normally associated with totalitarian rule: an attempt to transform society; a dictatorship that demanded abject loyalty, obedience, and self-sacrifice; an all-encompassing creed that rationalized, explained, and justified state actions; press censorship; and secret police, show trials, summary executions, and holy wars.

Eventually, no aspect of life in Iran lay outside governmental control. Teachers, textbooks, education, entertainment, the legal system, even courtship and sexual mores were made to conform to fundamental Islamic beliefs. The regime declared war on civil servants, intellectuals, professional and entrepreneurial elements of the middle class, and all others who had endorsed modern Western ways and culture.

After Khomeini's death, his successors relaxed some of the strict moral and social controls but maintained a rigidly theocratic police state fiercely opposed to the West and, in particular, to the U.S. presence in neighboring Iraq and the Persian Gulf. In addition, Tehran launched a major nuclear research and development program, raising a general alarm in the international community and causing the United States to orchestrate a global campaign to stop Iran from building nuclear weapons.

When President Obama assumed office he lost little time in attempting to break the diplomatic impasse with Iran. During the 2008 presidential campaign, Obama had roundly criticized President Bush for refusing to engage in direct talks with Tehran. In early 2009, the new administration expressed a willingness to meet with Iran "without preconditions," and on April 16, 2009, Iran's hard-line President Mahmoud Ahmadinejad declared in a televised speech, "We have prepared a package that can be the basis to resolve Iran's nuclear problem. It will be offered to the West soon."[49]

The Iranian case demonstrates three important points. First, totalitarian regimes, like democracies and traditional dictatorships, can share a single essence and assume many different guises. Second, although totalitarian regimes appear to be rigid and unchanging on the outside, they are, in fact, not impervious to change on the inside. Third, in the modern world of the twenty-first century, totalitarian regimes cannot succeed *economically* in isolation—that is, without access to global markets, the latest technological advances, and sources of investment capital.

Ironically, as totalitarianism disappeared in Russia and Eastern Europe, it sprang up in Afghanistan—a country the Soviet Union had invaded in 1979. It is generally accepted that the protracted and costly conflict in Afghanistan hastened the demise of the totalitarian Soviet state. It turned out to be Moscow's Vietnam, but with more dire consequences.

In the 1990s, totalitarianism in a different guise arose from the ashes of the war that had ravaged Afghanistan during the previous decade. That regime—the Taliban—captured the world's attention after September 2001 because the mastermind behind the 9/11 operation, the actual perpetrators, and the organization that carried it out were all based in Afghanistan. The Taliban was providing sanctuary for Osama bin Laden, who had set up training camps for his stateless "army."

But the Taliban was not only *harboring* a terrorist organization; it was itself a terrorist organization—a full-blown totalitarian regime complete with a single all-powerful ruling clique, harsh and arbitrary laws, kangaroo courts, predictable (guilty) verdicts, summary executions turned into public spectacles, severely restricted personal freedoms, closed borders, and a captive population. Afghans were not allowed to emigrate or travel abroad. Girls were not allowed to go to school. Boys were not allowed to fly kites. Women had no rights, had to be completely covered in public, and could not work outside the home. Wife beating, no matter how severe, was not a crime—not even when the victim died.

THE SHORT LIVES OF THE WORST REGIMES

Hitler boasted that his would be a thousand-year empire, but it lasted less than a decade. In fact, in stark contrast to the great autocratic empires of ancient history, totalitarian regimes are short-lived. They tend to burst on the scene like a meteor and burn out. Why?

Fatal wars with other nations, such as Hitler's defeat by the Allies in World War II, can bring a sudden end to totalitarian states. The death of a particularly charismatic or successful ruler—Mao or Stalin, for instance—can precipitate an extended downward spiral. Drab, indistinguishable successors who rule by coercion and terror rather than by consent may undermine the economic efficiency, moral vitality, and political idealism on which legitimate political power ultimately rests. Thus, the collapse of the Soviet Union was preceded by both a prolonged period of economic disintegration and a widespread loss of faith in the regime and its political ideals; a period of "totalitarianism in decline."[50]

Today, the Peoples' Republic of China is "Communist" in name only. In fact, it has metamorphosed into a one-party authoritarian system with a transitional capitalist economy that by its very nature sets limits on the exercise

theocracy
A government based on religion and dominated by the clergy.

of state power. Iran after Khomeini remains a **theocracy** with limited personal freedoms but it cannot in fairness be called totalitarian. North Korea alone still qualifies as unambiguously totalitarian. The totalitarian regimes in Kampuchea and Ethiopia are long gone—only their cruel legacies remain. But unfortunately, totalitarian dictatorships need only a little time to do incalculable damage.

 GATEWAYS TO THE WORLD: EXPLORING CYBERSPACE

www.historyplace.com/worldwar2/riseofhitler/index.htm

This site offers a 24-chapter history on the rise to power of Adolf Hitler, as well as biographies of Adolf Eichmann, Rudolf Hess, and Reinhard Heydrich; also a photo-rich timeline of the Holocaust.

www.thecorner.org/hist/total/total.htm

Focuses on the history of totalitarianism in Europe during the turbulent interwar period (1919–1939).

www.kirjasto.sci.fi/mao.htm

Succinct political biography of Mao Zedong as well as a number of useful links.

www.marxists.org/subject

Marxist Internet Archive; as the name suggests, it is a treasure trove of information on Marxism and Marxists.

www.yale.edu/cgp/

Yale University's Website for the Cambodia Genocide Program; contains a variety of links to resources of great value to students and scholars wishing to learn more about this tragedy, the murderous fanatics who carried it out, and the totalitarian impulse behind it.

SUMMARY

Totalitarian states attempt to realize a utopian vision and create a new political order. Like authoritarian states, totalitarian states are nondemocratic. Yet these two regime types differ in several important respects. In particular, totalitarian regimes seek total control over all aspects of their citizens' lives and demand active participation, rather than passive acquiescence, on the part of the citizenry.

The three major totalitarian states of the past century—Soviet Russia, Nazi Germany, and Maoist China—appear to have gone through several distinct stages of development. The first stage coincides with a period of violent revolution. The five major elements necessary for a successful revolution are charismatic leadership, ideology, organization, propaganda, and violence. During the second stage, power in the hands of the totalitarian ruler is consolidated, opposition parties are eliminated, the party faithful are put in charge, and real or imagined rivals within the party are killed.

The third stage attempts to bring about the total transformation of society. In the Soviet Union, Stalin launched this effort in 1928 with the first Five-Year Plan. In Nazi Germany, Hitler's goal of "racial purification" provided the rationale for a totalitarian drive that culminated in World War II and the Holocaust. In Maoist China, the first attempt to transform Chinese society, the Great Leap Forward, failed miserably in the late 1950s and was followed by the Cultural Revolution of the 1960s.

The human costs of totalitarianism have been staggering. Actual numbers cannot be verified, but even the roughest estimates suggest the totalitarian experiments of the twentieth century brought death or appalling hardship to many millions of people.

Totalitarian states appear in many guises, and there is no guarantee new ones will not emerge in the future. Indeed, the ousted Taliban regime in Afghanistan qualified as a new form of totalitarianism that used a perverted form of Islam as a political ideology.

KEY TERMS

totalitarianism
rectification
cells
partiinost
Gleichschaltung
propaganda
salami tactics

Kuomintang
purges
Gestapo
kulaks
collectivization
gulag archipelago

Hundred Flowers
  campaign
Great Leap Forward
Great Proletarian
  Cultural Revolution
theocracy

REVIEW QUESTIONS

1. What sets totalitarianism apart from other nondemocratic forms of rule?
2. What is required for a successful total revolution to take place?
3. How do totalitarian states consolidate power?
4. What are the basic characteristics of the totalitarian system of rule?
5. What were the primary aims of Stalin's drive to transform Soviet society in the 1930s? What methods did he use?

6. How and why did Hitler try to reshape German society?

7. What was the impetus behind the Great Leap Forward and the Cultural Revolution? What methods did the Maoists employ? What kind of a society did they envisage?

8. What have been the costs of totalitarianism, as measured in human terms?

9. "Totalitarianism passed away with the deaths of Hitler, Stalin, and Mao." Comment.

10. Name two or three recent examples of totalitarianism. Which one(s) are still in existence? Write a short essay on an existing totalitarian state, answering the following three questions. Who rules? How? To what ends?

11. Hitler's totalitarian state ceased to exist after a crushing military defeat. Does the evidence suggest that totalitarian regimes can ever change from within—that is, without being defeated in war—or not? Comment.

12. "As the world's oldest democracy, the United States government should never engage in direct talks with totalitarian states." Do you agree or disagree? Explain your position.

RECOMMENDED READING

Alpers, Benjamin J. *Dictators, Democracy, and American Political Culture: Envisioning the Totalitarian Enemy, 1920s–1950s*. Chapel Hill: University of North Carolina Press, 2003. A look at how totalitarianism was portrayed in U.S. books, movies, the news media, academia, and the political arena when it posed the greatest threat to Western-style democracy.

Arendt, Hannah. *Totalitarianism*. San Diego: Harcourt, 1968. A theoretical analysis of Nazi Germany and Stalinist Russia that spotlights totalitarian states' emphasis on terror, persecution, and mass murder.

Bracher, Karl Dietrich. *The German Dictatorship*. New York: Holt, 1972. A definitive study of Hitler's totalitarian state.

Browning, Christopher. *Ordinary Men: Reserve Police Battalion 101 and the Final Solution in Poland*. New York: HarperCollins, 1992. This study of a civilian Nazi police force engaged in mass murder argues that human beings commit the most evil acts imaginable when faced with tremendous social pressure to conform.

Bullock, Alan. *Hitler and Stalin, Parallel Lives*. New York: Knopf, 1992. A comprehensive and definitive account of the lives and character of these two tyrants.

Cassinelli, C. W. *Total Revolution: A Comparative Study of Germany under Hitler, the Soviet Union under Stalin, and China under Mao*. Santa Barbara, CA: Clio Books, 1976. The writer argues that these regimes are fundamentally similar.

Chirot, Daniel. *Modern Tyrants: The Power and Prevalence of Evil in Our Age*. New York: Free Press, 1994. Hitler and Stalin are presented as the prototype of a new kind of ideological tyrant, who seeks to mold society according to specific "scientific" theories about how society should be constructed.

Conquest, Robert. *The Great Terror: A Reassessment*. New York: Oxford University Press, 1991. A detailed, carefully researched book that provides the definitive scholarly account of Stalin's bloodiest days.

———. *The Harvest of Sorrow: Soviet Collectivization and the Terror-Famine*. New York: Oxford University Press, 1987. A chilling account of Stalin's war against the kulaks and the Ukrainians.

Friedrich, Carl, and Zbigniew Brzezinski. *Totalitarian Dictatorship and Autocracy*. New York: Praeger, 1965. A pioneering effort that attempts to classify and describe totalitarian states.

Hoffer, Eric. *The True Believer: Thoughts on the Nature of Mass Movements*. New York: Harper & Row, 1951. A perceptive examination of individuals who form the nucleus of mass movements.

Hosseini, Khaled. *The Kite Runner*. New York: Riverhead Books, 2003. A gripping novel of growing up in Afghanistan with the unmistakable ring of authenticity. As good an introduction to the cruel and austere world of the Taliban as you will find anywhere. The movie is good; the book is better.

Kiernam, Ben. *The Pol Pot Regime: Race, Power, and Genocide in Cambodia under the Khmer Rouge, 1975–79*. New Haven, CT: Yale University Press, 1996. This detailed examination of one of the darkest periods of human history makes the controversial argument that race, and not ideology, motivated the Cambodian genocide.

Koestler, Arthur. *Darkness at Noon*. New York: Bantam Books, 1984 (First publication, 1940). A classic work of fiction about a totalitarian system in which a Bolshevik loyalist and true believer is put on trial for treason, while his all-powerful tormentor, identified only as Number One, remains anonymous and without mercy.

Menand, Louis. "The Devil's Disciples," *The New Yorker*, July 28, 2003. Accessed at <www.newyorker.com/critics/books/articles/030728crbo_books?030728crbo_books> on January 15, 2007. An excellent review of old and new books on totalitarianism that begins with this tantalizing observation: "Few puzzles in political philosophy are more daunting than the Problem of the Loyal Henchmen."

Orwell, George. *Nineteen Eighty-Four*. New York: Knopf, 1992. The classic fictional caricature of Stalinist Russia that is full of insights regarding the nature of totalitarian societies.

Ponchaud, François. *Cambodia: Year Zero*. New York: Holt, 1978. A chilling historical account of Pol Pot's rule in Kampuchea.

Shapiro, Leonard. *Totalitarianism*. New York: Praeger, 1972. An evenhanded and informative discussion of the scholarly controversy that surrounds the concept of totalitarianism.

Solzhenitsyn, Aleksandr. *One Day in the Life of Ivan Denisovich*, translated by H. T. Willetts. New York: Farrar, Straus and Giroux, 1992. A description of the Soviet labor camps that became a cause célèbre in the Soviet Union during Nikita Khrushchev's de-Stalinization program.

Stewart, Rory. *The Places in Between*. Orlando: Harcourt, Inc., 2004. The true account of a young Scotsman's solitary walk across Afghanistan from Herat to Kabul in the winter of 2002, surviving on tribal hospitality and sharing meals with villagers, soldiers, Taliban commanders, and foreign-aid workers.

Wiesel, Elie. *Night*. New York: Bantam Books, 1982. A poignant autobiographical account of the suffering of the victims of totalitarian rule—in this case, the Jews under Hitler.

Queen's Guard at Windsor Castle—Tradition remains a powerful force in British politics.

©ALAMY LIMITED

Parliamentary Democracy

Great Britain: Mother of all Parliaments

A Mixed Regime

Fusion of Powers

Indefinite Terms of Office

Disciplined Parties

Are Two Heads Better Than One?

A Model with Legs

France: President Versus Parliament

The Fifth Republic: A Hybrid System

The Executive

Reduced Role of the National Assembly

Rival Parties and Seesaw Elections

Constitution under Pressure: Testing the Balance

Justice à la Française

The Balance Sheet

Germany: Federalism Against Militarism

The Weimar Republic

Divided Germany: The Cold War in Microcosm

The Great Merger: Democracy Triumphant

German Federalism

The Executive

We have not only to study the ideally best constitution. We have also to study the type of constitution which is practicable [that is, the best for a state under actual conditions]—and with it, and equally, the type which is easiest to work and most suitable to stages generally. . . . The sort of constitutional system which ought to be proposed is one which men can be easily induced, and will be readily able, to graft onto the system they already have.

Aristotle, *The Politics*[1]

The British system has its origins in horticulture, not architecture—that is, rather than resulting from a blueprint devised by rational minds, like the U.S. Constitution, it simply grew from the fertile soil of British political life. The organic nature of the British parliamentary system raises an obvious question about whether it can be transplanted, but first we take a closer look at this unique representative democracy.

GREAT BRITAIN: MOTHER OF ALL PARLIAMENTS

The political system that formed after the American Revolution represented a sharp break with the European autocratic tradition, and it required a fresh political theory. Although there is no British counterpart to *The Federalist Papers*, we find a sort of homegrown theory of British-style democracy in the writings and speeches of Edmund Burke. Burke detailed Britain's long unbroken

The United Kingdom's Queen Elizabeth II is a beloved monarch who reigns but does not rule. As the ceremonial chief of state, she has served a nation proud of its traditions with dignity and grace since 1952.

© AP PHOTOS

chain of political development, during which, significantly, economic equality and political liberty expanded together. As the monarchy declined in power, British government became increasingly democratic, evolving into a **parliamentary system.** It was gradually established that the British monarch would automatically accept Parliament's choice of prime minister (PM). In time, the PM eclipsed the monarch as the head of government. Today, the monarch Queen Elizabeth II is the head of state with no executive power—a beloved figurehead.

parliamentary system
A system of democratic government in which authority is concentrated in the legislative branch, which selects a prime minister and cabinet officers who serve as long as they have majority support in the parliament.

mixed regime
A nation in which the various branches of government represent social classes.

A Mixed Regime

From the seventeenth century on, the British parliamentary system became a prime example of what Aristotle called a **mixed regime,** in which different institutions represent different classes. The House of Lords represented the interests of the traditional governing classes, whereas the House of Commons gradually came to represent the interests of the general electorate, expressed through free elections and increasing suffrage.

Great Britain's mixed regime historically promoted stability by providing representation for classes that otherwise might have become openly hostile toward one another. Today, what we call the British welfare state has evolved into an elaborate system of income redistribution designed to perpetuate a large middle class. The traditional representation of separate social classes has become largely irrelevant, although the image of the two major parties—the Conservative Party (or Tories) and the Labour Party—continues to reflect the class consciousness that has always been present in British politics. The marginalization of the Peerage (nobility) is mirrored in the historical ascendancy of the popularly elected House of Commons over the aristocratic House of Lords. The House of Lords comprises about 1,100 people holding aristocratic titles (gained, in most cases, through inheritance), but only about 300 are eligible to actively participate.[2] The Parliament Acts of 1911 and 1949 made it impossible for the House of Lords to kill legislation passed by Commons; according to these acts, the Lords can do no more than delay a bill from taking effect for 1 year.

Fusion of Powers

Under the British parliamentary system, the executive branch—the prime minister and the cabinet—is formed after each election and consists of the leaders of the victorious party within the House of Commons, endorsed by the Parliament and appointed by the queen. Although all members of Parliament, including those in the opposition party, are free to question and criticize, the government is assured of getting its legislative program passed, because in the British system, there is always a clear majority for reasons peculiar to the "first-past-the-post electoral system" explained later in this chapter.

Most parliamentary systems function in much the same manner as the British system, but in countries with multiple parties and proportional representation (see Chapter 11), the government often cannot count on a clear parliamentary majority. Where there are five or six parties in parliament—and none with a popular base to match either of Britain's two major parties—it often happens that no single party has enough seats to form a government. In this event, coalitions, or two or more parties joining forces, are necessary. Sometimes coalition governments work fairly well; in the worst cases such as Italy, however, parliamentary rule can be unstable and even chaotic.

Indefinite Terms of Office

When a victorious party leader takes over in the United Kingdom, it is understood the new government will serve for *no more than* 5 years before seeking a new mandate from the voters. A British PM's job security entirely depends on his or her ability to maintain "confidence"—an elusive but vital intangible in British politics. Here, too, the British and U.S. systems differ significantly. U.S. elections are held at regular intervals that never change; voters always know exactly when the next election will be held. Not so in the British system. Parliament is required to stand for election every 5 years, but the prime minister can call for elections earlier if it looks as though the mood of the electorate momentarily favors the ruling party. By the same token, Parliament can force the government to resign by a vote of "no confidence." In this event, either a new government is formed under new leadership or the queen dissolves Parliament and calls new elections.

The authority to decide when to call new elections can be a big advantage for the party in power. Prime Minister Margaret Thatcher made particularly shrewd use of this authority in 1983, for example. After serving only 4 years, the "Iron Lady" (as she was often called) capitalized on a surge of British patriotism, spurred by a war with Argentina over the Falkland Islands, to renew the Conservative Party's mandate to rule for another 5 years. In 1987, she again called for an election 4 years into her term and won.

But 3 years later, Thatcher's popularity fell as a result of her support for a poll tax that many Britons considered regressive and unfair. Under intense attack within her Conservative Party, she resigned as party leader and prime minister, turning over the reins of government to her successor, John Major. Thatcher had served continuously for more than a decade—a twentieth-century record.

More recently, Prime Minister Tony Blair was forced to resign due to his unstinting support for the U.S.-led war in Iraq—a war strongly opposed by the vast majority of British voters. In the summer of 2007, Blair gave way to his chief rival in the Labour Party, Gordon Brown. The resignation of a British head of government is neither surprising nor unprecedented. Rather, when a leader has lost public confidence it is expected. Prime Minister Neville Chamberlain (1869–1940) resigned in 1940, despite the fact that his party still commanded a majority in the House of Commons. So widespread was his unpopularity after his "appeasement" of Adolf Hitler at Munich that he

FIGURE 7.1   Map of UK showing the 2005 election results by region. The Labour Party kept its majority in the House of Commons but lost 47 seats while the main opposition Conservative party gained 33 seats. Both main parties could (and did) claim victory.

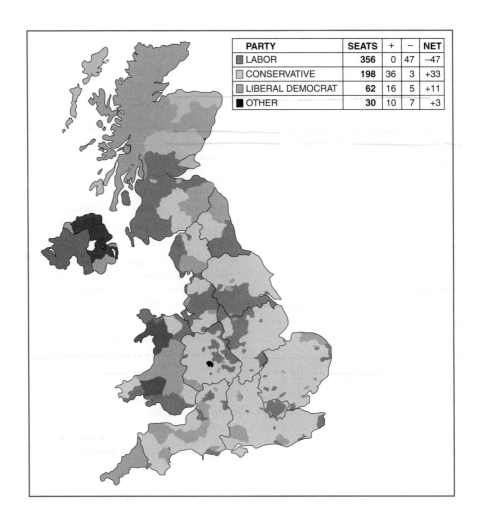

PARTY	SEATS	+	−	NET
LABOR	356	0	47	−47
CONSERVATIVE	198	36	3	+33
LIBERAL DEMOCRAT	62	16	5	+11
OTHER	30	10	7	+3

stepped aside and let another prominent Tory leader—Winston Churchill—take charge. Churchill, of course, proved to be one of history's great wartime leaders.

Other circumstances may cause a government to fall before its 5-year term has expired. If the majority party's policy is unpopular or if the government becomes embroiled in a scandal, a motion of no confidence can be introduced. If the motion passes in a **no-confidence vote,** the government resigns. The prime minister then asks the monarch to dissolve parliament and call for new elections. In countries with multiparty parliamentary systems, governments come

no-confidence vote
In parliamentary governments, a legislative vote that the sitting government must win to remain in power.

© LEFTERIS PITARAKIS/AP PHOTO

Gordon Brown succeeded Tony Blair in 2007. As a former Chancellor of the Exchequer, Brown is an expert on public finance and economics. He needed to draw on all his knowledge and experience to stabilize the British economy in the global recession of 2008–2009.

and go frequently in this manner, but it is rare in the United Kingdom, where it has not happened since Prime Minister James Callaghan lost a no-confidence motion in 1979.

Disciplined Parties

Party discipline in the United Kingdom manifests itself in a ritual show of public unity, coherent party platforms, and bloc voting. British parties differ sharply in this respect from U.S. parties, which are more loosely organized and often less important to voters than are the personal traits of the candidates.

In Parliament, the government demands unwavering support from its majority-party members. Strong party discipline does not mean that MPs never cross the aisle to vote with the opposition, however. They can also abstain on an important vote or even engineer a major party realignment. In the early 1900s, for example, when the trade union movement transformed the British working class into a powerful political force, the Labour Party eclipsed the old Liberal (or Whig) Party as the Conservative (or Tory) Party's chief rival.

The party-out-of-power—formally called Her Majesty's **Loyal Opposition**—criticizes the majority's policy initiatives and holds the government accountable for its actions. Criticism is usually tempered by civility, because the Opposition "thinks of itself as the next government, and a wise Opposition operates within those limits which it hopes its own opponents will respect when the tables are turned."[3] As one expert observer pointed out,

> Organized opposition is not now considered subversive or treasonable. Indeed, since 1937, the Leader of the Opposition has been paid a special salary out of public funds, and people often talk about *"Her Majesty's Opposition,"* because the existence of an Opposition is thought to be an essential part of the Queen's government.[4]

party discipline
In a parliamentary system, the tendency of legislators to vote consistently as a bloc with fellow party members in support of the party's platform.

Loyal Opposition
The belief, which originated in England, that the out-of-power party has a responsibility to formulate alternative policies and programs; such a party is sometimes called the Loyal Opposition.

Are Two Heads Better Than One?

Unlike the United States, where one chief executive (the president) serves as both the head of state and the head of government, Great Britain separates these functions. The British head of state is the reigning monarch. Queen Elizabeth II,

The British Agenda: A Sampler

The Economy

Under Labour leadership, Britain developed a model welfare state in the 1950s and 1960s but was stricken by stagflation, or simultaneous recession and inflation, in the 1970s. In 1979, Margaret Thatcher led the Conservative Party to victory and set about re-privatizing state-run industries and systematically deregulating the British economy.

Voters turned the Conservatives out of office in 1997 for the first time in 18 years. Under Labour PM Tony Blair's market-friendly policies, the British economy outperformed Europe's other major economies—Germany, France, and Italy. As Chancellor of the Exchequer, Gordon Brown was in charge of economic policy prior to becoming Prime Minister in 2007. Brown's popularity fell a precarious level in 2008. Then global financial crisis hit. Public confidence in Brown's economic crisis-management skills at first boosted his standing in opinion polls. But with national elections approaching in 2010, the deepening recession and growing public discontent worked against Brown's hopes of leading the Labour party to a third consecutive victory at the polls.

The European Union

Great Britain joined the European Union in 1973. However, its policy toward the EU has been characterized by continuing ambivalence. In the 1990s, when the adoption of the euro went into effect, British popular opinion was strongly against a common currency, and London opted out.

Support for U.S. Foreign Policy

In the aftermath of the September 11, 2001, terrorist attacks, Blair strongly backed the U.S. war on terror. The British played a key role in the bombing of Afghanistan and in the invasion of Iraq in 2003. The failure to find any evidence of "weapons of mass destruction" in Iraq intensified Britons' opposition to the war, moving Blair to step down as prime minister in May 2007.

Northern Ireland

The four options for settling the decades-old civil war in Northern Ireland (Ulster) are (1) reunification of Ulster with Ireland, (2) independence from Britain, (3) devolution (home rule), or (4) integration with Britain. Before a 1994 cease-fire, the provisional Irish Republican Army (IRA) repeatedly carried out terrorist attacks in an effort to force the British from Northern Ireland and made bold attempts to assassinate both Thatcher and Major. By the time of the cease-fire, some 3000 people had been killed on both sides—Catholic and Protestant.

Northern Ireland has been relatively calm, but when two soldiers and a policeman were murdered there in March 2009, two IRA splinter groups claimed responsibility—a grim reminder that peace in that troubled land is fragile. However, thousands attended rallies in Northern Ireland as a show of anger and outrage over the killings. Any lasting solution will have to take into account the claims of British-backed Protestants, who outnumber Catholics in Northern Ireland, and of Catholics, who constitute an overwhelming majority in the Irish Republic.

"arguably the most famous person in the world," has occupied the British throne for over half a century. The monarch is a national symbol and a source of unity, personifying the state but not wielding its powers.

The actual head of the government is the prime minister, who, in close consultation with key cabinet members (often called the *inner cabinet*), sets domestic and foreign policy. National policy emerges from this leadership core, which then presents it to the cabinet as a whole. Cabinet members who are out of step with the government on an important policy matter are expected to resign quietly.

A Model with Legs

Most European democracies are patterned after the British system, although with mixed results. France under the Third and Fourth Republics (1876–1958) and Italy since World War II came to be dominated by political parties and a parliament. The political party system became fragmented, internal party discipline broke down, and the government fell victim to never-ending legislative skirmishes. Strong executive leadership was often missing in France before 1958 and remains a chronic problem in Italy to this day.

Such conditions have led to political stalemate in both countries at different times. In France, during the entire life span of the Third and Fourth Republics, no single party ever won a majority of seats in the National Assembly, and no fewer than 119 governments ruled the country, each with an average life of less than a year. A similar malaise has plagued Italy, which had more than 40 prime ministers between 1945 and 1986 (one per year on average). Yet today, parliamentary governments are found all over Europe, with rare exceptions—a major triumph in a region divided by war, revolution, and totalitarian rule until recently. In a real sense, parliamentary government is Great Britain's gift to Europe—a model with "legs."

FRANCE: PRESIDENT VERSUS PARLIAMENT

The U.S. presidential and British parliamentary systems represent two different approaches to democratic government. Under the Fifth Republic, France has fashioned a form of representative democracy that successfully combines elements of both systems.

The Fifth Republic: A Hybrid System

The Fifth Republic, created in 1958, was meant to overcome what its founder, Charles de Gaulle, understood to be the great nemesis of French politics: impotent executives dominated by fractious legislatures (see Figure 7.2). As de Gaulle was fond of pointing out, France's first three experiments in republican government all ended in dictatorship.

Under the Fourth Republic (1946–1958), governments had lasted an average of 6 months. A profusion of political parties, some of fleeting duration,

FIGURE 7.2   Map of France. Divided into 22 regions, 95 departments, and 36,851 communes, France is a political-administrative jigsaw puzzle. Mayors of major cities often become prominent national politicians; in fact it is quite common for a mayor also to be a member of the National Assembly (the French parliament) at the same time.

turned France's parliamentary system into a travesty. Worse, parties at opposite ends of the political spectrum—Gaullists on the right and Communists on the left—both sought to undermine the Fourth Republic's constitution and force the resignation of weak coalition governments.

The Fifth Republic's constitution was short and simple. Its provisions were guided by de Gaulle, who, in a famous address 12 years earlier, declared:

> The unity, cohesion, and internal discipline of the Government of France must be sacred objects or else the country's leadership will rapidly become impotent and invalid. . . . The executive power should, therefore, be embodied in a Chief of State, placed above the parties . . . to serve as an arbiter, placed above the political circumstances of the day, and to carry out this function ordinarily in the Cabinet, or, in moments of great confusion, by asking the nation to deliver its sovereign decision through elections. It is his role, should the nation ever be in danger, to assume the duty of guaranteeing national independence and the treaties agreed to by France.[5]

In sum, the centerpiece of the constitutional system, de Gaulle insisted, would be a strong executive branch to counterbalance the perennially divided parliament. The centerpiece of the executive, however, would be the chief of state (president) rather than the prime minister.

France's Dual Executive

The basic elements of de Gaulle's diagnosis are etched into nearly every provision of the 1958 constitution that pertain to the organization of public powers. In accordance with the parliamentary model, the French executive is divided (i.e., **dual executive**). On paper, the prime minister (or *premier)* is the head of government; the president is head of state. Unlike the British monarch, however, the French president is democratically elected and wields executive powers similar, though not identical, to those of the U.S. president. As France's leading political figure, the president is independent of the legislative branch, possesses a wide array of powers, and serves a fixed term in office (7 years from 1962–2000, but now 5 years).

France's constitution positioned the president as the arbitrator of conflicting interests and competing political parties. As the nation's chief diplomat and foreign-policy decision maker, the president appoints and dismisses the prime minister, dissolves the legislature, calls for new elections, declares a state of emergency, issues decrees having the force of law, and presides over cabinet meetings. In addition, the president can call for a national referendum, a device used a number of times since the 1960s. For example, in 1962, de Gaulle's popular referendum to replace the electoral college with direct election of the president passed by an overwhelming majority. In a democratic age, nothing gives a political leader more legitimacy or moral authority than a mandate from the voters.

Compared with the president, France's prime minister generally exercises less power and influence, although there is now a greater balance between these two offices than there was in de Gaulle's time. As head of the government, the prime minister presides over the cabinet and is responsible to the legislature. Together, the prime minister and the cabinet oversee the running of government and the bureaucracy.

dual executive
In a parliamentary system, the division of the functions of head of state and chief executive officer between two persons; the prime minister serves as chief executive, and some other elected (or royal) figure serves as ceremonial head of state.

In general, however, the constitution of the Fifth Republic does not clearly delineate which powers or functions belong to the president and which belong to the prime minister. Due to his unrivalled stature in French politics, de Gaulle enjoyed considerable latitude in interpreting the constitution. Thus, during his tenure, the presidential powers were elastic—de Gaulle could, and did, stretch them to fit the needs of the moment.

No president after de Gaulle, however, has so dominated French politics. Although Socialist François Mitterrand served as France's president for 14 years (1981–1995), he was no de Gaulle. Neither was his center-right successor, Jacques Chirac. Not until the election of Nicolas Sarkozy in 2007 did France have a charismatic center-right president with the ego and ambition to match de Gaulle's. By that time, France had endured (and the Fifth Republic had survived) three periods of **cohabitation**—a political word for a divided executive (a president and prime minister from opposing parties).

cohabitation
In France, the uneasy toleration of a divided executive.

Reduced Role of the National Assembly

If the presidency was clearly the big political winner under the Fifth Republic, the legislature was the loser. France's parliament is divided into two houses, the Senate and the National Assembly. The French Senate, which has only limited powers, is indirectly elected. The **National Assembly**, its parliament, is popularly elected from multimember districts in a double ballot (two-stage) election process. As the focal point of legislative power, the National Assembly must approve all proposed laws. However, the word *law* is rather narrowly defined by the 1958 constitution; in fact, many matters are left to the executive branch, which has the power to issue "decree laws."

National Assembly
Focal point of France's bicameral legislative branch that must approve all laws.

The National Assembly is more interesting for the powers it does *not* have. For example, the French parliament has no power to introduce financial bills. If it fails to approve the government's budget by a certain deadline, the executive can enact the budget by fiat (presidential decree).

Rival Parties and Seesaw Elections

Unlike the United States, France has a wide spectrum of political parties. Rival parties exist on both the left and the right, as well as in the center, and both the Far Right and the Far Left often play a significant role in elections.

The two most important parties of the Left are the Communist Party and the Socialist Party. When left-leaning voters began turning away from the Communists in the late 1970s, the Socialist Party was the primary beneficiary on the left. In 1981, the Socialists won a resounding victory at the polls, and Socialist leader Mitterrand was elected president. Although the Socialists lost the 1986 elections, they made a comeback in 1988, when Mitterrand was reelected and the Socialists again became the strongest party in parliament (although they did not have a clear majority).

In 1993, however, the center-right won a landslide victory, retaking control of the National Assembly. Two years later, the Neo-Gaullist candidate Jacques

Chirac was elected president. Combined with the decisive center-right triumph in Senate elections that same year, Chirac's election put the conservatives back in the driver's seat—but not for long. In the June 1997 elections, parties of the Left, again led by the Socialists, won overwhelmingly. Chirac bowed to the will of the electorate and named Socialist Party leader Lionel Jospin the new prime minister.

In 1997, Jean-Marie Le Pen's far-right National Party received more votes than the Gaullist UDF (Union for French Democracy)—14.9 percent to 14.2 percent—and nearly as many as Chirac's RPR, which had 15.7 percent. Yet the two center-right parties garnered 242 seats in the National Assembly, while the National Party won but a single seat. The reason for this anomaly is that France's electoral system stacks the deck against fringe parties by requiring a second round of balloting when no candidate receives an absolute majority of votes in the first round. In practice, this means that parties with similar (and less uncompromising) ideological stances can, and do, form temporary alliances between the two balloting rounds. As a result, the influence of fringe or extremist parties is greatly diminished.

French voters reversed the tide again in 2002, giving Chirac's new center-right umbrella party called Union for a Popular Movement (UMP) a clear majority in the National Assembly (357 seats, or 62 percent of the total) in the second round of balloting. But the final result was misleading: The UMP, despite the pre-election realignment that merged three center-right parties into one, had received only 33 percent of the votes in the first round (just 7 percent more than the Socialists). The election outcome thus underscored the way France's two-step electoral process produces a parliamentary majority out of a fragmented party system. When center-right candidate Nicolas Sarkozy was elected president in May 2007, attention quickly turned to the upcoming parliamentary elections in June. Would the French voters give Sarkozy a "presidential majority" in the National Assembly, or would they effectively tie his hands by voting for opposition parties on both the left and the right?

The answer: French voters gave the center-right a solid majority, but little reason to celebrate—the Socialists realized a net gain of forty-six seats while the UMP actually lost forty-four seats. Likewise, in 2008 local and regional elections, the UMP suffered another serious blow, losing numerous city mayoral races and eight departmental presidencies.

Constitution under Pressure: Testing the Balance

The Fifth Republic has brought stable democracy to France for half a century now.[6] De Gaulle's influence has extended well beyond his presidency, and his broad interpretation of presidential powers prevails to this day. De Gaulle's preference for a strong national economy that mixes a large role for the state (a French tradition) with a healthy respect for free-market principles remains firmly fixed as a part of his legacy. Nonetheless, without de Gaulle's firm hand on the tiller, "long-range programs gave place to expediency, and party alignments obeyed the logic of electoral tactics rather than policy making."[7]

divided executive
Situation in French government in which the president and the prime minister differ in political party or outlook.

From the start of the Fifth Republic, France faced the danger of a **divided executive**: when the president and prime minister represented two different parties, embraced different ideologies, and advanced different policies. Although a deadlocked government remains a hazard in France's dual-executive system, France has survived three periods of cohabitation, most recently from 1997 to 2002.

Justice à la Française

The French judicial system is divided into two basic types of courts—ordinary courts and administrative courts—with different jurisdictions. Despite this

The French Agenda: A Sampler

The Economy

High taxes, chronic double-digit unemployment, mounting public debt, and a generally sluggish economy plagued France even before the 2008 global recession brought a sharp downturn in the national economies of all the European Union's member states. Many French perceive a close link between unemployment and immigration, as immigrants willing to work for low wages crowd into cities and compete for scarce jobs.

The Welfare State

In the 1990s, Socialist Prime Minister Lionel Jospin reduced the work week from 39 to 35 hours without reducing anyone's pay. Although such measures are popular for obvious reasons, they also place France at a competitive disadvantage. According to critics, France is paying the price for profligate spending and pandering to labor unions, farmers, pensioners, and other special interests. Without a major overhaul of pensions—a highly charged political issue—the French treasury faces a rising tide of red ink. President Sarkozy talks tough about the need for fundamental reforms in the economy. Easier said than done—especially in the face of rising social discontent as the recession takes its toll.

Immigration and the Far Right

The Far Right National Front, led by Jean-Marie Le Pen, has taken up the immigration issue most stridently. There are an estimated 14 million French citizens of foreign ancestry (about 23 percent of the total population) and more than three million Arabs, mostly from Algeria, Morocco, and Tunisia. Unemployment and urban decay have eroded traditional French hospitality toward political exiles, refugees, and asylum seekers. The election of Nicolas Sarkozy, a hard-liner on immigration, as president in May 2007 momentarily robbed the Far Right of its one big issue.

France and the United States

France joined the U.S.-led campaign against the Taliban regime in Afghanistan after the 9/11 attacks, but President Chirac opposed the invasion of Iraq in 2003, defiantly blocking U.S. efforts in the UN Security Council to get the United Nations to endorse the action. Reversing a time-honored French stance, President Sarkozy has sought to establish a close relationship with Washington. After a 40-year absence, France rejoined the NATO integrated military structure in 2009.

Nicolas Sarkozy, France's charismatic president, was elected in May 2007.

© EC.EUROPA.EU

rather routine distinction, France's legal system has some interesting twists. For example, the High Council of the Judiciary, chaired by the president, decides on judicial promotions and discipline, whereas the High Court of Justice has the power to try the president for treason and members of the government for crimes related to abuses in office.

The Constitutional Council is composed of nine justices—three nominated by the president of the republic, three by the president of the National Assembly, and three by the president of the Senate—plus all the past presidents of the republic. This judicial watchdog plays several vital roles in the French system. It supervises presidential elections and can investigate and resolve contested legislative races. Under certain conditions, it can also render opinions on laws and the constitution. The cases that come before the Council deal with political issues brought by either the president of the republic, the prime minister, the two presidents of the legislature, or at least 60 members of the National Assembly or the Senate.

The Balance Sheet

France has taken a troubled and tortuous road to democracy, but in the past half-century it has enjoyed the most stable government for the longest period since the French Revolution. The big question now is not whether its democracy is viable, but whether the French economy is sustainable without dismantling the welfare state that has the government forever teetering on the brink of insolvency.

GERMANY: FEDERALISM AGAINST MILITARISM

Modern Germany burst onto the European scene with two impressive military victories: over Austria in 1866 and France in 1871. Following two world wars and two defeats, Germany was partitioned from 1949 until 1989, when the Berlin Wall was dismantled and the country reunited after the communist regime in East Germany collapsed. To understand Germany's turbulent history in the first half of the twentieth century, it is necessary to go back to the bitter (for Germans) legacy of World War I.

The Weimar Republic

Weimar Republic
The constitutional democracy founded in Germany at the end of World War I by a constitutional convention convened in 1919 at the city of Weimar; associated with a period of political and economic turmoil, it ended when Hitler came to power in 1933.

Hitler's Third Reich sprang from the ashes of the **Weimar Republic,** Germany's first experiment with constitutional democracy. The Weimar Republic was ill fated from the moment of its inception because it was associated with Germany's humiliating defeat and the harsh peace terms imposed by the Allied powers after World War I. Burdened by punitive reparations, Germany fell victim to high unemployment, widespread business failures, and rampant inflation.

In the face of such turbulence, German society became polarized between the extreme Right and the extreme Left. In the words of one authority, "Stable democratic government was in jeopardy throughout the life of the Weimar Republic. The country was governed . . . by unpopular minority cabinets, by internally weak Grand Coalitions, or finally, by extra-parliamentary authoritarian Presidential Cabinets."[8] Between the two world wars (1919–1939) the country's fragile political institutions were put to a test that proved fatal.

Given this background, the founding of the Federal Republic of Germany in 1949 was risky. Whether democracy could ever be made to work in a country that had only recently bowed to a deranged dictator, served a totalitarian state, and looked the other way while millions of innocent people were systematically murdered was an open question.

Divided Germany: The Cold War in Microcosm

World War II destroyed Germany. The nation and its capital, Berlin, were subsequently bifurcated into the German Democratic Republic (GDR), or East Germany, and the Federal Republic of Germany (FRG), or West Germany. From 1949 to 1990, Germany and Berlin, the historical capital, became powerful symbols of the Cold War—the ideological rivalry between the United States and the Soviet Union—and the unbridgeable East–West divide.

The West German "economic miracle" in the 1950s was unmatched. In the 1960s it was the main engine driving the newly established Common Market, a six-nation trading bloc that in time evolved into the world's largest single economy—the European Union. West Germany's success stood in stark contrast to the dismal Stalinist state of East Germany. The dramatic difference between the two Germanys was highlighted by the building of the Berlin Wall in 1961, which was to keep East Germans (and other Eastern Europeans) from escaping to the West through West Berlin. The Berlin Wall became a metaphor for the struggle between freedom and tyranny.

The Great Merger: Democracy Triumphant

For three decades, East Germans, who endured far lower living standards than West Germans, had not been allowed to emigrate or even to visit relatives across the border. It was the reform-minded Soviet leader Mikhail Gorbachev who opened the floodgates.

East Germany's end came at a time when rebellion was rife in central and Eastern Europe: Poland and Hungary had already taken giant steps toward dismantling communist rule, and Czechoslovakia, Romania, and Bulgaria were not far behind. For East German communism, the unraveling started with a mass exodus and ended with the bulldozing of the Berlin Wall following the collapse of the East German regime in late 1989.

Following free elections in the former GDR in the spring of 1990, the two Germanys entered into a formal union, with Berlin restored as the capital. Together, the nearly simultaneous collapse of Soviet power and German reunification set the stage for the eastward expansion of the European Union.

© GETTY IMAGES

During the Cold War the Berlin Wall was a symbol of the political and ideological divide between East and West. When German citizens jubilantly tore down the wall in 1989 it signaled the end of an era in European and world history.

The remaking of Germany carried a big price tag. West Germans paid for the economic rehabilitation of East Germany with a 7.5 percent income tax surcharge and a higher sales tax. Nonetheless, unemployment in eastern Germany has hovered around 18 percent, nearly twice the rate in western Germany.

German Federalism

Prior to 1989, the Federal Republic of Germany consisted of ten states, or *Länder* (singular, *Länd)*, plus West Berlin. It was about equal in size to the state of Oregon. The merger of the two German states in 1989 added six new *Länder* to the federal structure. Even so, no fewer than twenty-five countries the size of the united Germany would fit comfortably into the territory of the United States.

The main reason for German federalism is political rather than geographic— namely, to act as a barrier to over-centralization of power. The primary responsibility of the *Länd* or state governments is to enact legislation in specific areas, such as education and cultural affairs. They alone have the resources to implement laws enacted by the federal government, exercise police powers, administer the educational system, and place (limited) restrictions on the press. The federal government in Berlin has the exclusive right to legislate in foreign affairs, citizenship matters, currency and coinage, railways, postal service and telecommunications, and copyrights. In other areas, notably civil and criminal law, as well as laws regulating the economy, the central government and the *Länder* have shared powers, although the European Union plays a large and ever-greater role in regulating the economies of its twenty-seven member-states.

The *Länder* are more powerful and receive a larger proportion of tax revenues than U.S. states do. For example, individual and corporate income taxes are split between Berlin and the *Länder* in equal 40-percent shares; the remaining 20 percent goes to the cities. The *Länder* also receive one-third of the value-added tax, the large but hidden sales (or turnover) tax used throughout Europe.

The Executive

Germany has a parliamentary form of government with a divided executive. The most important government official is the chancellor, akin to a prime minister. The head of the majority party in the lower house of parliament becomes the chancellor; if no one party enjoys an absolute majority, as has often been the case, a coalition government chooses the chancellor. The chancellor, with parliamentary approval, appoints and dismisses cabinet members. In case of a national emergency, the chancellor becomes commander-in-chief of the armed forces (which are integrated into the NATO alliance structure) and is responsible for the formulation and implementation of public policy. In November 2005, Angela Merkel became the first woman chancellor in German history.

The president, as the titular head of state, serves a largely symbolic function, except in the event of political stalemate in parliament. Chosen indirectly for a 7-year term, the president is, like the king or queen of Great Britain, above party politics.

The Legislature

The legislative branch of the German government is divided into a lower house, known as the **Bundestag,** and an upper house, called the **Bundesrat.** In this bicameral setup, as in France and Britain, the lower house is the more important of the two. In Germany, however, the upper house is a far bigger player than in France and Britain.

The Bundestag The presiding officer of the Bundestag is always chosen from the leadership of the majority party. Procedural matters are governed by rules inherited from the Reichstag, the prewar legislature. Important decisions regarding committee assignments, the scheduling of debates, and other questions of day-to-day parliamentary policy are made through the Council of Elders. This body consists of the president of the Bundestag, the three vice presidents (representing the two major parties—the Christian Democratic Union and the Social Democratic Party—and the smaller Free Democratic Party), as well as several other members chosen by each of the parties. Elections to the Bundestag are normally held every 4 years.

In Germany, the Basic Law (the constitution) requires a "constructive vote of no confidence," meaning a chancellor cannot be ousted by a no-confidence vote unless the Bundestag simultaneously chooses a successor. This provision was intended as insurance against a recurrence of the governmental instability associated with Hitler's rise to power.

Because the most important work is done in legislative committees, it is especially vital that political parties gain enough seats for a *Fraktion*, a block of at least fifteen legislative seats. It is only through this unit that deputies can be assigned to committees and political parties can receive formal recognition.

The Bundesrat The upper house must pass to the lower house any measure that would alter the balance of powers between the national government and the *Länder*. Bundesrat members are appointed by the *Länder* governments rather than being elected, and they must vote as a bloc. This gives the German states a powerful weapon to protect themselves against federal encroachment and makes the Bundesrat one of the most important upper houses anywhere in the world. Germany's state governments play a primary role in implementing federal policy as well as in helping to shape that policy in the concurrent areas designated under the Basic Law.

Political Parties

Germany's political party system was consciously designed to keep the number of parties from getting out of hand and to prevent tiny extremist groups from

Bundestag
The lower house in the German federal system; most legislative activity occurs in this house.

Bundesrat
The upper house in the German federal system; its members, who are appointed directly by the Länder (states), exercise mostly informal influence in the legislative process.

playing a significant role in the country's political life. To gain Bundestag representation, parties must receive a minimum of 5 percent of the national vote and must win seats in a minimum of three electoral districts.

Another factor strengthening the major parties is the mode of elections to the Bundestag. Each voter casts two votes, one for the individual and another for a *list* of names determined by the party. This method of election gives the major parties a significant role in determining the future of those who aspire to careers in politics and public service, because fully half the members of the Bundestag are elected from party lists in multimember districts by proportional representation.

Since 1949, the German Federal Republic has had two major parties—the center-left Social Democratic Party (SPD) and the conservative Christian Democratic Union/Christian Socialist Union (CDU/CSU). Because the two major parties have frequently evenly divided the popular vote (and the seats in the Bundestag), the small Free Democratic Party (FDP) has often held the key to forming a government. Both the SPD and the CDU/CSU have courted the FDP at different times but for the same reason. As a result, the FDP has had power disproportionate to its popularity at the polls and has been a junior partner in several coalition governments.

In recent years, the Green Party, which started as a social protest movement emphasizing environmental issues, has gained in popularity. In 1998, when the SPD defeated the CDU/CSU but failed to win a majority of the seats in the Bundestag, the Social Democrats, then led by Gerhard Schröder, entered into a coalition with the Green Party to form a center-left government. Schröder, who succeeded Christian Democrat Helmut Kohl (and preceded Angela Merkel) as chancellor, named Green Party leader Joschka Fisher as his foreign minister.

In 2005, Angela Merkel, leader of the Christian Democratic union, became the first female chancellor in German history. Chancellor Merkel's party won a major victory in national elections held in the fall of 2009, thus greatly strengthening her hand in dealing with Germany's problems, including a sluggish economy.

© EC.EUROPA.EU

The Judiciary

Besides its ordinary judicial functions, the German court system is designed to act as a barrier against abuses of executive or legislative power and as a guardian of civil liberties. The regular judiciary, headed by the Supreme Court, operates alongside a set of four specialized federal tribunals, Labor Court, Social Court, Finance Court, and Administrative Court. From a political standpoint, the most important judicial structure is the Constitutional Court, which deals exclusively with constitutional questions and has the express power to declare the acts of both federal and *Länd* legislatures unconstitutional.

The German Agenda: A Sampler

Reunification and Its Aftermath

Merging the two German states in the 1990s was costly. East Germany's infrastructure was in disrepair, factories operated with obsolete equipment, unemployment was high due to plant closings. Two decades after the Berlin Wall came down, former West Germany still accounts for 90 percent of the nation's total GDP.

Welfare State Versus Competitive Economy

The German economy stalled in the mid-1990s and unemployment hit a post-war high of 12.8 percent in 1998, helping the Social Democrats win control of the government. By 2005, some 5.2 million Germans were jobless—a post-World War II record. German voters brought the center-right Christian Democrats back to power. In recent years, major labor-market and pension reforms have helped restore German industry's competitiveness. In 2009, economists expected Germany's economy to shrink—along with that of the rest of the EU nations.

Foreign Workers, Illegal Immigrants, and Skinheads

Germany has been a magnet for temporary workers and illegal immigrants from Eastern Europe and elsewhere. Of the ten countries that joined the EU in 2004, eight are in Eastern Europe, where with few exceptions per capita income and living standards remain relatively low. Xenophobic extremists, including neo-Nazis and "skinheads," have tried to capitalize on popular fears over immigration—so far with little success.

Boosting the European Union

Germany remains a staunch supporter of European integration. Like France, it favors movement toward a "wider and deeper" Europe. The idea of one Europe appeals to many Germans for historical reasons—to allay any lingering fears of a resurgent Germany bullying the rest of Europe. With the 2004 and 2007 enlargements, Europe's single economy now embraces some 500 million consumers, creating new opportunities for German businesses and industries.

Germany's Changing Role in Europe and the World

Germany is in transition. When it participated in the UN peacekeeping mission in Bosnia in the mid-1990s, it was the first time German soldiers had been sent abroad since World War II. In 1999, Germany contributed 8,500 combat troops to the NATO operation in Kosovo (Serbia), and after 9/11, it sent 2,000 troops to Afghanistan. Germany's opposition to the U.S.–British invasion of Iraq in 2003 was the first time Germany openly opposed the United States on a major foreign policy issue since World War II. Most Germans alive today were born after 1945 and thus have no direct experience or recollections of World War II.

The Bundestag elects half the judges for the Constitutional Court, and the Bundesrat elects the other half. Most judges, however, are chosen on the basis of competitive civil service-type examinations and are appointed for life by the minister of justice, with the assistance of nominating committees selected by the federal and *Länd* legislatures. Indefinite terms help ensure judicial independence.

FIGURE 7.3   Map of Germany. Note that Berlin, once again the capital, is located in the state of Brandenburg. During the Cold War and before Germany reunification in 1990, it was deep inside East Germany. The provinces (now federal states) that comprised the former East Germany were Brandenburg, Mecklenburg-Vorpommern, Saxony-Anhalt, Saxony, and Thuringia.

In some eyes, the Constitutional Court is Germany's most powerful institution. It is certainly the most popular: almost 80 percent of Germans trust it, while fewer than half express confidence in the federal government and the Bundestag. One big reason: the court is widely seen as being above politics. Any German citizen can bring a case before the Constitutional Court, "an antidote to Nazi notions of justice, and some 6,000 a year do so."[9]

The Basic Law and Civil Liberties

In the realm of civil liberties, as one student of German politics declared, "The relevant historical experience was that of the Third Reich, with its oppressive flouting of all human liberties."[10] The first 19 articles of the Basic Law—Germany's constitution—are devoted to a careful elaboration of the unalienable rights of every German citizen.

All forms of discrimination, including religious and racial discrimination, are expressly prohibited. Freedom of speech, movement, assembly, and association are guaranteed, except when used "to attack the free democratic order." This last proviso was clearly aimed at the two extremes—Communism on the left, Nazism on the right. Fear of a right-wing resurgence has never been far beneath the surface. Indeed, in postwar Germany, neo-Nazi activity has generally been interpreted as constituting an "attack on the free democratic order."

Does Democracy in Germany Work?

One of the principal purposes behind the Basic Law was to arrange the institutional furniture in the "new Germany" to preclude a repeat performance of the "old Germany." By any standard, Germany's performance since World War II was been impressive.

JAPAN: BETWEEN EAST AND WEST

Like other Asian societies, Japan had no democratic traditions prior to 1947. In fact, its history and culture often worked against Western democratic ideas. Yet today, Japan is one of Asia's oldest parliamentary democracies (the other, India, came into being at the same time but under very different circumstances). To see how this remarkable transformation came about, we must first sketch Japan's historical background.[11]

Historical Background

Japan's feudal era lasted until the **Meiji Restoration** in 1868. At that time, under the guise of recapturing ancient glories, Japan crowned a new emperor, of the Meiji dynasty, and embarked on the path to modernization. Meiji Japan remained oligarchic, paying lip service to democracy. A group of elder

Meiji Restoration
The end of Japan's feudal era, in 1868, when a small group of powerful individuals crowned a symbolic emperor, embarked on an economic modernization program, and established a modern governmental bureaucracy.

FIGURE 7.4   Japan: Note Japan's proximity to the Korean peninsula and, in the north, to Russia.

statesmen, or *genro*, dominated the government, and the emperor, worshiped as a flesh-and-blood deity, personified national unity. He probably also played an important role in decision making on crucial issues.[12]

Domestically, Japan made great progress during the latter part of the nineteenth century. A modernizing elite promoted, protected, and subsidized a Western-style economic development program. Despite periodic opposition from rural landowners, the government force-fed the economy with infusions of capital designed to promote heavy industry. Only basic or strategic industries were state owned. Within a few decades, the leaders of the Meiji Restoration, according to one authority, "abolished feudal institutions, legalized private property in land, started a Western-style legal system, established compulsory education, organized modern departments of central and local government, and removed the legal barriers between social classes."[13]

After World War I, Japan entered a new phase of political development. Nationalism, taught in the schools, became a kind of religion. Governments blossomed and withered in a rapid and bewildering succession. All attempts at instituting democratic reforms were submerged in the tidal wave of militarism that swept over Japan in the 1930s. Charging that effete politicians infatuated with democracy had kept Japan down, ultranationalists looked to a strong military for leadership. Japan had never truly embraced Western concepts of constitutionalism and liberal democracy. Sovereignty, according to popular belief, issued from the emperor-deity, not from the people. Thus, prior to 1945, Japan had dallied with democracy in form but not in substance.

The 1947 Constitution

The 1947 Japanese constitution, imposed by the victors after World War II, sought to remake Japan's political system. Henceforth, sovereignty would reside in the Japanese people, not in the emperor. U.S. influence on the new Japanese constitution is readily apparent in its preamble:

> We, the Japanese people, acting through our duly elected representatives in the National Diet, determined that we shall secure for ourselves and our posterity the fruits of peaceful cooperation with all nations and the blessings of liberty throughout this land, and resolved that never again shall we be visited with the horrors of war through the action of government, do proclaim that sovereign power resides with the people and do firmly establish this Constitution. . . . Government is a sacred trust of the people, the authority for which is derived from the people, the powers of which are exercised by representatives of the people, and the benefits of which are enjoyed by the people.

Like weavers of a fine tapestry, the framers of the 1947 constitution sought to construct an elaborate system of representative democracy. Among the fundamental rights guaranteed by the constitution were the rights to receive an equal education and to organize and bargain collectively. In another extraordinary feature, the Japanese constitution explicitly renounced war and pledged that "land, sea, and air forces, as well as other war potential, will never be maintained." (This provision has not, however, prevented the government from building limited "self-defense forces.")

Parliament Above Emperor

The constitution establishes a parliamentary form of government. The emperor remains the head of state, although as a merely ceremonial figure. The prime minister is the real head of government. The authors of the constitution, however, placed a preponderance of *formal* power in the new bicameral legislature. That body, called the Diet, was divided into a 480-member House of Representatives elected at least every 4 years (elections can be more frequent when the House is dissolved) and a relatively less powerful House of Councilors, whose 252 members serve 6-year terms (half being elected every other 3 years).

Originally, members of each house were elected by universal suffrage from multimember districts in which voters made only one selection. This system endured until 1994, when calls for election reforms led to the redrawing of district boundaries and the altering of the election process for the lower House. Now there are 300 single-seat constituencies; the remaining 200 seats are decided by proportional representation.

The constitution explicitly states that popular sovereignty is to be expressed through the Diet, the only institution of the government empowered to make laws. Whereas in the past the prime minister and cabinet were responsible to the emperor, they are now responsible to the Diet, the "highest organ of state power." Japan's Supreme Court is empowered to declare laws unconstitutional (which it rarely does), and justices are to be approved by the voters every 10 years after their appointment, a process that has become virtually automatic.

As we shall see, however, the Japanese have adapted Western institutions to fit Japan's own rich and resilient cultural traditions. The result is a unique system that combines democratic politics and market economics—the new—with political hierarchy, economic centralization, and social discipline—the old.

The Party System

With one brief exception in 1993–1994, the Liberal Democratic Party (LDP) dominated Japanese politics from 1955 to 2009. Among the smaller parties, the Socialists and Communists occasionally garnered significant numbers of votes, but their legislative role was to provide parliamentary opposition. For four decades, the actual governing of the country fell almost exclusively to the LDP.

When a single party retains a majority of seats in a freely elected legislative assembly over an extended time, it usually means the party has satisfied a broad range of social interests. In Japan, the LDP succeeded because it embraced pragmatism over ideological purity, enjoyed the backing of powerful special interests, and benefited from the sheer force of political inertia. According to two authorities,

> The changes they [the LDP] made toward a more strongly centralized system of government corrected some of the most obvious mistakes of the Occupation. The Liberal Democratic Party, being in power, also controlled a considerable amount of patronage and had the advantage when seeking the support of economic and professional interest groups. With the support of the majority of the rural vote and access to the resources of the business community, the party was in a strong position. It was on intimate terms with the bureaucracy, . . . [but these efforts] were not sufficient. . . . Beginning in 1955, the Liberal Democratic Party attempted to build up a national organization with mass membership.[14]

The LDP's consensus-building role became a defining feature of Japanese politics. The party leader, the president, is chosen by delegates to the LDP conference before a national election. Until the 1990s, the LDP leader was assured of being elected prime minister. Getting elected president of the party, however, is not easy: A victor emerges only after intense bargaining by party factions, each of which has its own leader, its own constituencies to protect, and its own interests to promote.

The LDP nearly self-destructed in the early 1990s, after a series of political scandals severely tarnished the party's image. A rising tide of social discontent over the rigors of daily life, high prices, long workdays, and a sluggish economy also contributed to the party's unprecedented defeat in the historical national elections, shattering the one-party-dominant system. What followed was a chaotic period during which Japan would see five different governments come and go. The LDP was the clear loser, but there were no clear winners.

In the fall of 1996, disgruntled voters handed the LDP a slim victory at the polls, but control of the party remained in the hands of a change-resistant old guard, and the LDP again fell out of favor with the public as the economy continued a downslide throughout the 1990s. The promise of change came in 2001, when Junichiro Koizumi, an LDP maverick, won a hard-fought battle to become the LDP's new president. He was reelected by a large majority in September 2003. Reform-minded and opposed to cronyism, Koizumi did not enjoy the support of his own parliamentary party, but the party rank and file (and the public in general) responded enthusiastically to his personal charm, fresh ideas, and candor.

Promising reform "without any sacred cows," Koizumi was rewarded for his efforts as the country's economy revived. However, his prize proposal—privatization of Japan's massive postal savings system—was opposed by many members of his own party in the Diet. When the bill was defeated in the upper house in 2005, Koizumi dissolved the Diet and called new elections. The vote, which the LDP won by the largest majority since 1986, was a referendum on Koizumi's leadership *and* the postal privatization issue. The bill passed in 2005.

© KATSUMI KASAHARA/AP PHOTO

Junichiro Koizumi, former leader of the Liberal Democratic Party, became prime minister in April 2001 and led the LDP back to a position of dominance in Japanese politics, winning one of the largest parliamentary majorities in modern Japanese history in 2005. He stepped down as LDP party leader and prime minister in 2006.

After serving five years as LDP party leader and prime minister, Koizumi stepped down in 2006 having won his biggest political battle: Japan's postal system was privatized in 2007. Although Japan has never fully recovered from the 1990-91 stock market crash there (see "The Japanese Agenda" below) and the subsequent implosion of its "bubble economy," it still boasts the world's third largest GDP—behind only the European Union and the United States.

Patron–Client Politics

Japanese democracy is a unique blend of imported democratic ideals and native culture—in particular, Japan's traditional patron–client system that has long characterized Japanese politics. Factional leaders called patrons attract loyal followers or clients. The leader is expected to "feed" his faction, mainly by doling out campaign funds; in turn, faction members are obliged to vote as a solid bloc in the party conference and Diet.

Personal loyalty is the basis of financial support, intraparty power, and the prestige of individual leaders within the LDP. The vaunted political reform of 1994 that changed the electoral system temporarily disrupted the traditional behind-the-scenes collusion among government, bureaucracy, and the business elite, but it did not fundamentally change the patron–client system or practices. Nor is it likely to change the nation's preference for consensus seeking:

> This method rests on the premise that members of a group—say, a village council—should continue to talk, bargain, make concessions, and so on until finally a consensus emerges. . . . Despite the spread of democratic norms, this tradition of rule by consensus still has its appeal and sometimes leads to cries against the "tyranny of the majority"—for example, when the ruling party with its majority pushes through legislation over the strong protests of the opposition.[15]

After an 11-month hiatus in 1993–1994, the LDP regained control of the government. But then a new rival party emerged—the Democratic Party of Japan (DPJ). In the 2007 upper-house elections, the DPJ outpolled the LDP 39% to 21%, but the LDP still had a large majority in the Diet (300 seats to the DPJ's 113). The LDP's long run as Japan's ruling party ended in August 2009 when Japanese voters handed the DPJ a decisive victory, leaving the LDP with just 119 seats to the DPJ's 308. Voters rejected rule by Japan's "iron triangle" of party bosses, bureaucrats, and business elites—a closed and corrupt system that was tolerated so long as Japan's economy was robust. When Japan's economic miracle gave way to a severe and prolonged slump in the 1990s, the LDP's popularity faded with it.

The Judiciary and Japanese Culture

The Japanese judicial system displays a curious combination of U.S. and European influences. The U.S. influence is evident in the name of Japan's highest judicial body, the Supreme Court. The Chief Justice is appointed by the Emperor but is nominated by the government; all other justices are appointed by the cabinet. The Supreme Court, like its U.S. counterpart, enjoys the power of judicial review, meaning it can declare acts of the legislature unconstitutional. Few other constitutional democracies permit judges to second-guess legislators.

Japan's legal system as a whole is modeled after the European civil law system, but again with some U.S. influences. Culturally, the Japanese are far less prone to sue each other than are U.S. citizens. They are also less likely to resort to the courts as a means of settling civil disputes or to seek redress for alleged injuries and injustices. In Japan, social, rather than judicial, remedies are still the norm. Often, successful intervention by a respected member of the community, the head of a family, or a supervisor at work makes legal action unnecessary.

Does Democracy in Japan Work?

Despite the turbulence of the 1990s, Japan has successfully blended Western political forms and Japanese political culture. As in Germany, economics played a key role in the success of the nation's shotgun democracy. ("Shotgun" because it was the result of defeat in war and military occupation.)

Japan's economic revival after World War II was hardly less miraculous than Germany's, as bombed-out cities, symbolized by Hiroshima and Nagasaki, were turned into models of efficient and innovative industrial production. Deliberate planning by a modernizing entrepreneurial elite was important to Japan's resurgence; a rising volume of world trade and massive U.S. purchases during the Korean War (1950–1953) were also crucial. Within two decades, Japan's export-oriented, mercantilist economic strategy produced huge advances in heavy industry—notably, automobile manufacturing, robotics, and consumer electronics. Despite "the loss of 52 percent of Japan's prewar territories, the return of five million persons to a country about the size of California, the loss of 80 percent of Japan's shipping, and the destruction of one-fifth of [its] industrial plants and many of [its] great cities,"[16] Japan is now a major global economic power. China, with a population more than ten times larger, is only now beginning to catch up with Japan in GDP; India, despite its impressive strides in recent times, remains far behind.

After the 1980s "bubble" burst, Japan's economic growth rate slowed dramatically under the impact of four recessions in a dozen years. When the 1997 "Asian flu" financial crisis hit, Japanese banks were trapped in circumstances they themselves had done much to create by lending vast sums for speculative investments in construction, real estate, and retail trade with little security or scrutiny—like a dress rehearsal for the global financial meltdown that started on Wall Street in September 2008.

Japan is and will remain a major economic power, but its technological sophistication no longer sets it clearly apart from its Asian competitors. Reforms aimed at lifting the economy out of its malaise were derailed by the global recession in 2008 and 2009. Prime Minister Taro Aso was elected president of the LDP on September 22, 2008—only 6 days after Wall Street collapsed. In February 2009, Aso had the distinct honor of being the first foreign leader to meet with newly elected President Barack Obama at the White House.

The Japanese Agenda: A Sampler

Asian Challengers

Japan has largely lost its position as the pre-eminent economic power in Asia. In the 1980s, its main challengers were the so-called newly industrialized countries (NICs)—South Korea, Taiwan, Singapore, and Hong Kong. More recently, the surging economy of the People's Republic of China has registered double-digit annual growth rates and will soon overtake Japan in absolute GDP size; India's economy is also growing rapidly; with a population of over 1 billion, and therefore an abundant supply of comparatively cheap labor, India is also a potential economic superpower. Indonesia, Malaysia, and Vietnam are three other countries in the region capable of competing with Japan in major export markets.

Maintaining Close Relations with the United States

The United States is Japan's most important ally and trading partner. As Japan's largest export market, the United States is vital to Japan's economic health (and vice versa). The U.S. air and naval bases in the western Pacific, as well as the massive U.S.

Pacific Fleet, have enabled Japan to concentrate on development of high-technology consumer industries and overseas markets while spending less than 1 percent of its GDP on defense.

Sustaining a High Standard of Living

Despite its prolonged economic downturn, Japan remains an affluent society. Even so, it is a small, mountainous country with a large population and relatively little land suitable for agriculture or settlement. The problems of over-development—stress-related health problems, rush-hour crowds, traffic congestion—are readily apparent in present-day Japan.

Balancing Tradition and Modernity

To the casual observer, Japan appears the epitome of modernity. But most Japanese have great respect for tradition and custom, and theirs is an open society with a closed culture impenetrable by outsiders. Grasping this paradox is the secret to understanding how Japan has managed to change on the outside while staying the same on the inside.

INDIA AND ISRAEL: CHALLENGED DEMOCRACIES

Moghuls
Muslim invaders who created a dynastic empire on the Asian subcontinent; the greatest Moghul rulers were Babur (1526–1530), Akbar (1556–1605), Shah Jahan (1628–1658), and Aurangzeb (1658–1707); Shah Jahan was the architect of the Taj Mahal.

Even if parliamentary rule works in Europe, where it started, and in Japan, where it was imposed by an occupying military power, can it work in other nations and regions where representative government has no roots in native traditions, or even in a country that finds itself in a perpetual state of war with its neighbors? The experiences of India and Israel suggest that it can.

Amazing India: A Parliamentary Miracle

India is home to an ancient Hindu civilization and great empires, including that of the **Moghuls** or Muslim conquerors. Colonized by Great Britain in the nineteenth century, India regained its independence after World War II. The questions then were: Would the former colony become one country or two? Or would it fragment into a dozen or more ethno-linguistic states?

India is a paradox—an immense and extremely diverse established democracy in which poverty and illiteracy remain widespread despite great progress in recent times. With a population of 1.1 billion, it is the world's second most populous country. Some 70 percent of India's people still live in villages, making India a rural society in a postindustrial world. Most children in rural India lack schools and the basic skills (reading, writing, and arithmetic) necessary to find productive work in a modern, urban economy. About two in five will be physically stunted by malnutrition. Roughly half of all Indian women are still illiterate, compared with a ratio of about one in seven in China. Although a recent five-year growth spurt saw India's economy grow by nearly 9 percent a year, China's GDP was still 3.5 times larger than India's in 2008–2009.

Two large and distinct populations—the larger one Hindu and the other Muslim—inhabited the subcontinent of India. The heaviest concentration of Muslims was in the northwestern and eastern parts, whereas the vast lands in between, constituting the bulk of the territory under the **British Raj,** the colonial ruler, were dominated by Hindus. To avoid conflict between these two religiously distinct communities, the retreating British created two states—India and Pakistan. The western part of Pakistan was separated from the eastern part with India in the middle (see Figure 7.5).

This geographic anomaly was only one of the problems the British left unresolved. Another was the Hindu-Muslim split within India: Although most

British Raj
British colonial rule on the Asian subcontinent from the eighteenth century to 1947, when India and Pakistan became independent.

FIGURE 7.5 Pakistan at independence in 1947: Note that West and East Pakistan (present-day Bangladesh) were on opposite sides of India.

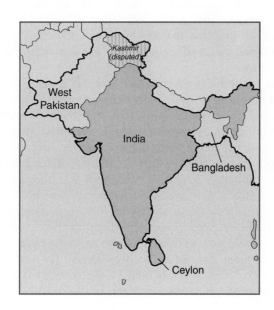

Muslims inhabited the territory of Pakistan, a large Muslim minority remained within the territory of the newly independent state of India. Even more problematic was the fact that India is a mosaic of diverse ethnic and cultural minorities, each speaking a different language. There were also several religions, including Sikhism, Jainism, and Christianity, as well as Hinduism and Islam.

Finally, no account of contemporary India is complete without mentioning poverty and population. Next to China, India is the most populous country in the world, with more than one billion souls. To this day, tens of millions are illiterate, and hundreds of millions are desperately poor, living in rural areas with little or no access to basic services, schools, health clinics, jobs, and the like. Village life is not a romantic idea in modern-day India: for more than two-thirds of India's population, it is a harsh reality.

But India is changing. After decades of sluggish growth (averaging roughly 3 percent per year and called the "Hindu" growth rate), which for a time barely exceeded the rate of population increase, economic reforms put in place by Prime Minister Manmohan Singh in the 1990s galvanized the Indian economy. "The Indian tiger is on the prowl," wrote the *Economist* in 2007, and "at some point, India's growth rate could even outpace China's; and if you measure things by purchasing power parity, India should soon overtake Japan and become the third-biggest economy, behind only America and China."[17] In fact, India's economy was growing almost as fast as China's before the global recession slowed both economies in the fall of 2008.

Despite all its recent achievements, however, India still faces huge challenges. Communal conflict among Hindus, Muslims, and Sikhs and ethnic violence have plagued the country since independence. Nor has trouble been strictly internal; India has fought wars with both China and Pakistan. The bitter dispute between India and Pakistan over the territory of Kashmir (see the map) has never been resolved, turning the two countries into perennial foes. One of the most dangerous moments came in the early 1970s, when East Pakistan broke away and became the present state of Bangladesh. India and Pakistan both possess nuclear weapons. India's border dispute with China has included military confrontation and conflict in the past but is now on the back burner, if not entirely forgotten.

As for India's economic prospects, the picture is brighter but far from rosy. India's sustainable rate of growth is probably lower than its historically high rates in 2006–2008. Despite clear signs that the country is on the move, modernization and the rise of a prosperous middle class have done little, so far, to pull hundreds of millions at the bottom out of poverty. People in rural India still "waste hours queuing for drinking water," children still have no chance to go to school, and "around half of all Indian women are still illiterate."[18]

And yet, there it is: a parliamentary democracy (see Box 7.1), functioning for more than half a century in a society faced with staggering challenges and presented with such extremes of size and diversity that its very existence for five decades as a single state under a single form of government—*any* form of government—is nothing short of miraculous. Except for one brief interlude in the late 1970s, when Prime Minister Indira Gandhi declared a state of national emergency and assumed dictatorial powers, India's leaders, starting with the

Lok Sabha
The lower house of India's Federal Parliament; the directly elected House of the People; in India, as in the United Kingdom and other parliamentary systems, governments are formed by the majority party (or a coalition of parties) in the lower house following national elections (see also Rajya Sabha).

Rajya Sabha
The upper house of India's Federal Parliament; the indirectly elected Council of States (see also Lok Sabha).

BOX 7.1 FOCUS ON India's Federal Government

India is a federal system with an indirectly elected president who plays an essentially ceremonial role in the government. The real power resides in a freely elected parliament and a prime minister who is the leader of the majority party (as in other parliamentary systems). The prime minister chooses a cabinet that is presented for approval to the **Lok Sabha,** the lower house. The **Rajya Sabha** or upper house is indirectly elected; it plays second fiddle to the lower house, but it debates and can delay passage of legislation, thus giving its members a real voice in the policy-making and law-making processes.

great Jawaharlal Nehru, have operated within the framework of a British-style parliamentary democracy.

In the May 2009 national elections, with some 300 parties and independent candidates vying for votes, over 417 million ballots were cast across India during a period of several weeks. The turnout rate was an impressive 58% (in contrast to the 2009 European Union elections in which the turnout rate was a mere 43%). The outcome: Prime Minister Manmohan Singh's Congress party won a large plurality of the votes, by far the biggest bloc of seats in parliament, and thus retained control of the government.

Israel: A War Republic

Like India, Israel came into being after World War II. Unlike Indians, most Israelis are relatively recent immigrants to the territory once known as Palestine. Also in stark contrast to India, Israel's population and territory are tiny—thus, the problem Israel faced was being too small, not too large. From its inception as a state, Israel was awash in controversy and surrounded by hostile Arab neighbors. In fact, Israel's very birth was violent, resulting from a bitter and prolonged struggle with the indigenous population of Palestinian Arabs.

Israel is a secular state but a Jewish society. A great influx of Jews into Palestine followed on the heels of Hitler's rise to power in Germany in the 1930s; however, the movement for a Jewish state in the modern era dates back to the 1890s. **Zionism,** as this movement was called, gathered momentum in 1917 with the famous **Balfour Declaration,** named for the then British foreign minister who authored the first official endorsement of the idea of a Jewish state. (At the time, Palestine was a virtual colony of Great Britain.)

Israel and the Holocaust are inextricably intertwined. The original idea backed by the United States, the United Kingdom, and the United Nations after World War II was to carve two states out of the historic territory of Palestine—one for Jews and the other for Palestinian Arabs—and to make Jerusalem, sacred to three religions (Judaism, Christianity, and Islam), an international city under

Zionism
The movement whose genesis was in the reestablishment, and now the support of, the Jewish national state of Israel.

Balfour Declaration
Named for the British foreign secretary who, in 1947, declared that the United Kingdom favored "the establishment in Palestine of a national home for the Jewish people" and pledged to "facilitate the achievement of this object, it being clearly understood that nothing shall be done which may prejudice the civil and religious rights of the existing non-Jewish communities in Palestine or the rights and political status enjoyed by Jews in any other country."

FIGURE 7.6   Israeli Jews and Palestinian Arabs claim the same historic land of Palestine, which has been at the epicenter of the Middle East conflict since the state of Israel was founded in 1947.

the auspices of the United Nations. That idea died when the Palestinian Arabs rejected the deal they were offered in 1947—though the Jewish side accepted it. As a result of the ensuing war, most Palestinian Arabs were displaced by Jewish settlers and became refugees living in squalid camps in the Gaza Strip, the West Bank of Jordan, and Lebanon.

This situation left a legacy of bitterness and despair that has inscribed itself indelibly in modern Middle Eastern history, pitting the Arab-Islamic world against a diminutive but invincible Jewish state. Facing hostile Arab neighbors on all sides, Israel fought and won three wars of self-defense with Egypt, Syria, Jordan, and Lebanon: the Suez Crisis in 1956, the Six Days' War in 1967, and the Yom Kippur War in 1973. In the 1967 war, Israel seized and kept control of the Gaza Strip and the Sinai Desert (Egypt), the West Bank (Jordan), and the Golan Heights (Syria). In the 1973 war, Israel was in a position to conquer all of Egypt but—under heavy diplomatic pressure from the United States—decided against doing so. In 1978, President Jimmy Carter brokered the **Camp David Accords**—a peace treaty between Egypt and Israel. This historic deal included large U.S. subsidies to both parties, but it worked: Egypt and Israel have not exchanged blows since 1973.

Camp David Accords
A 1979 agreement by which Israel gave the Sinai back to Egypt in return for Egypt's recognition of Israel's right to exist; the two former enemies established full diplomatic relations and pledged to remain at peace with one another.

Sadly, the Middle East in general and Palestine in particular continue to be turbulent and violent. In the 1980s and 1990s, a protracted Palestinian uprising, the **intifada,** in the occupied territories (disputed Arab lands seized by Israel in the 1967 Six Days' War) caused deaths and suffering on both sides. Although it is common to speak of two such uprisings, it was really one that was interrupted during part of the 1990s when the hope of a peace settlement hung in the balance.

The intifada that never really ended only got worse after the military group, Hamas, won parliamentary elections in the "state" of Palestine (the territory under the control of the Palestinian Authority) in January 2006. This upset victory set the stage for a struggle within the Palestinian territories between Hamas and the more moderate Fatah. The struggle split the territories politically, with Fatah controlling the West Bank (under the leadership of Palestinian President Mahmoud Abbas) and Hamas controlling Gaza.

Thereafter, Israel was hit by rocket attacks from Gaza; at the end of 2008, after stern warnings to Hamas, Israel invaded Gaza, killing many militants and some civilians; destroying buildings, including residences, thought to be harboring Hamas fighters; and leaving an otherwise poor and isolated Gaza in ruins. In 2009, parliamentary elections in Israel resulted in a virtual tie between Tzipi Livni, the centrist leader of the Kadimi party, and Benyamin Netanyahu, the right-wing leader of Likud. The hawkish Netanyahu, who as prime minister in the 1990s had turned his back on a possible peace settlement with the Palestinians, was subsequently elected prime minister. In the Middle East, the more things change, the more they stay the same.

Despite all, Israel has been governed as a parliamentary democracy without interruption since its founding. Like the United Kingdom, it does not have a written constitution. The reason is that security takes precedence over all other values in Israel, including the rule of law: thus, to protect the 5.7 million Jews who comprise the 75 percent majority, there are severe restrictions on the civil liberties of the roughly 1.14 million Arabs who are also citizens of Israel but now constitute only 20 percent of the population. Nonetheless, all Israeli citizens enjoy the right to vote in free elections, criticize the government, engage in peaceful protests, and emigrate.

Indeed, Israel at times is almost too democratic for its own good: Elections based on a wide-open system of proportional representation, in which even small upstart parties can often win a few seats, mean Israel's **Knesset** or parliament is a free-for-all that is often confusing and chaotic. Governments are forged from coalitions ranging from the center-left to the far right, depending on the mood of the country, the state of relations with Arab neighbors, and the outcome of the most recent election. The occurrence of one crisis after another has probably saved Israel from the consequences of a contentious political culture and a chaotic party system—among them a great deal of governmental instability.

Nonetheless, Israel remains a marvel of economic and political survival in a hostile environment. The examples of India and Israel as parliamentary democracies functioning under extremely adverse circumstances do not prove that popular self-government can work everywhere, but they demonstrate it can work in some very unlikely places.

intifada
An Arabic word meaning "uprising"; the name given to the prolonged Palestinian uprising against Israeli occupation in the West Bank and Gaza in 1987–1993 and again in 2001–2002.

Knesset
The unicameral Israeli parliament.

THE ADAPTABILITY OF DEMOCRACY

The examples of France, Germany, Japan, India, and Israel suggest that democracy is surprisingly adaptable. There are always idealists and dreamers who choose to believe it can be made to work everywhere, but that is probably not the case. Nor can democracy be imposed on a society, which we ought to know from our own bloody experience in Vietnam, for example. In 2009, it remains a wide-open question whether the lasting legacy of the Bush administration in Iraq and Afghanistan will be democracy, dictatorship, or never-ending civil war.

Virtually every government in the world today, no matter how tyrannical, tries to give the *appearance* of constitutionalism and claims to be democratic. Indeed, democracy is, by definition, popular. It is no surprise that the idea of government "of the people, by the people, and for the people" has a kind of universal moral appeal.

So democracy is unquestionably the best form of government, right? The answer is not as simple as flag-waving patriots in our midst would have us believe. The Islamic societies of North Africa, the Middle East, and South Asia, for example, have religion-based cultures and legal systems incompatible with the individualism, secularism, religious tolerance, and permissiveness inherent in the idea of liberal democracy. It is impossible to force people to be free. By the same token, starving people cannot eat freedom. The wretched masses in desperately poor nations plagued by overpopulation, chronic food shortages, and corrupt officials are apt to view constitutionalism as a vague and meaningless abstraction. For people living on the edge, any government that can alleviate the misery of daily existence even a little bit is a good government.

But it would also be a mistake to sell democracy short. Democracy now flourishes in Germany and Japan where dictatorship was once the rule. Many commentators attributed the failure of Germany's Weimar Republic to an allegedly ingrained antidemocratic passion for order and authority among the Germans. By the same token, Japan had virtually no experience with democracy before World War II, and its consensus-based patron–client culture appeared to be at odds with the basic principles of democracy. And who would have thought democracy had any chance of succeeding in India?

Are these nations exceptions that prove the rule? The experiences of such diverse countries as France, Germany, Japan, India, and Israel suggest that constitutional democracy is a surprisingly adaptable form of government that can work in a variety of social, cultural, and economic contexts. But the fact that it has yet to take root in the Islamic world or Africa is a cautionary note—one we ignore at our own peril.

PRESIDENTS VERSUS PARLIAMENTS: A BRIEF COMPARISON

The following section briefly compares presidential and parliamentary government. For simplicity's sake, we will focus on the U.S. and British models.

The Legislature

The purpose of legislatures is to enact laws. Beyond that general similarity, however, the British legislative branch is surprisingly unlike its U.S. counterpart.

In the British tradition, Parliament is sovereign. According to Sir William Blackstone (1723–1780), the famed British jurist, Parliament can do "everything that is not naturally impossible." In the words of another authoritative writer, "This concept of **parliamentary sovereignty** is of great importance and distinguishes Britain from most other democratic countries. Parliament may enact any law it likes, and no other body can set the law aside on the grounds that it is unconstitutional or undesirable."[19] In contrast, the U.S. system places the Constitution above even Congress. Ever since the 1803 case of *Marbury v. Madison*, the U.S. Supreme Court has successfully asserted its right and duty to overturn any law passed by Congress that it deems unconstitutional.[20]

In both systems, of course, legislatures can pass or defeat proposed new laws, both confirm new cabinet ministers, and both have oversight powers. But there is nothing in the U.S. Congress to compare with the **Question Time** in the British Parliament, when the various government ministers are required to answer questions submitted by MPs. Question Time occurs Mondays through Thursdays. On Wednesdays, the prime minister answers questions from 12:00 to 12:30 P.M. The questions, which run the gamut from the trenchant to the trivial, are aimed at clarifying issues, focusing public attention, eliciting information, and holding the government accountable for its actions (or its failure to act). Question Time is when the Opposition can and does go on the attack. It is representative democracy at its best.

Legislative Independence In theory, U.S. legislators have more latitude for independent action than do British MPs. Because senators and representatives are elected as individuals rather than on party tickets, the U.S. Congress is an assembly of 535 potential prima donnas. Political parties wield some influence, but they are loosely organized and poorly disciplined, at least by European standards. U.S. lawmakers tend to be oriented toward special interests and local, rather than national, constituencies. They are elected to advance local interests and are usually beholden to powerful special interests that contribute generously to the campaign coffers of virtually all incumbents.

Former Speaker of the House Tip O'Neill's famous quip that "All politics is local" was probably true at one time. But in today's Washington, all politics—no matter how "local" in appearance—is actually financed by out-of-state political action committee (PAC) money. Powerful special interests seeking influence over future legislation want to have as many "friends" on Capitol Hill as money can buy, and most candidates seeking high office cannot raise enough money locally to run the kind of high-priced, media-based campaign necessary to win. Thus, money, not party affiliation, now dictates how legislators vote on most issues most of the time (see Box 7.2).[21]

Most parliamentary systems display far greater party discipline than we find in the United States, especially in countries with electoral systems based on proportional representation. In these countries, legislators are chosen in multimember districts from party lists. The party organization decides who to put

parliamentary sovereignty
In the United Kingdom, the unwritten constitutional principle that makes the British parliament the supreme lawmaking body; laws passed by Parliament are not subject to judicial review and cannot be rejected by the Crown.

Question Time
In the United Kingdom, the times set aside Monday through Thursday every week for Her Majesty's Loyal Opposition (the party out of power) to criticize and scrutinize the actions and decisions of the government (the party in power); twice each week, the prime minister must answer hostile questions fired at him or her by the opposition.

BOX 7.2 FOCUS ON   The Best Government Money Can Buy

WASHINGTON, September 26, 2006—In the 2004 federal races, more than $1.85 billion flowed through a professional corps of consultants whose influence plays an important, though largely unexamined, role in the unrelenting escalation of campaign spending, a groundbreaking Center for Public Integrity study has found. The money going to these consultants amounted to about half of the total spending by presidential candidates, national party committees, general election candidates for Congress, and so-called 527s—independent political groups. In the 2008 U.S. presidential race, total spending by all presidential candidates exceeded $1.3 billion.

SOURCES: Center for Public Integrity, accessed at <www .publicinteqrity.orq/ consultants> on February 10, 2007; OpenSecrets.org, Center for Responsive Politics, accessed at <http://www.opensecrets.org/pres08/totals. php?cycle=> on April 3, 2009, and updated by the author.

on the ballot and in what position (first, last, or somewhere in between). The candidate at the top has the best chance of winning a seat. Moreover, because campaigns are shorter, operate under stricter rules, and cost far less than in the United States, money is a less obtrusive (though not insignificant) force in European elections. Then, too, parliamentary systems often subsidize political campaigns directly or indirectly, for example by requiring radio and television stations to set aside free time for political advertising in the run-up to elections. The fact that governments can (and often do) rise and fall on votes in parliament also reinforces party discipline in parliamentary systems, because defeat of any bill proposed by the government can be a vote of no confidence, forcing the government to resign and call for new elections.

Structural Complexity In contrast to the complex committee system in the U.S. Congress, there are only six standing committees in the House of Commons. These committees, each with twenty to fifty members, are not specialized and consider bills without reference to subject matter. They do not have the power to call hearings or solicit expert testimony, and they cannot table a bill; at most, they can make technical adjustments in its language. This system affords special interests relatively limited opportunities to lobby.

Both the U.S. House and Senate have more than fifteen specialized committees with numerous subcommittees, each charged with even more specialized tasks. Moreover, committees and subcommittees have the power to hold hearings and subpoena witnesses as part of routine investigations into executive branch programs and operations.

Until recently, it was a given that Congress played the role of a critical constitutional watchdog in the U.S. system of government. Students were taught that oversight occurs at many points in the legislative process (during the authorization and appropriation phases of the budgetary process, for example, or by means of investigations and hearings); that lawmakers who have large professional staffs regularly conduct program evaluation and policy review; and that these staffers are often powerful, behind-the-scenes operators on whom legislators rely for advice and counsel. However accurate this picture may have been, it is not the way Congress works today. Whether Congress will reclaim its rightful constitutional role, now that the United States has a reform-minded president and a Congress with a majority-party led by politicians who talk a good game, remains to be seen. In early 2009, however, Congress still appeared to be a "broken branch" of government.[22]

The Executive-Legislative Nexus A key difference between the two political systems lies in the extent to which the legislature determines the makeup of the executive branch. As we noted earlier, the prime minister is the leader of the majority party in Parliament. Government ministers—the cabinet—are prominent members of the majority party. Because the parliamentary system blurs distinctions between legislative and executive powers, it is often difficult to determine where the authority of one branch begins and that of the other leaves off.

No such fusion of powers exists under the presidential system of government. Unlike senators and representatives, presidents enjoy a *national* popular mandate, and the presidency derives its powers from a separate section of the Constitution. Nonetheless, Congress does have some influence over the staffing of the executive branch, because the Senate must confirm all cabinet and many other high-level appointments. If there are abuses of power or if the White House lies to the public or tries to cover up wrongdoing, Congress can hold public hearings, subpoena government officials to testify, and censure those who violate the law or the public trust—at least that is how it works in theory.

Unlike Parliament, however, Congress does not have the power to bring down the executive by a vote of no confidence. Even if Congress votes down a key program proposed by the White House, the president will normally remain in office for a full 4-year term. Unless a president dies in office or resigns, he or she can be removed only by impeachment, and no U.S. president has ever been impeached *and* convicted (see below).

The Executive

The executive branch of government comprises the head of government and the head of state, the cabinet, and the bureaucracy. In the U.S. system, the president is the head of government *and* the chief of state; in the British system, the executive is divided between the prime minister (head of government) and the monarch (head of state).

Presidents in the United States also enjoy the security of a fixed term. By contrast, the British prime minister's position depends on his or her ability to retain the confidence of a majority in the House of Commons. Prime ministers frequently are forced to step down either because public opinion turns against them or because they lose on a key vote in Parliament.

Only the voters can force a sitting president out of office, except in extraordinary circumstances involving grave misconduct ("high crimes and

© AP PHOTO/KEVIN WOLF

As both head of the government and head of state, the U.S. president delivers the annual State of the Union address to Congress and the people.

misdemeanors"). Andrew Johnson and Bill Clinton were both impeached, but neither was convicted. Richard Nixon resigned rather than face impeachment.

In the U.S. system, the president is the nation's commander in chief, chief legislator (not only because of the veto power, but also because of the significant amount of legislation presidents propose), and chief diplomat. The president's power, authority, and prestige are thus unsurpassed among democratically elected chief executives.

In at least one area, however, British prime ministers have an advantage over U.S. presidents, and that is in party leadership. As head of the government *and* head of the majority party, a British prime minister holds the key to success. The fortunes of the government and the majority party rise and fall together. If the government succeeds, the party in power will be rewarded at the polls. If not, it will find itself in opposition after the next election. Only through the party can a British prime minister govern, and only through governing can a party achieve its aims. Not surprisingly, British MPs seldom cross the aisle in the House of Commons.

The Judiciary

Despite significant differences in the structures of their court systems, both the United States and Great Britain share what is generally known as the common law tradition. **Common law** is based on decisions made by judges rather than laws promulgated by legislatures. The idea dates back at least as far as

common law
In Great Britain, laws derived from consistent precedents found in judges' rulings and decisions, as opposed to those enacted by Parliament. In the United States, the part of the common law that was in force at the time of the Revolution and not nullified by the Constitution or any subsequent statute.

the twelfth century, when Henry II sought to implement a system by which judges were charged with enforcing the king's law while taking into account local customs. In the process of resolving disputes, each judge made, and sent to London, a record of the legal proceedings. Over the years, certain common themes and legal principles emerged from these records, and magistrates turned to certain celebrated judicial decisions for guidance. In time, these precedents and decisions were codified by judicial commentators—the most famous being William Blackstone—and were carried to all corners of the globe, including the American colonies.

Notwithstanding this shared common law background, the legal systems of the United States and Great Britain differ with respect to selection of judges, organization of the judiciary, powers of judicial review, and other key structural matters.

Selection of Judges Great Britain has two kinds of law schools. In the lower-level law schools, one studies to become a **solicitor**, a legal counsel who prepares cases for court, advises clients, and draws up contracts, wills, and other legal documents. More exclusive law schools produce **barristers**, who can do everything solicitors do but can also enter a court and plead cases. In the British system, judges are appointed only from the ranks of barristers. To be recommended for a judgeship, a barrister must have achieved a high-class rank in law school and performed several years of outstanding legal service.

U.S. judicial selection is *much* more political and open to abuse.[23] A judge may be appointed on the basis of high marks at a prestigious law school or after years of distinguished legal practice, but not necessarily. More often, appointments to the federal bench are based on transparent political calculations—to reward an individual for favors; to appease a powerful senator, representative, or local party boss; or to achieve a certain geographic balance in the distribution of judgeships. At the state and local levels, judges are sometimes elected. The political nature of "justice" in the U.S. system was on display in 2007 when then–Attorney General Alberto Gonzales came under heavy pressure to resign after he summarily fired six federal prosecutors on grounds apparently unrelated to competency or objective standards of job performance. Gonzales finally did step down in September 2007.

Federal Versus Unitary Courts The U.S. judicial system is organized on a federal basis. There are actually fifty-one separate court systems. The federal court system adjudicates legal questions in which either the federal government is one of the parties or a federal law is invoked. The federal judiciary is subdivided into **district courts**, in which most cases originate; **appellate courts**, which review cases on appeal from district courts; and the **Supreme Court**, which acts primarily as a court of last resort, settling cases that raise particularly troublesome questions of legal interpretation or constitutional principle.

Coexisting with this federal court system are fifty state court systems, most of which also feature a three-tier structure. The state courts are not completely separated from the federal courts in the U.S. judicial system. The U.S. Supreme Court frequently accepts cases on appeal from the highest courts of the various states when legal questions raised there have constitutional implications.

solicitor
In Great Britain, an attorney who can prepare court cases and draw up contracts and other legal documents but cannot plead cases or become a judge.

barristers
In Great Britain, an attorney who can plead cases in court and be appointed to the bench.

district courts
The court in which most U.S. federal cases originate.

appellate courts
A court that reviews cases on appeal from district courts.

Supreme Court
The U.S. federal Court of last resort, setting cases that raise particularly troublesome questions of legal interpretation or constitutional principle.

The British court system is more streamlined, reflecting Britain's unitary government. The absence of state courts means many of the jurisdictional and procedural complexities that plague the U.S. judiciary are lacking in Great Britain.

Judicial Review   Perhaps the most important *political* difference between the two judicial systems is visible in **judicial review,** the power of the courts to uphold or strike down legislative or executive actions. In the United States, both state and federal courts review the acts of the other branches of government—state courts on the basis of state constitutions and federal courts on the basis of the U.S. Constitution.

> **judicial review**
> The power of a court to declare acts by the government unconstitutional and hence void.

This power of judicial review is greatly enhanced by the existence of written constitutions, which often provide a highly authoritative yardstick by which to measure ordinary (statutory) law. To some extent, the mere existence of federalism made judicial review necessary in the United States. If state courts could decide for themselves how to interpret federal law, no national body of jurisprudence would have much meaning.[24] The need for legal uniformity, and the belief that there are certain higher principles of law to which governmental action at all levels must conform, lie at the core of the concept of judicial review, not only in the United States but also in most other constitutional democracies.

In contrast, British judges play only a limited role in governing the nation. Whereas the question of constitutionality hovers over every legislative and executive act in the United States, in Great Britain the judiciary does not possess the power to overturn an act of Parliament. Nor do British judges act as constitutional guardians of civil liberties, as U.S. judges do whenever they assert the primacy of individual rights over legislative acts. Only rarely do British judges rule that the executive branch has overstepped its legal bounds. In the words of one authority,

> The powers of the British government are constrained in spite of rather than because of formal institutions of the laws. Englishmen voice fewer complaints about the denial of civil liberties or due process of the law than do citizens in many countries with written constitutions, bills of rights, and established procedures for judicial review.[25]

The British court system is headed by a member of the cabinet, known as the Lord Chancellor, who presides over the House of Lords and makes recommendations on judicial appointments. Theoretically, the high court of Britain *is* the House of Lords, though in actual operation, it comprises only a small number of lords with distinguished legal backgrounds. The fusion of powers characteristic of the British parliamentary system thus intermingles legislative and judicial powers in the upper house, just as it meshes legislative and executive powers in the lower house.

Strengths and Weaknesses of the Two Systems

In the words of one U.S. academic, "The parliamentary system is a Cadillac among governments." The same author referred to the U.S. presidential system as a "Model T."[26] Parliamentary systems are often credited with being highly responsive to voters. Political parties campaign on distinct, well-defined platforms. If the election outcome results in a strong mandate for one party, the resulting government is likely to succeed in pushing its program through the parliament. If government policies prove unpopular or impracticable or if the government falls into disrepute for any reason whatsoever, the prime minister or the ruling party can be replaced with no major shock to the political system as a whole. Finally, the British parliamentary system's greater party discipline makes it more efficient than the presidential system.

The U.S. presidential system, critics have asserted, is too often marked by deadlocks stemming from the checks and balances built into its tripartite structure. Too often, one party controls the presidency and another controls the Congress. Moreover, it is very difficult to remove an incompetent or unpopular president from office. In addition, an ossified two-party system leaves many groups and interests underrepresented in the Congress. Finally, the so-called popular election of the president is a farce. In critics' view, the archaic practice of choosing electors on a winner-takes-all basis means the will of the majority may not carry the day—witness the 2000 election in which Al Gore won the popular vote but George W. Bush won the White House.

GATEWAYS TO THE WORLD: EXPLORING CYBERSPACE

www.ukpol.co.uk

This site takes an extensive look at British political parties and government, including information about individual members of parliament, party platforms and manifestos, election results and analysis, and links to other sites.

library.byu.edu/~rdh/wess/fren/polygov.html

An excellent starting point for information on French government and politics.

www.germany-info.org

A general information site on Germany, including a collection of contacts' addresses and phone numbers from various levels and sectors of the German government, vital statistics on Germany, and links to other sites. Some of the referenced sites are available only in German, whereas others have an English translation.

mofa.go.jp

This is the official Website of the Ministry of Foreign Affairs of Japan. It is updated daily with press releases, news, and other information related to the government and foreign policy of Japan. There are links to general information sites as well.

http://india.gov.in/

The national portal for India. A useful source of basic information about India's government, society, and economy. Also, check out the "Overseas" feature, which offers "a wide range of options to travel and study in India."

www.asianinfo.org/asianinfo/india/politics.htm

This site claims to be "Your complete resource on Asia"—an extravagant claim but definitely not a bad place to look for information on politics and government in India, as well as other Asian countries.

http://www.goisrael.com/tourism_eng

The official Website of the state of Israel. At first glance, it appears this website is devoted exclusively to tourism, but that is not the case. Click "Discover Israel" and you will find all sorts of information about Israeli society, government, history, the economy, and much more. Also, be sure to look in the "Article Archive."

SUMMARY

The British parliamentary model features a fusion of powers, indefinite terms of office, disciplined parties, and a dual executive. This model of constitutional democracy has been imitated more widely (except in Latin America) than the U.S. model. It is especially influential in Europe, where it has inspired most of the constitutional democracies in existence.

France is a hybrid form of constitutional democracy, combining features of both the U.S. and the British systems. Germany features a parliamentary system but differs from both France and Great Britain in that it is federal (comprising states called *Länder*), rather than unitary. Japan is also a parliamentary democracy. Politically, it differs from Europe in its political culture rather than its political structure. Japan has incorporated a consensus-based society with informal, highly personal networks of political power based on patron–client relations into a set of political institutions that, on the surface, appear to be made in Europe. (Actually, they were made in America during the U.S. occupation after World War II.)

India and Israel are two unlikely candidates for republican rule, yet they have both survived as parliamentary democracies for more than half a century. Their examples suggest the parliamentary model is highly adaptable and has wide application, even in places that appear too troubled or turbulent for elections to occur or stable governments to endure.

The U.S. and British systems invite comparisons and offer provocative contrasts in the legislative, executive, and judicial areas. It is difficult to say which system is better in the abstract; the answer exists only within the specific context and circumstances of each nation.

KEY TERMS

parliamentary system
mixed regime
no-confidence vote
party discipline
Loyal Opposition
dual executive
cohabitation
National Assembly
divided executive
Weimar Republic
Bundestag

Bundesrat
Meiji Restoration
Moghuls
British Raj
Lok Sabha
Rajya Sabha
Zionism
Balfour Declaration
Camp David Accords
intifada
Knesset

parliamentary
  sovereignty
Question Time
common law
solicitor
barristers
district courts
appellate courts
Supreme Court
judicial review

REVIEW QUESTIONS

1. Why is the British political system often considered a model of parliamentary democracy?
2. What are the basic operating principles of the parliamentary system?
3. How can the British manage without a written constitution?
4. When did the current French republic come into being and under what circumstances?
5. Compare and contrast democracy in France with democracy in the United States and the United Kingdom. (Trick question: Which country did France model its own political system after?)
6. When did Japan adopt the parliamentary system and under what circumstances?
7. Compare and contrast democracy in Japan with democracy in France and Great Britain.
8. Comment on the significance of parliamentary democracy in India and Israel.
9. Compare the strengths and weaknesses of parliamentary versus presidential rule.

RECOMMENDED READING

Bailey, Sydney. *British Parliamentary Democracy*, 3rd ed. Westport, CT: Greenwood, 1978. A comprehensive introduction to the functioning of the British democracy.

Birch, Anthony. *Concepts and Theories of Modern Democracy*, 3rd. ed. New York: Routledge, 2007. The title says it all.

Diamond, Larry. *The Spirit of Democracy: The Struggle to Build Free Societies Throughout the World*. New York: Holt, 2009. A hopeful and optimistic book about the prospects for democracy in the world by a highly respected political scientist whose intelligent and well-researched argument will make most readers want to stand up and cheer.

Diamond, Martin, Winston Fisk, and Herbert Garfinkel. *The Democratic Republic: An Introduction to American National Government*. Skokie, IL: Rand McNally, 1970. An introductory text that contains an extraordinarily insightful discussion of the relationship between the American Founders and political institutions.

Dicey, A. V. *Introduction to the Study of the Law of the Constitution*. Indianapolis: Liberty Fund, 1982. A classic account of the British political tradition.

Magstadt, Thomas. *Nations and Governments: Comparative Politics in Regional Perspective*, 5th ed. Belmont, California: Cengage/Wadsworth, 2005. The 6th edition of this book, which deals in greater depth with the European democracies covered in this chapter, is forthcoming in 2010.

Ornstein, Norm E., and Thomas G. Mann. *The Broken Branch: How Congress Is Failing America and How to Get It Back on Track*. New York: Oxford University Press, 2006. The authors argue cogently that Congress no longer performs its critical constitutional functions and offer a well-conceived prescription for change.

Tilly, Charles. *Democracy*. New York: Cambridge University Press, 2007. A comparative study of the processes of democratization at the national level over the past several hundred years. The author explores the processes in both the rise and fall of democracies.

Wen Jiabao is the Premier of the People's Republic of China. As head of the government, he shares power with President Hu Jintao—significantly, both are engineers by profession, reflecting the pragmatism of China's new generation of leaders. Wen (pictured here), for example, has an advanced degree from the Beijing Institute of Geology.

States and Economies in Transition
Between Democracy and Yesterday

The Collapse of Communism

Russia: Old Habits Die Hard

The Superpower that Wasn't

The Politics of Reform

The Collapse of the Soviet Empire

Contemporary Challenges

Putin: President or Constitutional Czar?

Future Prospects

Eastern Europe: Two-Track Transition
China: Police-State Capitalism

Mao in Command

Changing of the Guard

China's Pragmatic "Communism"

Market-Oriented Reforms

Expanded Personal Freedoms

Political and Religious Repression

New Social Disorders

China as a Global Power: Rival or Partner?

Two Asian Tigers: Still Role Models?

South Korea: Crisis-Prone but Resilient

Taiwan: Asia's Orphan State

Latin America: Waiting for the Curtain to Go Up

The ABCs of Reform: Argentina, Brazil, Chile

Mexico

On December 31, 1991, the Soviet Union, one of two superpowers that had dominated world politics for nearly half a century, ceased to exist. The demise of this communist behemoth stands as one of the most momentous political events of the twentieth century. Although the end came as a surprise, it was not without warning signs; on the contrary, the Soviet Union had been going through a fascinating but turbulent period of change since 1985, when Mikhail Gorbachev, the country's charismatic leader, launched a series of bold reforms.

The disintegration of the Soviet order ushered in a new era in world politics. It also drew attention to the problems facing Russia and Eastern Europe. As major actors on the world stage, Russia and China are featured in this chapter. In both the process of transition is incomplete, as we shall see. The transition of Communist systems actually started in China, not Russia, more than a decade before the tearing down of the Berlin Wall. In Russia, as we shall see, the reform movement got underway in the mid-1980s before the collapse of the Soviet state, faltered in the 1990s, and failed in the 2000s—a failure manifested in a re-centralized political system and an economy precariously dependent on oil and gas exports. By contrast, China's market-oriented reforms have transformed the economy while leaving the monolithic party-state system largely intact. Only in Eastern Europe has the transition from Communism to a post-Communist order resulted in a full-fledged systemic transformation—political, economic, and social.

The problems of transition in these countries are also, to some extent, problems of political and economic redevelopment. Transition and development (discussed in the following chapter) are closely related; the issues facing societies in transition intersect with development issues at many points. Moreover, as we will see, the whole concept of "states in transition" applies to many countries in virtually every region of the world today. Following a look at the problems facing the former communist states, primarily in Eastern Europe, we take a brief look at several Asian and Latin American countries in various stages of transition toward market-based liberal democracy.

THE COLLAPSE OF COMMUNISM

What we once called the Communist world no longer exists; Communism as a political force on both the national and international levels has receded nearly everywhere in the world with a few notable exceptions. In 1988, before the end of the Cold War, fifteen states could be classified as Communist. One short decade later, the number had shrunk to only five or six states—China, Cuba, Laos, North Korea, Vietnam, and perhaps Cambodia—each pursuing relatively independent policies. Today, the People's Republic of China (PRC) is Communist in name only; Vietnam is imitating China; Laos and Cuba are going nowhere (the United States established normal trade relations with Laos in 2005, but has yet to do so with Cuba); and Cambodia is a fledgling parliamentary democracy. Only North Korea remains an unreconstructed Stalinist state. Indeed, it no longer makes any sense to talk about a communist bloc. What happened?

Eastern Europe abruptly abandoned Communist rule in 1989, ahead of the collapse of the Soviet Union in 1991. Thereafter, democracy and privatization (the process of turning formerly state-run enterprises over to the private sector) advanced rapidly in Poland, Hungary, the Czech Republic, and Slovakia, as well as in the Baltic states (Latvia, Lithuania, and Estonia). Romania and Bulgaria have followed suit, but at a slower pace. The former East Germany is a special case, having merged with West Germany in 1990.

In Asia, Communist regimes have proven somewhat more resilient. The People's Republic of China softened its totalitarian rule and liberalized its economy after Mao's death in 1976. But it remains a repressive state by Western standards. It has continued to pursue market-friendly reforms, which have stimulated rapid economic growth, especially in its coastal regions. North Korea, true to its long-standing reputation for Stalinist rigidity, has displayed a familiar tendency toward xenophobia, extreme secrecy, and self-imposed isolation, even as its people have suffered famine and hardship. In Cuba, an aging Fidel Castro in failing health relinquished the presidency to his brother Raúl in 2008 but continues to hang on as Secretary General of the Communist party. As president, Raúl has avoided the incendiary rhetoric so characteristic of Fidel, but only time will tell whether Cuban policy will change enough to bring about a normalization in relations with the United States—an eventuality the new Obama administration would almost certainly welcome.

RUSSIA: OLD HABITS DIE HARD

As the 1990s began, the Soviet Union stood as one of the last of the world's great empires (the United States and Communist China were two others). The Stalinist state that remained in place until 1991 displayed all the classic features of totalitarian rule, including centralized control over the armed forces, the media, and the economy; a dominant monopoly party; an official ideology; and a systematic program of terror against suspected political opponents and the mass murder of innocents deemed unworthy (or dangerous) by the regime. The story of how the Soviet Union emerged from the long dark winter of totalitarianism provides the essential background for understanding the nature of Russian politics today.

A newly downsized Russian state emerged from the ashes of the extinct Soviet Union. The post-Soviet government, headed by Boris Yeltsin, appeared to represent a sharp break with the past, initially seeking to establish a constitutional democracy. It then created a very loose confederation, the **Commonwealth of Independent States** (CIS), which included Russia and the former Soviet republics minus the Baltic States (Estonia, Latvia, and Lithuania). To understand what happened in Russia under Yeltsin, however, we need to go back one step to the period immediately preceding the fall, a time that changed everything—and nothing.

Commonwealth of Independent States (CIS)
A loose federation of newly sovereign nations created after the collapse of the Soviet Union; it consisted of almost all the republics that previously had made up the USSR.

The Superpower that Wasn't

When Mikhail Gorbachev, at age 54, became General Secretary of the Communist Party in 1985, he faced daunting political and economic problems. Gorbachev realized the Soviet Union was falling behind the West and could not survive without radical reforms; and because the Communist Party exerted total control over the state and society, he made a fateful decision to reform Communism—in order to save it.

From the time Lenin assumed power in 1917, the Soviet Union had featured a *planned economy*—also known as a *command economy*—in which all-important economic decisions (such as what and how much was to be produced and so on) were made at the uppermost level of the Communist Party. Competition, the pursuit of profits, and most forms of private ownership were forbidden as inconsistent with the tenets of Communism.

This system of central planning succeeded in making the Soviet Union a first-rate military power, but at a crushing cost to the consumer economy, which was all but nonexistent. Grossly distorted budget priorities and mounting debt were disguised by artificial prices, press censorship, and secrecy. By the mid-1980s, central planning had produced a stagnating economy. The Soviet Union was at a huge competitive disadvantage with industrialized democratic nations such as the United States, Japan, and the members of the European Union, and it was falling further behind all the time.[1]

Most Soviet citizens led relatively austere lives with few of the conveniences Westerners took for granted. Store shelves were often empty and spare parts

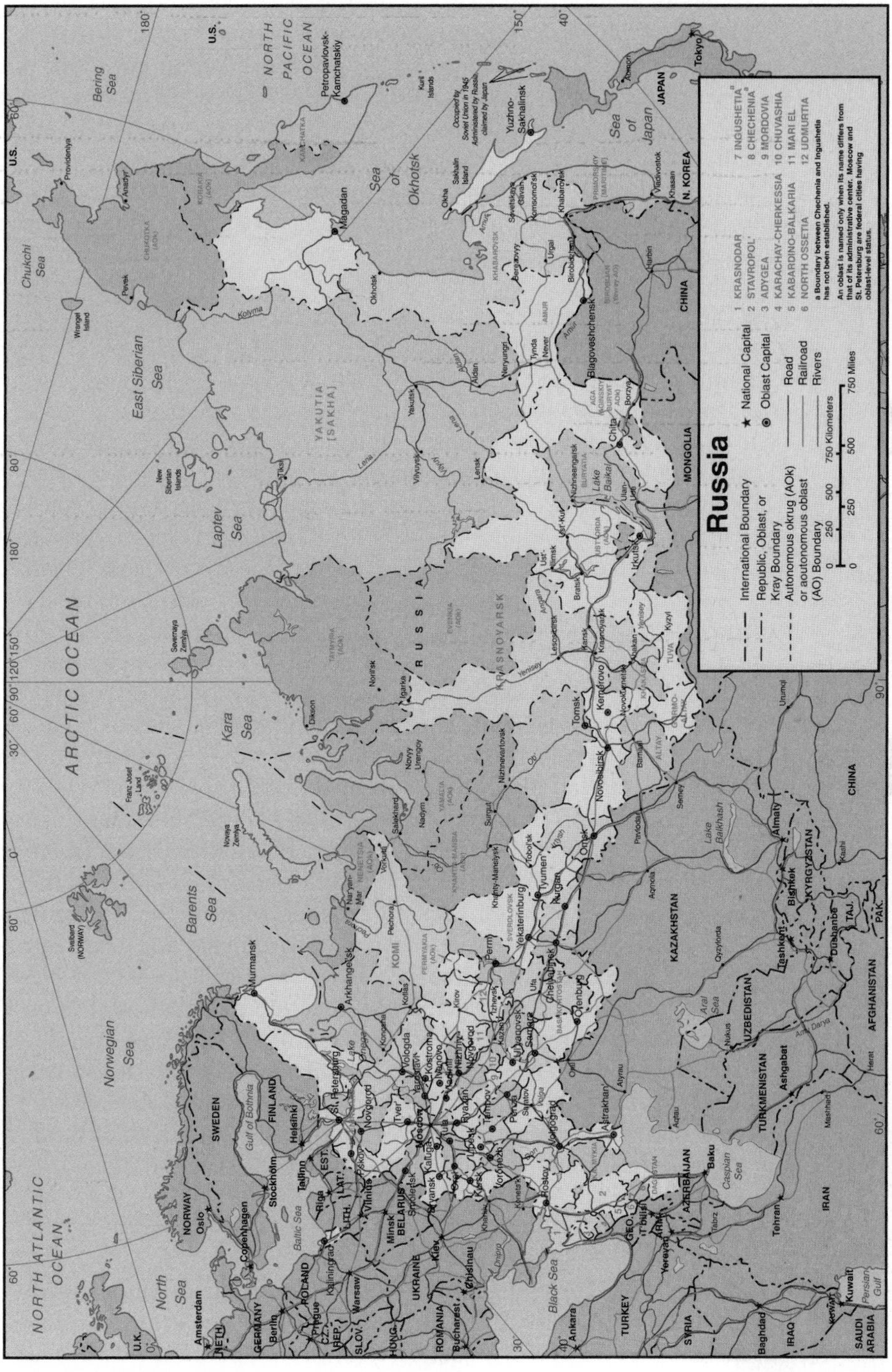

FIGURE 8.1 Russia and the Republics

unavailable. According to one estimate, women spent an average of two hours a day, seven days a week, waiting in line to purchase the few basic goods available.[2] By the end of the 1980s, an estimated 28 percent of the Soviet population lived below the official Soviet poverty line.[3]

In the realm of agriculture, Soviet economists estimated that about one-fourth of all grain harvested each year was lost before it got to the market. As a result, meat and dairy consumption for the average Soviet citizen declined 30 percent in fewer than 20 years.[4] While the Soviet economy decayed and the quality of life for the general populace deteriorated, growing social problems threatened the very fabric of Soviet society. Among the worst were alcoholism and corruption. Another major problem was a widening technology gap. Soviet managers had little encouragement to invest in new technologies (computers, cell phones, robotics), and the party feared (rightly, it turned out) that the coming Digital Age and Internet (already on the horizon in the 1980s) would jeopardize its information monopoly.

At the root of most of these problems was central planning, which discouraged initiative. Plant managers and directors of government-run farms remained tied to a central plan that imposed rigid quotas on factory and farm production. Plan fulfillment was the highest priority for all Soviet economic administrators. The Stalinist system sacrificed quality for quantity. Because of relentless pressures to meet overly ambitious production quotas, managers often took shortcuts and cooked the books to conceal failures or paper over problems.

The cynicism of the managers was matched by the low morale of the Soviet workers, who were underemployed, unhappily employed, or simply not motivated to work. The result was appallingly low productivity caused by the absence of dependable and efficient workers. Worker cynicism was reflected in popular Soviet sayings, such as "The party pretends to pay us, and we pretend to work." This cynicism was fed by the hypocrisy of high party officials, who espoused egalitarian ideals but lived in secluded luxury while the proletariat they glorified had to stand in long lines to buy bread and other staples.[5]

A privileged, entrenched elite known as the **nomenklatura** occupied all the top positions in the Soviet system.[6] It included members of the political bureaucracy (apparatchiki), senior economic managers, and scientific administrators, as well as certain writers, artists, cosmonauts, athletes, and generals who represented the Soviet state and enhanced its reputation. Their largely hidden world of luxury apartments, specialty shops, vacation resorts, hospitals, health spas, and schools stood in sharp contrast to the bleak existence of ordinary Soviet citizens and made a mockery of the "classless society" Marx had envisioned.

This moribund system is what Gorbachev inherited in the mid-1980s. He faced a stark choice: push reforms or preside over the death of the Soviet state. In the end, he did both.

The Politics of Reform

Gorbachev therefore undertook policies that became famous in the West as **perestroika**, restructuring, and **glasnost**, transparency. These, in turn, were to be accompanied by a democratization of the Soviet political system. Clearly, what

nomenklatura
The former Soviet Communist Party's system of controlling all important administrative appointments, thereby ensuring the support and loyalty of those who managed day-to-day affairs.

perestroika
Term given to Mikhail Gorbachev's various attempts to restructure the Soviet economy while not completely sacrificing its socialist character.

glasnost
Literally "openness"; this term refers to Mikhail Gorbachev's curtailment of censorship and encouragement of political discussion and dissent within the former Soviet Union.

Gorbachev had in mind was nothing less than a state-controlled revolution from above. Unfortunately, the revolution spun out of control.

The goal of perestroika was to revitalize the ossified system of central planning. Gorbachev hoped to accomplish this ambitious goal by attacking the political and social causes of the country's economic problems—that is, by reducing the power of the nomenklatura and the party apparatchiki while simultaneously improving the efficiency of Soviet workers. Ironically, either Gorbachev did not understand or he refused to face the need for radical change in the nation's underlying economic structures. Hence, perestroika became a catchy political slogan rather than a coherent economic policy. By 1989, the Soviet economy was rapidly disintegrating, and within two years it had plunged into a depression.

Gorbachev's policy of glasnost constituted the most extensive relaxation of media censorship in Soviet history. For a time, this openness won popular sympathy for Gorbachev and distracted public attention from the dislocations resulting from economic reform. It also held a wide appeal beyond Soviet borders, making Gorbachev the darling of the world press and a popular figure in many Western countries.

Despite its foreign policy advantages, however, glasnost was primarily an instrument of domestic policy. Its initial intention was to expose the official corruption and incompetence that Gorbachev blamed, in part, for the Soviet Union's economic malaise. He wanted to shake the change-resistant Soviet bureaucracy out of its lethargy and goad the working class into working. But glasnost quickly assumed a life of its own. Previously censored books and movies flourished; the state-controlled mass media dared to criticize the government; newspapers and magazines published scorching articles challenging the official version of history and current events. The Soviet Union had transformed itself virtually overnight from a country that permitted no public dissent to one where

Shown here visiting Finlad in 1989 with his wife, Mikhail Gorbachev instituted bold political and economic policies to reform communism and the Communist Party during his leadership from March 1985 until August 1991. Ultimately, these initiatives exacerbated the crisis of the Stalinist state and helped precipitate the downfall of communism throughout Eastern Europe.

© MARKKHU ULANDER/WOODFIN CAMP & ASSOCIATES

glasnost was rapidly undermining the legitimacy of both the Communist Party and the political system that had long served as the instrument of its rule.

Finally, Gorbachev also called for **democratization** of the political system, including elections that allowed voters a limited choice at the polls. These reforms, in effect, let the genie out of the bottle. The "genie" might be mob rule or popular democracy—which would it be?

The Collapse of the Soviet Empire

Gorbachev's efforts to reformulate the political and economic system of the Soviet Union failed. Virtually every social, political, and economic problem he inherited had worsened by the time he stepped down a little more than six years later. Popular expectations rose while living standards fell dramatically, creating a politically volatile situation. Galloping inflation and labor strikes, both previously unheard of, dangerously destabilized the Soviet state.

As the end of the Soviet empire drew near, the so-called Nationality Question loomed ever larger. In 1991, the seventeen largest nationalities accounted for more than 90 percent of the Soviet population (about 294 million people). The majority Russians accounted for only slightly more than half the total. Some twenty ethnic groups numbered more than one million. Among the largest were the fifteen nationalities for whom the union republics are named, plus the Tatars, Poles, Germans, Jews, and others less familiar to the outside world (see Table 8.1).

democratization
Mikhail Gorbachev's policy of encouraging democratic reforms within the former Soviet Union, including increased electoral competition within the Communist party.

TABLE 8.1   Major Nationalities in the Soviet Union at the Time of Its Demise (1989)

Nationality	Percent of Total Population[a]	Nationality	Percent of Total Population[a]
1. Russian	50.78	11. Moldovan	1.17
2. Ukrainian	15.47	12. Lithuanian	1.07
3. Uzbek	5.84	13. Turkish	0.95
4. Belarusian	3.50	14. Kirgiz	0.85
5. Kazakh	2.84	15. German	0.71
6. Azerbaijani	2.38	16. Chuvash	0.64
7. Tatar	2.32	17. Latvian	0.51
8. Armenian	1.62	18. Jew[b]	0.50
9. Tajik	1.48	19. Bashkir	0.50
10. Georgian	1.39	20. Polish	0.39

[a]The figures are adapted from the last official census of the Soviet Union.

[b]The former Soviet Union classified Jews as a nationality.

SOURCE: *Population Today*, November 1991, Population Reference Bureau. Reprinted by permission.

In total, the Soviet Union encompassed more than 100 different nationalities, speaking some 130 languages.

Historically, the Soviet government used force to assimilate non-Russian groups. Another primary instrument of state policy was the education system. All schoolchildren throughout the Soviet Union were required to learn Russian, ensuring that most non-Russians could speak the language fluently.

Gorbachev's reforms created a climate in which the non-Russian nationalities could dare to strive for self-determination and independence. Glasnost, in particular, encouraged local criticism of the government and the Communist Party. The independence movement surged in the Baltic States first. Lithuania, Latvia, and Estonia, which had been independent for a time before they were seized by Stalin in 1939, pushed the pace of reform further and faster than Gorbachev intended. The Baltic States, led by Lithuania, were the first to break away. Nationalistic demonstrations, riots, and rebellions rumbled across the Soviet empire, as republic after republic declared its independence.

In August 1991, a group of eight hard-line Communist Party traditionalists with ties to the army and the KGB (the Soviet secret police) staged a coup, which ultimately failed. Boris Yeltsin, the president of the Russian republic, saved the day, rallying demonstrators who had taken to the streets to fight for democracy. The Soviet Union ceased to exist on the last day of 1991; it was succeeded by the Russian Republic, a truncated version of the defunct Soviet state.

As Russia's first elected president, Yeltsin turned out to be a colorful but quixotic character, ill suited to run a country going through the transition from totalitarian tyranny to liberal democracy. His successor, Vladimir Putin, is the exact opposite: a no-nonsense political boss. Putin is immensely popular with the vast majority of Russians for precisely this reason (see Box 8.1).

Contemporary Challenges

With three-fourths the landmass, about half the population, and approximately three-fifths the GNP of its predecessor, Russia is significantly reduced by any and all measures. However, it remains by far the world's largest country, encompassing an area roughly twice the size of Canada, the United States, or China. Across this vast territory, Ukraine, Kazakhstan, and Belarus all fell heir to the nuclear weapons the former Soviet government had deployed in the Soviet republics (SSRs). As a result, the world suddenly had several new nuclear powers; at the same time, the weapons heightened tensions among the newly independent nations. As a matter of policy, Russia sought to gather all the nuclear arms of the former Soviet state into its own arsenal. Both Ukraine and Kazakhstan promised to relinquish control of these inherited weapons, but before doing so, they sought economic and financial concessions from Moscow, as well as security guarantees from the West. By 1996, all nuclear weapons had reportedly been removed to Russia, including those in Belarus. The security of Russia's huge arsenal of chemical and biological weapons of mass destruction was also a matter of great concern in the West. The 9/11 terrorist attacks on the United

BOX 8.1 FOCUS ON   Vladimir Putin: Russia's "Black Belt" Tsar

When Vladimir Putin was elected to succeed Boris Yeltsin as Russia's president, he faced three major problems: a sick economy, a society still riddled by corruption and violent crime, and a smoldering war in the breakaway republic of Chechnya. A former KGB agent with a Black Belt in karate, Putin is ruthless, tough-minded, and smart.

Several examples illustrate his no-nonsense style of leadership: Putin withdrew from the START II treaty in June 2002, one day after the United States withdrew from the antiballistic missile (ABM) treaty.[7] (SALT II was the successor to the original Strategic Arms Limitation Treaty, or SALT I, between the United States and the Soviet Union in 1972, cutting the number and type of nuclear weapons each side could deploy.) In October 2002, when fifty Chechen rebels seized 800 hostages inside a Moscow theater, Putin ordered Russian special forces to move in, using poison gas to incapacitate the guerrillas. Nearly all the guerillas died, as well as 129 hostages. Putin backed the U.S.-led war in Afghanistan in 2001, but he sided with Germany and France against the United States in blocking UN Security Council endorsement of the 2003 invasion of Iraq. In October 2003, Putin ordered Mikhail Khodorkovsky, the richest man in Russia at the time, arrested and jailed on charges of tax evasion. Khodorkovsky was sentenced to nine years in prison in 2005. However, critics suggest the move was political; Khodorkovsky had been a potential candidate for president.

Putin won re-election in 2004 by a landslide. Under the Russian constitution, a sitting president can serve no more than two consecutive terms. In 2008, Putin's protégé, Dimitry Medvedev, was elected to succeed his boss, winning about 70 percent of the popular vote with Putin's endorsement. Medvedev then named Putin prime

© AP PHOTOS

Vladimir Putin is Russia's second president since the fall of Soviet communism. When Yeltsin named him premier in 1999, Putin was an obscure figure who had served for many years as a KGB recruiter. In 2001, this former Soviet spy became an important U.S. ally in President George W. Bush's war on terror. However, relations soured after the U.S. invasion of Iraq, and at the Munich Security Conference in February 2007, Putin bitterly denounced the United States for allegedly provoking a new global arms race.

minister—a convenient arrangement that honored the letter of the law but left Russia's "Black Belt" Tsar firmly in charge.

States raised new fears that some of these lethal materials, including anthrax, might fall into the hands of international terrorists based in Afghanistan and elsewhere.

Economic Dislocations In the 1990s, the failing economy brought new hardships to the vast majority of Russians, who naturally blamed democracy for the deteriorating situation. Not a few looked back nostalgically to the "good old days" of Communist rule. Things went from bad to worse in Russia, with industrial production, retail sales, and national income plummeting and budget deficits soaring. By the middle of the decade, output in Russia had dropped by one-third.[8] These economic failures were accompanied by severe and widespread inflation.

President Yeltsin did not stay focused on the fundamental problems of managing an economy in the throes of transition. The basic elements of his reform program sounded good in theory, but their execution was half hearted. Despite progress in cutting inflation and stabilizing the ruble, the economy was still failing. Both GDP and industrial output continued to decline, if not as fast as before.[9] Failure to crack down on organized crime was partially to blame, as was official corruption that, among other things, turned the privatization program into a bonanza for crooks.

Rather than making the Russian people stakeholders in the promised new market economy, the government's privatization plan allowed venal wheelers and dealers, operating behind the scenes and using political connections in the Kremlin, to manipulate the divestiture of state assets and thus gain control of huge chunks of the Russian economy. In this way, the sell-off of state assets at bargain-basement prices behind the smokescreen of privatization created instant multimillionaires, and even billionaires, while most Russians sank deeper into poverty. Among a host of other deficiencies, Russia lacked clearly defined stockholders' rights, laws to encourage development of real estate markets, and a social safety net allowing enterprises to lay off workers and cut operating costs.

Most Russians under Yeltsin perceived they were worse off with each passing year. One-fourth of the population, or 36.6 million people, were living below the poverty level; a decade later under Putin's leadership, inflation was slowing (eventually stabilizing at around 12 percent), the economy was growing (6 to 7 percent annually), the ruble was stable, and the trade balance was strongly positive. At under 7 percent, unemployment was considerably lower than in France and Germany and slightly lower than the EU average.[10]

But there is less to the revival of the Russian economy than meets the eye. In fact, Russia's economic growth can be attributed to a single factor: the steep rise in oil and natural gas prices on the world market in the post-9/11 period. As a major producer and exporter of fossils fuels, Russia was reaping windfall profits before the global recession drove world oil prices down in 2008.[11] By becoming the world's largest oil producer and second-largest oil and natural gas exporter, Putin's Russia paid off its international debt and accumulated the world's third-largest holdings of foreign currency.

But Putin pointedly failed to use Russia's energy-export windfall to diversify the Russian economy or to create a business environment attractive to foreign investors. The extreme dependence on energy exports put Russia's economy in dire straits when world oil and gas prices collapsed and export revenues plummeted in 2008–2009. One lucky consequence was that the West's fears of a resurgent Russia bent on reincorporating the former soviet republics—fears that were pushed to new heights after the Kremlin invaded Georgia in August 2008 (see below)—rapidly receded.

Ethnic Conflict The Soviet breakup in 1991 was accompanied by civil war, religious persecution, and ethnic strife in many parts of the Old Empire. Russia remains an ethnically diverse state trying to overcome the powerful centrifugal force of conflicting ethnic groups, some of which have sought sovereign independence. Integrating these groups successfully into the Russian state remains unfinished business.

Under the 1993 constitution, ethnic groups form the basis for the twenty-one republics in the new Russian Federation (successor to the USSR). These federal units, similar to state governments in the United States, are represented as *republics* in the upper house of the Russian legislature. Yet no constitution can resolve the issue of ethnic tension within Russia—time, mutual respect, and economic success are among the ingredients in any recipe for long-term stable relationships between the dominant Great Russians and the nationalities on the periphery, both inside and outside Russia's borders.

The political problem posed by Russia's ethnic republics came to the fore in December 1994, when Russia attacked Chechnya, a Connecticut-sized, ethnic Muslim republic within its borders, situated in the north Caucasus between the Black and Caspian seas. Chechnya had declared independence from Russia shortly after the Soviet Union collapsed in 1991. Determined to end its defiance, however, President Yeltsin sent Soviet troops to put down the revolt. In the

The wars in Bosnia and Chechnya are often called "dirty wars" because uniformed soldiers (not insurgents or "terrorists") as a matter of strategy and policy deliberately attacked and targeted civilians. Such acts are outlawed under the rules and conventions of warfare going at least as far back as the Geneva Convention of 1864. No wars are civilized; the wars in Bosnia and Chechnya were particularly barbaric (hence the term "dirty").

© GETTY IMAGES

ensuing war, Russian warplanes heavily bombed the Chechen capital of Grozny. Chechen fighters were highly motivated, whereas the Russian troops, reflecting widespread public skepticism (and perhaps mindful of Russia's disastrous war against Afghanistan in the 1980s), were more reluctant to go into battle and suffered heavy casualties.

Yeltsin sought to end the dirty war in Chechnya. A truce signed in late 1996 gave Moscow until 2001 to decide how to handle Chechnya's claim to independence; it thus settled nothing. In 1999, when fighting broke out again, Yeltsin called upon his deputy, Vladimir Putin, to orchestrate a brutal crackdown on the rebels. Putin's success made him a national hero to millions of Russian patriots.

Ethnic tensions between Russia and many of the newly independent republics of the former Soviet Union raise a different set of problems. Thus, although Russia and Ukraine are both members of the Commonwealth of Independent States, they have sometimes been at odds. In December 2005, in the middle of winter, Russia threatened to cut off natural gas supplies to Ukraine unless Ukraine agreed to a fourfold increase in gas prices. Ukraine balked. Under pressure from the EU and European heads of state, President Putin, who was also widely suspected of trying to interfere in Ukraine's internal politics, agreed to a compromise. But Russia again cut off natural gas supplies to Ukraine in the winter of 2008–2009.

Tensions between Russia and Ukraine are based on history as well as economics. Ukraine, and specifically the city of Kiev, is the ancient birthplace of Russia. It is one of the largest countries in Eastern Europe, with a population of approximately 40 million, roughly the size of neighboring Poland's population. Within Ukraine, situated on a strategic peninsula, is the Crimea, an important piece of real estate on the banks of the Black Sea.

Crimea's current inhabitants are Great Russians, who replaced the indigenous population after Stalin sent the Crimean Tatars (famous as formidable warriors) into internal exile to Siberia in the 1930s. A dispute in the mid-1990s over control of former Soviet naval facilities and forces at Sevastopol, a historic Crimean port city, arose from ambiguities and conflicting interests. Although it was resolved peacefully in 1997 (Russia got 80 percent of the fleet but conceded the port to Ukraine), it re-surfaced again in 2008 during Russia's war with Georgia (see Box 8.2).

Kazakhstan is another large former Soviet republic, now independent and home to a large Russian minority who make up nearly one-third of its population. The tension between them and the Kazakhs, just over half the population, raises the possibility of future conflict. Moldova, a state bordering Romania on Russia's western border, is another case in point. In the 1990s, Russia's support of internal territorial claims by ethnic Russians in Moldova (13 percent of the population) led to bitter dissension between Russians and native Moldovans (65 percent of the population).

Kazakhstan and Moldova are but two examples among many. Troubled ethnic relations in the former Soviet republics are also mirrored by ethnic politics *inside* the Russian Republic. In 15 of the 21 ethnic republics in Russia today, the titular nationality is in the minority.[12]

BOX 8.2 FOCUS ON   Russia's War on Georgia

Russia's military invasion of Georgia, a small country of less than 5 million on its southern flank, rekindled memories of the Cold War when the United States and the Soviet Union were bitter rivals. In happier times, the United States made a show of promising Georgia it would not stand alone as it embarked on the path of democracy. But when Russia attacked in August 2008, the United States was not in a position to do anything but issue a statement denouncing this act of aggression.

The United States did not have the military or economic wherewithal to get into a shooting war with Russia on its own periphery in the fall of 2008. It would have been extremely risky in the best of circumstances, given Moscow's huge nuclear arsenal, even if the United States had not been stuck in two quagmires—Iraq and Afghanistan. Meanwhile, Georgia's army of 30,000 was no match for Russia's million-man juggernaut.

Ironically, Georgia was desperately trying to get into NATO—one reason Moscow attacked. Most of the former Warsaw Pact countries are now members of both NATO and the European Union. The Baltic states of Estonia, Latvia, and Lithuania—like Georgia, former Soviet Socialist Republics—are also in NATO and the EU. Viewed from the Kremlin's vantage point, this geostrategic encroachment on Russia's periphery is a Western provocation. So the attack on Georgia put the West on notice: No (more) trespassing!

Nor was the war just about Georgia. It was also about control of vital oil and natural gas pipelines to the West, about Russia's debut as a post-Soviet global power (which it clearly is by any geopolitical reckoning), and about drawing a line in the sand on Russia's western and southern frontiers. Georgia always has been important to Russia because of its strategic position on the Black Sea, the gateway to the Mediterranean, and its proximity to Iran, Turkey, and the Middle East.

What's far more significant than Georgia, though, is Ukraine, a large country with a population of 46.5 million—larger than either Spain or Poland. By invading Georgia, Russia has also served notice that it will oppose Ukraine's bid to join NATO and the EU by any and all means necessary.

Meanwhile, Russia's use of force against a sovereign state friendly to the West threatened to start Cold War II. As such, it made Russia appear once again in the guise of Public Enemy #1 in Europe. But words of wisdom are small consolation when one's country is being bombed and foreign troops are streaming across the border. Ask any Georgian.

SOURCE: Adapted from my op-ed article in the *Kansas City Star*, August 18, 2008, p. B6.

State Building Putin re-centralized government at great cost to Russia's fragile democratic institutions. We can summarize the effect of his reverse reforms as follows:

- *A Tattered Constitution.* Adopted in 1993, the Russian constitution strengthened the executive in relationship to the legislature. Putin shifted power even more decisively in favor of the president or prime minister. In so doing, he has stabilized the political system, but also set back the cause of Russian constitutionalism and respect for human rights, while complicating Russia's relationships with Europe and straining its ties with the United States.

- *Feeble Parties and Fewer Elections.* The Russian party system is highly fragmented. In the December 1995 election to the **Duma**, the lower house of the **Federal Assembly**, Russia's national legislature, forty-two parties appeared on the ballot. As president, Putin placed formidable obstacles in the path of political parties and party leaders who dared to oppose his policies and abolished elections for regional governors altogether (these positions are now appointed by the president).

- *Organized Crime.* According to one estimate, organized crime in the mid-1990s employed some three million people and had infiltrated the Russian police and bureaucracy, as well as those of other republics. The Russian mob's influence was everywhere; it intruded "into every field of Western concern, the nascent free market, privatization, disarmament, military conversion, foreign humanitarian relief and financial aid, and even state reserves of currency and gold."[13] Organized crime remains a major blight on civil society in Russia to this day.

- *Disrespect for the Law and the Police.* The rise of organized crime, the emergence of localized political bosses, the prevalence of corruption, and a broad spectrum of social ills such as ordinary crime, prostitution, and drug abuse all eat away at the social fabric. Widespread lawlessness also reflects the Russian government's inability to maintain law and order. One consequence of these problems is a disrespect for the very idea of law that, for good reason, has been called "Russia's biggest blight."[14]

Putin: President or Constitutional Czar?

In August 1999, then-President Yeltsin named Putin to be his new prime minister. None of Yeltsin's first four prime ministers had lasted long in office, so Putin's sudden elevation to this post might not have been significant. But it was: eight months later Putin was the newly elected president of Russia.

Putin quickly moved to put his personal stamp on Russia's domestic and foreign policies. At home, he moved against Russia's notorious "oligarchs" (wealthy tycoons who gained control over gigantic pieces of the old Soviet economy in the botched privatization program carried out during the Yeltsin era). Abroad, he gave Russia's foreign policy a new look, strongly backing the U.S. campaign against terrorism in the fall of 2001.

Putin also paid tribute to economic reforms, including changes in the tax laws and creation of a financial intelligence service to fight money laundering. Buoyed by high oil prices, the Russian economy revived (see Table 8.2). But the basic structures of Russia's protectionist, cartel-dominated, red tape-ridden economy, including such key sectors as utilities, banks, and state-owned enterprises, remain largely unchanged.

Nor has the political landscape changed fundamentally. Putin remains in charge—changing hats but little else as he became Russia's prime minister rather than president. Not only has he eviscerated the independent news media; he also has turned to the so-called *siloviki* (antidemocratic hard-liners from the old KGB, police, and the army) to run the country.

Duma
Officially called the State Duma, it is the lower house of the Federal Assembly, Russia's national legislature, reestablished in the 1993 constitution, after having been abolished in 1917. It comprises 450 members, half of whom are elected from nationwide party lists, with the other half elected from single-member constituencies.

Federal Assembly
Russia's national legislature, a bicameral parliament, established under the 1993 constitution, comprising a lower chamber (State Duma) and an upper chamber (Federation Council).

The independent press in Russia gets little or no protection from the state. Being an investigative reporter or a muckraking media personality can be dangerous. The mysterious poisoning of Alexander Litvinenko in a London restaurant in November 2006 demonstrated to the satisfaction of many observers that the Kremlin under Putin had reverted to the cloak-and-dagger practices of the Soviet era. Litvinenko, who had defected to the United Kingdom six years earlier, was a former colonel in the Russian secret service (the FSB, successor to the KGB) and a vitriolic critic of Putin. He died on November 23, 2006, in a London hospital. A month earlier, Anna Politkovskaya, a crusading and often polemical Russian journalist and, like Litvinenko, a fierce critic of Putin, was shot dead in Moscow in what many believed to be a contract killing. Thus, long after the lifting of the veil of Communist rule, Russia remains a riddle to the West and the world.

Future Prospects

Does Russia represent the remains of a great empire in decay or will it reemerge as a major world power? Is it unalterably authoritarian? The answer to the first question is probably "neither"—Russia will neither self-destruct as the Soviet Union did nor will it recapture the status of world-class superpower the Soviet Union achieved. The answer to the second question is probably "yes"—there is little reason to believe Russia's political culture will change any time soon.

Dissident journalist Anna Politkovskaya was shot dead in the elevator of her apartment building in October 2006. No one has ever been charged with the murder, which appeared to be the work of professionals.

© CORBIS

TABLE 8.2 Russian Economic Performance, 1992–2008 (% annual change)

	1992	1994	1996	1998	2000	2002	2004	2006	2008
GDP	−14.5	−12.6	−6.0	−5.0	9.0	4.0	6.4	7.5	6
Inflation	2323	202	21.8	82.0	20.2	14.0	12.7	9.2	14.1

SOURCE: World Bank and *The Economist* ("Emerging Market Indicators"), July 1, 2000; December 7, 2002; March 27, 2004; February 19, 2005; and December 2, 2006. Data for 2008 from Economist Intelligence Unit estimate, *The Economist*, January 31, 2009, p. 101.

The very possibility of liberal democracy in Russia has always been, at best, an uncertain prospect, given centuries of despotism and centralized rule. Still, in the early 1990s, many dared to hope that Russia was finally shedding its authoritarian habits. By the late 1990s, however, that hope appeared distant, if not naive. A decade later, with Putin at still the helm, it appeared dead on arrival—a victim of an autocratic Kremlin boss who re-centralized the political system and restored order, but utterly failed to take advantage of windfall profits from Russia's oil and gas exports to modernize and diversify the Russian economy.

We turn next to a brief look at Eastern Europe, a region of nations in transition. No two countries have approached the problems of political and economic reform in exactly the same way, and there is a widening gap between the most and least successful countries.

EASTERN EUROPE: TWO-TRACK TRANSITION

Without exception, the newly independent states of Eastern Europe were Communist-ruled during the Cold War era, which lasted for more than four decades. All were saddled with centrally planned economies patterned after that of the Soviet "Big Brother." Just as central planning did not work in the long run in the Soviet Union, neither did it work anywhere else. But it is easier to demolish than to construct—for rebuilding, Eastern Europe had to look to the West. The West stood ready to help, but first the former Communist states would have to create democratic institutions and market-based economies.

The boldest reforms were adopted in Poland, the Czech Republic, and Hungary. Poland showed the way, launching "shock therapy" policies designed to create a functioning market and to privatize the notoriously inefficient state enterprises that were a legacy of Communist rule. Unlike the Soviet Union, Poland had never banned small-scale private enterprise, and a decade after its democratic revolution, private enterprise was flourishing as never before (with some two million registered businesses).

Poland's tough approach to reform yielded impressive results in the 1990s, when its economy grew faster than that of its ex-Communist neighbors, averaging over 5 percent a year between 1995 and 2000. Poland also managed to tame inflation, a major threat to social and economic stability throughout the region. As a direct result of these market-friendly reforms, Poland attracted infusions of foreign investment that were, in turn, a tonic to its reviving economy.

But relatively high unemployment (still hovering near double digits in 2009) was a nettlesome issue, especially in a country where jobs had been guaranteed to all adults during two generations of Communist rule. A growing social disparity was also a problem, as the relatively poor rural population lagged behind the burgeoning urban middle class. Because Polish agriculture was never collectivized (as in the Soviet Union), many of Poland's impoverished villagers still live and work on its two million family farms.[15]

Although polls show crime and official corruption have undermined public confidence in government, the Polish economy has continued to improve year after year, turning in steady growth rates (5–7 percent) with modest inflations (2–4 percent). The fact that Poland became a member of the EU in 2004—and is by far the biggest of the EU's twelve new members—also bodes well for the future.

In the Czech Republic, Prime Minister (now President) Václav Klaus extolled the virtues of the marketplace and implemented an ambitious coupon-redemption scheme that theoretically gave all Czech citizens shares of newly privatized (formerly state) enterprises. But the distribution was done without adequate safeguards and thus failed to accomplish one of its primary aims—to give Czechs a stake in the new market economy. In fact, crooks and insiders (a distinction without a difference in Czech politics) grabbed up the high-quality stocks, most of which never became available to the public, and used connections to get operational control of the "hottest" properties.

Ironically, this bungled attempt at reform soured ordinary Czechs toward democracy and capitalism rather than solidifying popular support as it was intended to do. Inflation, fear of job losses, corruption in high places, a growing gap between the *nouveaux riche* and the majority, and a heightened awareness of how far behind the West Eastern Europeans in general—and Czechs in particular—had fallen all contributed to a deepening disillusionment. In the eyes of the people, the shady entrepreneurs and self-aggrandizing politicians became synonymous with "the system."

Despite popular dissatisfaction with "politics" and the pace of improvement in the general standard of living, the Czech Republic is again a true republic. (Czechoslovakia came into being after World War I as a full-fledged parliamentary democracy—the only instance of popular self-government in Eastern Europe prior to 1989.) In addition, the Czech economy, having stumbled along for most of the 1990s, made a relatively strong recovery following the recession of 1997–1999. Structural reforms (for example, in the banking sector) helped achieve this result. Voters strongly endorsed the Czech Republic's entry into the EU in 2004, a move that opened Europe's huge Single Market to Czech-built automobiles, armaments, machinery, and other exports and could well make the Czech Republic a magnet for foreign investment.

In 2008, Czech GDP grew at a respectable rate of 4.2 percent; unfortunately, inflation climbed to 6.5 percent. The manufacturing-based economy was especially hard-hit by the global recession in 2008–2009—industrial output fell by over 17.4 percent in November 2008, the highest of any EU country. (Spain was close, but the overall drop in industrial activity for the EU as a whole was a less dramatic 7.7 percent.)

Nonetheless, as in Poland, polls consistently show that after more than a decade of freedom and independence, many Czechs do not trust the government or politicians. And for good reason: the Czech political party system is fragmented, parliament is fractious, and coalition governments are unstable. In March 2009, the Czech Republic embarrassed itself in the eyes of Europe and the world when the government of Mirek Topolanek was forced to resign following a vote of no confidence—at a time when the Czech Republic held the six-month presidency in the European Council (the supreme decision making body of the EU). Thus, Topolanek was president of the EU when he was ousted as prime minister of the Czech Republic. In April 2009, a caretaker prime minister was named to replace Topolanek pending early elections in the fall, but he did not take office until May, so the country actually had two lame-duck prime ministers at the same time. Meanwhile, the Czech Republic remained the only EU member-state besides Ireland that had not ratified the Reform Treaty, which Václav Klaus outspokenly opposed. Despite the often farcical nature of Czech politics, however, the level of dissatisfaction among the rank-and-file is not high enough to prefer a return to the days of Soviet-backed Communist rule.

Hungary experimented with economic reforms well before the fall of Communism. In 1968, the same year as the tumultuous Prague Spring in Czechoslovakia, when a reform-minded Communist Party leader named Alexander Dubcek called for "socialism with a human face" and led an inspired popular liberalization movement that was ultimately crushed by Soviet tanks, the Budapest government launched the New Economic Mechanism (NEM). The NEM, aimed at limited decentralization of the economy and other market-oriented reforms, was a promising experiment in the early going. Production of consumer goods (always a low priority in Soviet-type economies) rose, and the quality of life for Hungarians generally improved. But hard-line Communists at home and abroad (particularly in the Soviet Union) opposed these reforms, and in the 1980s, the NEM was abandoned.

Even so, as the economy steadily declined, Hungary turned to the West for trade, aid, and investment. The liberalization that accompanied this policy included a new tolerance of private businesses and partnerships with foreign multinational companies. Thus, Hungary's reform efforts—though limited in scope and scale by a combination of politics, ideology, and Soviet interference—gave it a head start when Communism self-destructed at the end of the 1980s.

After 1989, Hungary's popularly elected government accelerated the pace of free-market reforms. In particular, as the leading emerging market in the region, Hungary attracted more than half of all direct foreign investment in Eastern

Europe, even though its population (about 10 million) was a mere 25 percent of Poland's (42 million) and a tiny fraction of Russia's (147 million). Post-Communist Hungary moved swiftly to break up and privatize its huge state-owned enterprises; by 1993, the private sector's share of the GDP was about 50 percent. The pace of privatization slowed temporarily when the socialists gained a majority in the parliament in 1994, but the following year, the same parliament passed legislation to speed the sale of state-owned enterprises and to prepare to sell off public utilities and strategic industries such as steel and electricity.

Despite these bold restructuring efforts, however, Hungary has suffered high levels of inflation and unemployment unknown in Communist times. In 2008, Hungary's economy grew by less than one percent, inflation was over 6 percent, and unemployment was close to 8 percent. In 2009, the economy was in dire straits as demand for the country's manufactured goods crumbled—exports account for about 80 percent of Hungary's GDP and industrial output fell by almost 30 percent in February. Also, Hungary's currency, the Forint, dropped sharply. Because it depends so heavily on exports to the EU (and especially Germany), Hungary was especially vulnerable as Europe and the globe sank into a severe recession in 2009.

On the positive side, Hungary is now a stable parliamentary democracy. In the first three free elections after 1989, a different party won control of the government each time—a sign of party competition and political pluralism at work. Moreover, this frequent changing of the guard has led neither to sharp lurches to the Left or Right nor to political paralysis. Also, like Poland and the Czech Republic, Hungary joined the EU in 2004.

Other former Communist states in Eastern Europe that have joined both NATO and the European Union include Slovakia, Slovenia, the Baltic states (Estonia, Latvia, and Lithuania), Bulgaria, and Romania. Tiny Slovenia (population: 2 million) has outshined all the others, achieving a per capita GDP that puts it well ahead of the Czech Republic, Poland, and Hungary—and even one Western European country, Portugal. All have made—or are in the process of making—the transition from authoritarian one-party rule and Soviet-style command economies to pluralistic representative democracy and market economies. The reward and incentive for these countries to institute sweeping reforms has been admission to NATO and the European Union. Among the countries expected to join the West in the near future are Albania, Croatia, and Montenegro. Serbia and Ukraine have expressed a desire to join both NATO and the EU as well. But the question of Kosovo's independence stands in the way of Serbia's joining the EU at this time, and Russia has threatened Ukraine with dire consequences if it joins NATO.

In sum, Communism has largely disappeared from the map of Europe, although Communist parties (often with changed names) are still around. Free and fair elections are held nearly everywhere, and genuine parliamentary democracy is by far the most common form of government. We turn next to a look at the transition in Communist China, where political change has been set aside in favor of economic transformation. The results have been nothing short of spectacular, but less than satisfying in the eyes of the West.

CHINA: POLICE-STATE CAPITALISM

In the past three decades, China has transformed from an isolated pariah state with a dysfunctional command economy to a global power with a dynamic economy, achieving export-driven, double-digit growth rates year after year since the early 1990s. China's economic "miracle" is the result of a vast supply of cheap labor, pragmatic policies devoid of ideological content, skillful diplomacy aimed at opening mass consumer markets in the West, and the creation of special economic zones (SEZs) to attract and protect foreign investment capital. The SEZs combine liberal foreign-ownership policies with generous tax incentives. It is said that imitation is the sincerest form of flattery—25 years after China demonstrated the potential of SEZs to stimulate economic development and boost exports, India, Asia's other demographic giant, decided to follow suit (see Chapter 9).[16]

But China, like India, remains a poor country compared to Japan, South Korea, Singapore, and its two largest trading partners, the United States and the European Union. And while most observers would agree it has shed its legacy of Maoist totalitarian rule (see Chapter 6), China continues to be a monolithic, one-party police state.

The path to power for Mao's Chinese Communist Party differed sharply from that of Lenin's Bolsheviks. Because Mao's victory followed a protracted guerrilla war against the Japanese and the Chinese Nationalist government of

FIGURE 8.2   The People's Republic of China: Note that many of China's greatest cities are in the east; note where Taiwan is located; note also the close proximity of Japan to the Korean Peninsula.

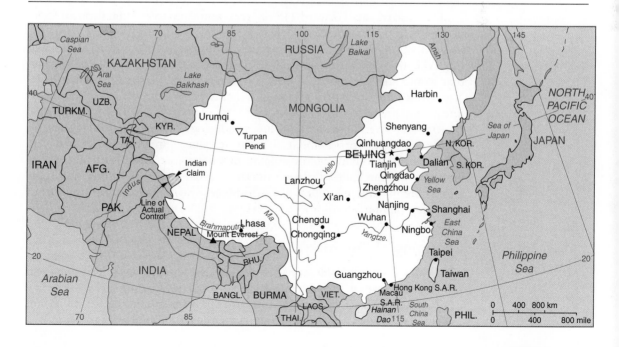

Chiang Kai-shek, the army played a much greater role in Mao's theory and practice of revolution than in Lenin's. When the Chinese Communists came to power in 1949, the army and the party were fused into a single organization.

Acting as a virtual government, the army was charged not only with fighting but also with administration, including maintenance of law and order, construction and public works, management of the economy, and education and indoctrination. In effect, the army became the nucleus of the People's Republic, the new government of China.

Mao in Command

In the early 1950s, the People's Republic of China (PRC) was heavily dependent on political, economic, and military assistance from the Soviet Union, a dependency heightened by the Korean War (1950–1953) that saw U.S. military forces cross the 48th Parallel and advance almost all the way to the Yalu River—China's border with North Korea. The USSR, ruled by the aging Stalin, insisted the fledgling Communist government in Beijing emulate the Stalinist model. Thus, the political structures of the Chinese state, as well as the thrust of Chinese economic and foreign politics, closely resembled those of the Soviet Union. Everything from collectivization of agriculture and a lopsided emphasis on industrial investment to the Soviet educational system was borrowed, almost without modification.

The turning point came when Stalin's successor, Nikita Khrushchev, made his famous speech at the Twentieth Party Congress in 1956, in which he denounced the crimes of Stalin and proclaimed the advent of peaceful coexistence with the West. From that point on, the Chinese Communists, under Mao's erratic leadership, went their own bizarre way.

The Great Leap Forward (1958) represented Mao's declaration of independence from the Soviet model of industrial development. In place of the Stalinist emphasis on heavy industry, especially large-scale mining and metallurgical complexes, the Great Leap stressed decentralized industrial production that would take advantage of China's greatest natural resource: human labor. Numerous small-scale backyard steel furnaces became the symbol of this labor-intensive approach.

Mao's believed with the right mix of ideology and inspiration, the masses could and would bring about the revolutionary transformation of society he so ardently desired. Mao's utopian obsession led to the launching of the Great Proletarian Cultural Revolution in 1966, designed to utterly smash the party-state bureaucracy. For China, the Soviet system had become a model of counterrevolution.

Changing of the Guard

The deaths of Chou En-lai and Mao Zedong, the People's Republic's two great founders, made the year 1976 a watershed in modern Chinese history. According to one China scholar, "Mao's death marked the end of an era; what was not clear was who would lead China and in what direction in the era to come."[17]

Hu Jintao, who became Communist China's top leader in 2002, was a protégé of his predecessor, Deng Xiaoping, China's pre-eminent economic reformer; like Deng (and in sharp contrast to Mao), he is a pragmatist who places economic success above ideology.

After two years of halting reforms, the nation's post-Mao leadership under the direction of Deng Xiaoping (who had twice been purged by Mao for his alleged lack of revolutionary zeal) "mounted a major campaign to abandon ideological dogma and to adopt pragmatism—symbolized by the slogans 'practice is the sole criterion of truth' and 'seek truth from facts.'" Economic development replaced class struggle, and a welcome mat replaced the "no trespassing" sign that had impeded China's trade relations with the West for nearly three decades.

Banished were the mass campaigns, crash programs, hero worship, and ideological fanaticism that had been the hallmarks of Maoism. Expanding trade, especially with the industrial democracies, became a principal aim of Beijing's diplomacy. Deng's economic reforms—notably, the SEZs mentioned above—were gradually implemented between 1978 and 1982, as he carefully and patiently consolidated his power within the ruling **politburo**—the Kremlin's supreme decision-making body. By the fall of 1982, the reform-minded Deng was in full command.

Deng remained China's paramount ruler until his death, at the age of 92, in early 1997. His successors—first Jiang Zemin and, since 2003, Hu Jintao—have continued Deng's pragmatic political and economic policies.

China's Pragmatic "Communism"

The Communist Party continues to govern China. Party members, about 5 percent of the population, constitute a political elite that enjoys special

politburo
A small clique that formed the supreme decision-making body in the former Soviet Union. Its members often belonged to the Secretariat and were ministers of key governmental departments.

privileges—but the emergence of a class of *nouveau riche* entrepreneurs and a burgeoning middle class are changing the face of Chinese society, though with little impact on the political system thus far. High party ranking remains a prerequisite to the exercise of political power.

Before 1978, Maoism, a radical peasant-based brand of Communism that glorified revolution as a form of moral purification, was the official ideology of China. After 1978, Deng's pragmatic view prevailed—that economic growth, and not class struggle, ought to be the main measure of success for both the party and the state. In Deng's own words, "It matters not if a cat is black or white, as long as it catches mice." No longer would the party invoke Marxist ideology to justify its programs or policies or to legitimize the party's rule.[18]

A Communist Party that distances itself from Communism is not only a novelty, but also an anomaly—one that leads us to ask how long China's leadership can continue the charade now that computers and the Internet have so greatly multiplied and diversified the sources of information available to the masses. At the same time, China's engagement in the global economy has necessitated opening Chinese society to outsiders. Even so, while the world now has a window into China, the political process remains off limits and shrouded in secrecy.

Market-Oriented Reforms

In the post-Maoist era, Beijing has boldly sought foreign loans and direct foreign investment, primarily from the West, thus violating a long-standing ideological taboo. The approach worked wonders; Western investment and loans began pouring into the country in the 1980s and continued thereafter, providing much-needed capital for China's modernization drive (see Figure 8.3).

At the same time, agriculture underwent de-collectivization—that is, a kind of re-privatization of farming. Under this system, the state makes contracts with individual households to purchase specified products; farmers can also sell produce in private markets. The reforms proved remarkably successful in boosting agricultural productivity. In industry and commerce, too, China has moved toward a greater reliance on market forces. One statistic is remarkably revealing. In 1978, there were no privately owned businesses in China; by 1995, approximately one-third of all businesses were privately owned (see Figure 8.4).

The results of China's agricultural and industrial revolution have been impressive. After decades of induced turmoil under Mao, China's economy has revived. In fact, China was one of the world's fastest-growing economies during the past two decades. By 2008–2009, when China's economy (like everyone else's) slowed in the face of a severe global recession, China boasted the third largest national economy in the world, behind only the United States and Japan. It was on a pace to overtake Japan in 2010.

For all its recent success, China is still poor in terms of per-capita wealth. In 2009, China's total GDP by one common measure was still smaller than Japan's, and Japan's per capita income was nearly twelve times that of China ($42,300 versus $3,600). Even so, during the 1990s alone, between 150 and

FIGURE 8.3 Foreign Capital Inflows to China, 1989–2006 (billions of U.S. dollars)

SOURCE: *The Economist*, February 22, 1997, p. 22; *2000 World Bank Atlas* (Washington, DC: World Bank 2000), 56; World Bank, 2008.

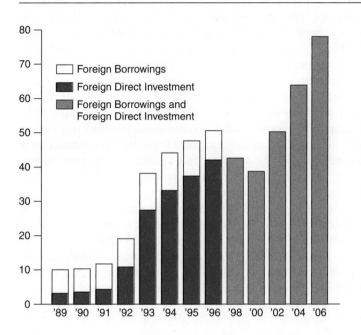

FIGURE 8.4 An Emerging Private Sector: Private ownership of business in China increased dramatically after Mao Zedong's death in 1976.

*Partly government owned

SOURCE: *Newsweek*, March 3, 1997, vol. CXXXIX, no. 9, p. 27. The research is attributed to the Heritage Foundation and IMF, conducted by Anna Kuchment and Dane Chinni. Newsweek, Inc. All rights reserved. Reprinted by permission.

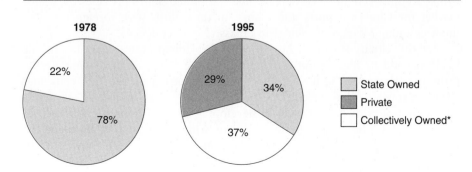

200 million Chinese people, equal to half the population of western Europe, escaped debilitating poverty, according to some estimates. In addition, although the 800 million or so Chinese who live in the interior rural areas remain poor, farm incomes rose significantly after agricultural reforms were put in effect.[19]

Despite huge strides, China officially acknowledged that 80 to 100 million people were living in poverty in the late 1990s; other estimates, such as those made by the World Bank, placed the figure much higher at 350 million.[20] One reason these numbers vary so much is that there is no universally accepted definition of poverty, and where the official "poverty line" is drawn can be (and often is) more a matter of politics than economics. But everyone agrees that by any measure, poverty in China—especially rural poverty—has been reduced by a huge margin in the last 30 years, and while it has not disappeared, it is rapidly receding. China has "witnessed the most astonishing economic transformation in human history," according to *The Economist*. "In a country that is home to one-fifth of humanity some 200 million people have been lifted out of poverty."[21]

Exports continue to be a major source of China's economic dynamism. By 2003, China's trade surplus with the United States had surpassed Japan's. The overall U.S. trade deficit with China alone accounted for about one-fourth of the total. By 2008, this imbalance had jumped from $124 billion in 2003 to $266 billion, and China was garnering the largest trade surpluses in the history of the world. This lopsided trade relationship is one indication that China's currency (the yuan) is undervalued (making its goods cheaper, and thus more competitive, in foreign markets than they should be).

Understandably, Beijing has resisted international pressure to revalue its currency. In fact, in early 2009 China's Ministry of Finance issued a report arguing that the central bank should actually *devalue* its currency. Because its economy is extremely export-dependent, China was eager to counteract any fall off in global demand due to the worldwide recession—despite the fact that China reported a trade surplus of $39 billion in January 2009, the second highest on record.

sovereign wealth funds
A state owned investment fund made up of financial assets such as stocks, bonds, precious metals, and property; such funds invest globally. China, for example, has invested huge sums in the United States via its sovereign wealth fund.

China's huge trade surpluses have resulted in vast state holdings of foreign reserves, in so-called **sovereign wealth funds** that totaled more than $1.7 trillion in 2008. China has invested most of its vast foreign-exchange reserves in U.S. Treasury bonds and T-Bills, in the process becoming the U.S. government's second-biggest creditor (behind Japan). As a consequence, the United States and China are now economic co-dependents: the United States provides the major market for China's exports and China, in turn, flush with foreign reserves, finances a major part of Washington's massive budget deficits.

But this situation cannot last forever: the United States cannot continue living beyond its means, outsourcing and losing jobs to China while saving little or nothing for the future; and China cannot expect the U.S. consumer spending spree that has fueled the Chinese economy to go on indefinitely, while China continues to drag its feet in developing its own domestic markets. In other words, China cannot go on producing without consuming more and the United States cannot go on consuming without producing more—this is one of the lessons we ought to take away from the banking crisis and the deep global recession it triggered in 2008–2009.

BOX 8.3 FOCUS ON   China's Rise: Economic Miracle or Environmental Nightmare?

The following excerpt from an article by David Lynch describes warning signs that suggest the Chinese economy is on a collision course with the environment. If China's rulers continue to ignore the environment, today's economic policies aimed at maximizing current growth rates may, ironically, become a drag on tomorrow's prosperity and social progress.

Over the past two decades, China's economy has grown at an average annual rate of more than 9%. But the economic cost of environmental harm, measured in public health, worker absenteeism, and remediation efforts, is becoming prohibitively high. "This miracle will end soon because the environment can no longer keep pace," Pan Yue, deputy director of China's State Environmental Protection Administration, told the German magazine *Der Spiegel*.

Environmental injury costs China 8% to 15% of its annual gross domestic product, Pan said. In the north, encroaching deserts are prompting human migrations that swell overburdened cities. In the south, factories have closed periodically for lack of water, according to [Elizabeth] Economy [of the Council on Foreign Relations], who wrote a book last year on China's environmental woes. The World Bank estimates such shutdowns cost $14 billion annually in lost output.

Since this article appeared, scientific evidence has mounted of global warming caused by excess carbon emissions released into the atmosphere. The international community has become increasingly alarmed about warnings that Earth is reaching a fateful tipping point—the moment when it will become impossible to reverse climate changes, and polar icecaps and glaciers will melt at an accelerating pace with disastrous consequences for the ecosystem. Meanwhile, in 2009 China and India—the two most populous countries in the world—were both continuing to build dozens of new carbon-emitting coal-fired power plants each year to supply electricity for construction, transport, and industry.

SOURCE: From David J. Lynch, "Pollution Poisons China's Progress," *USA Today*, July 4, 2005 (electronic edition). For an in-depth analysis of this problem, see Elizabeth Economy, "The Great Leap Backward: The Costs of China's Environmental Crisis," *Foreign Affairs*, vol. 86, no. 5, September/ October 2007, pp. 38–59; see also, Carin Zissis and Jayshree Bajorie, "China's Environmental Crisis," *Foreign Affairs*, updated August 4, 2008 accessed online at http://www.cfr.org/publication/12608/.

Beijing faces other economic challenges as well. Conspicuous income disparities exist for the first time since the Communist takeover in 1949. The coastal provinces of the east—Shanghai is a particularly striking example—are growing much faster than the rural provinces of central and western China and produce two to four times the income, according to official statistics.[22] The costs of this rapid development include appalling air pollution in China's teeming cities, rivers that run thick with silt, industrial waste and sewage, and scenes of great natural beauty lost forever to construction of dams and reservoirs needed for hydroelectric power generation to keep the engines of economic development going at full tilt (see Box 8.3).

In sum, market-friendly reforms have produced a vibrant economy, rising incomes, and a new class of millionaires, but at the price of growing income disparities and immeasurable damage to the environment. In response to China's turn toward a more liberal economy, the United States dropped its opposition to Chinese membership in the World Trade Organization (WTO). When China formally joined the WTO in 2001, the *Economist* asserted, "China's accession to the WTO . . . will be its biggest step since Communist rule began more than 50 years ago toward the integration of its economic system with that of the capitalist West."[23]

Expanded Personal Freedoms

One mark of totalitarianism's demise is that China "has become freer in terms of daily life for large numbers of people."[24] People can now change jobs, move from one part of China to another, exhibit greater individuality in dress and expression, and exercise free choice in such important personal matters as whom to marry and divorce—individual liberties unknown in Mao's China. These new freedoms, however, stop far short of constitutional rights common in the West. For instance, couples are still limited by the government to having only one child. And, as we shall see, political and religious freedoms are nonexistent.

Political and Religious Repression

Despite liberalization in the economic and social spheres, political and religious persecution continues in China. Not long after the death of Mao Zedong, in 1978, a phenomenon known as the **Democracy Wall** captured world attention. On a wall in the heart of Beijing, opinions and views at variance with the official line—including blunt criticisms of the existing system and leaders—were displayed with the government's tacit approval. But a government crackdown in 1979, complete with arrests and show trials, put an end to Beijing's brief dalliance with free speech. A decade later, the **Tiananmen Square massacre** came to epitomize the Chinese government's persistent hostility to human rights (see Box 8.4).

Tiananmen Square continues to symbolize China's persecution of critics and dissidents. Related issues are the harsh treatment of political prisoners, routinely forced to work as slave laborers in factories that produce cheap goods for export, and the persistent persecution of religious practitioners. To some extent, the government's imprisonment of religious followers is a remnant of Marxism's ideological mistrust of, and hostility to, religion. It represents the party's continuing perception that religion poses a political threat to the continuity and health of the regime.

For the most part, the government controls religion by licensing and monitoring churches, monasteries, mosques, and other religious institutions. Beijing has been particularly ruthless in Tibet, according to Human Rights Watch and many other non-governmental organizations (NGOs), where it has closed

Democracy Wall
A wall located in the heart of Beijing on which public criticism of the regime was permitted to be displayed in 1978.

Tiananmen Square massacre
In 1989, unarmed civilian workers and students marched in Tiananmen Square in Beijing to demand democratic freedom and government reforms. Army troops responded with force, killing 1,500 demonstrators and wounding another 10,000.

BOX 8.4 SPOTLIGHT ON   The Tragedy of Tiananmen Square

In May 1989, students and workers staged a mass march in Beijing to protest party privilege and corruption and to demand democratic reforms. The protest grew as throngs of demonstrators camped in Tiananmen Square, making speeches and shouting slogans. The rest of the world watched in rapt attention as the drama unfolded before Western television cameras. The fact that Mikhail Gorbachev, the father of "reform Communism," visited Beijing that same month for the first Sino-Soviet summit in three decades only added to the sense of high drama. When unrest spread throughout the country, Beijing declared martial law, but to no avail.

Army troops entered the Chinese capital with tanks and armor on June 3; it soon became apparent that the show of force was not a bluff. The crackdown that ensued brought the democracy movement to a bloody end as hundreds, possibly thousands, of protesters were killed or injured and many more arrested. Security forces later rounded up thousands of dissenters, and at least thirty-one were tried and executed. The atrocities against unarmed civilians in the Tiananmen Square massacre proved that China was still, at its core, a repressive state.

Buddhist monasteries, jailed and executed worshippers, and exiled Tibet's religious leader, the Dalai Lama.

New Social Disorders

China suffers some of the same problems affecting Western democracy. Theft and robbery have become particularly common in cities, while drug-related crimes and prostitution are also on the increase—all representing the underside of China's economic expansion.[25] Corruption is also rampant. With the blurring of the line between the public and private spheres, and with vast amounts of money circulating through China's burgeoning economy, business and politics have become tainted by routine acts of bribery, nepotism, and "unofficial favoritism."

China as a Global Power: Rival or Partner?

China is now a global power. With the world's largest population, it has no difficulty finding conscripts for its armed forces, which total some three million troops. Since the late 1970s, China has sought to modernize its military capabilities. Today, it has the fastest-rising arms expenditures of any major world power. China also continues testing nuclear weapons and selling high-tech armaments on the international market (in some instances, to customers the United States regards as a threat to peace and order).

China's growing military power has not gone unnoticed, especially in Asia.[26] Thus, India's reluctance to forgo its nuclear weapons programs can be traced, in part, to its distrust not only of Pakistan, but also of China. By the same token, Japanese leaders have viewed China's military modernization with ill-concealed alarm, and the Vietnamese have not forgotten the 1979 border war with China. The Philippines, long a staunch U.S. ally in the western Pacific, have an unresolved dispute with China over potentially oil-rich islands in the South China Sea.

And then there is a longstanding dispute over Taiwan (see below): Beijing considers Taiwan a breakaway province of China, while the United States continues to back Taiwan's independence. Periodic Chinese naval exercises have reinforced this point, although Taiwan has continued to hold firm, buttressed by the U.S. Navy. But the meaning of China's emergence as a global power is far from certain. One thing is clear: China continues to face huge challenges at home and to present huge challenges abroad.

TWO ASIAN TIGERS: STILL ROLE MODELS?

China is not the only country in Asia with a dynamic economy in recent times. South Korea, Taiwan, Singapore, Thailand, Malaysia, and Indonesia all compete with Japan—and now China—for export markets. Unlike China, they have also taken steps toward political liberalization.

South Korea: Crisis-Prone but Resilient

The economic transformation of South Korea, from a poor country dependent on agriculture to a modern industrial state powered by a technologically advanced manufacturing sector, was complete by the turn of the twenty-first century.

South Korea's per capita national wealth (GDP) was roughly 5 times mainland China's and twenty times that of Pakistan in 2008. To put South Korea's achievement in even better perspective, South Korea's GDP per capita is nearly double that of Chile, currently the richest country in Latin America, and three times larger than that of Brazil, the region's largest country.

Still, South Korea lags well behind the two poorest countries in Western Europe, Greece and Portugal. It has come far in the half-century since World War II and the Korean War left its economy in a shambles and its people traumatized and destitute. But it has a long way to go to catch up with Japan. Indeed, Japan's GDP per capita (estimated at roughly $39,000 in 2007) is three times larger than South Korea's, putting Japan's economy in the same league as those of Germany, France, and the United Kingdom.

In the 1990s, huge industrial conglomerates and largely unregulated big banks dominated South Korea's economy. These special interests had become so powerful and entrenched as to stifle competition. Although Asia's financial crisis of 1997–1998, known as the **Asian flu**, did not start in South Korea, it had a devastating impact there. Big banks had been lending money to big business without regard to the underlying financial condition of the borrowers. This situation, as well as the general need to revitalize the country's economy, compelled South Korea's popularly elected president to undertake aggressive state intervention—not to put the government in control of the economy but to give greater play to free-market forces. Seoul launched a program of bold reforms in the late 1990s designed to resuscitate the economy after it contracted by over 6 percent in 1998. The reforms proved to be a tonic: Although the country experienced a recession in 2003, South Korea's economy grew at an average annual rate of 4.4 percent in the decade 1995–2005.

To what extent was this second transition political as well as economic? No doubt politics played an important role. Korea's political traditions are authoritarian. North Korea has been Communist-ruled since World War II, while South Korea, a close ally of the United States, is anti-Communist. Even so, South Korean "democracy" was little more than a façade for a pro-Western police state until 1997, when Kim Dae Jung became the first opposition candidate ever

Asian flu
A term used to describe the widespread financial turmoil in Asian stock markets, financial institutions, and economies in 1997.

FIGURE 8.5   South Korea: Note the vulnerable geostrategic location of the captital, Seoul, perilously close to the Demarcation Line (border zone) with South Korea's archenemy, North Korea.

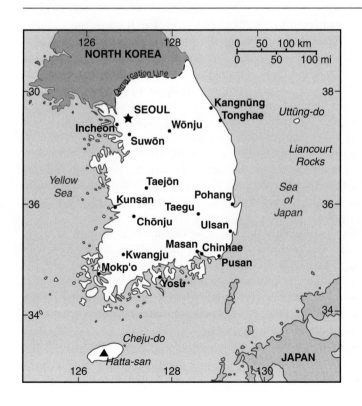

elected in South Korea. He won the Nobel Peace Prize in 2000 for his valiant efforts to improve relations between the two Koreas.

But South Korea's democracy is still relatively fragile. Kim Dae Jung's successor, Roh Moo Hyun, won the 2002 presidential election but immediately faced a recalcitrant legislature controlled by opposition parties. Dissension within the ruling party led to a split, weakening it badly in the run-up to parliamentary elections in April 2004. In these tumultuous circumstances, Roh Moo Hyun called for a referendum on his presidency, giving rise to speculation that without a strong popular mandate he might resign. In March 2004, the National Assembly, in a recriminatory and unprecedented move, impeached him. After a 63-day hiatus, the Korean Constitutional Court overturned the impeachment action and reinstated Roh, thus ending a perilous political crisis in one of East Asia's pivotal states.

Business executive and former mayor Lee Myung-bak won the December 2007 presidential election and was inaugurated on February 25, 2008. Although Korea remains a divided country, South Korea has made the transition from an authoritarian state with a democratic veneer to a political system based on regular elections, civilian authority, and the rule of law.

Taiwan: Asia's Orphan State

Taiwan is another of Asia's success stories, but it exists in a kind of diplomatic twilight zone. For more than three decades, despite determined efforts by the People's Republic of China to isolate it on the global stage, Taiwan has managed to prosper.

Taiwan became an independent state after World War II when the Chinese Communists, led by Mao Zedong, defeated Chiang Kai-shek's Kuomintang. Until 1972, the United States recognized Taiwan as the legitimate government of China, although it was clear the Communist regime in Peking was in control of the mainland. In 1972, the People's Republic of China replaced Taiwan at the United Nations, and the United States decided to "derecognize" Taiwan in order to restore full diplomatic ties with Beijing for the first time since 1949.

The decision was a devastating blow to Taiwan. Although it has remained independent, it no longer enjoys diplomatic recognition by other sovereign states and is no longer a member of the United Nations. The reason for this unique state of affairs is that the People's Republic of China has successfully pressed its claim that Taiwan is part of China, that there is only one China, and that Beijing is its capital.

Nonetheless, Taiwan—officially the Republic of China– continues to enjoy the military protection and diplomatic goodwill of the United States, as well as close economic ties. Taiwan's economy is one of the most dynamic in Asia, outpacing even South Korea's. If Taiwan were in Europe, it would rival Portugal and Greece and would outrank nearly all the EU's new members, including the Czech Republic, Hungary, and Poland. Its economic success is nothing new, but its movement toward liberal democracy *is*.

In 1988, Lee Teng-hui became the first native Taiwanese leader to assume the office of the presidency, and in the 1996 election he became the first popularly elected president in Taiwanese history. Lee instituted sweeping political reforms during his 12-year tenure, continuing a process initiated in the mid-1980s by his predecessor, Chiang Ching-kuo (Chiang Kai-shek's son). In 2000, Taiwan's voters elected Chen Shui-bian president—the first time ever that the Taiwanese government was not headed by the leader of the Kuomintang.

With the formation of the Kuomintang-led Pan-Blue Coalition of parties and a Pan-Green Coalition led by the ruling Democratic Progressive Party, politics in Taiwan has become polarized. The Pan-Blue Coalition favors eventual Chinese reunification, while the Pan-Green Coalition favors an official declaration of Taiwan independence. In September 2007, the Democratic Progressive Party approved a resolution asserting Taiwan's separate identity from China, expressing a desire to become a "normal country" under a new constitution, and calling for general use of "Taiwan" as the island's name.

Chen assumed office pledging to clean up government. But his tenure was marred by allegations of corruption that came against a background of public discontent over a slowing economy and legislative gridlock. Chen and several family members allegedly embezzled millions of dollars while he was in office, charges that led to a high-profile trial in March 2009. If convicted, Chen faces life in prison.

The Kuomintang increased its majority in Taiwan's parliament in January 2008, and its nominee Ma Ying-jeou won the presidency in March of that year, taking office in May. Ma's campaign platform promised more robust economic growth and better ties with the People's Republic of China.

Former president of Taiwan, Chen Shui-bian, was elected on a promise to root out corruption in government, but now stands accused of stealing public funds.

© GETTY IMAGES

LATIN AMERICA: WAITING FOR THE CURTAIN TO GO UP

Whereas Asia's transitional states started with economic reforms, Latin America's led with political change. Democracy has finally taken root, but most countries in Latin America still have not found a recipe for economic revitalization.

The states of Latin America (formerly colonies of Spain or Portugal) gained independence in the 1820s—long before Europe's colonial empires were dismantled elsewhere. With few exceptions, military-bureaucratic rule was the norm in Latin America until quite recently. Only in a few countries, such as Colombia, Venezuela, and Costa Rica, had popularly elected civilian government ever succeeded. The wave of liberalizing reforms that swept across Latin America in the 1980s ushered in a whole new age in the region's history and opened a fresh page in its politics.

The ABCs of Reform: Argentina, Brazil, Chile

In the 1980s, one Latin American military dictatorship after another stepped aside in favor of a democratically elected civilian government. Today, virtually every government in the region qualifies as a liberal democracy. What drove these regime changes was the need for economic reforms, evidenced, above all, in the huge foreign debts many Latin American countries had amassed. The burden of these debts, combined with outmoded economic structures and uncompetitive (protected) industries, high inflation, mass unemployment, widespread poverty, and gross inequality between the rich and poor, plunged the region into a crisis of self-confidence and under-consumption. Millions of people, especially *campesinos* (peasants) in rural areas, continue to struggle to survive at a bare subsistence level.

Chile has led the way in reforming its economy. Although in most of Latin America political change preceded economic reforms, Chile instituted market reforms *before* it democratized its political system. Under General Augusto Pinochet, who seized power in a bloody coup in 1973 by overthrowing the elected Marxist government of Salvador Allende, was one of the harshest military dictatorships in the region. During Pinochet's long rule, more than 3,200 people were executed or disappeared. Yet despite this reign of terror, the Chilean economy—spurred by market forces and a cozy relationship with the United States—performed remarkably well.

Chile is now the most prosperous country in South America, and despite a corrupt civil service and deep social divisions, its economy continues to grow. Exports, a major factor in this success story, rose sharply in subsequent years. In addition, Chile signed free-trade agreements with the EU in 2003, and similar agreements with the United States and South Korea went into effect in 2004.

Pinochet gradually eased his iron grip on the Chilean political system in the 1990s. Today, Chile holds free elections and civilians run the government. In 2006, Michelle Bachelet, running as the candidate of the Socialist Party of Chile, won in a run-off to become Chile's fourth elected president since the end of the Pinochet era. Chile is set to hold presidential elections again in 2009. A

Michelle Bachelet, elected president of Chile on the Socialist Party ticket in 2005–2006.

© GETTY IMAGES

leading candidate to succeed Bachelet is the man she narrowly defeated in the 2005 presidential election, billionaire businessman Sebastián Peñera, leader of the opposition Alianza coalition.

In Brazil, the generals finally relinquished control of the government in 1985. Three years later, the country adopted a new constitution that provides for a direct election of the president.

President Fernando Henrique Cardoso was an economist by training who tried to reform and restructure Brazil's economy. Despite his best efforts, Brazil continued to be plagued by heavy external debts, chronic budget shortfalls, extensive rural poverty, and glaring inequalities.

Brazil's current president is Luis Inácio Lula da Silva, a charismatic union leader and reformer known simply as "Lula" to millions of Brazilians. Lula campaigned for the presidency promising to tackle the country's problems. In office, he has tried to balance two competing needs: economic reforms and social justice. The voters rewarded Lula's efforts by re-electing him to a second term in 2006.

Bureaucratic obstruction, corruption, poverty, illiteracy, and inequality remain major obstacles to a Brazilian economic miracle. But Brazil has a lot going for it. Measured by both population and land mass, it is the fifth-largest country in the world. Measured by GDP at purchasing-power parity, it ranked as the ninth-largest economy in the world in 2008. Brazil now has a large, diversified service sector and modern industries including automotive, aeronautical, and electronics.

Argentina's military rulers bowed out in 1982 after the country's humiliating defeat by the British in the Falklands War. Argentina was then the richest country in South America in per-capita GDP, but in the years that followed, corrupt politicians and economic mismanagement reduced its economy to ruins.

FIGURE 8.6   Brazil: With the exception of Ecuador and Chile, every country in South America borders on Brazil, the fifth-largest country in the world by total land mass.

To hold down inflation and budget deficits, the government had little choice but to adopt unpopular policies, including high taxes and spending restraints. This policy of fiscal austerity, in turn, led to rising unemployment and social unrest. But the government feared that if it relaxed fiscal discipline, foreign investors would turn away. This dilemma led to a political crisis in 2001 as the slumping economy went from bad to worse. With the country on the verge of economic collapse, popular anger boiled over. Argentina became the scene of widespread riots and looting. Then it defaulted on its $155 billion foreign debt payments—the largest default of its kind in history. One president resigned, another could not calm the storm; finally, in 2003, Néstor Kirchner, the governor of Santa Cruz, was elected president.

Kirchner vowed to reform the courts, police, and armed services and to prosecute perpetrators of the dirty war (see Box 8.5). Argentina's economy rebounded after 2001, growing at an impressive rate of 8 percent a year under Kirchner's guidance. In March 2005, Kirchner announced the successful restructuring of the country's debt. In January 2006, Argentina paid off its remaining multi-million IMF debt ahead of schedule.

BOX 8.5 FOCUS ON   Argentina's Dirty War

Following a military coup in 1976, Argentina's junta (ruling clique) declared martial law and began the "dirty war" to restore order and eradicate its opponents. No one knows or will ever know for certain how many people perished in this brutal campaign of repression, but the Argentine Commission for Human Rights charged the junta with 2,300 political murders, over 10,000 political arrests, and the disappearance of 30,000 people.

Blanket amnesty laws protected the perpetrators for many years. In July 2002, former junta leader Leopoldo Galtieri and forty-two other military officers were arrested and charged with the torture and execution of twenty-two leftist guerrillas during the country's seven-year military dictatorship (1976–1983). In June 2005, the Supreme Court ruled the amnesty laws unconstitutional. The following year, numerous military and police officials went on trial. But it was too late to save the victims or to find any trace of the "disappeared."

The problems facing Brazil and Argentina are fairly typical of the entire region. In Latin America, political reform toward democratization has proven considerably easier than economic reform and revitalization, as attested to by the left-wing governments in Venezuela, led by Hugo Chávez, and in Bolivia, led by Evo Morales. Both countries are examples of a transition *away* from the market economy model.

The reasons are many and varied; the most intractable problems, however, are essentially social and cultural. Latin American society has long been exceedingly elitist and unjust. Inequalities are so great and wealth so highly concentrated that most people do not have enough purchasing power to be "consumers" in any meaningful sense of the word.

Chávez was re-elected president of Venezuela in 2006. In 2007, he proposed a package of sweeping reforms as part of a constitutional revision, including an end to presidential term limits, greater state control over the central bank, wider state expropriation powers, and public control over international reserves. These proposed changes were approved by the National Assembly but ultimately rejected by a narrow margin in a referendum held in December 2007.

Mexico

Last, we turn to Mexico, the United States' "distant neighbor" to the south.[27] Mexico is a good example of the historical contradiction found in so many Latin American countries—a romantic attachment to democratic ideals coexisting with an authoritarian regime disguised as a republic.

On paper, Mexico has been a liberal democracy since World War I. In reality, however, there has rarely been anything resembling genuinely competitive elections in Mexico—until 2000. Finally, after decades of one-party rule under the **Institutional Revolutionary Party (PRI)**, Mexican voters were given a real

Institutional Revolutionary Party (PRI)
The dominant political party in Mexico from 1929 to the present. The PRI had never lost an election until 2000, when Vicente Fox of the National Action Party won the presidency.

National Action Party (PAN)

The main opposition party in Mexico; the PAN's candidate, Vicente Fox, was elected president in 2000.

North American Free Trade Agreement (NAFTA)

Agreement signed in 1994 by the United States, Mexico, and Canada that established a compact to allow free trade or trade with reduced tariffs among the three nations.

choice. The result was a bombshell: opposition candidate Vicente Fox, representing the **National Action Party (PAN)**, won in a runoff election.

The **North American Free Trade Agreement (NAFTA)** boosted Mexico's economic prospects in the 1990s, but internal market reforms had been half-hearted, at best, due to Mexico's inefficient state-owned companies (for example, PEMEX, the oil monopoly), entrenched interests, and a corrupt bureaucracy fearful of losing its privileges. Membership in NAFTA gave Mexico easy access to U.S. markets, but it also gave the United States leverage to pressure the Mexican government into accelerating economic reforms.

President Fox came into office vowing to do just that. It would not be any easier in Mexico than elsewhere in Latin America, but Mexico had to agree if it wanted to compete as an equal NAFTA partner with the United States and Canada. The 2003 national elections produced no clear majority in Mexico's federal legislature—for the third time in a row.[28] President Fox's efforts to reform Mexican government and economy were effectively blocked. In 2006, the PAN candidate, Felipe Calderón, was elected president in the closest Mexican election ever, with a .58% lead over a center-left opponent. Calderón pledged to fight crime and corruption. If history is any guide, his campaign slogan, "Clean hands, firm hands," will become grist for the mill—for comedians and cartoonists.

The portrait of official corruption and economic mismanagement that have dogged efforts to boost living standards in Mexico fits many other countries in Latin America as well. When people do not have good jobs or benefits or steady income, they lack the kind of security we tend to take for granted. Without a circulation of wealth throughout the whole society, it is difficult, if not impossible, to complete the transition from a rural-based, slow-growth, inward-looking protectionist economy to a modern, urban, market-based, mass-consumption, export-oriented economy. The latter appears to be Latin America's destiny, but for the region's impoverished masses, it is taking way too long to get there.

In sum, Latin America has made a turn toward political pluralism, but the transition is both ambiguous and incomplete. For the vast majority of Latin Americans, the promise of a better life is still an empty one.

GATEWAYS TO THE WORLD: EXPLORING CYBERSPACE

www.valley.net/~transnat

This site, called "Russia on the Web," provides quick, easy access to all sorts of information on Russia, past and present, categorized by subject matter.

www.praguepost.com

An English-language newspaper published in Prague; a good source of current information on news and views in the Czech Republic and other Eastern European states.

www.chinasite.com

This site contains a comprehensive list of Web links and online sources of information on China.

www.kimsoft.com/korea.htm

This site is self-described as a nonpartisan "educational web" devoted to providing accurate information on politics and society in the two Koreas.

www.economist.com/countries/Taiwan

Features point-and-click access to *The Economist*'s recent articles on Taiwan, as well as a country fact sheet, the most recent economic forecast, and so forth.

http://lanic.utexas.edu/

This is the Latin American Information Network site maintained by the University of Texas. Lots of links. It helps to read Spanish and Portuguese, of course, but at many of the links are in English or can be clicked into English.

http://pdba.georgetown.edu/

The Political Science Database of the Americas maintained by Georgetown University. Essential for students and scholars doing research on Latin America.

SUMMARY

With the demise of the Soviet Union in 1991, Communist rule ended nearly everywhere in the world. Nonetheless, a few exceptions remain, including China, Cuba, and North Korea. The collapse of Communism brought the problems of transition in the former Soviet-bloc states to the fore. Other countries launched major political and economic reforms in the 1990s, including South Korea and Taiwan in Asia and Argentina, Brazil, and Chile in Latin America.

The Soviet political system was an outgrowth of the Stalinist totalitarian model. In trying to reform and restructure this system, Mikhail Gorbachev followed in the footsteps of an earlier Soviet leader, Nikita Khrushchev. In the Soviet system, the Communist Party ruled, and a person's ranking in the party was the best indication of that individual's political power. When Gorbachev rose to the top post in the Communist Party in 1985, he faced both acute economic problems and associated social problems, each related to the failure of central planning.

Gorbachev's reforms proved inadequate to save the former Soviet Union. His successor, Boris Yeltsin, failed to guide Russia through a smooth transition. His successor, Vladimir Putin, inherited a mess—economic dislocations, ethnic fragmentation, and poorly established state institutions. Putin turned out to be a decisive leader who was twice elected by large majorities but has ruled as a traditional strong Russian boss.

China instituted major free-market reforms and downplayed much of its Communist ideology after Mao's death, but remains a country headed by a single party that brooks no political or religious dissent. As China modernizes its armed forces and attempts to become a world power, it faces increasing social problems as well as economic and border tensions among its provinces.

India, South Korea, and Taiwan are three other examples of Asian societies in transition. All three countries made the transition to market-based (though semi-protectionist) economies first, but have more recently instituted meaningful political reforms.

The transition process in Latin America is the reverse of the pattern found in Asia. Argentina, Brazil, Chile, and Mexico are four key countries in the region. Except in the case of Chile, political reforms (aimed at establishing liberal democracy) in these countries came before economic reforms (aimed at creating a more competitive domestic market). In Venezuela and Bolivia, the transition process has gone against market reforms—a reversal of what has happened elsewhere in the region and world. The extremely unequal distribution of wealth in Latin America remains a barrier to both reform and development.

KEY TERMS

Commonwealth of
   Independent States
   (CIS)
nomenklatura
perestroika
glasnost
democratization
Duma

Federal Assembly
politburo
sovereign wealth
   funds
Democracy Wall
Tiananmen Square
   massacre
Asian flu

Institutional
   Revolutionary Party
   (PRI)
National Action Party
   (PAN)
North American Free
   Trade Agreement
   (NAFTA)

REVIEW QUESTIONS

1. What problems did the Soviet Union face in 1985, when Mikhail Gorbachev came to power and how did Gorbachev respond? With what consequences?
2. "One of the most important questions facing Russia today is whether it can become a stable democracy." What do you think? Explain.
3. What countries in Eastern Europe, Asia, and Latin America have made the most successful transitions so far? Explain your choices.
4. Comment on the economic transition in China since Mao's death. What reforms did Mao's successors institute and with what results?
5. Compare and contrast the transitions in Eastern Europe on the one hand and Latin America on the other relative to: (a) economic reforms; (b) political stability; (c) the rule of law; and (d) human rights.
6. Compare and contrast the transitions in Asia on the one hand and Latin America on the other relative to: (a) economic reforms; (b) political stability; and (c) the rule of law; and (d) human rights.

7. What region of the world has experienced the most success in making the transition from dictatorship to democracy in the past two decades? Justify your view.

8. Has Russia or China been more successful in making the transition from a centrally planned economy to a market-oriented economy? Compare and contrast the way the two countries have approached problems and assess the economic reform strategies of each. Which country has had a better outcome so far? What is the evidence?

RECOMMENDED READING

Baker, Peter, and Susan Glasser. *The Kremlin Rising: Putin's Russia and the End of the Revolution.* New York: Scribner, 2005. A highly readable account of Russian politics in the Putin era written by two former *Washington Post* bureau chiefs.

Bernstein, R., and R. H. Monroe. *The Coming Conflict with China.* New York: Knopf, 1997. A warning about the dangers posed by China's rapid rise.

Camp, Roderic et al. *Politics in Mexico: The Democratic Transition*, 4th ed. New York: Oxford University Press, 2003. A rich introduction to Mexican politics that continues to withstand the test of time.

Goldman, Marshall. *Petrostate: Putin, Power, and the New Russia.* New York: Oxford University Press, 2008. Argues that Russia has become an energy superpower and explores the implications and consequences. Author also notes the inherent dangers, for Russia and the world, of Russia's extreme dependence on a single export to sustain its otherwise bleak and weak economy.

Kynge, James. *China Shakes the World: A Titan's Rise and Troubled Future—and the Challenge for America.* New York: Houghton Mifflin, 2006. A treasure trove of information and insight into contemporary China by a former *Financial Times* bureau chief in Beijing.

Lucas, Edward. *The New Cold War: Putin's Russia and the Threat to the West.* New York: Palgrave Macmillan, 2009. A timely and well-constructed study of a resurgent post-Soviet Russia, originally published before world energy prices plummeted in 2008, but quickly revised and updated.

Malia, Martin. *The Soviet Tragedy: A History of Socialism in Russia, 1917–1991.* New York: Free Press, 1994. Views the actions of the USSR as directed by utopian ideology, not by an effort to overcome historical backwardness.

Page, Joseph. *The Brazilians.* Boston: Addison Wesley, 1996. Everything the reader wants to know about Brazil (and quite possibly more), this book is slightly dated now but continues to paint a vivid picture of Brazilian culture, politics, economics, and history.

Politkovskaya, Anna. *Putin's Russia: Life in a Failing Democracy.* New York: Henry Holt, 2004. Reprinted in 2007 in paperback (Owl Books) after the author, one of Russia's best-known dissident journalists, was murdered in what appeared to be a contract killing. This book is a no-holds-barred attack on Putin's allegedly authoritarian policies, official corruption, and the Kremlin's brutal conduct of the war in Chechnya.

Preston, Julia, and Samuel Dillon. *Opening Mexico: The Making of a Democracy.* New York: Farrar, Strauss, and Giroux, 2005. A good read by two former *New York Times* Mexico bureau chiefs.

Shirk, Susan. *China: Fragile Superpower.* New York: Oxford University Press, 2008. One of the best new books on contemporary China. The author gives an insider's view of the challenges facing China's current generation of leaders. A sobering and realistic treatment from cover to cover.

Wilpert, Gregory. *Changing Venezuela by Taking Power: The History and Policies of the Chavez Government.* New York: Verso, 2006. The title captures the book's contents. There are lots of recent books about Chávez in English, many highly critical; this one, by a freelance journalist and former Fulbright scholar in Venezuela, is readable, well informed, and strikes a better balance than some.

© AP PHOTOS

Developing countries have one foot in the modern world and one foot in traditional society. Rapid social and economic change is what the Western world calls progress. But throughout much of the non-Western world such change can be highly disruptive and is often accompanied by rising political instability. Overpopulation contributes to problems such as global warming, pollution, and pandemics, which also pose a threat to developed countries—and greatly complicates the search for solutions.

The Other World
Development or Anarchy?

Until recently when we looked at the world beyond our shores we saw not one world, but three. The First World, the West, was epitomized by the United States and included rich countries with stable societies and well-established democratic political institutions. The citizens of these fortunate states were free to criticize the government, but the vast majority were generally content. By contrast, the Second World of Soviet Russia and Eastern Europe was bleak and repressive; the people of these "captive nations" were downtrodden and deprived but did not dare to dissent. In this convenient if oversimplified model, the former colonial areas that did not belong in either the First or the Second World were lumped together as the Third World—the "underdeveloped" or "less-developed" countries.

Eventually, it became politically incorrect to use such pejorative terms. Today, we often use the term **developing countries** to refer to the former colonies—never mind that *all* countries are developing, no matter how rich or how poor. Indeed, if some countries are not developed enough to sustain themselves, other countries are, arguably, not sustainable for the *opposite* reason: development driven by the latest advances in science and technology has given rise to unanticipated and perhaps insoluble problems.

This chapter focuses on the problems arising in the context of too little development too late, rather than too much too soon. Developing countries by definition display all or most of the following features: endemic poverty; ethnic, religious, or tribal conflict; widespread illiteracy; political turmoil; and glaring inequalities. Although the picture is changing in much of Asia and, to a lesser extent, in Latin America, most sub-Saharan African nations continue to face great obstacles on the path to full political, economic, and social development.

In the worst cases, the economy goes into a tailspin, the government collapses, societies erupt, and entire populations are plunged into anarchy. In the 1990s, this chilling possibility became a reality in places like the former Yugoslavia, Rwanda, Sierra Leone, and the Côte d'Ivoire (Ivory Coast); more recently, civil violence has engulfed Iraq, Afghanistan, Sudan, and Somalia. In 2009, Pakistan, a big country (population: 170 million) of incalculable strategic importance and located in one of the most volatile regions of the world, appeared dangerously close to the political boiling point. Pakistan's per capita GDP in 2008 was roughly $900 (purchasing power parity of $2,700), lower than India's and roughly one-tenth that of New Zealand or South Korea. (Purchasing power parity, or PPP, in essence equates incomes and prices in other countries with the US$. If a US$ at the going exchange rate buys twice as much in Country X as it does in the United States, Country X's PPP will be twice what its nominal GDP is. Thus PPP is actually a much more meaningful number than nominal GDP. Obviously, people making, say, $2 a day in the United States could not survive. But $2 can keep a family from starving in many of the poorest developing countries.)

With few exceptions, endemic poverty is the root cause of the worst problems facing most developing countries—some 3 billion people, almost half the world's population, live on less than $2.50 a day (see Figure 9.1). According to the World Bank, the poorest 40 percent of the world population accounts for 5 percent of global income; the richest 5 percent account for three-quarters. According to UNICEF, some 25,000 children die *every day* due to poverty. About two-thirds of the 27–28 percent of all children in developing countries

developing country
Term used loosely to denote any country that has not achieved levels of economic prosperity and political stability found in North America, the European Union, Australia, New Zealand, and parts of Asia (particularly Japan, South Korea, Taiwan, Hong Kong, and Singapore); in general, a country where the ratio of population to land, jobs, and other factors (private capital, infrastructure, education, etc.) is unfavorable and where political stability, public services and individual safety are lacking. Developing countries are found mainly in Africa, Asia, the Middle East, and Latin America and are characterized by high levels of unemployment, widespread poverty and malnutrition, highly restricted access to education and medical care, official corruption, and social inequality.

FIGURE 9.1   **Percent of People in the World at Different Poverty Levels, 2005**
How many people in this world are poor? The answer depends on who is
counting and how national governments and international organizations define
poverty. At $1.00 a day "only" about 880 million people were poor in 2005; but if
we draw the poverty line at $2.00, that number climbs to 2.6 billion.
SOURCE: World Bank Development Indicators, 2008.

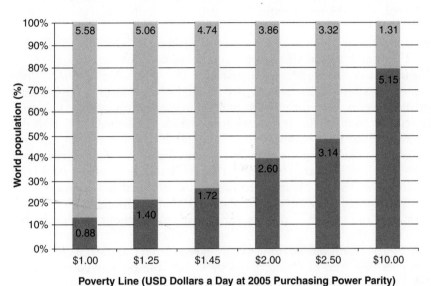

Poverty Line (USD Dollars a Day at 2005 Purchasing Power Parity)
Numbers inside bars are world population at that indicator, in billions

■ Below the poverty line   ■ Above the poverty line

who are stunted or underweight due to chronic malnutrition live in South
Asia or sub-Saharan Africa—two of the most conflict-ridden regions on the
planet.

Nearly one billion people entered the twenty-first century unable to read or
write, but the correlation between poverty and illiteracy is just part of the story.
In developing countries unemployment is the norm and only the most fortunate few have access to a health clinic or doctor. Preventive health care is also
beyond reach. The lack of mosquito nets is a major reason why there are half a
billion new cases of malaria and as many as 2 million deaths, mostly children,
in developing countries each year. Add an estimated 50–100 million cases of
dengue fever and approximately 25,000 deaths annually, and the magnitude of
the problem of poverty becomes all too apparent.[1]

World poverty, of course, raises moral issues, but this chapter is predicated
on two political questions. First, what are the causes of poverty and instability
in developing countries? Second, is a world divided into rich ("us") and poor
("them") sustainable—otherwise put, can the problems of poverty be contained
or will they inevitably spill over? A look at the context of politics in the so-called
Third World will shed light on the extreme challenges these countries face.

CLASSIFYING DEVELOPING COUNTRIES

During the Cold War, developing nations were also called "the South," which highlighted the great disparities between the industrially developed states in temperate climates (North) and the less-developed states in tropical and semitropical zones (South). According to a view known as neo-colonialism, the rich nations of the North continued to exploit the poor nations of the South even after the latter gained independence in the post-World War II period.

This view was promulgated by several prominent **Third World** figures in the 1950s and 1960s. Ghana's Kwame Nkrumah, for example, popularized it in a book entitled *Neo-Colonialism, The Last Stage of Imperialism* published in 1956. According to neocolonialism, the great and growing disparity between the world's rich and poor was an open invitation to a North–South conflict. But in the ensuring decades this dire prediction did not come to pass. It now appears that lumping developing nations into one category was an oversimplification that obscured more than it explained and that the imagined solidarity among the former colonies does not exist (and never did). Too, the problems of economic and political development seem more often rooted in internal than external circumstances, and economic performance and political stability vary greatly throughout the developing countries.

The North–South distinction was thus flawed from the start. As we know, the People's Republic of China, formerly among the poorest countries, has emerged as one of the world's fastest-growing economies (see Chapter 8), as has India in recent years. In both countries millions are still poor, but hundreds of millions have been lifted out of poverty. The poverty rate in China alone has fallen by over 600 million in the past two decades, accounting for roughly 90 percent of the total reduction in world poverty. India, too, has made major strides in alleviating poverty and creating the conditions for sustainable growth, as we'll see below.

What exactly does the term *developing* mean in a global economy undergoing such rapid change? For better or worse, the yardstick is a Western measure of economic and political success, a Western way of looking at development rooted in the Western experience. That does not make it good or bad, right or wrong, but it does raise questions about its applicability and acceptability outside the West.

In the **poorest developing countries** (what we will call PDCs), the vast majority still do not enjoy access to education, jobs, health care, or any of the other good things in life that are the hallmarks of modernity in the West. Moreover, few PDCs have governments that are accountable, stable, and clean (as opposed to corrupt). When we in the West say a country is "developing," we are usually thinking of a PDC, and what we mean is that it is not *yet* truly modern—that is, resembling the Westernized world. Westerners tend to assume that as, or if, these countries develop, they will look increasingly like us—urbanized, secularized, materialistic, and technology-dependent—and will want what we want.

Third World
Collectively, the developing nations of Asia, Africa, and Latin America, most of which were once European colonies; Third World nations tend to be poor and densely populated.

poorest developing countries (PDCs)
The 20 or so countries with the lowest per capita income in the world; all are located in sub-Saharan Africa with the exceptions of Afghanistan and Nepal.

UNDERSTANDING DEVELOPING COUNTRIES

Developing nations defy simple generalizations. There is no easy way to categorize countries that account for more than half the world's surface and hold about 85 percent of the world's population. With a few notable exceptions (such as Japan and South Korea), we can classify most states in Asia, sub-Saharan Africa, and Latin America as developing countries; however, we find most of the PDCs in South and Southeast Asia and sub-Saharan Africa, although some are in Latin America and the South Pacific.

Developing countries come in all shapes and sizes. Some are huge—Brazil has a territory of 3 million square miles (larger than the continental United States) and a population of 160 million; India's territory of 1 million square miles supports a population of more than 1 billion. Others are tiny—for example, Barbados in the Caribbean (territory, 166 square miles; population, 252,000) and Kiribati in the Pacific (territory, 266 square miles; population, 61,000). The Pacific island of Nauru wins the prize: It has 8,000 people living on 8 square miles of land.

Nauru is small but not poor, thanks to a brisk trade in phosphate exports. Most of the poorest developing economies depend primarily on agriculture. PDCs are often dependent on a single commodity or raw material for export, but a few, such as the oil-rich states of the Persian Gulf—Bahrain, Kuwait, Oman, Qatar, Saudi Arabia, and the United Arab Emirates—rely largely on a single natural resource, as does Russia, a country much poorer than Saudi Arabia and the others. Russia fits the definition of a developing country better than they do. The developing nations—especially the PDCs—have the world's highest population growth rates. Between 1969 and 2009, the world's population more than doubled to 6.7 billion. As Figures 9.2 and 9.3 show, population growth rates

FIGURE 9.2 World Population Growth Rates, 1950–2050
SOURCE: U.S. Census Bureau, International Data Base, December 2008 Update.

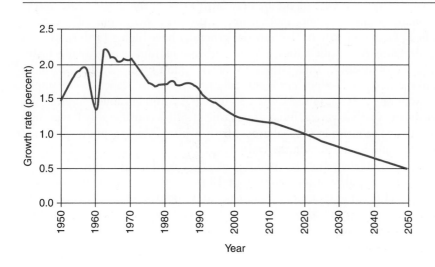

FIGURE 9.3   World Population, 1950–2000
SOURCE: U.S. Census Bureau, International Data Base, December 2008 Update.

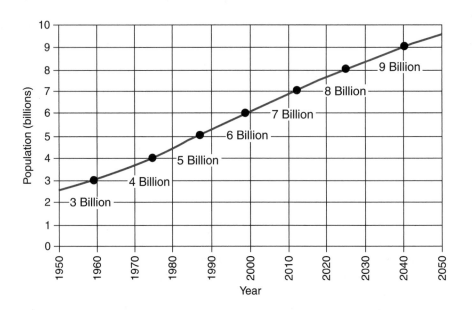

have been steadily declining since the 1960s, but the world's total population has continued to climb, more than doubling from 3 billion to 6.7 billion and heading for 9 billion by 2050.

Population pressure places onerous burdens on economic, social, and political structures in many poor countries, but comparisons can be misleading and often yield surprises. One of the highest birth rates in the world (3.42 births per woman of child-bearing age) occurs in the Gaza Strip, one of the most wretched places on earth. Arab countries generally have higher birth rates than Asian or Latin American nations. Lebanon's population was growing faster than Mexico's in 2008. Today, the only other region of the world with birth rates in the range of 3–4 percent is sub-Saharan Africa. In France, for example. the growth rate is 0.57, in the United States 0.97. Although much higher than in Europe or North America, India's birth rate (1.58) is considerably lower than that of many countries in sub-Saharan Africa, while China's is about the same as France's (and lower than in the United States).

Asia, the most densely populated region of the world, has about 57 percent of the world's population but only about 18 percent of its landmass, much of which is arid or mountainous. Apart from Asia (and with a few exceptions, such as Egypt, whose population is clustered around the Nile River), population density in developing countries is relatively low. Africa's average population density is only 24 per square kilometer, as opposed to India's 296, the United

Kingdom's 646, Japan's 880, and Singapore's 5,571. Africa also has more arable land per capita than any other developing region.

Of course, developing countries are not the only places where social, economic, and political development is occurring. Indeed, both development and decay are constants in this world. But, as we noted earlier, development takes place unequally; some nations, such as Afghanistan, Albania, Bangladesh, Belarus, Burundi, Chad, Congo, Eritrea, Ethiopia, Guinea-Bissau, Mali, Malawi, Burma, Rwanda, Sierra Leone, Somalia, and Sudan, are extremely poor and mired in misery. Note how many of PDCs on this list (the "poorest of the poor") are located in sub-Saharan Africa. Why are poor countries poor? We turn next to a consideration of this question.

THE LEGACY OF COLONIALISM

Only 23 countries among the current United Nations membership were independent in 1800. More than half these states were in Europe, with Afghanistan, China, Ethiopia, Japan, Iran, Nepal, Oman, Russia, Thailand, Turkey, and the United States rounding out the list.[2] Since then, the number of independent states has increased more than eightfold and now stands at 192. World War II (1939–1945) was a watershed, because it led to the rapid deconstruction of the European colonial empires (see Box 9.1). Most of the countries existing today came into being during this recent period, and all but a few were developing countries. Also, the breakup of the Soviet Union led to the creation of some 25 new independent states in Eastern Europe, Transcaucasia, and Central Asia by 1994.[3]

© REUTERS NEWSMEDIA, INC./CORBIS

To some extent, ethnic warfare between the Hindu Tamils and Buddhist Sinhalese in Sri Lanka, which began in 1983 when Tamil rebels demanded independence for the Sri Lanka northeast, reflects the imposition and policies of Britain's colonial rule. Ethnic strife is an all-too-common legacy of colonialism and remains a problem for many developing nations.

BOX 9.1 SPOTLIGHT ON   The Age of Imperialism

FIGURE 9.4   The World in 1914: Note how many European countries, including small countries such as Belgium, Denmark, and Holland (the Netherlands), had far-flung colonial empires at the beginning of the twentieth century. Note also that these empires encompassed nearly all of Africa and much of Asia but had all but disappeared from Central and South America.

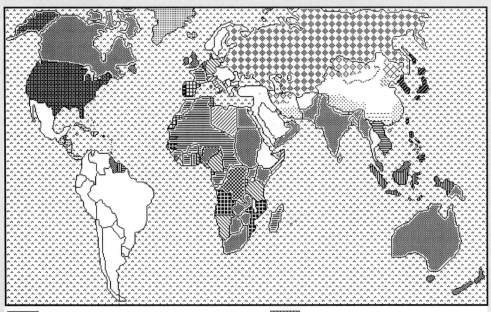

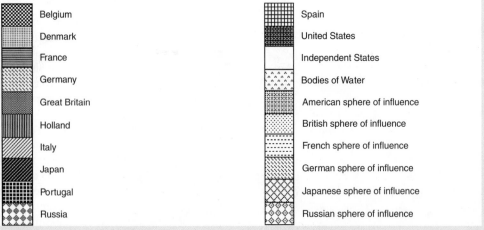

Belgium	Spain
Denmark	United States
France	Independent States
Germany	Bodies of Water
Great Britain	American sphere of influence
Holland	British sphere of influence
Italy	French sphere of influence
Japan	German sphere of influence
Portugal	Japanese sphere of influence
Russia	Russian sphere of influence

BOX 9.1: SPOTLIGHT ON *(Continued)*

A new wave of European colonial expansion occurred in the second half of the nineteenth century, sometimes called the Age of Imperialism. Earlier in that century, popular revolutions in the Americas against England, Spain, and Portugal had led to disillusionment with empires and colonies. Industrialization diverted attention from external expansion in favor of internal development, and the new emphasis on free trade removed much of the rationale for global empire building. British Prime Minister Benjamin Disraeli expressed the tenor of the times in 1852. "These wretched colonies," he said, "will all be independent too in a few years and are a millstone around our necks."

But as industry grew, Europe's economic and political leaders began to seek new sources of raw materials and new markets for their products. After 1870, free trade gave way to protectionist policies, and soon a race for new colonies began (see Figure 9.4). Various theories defending colonial expansion were expounded. Alfred T. Mahan's geopolitical concepts were used to "prove" great powers could not survive without overseas possessions. Charles Darwin's concept of the survival of the fittest was used to "prove" colonialism was in accordance with the inexorable laws of nature. Rudyard Kipling wrote about the "white man's burden" of spreading civilization to a benighted world. Even U.S. President McKinley claimed God had spoken to him on the eve of the Spanish-American War (1898), commissioning the United States to take the Philippines and Christianize "our brown brothers."

By the end of the nineteenth century, all Asia and Africa had been colonized. Even China had lost its sovereign status: It was subjugated through a series of treaties that gave various European powers special rights and prerogatives. Africa in 1914 was under the colonial sway of no fewer than seven European nations—Belgium, France, Germany, Great Britain, Italy, Portugal, and Spain. In fact, only two independent nations remained—Ethiopia and Liberia.

For centuries, the great powers of Europe competed for colonial holdings, ruling and administering over weaker and technologically less-advanced peoples and territories located in faraway places around the globe. These colonial empires were a source of great prestige and wealth. In the nineteenth century, European powers scrambled to colonize Africa. At the beginning of the twentieth century, Britain, France, Belgium, Germany, Portugal, Holland, Italy, Spain, and Turkey all possessed overseas colonial empires (see Box 9.1). This European intrusion—which came to be known as **colonialism** or **imperialism**—became synonymous with subjugation and exploitation in the minds of the indigenous peoples.

Colonialism *did* include Europeans dominating native peoples, and it *was* based on implicit or explicit notions of racial superiority or religious zeal (or both). However, there were great differences in the methods and means employed by the colonial powers. For instance, the British approach was far milder than Spanish colonial rule, which was notorious for its rapacity and cruelty. The Portuguese and French tried to assimilate colonized peoples. France even granted Algerians seats in the national legislature and positions in the

colonialism
The policy of seeking to dominate the economic or political affairs of underdeveloped areas or weaker countries (see also imperialism).

imperialism
A policy of territorial expansion (empire building), often by means of military conquest; derived from the word *empire*.

BOX 9.2 FOCUS ON   Never Ending Talk: The Doha Round

In 2001, the 150-member World Trade Organization (WTO) focused on agricultural protectionism in the **Doha Round** of trade negotiations. The developing countries (the **G33** nations), many heavily dependent on agricultural exports, feared rising protectionist sentiment in the West would cut off vital markets. Therefore, the G33 nations urged the United States and Europe to eliminate or greatly reduce tariffs and farm subsidies. But for political reasons—mainly the influence of powerful farm lobbies—the talks stalled. In July 2008 it appeared a compromise agreement was finally in the works. But the talks broke down and protectionism was once again on the rise following the near-collapse of the global banking system in the fall of 2008. The rich debate; the poor wait. Some things never change.

national cabinets. The Dutch in Indonesia allowed native rulers to remain in power. Great Britain pursued both strategies, relying on local authorities to maintain law and order and allowing natives to pursue careers in public administration, attend British schools and universities, and enter the professions.[4]

Nonetheless, the idea of being governed by a distant country was repugnant to most colonial peoples. In many instances, they finally gained independence by resorting to various forms of violence. In India, however, Mahatma Gandhi led a nationwide mass campaign of **nonviolent resistance** (*satyagraha*), a strategy later adopted by Martin Luther King, Jr. in the United States. (Ironically, both Gandhi and King were assassinated.)

nonviolent resistance
A passive form of confrontation and protest; also called civil disobedience at times.

Colonialism's legacy remains controversial. Europeans did introduce elements of modernization, including modest advances in health (hospitals), education (schools), and transportation (roads). But any gains often came at a high price for the native peoples—including disruption of traditional ways of life and epidemics caused by the introduction of European germs into populations with no resistance.[5]

The extent to which developing nations *after* independence continued to be exploited by rich Western countries is debatable, although with the ending of the Cold War this issue faded into the background. Today, trade issues top the political agenda in relations between the rich and poor countries. Although agriculture constitutes only 8 percent of the world's total merchandise trade, it is this segment of the market that is most important to poor countries and most distorted by protectionist policies of rich countries (see Box 9.2).

Doha Round
The trade negotiations within the framework of the World Trade Organization (WTO), formerly the General Agreement on Trade and Tariffs (GATT).

G33
A group of 33 developing countries that attempt to coordinate trade and economic development policies.

The consequences of colonialism continue to disrupt the contemporary world. Colonial empires were created without regard to the preexisting ethnic identities, territorial boundaries, or loyalties of native populations. When the European powers withdrew, they typically created a crazy quilt of new states with borders that made no sense, because they cut across traditional religious, ethnic, and tribal territorial lines. (Iraq is a prime example.) Chronic political instability, coups, revolutions, civil wars, and even genocide—these are bitter fruits of colonialism. Simply listing *some* of the developing countries that have been wracked by conflict in recent years proves the point: Afghanistan, Angola, Burma, Burundi, Cambodia, Chad, Congo (formerly Zaire), Côte d'Ivoire, Ethiopia, Iraq, Liberia, Nigeria, Pakistan, Rwanda, Sierra Leone, Somalia, Sudan, and Sri Lanka.

The fragility of these societies has led to dire warnings about the "coming anarchy" in Africa and elsewhere.[6] But perhaps raising the specter of anarchy is too pessimistic, although Somalia, to cite one example, has existed in a state of anarchy for nearly two decades. Pakistan is another extremely fragile country in 2009—one teetering on the edge. Except for the presence of Western military forces, anarchy would also be a distinct possibility in Iraq and Afghanistan.

POLITICAL DEVELOPMENT: FOUR CHALLENGES

What is **political development**? Rich countries often display certain common traits: a stable government, a merit-based civil service system, basic public services (police and fire protection, education, health, and sanitation), and legal structures (law codes and courts). All these traits are typically lacking in poor countries. Imagine growing up in a society where not only schools but also drinking water and basic sanitation do not exist. How can people who have no money, no police protection, and who cannot read or write lift themselves out of poverty or demand decent government?

By its very nature, the development process is destabilizing. It is therefore no great surprise that governments in developing countries are often authoritarian, prone to coups, and beset by crises. Poor countries typically face four fundamental developmental challenges: nation building, state building, participation, and distribution.[7]

The first and most basic challenge is **nation building**—the process by which all the inhabitants of a given territory, regardless of individual ethnic, tribal, religious, or linguistic differences, come to identify with the symbols and institutions of the state and to share a common sense of destiny. The countless conflicts in Africa and Asia in the post–World War II era testify to the extreme difficulty (if not impossibility) of artificially "building" something as natural as a nation.

Having a *charismatic* leader present at the creation is a key variable in the initial nation-building stage (try to imagine the founding of the United States without George Washington). Notable Third World examples include Egypt's Gamal Abdel Nasser (who ruled from 1954 to 1970), Kenya's Jomo Kenyatta (1964–1978), India's Jawaharlal Nehru (1947–1964), Indonesia's Sukarno (1945–1967), and Libya's Muammar el-Qaddafi (still in power). Flags and celebrations also help instill a sense of national identity, and threats from a neighboring state—real, imagined, or manufactured—can galvanize unity, at least until the perceived danger subsides.

political development
A government's ability to exert power effectively, to provide for public order and services, and to withstand eventual changes in leadership.

nation building
The process by which inhabitants of a given territory—irrespective of ethnic, religious, or linguistic differences—come to identify with symbols and institutions of their nation-state.

state building

The creation of political institutions capable of exercising authority and allocating resources effectively within a nation.

The second challenge, **state building**, is the creation of political institutions—in particular, a central government—capable of exercising authority and providing services throughout the length and breadth of society. A functioning state bureaucracy promotes economic development and social unity by such mundane means as creating the infrastructure (roads, bridges, telephone lines) necessary for an integrated national economy. To achieve this, the government must be capable of levying and collecting taxes. But in countries with traditional economies based on subsistence agriculture, there is often little or nothing to tax, which leads to a vicious cycle that can only be broken with infusions of foreign capital (trade, aid, and investment). However, foreign investment (an external variable) depends on political stability (an internal variable). It turns out that in developing countries, there are all sorts of vicious cycles.

A third challenge facing developing countries is **participation**. For new societies to prosper and grow economically, the people must be actively engaged in the development process. This kind of mobilization gives rise to a political dilemma: As people become more actively involved and feel the effects of government (good and bad), they begin to demand a greater voice in determining who governs and how. But what if rising expectations strain the capacity of the state to respond? Hence, the challenge of participation is how to harness popular energies without setting in motion the forces of political disintegration or revolution?

A fourth major development challenge is **distribution** to reduce the extreme inequalities that often characterize **traditional societies**. Extremes of wealth and poverty can easily lead to a pervasive sense of injustice and, in turn, to mass revolt (see Chapter 14), as Marxism's popular appeal in the Third World during the Cold War demonstrated. In some cases, Third World governments have attempted to address the challenge of distribution through land reform, but often only half-heartedly. Readjusting tax burdens and instituting income redistribution are two other obvious approaches to this problem, but the cost of Western-style social welfare programs is prohibitive for most developing countries.

DEMOCRACY AND DEVELOPMENT

As we have seen, political development and popular participation often go hand in hand. But not all forms of popular participation are bottom-up (democratic); some are top-down (coercive). The latter are associated with authoritarian or totalitarian regimes. Democratic states are, by definition, limited in what they can do by constitutions, laws, and public opinion. For this reason, democracy and development often do not easily coexist, and dictatorships have been (and still are) all too common in the Third World.

To say that democracy is a sign of development is true, but it begs the question: what explains development? In fact, democracy is a sign of wealth. Not all democracies are rich (although most are), nor are all rich nations democratic (although again, most are). But there are very few examples of democracy and poverty co-existing for very long.

The Correlates of Democracy

One useful way to gauge a developing nation's potential to achieve democracy is to focus on **democratic correlates**. Where these correlates exist in the greatest number and measure, the probability of democracy is greatest; conversely, where they are largely absent, democracy has the smallest chance of succeeding.[8] Major economic correlates include:

- *National Wealth*. Prosperity generally correlates with democracy. Conversely, poverty is not conducive to democracy. But if democracy is a luxury poor nations cannot afford, how do we explain India, which has been democratic, extremely diverse, and very poor since independence?
- *A Market or Mixed Economy*. Market economies allow both public and private ownership of the means of production and distribution. They also have the flexibility to combine elements of a market economy with varying types and degrees of governmental intervention. Most important, however, is what such economies do *not* allow: Large-scale centralized state planning of the economy is excluded, and economic decisions, especially those about the production and distribution of products and services, are left primarily to private enterprises and consumers.
- *A Middle Class*. This correlate stresses not the amount of wealth in a nation but rather its distribution. A sharp class division with no "buffer" between the very rich and the very poor is not conducive to the success of representative democracy.
- *The Internet*. Access to knowledge and information has always been important to economic growth and development; in the age of globalization, access to the Internet is essential.

> **democratic correlates** A condition or correlate thought to relate positively to the creation and maintenance of democracy within a nation.

Significantly, freedom of communication is also a *political* correlate of democracy. Other political correlates include civilian control over the military, a strong independent judiciary, and the existence of a differentiated civil society (civic clubs, trade unions, business organizations, and the like).[9] *Cultural* correlates are needed as well: tolerance of diversity, respect for the rule of law, and belief in democracy. Finally, *history and geography* also matter. Democracy has a better chance of succeeding in countries with previous democratic experience. Having democracies in neighboring states also appears to be an advantage. In general, the greater the distribution of wealth and education in a given society, the more likely that the seeds of democracy will sprout and freedom will flourish.[10]

The Strategy of Development

Which comes first, democracy or development? The stunning success of China in reducing poverty argues for a strategy of *economic* reforms first—indeed, civil rights are hardly a top priority for people who are starving, sick, or homeless.[11] A vibrant economy is far more likely to have an immediate impact on the quality of life, social services, infrastructure, and educational opportunity than, say, free elections.

The reforms necessary to spur economic development inevitably have spillover effects on society and the political system. Thus, privatization and foreign investment give rise to a nascent middle class. To be competitive, it is necessary to cultivate a professional class with the same type of educational opportunities and financial rewards. To gain access to foreign markets, developing countries face pressures to open up its their own markets. Western products and services—from music to fashion—give rise to individualism, materialism, and a desire for freedom of expression, especially among the youth. In these and countless other ways, market-oriented economic reforms impart a bias toward democratization. Where such reforms bring new hope and prosperity, they help ensure that if and when democracy finally arrives, it does so without plunging society into a state of anarchy.[12]

Africa: Democracy's Dustbin?

Between 1974 and 1990, more than 30 countries in southern Europe, Latin America, East Asia, and Eastern Europe replaced authoritarian with democratic governments. One noted observer wrote that it was "probably the most important political trend in the late twentieth century."[13] Everywhere, that is, except Africa.

Then, in the early 1990s, a democracy wave rolled across sub-Saharan Africa, where at least nine countries—including Benin, Cape Verde, and Gabon in West Africa—held free elections, in most cases for the first time ever.[14] It was South Africa that witnessed the most stunning changes, however, as black majority rule supplanted apartheid (white-supremacist rule). Democratic reforms were changing the face of politics in Benin, Botswana, Guinea-Bissau, Madagascar, Mali, Namibia, and Sao Tome as well during this time.[15]

Elsewhere in Africa, however, things fell apart. In 1993, Nigeria's military rulers rescinded election results that displeased them. Côte d'Ivoire's government did the same. Elections in Kenya, the Cameroon, and Gabon were marred by irregularities and corruption. Rwanda was the scene of genocidal violence in 1994. In 1996, military governments in Chad, Gambia, and Niger rigged national elections to achieve the outcomes they desired. During the 1990s, Somalia sank deeper into chaos and anarchy. Bloody civil wars wrought havoc in Liberia and Sierra Leone, and conflict in the Democratic Republic of the Congo (formerly Zaire) was accompanied by unspeakable atrocities. More than a decade later, the Congo is still a war zone. Thus, despite democratic gains, clan or tribal tensions destabilized much of sub-Saharan Africa in the 1990s.[16]

THE DEVELOPMENT STEEPLECHASE

The steeplechase is a challenging track-and-field event, of course, a race over fences and ditches and hurdles—in a word, an obstacle course. As such, it is an excellent metaphor for the problems facing developing nations. They, too, are in a race—against the clock and the competition. And they, too, face all sorts of obstacles.

© HOWARD DAVIES/CORBIS

Wars, revolutions, ethnic rivalries, droughts, and epidemics (e.g., AIDS) cause widespread human misery while also threatening the democratic future of numerous countries. Pictured here are refugees escaping from a bloody civil war that consumed Rwanda in 1994.

Development and Conflict: Deadly Diamonds

Wars interfere with a nation's development efforts by diverting the government's attention and sapping its limited resources. Nearly all the wars since World War II have been fought in the Middle East, Africa, and Asia. Rivalries in the Middle East and Asia have also culminated in wars at various times, including those between Iran and Iraq, Pakistan and India, Vietnam and China, and China and India. Many Latin American countries also have longstanding disputes and rivalries with neighbors. Chile, for example, has engaged in military clashes with all three adjacent states: Argentina, Bolivia, and Peru.

In the 1980s, a conflict between Ethiopia and Somalia over the Ogaden region, worsened by a famine that spread across the Horn of Africa, led to a humanitarian crisis for some 1.5 million Somali refugees. This conflict was the background for the ill-fated 1992–1994 intervention by U.S. military forces, which was ostensibly to safeguard food deliveries to the starving (see discussion later in this chapter). Anarchy stalked West Africa during these years.[17] In Sierra Leone, violence was driven by the diamond trade. For years, so-called "conflict diamonds" from rebel-held mines allowed the brutal Revolutionary United Front (RUF) to arm and equip armies (see below).[18]

Between 1994 and 2007, sub-Saharan Africa was the scene of four major wars (conflicts causing at least 800,000 deaths each)—in Rwanda, Sudan, Congo, and Angola—and eighteen smaller wars. Armed conflicts in sub-Saharan Africa have not only taken a terrible toll in human life; they have also destroyed and disrupted fragile economies.

Development and Ethnicity: Deadly Differences

Many developing countries were carved out of former colonial holdings with little concern for the geography or history of the area or indigenous ethnic, religious, tribal, or linguistic patterns. Too often the result has been interethnic strife and even civil war.

Modernization (another name for development) poses daunting problems for indigenous peoples. Western concepts of "nation" and "nationalism" have little relevance, and yet success in forging a single national identity is crucial. Often, militant groups or movements hostile to social integration and modernization (Westernization) obstruct efforts at nation building. For example, Islam's emphasis on piety, devotion to Allah, prayer five times each day, and strict rules of moral conduct are at odds with secularization, the sexual revolution, materialism, and self-gratification. In other words, the kinds of social change associated with modernization in the West.

Specific examples best illustrate the practical problems associated with diverse populations. Nigeria and India are both developing countries with very diverse populations.

Nigeria: World's Poorest Oil-Rich Country

A large country in West Africa (population 135 million in 2007), Nigeria includes several distinct ethnic groups that predominate in different parts of the country. There are also many smaller tribes, and nearly 400 distinct languages are spoken.[19] Tensions simmer between Christians and Muslims. Regional animosities, exacerbated by religious, ethnic, and linguistic differences, erupted in a bloody civil war in 1967, when eastern Nigeria seceded as the independent state of Biafra. The war, which lasted about 3 years and ended in defeat for the rebels, claimed at least 600,000 lives.

For most of the period after 1967, corrupt military regimes ruled Nigeria. Despite huge state-owned oil reserves that produced a steady flow of export revenues, Nigeria's economy sank deeper and deeper into a morass, and the vast majority of the population was forced to live from hand to mouth. The average per capita income in oil-rich Nigeria (about $1,260 in 2009) is only slightly larger than that of India, an oil-importing country with a population more than six times larger. High world oil prices have boosted Nigeria's oil-dependent economy in recent years, but most Nigerians have experienced few benefits.

Corrupt military regimes ran the country almost continuously from 1967 to 1999. The generals would promise—and occasionally stage—a national election, but it would turn out to be a sham (as in 1993). Mounting international pressure no doubt played a large role in compelling Nigeria's military rulers to allow free elections in 1999 and to permit the results—the election of the first popular presidential candidate in nearly 20 years—to stand.

But corruption did not end with the return of civilian government, and a decade later, the morally debasing effects of easy money from a grossly mismanaged oil industry with few links to the national economy were still everywhere apparent. Indeed, for a time Nigeria—the richest poor country in Africa—was actually *importing* gasoline.

India: Elephant or Cheetah?

With its 1.14 billion people—17 percent of the world's population—India accounts for only about 2 percent of global GDP and about 1 percent of trade,[20] although it is experiencing an impressive growth spurt in recent years (Box 9.3). India is the second-largest country in the world and one of the most diverse. The Indian constitution recognizes 16 languages, though census data indicate more than 1,500 languages are spoken, including dialects. The "big three" official languages are English, Hindi, and Urdu. Hindi is spoken by about one-third of all Indians. English is the elite language, spoken by all university-educated Indians. Urdu is the language of Indian Muslims, the nation's largest minority group.

India is also home to various religions. Hinduism predominates, but there is also a large Muslim population (about 12 percent of the total), as well as Sikh, Jain, Parsi, Buddhist, and Christian minorities. Since Indian independence in 1947, communal violence—between Hindus and Muslims or Hindus and

FIGURE 9.5   India: Note India's lengthy border with Pakistan; note also the geographical triangle formed by New Delhi (north central) and Mumbai (formerly Bombay) on the Arabian Sea and Calcutta on the extreme eastern edge by the Bay of Bengal.

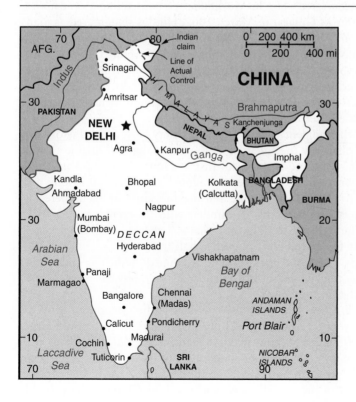

Sikhs—has erupted periodically. In some instances, members of one religious group have massacred members of another. In 1984, Prime Minister Indira Gandhi, a Hindu, was assassinated by her Sikh bodyguards. In 1991, her son, former Prime Minister Rajiv Gandhi, was assassinated while campaigning to regain office.

The traditional caste system in India also created a barrier to development—everyone was born into a particular caste and remained there for life. Professions, occupations, and social status were all governed by the rules of the caste system. Members of a lower caste could not aspire to a profession or occupation reserved for a higher caste, nor could anyone marry outside his or her caste. Obviously, this rigid framework greatly impeded social mobility—the very mobility needed to transform a traditional society into a modern one. A vast underclass, called the untouchables, had no rights or opportunities in traditional India. The Indian government has since outlawed untouchability, but old attitudes die slowly, especially in tradition-bound rural societies. (Seven in 10 Indians still live in small villages.)

Societal divisions tend to be reinforcing rather than crosscutting. Thus, Indian Muslims not only practice their own distinct religion but also live in their own insular areas, have a distinct ethnic heritage, and speak their own language. Much the same can be said of Sikhs, Jains, and other groups. In extreme cases, these divisions can lead to calls for separatism or communal violence. Militant Sikhs have called for an independent state in northwestern India (where they are concentrated). Hindu-Muslim hatred has led to periodic massacres. Thus, in the state of Gujarat in March 2002, Hindus slaughtered as many as 2,000 Muslims. In August 2003, two bombs blamed on Muslim militants killed 52 people in Mumbai (formerly Bombay). On November 26–29, 2008, ten coordinated shooting and bombing attacks occurred in Mumbai, killing at least 173 people and injuring more than 300. The split between Hindus and Muslims continues to destabilize India—and therefore South Asia as a region—more than six decades after independence.

India was long the indigent giant of Asia, a society with a rich history and a civilization symbolized by the splendor of the Taj Mahal but unable to cope with the challenges of the modern world. Just as Hong Kong, Taiwan, South Korea, and Singapore were often called "dragons" or "tigers" not long ago, India was likened to an elephant—huge and magnificent, but encumbered by the weight of its massive body. Anyone familiar with the contemporary Asian scene, however, is more likely to think of India as a cheetah than an elephant. Neither image quite fits; paradoxically, each is half true.

India is the world's second most populous country. India's population is growing much faster than China's. Until recently, demography has overwhelmed development in India.

Although a recent five-year growth spurt saw India's economy grow by nearly 9 percent a year (see Box 9.3), China's GDP was still 3.5 times larger than India's in 2008–2009. China needs 8 percent annual growth to provide jobs for the roughly 7 million new members of its workforce each year; India's workforce is growing by about 14 million a year—that is, it is producing about 25 percent of the world's new workers. Like China, India is highly

BOX 9.3   India: Moving Up in the World

India's achievements since Independence (1947):

- Maintaining parliamentary democracy
- Reducing absolute poverty by more than half
- Dramatically improving literacy and health care delivery
- Becoming one of the world's fastest-growing economies, with average growth rate of 9 percent over the past four years
- Emerging as a global player in information technology, business process outsourcing, telecommunications, and pharmaceuticals

SOURCE: The World Bank, "India Country Overview 2009."

As India's finance minister, Manmohan Singh authored the country's successful economic reform program in 1991. He became India's Prime Minister in 2004, the first Sikh ever to head an Indian government.

© GAUTAM SINGH/AP PHOTO

vulnerable to a drop in global demand for its exports. The global financial crisis caused the Indian economy to slip dramatically to 5.3 percent in the last quarter of 2008. Unlike China, India was severely limited in its efforts to stimulate the slowing economy due to a budget deficit approaching 8 percent of GDP.[21]

Today's India is a study in contrasts. In the 1990s, Manmohan Singh, now the prime minister, opened up India's economy by privatizing publicly owned enterprises, easing protectionist trade practices, cutting red tape, and making it possible for foreign firms in certain sectors to set up operations in India for the first time since independence. India's current five-year plan (2007–2012) called for a sustained growth rate of 9 percent, which looked ambitious but not unrealistic until the downturn in 2008–2009. Even before the global financial meltdown, India's economic miracle was in danger of being derailed by galloping inflation, overextended commercial bank credit, widening current account (foreign trade) deficits, and mushrooming budget deficits.

Sri Lanka: Sinhalese versus Tamils

Although we have focused on India and Nigeria, many other developing countries face similar problems. Sri Lanka, for example, is split between the majority

Sinhalese (74 percent), who are mostly Buddhist, and the Tamils (18 percent), who are mostly Hindu and predominate in the northern and eastern parts of the country. Militant Tamil groups seeking to secede—notably the Tamil Tigers—have carried out terrorist acts and conducted guerrilla warfare against the central government since 1983, when an outbreak of communal riots left at least 2,000 Tamils dead.[22] After a quarter-century of civil war, Sri Lanka has still not defeated this insurrection, but in February 2009, the United States, the European Union, Japan, and Norway issued a joint statement saying it was "just a short time before the Tigers lost all the territory still under their control." Like India, Sri Lanka displays a pattern of cultural diversity that impedes the search for a national consensus.

In sum, ethnically diverse societies are the rule in the Third World. Over half of the nations created by de-colonization in the postwar period are home to more than five major ethnic groups.[23] This ethnic diversity has made the problems of nation-building in these countries complex and conflict an all-too-common occurrence.

Development and Identity: Paradise Lost

When modernization occurs, traditional ties are undermined, people are uprooted, and beliefs are challenged. Villagers tend not to trust strangers; social interaction is generally confined to family, clan, or village members. Fear of the unfamiliar, fatalism in the face of nature's accidents, and a low sense of individual efficacy combine to make traditional peasants and villagers averse to risk taking. Modernization often forces villagers to move to cities in search of work; to interact with strangers; and to redefine themselves. Traditional people are less time-conscious than modern urbanites. Punching a clock is alien. Personal success and the spirit of free enterprise associated with entrepreneurship and competition are also alien to people accustomed to thinking in group terms (family, clan, or tribe).

ascriptive societies
A society in which an individual's status and position are ascribed on the basis of religion, gender, age, or some other attribute.

Status in traditional societies is **ascriptive**, that is, it is *ascribed* by society on the basis of religion, age, and the like. In contrast, modern societies are (or claim to be) merit based. The Indian caste system is an extreme example of ascriptive status.

Gender is another key status factor. Male dominance is prevalent in most traditional societies, where a low level of technology, ranging from the lack of modern machines to absence of birth control, combines with high infant mortality rates to reinforce traditional gender roles and attitudes. Thus, in developing nations, the communal nature of traditional life precedes, and often precludes, individualism, entrepreneurship, and self-expression.

Development and Poverty: How Green Is the Revolution?

Despite significant differences in economic development and national wealth, many developing nations are still poor more than a half century after independence. Why?

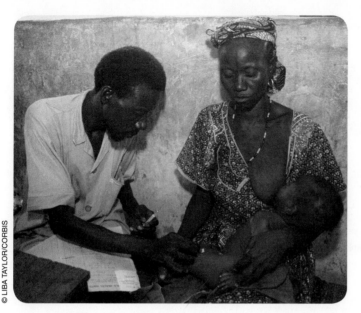

© LIBA TAYLOR/CORBIS

Traditional people tend not to trust strangers and often do not understand modern technology, including basic health care, which is considered routine in the developed world. Although such reactions are natural, they can impede modernization.

Pre-modern economies are based on agriculture and mining. Excessive dependence on agricultural commodities and raw materials makes these societies vulnerable to the ups and downs of global markets. Some developing countries raise only one major export crop. Bangladesh, for example, produces nothing but jute for export. When the price of jute declines, Bangladesh—one of the poorest developing nations—has nothing to fall back on. Ethiopia's monoculture economy is based on coffee exports; Cuba mainly produces sugar for export; Honduras exports bananas, and so on. Some developing countries are economically addicted to illegal cash crops: peasants in Colombia, Ecuador, and Peru, for example, produce coca (cocaine) for export; Afghanistan is the world's primary source of heroine (made from poppy seeds). Though many PDCs have more than one crop or mineral resource, few are highly diversified in both agriculture and industry. As a result, great economic disparities still exist, not only from one country to another but also from region to region (see Table 9.1).

To modernize, poor developing countries need to import industrial goods. To pay for manufactures, PDCs need to export food, fiber, and minerals. But the **terms of trade** tend to work against them—the price of industrial goods is high, while the price of agricultural products and raw materials is often low. Commodity prices on the world market fluctuate wildly at times, creating uncertainties and mounting foreign debt.

Some developing countries also face a serious population problem. The industrial democracies have population growth of less than 1 percent, and several western European countries reached zero or negative population growth by 1990. By contrast, many of the poorest developing countries still have birthrates in the range of 2–3 percent annually (compare Figures 9.6 and 9.7). In some African countries (Niger and the Democratic Republic of the Congo), as well

terms of trade
In international economics, the valuation (or price) of the products (commodities, manufactures, services) that countries buy on the world market relative to the valuation of the products they sell; the structure of prices for different kinds of goods and services in international trade—for example, if manufactures are generally high-priced relative to minerals and agricultural products, then the terms of trade are unfavorable for countries that produce only farm commodities or raw materials.

TABLE 9.1   Per Capita Gross National Income by Region (Purchasing Power Parity)

Region	Per Capita GNI (in U.S. dollars)
Sub-Saharan Africa	1,870
North America*	45,850
Latin America and the Caribbean	9,321
Asia	5,960
East Asia and Pacific	4,937
EURO area	32,508

*This number is for the United States; Canada's per capita GNI was around $35,000, but Canada represents less than 7 percent of the population of North America.

SOURCE: The World Bank 2009.

as in parts of the Middle East (notably the Palestinian territories and Yemen), annual birthrates are greater than 3 percent.

Rapid urbanization poses acute problems, because PDCs do not have the resources to support public services and create new schools, hospitals, housing complexes, and most important, jobs. The **Green Revolution**, the application of agricultural technology and modern irrigation and synthetic fertilizers to produce high-yield strains of wheat, rice, and corn, has helped ease the food-population crisis in India, Mexico, the Philippines and elsewhere, but as we now know, at a high cost to the environment.[24] The promise of ending world hunger through modern technology has yet to be fulfilled (see Box 9.4).

People who subsist on severely limited diets do not have the energy to be productive, leaving many developing nations caught in a vicious cycle: they are poor because they are not productive enough, and they are not productive enough because they are poor.

Land tenure also poses a significant problem in many developing countries. In some areas, land ownership—and local power—is highly concentrated; in others, land is fragmented into parcels too small to be profitable. In Africa, communal ownership of rural land is (or was) common. But as commercial plantations encroach on village land, cash crops such as maize, rice, and coffee replace traditional food crops. Young men and women are forced leave in search of work. Many become migrant farm workers, earning paltry wages during the crop-growing season.

Finally, damage to the environment is an ever-growing problem in the developing countries. Native plants and animals are disappearing in many places, water and air pollution is rising, soil degradation and deforestation are occurring at an alarming rate from Indonesia to Brazil and in many parts of sub-Saharan Africa, causing floods, soil erosion, and loss of wildlife habitat.

Green Revolution
A dramatic rise in agricultural output, resulting from modern irrigation systems and synthetic fertilizers, characteristic of modern India, Mexico, Taiwan, and the Philippines.

FIGURE 9.6   World Population, 1995: 5,692,210,000.

SOURCE: © 1997 *The Washington Post*. Reprinted with permission.

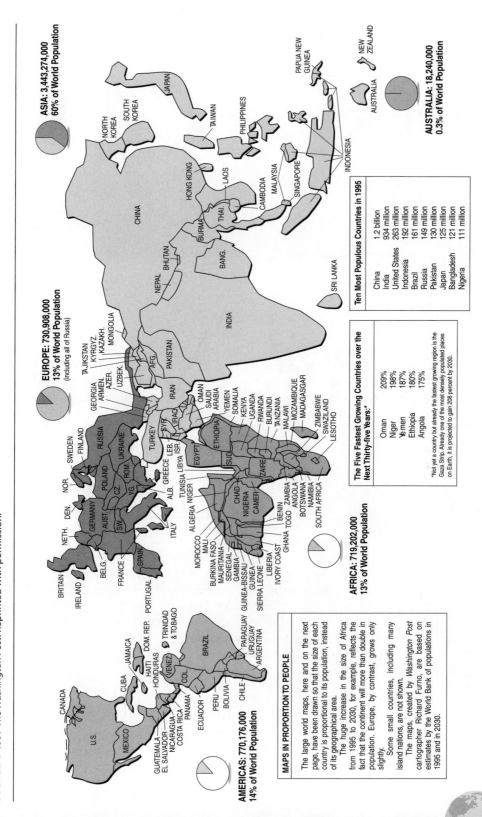

ASIA: 3,443,274,000
60% of World Population

EUROPE: 730,908,000
13% of World Population
(including all of Russia)

AMERICAS: 770,176,000
14% of World Population

AFRICA: 719,202,000
13% of World Population

AUSTRALIA: 18,240,000
0.3% of World Population

Ten Most Populous Countries in 1995

China	1.2 billion
India	934 million
United States	263 million
Indonesia	192 million
Brazil	161 million
Russia	149 million
Pakistan	130 million
Japan	125 million
Bangladesh	121 million
Nigeria	111 million

The Five Fastest Growing Countries over the Next Thirty-five Years:*

Oman	209%
Niger	198%
Yemen	187%
Ethiopia	180%
Angola	175%

*Not yet a country but already the fastest growing region is the Gaza Strip. Already one of the most densely populated places on Earth, it is projected to gain 208 percent by 2030.

MAPS IN PROPORTION TO PEOPLE

The large world maps, here and on the next page, have been drawn so that the size of each country is proportional to its population, instead of its geographical area.

The huge increase in the size of Africa from 1995 to 2030, for example, reflects the fact that the continent will more than double in population. Europe, by contrast, grows only slightly.

Some small countries, including many island nations, are not shown.

The maps, created by *Washington Post* cartographer Richard Furno, are based on estimates by the World Bank of populations in 1995 and in 2030.

FIGURE 9.7   World Population, 2030: 8,474,017,000 (a 49 percent increase from 1995 world population). These two maps show the projected change in population growth between 1995 and 2030. The maps have been drawn so that each country's size is proportional to its population. As these maps dramatically illustrate, much of the projected population increases will occur in developing nations.

SOURCE: Boyce Ransberger, "Damping the World's Population: Birthrates Are Falling Now but More Needs to Be Done in the Long Term," *Washington Post National Weekly Edition.* September 12–18, 1994, 10–40. ©1994 *The Washington Post.* Reprinted with permission.

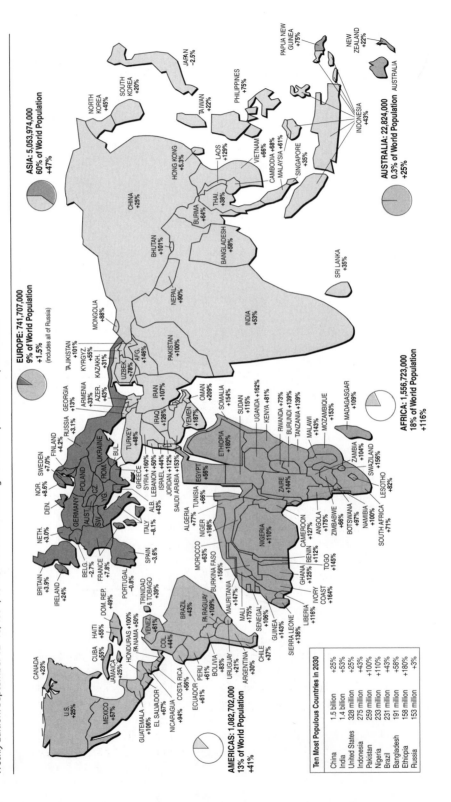

Ten Most Populous Countries in 2030

China	1.5 billion	+25%
India	1.4 billion	+53%
United States	328 million	+25%
Indonesia	275 million	+43%
Pakistan	259 million	+100%
Nigeria	233 million	+110%
Brazil	231 million	+43%
Bangladesh	191 million	+58%
Ethiopia	158 million	+180%
Russia	153 million	+3%

Box 9.4 FOCUS ON   **World Hunger**

- Across the world, 63 million people are hungry.
- Every day, almost 16,000 children die from hunger-related causes—one every five seconds.
- Poor nutrition and calorie deficiencies cause nearly one in three people to die prematurely or develop disabilities, according to the World Health Organization.
- Hunger manifests itself in many ways other than starvation and famine. Most poor people who battle hunger also deal with chronic undernourishment and vitamin or mineral deficiencies, which result in stunted growth, weakness, and heightened susceptibility to illness.
- Countries in which a large portion of the population goes hungry are usually poor and lack

social safety nets; when a family cannot grow enough food or earn enough money to buy food, there is nowhere to turn for help.

- In 2006, about 9.7 million children died before they reached their fifth birthday. Almost all these deaths occurred in developing countries, four-fifths of them in sub-Saharan Africa and South Asia, the two regions that suffer the highest rates of hunger and malnutrition.
- In the developing world, 26 percent of children under 5 are moderately to severely underweight and an overwhelming 32 percent are moderately to severely stunted.

SOURCE: Adapted from Bread for the World Website at <http://www.bread.org/learn/hunger-basics/hunger-facts-international.html>, accessed on April 28, 2009.

When Development Fails: The Lessons of Darfur

We in the West believe in progress and tend to see history as a record of linear development. Change in this view goes in one direction—from worse to better. But societies in the throes of modernization are also, paradoxically, among the most vulnerable to disintegration and decay—from better to worse. "Modernization in practice," noted political scientist Samuel Huntington, "always involves change in and usually the disintegration of a traditional political system, but it does not necessarily involve significant movement toward a modern political system . . . Yet the tendency is to think that because social modernization is taking place, political modernization must also be taking place."[25]

Thus, Rwanda and Burundi became genocidal killing fields in 1993–1994 as a result of hatred and mistrust between Hutu and Tutsi tribes. Between 2003 and 2007, a tragedy of similar proportions unfolded in eastern Sudan, where a government-sponsored campaign to crush rebels turned into a policy of **ethnic cleansing**, the unconscionable practice of rape, pillage, and mass murder, in the remote Darfur region. As many as 2.5 million refugees—mostly women and children who managed to escape mass murder—had reportedly been displaced as of October 2006. Development is necessary, but it is no guarantee of peace or prosperity.

ethnic cleansing
The practice of clearing all Muslims out of towns and villages in Bosnia by violent means; the term has also been used to characterize genocidal assaults on minority populations in other parts of the world, including the Darfur region of Sudan.

DYSFUNCTIONAL STATES

In recent times, we have seen states and societies self-destruct, destabilizing neighboring states in the process and even threatening world peace. Dysfunctional states are wretched places where extremes are the norm, where government is either repressive or too weak to maintain a modicum of law and order. Under such circumstances, the most violent elements in society take over. Both criminal and political violence stalk the city streets and threaten villages unprotected by police or a vigilant free press. When the world is not watching, atrocities can go unnoticed for days, weeks, even months. This image may be disturbing, but it is all too real. In this section, we look at four examples of political systems that are (or were) dysfunctional: Somalia, Sierra Leone, Afghanistan, and Zimbabwe. These examples by no means exhaust the list of candidates. A complete list would, of course, include Russia and the Central and Eastern European countries before the collapse of Communism in 1989–1991, as well as the former Yugoslavia.

Somalia

The Horn of Africa is home to several of the poorest countries on earth, including Sudan, Somalia, Eritrea, and Ethiopia. In the 1980s and 1990s, this region was afflicted by drought, famine, international conflict, civil wars, and all manner of violence. In the early 1990s, the most critical food shortages occurred in Somalia, where civil war and drought conspired to cause terrible human suffering. In August 1992, the United Nations Children's Fund (UNICEF) triggered a massive international relief effort when it warned that two million Somalis, of a total population of slightly more than eight million, faced starvation within 6 months.

Against this backdrop of violence and misery, rebels ousted Somalia's longtime dictator, Siad Barré, in January 1991. Fighting and famine followed, leaving 300,000 people dead and millions at risk of starvation. A near-total breakdown of law and order plunged the country into anarchy and placed women and children at the mercy of armed bandits, who disrupted relief efforts by international agencies, stole food intended for starving children, and murdered relief workers. At the end of 1992, outgoing U.S. President George H. W. Bush ordered a military intervention to safeguard relief supplies and workers. The scene was so chaotic that restoring law and order proved impossible. Long after the U.S.-led UN forces departed in March 1995 (following the brutal killing of several U.S. soldiers), Somalia remained a country without a national government. Maps showing which areas were controlled by which factions looked more like a jigsaw puzzle than a political configuration.

Somalia was one of the poorest countries in Africa in the 1990s, with a per capita GNP of less than $500 and an illiteracy rate of more than 75 percent. Moreover, it is underdeveloped both politically and economically. The structure of Somali society is based on kinship ties, or clans—in fact, the civil war was a clan war. If Somalia cannot find a formula for political stability, it cannot rebuild its economy. The reverse is also true: stability depends on economic and social progress.

Somalia today remains a failed state. Anarchy is a boon to thieves, and Somalia is the world's number-one haven for pirates. In 2009 it once again became the focus of world attention when Somali pirates seized a merchant ship flying the U.S. flag and held the captain hostage, provoking President Obama to authorize the use of force if it appeared the captain's life was in imminent danger. Three of the hostage takers were killed by sharpshooters and a fourth was captured and brought back to the United States to face trial on criminal charges. The rescue operation succeeded: the captain's life was saved. But who will rescue Somalia?

Sierra Leone

We've seen that functioning democracy is rare in sub-Saharan Africa. Even where it once appeared to be working, it has failed—in some cases miserably, and nowhere more so than in Sierra Leone.

When legislative elections were held in Sierra Leone in 1986, the aptly named All People's Party approved 335 candidates to contest 105 elective seats. The party typically offered at least three contestants for each seat, a common practice among one-party states in sub-Saharan Africa. Voters in Sierra Leone actually had more choices—relative to personalities, at least—than voters in most U.S. legislative races.

Nonetheless, in the 1990s, Sierra Leone began a steady descent into anarchy. Between 1996 and 1998, the government changed hands four times. Then all hell broke loose, and rebel members of the so-called Revolutionary United Front began chopping off hands right and left. They chopped off heads, too. They kidnapped small boys and girls and abused them in unspeakable ways. The RUF was notorious for turning boys into drug-addicted killers and sex slaves—so-called "child soldiers." Kidnapped girls became sex slaves and sometimes fighters as well.

The conflict officially ended in January 2002. It is estimated that 50,000 people were killed in the decade-long civil war, but there is no way of knowing for sure and no way of measuring the cost in shattered lives. The United Nations installed a peacekeeping force of 17,000 troops—the largest ever. The incumbent president, Ahmad Tejan Kabbah, was reelected with 70 percent of the vote in May 2002. The disarmament of 70,000 soldiers was completed in 2004, and a UN-sponsored war crimes tribunal opened.

In September 2007, voters in Sierra Leone elected a new president, handing the governing party a surprising defeat. It was at least a minor victory for democracy, the first elections since the departure of the United Nations peacekeeping force in 2004.

Also in 2007, the ongoing trial of Charles Taylor, the former Liberian president, for "crimes against humanity"—specifically, abetting the violent rebel group (RUK) mainly responsible for the atrocities committed in the civil war—began at a UN criminal court at The Hague. In June 2007, three former rebel leaders were found guilty of rape and enlisting child soldiers—the first time an international tribunal ruled on the recruitment of child soldiers under age 15.

The UN has listed Sierra Leone as the world's "least livable" country for the past several years, due to widespread poverty and what can only be described as the abysmal quality of life endured by its citizens. Sierra Leone is an object lesson in what can happen when a dysfunctional state sinks into anarchy. Neither the civil institutions nor the political culture necessary to support and sustain democracy were present. For several decades, the appearance of democracy masked the reality of a society capable of erupting into volcanic civil violence at any moment.

Afghanistan

As everyone knows, the United States invaded Afghanistan when it became known that the 9/11 attacks were carried out by a militant Islamic group called al-Qaeda and that the Taliban, Afghanistan's fundamentalist political regime, was allowing al-Qaeda's leader, Osama bin Laden, to use Afghanistan territory as a base of operations. What was less well known at the time (and what decision makers in Washington appear to have forgotten or overlooked) is the historical background. For nearly three decades prior to the landing of U.S. Special Forces on Afghan soil, Afghanistan had been one of the world's most dysfunctional states. Even prior to the overthrow of the monarchy in the 1970s, the country was poor and backward, but thereafter it spiraled into two decades of bloody turmoil. By 2001, the entire country was a shambles and millions of people—especially women and children—were living on the very edge of a precipice.

Home to many ethnic groups, Afghanistan reflects the disparate populations around its periphery—Pakistan, Iran, Turkmenistan, Tajikistan, Uzbekistan, and China. The largest group, the Pashtuns, constitute about 40 percent of the total population (about 26 million people). Thus, there is no majority group, only minorities of different sizes. Roughly 99 percent of all Afghans are Muslims; about 15 percent are Shi'ite Muslims (as are most Iranians).

Afghanistan was a monarchy from 1747 to 1973, when the country came apart at the seams. Various factions fought for supremacy after 1973, until the Soviet Union made the fateful decision to intervene on behalf of its favorite thug (a Communist) in 1979. A brutal and protracted war ensued; the Soviet Union finally withdrew in defeat in 1989 after a decade of debilitating (and humiliating) warfare. The United States had secretly backed the Islamic resistance, called the mujahedeen, by supplying weapons and other aid to the rebel forces. Amazingly, the United States and Osama bin Laden were fighting side by side at this time.

Opponents overthrew the Communist regime and seized power in 1992. The new strongman refused to relinquish power when his term officially expired, but Taliban forces assaulted the capital and ousted him in 1996. The Taliban regime instituted a totalitarian system of rule couched in the language and concepts of Islam but based on a perversion of the Qur'an (holy scripture) and Sharia law (based on the teachings of Muslim clerics or mullahs). Women and girls were forced to wear the burka (a one-piece, head-to-toe garment) in public and were forbidden to work outside the home, to go to school, or to express opinions at variance with the government. The government banned television, movies, music, dancing, and most other forms of "decadent" entertainment.

The Taliban was a brutal and repressive regime that clearly did not enjoy the support of the people. It seized control of a fragile and dysfunctional state and turned it into a tool of domestic and international terrorism. Instability in Afghanistan poses a grave danger to neighboring Pakistan as well. As a failed state, Afghanistan illustrates a stark and sobering lesson: dysfunctional states can become a threat to regional stability and even to world order. The solution—economic growth and development—is obvious but elusive.

Zimbabwe

In March 2007, a popular opposition leader named Morgan Tsvangirai was beaten and hospitalized in Zimbabwe after the country's 83-year-old virtual dictator, Robert Mugabe, ordered police to break up a protest rally in the capital of Harare. Despite all, Tsvangirai defeated Mugabe in the 2008 presidential elections, but Mugabe refused to relinquish power, eventually agreeing to a power-sharing scheme which he quickly violated (see Chapter 5).

During his 27 years in power, Mugabe has plunged Zimbabwe into utter ruin. When he finally goes, he will leave a bitter legacy of chronic unemployment, hyperinflation (the highest in the world), and an impoverished society where the oft-repeated promise of democracy was repeatedly broken.

Mugabe is an example of the kind of corrupt and incompetent leadership that has plagued sub-Saharan Africa since the end of the colonial era. Sadly, at the end of the first decade of the twenty-first century, what distinguishes Zimbabwe's government from that of most other countries in the region is a difference in degree, not in kind.

Development is generally a good thing. Next we ask, is it possible to get too much of a good thing?

OVERDEVELOPMENT: THE ENEMY WITHIN

All societies are in a constant state of flux, rising or falling, but never standing still. They develop in different ways, at different rates, and at different times. In the modern era, Western societies have led the way—they developed economically and technologically along lines congruent with the political institutions that evolved at the same time. In this sense, development, as defined in the contemporary world, was a natural process that originated within these societies.

For developing countries, development is often just the opposite: an alien process that originates from the outside—that is, from world market forces, International Monetary Fund pressures, foreign capital looking for cheap labor, and the like. Development is always disruptive, but even more so when it is forced on societies, whether by foreign powers or by external circumstances.

The story of development does not end with the arrival of the postindustrial state. Western countries have developed beyond the agricultural stage, beyond the industrial stage, and are now high-tech economies offering a vast array of commercial and financial services. Of course, they are still engaged in agriculture, mining, and industry, but these sectors of the economy have been eclipsed in importance by high-tech goods, such as computer software, science- and research-based products such as pharmaceuticals, and financial services. These new products bring a higher quality of life to consumers who can afford them, but they come with a price—congestion and crowding in cities, air and water pollution, stress-related illnesses, illegal drug use, overconsumption, energy shortages, waste disposal problems, global warming, extinction of countless plant and animal species, and many other maladies commonly associated with development.

Thus late-stage development is no more free of challenges than early-stage development. The challenges are different, but no less daunting. Overdeveloped countries—where development has outrun society's capacity to deal with undesirable side effects of rapidly accelerating technological and social change—might do well to focus more attention on solving the problems they face and less on telling so-called underdeveloped countries what to do and how to do it.

Development and democracy are often viewed as synonymous in the West, and the language of political science and the literature of development suggest all aspects of development are desirable. Sometimes, in an effort to be politically correct, political scientists use the term *pre-modern* to describe societies in an early stage of development. Development theory thus *assumes* development is good—always and everywhere—and that tradition and superstition, the "dead hand of the past," are impediments to progress. But some critics point out that musings on development often amount to little more than praise for all things Western, and that Western experts on the subject are guilty of ethnocentrism.[26]

In fact, Western philosophers have long struggled with this problem. Thus, in 1750, the French philosopher Rousseau declared, "Our souls have been corrupted in proportion to the movement of our sciences and arts towards perfection."[27] Much of Rousseau's political philosophy indeed springs from the notion that modern civilization has eroded, rather than enhanced, our humanity. As each passing day brings more scientific evidence of the dark side of development—over-population, climate change, pandemic influenza, and other infectious diseases—Rousseau is looking more and more like a prophet.

GATEWAYS TO THE WORLD: EXPLORING CYBERSPACE

www.undp.org

This is the UN Development Program site, which includes news features on developing countries, pages for various UN development programs, and the UN's poverty clock.

http://www.bread.org/learn/hunger-basics/

This is the world hunger page at the Bread for the World Website. A good source of basic facts and information about a killer rooted in poverty that stalks hundreds of millions of people.

www.globalservicecorps.org

This Website of the Global Service Corps provides information for prospective volunteers in various developing countries and an online newsletter addressing current events and issues in the developing world.

http://www.worldbank.org/

The World Bank's gateway to its extensive data bases on all member states. On the front page just click on "Countries." Also, check out "Data and Research."

www.g77.org

The Group of 77 Website includes a description of the organization's composition, aims, membership, and special programs.

www.fundforpeace.org/programs/fsi/fsindex.php

This is the site of the "Failed States Index," first introduced by the Fund for Peace in 2005.

http://www.census.gov/ipc/www/idb/summaries.html

This is the U.S. Census Bureau International Database. A quick and easy way to get country-by-country demographic data in a standard format.

www.wto.org/english/thewto_e/whatis_e/tif_e/org6_e.htm

Visit the Website of the World Trade Organization to learn about current trade talks and ponder whether global markets are mainly driven by economics or politics.

SUMMARY

Developing countries are so named because they are less developed economically and less modernized socially than are Western liberal democracies. Although some generalizations about developing countries are possible (for instance, most are poor, have high population growth, and rely on agriculture), these nations are highly diverse. The historic legacy of developing nations—especially European colonialism—is a political map that makes little sense, including borders that do not reflect indigenous ethnic, religious, and tribal patterns and thereby have fostered political instability, including riots, rebellions, civil wars, and even genocide.

Political development requires that leaders effectively unify the population (nation building), provide for government institutions that respond to people's needs (state building), encourage citizen participation, and ensure an adequate distribution of wealth, power, and property. Specifically, political development requires a government that can govern effectively and transfer political power smoothly. Usually, political development also assumes movement toward democratic government. Democracy in developing countries correlates with the existence and distribution of certain identifiable economic, political, social, and attitudinal variables. To institute democratic reforms, a nation may start with either political or economic reforms, but an economy-first strategy provides the more likely prospect for success. Many developing nations have adopted democratic reforms in recent decades, but this trend is reversible.

Development can be an arduous task. Developing nations are motivated to undertake development programs by economic hardships, political rivalries, and rising expectations; however, in the process, they encounter significant barriers. Socially, populations are often fragmented. Psychologically, individuals are heavily dependent on tradition and frequently oppose change. Economically, problems range from unfavorable terms of trade and high foreign debt to rapid population growth, a low level of technology, entrenched land tenure problems, and environmental difficulties. When leaders cannot successfully meet the social, economic, and political demands of development (for any number of reasons), development fails and nations disintegrate.

Some societies decay and disintegrate rather than develop. The Soviet Union provides the most stunning example; others include Afghanistan, Congo, Ethiopia, Haiti, Lebanon, Liberia, Sudan, Somalia, Sierra Leone, and Yugoslavia.

Overdevelopment (the opposite of "underdevelopment") is a problem afflicting many Western societies today. Contemporary ideas about development tend to assume its desirability despite such postindustrial problems as pollution, congestion, and drug addiction, as well as over-population, climate change, and pandemic diseases.

KEY TERMS

developing countries	G33	state building
Third World	Doha Round	democratic correlates
colonialism	poorest developing	ascriptive
imperialism	countries (PDCs)	Green Revolution
nonviolent resistance	political development	ethnic cleansing
terms of trade	nation building	

REVIEW QUESTIONS

1. What are the salient characteristics of the so-called Third World? How do these relate to the development process?
2. Are most WTO members rich or poor? Do the majority of the world's nations and peoples have fair access to global markets?
3. Elucidate the correlates of democracy. How compelling is this line of analysis? Comment.
4. What are the incentives for modernization? What sources of resistance can you identify?
5. Does development always lead to democracy? Is the reverse true? List some examples.
6. All things considered—India's political system, the current state of the Indian economy, and the broader question of social justice—would you say India's successes outweigh its failures or vice versa? Explain.
7. Nigeria is most likely to become sub-Saharan Africa's first major global power. Do you agree or disagree with this statement? Explain.
8. What are the barriers to development? If development is so difficult, why do nations undertake it?
9. How are development and decay related? Are states and societies ever static? Comment.
10. Name three dysfunctional states and use one as an example to illustrate the nature of this type of state.

RECOMMENDED READING

Beah, Ishmael. *A Long Way Gone: Memoirs of a Boy Soldier.* New York: Sarah Crichton Books, 2007. A shocking firsthand account of the horrors of Sierra Leone's descent into anarchy in the 1990s and how children were both innocent victims and brutal perpetrators of violence. The factual accuracy of the author's account has been called into question, but not the authenticity of his ordeal.

Binder, Leonard. "The Crises of Political Development." In *Crisis and Sequences in Political Development*, edited by Leonard Binder et al. Princeton, NJ: Princeton University Press, 1971. A groundbreaking study that identifies five "crises of development": identity, legitimacy, participation, distribution, and penetration.

Brass, Paul. *The Politics of India Since Independence.* New York: Cambridge University Press, 2008. A concise but broad study of political, economic, and culture change in India over the past half century.

Casper, Gretchen. *Fragile Democracies: The Legacies of Authoritarian Rule.* Pittsburgh, PA: University of Pittsburgh Press, 1995. Relying on numerous examples from developing countries, the author explores why democracy "remains problematic" in such states.

Chomsky, Noam. *Failed States: The Abuse of Power and the Assault on Democracy.* New York: Henry Holt and Company, 2006. A leading intellectual offers a scathing critique of U.S. policy toward the Third World: Washington has repeatedly asserted the right to intervene against "failed states," but, ironically, the United States is *itself a* failed state—and the most dangerous one of all.

Collier, Paul. *The Bottom Billion: Why the Poorest Countries are Failing and What Can Be Done About It*. New York: Oxford University Press, 2008. A book on world poverty variously described by reviewers as "thought-provoking," "path-breaking," and "insightful."

Diamond, Jared. *Guns, Germs, and Steel: The Fate of Human Societies*. New York: Norton, 1999. In this fascinating bestseller, Diamond argues that geography and environment are the critical variables that determine winners and losers in world history. His penetrating analysis flies in the face of theories that stress biological factors. If Diamond is correct, Western civilization flourished for reasons that had nothing to do with the racial superiority; Europeans were (are) no stronger or smarter than the peoples they colonized—just luckier.

_____. *Collapse: How Societies Choose to Fail or Succeed*. New York: Viking Penguin, 2005. In this sequel to *Guns, Germs, and Steel*, Diamond turns the question around and asks, What causes great civilizations and thriving societies to decline or disintegrate?

Easterly, William. *The White Man's Burden: Why the West's Efforts to Aid the Rest Have Done So Much Ill and So Little Good*. New York: Penguin, 2007. An incisive analysis of failed Western aid policies in the Third World by a former senior economist at the World Bank.

Ghani, Ashraf and Clare Lockhart. *Fixing Failed States: A Framework for Rebuilding a Fractured World*. New York: Oxford University Press, 2008. The authors rely heavily on management theory and make policy recommendations based on practical real-life experience.

Godwin, Peter. *When a Crocodile Eats the Sun: A Memoir of Africa*. New York: Little, Brown and Company, 2008) This is a book about the death of the author's father and of the country the author knew as a child growing up in Zimbabwe during it war of independence. It is also a book about Robert Mugabe, the violent self-proclaimed president-for-life who is to blame. A gripping personal account written by a professional journalist.

Guha, Ramanchandra. *India after Gandhi: A History of the World's Largest Democracy*. New York: Harper Perennial, 2008. This elegant history of India since 1947 not only chronicles the nation's trial and tribulations but also celebrates its achievements.

Huntington, Samuel P. "How Countries Democratize." *Political Science Quarterly* 106 (1991–92): 578–616. Examines how various nondemocratic regimes (classified as one-party systems, military regimes, and personal dictatorships) democratized between 1974 and 1990, with an emphasis on Third World nations.

Kaplan, Robert D. *The Coming Anarchy*. New York: Vintage Books, 2001.

_____. "Will More Countries Become Democratic?" *Political Science Quarterly* 99 (1984): 193–218. Articulates the economic, cultural, and social factors assumed to be associated with democracy.

Kaplan, Seth. *Fixing Fragile States: A New Paradigm for Development*. Westport, CT: Praeger Security International, 2008. Argues for placing policy emphasis on institution building instead of sending troops and foreign aid. Gives special attention to seven dysfunctional places, including West Africa.

Lipset, Seymour. *American Exceptionalism: A Double-Edged Sword*. New York: W. W. Norton, 1996. The thesis that the United States was "born modern," having shed all vestiges of feudalism at birth, and that it remains fundamentally different from European societies.

_____. *Political Man: The Social Bases of Democracy*, rev. ed. Garden City, NY: Doubleday, 1983. A wide-ranging discussion of politics and nation-states arguing compellingly that national wealth is the most reliable predictor of democracy.

Luce, Edward. *In Spite of the Gods: The Strange Rise of Modern India*. New York: Doubleday, 2007. A good, balanced account of contemporary India's emerging economy, the problems India still faces in its modernization drive (including pervasive corruption and criminality in government and society alike), and the sheer complexity of this wondrously diverse society.

Rostow, Walt Whitman. *The Stages of Economic Growth: A Non-Communist Manifesto*, 3rd ed. Cambridge: Cambridge University Press, 1991. A provocative study posits that all developing economies go through basically the same stages, beginning as traditional societies and progressing through self-sustaining growth to the age of mass consumption. The theory suggests that eventually all societies will become industrialized, capitalist, and democratic.

Sachs, Jeffrey. *The End of Poverty: Economic Possibilities for Our Time*. New York: Penguin, 2006.
An exploration of how societies emerge from poverty by an internationally renowned scholar.
Sachs is the director of Columbia University's Earth Institute. *Time* magazine has called him
"the world's best-known economist."

Wolpert, Stanley. *A New History of India*, 8th ed. New York: Oxford University Press, 2008.
Perhaps the best and still the most readable and popular history of India.

© TOM MAGGART

Patriotism is a civic virtue. From an early age, we are taught to show reverence for national symbols like the flag.

Political Socialization
The Making of a Citizen

The year is 1932. The Soviet Union is suffering a severe shortage of food, and millions go hungry. Joseph Stalin, leader of the Communist Party and head of the Soviet government, has undertaken a vast reordering of Soviet agriculture that eliminates a whole class of landholders (the *kulaks*) and collectivizes all farmland. Henceforth, every farm and all farm products belong to the state. To deter theft of what is now considered state property, the Soviet government enacts a law prohibiting individual farmers from appropriating any grain for their own private use. Acting under this law, a young boy reports his father to the authorities for concealing grain. The father is shot for stealing state property. Soon after, the boy is killed by a group of peasants, led by his uncle, who are outraged that he would betray his own father. The government, taking a radically different view of the affair, extols the boy as a patriotic martyr.

Stalin considered the little boy in this story a model citizen, a hero. How **citizenship** is defined says a lot about a government and the philosophy or ideology that underpins it.

THE GOOD CITIZEN

Stalin's celebration of a child's act of betrayal as heroic points to a distinction Aristotle originally made: The *good citizen* is defined by laws, regimes, and rulers, but the moral fiber (and universal characteristics) of a *good person* is fixed, and it transcends the expectations of any particular political regime.[1]

citizenship
The right and the obligation to participate constructively in the ongoing enterprise of self-government.

Good **citizenship** includes behaving in accordance with the rules, norms, and expectations of our own state and society. Thus the actual requirements vary widely. A good citizen in Soviet Russia of the 1930s was a person whose first loyalty was to the Communist Party. The test of good citizenship in a totalitarian state is this: Are you willing to subordinate all personal convictions and even family loyalties to the dictates of political authority, and to follow the dictator's whims no matter where they may lead? In marked contrast are the standards of citizenship in constitutional democracies, which prize and protect freedom of conscience and speech.

Where the requirements of the abstract good citizen—always defined by the state—come into conflict with the moral compass of actual citizens, and where the state seeks to obscure or obliterate the difference between the two, a serious problem arises in both theory and practice. At what point do people cease to be real citizens and become mere cogs in a machine—unthinking and unfeeling subjects or even slaves? Do we obey the state, or the dictates of our own conscience?

This question gained renewed relevance in the United States when captured "illegal combatants" were subjected to "enhanced interrogation techniques"—an Orwellian euphemism for torture—during the Bush administration's war on terror from 2002 to 2008. One prisoner was waterboarded 183 times (strapped to a board with towels wrapped around his head while water was poured slowly

© ALAMY LIMITED

After the Bush administration seized and incarcerated "illegal combatants" in a special military prison (known as "Gitmo") at Guantanamo Bay, Cuba, President Obama faced the question whether citizens who are also soldiers in the U.S. military can commit torture as part of the interrogation process and whether the fact that they were merely following orders is a defense.

onto the towels until he smothered).[2] Other harsh interrogation methods were also used.

Torture is outlawed by the Third Geneva Convention (1949), to which the United States is a party, as well as by the U.S. Code (Title 18, Chapter 113C). In addition, torture is a gross violation of the *moral* code we are taught to observe in our everyday lives from earliest childhood. As a presidential candidate, Barack Obama denounced torture and the use of "extraordinary" methods and procedures in the war on terror. As president, he ordered the closing of the Guantanamo Bay detention camp (Gitmo) and an end to waterboarding and other extremely harsh interrogation techniques practiced there and elsewhere.

Question Number One: Can anyone in any position of authority who orders the use of torture be justified in so doing? Question Number Two: Can anyone who carries out such an order be a good citizen? Question Number Three: Is it ever right to obey orders that are wrong—that is, illegal and (or) immoral? Keep these questions in mind as you read on.

Defining Citizenship

Throughout history, people of diverse moral character have claimed to be models of good citizenship. The relationship between the moral character of citizens and different forms of government underscores Aristotle's observation that the true measure of a political system is the kind of citizen it produces. According to this view, a good state is one whose model citizen is also a good person; a bad state is one whose model citizen obeys orders without regard for questions of good or evil. Simple though this formulation may sound, it offers striking insights into the relationship between governments and citizens, including, for example, the fact that we cannot divorce civic virtue or public morality from our personal integrity or private morality.

It is little wonder that different political systems embrace different definitions of citizenship. In many authoritarian states, people can be classified as citizens only in the narrowest sense of the word—that is, they reside within the territory of a certain state and are subject to its laws. The relationship between state and citizen is a one-way street. Ordinary citizens have no voice in deciding who rules or how, or even whether they have a vote. In general, the government leaves them alone as long as they acquiesce in the system.

By contrast, in totalitarian states, where the government seeks to transform society and create a new kind of citizen, people are compelled to participate in the political system. From the standpoint of citizenship, however, their participation is meaningless because it is not voluntary and stresses duties without corresponding rights. Loyalty and zealotry form the core of good citizenship, and citizens may be forced to carry out orders they find morally repugnant.

In democratic societies, people define citizenship very differently. In elementary school, the good citizenship award typically goes to a pupil who sets a good example, respects others, plays by the rules, and hands in assignments on time. Adults practice good citizenship by taking civic obligations seriously, obeying the laws, paying taxes, and voting regularly, among other things. In a democracy, the definition of good citizenship is found in the laws, but the legislators who write the laws are freely elected by the people—in other words, a true republic at its best erases (or at the very least eases) the tension between citizenship and moral conscience.

Many individuals, including civil libertarians, emphasize that the essence of citizenship lies in individual rights or personal liberties. The formal requirements of citizenship in the United States are minimal (see Box 10.1), even though people the world over envy its rewards (hence the steady flow of immigrants into the United States, compared with the trickle of U.S. citizens emigrating to other countries). According to the Fourteenth Amendment, "All persons born or naturalized in the United States, and subject to the jurisdiction thereof, are citizens of the United States and of the State wherein they reside." Note that citizens of the United States are distinguished from aliens not on the basis of how they act or what they have done but simply on the basis of birthplace—to be born in the United States is to be a U.S. citizen. Moreover, the presumption is once a citizen, always a citizen, barring some extraordinary misdeed (such as treason) or a voluntary renunciation of citizenship.

A Classical View

The minimalist view of citizenship described in Box 10.1 may provide a convenient way of distinguishing citizens from aliens (foreigners), but it does not do justice to a time-honored concept in Western civilization. To the ancient Greeks,

BOX 10.1 FOCUS ON   Citizenship and War: Democracy and Duty

In the United States, apart from paying taxes, the demands of citizenship are quite limited. They became especially limited once the United States switched to an all-volunteer army in 1972, largely as a response to the backlash against the **Selective Service** System (often called "the draft") many considered unfair during the Vietnam War. Since then the law has been changed—citizenship no longer entails the duty of all males over the age of 18 to register for the draft or, in the event of war, to defend the country.

Defenders of an all-volunteer army argue that it is more professional and proficient, that willing recruits are likely to make better soldiers than are conscripts, and that the military provides excellent opportunities for young men and women from minority and low-income groups to acquire the self-confidence, discipline, and technical skills that can lead to high-paying jobs in the civilian economy.

Many veterans of past U.S. wars, among others, decry the ending of the draft. Others advocate making at least one year of national service mandatory for young adults who do not enlist in the armed forces.

Some who argue for bringing back the draft do so on the surprising grounds that it would make war less likely. Why? Because voters are often apathetic when an issue does not affect them directly and too easily swayed when patriotism is invoked—as it always is in war. This issue resurfaced in 2003 when President George W. Bush, in effect, declared a "presidential war"—defined as the use of force outside the United States without a formal declaration of war by Congress as required under the Constitution—on Iraq.

Was President Bush justified in ordering U.S. troops to invade a country that did not (and could not) attack the United States? Is it right to send the sons and daughters of minorities and the poor to fight our wars, while the children of the rich who run the country's corporations and have close ties to the power elite never have to serve if they don't choose to? What kind of society starts wars, kills countless people in a foreign country, and calls upon the vast majority of its own people to make no sacrifices? Why not reinstitute the draft, or at least a universal national service of some sort? Questions of this nature help explain why the United States has been so deeply divided over politics in the post-9/11 era and why the war in Iraq figured so prominently in the 2008 presidential election.

© LIBRARY OF CONGRESS

I WANT YOU FOR U.S. ARMY
NEAREST RECRUITING STATION

After the unpopular Vietnam War, the United States abolished the draft in favor of an all-volunteer armed forces.

the concept of citizenship was only partly related to accidents of birth and political geography; rather, responsible and selfless participation in the public affairs of the community formed the vital core of citizenship. Aristotle held that a citizen "shares in the administration of justice and in the holding of office."[3] The Athens of Aristotle's time was a small political society, or city-state, that at any given time accorded a proportionately large number of citizens significant decision-making power (women and slaves were excluded). Citizenship was the exalted vehicle through which public-spirited and properly educated free men could rule over, and in turn be ruled by, other free men and thereby advance civic virtue, public order, and the common good.

In eighteenth-century Europe, the Greek ideal reemerged in a modified form. *Citizen* became a term applicable to those who claimed the right to petition or sue the government. Citizens were distinguished from slaves, who had no claims or rights and were regarded as chattel (property). Citizens also differed from subjects, whose first and foremost legal obligation was to show loyalty to and obey the sovereign. According to the German philosopher Immanuel Kant (1724–1804), citizens, as opposed to slaves or subjects, possessed constitutional freedom; that is, the right to obey only laws to which they consented. Kant also contended that citizens possessed a civil equality, which relieved them of being bound by law or custom to recognize any superior among themselves, and political independence, meaning a person's political, status stemmed from fundamental rights rather than from the will of another.[4] No longer were citizens to be ruled arbitrarily by the state.

Republican government came the closest to this ideal of citizenship. In the final analysis, as Kant and other eighteenth-century thinkers recognized, the freedom and dignity of the individual inherent in the concept of citizenship could flourish only under a republican government, and such a government could function only if its rank-and-file members understood and discharged the responsibilities of citizenship.

One distinguishing feature of the modern era is the *extension* of citizenship. In the United States, for instance, it took many years for racial minorities, women, and individuals without property to gain the right to vote and the right to protection under the law in the exercise of their civil rights. Yet, as the number of citizens (and of people in general) has risen, *effective* political participation for individuals has often become more difficult. It is one thing for society to embrace ideas such as citizenship for all and equal rights in theory; it is quite another to provide the civic education and social development necessary to make the *ideal* of a society of equals a practical reality.

POLITICAL CULTURE: DEFINING THE GOOD

The Greek view of what constituted the good citizen was a reflection of the way the Greeks defined the word *good*. Every language in the world has a word meaning "good," and it is arguably the most important word in any language. But every language is embedded in a culture, and no two cultures are identical.

We are all products of the culture into which we are born. From our earliest infancy, and long before we know how to read or write, we learn to talk.

Along with the language, we also learn about our environment, which includes both tangible and intangible things. Among the most important intangibles are values—that is, what our parents or other guardians say is "good" or "bad." In the process of learning the difference between good and bad (picking up our toys is "good" and not eating our vegetables is "bad"), we also learn about right and wrong. Crossing the line from "good" and "bad" in word and deed to "right" and "wrong" in thought and sentiment is a giant step across a great chasm—it is the difference between outward behavior and inner motives, beliefs, and desires. Culture, in the sense that anthropology and political science use the word, is all about established norms, customs, and traditions—in other words, how *society* defines right and wrong and about what "the good life," or the word *good* itself, means in a given place and time. There is no universally accepted definition of "the good life" in this world for the simple reason that there is no universal culture.

Culture has many meanings. Here we are interested primarily in the aspects of culture that are related to politics—what scholars often call **political culture**. Political culture encompasses the prevailing moral values, beliefs, and myths people live by and are willing to die for. It also includes the **collective memory** of a society—the history we learn about in grade school; what we come to know about our leaders, about crises we have survived as a nation, and about wars we have fought. Virtually anything and everything that shapes our shared perceptions of reality is part of our political culture. This collective memory and these shared perceptions differ depending on the specifics of geography, climate, terrain, and other physical circumstances, as well as certain accidental factors—for example, the presence or absence of hostile and aggressive neighbors.

Small nations often have a history of being subjugated by powerful neighbors. Island peoples, such as the British and the Japanese, have a history that differs in fundamental ways from landlocked nations, owing to the absence of shared borders. The success of the thirteen American colonies in breaking away from the British Empire, as well as the United States' historic isolationism, would not have been possible without the benevolent presence of two great oceans.

Religion has played a major role in shaping political culture (for example, the Puritans of colonial times and the Religious Right today). We cannot understand Western civilization without reference to Roman Catholicism, the Reformation, and Christianity. By the same token, Islam forms the moral core of life in the Arab Middle East, as well as in much of South, Central, and Southeast Asia (see Figure 10.1). The same is true of Hinduism in India; Buddhism in Cambodia, Tibet, and Thailand; Taoism and Confucianism in China; and Shinto, as well as Buddhism, in Japan. Even where secularization has eroded religious beliefs (as in the West), the stamp of religion on political culture is both undeniable and indelible (see Box 10.2).

We are often bemused, perplexed, or outraged by the reactions and perceptions of others. We wonder what they must be thinking. How could anyone, for example, condone the actions of terrorists whose victims are often innocent bystanders? We tend to think those whose take on reality is different from our own are ignorant,

political culture
The moral values, beliefs, and myths people live by and are willing to die for.

collective memory
The things we learn about in grade school—what we come to "know" about our leaders, about crises we have survived as a nation, and about wars we have fought.

BOX 10.2 SPOTLIGHT ON   The United States, Islam, and the Tao

In his provocative little book *The Abolition of Man* (New York: Macmillan, 1947), C. S. Lewis argued that "the Tao" could be found in civilizations, cultures, and religions the world over. Taoism originated in China in ancient times. The Tao is "the way"—the source of all knowledge about nature and truth, the key to inner peace and social harmony. Lewis noted that this type of metaphysical reasoning and the moral values it fostered are found in religions and ethical systems all over the world. He cites many "Illustrations of the Tao" drawn "from such sources as come readily to the hand of one who is not a professional historian."

Lewis makes a powerful case for humanistic education—that is, for teaching people to love truth and justice. Learning to love truth and justice, Lewis suggested, is the key to civil society, because people are not simply rational beings and do not naturally behave according to reason. It is necessary, therefore, that society finds ways to link human emotions with positive attitudes and good acts, which brings us back to the Tao. What Lewis called the Tao teaches respect for authority, humility, honesty, charity, generosity, and so forth—in short, the way to live in harmony with oneself, others, and nature.

Political culture cannot be distilled from moral and religious teachings alone; indeed, politics is not what Lewis's book is about. But his views on the role of public education in developing a sense of right and wrong—a civic culture that supports democratic processes and institutions—have significant implications for students of politics.

The prevalence and intensity of faith-based politics in today's world serves to remind us that the nexus between education and values, the province of religion and morality, remains an important question—one involving a battle for control over not only the Islamic world's political culture but also the political culture of the United States.

FIGURE 10.1   Religion exerts a powerful influence on the political ideas, values, and aspirations of people all over the world. With an estimated 1.5 billion adherents, Islam is the second-largest body of believers in the world. (Christianity is the first, with roughly 2.1 billion.)

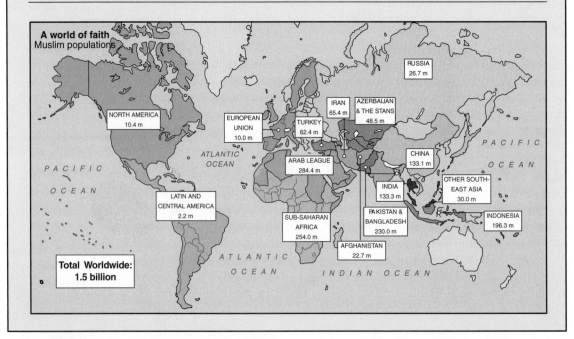

misguided, or even depraved. In fact, profound differences in perception, outlook, and behavior can often be traced to differences in political culture.

A political culture is like a filter for our personal experiences—without it we lack any common interpretation of reality. Without a shared reality, we lack the basis for a community or society.

We can study political culture in several different ways. We can look at its sources in society (geography, climate, history, religion, and the like); at its manifestations (attitudes, perceptions, beliefs, and prejudices); or at its effects (actions and public policies). As is often the case, however, the closer we look, the more complicated the picture becomes.[5]

Another way to think about political culture is in terms of one national political culture and many regional and local political *subcultures*. College students have an opportunity to research this question themselves by simply engaging classmates from different states or regions of the country—and from different countries—in conversations about growing up. Comparing your own upbringing with those of others from different backgrounds can be both fun and enlightening.

In the next section, we look at the ingenious ways societies sow the seeds of political culture. Consider this: are our ideas about "first things" (good and bad, right and wrong) really *our* ideas at all—or were they implanted at a young age, long before we had any idea of them?

POLITICAL SOCIALIZATION: FORMING CITIZENS

Though we can dispute the proper definition of citizenship, most people agree that good citizens are made, not born. Children grow up to be responsible citizens through the interplay of various influences and institutions—including family, religion, school, peer groups, the mass media, and the law. The process of being conditioned to think and behave in a socially acceptable manner is called *socialization*.

Every self-sustaining society inculcates in its citizens certain basic values necessary to establish and perpetuate a political order. Even as staunch an individualist as the British philosopher John Stuart Mill (1806–1873) acknowledged that the sense of citizen loyalty or allegiance "may vary in its objects and is not confined to any particular form of government; but whether in a democracy or in a monarchy its essence is always . . . that there be in the constitution of the state something which is settled, something permanent, and not to be called into question; something which, by general agreement, has a right to be where it is, and to be secure against disturbance, whatever else may change."[6]

Political socialization is the process whereby citizens develop the values, attitudes, beliefs, and opinions that enable them to support the political system.[7] This process begins with the family.

political socialization
The process by which members of a community are taught the basic values of their society and are thus prepared for the duties of citizenship.

The Family

The family exerts the first and most important influence on the formation of individual values. Different political regimes view the family in different ways. Some governments support and nurture the family; others choose to remain indifferent toward it; a few seek to undermine it and regard the love and loyalty that flow from family ties as subversive to the state. Despite these varying reactions, all governments recognize the importance of the family in the socialization process.

Even nations that publicly proclaim the value of the traditional family, however, may not be able to ensure its success in society. The number of children living in single-parent households in the United States, for example, has risen dramatically since the 1960s, due to rising divorce rates, changes in sexual mores, teenage pregnancies, and other social changes. Whereas in 1970 about 12 percent of all children were living in single-parent households, by the mid-1990s (according to Census Bureau data) that figure had more than doubled to 28 percent. In 1998, some 20 million children in the United States were living with a single parent. These numbers have since leveled off, but the likelihood of living with two married parents for a child in the United States had declined from 85 percent to just over 67 percent in 2006.

Poverty and lack of education are major causes of divorce. Moreover, the problem is self-perpetuating. Studies confirm that children raised in single-parent families are at greater risk than those in two-parent families to drop out of school, to become involved with crime and illegal drugs, to be unemployed (or underemployed) and poor, and to have failed marriages and personal relationships as adults—a vicious cycle.[8] Of course, single-parent families are often successful, and many children raised by single parents become well-adjusted adults. Indeed, if one parent is physically or emotionally abusive, it is often better for a child to be nurtured (and protected) only by the parent who is not.

Children are first socialized at home, within the family structure, learning what is and what is not permissible, with rewards and punishment to reinforce daily behavior. In this manner, parents make the obligations of children to the family and to others clear. Slowly, children become citizens of the family, often with clearly defined responsibilities and occasionally with rights or privileges. Parents emphasize moral ground rules, even if they don't always specify the reasons for them ("Do it because I said so"). Trust, cooperation, self-esteem, respect for others, and empathy, each rooted in family relations, bear on the behavioral and moral development of individuals.[9]

Where discipline is lacking and parents are overly permissive, children are given rights and privileges with few if any responsibilities. In such cases, socialization is impeded to the extent it fails to produce behaviors conducive to social harmony, civility and civic duty, or leads to narcissism, self-promotion, and a tendency to exploit others.

The family also helps determine the direction the ultimate political socialization of children takes and how successful it will be. Party orientation and even affiliation often derive from the family, especially when both parents belong to the same party. In the United States, about 70 percent of children whose parents both have the same party affiliation favor that party too.[10] In addition, the family exerts a powerful influence on religious persuasion, which tends to correlate highly with party affiliation, as well as with certain political opinions (fundamentalist Protestants tend to oppose abortion; Jews tend to support Israel; and so on).[11] However, studies indicate that when it comes to opinions about more abstract political issues, parental influence is quite limited.[12] As adults, we often find ourselves at odds with our parents' ideas about politics (among other things), a fact often attributed to "generational" differences.

Social Class and Minority Status Family interest in politics tends to increase with social standing. Middle- and upper-class children are most likely to become actively engaged in politics; children from lower-class families are typically uninformed about politics and participate less often.[13] There are many exceptions, however—four famous examples are Abraham Lincoln, Harry S. Truman, William Jefferson Clinton, and Barack Obama, all arising from humble origins to become president of the United States. Former Secretary of State Madeleine Albright, current president of Liberia Ellen Johnson Sirleaf, and Josephine Baker, the first African American female to star in a major motion picture, are examples of women not born to privilege who rose to great heights. Josephine Baker was born in St. Louis in 1902 and dropped out of school at the age of 12. She is best known as a recording artist and stage performer, but she was decorated for her undercover work in the French Resistance during World War II. When she died in Paris in 1975, she became the first American woman to receive French military honors at her funeral.

Minority status can play a significant role in political socialization. Some researchers have found that in the United States, African-American children tend to place less trust in government, and to feel less confident of influencing it, than do white children.[14]

Not surprisingly, such attitudes correlate with political opinions; thus, holding social-class differences constant, black adults in the United States tend to be less conservative than whites on most economic and foreign policy issues, although not on the issue of crime. Politically, though not necessarily socially and culturally, Asian Americans tend to resemble white ethnic groups more closely than black groups, particularly on domestic social issues. Hispanic Americans

© BROOKS KRAFT/CORBIS NEWS/CORBIS

The current president of Liberia, Ellen Johnson Sirleaf became Africa's first elected female head of state in her country's 2005 elections. Her parents were born in poverty, but she was able to earn bachelor's and master's degrees in the United States before returning to her homeland to enter the government in 1971.

© U.S. NAVY PHOTO BY PHOTOGRAPHERS MATE 1ST CLASS ARLO K. ABRAHAMSON

A young boy awaits the arrival of the late president's funeral motorcade at the gate of the Ronald Reagan Presidential Library in Sim Valley, California, on June 7, 2004. This picture illustrates that children begin learning to be good citizens and to show respect for legitimate authority—important lessons in political socialization—at an early age.

tend to fall between blacks and whites. However, family socialization and the transmission of political beliefs have exerted an influence on Cuban Americans, who, as a group, tend to be more hard-line conservative, especially on foreign policy questions, than are other Hispanic-American groups, including Mexicans and Puerto Ricans. One reason is that after Cubans fled to the United States at the time of the Cuban Revolution, Cuban leader Fidel Castro confiscated their property and persecuted family members they had left behind.

Gender and Politics Like class and race, gender differences can be important independent correlates of political behavior and opinions. In the United States, the so-called **gender gap**—differences in the ways men and women think and vote in the aggregate—has gotten a lot of attention in recent decades. For instance, in the 1992 general elections, Bill Clinton won the women's vote by 8 points, but won the men's vote by only 3. Women thus helped a challenger defeat a sitting president. In 1996, the gender voting gap was even bigger. In 2008, women favored Barack Obama over John McCain by 7 points, despite the fact that McCain's running mate was a woman, Sarah Palin. But that number does not tell the whole story: in all, eight million more women voted for Obama than for McCain, and women voters accounted for 53 percent of all the votes cast. Obama thus received a double boost from women voters—a larger percentage of a bigger vote (Table 10.1; the figures here are from the same source). The pattern is different in congressional races, however, where the gender gap is seldom apparent.

gender gap
A term used to refer to differences in voting between men and women in the United States; this disparity is most obvious in political issues and elections that raise the issue of appropriateness of governmental force.

TABLE 10. 1   The Gender Gap and the 2008 Election

	Women (%)	Men (%)
Barack Obama	56	49
John McCain	43	48

Sources: **Center for American Women and Politics (CAWP), Eagleton Institute of Politics, Rutgers University, December, 2008; Edison Media Research and Mitofsky International.**

Some researchers tie gender differences to early family experiences and expectations; others contend there are innate differences in the way men and women develop moral and political awareness. One theory postulates that due to some combination of socialization and biology, women—as mothers and primary caregivers for children—tend to develop a moral and political perspective that emphasizes compassion and the protection of human life.[15] An alternate theory holds that gender-based political differences are rooted in *some* women's later life experiences.[16] For example, working women who have been paid less than men doing the same job are likely to vote for a party or candidate that stresses fairness and equal rights.

One important political difference between the sexes revolves around the government's use of force. Women tend to be more reluctant to support war, more opposed to capital punishment, and more inclined to support gun control. Women also tend to give more support to social welfare programs intended to help families, the working poor, and the economically disadvantaged. These differences help explain why the gender gap has aided Democrats in recent years. We turn now to a factor that has aided Republicans—especially George W. Bush.

Religion

Either the church or the state may present itself as the true source of moral authority, which makes religion particularly important in the socialization process. And just as religion can influence a young person's developing political opinions, so can politics decisively shape the role of religion within the family and the place it ultimately occupies within the larger political order.

Sometimes religion can legitimize existing practices and lend stability to a society in transition. Hinduism in India, for instance, has proved compatible with changing political institutions. Described by one expert as having "a multi-layered complexity allowing for the existence of many gods, many incarnations, many layers of truth,"[17] Hinduism has tended, historically, to support the status quo. Even when the status quo allowed systematic discrimination against a lower, "untouchable" class, Hinduism counseled patience and perseverance in anticipation of future lives to come. In other parts of the world, however, religious doctrine has ignited aggressive policies. In Libya and Iran, for instance, Islamic fundamentalism has helped fuel belligerent foreign policies and contributed to a periodic fervor for war.

Religion and politics sometimes conflict. In Nazi Germany, the government steamrolled the Lutheran and Catholic churches. In the former Soviet Union, the regime allowed the historically entrenched Russian Orthodox Church to continue functioning but restricted and monitored its activities, frequently persecuting believers.[18]

In the United States, religion and politics reinforce one another at a number of levels. Although the Supreme Court has interpreted the Constitution to prohibit government from directly supporting religion, the First Amendment also clearly prohibits government from denying an individual's free exercise of religion. Religion continues to flourish in the United States. In the mid-1980s, "More than 90 percent of all Americans identify with some religious faith, and on any given Sunday morning more than 40 percent are to be found in church." Furthermore, by "most measurable indices the United States is a more religious country than any European nation except Ireland and Poland."[19] But this picture appears to be changing. In 2008, in a nationwide survey 15 percent of the U.S. population claimed to have "no religion."[20]

The Judeo-Christian tradition continues to be dominant in the United States, yet there is significant diversity within that tradition. Census data show numerous Protestant denominations constitute about 51 percent of the population (with Baptists constituting the largest groups at about 16 percent); Roman Catholics, 24 percent; and Jews, 1.7 percent. After the terrorist attacks of September 11, both the public reaction and the mass media focused attention on the fact that there is also a Muslim minority in the United States, although it is relatively small (0.6 percent). There are more Buddhists in the United States than Muslims.

Important political differences correlate with these differences in religious orientation, some even arising from the religious doctrines themselves. Quakers and Mennonites tend to be pacifists, while, as previously mentioned, fundamentalist Protestants tend to oppose abortion and Jews generally favor Israel. By the same token, members of black Protestant churches tend to be more politically liberal than are Protestants affiliated with mainstream churches, and members of mainstream churches tend to be more politically liberal than their evangelical Protestant counterparts.

More generally, on a scale measuring political conservatism and liberalism, Protestants tend to be somewhat more conservative than Catholics and much more conservative than Jews. Jews and Catholics have historically identified more with the Democratic Party, while Protestants have leaned toward the Republican Party, though the correlation between religion and party affiliation appeared to be weakening until George W. Bush received 56 percent of the Protestant vote and Al Gore (the Democratic candidate) only 42 percent in the 2000 presidential election. Gore won among Catholic voters, however, with 50 percent to Bush's 47.

Arguably, religion also has a utilitarian political value in the United States. In this view, religion benefits public life by providing, in George Washington's words, an "indispensable support" for representative government. By teaching that everyone is equal in God's eyes, religion inculcates a private morality that can elevate public life.

The Rev. Martin Luther King, Jr. (1929–1968) mixed religion and racial equality in his message of unity and non-violence.

© CORBIS

Sometimes political leaders draw on religious imagery to unite citizens in a common understanding of the present or point them toward a more noble vision of the future.[21] For example, the famous U.S. clergyman and civil rights leader Martin Luther King, Jr. inspired the nation with his dream of a day "when all of God's children—black men and white men, Jews and Gentiles, Protestants and Catholics—will be able to join hands and sing in the words of the old Negro spiritual 'Free at last! Free at last! Thank God Almighty, we are free at last.'" The tragic assassination of King, like the assassination of Abraham Lincoln a century earlier, helped rally the U.S. people to the cause of racial equality.

The election of George W. Bush in 2000 elevated the importance of religion in national politics. As part of his so-called faith-based initiative program, Bush asked Congress to allow religious organizations to compete for government contracts and grants without a strict separation of religious activities and social service programs.

But it was the shock of September 11, 2001, that changed everything. Suddenly, the role of religion in world politics was on everyone's mind.

Osama bin Laden and his al Qaeda terrorist network gave the world a horrifying glimpse of religion's dark side in the fall of 2001, when they attempted to unite the world's 1.5 billion Muslims against the "Crusaders" (Christians and Jews) in a jihad, or holy war. Al Qaeda obliterated the distinction between religion and ideology and used Islam as an instrument of war against the West.

Schools

Schools play a vital role in **civic education**. In effect, the state uses schools as instruments of political socialization. Some governments merely prescribe one or two courses in civics or history, require students to salute the flag, and hang a few pictures of national heroes on school walls. Other governments dictate the entire school curriculum, indoctrinate the children with slogans and catch phrases,

civic education
The process of inculcating in potential citizens the fundamental values and beliefs of the established order.

heavily censor textbooks and library acquisitions, and subject teachers to loyalty tests.

Different regimes inculcate different values. Under some regimes (for example, the Soviet Union in the 1930s), blind obedience to authority is the norm. In others, patriotism is encouraged, but so is the habit of critical and independent thinking.

Socialization studies tell us a lot about how children learn civic values in school.[22] During the elementary school years, children develop positive *emotional* attachments to key political concepts such as liberty and democracy and respect for others. Young children also learn to think of the government in terms of an authority figure—a police officer, the president, and so on.

As we mature, *cognition* comes into play; we begin to grasp abstract concepts such as democracy. During adolescence and early adulthood, our attitudes toward authority often change radically. We cease to obey authority without question. Increasingly, we want to decide things for ourselves—a sentiment readily transferable to the political realm.

High school civics classes are probably less important than the total educational experience.[23] Lessons and stories on the nation's history, formal rituals such as reciting the Pledge of Allegiance, patriotic music, and extracurricular activities like sports, band, debate, and writing for the school newspaper all can convey the importance of responsible participation and working toward a common goal. Electing class officers and participating in student government is typically our first exercise in democracy.

In general, the higher the level of education, the greater the propensity to participate in politics—at a minimum, by voting. Also, higher education correlates positively with personal self-confidence and trust in others—personality traits that democratic political systems, based on citizen participation, require.[24]

In the United States, the college curriculum often represents a blend of vocational training and liberal arts—with the latter, which includes literature, philosophy, science, history, and linguistics, placing great emphasis on the development of critical thinking.[25] Advocates of the liberal arts stress the importance of education not only for citizenship, but also for leadership. What such an education does, at its best, is produce adults capable of *critical* thinking. Evidence suggests it tends to produce more *liberal* adults, as well.[26]

The ideal of **liberal education** fits easily with constitutional guarantees that protect the right to question authority. It also appears to predispose citizens to do so.[27] Significantly, it is only in democracies that independent thinking and dissent are actually encouraged. Recall that the Greek philosopher Socrates was considered subversive and sentenced to death, not for teaching his students *what* to think but for teaching them *how* to think.

liberal education
A type of education often associated with private colleges in the United States; stresses the development of critical thinking skills through the study of literature, philosophy, history, and science.

peer group
A group of people similar in age and characteristics.

Peer Groups

A **peer group** can refer either to a group of people who are friends, or to people of similar age and characteristics. The concept of peers itself arises from "the tendency for individuals to identify with groups of people like themselves."[28]

Peer groups exert considerable influence over our political activities and beliefs, but there has been little research on the influence of peer groups in politics.[29]

The relationship between gang membership and the development of anti-social attitudes by adolescent male lawbreakers, for example, is a matter of more than academic interest. Although it seems likely the linkage between peer groups and gangs is one key to understanding teenage crime, it is still not clear whether "good" boys (and girls) become "bad" because they join the wrong crowd or whether they join the wrong crowd because they are bad. We do know that membership in a gang increases the frequency with which the average teenager commits crimes. According to one study, peers and gangs "can affect the value a person assigns to the rewards of crime (by adding the approval of colleagues to the perceived value of the loot or the direct gratification of the act)."[30]

Psychologically, peer groups fulfill a member's need for approval, which affects the formation of political attitudes and beliefs. Generally speaking, peer groups are formed voluntarily and informally. If we expand the peer-group concept to encompass such organizations as the Girl Scouts, the Young Democrats, or a high school journalism club—and then of similar organizations that operate in other political contexts—we make an important discovery, one that tyrants like Hitler and Stalin deftly exploited. The state can create peer-group structures for youth, as well as adults. These involuntary associations are typically designed to infuse ideological fervor and abject loyalty into young hearts and minds. Under the Nazi Party, for example, German life was organized through an elaborate network of state controlled associations of peers to ensure that every German would, in time, adopt correct political attitudes and be properly socialized into the new Nazi order. Similarly, the Communist Party of the Soviet Union created an all-encompassing set of centrally controlled peer organizations in the guise of clubs and civic associations.

In democracies, peer groups form naturally and civic associations are independent of the state. The state plays a role in the socialization process, but does not control it.

The Mass Media

The media also play a significant role in political socialization. In nondemocratic states, the **mass media**—that is, television, radio, newspapers, and large-circulation magazines—are almost always owned or controlled by the state. Even some democratic governments monopolize radio and television broadcasting (as in Denmark) or own and operate television networks (as in Great Britain) but strive to ensure fairness and objectivity.

Television is popular even in some strict Islamic societies, where the state now uses this otherwise "decadent" source of Western pop culture to inculcate Islamic moral values. Thus, in Saudi Arabia, a traditional monarchy, state-owned television holds an annual "Miss Beautiful Morals" pageant that is the exact opposite of our beauty pageants—the physical appearance of the contestants is irrelevant (in fact, they are covered from head to foot). Rather, the

mass media
The vehicles of mass communication, such as television, radio, film, books, magazines, and newspapers.

winner is the contestant who is judged to have the most devotion and respect for her parents.[31]

In the United States, where the mass media are privately owned, the Federal Communications Commission (FCC) regulates radio and television. FCC rules are designed to discourage ideas, attitudes, or behavior the agency considers undesirable or unhealthy. For example, certain words cannot be uttered on television in the United States (see Box 10.3), full nudity is banned from 6:00 A.M. to 10 P.M. daily, and broadcasters are not permitted to air commercials for cigarettes. The FCC is also charged with promoting and preserving media competition, but in December 2007, it lifted the so-called cross-ownership ban in the twenty largest U.S. markets. Radio and television broadcasters are now allowed to own newspapers, as well.

Television has become a critical source of information as U.S. adults read fewer newspapers and attend fewer political party functions.[32] The high cost of television advertising—and, therefore, of running for office (see Table 10.2)—affects the quality of campaigns and candidates. Equally detrimental is the content—the vicious political attack ads—that are now a trademark of U.S. elections. Attack ads are intentionally unfair, misleading, and manipulative (see Box 10.4). They typically impugn the character and motives of the other candidate and often deliberately misrepresent his or her voting record.

The way news is presented, particularly on television, is also highly suspect. Some conservative critics contend that television news (and the media in general) often reflects the political agenda or ideas of journalists and broadcasters, who are predominantly liberal. But the media's emphasis on rumor and innuendo, as well as the right-wing bias of corporate media personalities such as Rush Limbaugh, Bill O'Reilly, and Sean Hannity, has blurred the difference between sensationalism and straight news. There is also justifiable criticism that media consolidation (especially for radio and newspapers) is leading to homogenized news, keyed to conservative audiences and corporate agendas. Critics fear the daily news will reflect right-wing biases while also becoming more and more like tabloid journalism or mind-numbing entertainment.

There is no denying radio and television are often exceedingly superficial and sensationalistic. They look for bad news rather than important news. Television coverage of election campaigns, for example, stresses candidates' attempts to gain strategic advantage, instead of focusing on the policies and ideas they stand for, often singling out inconsistencies and blunders. For example, a president falling down the steps of the presidential helicopter or vomiting at a formal state dinner in Japan. Meanwhile, anyone can exploit the new Internet technology, establishing websites and blogs that sometimes spread gossip while speculating about the private lives of public officials. It is little wonder the media are blamed for the sharp rise in public cynicism over the past four decades. Indeed, one mainstream political scientist argues "the United States cannot have a sensible campaign as long as it is built around the news media."[33]

Television executives know that conflict and confrontation are entertaining and that, as a rule, bad news makes good ratings. For this reason also, television almost always emphasizes the "horse race" aspect of presidential elections,

BOX 10.3 FOCUS ON   FCC vs. FOX TV—Unspeakable Words

The late comedian George Carlin created a sensation when he did a stand-up routine about the "seven dirty words" you cannot say on television. That routine secured Carlin's place as one of the most famous nightclub and television comedians in recent U.S. history. But it was more than a knee-slapping "shtick"; it was also political satire at its most biting, for Carlin was raising a serious question: Does the state's action in restricting indecent speech on television violent the citizen's right to free speech?

For several decades, the FCC's restrictions on indecent speech allowed a fleeting swear word or curse word—that is, so long as it was not repeated. In 2003, the FCC changed the rule to make even a fleeting indecent word impermissible, and to impose severe penalties in the form of steep fines for violations. FOX TV then sued the FCC and in November 2008 the case came before the U.S. Supreme Court. The issue: Whether the FCC provided an adequate explanation, or instead acted arbitrarily and capriciously, in changing its policy to permit isolated uses of expletives on broadcast television to be considered "indecent" under federal law. The broader issue to be decided is whether and under what conditions the state can censor speech on television.

dwelling on who is ahead, who gained, and who lost because of this gaffe or that revelation. The networks all want to be the first to call every contest. The race becomes an end in itself, and the "product" (where the candidates stand on the issues) takes a back seat to the process.

In one study of network news coverage between 1968 and 1988, the average length of presidential quotations shrank from 45 seconds to 9 seconds—truncated sound bites.[34] The old form of coverage—a short setup and a relatively long presidential comment—was reversed. By the late 1980s, reporters were regularly upstaging the president, commenting on his comments rather than letting him speak for himself. This trend continues, while the ratio of paid political ads to political news has also shifted dramatically. In 2006, a study at the University of Wisconsin-Madison found that "local newscasts in seven Midwest markets aired 4 minutes, 24 seconds of paid political ads during the typical 30-minute broadcast while dedicating an average of 1 minute, 43 seconds to election news

TABLE 10.2   The Best Government Money Can Buy

Campaign Spending in the 2008 Elections			
	House	Senate	President
Democratic Party	$489.7 million	$217.1 million	$1.12 billion
Republican Party	$442.5 million	$200.6 million	$630.3 million
Total	$936.8 million	$418.4 million	$1.75 billion

SOURCE: Open Secrets.Org at <http://www.opensecrets.org/overview/index.php>.

BOX 10.4 FOCUS ON   "Opposition Research"

Increasingly, the mass media broadcast negative political advertisements. These ads may or may not be entirely truthful, but they are often very effective. Sometimes viewed as a kind of political ambush, they are the product of extensive research into the backgrounds of political opponents and are aired at strategic times during the campaign. The Internet has made this kind of dirty work much easier for those who do it. Dirt diggers can request (and often obtain) telephone records, credit checks, and court records. Opposition research—or "oppo"—is a multimillion-dollar business employing investigators, consultants, lawyers, pollsters, and media experts.

Perhaps the best (or worst) example of oppo is the one that represents a turning point in U.S. political campaigns, namely the Willie Horton ad that helped defeated Michael Dukakis in the 1988 presidential race:

Michael Dukakis let Willie Horton out on a weekend furlough program that he supported and, of course, this murderer went on a rampage, and, of course, the rest is history. That really defined Michael Dukakis, and it really sunk his candidacy as well.

Most people old enough to vote in 1988 remembers this ad, which showed a picture of inmates, including a male African American (like Willie Horton), existed through a prison gate. What is seldom remembered is that in the fall of 1988, Dukakis had a 17-point lead over George H.W. Bush. Bush won by over 7 million votes (53.4 percent to 45.6 percent), carrying all but eight states.

SOURCE: Michele Norris, "Opposition Research: Know Thine Enemies," National Public Radio (NPR), *All Things Considered*, February 6, 2007, accessed May 7, 2009 at <http://www.npr.org/templates/story/story.php?storyId=7226716>.

coverage."[35] In-depth analysis, critics say, has become a casualty of Madison Avenue marketing techniques, the Nielsen ratings, and outright manipulation by highly paid professionals (see Box 10.5)—political gurus, media consultants, and spin doctors (public relations specialists).

In short, a drift toward tabloid journalism and the use of the airways as a vehicle for propaganda have severely compromised the integrity of television news reporting and talk radio. This type of coverage, pandering to prurience and prejudice, increasingly crowds out honest attempts to fulfill the vital "news and information" function of the mass media.[36] To make matters worse, newspapers—long the main source of information on current events for most citizens—are rapidly losing readership (see Box 10.6).

Consumers are also to blame for the state of the news. The news is "dumbed down" and entertaining because that is what attracts the largest number of viewers. Knowing the average viewer has a short attention span, television news directors spotlight the razzle-dazzle of video technology, flashy computer graphics, fast-paced interviews, and rapidly changing stories, locations, and camera angles. After a hard day's work, most viewers are not in the mood for an in-depth story or analysis that confuses, upsets, or makes them think too much. The problem is that the most important political issues tend to do all three.

BOX 10.5 FOCUS ON — Hunting for Votes, Targeting Voters*

The following is excerpted from an Internet article cited below.

Not only [do candidates] choose the content of the message, they choose the demographic that views it. Candidates can strategize and break down the population into race, age, religion, and education. . . . African Americans are most often concerned with social programs and issues of social justice. Thus candidates can target Black Entertainment Television in order to spread awareness . . . and increase the name recognition within this subset of the population. Similarly, candidates may target MTV to [reach] . . . young people or the Women's Entertainment (WE) channel for reproductive health issues. The element of control in selecting TV ad slots offers an appealing opportunity to gain support from large voting blocks.

Campaign websites and use of the internet can achieve a similar goal. Candidates and avid supporters can link the campaign website with a candidate's concise messages to special interest blogs, chat rooms, or purchase ad banner space on special interest website. . . . At the same time,

candidates may use RSS feeds, social networking updates, or even a blog on the campaign website to defend themselves from previous opposition attacks. While campaign websites may be confined initially to a single domain, the ease of copying and pasting the information into targeted demographic sites makes campaign websites an attractive proposition for candidates.

Television ads, on the other hand, increase name recognition which can encourage individuals to seek out additional information from alternative sources, i.e. the internet. Both elements work together to create a cohesive candidate image which is key to generating a honest, credible image.

Together these methods are considerably easier to disburse messages and garner support from large audiences, a significant advantage in comparison to face to face campaigning.

SOURCE: Sarah Spiker, "Political Advertising: The Appeal of Television and Web Campaigning" accessed at http://us-elections.suite.101.com. Reprinted by permission of the author.

The media's tendency to focus on negative news serves as a reminder that freedom of speech and criticism of the government are protected rights in liberal democracies. Indeed, the content and quality of the daily news in any given country is one indicator of how much freedom exists there. Where criticism of the government is allowed, freedom is usually the norm. In the final analysis, the mass media in democratic states are both gauge and guarantor of individual freedom.

The Law

The law plays an important role in socialization. Some laws are designed to promote public order (by having cars drive on the right side of the street, for example). Other laws prohibit violent or anti-social behavior society, such as murder, false advertising, theft, and racial discrimination. Equally important, the very idea of "law and order" is ingrained in us at an early age and the "rule

BOX 10.6 FOCUS ON   Media Trends: Who Needs Newspapers, Books, or Competition?

On this topic of vital interest to everyone in a democracy, the facts speak for themselves:

- In early 2009, the *Seattle-Post Intelligencer* shut its printing presses after 146 years in business; two weeks after, the *Rocky Mountain News* folded. The *Tucson Citizen* suffered the same fate.
- Daily print circulation has dropped from a peak of 62 million two decades ago to around 49 million. Online readership has risen faster, to almost 75 million people and 3.7 billion page views in January 2009, according to Nielsen Online.
- In the middle of the twentieth century, 80 percent of all newspapers were independently owned. By 2004, more than 7,000 cities and towns had no locally owned newspaper.
- There are 2,500 book publishers in the United States, but five giant companies produce most of the revenue.
- Two retail chains (Barnes and Noble and Amazon.com) accounted for well over half of all retail book sales in the United States in 2008.

- Four major companies account for half the movie business.
- Six companies account for at least 90 percent of all domestic music sales, and Apple (iTunes) became the biggest single U.S. music retailer in 2008 (19 percent), beating out Wal-mart (15 percent) for the first time.
- The 1996 Telecommunications Act doubled the number of local radio stations a single company can operate and removed all limits on how many one company can own nationwide.
- A single company—Clear Channel Communications—owns more than 1,200 radio stations.
- By one count, the 45 top-rated talk radio shows ran 310 hours of conservative talk to a mere 5 hours that were not patently right-wing in 2004.

SOURCE: NOW with Bill Moyers on PBS, February 13, 2004, http:// www.pbs.org, Digital Trends on the Internet at <http://news.digitaltrends.com/news-article/16263/apple-now-top-u-s-music-retailer> and author's updates.

of law" is an essential feature of liberal democracy. Thus, the law conditions our behavior in all sorts of subtle and not-so-subtle ways.

SOCIALIZATION AND POLITICAL BEHAVIOR

Fortunately, most citizens who participate in the political process choose, most of the time, to do so legally.

Political Behavior

Most of us participate in politics in largely symbolic, passive, or ritualistic ways—for example, by attending a political rally, responding to a political poll, watching a candidate on television, or putting a bumper sticker on our cars.

Participants in the Africa Action rally on September 9, 2006, are arrested for committing nonviolent civil disobedience by remaining immobile while holding signs in front of the White House—a federal crime.

© GERALD HERBERT/AP PHOTO

Some volunteer on political campaigns (witness the huge volunteer "army" that helped Barack Obama get elected in 2008) or join such liberal public interest groups such as the Sierra Club, the American Civil Liberties Union, or MoveOn. Org, or conservative ones such as the National Right to Life Committee, the National Taxpayers Union, or the Christian Coalition. Others participate in political protests of one kind of another.

In the United States, only 2 percent of those surveyed during the turbulent Vietnam War era believed violence was justified to achieve political aims.[37] Support for milder forms of unconventional participation is much higher, but this support falls off sharply as the action in question approaches the line between legality and illegality.

Illegal Political Behavior

Some illegal acts—in particular, those classified as civil disobedience—are intended to stir a nation's conscience. Taking his cue from Mahatma Gandhi, Martin Luther King, Jr. advocated civil disobedience in the struggle for racial equality in the 1960s. Civil disobedience stresses nonviolence and encourages demonstrators to accept the consequences of breaking the law, including arrest and detention.

Other forms of illegal political behavior include violence. **Terrorism** uses mass violence against civil society (noncombatants) for political aims. **Subversion** attempts to undermine a government, often with outside assistance. **Sedition** incites rebellious acts. In some troubled parts of the world, the line between legal and illegal is morally ambiguous. Where people are victimized by government or by a dominant class or ethnic group, the moral basis for law and authority often erodes. Even in the United States, illegal forms of political behavior have not always been considered "un-American."

terrorism
Political activity that relies on violence or the threat of violence to achieve its ends.

subversion
The attempt to undermine a government, often using outside assistance.

sedition
Inciting rebellion or other antigovernment acts; fomenting revolution.

Agitating for independence from Great Britain in colonial times, for example, was certainly illegal, if not treasonous. Had the American Revolution failed, Benjamin Franklin, Thomas Jefferson, and George Washington, among other leaders of the revolt, would probably have been hanged. Before the Civil War, the "underground railroad" that helped fugitive slaves escape bondage was a clear violation of federal law by many otherwise law-abiding citizens, especially in northern states like Massachusetts and New York. The underground railroad could not have existed without a network of activists who considered slavery a desecration of a "higher law," nor could these activists have themselves escaped prosecution without the cooperation of family, friends, and neighbors.

In sum, there are a few examples of illegal political behavior in our own history that we now celebrate. But, in general, actions directed against a representative government are, by definition, also directed against the majority.

WHEN POLITICAL SOCIALIZATION FAILS

A nation's political culture reflects the fundamental values its people hold dear. These values need not be entirely consistent and may even conflict at times. Nor will day-to-day political beliefs and actions of individual citizens always conform to the ideals people hold dear in the abstract.[38] But a steady state requires an established political culture consisting of shared values. In democracies, these values set a very high standard—too high, in fact, to be fully attainable. And yet the standard is keeping at the forefront and it is the striving for a perfection never achieved that, in many ways, defines democracy and distinguishes it from its alternatives.

In the United States, private values correlate highly with key public (or civic) values.[39] Accordingly, U.S. adults generally profess a strong belief in basic liberal values: personal freedom, political equality, private ownership of property, and religious tolerance. Not only are these values expressed in the nation's fundamental documents and writings, including the Declaration of Independence, the Constitution, and *The Federalist Papers*, but they are also instilled in U.S. youth by a variety of socialization strategies.

In other democratic societies, the process of socialization works the same way and serves the same purposes. But the *expression* of such core values as liberty, equality, security, prosperity, and justice (see Chapter 13), as well as the precise content and balance among them, vary significantly from one country to another. In Europe, "equality" is more often about class consciousness than civil rights. As a result, the state provides a much wider range of social services (including guaranteed universal health care) than in the United States. By the same token, love of liberty in Europe does not impede the police in criminal investigations the way it often does in the United States, nor does it entail the right of private citizens to own deadly weapons.

When a multiethnic nation fails to politically socialize large numbers of citizens as members of a single community—in effect, a new nation—the consequences are far-reaching. If there are multiple communities, there will be multiple processes going on and multiple political cultures being perpetuated. Members of the various sub-national communities will not be successfully integrated into the political system, and they will not share the norms, rules, and laws of the society.

Some citizens may never become fully socialized politically. A state's failure to socialize its citizens may result from its unequal or unfair treatment of them. Citizens may then become angry, cynical, or embittered, or they may even turn to crime or revolution. In extreme cases of unjust, tyrannical government, citizens' "crimes" may be viewed as actions taken justifiably. Thus, while the failure of political socialization is always detrimental to the government in power, the moral and political implications of that failure are not always as easy to evaluate.

GATEWAYS TO THE WORLD: EXPLORING CYBERSPACE

www.politicsol.com/quiz.html

Did this chapter make you think about how you have been socialized? How politically knowledgeable a citizen are you? This site provides a political IQ quiz geared specifically to U.S. politics.

www.icpsr.umich.edu/GSS

This site provides access to public opinion data from the General Social Survey. Here, students can examine—and even perform calculations on—actual data from the archives at the Inter-University Consortium for Political and Social Research (ICPSR.), housed in Ann Arbor at the University of Michigan.

www.electionstudies.org

The National Elections Studies website provides an excellent source of information about the demographic and behavioral aspects of the U.S. electorate and its development over time.

http://moneyline.cq.com/pml/home.do

CQ MoneyLine is an online service of Congressional Quarterly, Inc., containing a complete set of current "Money in Politics Databases" (see also CQPolitics.com).

SUMMARY

Different governments treat the concept of citizenship in different ways. All states demand adherence to the rules (laws), of course, and most treat birth in, or naturalization into, the political order as a requirement of citizenship. In democratic states, the concept of citizenship is also tied to the ideas of equality and liberty, as well as to meaningful participation in politics, such as voting in periodic elections. This ideal of democratic citizenship dates back to the ancient Greek city-states, which were small enough to permit direct democracy (self-representation of enfranchised adults through public assemblies and plebiscites).

Political socialization is the process whereby citizens develop the values, attitudes, beliefs, and opinions that enable them to relate to and function within the political system. Specific influences on the developing citizen include the family, religion, public education, the mass media, the law, peer groups, and key political values. Political socialization is of paramount importance; if a nation fails to socialize its citizenry on a large-scale basis, its political stability can be endangered.

KEY TERMS

citizenship
selective service
political culture
collective memory
political socialization

gender gap
civic education
liberal education
peer group
mass media

terrorism
subversion
sedition

REVIEW QUESTIONS

1. Why was the concept of citizenship of central importance to Aristotle and other political thinkers?
2. In what contrasting ways can we define citizenship? Which definition best describes your understanding of citizenship? Explain your choice.
3. It is sometimes argued that true citizenship can be found only in a democracy. What does this statement mean? Do you agree with it? Why or why not?
4. What factors influence the political socialization of citizens? Which ones do you think have been most influential on you? On your peers? Your parents?

RECOMMENDED READING

Almond, Gabriel, and Sidney Verba. *The Civic Culture: Political Attitudes and Democracy in Five Nations*. Newbury Park, California: Sage Publications, 1989. An influential comparative study of politics and political culture in the United States, Great Britain, former West Germany, Italy, and Mexico.

Alterman, Eric. *What Liberal Media? The Truth About Bias and the News*. New York: Basic Books, 2003. The author refutes the charge that the news has a liberal bias and makes a compelling (if controversial) argument that it reflects the corporate culture of the giant media conglomerates who control the industry.

Bennett, Lance W. *News: The Politics of Illusion* (8th Edition) (Longman Classics in Political Science). White Plains, NY: Longman, 2008. An intriguing analysis of television news. Raises the central question: How well does the news serve the needs of democracy?

Dalton, Russell J. *Citizen Politics: Public Opinion and Political Parties in Advanced Industrial Societies*. 5th ed. Washington, D.C.: CQ Press, 2008. A popular comparative study of political attitudes and behavior in the United States, Great Britain, France, and Germany.

Franken, Al. *Lies and the Lying Liars Who Tell Them: A Fair and Balanced Look at the Right*. New York: Dutton, 2003. A comedian turned political activist (and now the apparent winner of a recount in the pivotal 2008 Minnesota race for the United States Senate) gives the right-wing media a taste of its own medicine using his Harvard graduate students as research assistants to write a best-selling book that started out as a class project.

Graber, Doris. *Media Power in Politics*. Washington, D.C.: CQ Press, 2007. This book looks at recent scholarship on traditional and new (electronic) media and analyzes the role of "media power" in U.S. politics.

Glendon, Mary Ann, and David Blankenhorn, eds. *Seedbeds of Virtue: Sources of Competence, Character, and Citizenship in American Society*. Lanham, MD: University Press of America, 1995. Thoughtful essays discuss the role of virtue and values in the contemporary formation of the American character.

Holloway, Harry, and John George. *Public Opinion*, 2nd ed. New York: St. Martin's Press, 1985. A thoughtful general introduction to the U.S. political culture.

Jones, Jeffrey P. *Entertaining Politics: New Political Television and Civic Culture (Communication, Media, and Politics)*. New York: Rowman and Littlefield Publishers, 2004. Explores the role of political comedy and satire on television in shaping the way we think about candidates, issues, and politics.

Lipset, Seymour Martin. *American Exceptionalism: A Double-Edged Sword*. New York: Norton, 1996. According to Lipset, U.S. exceptionalism resides in its culture and its creed, including liberalism, individualism, egalitarianism, populism, voluntarism, and moralism.

Moore, Barrington. *The Social Origins of Dictatorship and Democracy: Lord and Peasant in the Making of the Modern World*. Boston, MA: Beacon Press, 1993. A classic study. The *New York Times Review of Books* calls it, "A landmark in comparative history and a challenge to scholars of all lands who are trying to learn how we arrived at where we are now."

Patterson, Thomas E. *Out of Order*. New York: Vintage, 1994. The author makes a convincing case that the media has distorted and undermined the integrity of U.S. elections.

Wald, Kenneth. *Religion and Politics in the United States*, 3rd ed. Washington, DC: CQ Press, 1996. A comprehensive account of the relationship between public life and religion in contemporary America.

Walzer, Michael. *Obligations: Essays on Disobedience, War, and Citizenship*. Cambridge, MA: Harvard University Press, 1982. A collection of philosophical essays dealing with the meaning of citizenship by one of the leading socialist thinkers in the United States.

Westin, Drew. *The Political Brain: The Role of Emotion in Deciding the Fate of the Nation*. New York: Perseus, 2007. A recent study on a topic of enormous relevance to the viability of democracy at a time when the spectacle of zealots taking center stage in politics is all too familiar—both at home and abroad.

Wilson, James Q. *The Moral Sense*. New York: Free Press, 1995. How is it that people come to act morally? Wilson fuses theory and social science research in the search for an answer.

© MARK RICHARDS/PHOTOEDIT

President Obama's response to the global recession in 2008-2009 called for sacrifices on the part of both big business and organized labor, but assembly-line shutdowns and job losses in the hard-hit auto industry, among others, gave rise to working class discontent. Peaceful street demonstrations, like the one depicted here, are a form of political participation guaranteed by the First Amendment as part of the Bill of Rights enshrined in the U.S. Constitution.

Political Participation
The Price of Influence

Defining Participation
Public Opinion

Polls

Elections

Electoral Systems

Direct Democracy

Rationalizing Participation: Why Vote?
Voting in the United States

Patterns of Participation

Private Pursuits and the Public Good

Affluence and Apathy

Participating as a Spectator: Outsiders

Participating as a Player: Insiders
Elitist Theories: Iron Laws and Ironies

Pluralists Versus Elitists

Participation and Political Parties
American Democracy: No Place for a Party?

General Aims

One-Party Dominant Systems

M any of us hold certain unexamined assumptions about democracy and political participation:

- The more citizens participate, the healthier the democracy.
- Participation is natural; that is, citizens want to participate.
- The average voter is knowledgeable; that is, participants know and understand the political choices they make.
- Public opinion matters.

These assumptions are worth examining, but first we look at the ways citizens participate in the political process.

DEFINING PARTICIPATION

Citizens in democracies participate in politics by expressing opinions and casting votes. Polls focus attention on public opinion and give it clear definition.

Box 11.1 FOCUS ON   Public Opinion: Just How Stupid Are We?

In his book entitled *Just How Stupid Are We?* (New York: Basic Books, 2008), historian Rick Shenkman asks, Why do we value polls when most citizens do not know enough to make a reasoned judgment? He is not alone in wondering.

"Americans are too ignorant to vote." That was the conclusion of a report from the Intercollegiate Studies Institute on the state of civic literacy in the United States, published in late 2008.* Nearly half the 2,500 voting-age adults in the study (including college students, elected officials, and other citizens) flunked a 33-question test on basic civics. Consider these results:

- Only 17 percent of college graduates knew the difference between free markets and central planning
- Only 27 percent of elected officials could name a right or freedom guaranteed by the First Amendment
- Asked what the Electoral College does, 43 percent of elected officials were stumped

- Almost half the elected officials (46 percent) in the study did not know the Constitution gives Congress the power to declare war.

The authors of this study recommend reforms in the higher-education curriculum to correct the problem. Shenkman, founder of George Mason University's History News Network, suggests requiring students to read newspapers and giving college freshmen weekly quizzes on current events. He would subsidize newspaper subscriptions and college tuition for students who perform well on civics tests.*

In the meantime, don't expect government to do anything about the problem. After all, most elected officials can't pass a basic civic literacy test themselves.

───────────

*Kathleen Parker, "Disheartening Finds about Civic Literacy," Washington Post, November 26, 2008, http://www.washingtonpost.com

Public Opinion

Politicians who swim against the tide of public opinion can find themselves out of a job come the next election. In theory, citizens thus have a powerful voice in shaping government policies. But in practice it is not so simple: **public opinion** is often divided, changes over time, varies from place to place, and is difficult to measure accurately. As we will see, it is also elusive—different polls on the same issue or candidate often produce conflicting results.

Politicians do pay attention to opinion polls, but is public opinion a reliable guide? (See Box 11.1.) Should elected officials decide where they stand on a given issue or how to vote on a legislative proposal based on what *we* say, or should they vote as *they* see fit and simply explain their reasons to us? As we will see in Chapter 12, this question is at the root of two opposing theories of representation.

What is public opinion? Is it a fine blend of collective wisdom, rational thought, and well-informed judgment, or a witch's brew of gut feelings, prejudices, and preconceptions based on scanty information? Answer: Both. (It was a trick question.)

public opinion
In general, the ideas and views expressed by taxpayers and voters; when a majority of the people hold strong opinions one way or the other on a given issue or policy question, it tends to sway legislators and decision-makers who know they will be held accountable at the next election.

Box 11.2 FOCUS ON   The Political Uses (and Abuses) of Polls

Traditionally, polls measured public opinion *after* political leaders took positions or enacted legislation. Increasingly in election campaigns, however, polling has become future oriented, to determine what positions candidates *ought* to take or how positions are to be advanced or what advertisements will project positive candidate images. This use of public opinion is *strategic polling*.

To gauge whether a political advertisement or position will be popular, *focus groups*, small numbers of people led by a professional communi-

cations expert, are asked to react to and discuss particular agenda items. Electronic polling has made possible the *dial group*, in which individuals use a dial to register instant approval or disapproval.

Strategic polling, even among incumbents, has become a fact of political life. In the 2008 presidential election, the Obama campaign was particularly adept in using polls to determine how to frame not only the issues but also the message, including slogans like "Yes, we can" and "Change you can believe in."

Polls

straw poll
Unscientific survey; simple, inexpensive poll open to all sorts of manipulation and misuse.

public opinion polling
Canvassing citizens for their views.

random sampling
A polling method that involves canvassing people at random from the population; the opposite of stratified sampling.

stratified sampling
A manner of polling in which participants are chosen on the basis of age, income, socioeconomic background, and the like, so that the sample mirrors the larger population; the opposite of random sampling.

The first attempts to measure public opinion were **straw polls**—unscientific opinion samples nineteenth-century newspapers used to predict a winner in the run-up to elections. Local news sources still sometimes use straw polls today.

But there is never any guarantee that the sample in such a poll is representative of the population as a whole. The *Literary Digest* poll that predicted Alf Landon would defeat Franklin D. Roosevelt in 1936 is a famous case in point. Although the *Literary Digest* had correctly predicted the outcome of the three previous presidential elections, in 1936 its poll missed by a mile: Roosevelt won big. Where did this particular poll go wrong? The names in the sample were taken from the telephone directory and automobile registration lists—two very unrepresentative rosters at the time, because only rich people could afford telephones and cars during the Great Depression. Incidentally, that was the end of the *Literary Digest*'s polling and, for all practical purposes, of the *Literary Digest* itself. In 1938, it went out of business.

Over the past few decades, **public opinion polling** has improved. In the preferred method, a **random sampling** of citizens is drawn from the entire population, or universe, being polled. (Statisticians have deemed a sample of 1,500 respondents ideal for polls of large numbers of people.) In a cross-section of this kind, differences in age, race, religion, political orientation, education, and other factors approximate those within the larger population.

Because it is not always possible to conduct hundreds of separate interviews, pollsters sometimes use smaller, pre-selected samples based on such key characteristics as age, religion, income, and party affiliation. This is **stratified sampling.** Exit polling, which permits television networks to predict political winners as the polls close by surveying departing voters, illustrates two levels of stratified polling. First, pollsters identify precincts that statistically approximate the

© HOWARD YANES/AP PHOTO

Students marching for freedom of speech in Caracas, Venezuela after President Hugo Chavez closed down a popular television channel. Note that many of the student demonstrators' hands are painted white as a sign of peaceful intentions, but the government nonetheless accused them of being violent.

larger political entity (a congressional district, a state, or the nation). Then they try to select a sample that reflects the overall characteristics of the precinct.

Tracking polls repeatedly sample the same voters during the course of a campaign to identify shifts in voter sentiment and correlate them with media strategy, voter issues, candidates' gaffes, and so forth. To discover which campaign strategies are working and which are not, candidates often use tracking polls in conjunction with focus groups and other campaign instruments (see Box 11.2).

Polls are useful predictive instruments, but they are not infallible. In general, they have a margin of error of 3 percent at the .05 level of confidence, which means 95 in 100 times the error is no more than 3 percent in either direction. The exact wording of a given instrument is important for issues about which most people do not have well-formed opinions. Given a choice between two policy alternatives (for example, "Should the federal government see to it that all people have housing, or should individuals provide for their own housing?"), some respondents can be so influenced by the order in which the policies appear that a 30 percent variance between them may result, depending solely on which comes first in the question.[1] The *way* a question is phrased can also make a big difference. For example, "Do you support the right to life?" is likely to produce very different results from, "Do you support the right to terminate a pregnancy in the first trimester?"

Polls not only *measure* public opinion but also *influence* it. A question that frames smoking in terms of freedom to exercise a personal choice will yield a higher rate of approval for smoking than a question that mentions the health risks of secondhand smoke. Candidates, corporations, and organized interest groups of all kinds can often obtain the results they want through careful phrasing of their questions. Unfortunately, stacking the deck this way is a common practice in both the public and the private sectors.

Today, literally hundreds of polls are taken in a presidential election year. More polls do not necessarily mean better results,[2] though in the last three

tracking poll
Repeated sampling of voters to assess shifts in attitudes or behavior over time.

presidential elections they have been quite accurate. Indeed, the "poll of polls" (the average of all the major surveys) in the 2008 presidential election was right on the money. Nearly two dozen polls taken on the eve of the election projected an Obama advantage of 7.52 percentage points on average; Obama's actual margin of victory was 7.2 percent.[3]

But even at its best, political polling presents certain hazards. First, polls are only snapshots of public opinion, and public opinion is subject to rapid change. Second, as polling has become more widespread and intrusive, citizens are becoming less cooperative (despite pollsters' assurances of anonymity) and probably less truthful as well. Third, there are important methodological differences among the various polls. The biggest is the way polling organizations count the "undecided" voter and how they predict who the "likely" voter will be.

A president's popularity as reflected in public opinion polls often weighs heavily in the relationship between the president and Congress. During President Obama's "First 100 Days," for example, the White House was able to push the largest economic stimulus package and largest federal budget in U.S. history through Congress, thanks in no small part to public opinion polls showing widespread voter approval of Obama's leadership.

Elections

Polls and elections are closely related. In fact, elections *are* polls—the most accurate ones of all because the "sample" includes everybody who actually votes. Free elections are tied to the concept of representation—indeed, *representative democracy* and *republic* are synonymous.

Limitations of Elections Ideally, elections should enable a democratic society to translate the preferences of its citizens into laws and policies. In reality, elections often produce disappointing or indecisive results for a long list of reasons, including the following:

- If public opinion is ill defined or badly divided, elected officials get mixed signals.
- The great expenditure of time and money required to run for public office gives a huge advantage to incumbents and discourages many potential challengers.
- To attract as many voters or interest groups as possible, candidates often waffle on issues, giving voters a choice between Tweedledee and Tweedledum.
- Powerful lobbies and a convoluted budget process preoccupy, and occasionally paralyze, Congress.
- Politicians frequently say one thing and do another.

Despite these limitations, elections are indispensable to democracy. Contrary to popular opinion, campaign promises are often kept.[4] Elected officials sometimes turn out to be duds or disappointments, but they are seldom surprises; often what you see is what you get. And when candidates do break election promises, they risk paying a heavy price.

Electoral Systems

Electoral systems vary greatly. We begin with the familiar and then look at some of the alternatives.

Winner-Takes-All Systems Most voters in the United States would have difficulty explaining how the U.S. electoral system works. Members of Congress are elected by plurality vote in single-member districts—that is, in the **winner-takes-all system**, which means that only one representative is elected from each electoral district, and the candidate who gets the most votes in the general election wins the seat. Because a state's two senators are elected in different years, entire states function as single-member districts. Finally, the 50 states are each single-member districts in the presidential race, because *all* the electoral votes in any state are awarded to the electors of the presidential candidate who receives the most popular votes in that particular state.

The practical implications of such a system are wide ranging. In any election within a single-member district, if only two candidates are seeking office, one of them necessarily will receive a **simple majority**, defined as the largest bloc of votes. If three or more candidates are vying for a seat, however, the one who receives the greatest number of votes is elected. In a five-way race, for example, a candidate could win with 25 percent (or less) of the votes. As we shall see, this method of election strongly favors the emergence of a two-party system.

The effects of winner-takes-all, also known as **first past the post**, electoral systems are graphically illustrated by the hypothetical U.S. congressional race depicted in Table 11.1. This system has at least one important advantage: It produces clear winners. A simple majority (or plurality) decides who will represent the district. In the table, John Liberal is the clear winner. But there is a price to be paid for this convenient result—a majority (57 percent of the electorate) did not

©GETTY IMAGES.

winner-takes-all system
Electoral system in which the candidate receiving the most votes wins.

simple majority
The largest bloc of voters in an election.

first past the post
An electoral system used in the United Kingdom and the United States in which legislative candidates run in single-member districts and the winner is decided by plurality vote; this system favors broad-based, entrenched political parties and tends toward a two-party configuration. Critics contend that it is undemocratic because it places a huge hurdle in the path of small or new parties and forces voters to decide between voting for a major-party candidate near the center of the political spectrum and wasting their votes on a third-party candidate who cannot possibly win.

At present, voters cast ballots in elections held all over the world, but the rules (for example, who is eligible to vote) and precise workings of electoral systems vary greatly from country to country.

TABLE 11.1   Hypothetical Political Race

Party	Candidate	Votes Received	Percent of Vote
Democratic	John Liberal	25,800	43
Republican	Jane Conservative	24,600	41
Independent	Ima Nothing	9,600	16

vote for him. For all it mattered, they might as well have stayed home. Neither the policies advocated by candidates Jane Conservative and Ima Nothing nor the preferences of the majority in this congressional district will be represented.

Under this system, one of the two major parties in every election invariably gains representation disproportionate to the actual size of the popular vote it receives, *at the expense of the other major party and any minor parties in the race.* Hence, a major party receiving 40 percent to 45 percent of the popular vote may win a clear majority of legislative seats, as normally happens in British elections. This type of distortion is so pronounced in the United Kingdom that a major party receiving fewer than half the votes can sometimes win in a landslide (an election resulting in a huge parliamentary majority).

In this way, the winner-takes-all electoral system encourages the emergence of two major political parties and hampers the growth of smaller political parties and splinter groups. The advantage is greater political stability, compared with many multiparty systems. Some critics feel, however, that such stability is achieved at the expense of representative democracy's very essence—that is, its emphasis on a government that reflects the will and preferences of the majority. Because the winner-takes-all system does not represent the total spectrum of voter opinions and interests, critics point out, it tends to magnify the legislative power of the major party or parties and stifle attempts of minor parties to secure a legislative toehold.

proportional representation (PR)
Any political structure under which seats in the legislature are allocated to each party based on the percentage of the popular vote each receives.

Proportional Representation Systems   The alternative to winner-takes-all is an electoral system based on **proportional representation**, designed to ensure the representation of parties in the legislature approximates party support in the electorate. Usually, under this system, the nation is divided into *multimember* electoral districts, with a formula awarding each district's seats in proportion to the fractions of the vote the various parties receive in that district.

Among the many countries using this system are Israel, Italy, Belgium, Norway, and Ireland. Germany also uses proportional representation to elect half the members of the Bundestag (the lower house of parliament). Candidates in a district win office if they receive at least a specified number of votes, determined by dividing the number of votes cast by the number of seats allocated. For example, assume in Table 11.1 that a proportional representation system is in place, the district has been allocated three seats, and 60,000 votes have been cast. A representative will thus be elected for every 20,000 votes a party receives. According to this formula, candidates Liberal and Conservative would both be elected, because each received more than 20,000 votes.

But no votes are wasted. The district's third representative would be determined by a regional distribution, which works like this: 5,800 Democratic votes, 4,600 Republican votes, and 9,600 Independent votes are forwarded to the region, to be combined with other districts' votes and reallocated. Where regional distributions fail to seat a candidate, a final *national* distribution may be necessary. In this manner, proportional representation guarantees that everyone's vote will count.

Some countries have modified this system to prevent the proliferation of small fringe parties, requiring that minor parties receive a certain minimum of the national vote to qualify for district representation. In Germany and Russia, this figure is 5 percent; in other countries, it can be 15 percent or even higher.

The **list system** is by far the most common method of proportional representation in use. A party may run as many candidates as it wishes in any particular electoral district, but it must rank its candidates on the ballot. If the party receives enough votes in the district to win only one seat, the candidate ranked first on the list gets that seat; if the party garners enough votes to elect two delegates from that district, the candidate ranked second also gets a seat; and so on. The list system strengthens political parties significantly, because citizens vote primarily for the party (as opposed to the candidate), and the party controls the ordering of the candidates on the ballot.

The **Hare plan,** one alternative to the list system, is based on a single, transferable vote and emphasizes individual candidates or personalities rather than parties. Voters indicate a first and second preference. A quota—the number of votes required to win a seat—is set, and when a candidate has met the quota, the remainder of votes cast for that candidate are transferred to the second preference on those ballots, and so on until all available seats have been awarded.

Electoral Systems Compared Proportional representation systems have certain advantages over the winner-takes-all method. Few votes are "wasted," more parties can gain seats in the legislature, and fairness—to voters, candidates, and parties—is emphasized, because seats are apportioned according to the vote totals that each party actually receives.

The winner-takes-all system has the advantage of stability. It effectively bars the door to upstart and single-issue splinter parties. It eliminates the need for **coalition governments,** because it stacks the deck in favor of two major parties. It also boils down choices for the voters, typically between two middle-of-the-road programs—one slightly center-right, the other slightly center-left.

Direct Democracy

Voters can be legislators. Perhaps the most easily recognized model of direct democracy is the New England town hall meeting. By providing for elected representatives, however, the U.S. Constitution rejects the idea of a direct democracy in favor of a representative one.

Today, direct democracy coexists with representational democracy in many places. In some democracies, such as Switzerland and Australia, as well as a number of U.S. states (see Figure 11.1), citizens can bypass or supersede the legislature by voting directly on specific questions of public policy in a **plebiscite.** In the United States, a plebiscite can take three forms, as illustrated in Figure 11.1.

list system
Method of proportional representation by which candidates are ranked on the ballot by their party and are chosen according to rank.

Hare plan
In parliamentary democracies, an electoral procedure whereby candidates compete for a set number of seats and those who receive a certain quota of votes are elected. Voters vote only once and indicate both a first and a second choice.

coalition government
In a multiparty parliamentary system, the political situation in which no single party has a majority and the largest party allies itself loosely with other, smaller parties to control a majority of the legislative seats.

plebiscite
A vote by an entire community on some specific issue of public policy.

FIGURE 11.1   Citizen-Initiated Initiative, Referendum, and Recall at the State Level.

SOURCE: From *Direct Democracy: The Politics of Initiative, Referendum, and Recall* by Thomas E. Cronin (Cambridge, MA: Harvard University Press). Copyright 1989 by the Twentieth Century Fund, Inc. Updated by Thomas Magstadt, 2002.

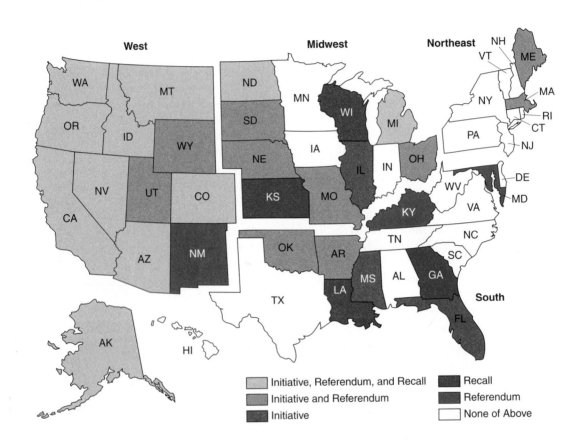

referendum
A vote through which citizens may directly repeal a law.

initiative
A mechanism by which voters act as legislators, placing a measure on the ballot by petition and directly deciding whether or not to make it a law on election day.

A **referendum** occurs when the state legislature or constitution refers a question of public policy to its voters. Sometimes the vote is merely advisory, indicating the electorate's preferences; in other cases, voter approval is required before a ballot item can be enacted into law. In an **initiative,** the voters themselves put a measure on the ballot by filing petitions containing a stipulated number of valid signatures (see Box 11.3). The **recall** is a political device intended to remove an elected official from office. It works much like an initiative and is also placed on the ballot by the signatures of a predetermined number of citizens.

Some major issues decided by direct vote in Europe include the following:

- French President Charles de Gaulle used a referendum to amend the French constitution to provide for the direct election of the president (de Gaulle himself) in 1962.

Box 11.3 FOCUS ON — Initiative and Referendum

There are two types of initiative—direct and indirect— and two types of referendum—popular and legislative. Legislative referendum is divided into two categories: amendments and statutes. Twenty-three states give their legislatures *discretionary power* to place statutes on the ballot. Delaware is the only state that does not *require* placement of *constitutional amendments* on the ballot.

- Twenty-seven states have some form of initiative or popular referendum.
- Twenty-four states have a form of initiative.
- Twenty-four states have popular referendum.
- Fifty states have some form of legislative referendum.
- The first state to hold a legislative referendum to adopt its constitution was Massachusetts, in 1778.

- The first state to adopt the initiative and popular referendum was South Dakota, in 1898.
- The first state to place an initiative on the ballot was Oregon, in 1904.
- The first state to allow cities to use initiative and popular referendum was Nebraska, in 1897.
- The first state to provide for initiative and popular referendum in its original constitution was Oklahoma, in 1907.
- Four states have adopted initiative or popular referendum since 1958.

SOURCE: Adapted from Initiative and Referendum Institute, "Quickfacts," http://www.iandrinstitute.org/factsheets/quickfacts.htm.

- The United Kingdom held its first referendum in 1973 to decide whether the nation should join the Common Market (a narrow majority voted in favor).
- Denmark, Ireland, and Sweden, among others, have put issues such as whether to join the **euro area**—the EU countries that have adopted the euro—on the ballot. (It was rejected by Danish voters, but Denmark plans to hold another referendum on it; Irish voters said yes, and Swedish voters said no.)
- Direct popular vote in several Central and East European countries determined whether they would join the European Union. (All countries invited said yes.)

We can trace the modern era of direct democracy in the United States to 1978 and California's passage of the famous Proposition 13, which not only halved property taxes there but also spurred many initiatives and referendums throughout the nation.

Many direct democracy measures remain controversial. In 1996 Proposition 209, a California Civil Rights Initiative, limited affirmative action programs by amending the state's constitution to prohibit discrimination against, or preferential treatment of, "any individual or group on the basis of race, sex, color, ethnicity, or national origin in the operation of public employment, public education, or public contracting." Opponents of the initiative challenged the new law in federal court on grounds it was unconstitutional, but they lost. Michigan voters passed a similar amendment in 2006.

recall
Direct voting to remove an elected official from office.

euro area
In the EU, the euro zone refers to the 12 member states that have adopted the euro, including Germany, France, and Italy, but not the United Kingdom.

Even more controversial is Proposition 8, another California ballot initiative—passed in the November 4, 2008, general election—that amended the state Constitution to restrict the definition of marriage to opposite-sex couples and eliminate same-sex couples' right to marry. The "yes" vote overrode portions of a California Supreme Court decision affirming marriage as a fundamental right earlier in 2008.

Direct democracy is often championed as a means of revitalizing public faith in government, improving voter participation, and circumventing corrupt, cowardly, or incompetent officeholders.[5] Opponents argue that money and special interests can too easily engineer the outcome of an initiative or referendum. They also say ballot measures are often so complex and technical, the average voter cannot understand the issues. At least one student of plebiscites disagrees: "On most issues, especially well-publicized ones, voters do grasp the meaning . . . and . . . they act competently."[6]

For opponents to argue that money distorts the outcome of referendums is disingenuous at best. Money is arguably *the* major factor in virtually *all* U.S. elections of any consequence today, so it follows that such critics ought to focus on the role of money in U.S. *politics*, not in plebiscites (direct democracy).

Still, too much democracy can perhaps be as bad as too little; if all laws had to be put to a vote of all the people all the time, government could never act quickly or expeditiously, even in a crisis or national emergency. When measures are numerous and issues complex, the opportunity for demagoguery grows, and the possibility of rational voter choice diminishes. For these reasons, direct democracy is, at best, a supplement to, rather than a substitute for, representative democracy.

RATIONALIZING PARTICIPATION: WHY VOTE?

The right to vote is not a foolproof defense against tyranny and oppression, but it is the best one available. Yet later generations often take for granted rights earlier generations won at a very dear price. The United States offers no exception.

Voting in the United States

Most voting-age U.S. adults do not bother to vote in midterm elections (when there is no presidential race). Even in presidential races, voter turnout has often been low by comparison with many European democracies. In 1996, a presidential election year, fewer than half voted (see Figure 11.2); by contrast in the 1960 Kennedy-Nixon election, nearly 63 percent of the adult population voted. In recent elections, however, turnout has climbed back up but still remains well below 60 percent.

In 2000, a slightly larger turnout in Florida (where less than half the voting age population cast a ballot) might have changed the outcome—and the course of U.S. history (see Box 11.4). In the hotly contested 2004 presidential election

FIGURE 11.2 Voter Turnout in U.S. National Elections 1996–2008.
Color indicates presidential election years.

Source: Federal Election Commission. Data drawn from Congressional Research Service reports, Election Data Services Inc., and state election offices.

Year	Voting age	Voter registration	Voter turnout	Voting-age turnout
2008	231,229,580	NA	132,618,580	56.8%
2006	220,600,000	135,889,600	80,588,000	37.1%
2004	221,256,931	174,800,000	122,294,978	55.3%
2002	215,473,000	150,990,598	79,830,119	37.0%
2000	205,815,000	156,421,311	105,586,274	51.3%
1998	200,929,000	141,850,558	73,117,022	36.4%
1996	196,511,000	146,211,960	96,456,345	49.1%

(George W. Bush vs. John Kerry), as the electorate became polarized over the war in Iraq, voter turnout climbed to 55 percent and in 2008 reached nearly 57 percent, the highest since 1968.

Midterm elections provide another measure of voting behavior in the United States. In general, turnout is dismal in these years (see Figure 11.3). Even in the highly charged 2006 midterm elections, only 37 percent of the voting age population turned out at the polls. Compared with other democracies, voter turnout in the United States is an embarrassment.[7] In Europe, voter participation in national elections typically averages over 80 percent. Imagine a U.S. presidential election with an 85 percent voter turnout—that was the actual turnout in France in April 2007.

The low participation is an enigma, because it has occurred against a backdrop of changes that ought to have brought voters to the polls. Laws and rules designed to block or burden access to the ballot, such as poll taxes, literacy tests, and lengthy residence requirements, are gone. The voting age has dropped to 18. The potential for virtually all U.S. adults to vote now exists.[8] Moreover, since passage of the **motor voter law** in 1993, new voters can register while obtaining or renewing their driver's licenses. In sum, low voter participation flies in the face of "broad changes in the population [that] have boosted levels of education, income, and occupation, all associated with enhanced rates of turnout."[9]

Who votes and who does not are key questions in any democracy (see Box 11.4). Perhaps even more important, however, is the question many nonvoters ask: Why bother? Unless the defenders of democracy can continue to give them a meaningful answer, there is always a danger that liberty itself will lose its hold on the popular imagination.

People who believe it is possible to make a difference, who are confident self-confident and assertive, are more likely to become engaged in public affairs, including political activity, than people who lack these attributes. Why then do

motor voter law
A statute that allows residents of a given locality to register to vote at convenient places, such as welfare offices and drivers' license bureaus; the idea behind laws of this kind is to remove technical obstacles to voting and thus promote better turnouts in elections.

Box 11.4 FOCUS ON   Who Decides Who Gets to Vote?

The 2000 presidential election came down to 537 official votes separating the "winner" (Bush) from the "loser" (Al Gore) in one state, Florida, where the chief election official, Katherine Harris, was also co-chair of the Florida Bush campaign. In that race, thousands of Florida voters were "wrongly purged" according to the *New York Times.**

Florida was the most notorious case of voting list irregularities in the 2000 election, but it was not the only one, nor was it the most egregious. The *New York Times* cited another example:

In Missouri, St. Louis, election officials kept an "inactive voters list" of people they had been unable to contact by mail. Voters on the list, which ballooned to more than 54,000 names in a city where only 125,230 voted, had a legal right to cast their ballots, but election officials put up enormous barriers. When inactive voters showed up to vote, poll workers had to confirm their registration with the board of elections downtown. Phone lines there were busy all day, and hundreds of voters travelled downtown in person, spending hours trying to vindicate their right to vote. The board admitted later that "a significant number" were not processed before the polls closed.

The same thing that happened in Florida and Missouri in 2000 could happen elsewhere. According to the *New York Times*, "Voters would have no way of knowing [if there was a problem] because of the stunning lack of transparency in election operations." Election board officials often make decisions about removing voters from the rolls without any written rules or procedures.

The power to decide who gets to vote has both social and political implications. In both Florida and St. Louis, disenfranchised voters were disproportionately black. In Florida, African Americans are one of the strongest Democratic voting groups.

What is to be done? The *New York Times* recommends a three-step remedy: (1) clear standards—the policy for purging voting lists ought to be based on clear, written guidelines; (2) transparency—the public has a right to know when voting list purges are under way; and (3) non-partisanship—election board officials should not be connected to candidates or parties.

---

*Editorial, "How America Doesn't Vote," New York Times, February 15, 2004, <http://www.nytimes.com/2004/02/15/opinion/how-america-doesn-t-vote.html?>

some people lack a sense of **political efficacy** and why do so many U.S. adults not even vote?

Patterns of Participation

political efficacy
The ability to participate meaningfully in political activities, usually because of one's education, social background, and sense of self-esteem.

It is ironic that U.S. adults take such pride in being citizens of the world's oldest democracy, because most of us are public-affairs averse.

A pioneering 1950 study by Julian L. Woodward and Elmo Roper revealed that about 70 percent of U.S. adults were politically inactive.[10] A later study found approximately 26 percent of the U.S. population could be classified as activists; the rest either limited participation to voting or avoided politics altogether.[11]

FIGURE 11.3   U.S. Midterm Election Turnout, 1962–2006, based on House Votes Cast (percentage of voting-age population).

SOURCE: Adapted from *Congressional Quarterly Weekly Report*, February 23, 1991, p. 484; and the United States Elections Project, Department of Public and International Affairs, George Mason University, http://elections.gmu.edu/Voter_Turnout_2006.htm.

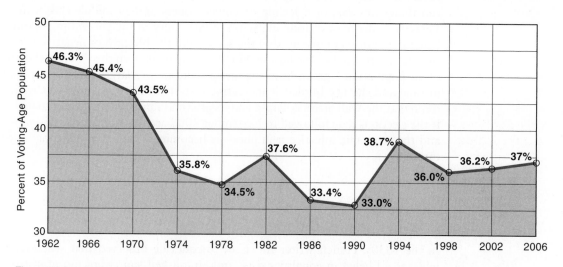

The voter turnout rate in midterm elections remains low. It fell abruptly after the voting age was lowered to 18 in 1971 and has trended downward, with a mild reversal in the recession year of 1982 and a significant upturn in 1994. In Tennessee, Mississippi, and Louisiana (where only one district was decided in November), the turnout rate did not reach 20 percent. In only four states did a majority of the voting-age population participate in voting for the House: Maine (55.6 percent), Minnesota (54.8 percent), Montana (54.6 percent), and Alaska (52.5 percent).

Who votes in the United States? According to U.S. census data, women are more likely to vote than men, and whites more likely than blacks or Hispanics. People over 65 are much more likely to vote than young adults 18–24. Midwesterners are more likely to vote than people in the South or West. People with a college education vote more than people who never finished high school, and white-collar workers vote more than blue-collar workers. Clearly, socioeconomic factors affect participation rates.

The 2008 general election, however, saw a marked difference in certain voting patterns. Minorities and youth voted in record numbers. African Americans cast nearly 3 million more ballots in 2008 than in 2004 (up 21 percent); 1.5 million more Latinos voted in 2008 than in 2004 (up 16 percent); and the youth vote (aged 18–29) climbed by 1.8 million votes (a 9 percent rise). The 2008 election was "the most diverse in U.S. history;" black women had the highest voter turnout rate (68.8 percent)—a first.[12]

Generational factors are increasingly important in U.S. elections. In the last three general elections—2004, 2006, and 2008—voters 18–29 have been "the Democratic party's most supportive age group. In 2008, 66% of those under age 30 voted for Barack Obama, making the disparity between young voters and other age groups larger than in any presidential election since exit polling began in 1972."[13]

Until recently, some observers blamed low voter turnout rates on the 1971 lowering of the voting age to 18, which brought into the electorate a group long thought not to vote. But this simplistic explanation overlooks potential voters' attitudes—for example a sense that wealthy elites (mostly white males) run things anyway, or a feeling of powerlessness among middle-class voters. There is evidence of a declining sense of civic duty in the general population. Lengthy political campaigns dull the senses and the blizzard of negative television ads deepen public disillusion. Finally, the gap between the rich and the rest of the population is growing, as the former take an ever larger share of national income and the tax burden is increasingly shifted onto the latter—a divisive trend that the Wall Street collapse and its aftermath in 2008 only accentuated.[14] If the elections that followed in November 2008 are any indication, this gap—and the economic injustice it implies—is becoming a factor in boosting voter turnout.

Private Pursuits and the Public Good

In the 1830s, French writer Alexis de Tocqueville observed that wherever a widespread belief in equality exists, and established sources of moral instruction like religion, family, monarchy, and tradition fail to carry the weight they once did, individuals tend to be morally self-reliant. For Tocqueville the resulting **individualism** was the moral equivalent of selfishness.

"Individualism," he wrote, "is a mature and calm feeling, which disposes each member of the community to sever himself from the mass of his fellow creatures; and to draw apart with his family and friends; so that, after he has thus formed a little circle of his own, he willingly leaves the society at large to itself."[15] Tocqueville's America was so populated by self-centered individuals that concern for the common good was in danger of extinction. In a society where success is defined as "keeping up with the Joneses," the people live in a state of constant agitation arising from personal ambitions. Thus, he noted, "In America the passion for physical well-being . . . is felt by all" and "the desire of acquiring the good things of this world is the prevailing passion of the American people."[16]

Tocqueville thought the detrimental effects of individualism were counteracted, to some extent, by the fact that in the United States, people belonged to an enormous number and variety of civic associations. These associations expanded the personal horizon of the average citizen while reinforcing democracy's underpinnings, encouraging social cooperation, and teaching respect for others' opinions.

But participation in group activities of all kinds has declined in the United States. Observing that the number of bowlers had increased 10 percent whereas league bowling decreased 40 percent between 1980 and 1993, Robert Putnam concluded in the mid-1990s that bowling symbolized life as we know it in the United States.[17] Putnam also pointed out that participation in organized religion, labor unions, the

individualism
According to Alexis de Tocqueville, the direction of one's feelings toward oneself and one's immediate situation; a self-centered detachment from the broader concerns of society as a whole. According to John Stuart Mill, the qualities of human character that separate humans from animals and give them uniqueness and dignity.

PTA, traditional women's groups such as the League of Women Voters, and service clubs, such as the Shriners and Masons, had declined during the past 30 years, as had volunteering. The implications are an eroding sense of community and a tendency to withdraw from public affairs. Inevitably, civil society is the loser.

In April 2009, President Obama signed a new national service bill into law. The Edward M. Kennedy Serve America Act dedicates $5.7 billion over five years to promoting volunteerism. It reauthorizes and expands national service programs run by the Corporation for National and Community Service, a federal agency created in 1993 that already engages four million volunteers each year, including 75,000 AmeriCorps members. Under the new law, this number will to rise by 250,000. AmeriCorps volunteers will receive a living allowance ($12,000 for 10 to 12 months of work) and staff programs for poor people, veterans, the environment, healthcare, and education.

Whether a new federal program to tackle a problem Tocqueville identified as a national trait so long ago can change a society set in its ways remains to be seen. But the fact that we are talking about spending billions of dollars to revive a sense of civic responsibility points to the persistence—and seriousness—of the problem.

Affluence and Apathy

Political apathy and indifference, expressed as a surprising lack of curiosity about what is going on in Washington or the world, persisted in the United States even after 9/11 and the invasion of Iraq. But that changed dramatically in 2008 when the financial crisis suddenly jeopardized the fortunes and future of millions of U.S. workers with investments in mutual funds and retirement plans. What it says about human nature when we are more concerned about our wallets than our wars is an interesting question, but not one we will try to answer here. Apparently, however, most of us believe we can afford to be nonchalant about politics, so long as we ourselves are not insecure or oppressed. In other words, political apathy is a luxury. Only in an affluent and stable society do people take the right to vote for granted or treat it as a trivial thing.

Political apathy is not necessarily a sign of decay or impending doom. The United States has functioned as a stable political system with a robust economy in spite of low voter turnout. When people who are normally apathetic suddenly begin to express high anxiety about politics, however, usually all is not well. In the 1850s, for example, apathy gave way to antipathy between North and South over slavery and states' rights, leading to secession and the Civil War. In the 1930s, the Great Depression galvanized the nation. Today, the deepest recession since the 1930s has banished our apathy.

In sum, participation is not always a good thing. But neither is apathy. If the only time we take a keen interest in politics is when we are personally affected, if our *only* motive is self-interest as opposed to the public interest or the common good, that points to a serious defect in our national character—one that, over time, will manifest itself in undesirable ways. Try explaining what went wrong on Wall Street in August 2008, for example, without mentioning greed.

political apathy
Lack of interest in politics resulting from complacency, ignorance, or the conviction that "my vote doesn't really count" or "nobody cares what I think anyway."

BOX 11.5 SPOTLIGHT ON   Australia's Mandatory Voting Law

Noted scholar and political observer Norm Ornstein wants to make voting mandatory in the United States. He believes lower turnout is the cause of "ever-greater polarization in the country and in Washington, which in turn has led to ever-more rancor and ever-less legislative progress." He makes a persuasive case:

With participation rates of about 10 percent or less of the eligible electorate in many primaries, to 35 percent or so in midterm general elections, to 50 or 60 percent in presidential contests, the name of the game for parties is turnout—the key to success is turning out one's ideological base. Whichever party does a better job getting its base to the polls reaps the rewards of majority status. And what's the best way to get your base to show up at the polls? Focus on divisive issues that underscore the differences between the parties.

Ornstein points out that several countries, including Austria, Belgium, and Cyprus, as well as Australia and Singapore, have adopted mandatory voting. In Australia (see Figure 11.4), "no-shows" at the polls pay a modest fine of about $15 the first time and more with each subsequent offense. The result: a turnout rate greater than 95 percent. "The fine, of course, is an incentive to vote. But the system has also instilled the idea that voting is a societal obligation." No less important, "It has elevated the political dialogue," and it places a premium on "persuading the persuadables."

Ornstein surmises, "If there were mandatory voting in America, there's a good chance that the ensuing reduction in extremist discourse would lead to genuine legislative progress." But, he argues, political reform is urgent: "These days, valuable congressional time is spent on frivolous or narrow issues (flag burning, same-sex marriage) that are intended only to spur on the party bases and ideological extremes. Consequently, important, complicated issues (pension and health-care reform) get short shrift."

Norm Ornstein is a scholar in residence at the American Enterprise Institute and the co-author (with Thomas Mann) of *The Broken Branch: How Congress Is Failing America and How to Get It Back on Track* (New York: Oxford University Press, 2006).

SOURCE: Norm Ornstein, "Vote—Or Else," *New York Times*, August 10, 2006 (online edition).

FIGURE 11.4   Australia is a continent as well as a country that is roughly the size of the "lower 48" (the continental United States minus Alaska). It is a parliamentary democracy with a mandatory voting requirement.

A steady and sober interest in public affairs stemming from a well-ingrained sense of civic duty is a healthy antidote to excessive individualism—and a far better solution to the problem of apathy than an aroused but ignorant majority (see Box 11.5).

PARTICIPATING AS A SPECTATOR: OUTSIDERS

In the competitive "game" of politics (see Box 11.6), outsiders—most of us—are at a disadvantage—not least because we do not understand the game very well. One study in the 1990s found nearly half of respondents did not know the Supreme Court has final authority to determine whether a law is constitutional, while three of four were unaware senators serve 6-year terms.[18] Can democracy work if the majority—the outsiders—do not know how it works?

Some feel the debate is much ado about nothing. First, whereas only a minority of the voting-age population votes, those who do vote generally are better informed than are those who do not. Second, U.S. adults as a whole probably know as much about politics today as they did in the 1940s.[19] Third, many find it more worthwhile to engage in private pursuits and leave politics to others.[20] Fourth, candidates often take no clear political stance, so many citizens may wonder, What's the point? Finally, many voters make reasonable judgments about issues and candidates despite being poorly informed.[21]

According to a theory called **low-information rationality,** ill-informed voters use shortcuts (for example, does a candidate look the part?) and simplifying assumptions (such as party identification) to make political judgments.[22] This theory assumes picking a candidate for office is like buying a car. But when voters go to the polls, they have a far narrower range of choices than car buyers and far less information about the "product"—problems that can be fixed only by elected representatives, who unfortunately often have a vested interest in *not* fixing them.

Why do supposedly rational voters almost always reelect incumbents while mistrusting Congress as an institution? According to rational actor theory (which holds that human behavior is a product of logical reasoning rather than emotion or habit), they are "voting for the devil they know rather than the devil they don't" and for representatives with seniority who have proven they can produce "pork" (federal funding) for local projects.

Enlightened or not, this type of voting behavior is rational in the short term and on the local level. The dilemma for democracy arises from the fact that "comfort zone" voting is not necessarily rational in the aggregate or in the long run—that is, on the national level, where the big-picture decisions, laws, and policies are made.

low-information rationality
The idea that voters can make sensible choices in elections even though they lack knowledge and sophistication about public policy, candidates, and current events.

Box 11.6 FOCUS ON   Wallets and Wars: Is Politics a Game?

Game theory treats politics as a game—not like Trivial Pursuit, but as an analytical tool. To say voters are spectators is not to deny they participate in the process. Fans at basketball games, for example, are spectators, but they also "vote" in various ways—from buying tickets to cheering or booing. At college games, fans at the visitors' end of the court often try to distract the free-throw shooter. It is doubtful whether a "home court" would exist without spectators. In fact, there might be no home court at all. Finally, some games have very high stakes—from big wallets to big wars. In sum, although outsiders (rank-and-file citizens) are not directly involved in the "game" most of the time, insiders (political elites) cannot ignore them; by the same token, because decisions made by the few directly affect the many, outsiders cannot afford to be ignored.

PARTICIPATING AS A PLAYER: INSIDERS

Some say a power elite controls the political process from top to bottom. The most popular version of this theory holds that ordinary citizens never exercise much influence, elections and public opinion polls notwithstanding, and the political system is manipulated from above rather than below. The manipulators are the power elite, a small group of individuals who go through a "revolving door" between the commanding heights of industry and the rarefied echelons of government, exercising enormous power over the nation's destiny. The status, wealth, and power of this self-perpetuating political class ensure that access to the levers of government is monopolized by the few to pursue private interests, not the public interest.

The close links between personal business interests of the Bush family and the oil industry gave new credence to this theory (especially after the ill-fated invasion of Iraq), as did the fact that Halliburton, the huge multinational corporation formerly headed by Vice President Cheney, was awarded billions of dollars in no-bid contracts to operate in Iraq.

Elitist Theories: Iron Laws and Ironies

elitist theory of democracy
In political thought, the theory that a small clique of individuals (a "power elite") at the highest levels of government, industry, and other institutions actually exercise political power for their own interests; according to elitist theories, ordinary citizens have almost no real influence on governmental policy.

Elitist theories of democracy hold that democracy is governed by neither the voters nor public opinion nor a variety of competing interests, but rather by a small number of wealthy individuals. This theory was propounded most influentially in the 1950s by sociologist C. Wright Mills.[23] By putting the power elite in the spotlight, Mills challenged the idea of "government by the people" and called into serious question whether it exists (or has ever existed) in the United States.

Robert Michels, a German sociologist, also advanced a theory of elitism, but his study applied to all modern bureaucratic organizations. His findings were distilled from an analysis of the German Social Democratic Party, which before the outbreak of World War I had been the largest socialist party in the world. Michels reasoned that because the party favored equality in wealth and status, it should be sufficiently committed to democratic principles to put them into practice. He found instead that elite groups that derived their power and authority from well-honed organizational skills ran the party.

This discovery led Michels to postulate his famous **iron law of oligarchy,** which holds that all large organizations, including governments, are run in the same fashion. He believed organizations naturally become increasingly oligarchic, bureaucratized, and centralized over time, as those at the top gain more information and knowledge, greater control of communications, and sharper organizational skills, while the great mass of members (or citizens) remain politically unsophisticated, preoccupied with private affairs, and bewildered by the complexity of larger issues. According to this view, the people, for whose benefit democratic institutions were originally conceived, are inevitably shut out of the political or organizational process as corporate officers or bureaucratic officials govern in the name of the rank-and-file shareholder or citizen.

In elitist theories, democracy is seen as a sham or a myth: it does not matter what the people think, say, or do, because they have no real influence over public policy. If most people believe public opinion matters, it is only because they are naive and do not really understand how "the system" works.

Most believe "democracy for the few" violates the very essence of government by consent, but a few theorists have argued the U.S. political system *is* dominated by the privileged few, and that we are all much better off for it because the people as a whole are unfit to govern themselves. The "masses are authoritarian, intolerant, anti-intellectual, atavistic, alienated, hateful, and violent."[24] The irony of democracy is then clear: allowing the people real power to rule will only result in the expression of antidemocratic preferences and policies.

iron law of oligarchy
According to this theory, the administrative necessities involved in managing any large organization, access to and control of information and communication inevitably become concentrated in the hands of a few bureaucrats, who then wield true power in the organization.

Pluralists Versus Elitists

The chief opponents of the elitist school of thought are known as pluralists. Pluralists and elitists alike accept that in any society there are gradations of power and certain groups or individuals exercise disproportionate influence. They disagree, however, about the basic nature of the political system itself.

According to pluralists, the U.S. political system is intricate and decentralized. They concede that various organized interest groups, by concentrating all their energies, resources, and attention on one issue, exert disproportionate influence in that specific policy area. They also admit that from time to time certain disadvantaged or unpopular groups may not be adequately represented. Nonetheless, no single individual or group can exercise total power over the whole gamut of public policy. The political system is too wide open, freewheeling, and institutionally fragmented to allow for any such accumulation of power. In the opinion of one prominent pluralist,

Demonstrators demand universal health care at a recent ACT UP rally in New York City.

© JENNIFER GRAYLOCK/AP PHOTO

The most important obstacle to social change in the United States, then, is not the concentration of power but its diffusion. . . . If power was concentrated sufficiently, those of us who wish for change would merely have to negotiate with those who hold the power and, if necessary, put pressure on them. But power is so widely diffused that, in many instances, there is no one to negotiate with and no one on whom to put pressure.[25]

Pluralists do not deny that those who hold the highest positions in government and business tend to have similar backgrounds and characteristics: Admittedly, many are males from well-to-do WASP (white Anglo-Saxon Protestant) families who have had Ivy League educations. However, that wealth, status, and education correlate closely with political influence and participation does not prove the system is closed and public policy predetermined, nor does it mean participatory democracy is a sham. Power is diffused, and there are many opportunities to exert political pressure at the local, state, and national levels. The public interest—defined as the aggregation of private interests—is generally better served under constitutional democracy than under any other system. So say the pluralists.

There is more than a grain of truth in elitist theory, as the concentration of wealth in the United States, with its market economy and business-friendly tax system, attests. Nonetheless, public policies *have* been affected by public opinion. Widespread and steadily growing popular sentiment against the Vietnam War was instrumental in pressuring the government to withdraw from that conflict. In 2006, growing opposition to the war in Iraq cost the Republicans control of the Congress. Public opinion in the United States is often fragmented, but that does not render it nonexistent or irrelevant. Whether elections are meaningful or the outcomes rational, however, are very different questions (ones we will take up later in this chapter).

PARTICIPATION AND POLITICAL PARTIES

Only when the voice of the citizenry is magnified many times is it likely to be heard in a process that political scientists sometimes call **interest aggregation**. Political parties and interest groups are two types of structures capable of performing this aggregation function. Their effectiveness in a particular society depends in large part on how much the government protects political and civil rights and is responsive to the demands of the people.

The purpose of a **political party** is to select, nominate, and support candidates for elective office. Political parties have become permanent fixtures in all liberal democracies, including the United States.

American Democracy: No Place for a Party?

The Constitution makes no mention of political parties; some Founders abhorred them. George Washington sought to avoid partisanship by forming a cabinet composed of the best available talent, including Thomas Jefferson as secretary of state and Alexander Hamilton as secretary of the treasury.

Washington's noble attempt to avoid partisan politics ultimately failed. Personal animosities developed between Jefferson and Hamilton, in large part due to conflicting understandings of government and public policy, and the two became fierce rivals. In the late 1790s, Jefferson and his followers founded a loosely organized Republican Party to oppose the strong anti-French policies of Federalists such as Hamilton and John Adams. Yet in 1789, Jefferson himself had written, "If I could not go to heaven but with a party, I would not go there at all."[26]

Why did so many statesmen of Jefferson's generation distrust political parties? In Jefferson's case, dislike stemmed from a peculiarly American brand of individualism that has survived to this day. "I never submitted the whole system of my opinions to the creed of any party of men whatever, in religion, in philosophy, in politics, or in anything else, where I was capable of thinking for myself," he observed, concluding that "such an addiction is the last degradation of a free and moral agent."[27] Other thinkers of Jefferson's generation believed political parties fostered narrow self-interest at the expense of the general or public interest. They saw parties as the public extension of private selfishness.

Only gradually did partisanship in U.S. politics lose this stigma. Even so, the sense that it is a necessary evil persists—witness constant but empty calls for a "bipartisan" approach to legislation in Congress, often by the very politicians who are the most uncompromising.

General Aims

Political parties strive to gain or retain political power; in practical terms, this means capturing control of the government. Because voters decide who rules,

---

interest aggregation
A term political scientists use to describe how the interests, concerns, and demands of various individuals and groups in society are translated into policies and programs; in constitutional democracies, a major function of political parties.

political party
Any group of individuals who agree on basic political principles, have shared interests, and on that basis organize to win control of government.

recall
Direct voting to remove an elected official from office.

euro area
In the EU, the euro zone refers to the 12 member states that have adopted the euro, including Germany, France, and Italy, but not the United Kingdom.

political parties concentrate on winning elections, but they also engage citizens as volunteers, recruit candidates, raise money, and launch media campaigns. In the party platform, proposals and policies are formulated to appease key interest groups, which, in turn, support the party's candidates with money and votes.

In the United States, candidates frequently appeal for votes by promising to deliver on bread-and-butter issues rather than taking strong stands on ideological issues or advancing bold domestic and foreign policy proposals. The idea is to build a consensus around a vague set of principles rather than detailed policies. The presidential candidate perceived to be closest to the political center is usually elected. An alternative is to offer voters clear alternatives, which is how elections are structured in most democratic countries—and how the Obama campaign won in 2008.

In Europe, multiple parties vie for votes and each formulates more or less distinctive policy alternatives. Party platforms are much more important than the personal popularity of individual candidates, because parties in parliamentary systems seek to capture and maintain a majority of seats in the parliament (see Chapter 7). There is obviously a premium on party discipline because the stakes are so high.

One-Party Dominant Systems

one-party dominant
One-party dominant systems are different from authoritarian one-party systems in that they hold regular elections, allow open criticism of the government, and do not outlaw other parties; until recently, Japan operated as a one-party dominant system, as did Mexico; South Africa is one current example.

Examples of **one-party dominant** systems include Mexico (the Institutional Revolutionary Party) until 2000, Japan (the Liberal Democratic Party) since the mid-1950s, post-independence India (the Congress), Taiwan (the Nationalist Party), and the U.S. Deep South (the Democratic party) for nearly a century after the Civil War. One-party dominant systems resemble the one-party systems found in authoritarian states, but they hold regular elections, allow open criticism of the government, and do not outlaw other parties.

However, the line between authoritarian and democratic rule is not always clear. In Mexico, the Institutional Revolutionary Party long maintained its dominant position through corruption, intimidation, and voting fraud. One-party dominant systems invite official interference in elections—including ballot box stuffing and other blatantly unfair practices. A virtual monopoly of political power encourages cozy arrangements among business leaders, bankers, entrenched bureaucrats, and top government officials. Thus, opposition parties have challenged single-party domination in Mexico, Japan, and Taiwan in recent years by campaigning on a "clean government" platform.

Japanese voters were reminded in the spring of 2009 that corruption is not confined to the dominant party. The political secretary of Ichiro Ozawa, leader of the main opposition Democratic Party of Japan, was indicted "for accepting illegal funds from a construction company with a history of lining politicians' pockets."[28] Until this scandal hit the newsstands in Japan, Ozawa's party appeared poised to win the upcoming general election, which would have upended a political system that has kept the Liberal Democratic Party in power—with one brief interruption—for more than half a century.

Competitive Party Systems

Under a two-party system, the vast majority of voters support one major party or the other, very few independents or minor party candidates ever win an election, and the opposition party is constitutionally protected from undue interference or intimidation by the government. In multiparty systems no political party is always in the majority; in any given election, any one of several parties may emerge with the largest number of seats, although often with less than an absolute majority.

One key advantage of two-party systems is political and governmental stability (the United States and the United Kingdom are prime examples). To some extent, continuity is ensured by the system itself, as the two major parties keep to the middle of the road to appeal to a broad range of middle-class interests.

The dynamic in multiparty systems is very different. Compromise on principles or consensus-seeking is less common and candidates take definite stands on issues of the day. The multiparty system sounds strange to those in the United States, but it is second nature to Europeans. It offers voters a wide range of choice, though it sometimes leads to unstable governments, as Italy in the post-World War II era demonstrated.

The Architecture of Democracy

Political parties allow citizen participation; they are thus an important part of the architecture of democracy. But this architecture is not entirely accidental—in fact, party systems reflect electoral systems. That is, the *rules* governing elections, sometimes spelled out in a constitution, limit the number of political parties that can exist and thus shape the choices available to voters. The success of minor parties is discouraged in systems based on single-member districts, where any candidate with a one-vote advantage (a plurality) wins the only available seat. Smaller parties find it difficult to attract voters simply because their candidates have such a small chance of winning. By contrast, in PR systems, where several candidates are elected from each district, minor parties enjoy a far greater chance of being elected. Thus, to repeat a key point, proportional representation is far more likely than the first-past-the-post system to produce a multiparty political system.

Another structural consideration is whether the political system is centralized or decentralized. Parties in federal systems organize themselves along the federal structure of the government. In the United States vote totals in presidential elections are determined nationally but counted (and weighted) state by state in winner-take-all contests. Thus George W. Bush won the 2000 election despite the fact that Al Gore received more total votes nationwide. U.S. presidential candidates, and the political parties they lead, face the challenge of winning not one election, but 50. And though the United States has only two major parties,

50 state parties exist alongside each *national* party. Historically, the Democratic Party in Massachusetts has borne little resemblance to the Democratic Party in Mississippi, for example. Strong state-level party organizations help elect senators, representatives, and state and local officials.

Structural factors are thus clearly important, but culture also influences a nation's form of government and the party system it adopts. Multiparty systems are most likely to thrive in countries that value ideology and group solidarity over compromise and stability.

Is the Party Over?

Many in the United States say neither major party any longer reflects the realities of U.S. life and society.[29] Others see the parties as evidence of a failed political system. The very idea of party politics or partisanship has sometimes come into conflict with the ideal of democracy.

At the same time, however, participatory democracy is here to stay. State primary elections, once the exception, have become the rule. States now compete to hold the earliest primaries. (The elections themselves have become a bonanza for some states, attracting revenue and wide media attention.) Other states hold party caucuses, where rank-and-file party members choose delegates who later attend state conventions that, in turn, select delegates pledged to support particular candidates at the party's national convention.

Such reforms make the average citizen at least *feel* a part of the party's nominating process and diminish the power of both state party and national party regulars. But there is a downside: U.S. presidential campaigns are costly and prolonged; the nomination and election process can last well over a year. (British parliamentary elections often last less than a month and cost a tiny fraction of what U.S. elections cost.) Fund-raising is a full-time endeavor, not only for presidential hopefuls but also for serious candidates in Senate and House races, prompting cynics to remark that U.S. elections have become nonstop events.

No other liberal democracy in the world spends so much time and treasure choosing its chief executive. Parties play a role in elections, but money plays a far bigger role. Where do candidates turn for financial backing? Next we look at the role of interest groups in contemporary U.S. politics.

PARTICIPATION AND INTEREST GROUPS

interest group
An association of individuals that attempts to influence policy and legislation in a confined area of special interest, often through lobbying, campaign contributions, and bloc voting.

Interest groups do not seek direct control over government nor do they recruit, nominate, and elect public officials. Instead, they concentrate on influencing legislation, policy, and programs in specific areas of special interest, including corporate taxes and subsidies for big business, banking regulations, farm subsidies, federal aid to education, or wildlife conservation, to name a few. Interest groups are also known as special interests, lobbies, pressure groups, and advocacy groups.

One way to categorize interest groups is to distinguish between those that represent **special interests** and those that represent the **public interest**. The Audubon Society, the Aspen Institute, Greenpeace, Friends of the Earth, the Sierra Club, The Fund for Peace, Worldwatch Institute, and the Earth Policy Institute are examples of familiar public interest advocacy groups in the United States. The Royal Society for the Protection of Birds, with more than a million members, is the largest advocacy group in Europe.

The focus of public interest groups is often very broad, for example the environment or human rights. Such groups promote causes they believe will benefit society as a whole. The Sierra Club, for example, lobbies for environmental causes and conservation policies. Although not everyone agrees with its goals, no one can accuse its members of pursuing narrow self-interest; all citizens benefit from clean air and pure water.

Interest groups differ not only in the issues they emphasize, but also in scope. Most ethnic groups (the National Italian American Foundation, for example), religious groups (the American Jewish Congress), occupational groups (the American Association of University Professors), age-defined groups (AARP), and a variety of groups that cannot be easily categorized (such as the Disabled American Veterans) are narrowly focused. Each fights for laws and policies that benefit the exclusive group it represents—for private rather than the public interest.

One common classification scheme distinguishes four basic types of interest groups.[30]

- Associational interest groups have a distinctive name, national headquarters, professional staff, and political agenda tied to specific group characteristics, goals, beliefs, or values. Examples include the National Association of Manufacturers (NAM), the National Rifle Association (NRA), the National Association for the Advancement of Colored People (NAACP), the United Auto Workers (UAW), the Christian Coalition of America (CCA), the Sierra Club, and AARP (formerly the American Association of Retired Persons).
- Non-associational interest groups lack formal structures but reflect largely unvoiced social, ethnic, cultural, or religious interests capable of coalescing into potent political forces under the right circumstances. Informal groups are most common in the developing countries of Asia, the Arab world, Latin America, and sub-Saharan Africa.
- Institutional interest groups exist mainly within the government, although some outside groups—major defense contractors, for example—are so intertwined in the operations of government that we can include them in this category. In the United States at the federal level, departments and agencies have vested interests in policies and programs for which they lobby from the inside, often out of public view. The Pentagon lobbies for new weapons systems, airplanes, warships, and the like, while Labor, Agriculture, and Education become captives of the special interests most directly affected by the programs they administer.
- Anomic interest groups sometimes develop spontaneously when many individuals strongly oppose specific policies. The nationwide student demonstrations against the Vietnam War in the late 1960s and early 1970s are one example. Political scientist Gabriel Almond suggested that street riots and even some assassinations also fit this category.[31]

special interest
An organization or association that exists to further private interests in the political arena; examples in the United States are the U.S. Chamber of Commerce or the National Association of Manufacturers (business), the AFL-CIO (labor), and the National Farmers Organization (NFO).

public interest
The pursuit of policies aimed at the general good or the betterment of society as a whole; in contrast to special interests that pursue laws or policies more narrowly favoring individuals or groups.

Sources and Methods of Influence

Interest groups attempt to sway public policy by influencing elected officials and public opinion at the national or state level, in three primary ways: (1) by seeking the election of representatives they trust, (2) by seeking access to elected officials, and (3) by mounting mass media campaigns.

Interest groups prize access to decision makers, especially on a one-on-one basis. Many employ **lobbyists,** who cultivate credibility and influence with legislators in various ways. They testify before legislative committees on the basis of their expert knowledge and arrange for intermediaries—close personal friends or constituents—to advance their viewpoints. Lobbyists also mount public relations, fax, telephone, telegraph, or Internet campaigns; cooperate with other like-minded lobbyists for common legislative objectives; and increase communication opportunities between themselves and legislators (for example, by throwing a party or sponsoring a charitable event).[32]

Two factors are vitally important in the success of interest groups—money and membership. Organizations representing a large and distinct group of citizens with identical interests have a clear advantage, especially when the issues are specific and keenly felt and no competing groups stress the same ones. AARP is a prime example, with a large number of like-minded members (some 36 million) and an issue monopoly (protecting and expanding governmental entitlement for senior citizens) that opposing organizations have seldom challenged successfully.[33] Roughly half of all U.S. adults over 50 (some 20 percent of all voters) belonged to AARP, making it the second-largest nonprofit organization in the country, trailing only the Roman Catholic Church. Employing 18 registered lobbyists and a staff of 1,800 people, maintaining a budget of nearly $600 million, and portraying itself as

lobbyist
A person who attempts to influence governmental policy in favor of some special interest.

Interest groups take many differ forms. Some, like labor unions, are formal and highly structured with dues paying members and professional staffs; others, like these demonstrators on behalf of health care reform, are informal, spontaneous, narrowly focused, and often short-lived.

SAMUEL PERRY, 2009/USED UNDER LICENSE FROM SHUTTERSTOCK.COM

the guardian angel of the U.S. elderly, AARP has become one of the nation's most influential interest groups.

The American-Israel Political Action Committee (AIPAC), the National Right to Life Committee (NLRC), and the National Rifle Association (NRA) are three powerful single-issue interest groups. Each focuses all its resources on one political objective: support for Israel (AIPAC), opposition to abortion (NLRC), and the right to bear arms (NRA).

Having a highly motivated mass membership is important, but having truckloads of money is even more important. Major corporations, interest groups, and wealthy private citizens can exert great influence on the political process by launching expensive media campaigns or contributing large amounts to political campaigns. In addition, the personal networks and political contacts of the super-rich are often advantageous in influencing elected officials.

Interest groups are sometimes closely tied to political parties. In Western Europe, the giant trade unions maintain close ties with working-class political parties. (The British Labour Party and Trades Union Congress have the support of some 85 percent of organized labor in Great Britain.)

In the United States, by contrast, interest groups increasingly bypass political parties entirely, providing direct financial support to candidates they favor. Some interest groups hedge their bets by contributing to both candidates in the same race. In the 2004 election, for example, 21 lobbyists gave money to both the Bush and Kerry campaigns.

Soliciting funds through computerized direct-mail appeals and the Internet is one key to interest-group success, but personal connections are also important. In Washington, it is often said, "It isn't *what* you know, but *who* you know that counts." Thus interest groups often compete to hire former presidential advisers, ranking civilian and military Pentagon officials, and members of Congress as "consultants." These lobbyists are paid handsomely by defense contractors, arms manufacturers, oil companies, and the like to open doors on Capitol Hill, at the Pentagon, and, yes, even in the White House (see Box 11.7).

Upon taking office, President Obama—striking a blow for clean government as he had promised to do in the campaign—laid down a marker for members of his administration: "If you are a lobbyist entering my administration, you will not be able to work on matters you lobbied on, or in the agencies you lobbied during the previous two years." When it was disclosed that Obama's choice for Secretary of Health and Human Services, former Senator Tom Daschle, had not paid all the income tax he owed, and that after leaving the Senate he had lobbied for clients in the field of health care, among others, Daschle resigned. President Obama accepted the blame, saying, "I screwed up" and promised not to let it happen again. It was a step in the right direction, though the path of reform in today's Washington can be tortuous and strewn with landmines.

The Great Race: Getting Ahead of the PAC

Although estimates differ significantly, experts agree the number of interest groups in the United States, and the lobbyists they employ, has increased by at least 50 percent over the past three decades. Today, lobbying is the third-largest

Box 11.7 FOCUS ON   The Best Congress Money Can Buy*

In January 2007, shortly after midterm elections in which Democrats wrested control of the U.S. Congress from Republicans, the House of Representatives, with Nancy Pelosi (D-Calif.) as the new speaker, announced a major drive to curb unethical ties between Washington lobbyists and legislators. Among other things, House Democrats pledged to bar or severely limit the use of corporate jets by members of Congress and to adopt stricter rules on gifts and travel. This move followed a bruising campaign in which Congressional corruption scandals included one that led to the imprisonment of super-lobbyist Jack Abramoff.

Not to be outdone, President George W. Bush, taking aim at the widespread use of "earmarks" by Congress, declared, "One important message we all should take from the elections is that people want to end the secretive process by which Washington insiders are able to get billions of dollars directed to projects, many of them pork

barrel projects that have never been reviewed or voted on by the Congress."

So who was really to blame for ethical lapses? Republicans or Democrats? Are lobbyists or earmarks the problem? The truth is, both Republicans and Democrats in Congress use lobbyists and earmarks to get what they want—re-election. Meanwhile, until Barack Obama gained the White House, nobody on either end of Pennsylvania Avenue talked about the real problem in Washington, namely that too often when a member of Congress finds out how much his vote is worth, he sells it to the highest bidder. (There are 449 males and only 89 females in Congress—that, too, is part of the problem.)

_____

*Based on Carl Hulse and David D. Kirkpatrick, "Ethics Overhaul Tops the Agenda in New Congress," *New York Times*, January 4, 2007 (electronic edition).

industry in Washington, D.C., behind only government and tourism. There were about 5,000 registered lobbyists in the Nation's Capital in 1956. One source estimated that in 1991 there were still fewer than 6,000.[34] That number jumped to 20,000 by 1994 and kept rising. In 2005, there were 34,750, whereas the fees lobbyists charged clients rose by as much as 100 percent.[35]

Why this population explosion? It results from the dramatic increase in government benefits, the declining influence of political parties, the increasing diversity of U.S. society, and the rise of single-issue movements.[36] At the same time, mass mailings and computer technology make new start-ups relatively easy. Higher levels of education have increased individuals' interest in such associations, and relative prosperity has made them better able to pay dues.

political action committee (PAC)
Group organized to raise campaign funds in support of or in opposition to specific candidates.

In the early 1970s, a new kind of interest group, known as **political action committees (PACs)**, became prominent in the United States. In 1971, Congress attempted to curb election abuses by prohibiting corporations and labor unions from contributing directly to political campaigns. However, the law did not prohibit special interests from spending money *indirectly* through specially created committees. The number of PACs rose dramatically until the mid-1980s, as shown in Figure 11.5. Interest groups with large and influential PACs include the American Medical Association; the National Association of Realtors; the National Automobile Dealers Association; the National Association of Letter Carriers; the American Institute of

Certified Public Accountants; the American Dental Association; and the American Federation of State, County, and Municipal Employees.

PACs have played a key role in financing candidates and causes at both the national and state level as the cost of elections, increasingly dependent on television advertising, has escalated. Dianne Feinstein, a Democratic senator from California, raised $22,000 a day during the 7 months before the 1994 election; if "Feinstein Inc. were a business, its projected revenue would place it among the top 5 percent of U.S. corporations."[37] Incredibly, Feinstein was outspent by her wealthy Republican opponent, Michael Huffington, who squandered $29 million of his own money in a losing campaign.

FIGURE 11.5   Special interests contribute huge sums to political campaigns in the United States. This chart shows the amounts contributed by various sectors of the economy to candidates for the U.S. House and Senate in 2005–2006; the percentages at the top of each bar indicate the sharp increases over the 2003–2004 election cycle, suggesting a trend that many consider incompatible with a healthy democracy and evidence of the urgent need for major campaign finance reform.

SOURCE: Figures obtained from PoliticalMoneyLine, April 6, 2007, http://www.fecinfo.com.

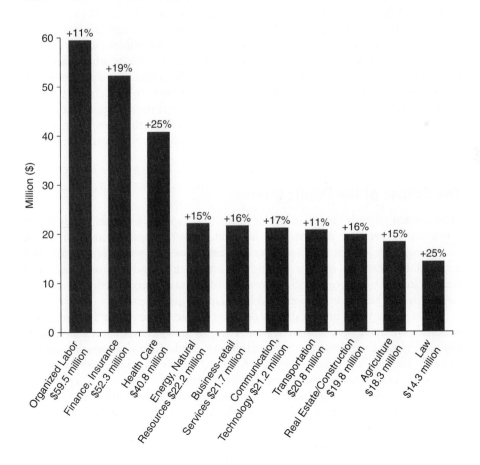

Given the high cost of campaigns, it is hardly surprising to find more, not less, PAC involvement in elections. In the 2005–2006 election cycle, industry-group PACs alone gave $311 million to federal candidates, an increase of $45 million since the 2003–2004 election cycle (see Figure 11.5).[38]

Many observers decry the growing influence of money in U.S. politics. Although money has always been a factor in politics, in recent decades it has become *the* factor without which winning is virtually impossible. The average cost of winning a House seat jumped from $73,000 in 1976 to $680,000 in 1996 and to roughly $1 million in 2004; for a Senate seat, it rose from $595,000 to more than $7 million during the same period.[39]

As a rule, Republicans raise more money than Democrats, and incumbents have a huge financial advantage over challengers. In 2004, 98 percent of House incumbents and 96 percent of incumbent senators won reelection. In 2008, five U.S. Senators lost their seats to challengers; but only 23 incumbents in the House of Representatives were defeated (6 Democrats and 17 Republicans), for a total of 435.

In the 2006 midterm election, the incumbent senators raised, on average, $11.3 million, compared with the average challenger's $1.8 million. In House races, incumbents raised an average of $1.27 million, compared with $283,000 for challengers. According to the Pew Charitable Trusts, "Money is the fuel that powers the current campaign system. In a circular fashion, interest groups, candidates, and parties raise money to pay consultants to launch expensive television ad campaigns."[40]

Interest groups are essential, but in the absence of any effective curbs on **soft money**—money given to political parties ostensibly for purposes other than campaigning and money spent independently *on behalf* of candidates or parties—they are increasingly drawn into a kind of systemic corruption for which there is currently no adequate legal or political remedies. To expect the very politicians who benefit most from this system to change it is unrealistic. Only when voters refuse to reelect incumbents who refuse to fix the system will the system get fixed.

The Eclipse of the Public Interest

Often, when citizens complain about influential "special interests," they mean lobbyists or pressure groups that advocate *other people's* interests. When those people or groups represent *our* interests, however, we both approve and applaud. For instance, interest groups that advocate extending work-study and student loan programs are praised by some of the same people (educators) who lament the undue influence exercised by such groups in general.

What problems do interest groups *objectively* pose to the public interest? Some critics argue that the proliferation of interest groups in the United States and Western Europe imposes a particular hardship on the most disadvantaged segments of society. The poor have too little influence and the rich have entirely too much. In this view, the ascendancy of interest groups in democracies has produced a system that promotes the most powerful interests in society at the expense of the weak and downtrodden.

Critics also express alarm at the number of government officials who leave high positions to work directly or indirectly for companies with whom they previously had dealings, such as former Pentagon officials employed by defense contractors, or former presidential advisers who become lobbyists,

soft money
Campaign contributions to U.S. national party committees that do not have to be reported to the Federal Election Commission as long as the funds are not used to benefit a particular candidate; the national committees funnel the funds to state parties, which generally operate under less stringent reporting requirements. Critics argue that soft money is a massive loophole in the existing system of campaign finance regulation and that it amounts to a form of legalized corruption.

media commentators, or some other high-salaried position and vice versa. (Vice President Cheney, a former secretary of defense, left his job as CEO of defense contractor Halliburton to become George W. Bush's running mate.) In 1978, Congress banned high-ranking, ex-government officials from any contact with the agencies for which they previously worked for a year and prohibited them from attempting to influence the government on policies for which they had "official responsibilities" for 2 years. But the rules did not prevent government officials from going back and forth between the public and private sectors, a practice with serious ethical issues involving conflicts of interest and the public trust. As mentioned earlier, one of Barack Obama's first acts as president was to issue an order barring members of his administration from engaging in this practice.

When a single-issue interest group champions a very specific regulation or law—one that most voters do not care about and pay no attention to—where is the incentive for lawmakers or bureaucrats to resist pressures from special interests? In a large country with numerous levels of government, important matters, especially tax laws in the United States, are decided with little debate or media attention.[41] When well-financed lobbies operating under the radar or behind the scenes push for laws and regulations that bear little, if any, relationship to the public interest, the policy process is likely to be corrupted.

The Obama Factor: Technology to the Rescue? The foregoing points to the conclusion that political participation in the United States today is all about money. To the extent that participation and democracy go hand in hand, it follows that the super rich can participate to a far greater degree than the rest of us. If so, and if the trend is toward ever greater concentration of wealth (as it has been at least since the early 1980s), then democracy becomes less and less meaningful for the vast majority of Americans who constitute the middle class—precisely the class that political philosophers since Aristotle have recognized as the backbone of democracy. Can anything reverse these twin trends toward ever greater concentration of wealth and power? Or is the coin of democracy in America destined to be further debased?

Some observers see possibilities for rejuvenating democracy in technology—especially information technology and the Internet. Few dispute that the Obama campaign changed politics, that presidential campaigns in America will never be the same. Thus, "by using interactive Web 2.0 tools, Mr. Obama's campaign changed the way politicians organize supporters, advertise to voters, defend against attacks and communicate with constituents."[42] Obama's campaign videos were watched on YouTube for 145 million hours. To buy the same amount of exposure on broadcast TV would cost $47 million.[43]

The same technology that has revolutionized political campaigns, increasing citizen participation exponentially, could also revolutionize the way the federal government works or the president governs. During the transition from Bush to Obama, the Obama team created a Website, Change.gov, to keep the public informed and get voter feedback. One proposal was to create a similar Website called MyWhiteHouse.gov to maintain a dialogue between citizens and the president. In fact, such a Website now exists at <http://www.whitehouse.gov> complete with the latest information on legislation, issues of the day, the federal budget, and the economy (at <ww.Recovery.gov>)—and, of course, a blog. Go check it out and decide for yourself.

GATEWAYS TO THE WORLD: EXPLORING CYBERSPACE

www.umich.edu/~nes/nesguide/nesguide.htm

From the Inter-University Consortium for Political and Social Research (ICPSR), housed in Ann Arbor at the University of Michigan, this site from the National Elections Studies provides an excellent source of information regarding political participation in the United States.

www.pollingreport.com

"An independent, nonpartisan resource on trends in American public opinion."

www.fecinfo.com

This Website from CQ MoneyLine (formerly PoliticalMoneyLine) claims to be "the leading independent source of campaign finance information."

www.opensecrets.org/bigpicture/stats.asp

This site, maintained by the Center for Responsive Politics, provides extensive information on PACS, political parties, and money in U.S. politics. Want to know who the top donors are? Who gets most of the money? How much it takes to win an election? You can find answers here.

plato.stanford.edu/entries/affirmative-action

www.washingtonpost.com/wp-srv/politics/special/affirm/affirm.htm

vote96.ss.ca.gov/bp/209.htm

www.landmarkcases.org/bakke/impact.html

These four sites provide information on the California Civil Rights Initiative (Proposition 209). Beyond the implications for California politics and society, the articles and links offer critical analyses and coverage of affirmative action in general.

www.pewtrusts.com

This is the Website of the Pew Charitable Trusts, a public interest foundation and policy think tank. Check out the links under "Informing the Public."

www.fec.gov/index.shtml

The official Website of the U.S. Federal Election Commission.

www.truthout.org

"Truthout is a full-service news agency dedicated to establishing a powerful, stable voice for independent journalism. The core of our mission is educational. We believe the biggest impediment to responsible decision-making is lack of information . . . We attempt to shed light on issues of vital interest to the community such as health care, the environment, international relations, and human rights."

SUMMARY

Citizens can participate in politics in a variety of legal ways: conventionally, by voting and taking part in public opinion polls; organizationally, by joining political parties or interest groups; or professionally, by working full time for such organizations. Some types of political participation are unconventional, such as engaging in protests or economic boycotts. Illegal participation goes beyond unconventional means—from deliberately nonviolent actions (civil disobedience) to extremely violent acts (terrorism).

Influencing the decision-making process includes aggregating individual opinions and interests into group opinions and interests. Public opinion can be expressed through polls, which influence the political process at various points and in a variety of ways. Elections, despite inherent limitations, represent the best means of translating mass preferences into public policy. Electoral systems vary, but the two major types are first-past-the-post systems (found in the United States and Great Britain) and proportional representation systems (used in most representative democracies). In democratic republics, voters elect legislators, chief executives, and sometimes judges. Direct democracy instruments include referendums, initiatives, and recalls, all intended to allow citizens to participate directly in the formulation of public policy.

Voting rates are low in the United States and have been declining. Voters are generally not very knowledgeable. Cynics argue that political participation by the masses is more illusory than real and that power is actually concentrated in the hands of a small, elite group of influential people. This elitist theory is disputed by Madisonian pluralists, who argue that in a democratic society, power is diffused rather than concentrated and that political phenomena are too complex to be reduced to the simplistic terms of elitist theory.

In the United States, political parties were originally regarded as divisive and dangerous, but it turns out they perform several key functions in republics. They facilitate participation, aggregate interests, recruit qualified candidates for office, raise money for political campaigns, and help organize governments by building a national consensus and offering alternatives, especially during the election process. One-party systems are generally associated with authoritarianism, although a few modified one-party systems exist in which one party is consistently backed by a majority of the voters. Multiparty systems typically offer voters clearer alternative than do two-party systems. The type of party system found in a given country is determined by its traditions, constitution, and culture.

A number of factors determine the effectiveness of interest groups, both public interest and private interest, including their size, the intensity of members' political opinions, their financing, and their leadership. Some observers fear these associations have recently become too influential, but others (Madison's intellectual heirs) believe they exist in sufficient numbers and kinds to offset one another and ensure a competitive political system.

KEY TERMS

public opinion

public opinion
  polling

straw poll

random sampling

stratified sampling

tracking poll

winner-takes-all
  system

simple majority

first past the post

proportional
  representation (PR)

list system

Hare plan

plebiscite

referendum

initiative

recall

euro area

motor voter law

political efficacy

individualism

political apathy

low-information
  rationality

elitist theories of
  democracy

iron law of
  oligarchy

interest aggregation

political party

one-party dominant

coalition
  government

interest group

special interest

public interest

lobbyist

political action committee
  (PAC)

soft money

REVIEW QUESTIONS

1. How do citizens participate in politics?
2. What are the different forms of electoral systems? What are the advantages and disadvantages of each?
3. Some say apathy is a problem in democratic societies. Do you agree or disagree? Explain.
4. How do the elitist theories of democracy differ from the pluralist model? What political implications follow from the elitist theories?
5. What assumptions do we generally make about political participation in democracies? Are they correct? Explain.
6. What kinds of party systems are found in democracies? How do they differ? Why do the differences matter? Finally, in your opinion, which one is best?
7. To what extent does the functioning of interest groups depend on the political system in which they operate?
8. Why has the power of interest groups increased as the power of political parties has decreased? To what extent are these two phenomena related?
9. What does this statement mean: "Not all interest groups are created equal"?

RECOMMENDED READING

Asher, Herbert. *Polling and the Public: What Every Citizen Should Know*, 7th ed. Washington, DC: CQ Press, 2007. A solid introduction to polling and polling techniques.

Caplan, Bryan. *The Myth of the Rational Voter: Why Democracies Choose Bad Policies*. Princeton, NJ Princeton University Press, 2008. If you want to know the answer, read the book. The author blows gaping holes in rational choice theory.

Cigler, Allan, and Burdett Loomis, ed. *Interest Group Politics*, 6th ed. Washington, DC: CQ Press, 2002. A comprehensive account of the roles and influences of interest groups in contemporary U.S. politics.

Cronin, Thomas. *Direct Democracy: The Politics of Initiative, Referendum, and Recall*. Cambridge, MA: Harvard University Press, 1999. A measured examination of the history, advantages, and disadvantages of direct democracy.

Dye, Thomas. *Who's Running America? The Bush Restoration*, 7th ed. Englewood Cliffs, NJ: Prentice-Hall, 2001. A detailed examination of the political and corporate elites who decisively influence U.S. politics.

Erikson, Robert, and Kent Tedin. *American Public Opinion: Its Origins, Contents, and Impact*, 7th ed. Englewood Cliffs, NJ: Prentice-Hall, 2004. An excellent summary and discussion of the literature.

Flanigan, William, and Nancy Zingale. *Political Behavior of the American Electorate*, 11th ed. Washington, DC: CQ Press, 2006. A general but comprehensive account of voting in the United States.

Gais, Thomas. *Improper Influence: Campaign Finance Law, Political Interest Groups, and the Problem of Equality*. Ann Arbor: University of Michigan Press, 1998. An advanced, empirical study that focuses on interest groups and PACs and argues that business PACs in particular are able to exercise excessive influence.

Goldwin, Robert, ed. *Parties U.S.A.* Skokie, IL: Rand McNally, 1964. A stimulating collection of essays that present important and contrasting interpretations regarding the theory and practice of U.S. political parties.

Hillygus, D. Sunshine, and Todd G. Shields. *The Persuadable Voter: Wedge Issues in Presidential Campaigns*. Princeton, NJ Princeton University Press, 2008. The authors identify persuadable voters and micro-targeting techniques and show how candidates and parties frame messages around wedge issues that elections often hinge on.

Hofstadter, Richard. *The Idea of a Party System: The Rise of Legitimate Opposition in the United States, 1780–1840*. Berkeley: University of California Press, 1969. A historical examination of the origins of the American party system.

Jacobson, Larry. *The Politics of Congressional Elections*. 7th ed. New York: Longman, 2008. This edition brings things up to date through the 2006 elections.

Lewis-Beck, Michael S., Helmut Norpoth, William G. Jacoby, and Herbert F. Weisberg. *The American Voter Revisited*. Ann-Arbor, Michigan: University of Michigan Press, 2008. This book argues that patterns of voting behavior in the United States have been consistent for the past half-century. The book is well worth reading for the elections between 1960 and 2004, but the analysis does not anticipate or predict the paradigm shift that appears to have occurred in the historic 2008 election.

Lippmann, Walter. *Public Opinion*. New York: Simon & Schuster, 1997. This book, written by one of the greatest American journalists of the twentieth century, explores the relationship between public opinion and democracy. A classic originally published in 1922, which has been republished many times over the years.

Maisel, Sandy. *American Parties and Elections: A Very Short Introduction*. New York: Oxford University Press, 2007. A little book on a big topic all-too-seldom taught in school or talked about at the dinner table.

Michels, Robert. *Political Parties*. Translated by E. Paul and P. Paul. New York: Free Press, 1966. The original study that produced the Iron Law of Oligarchy.

Mills, C. Wright. *The Power Elite*. New York: Oxford University Press, 1959. The original formulation of the power elitist thesis.

Ornstein, Norman J., and Thomas E. Mann, *The Broken Branch: How Congress Is Failing America and How to Get It Back on Track*. New York: Oxford University Press, 2006. A rigorous critique of the U.S. Congress by two highly respected experts on American politics; the title nicely captures the content and intent of the book.

Tocqueville, Alexis de. *Democracy in America*. New York: Schocken Books, 1961. A classic study of American democracy in the nineteenth century.

Wattenberg, Martin P. *The Decline of American Political Parties: 1952–1994*. Cambridge, MA: Harvard University Press, 1996. A scholarly study neatly capsulated by the book's title.

WORLD PEACE

WINSTON CHURCHILL

POSTAGE
20 AJMAN بريد
DIRHAMS ٢٠ درهما

©SHUTTERSTOCK

Sir Winston Churchill (1874–1965) was an indomitable wartime leader who opposed the policy of appeasement toward Hitler and, when his dire warnings turned out to be true, led his country through its darkest days to its finest hour. As bombs fell on London and other British cities, Churchill declared, "We shall not flag or fail. We shall go on to the end . . . We shall never surrender."

Political Leadership
The Many Faces of Power

The Ideal Leader

Statesmanship

The Lure of Fame

Four Exemplary Leaders

Rómulo Betancourt (1908–1981)

Winston Churchill (1874–1965)

Abraham Lincoln (1809–1865)

Anwar al-Sadat (1918–1981)

The Eclipse of Leadership?

American Demagogues

Aaron Burr (1756–1836)

Theodore Bilbo (1877–1947)

Huey Long (1893–1935)

Joseph McCarthy (1906–1957)

Tom DeLay (b. 1947)

Politicians

Legislators as Delegates

Legislators as Trustees

Solons

Citizen-Leaders

Václav Havel (b. 1936)

Martin Luther King Jr. (1929–1968)

Rosa Parks (1913–2005)

Perhaps more than any other group, politicians tend to be lumped together and stereotyped. Seldom does anybody have anything good to say about them in general or about politics as a profession. Most parents do not boast, "My daughter (son) wants to be a politician when she (he) grows up."

Nancy Pelosi is the first woman to become the Speaker of the House; in the 1990s, Madeleine Albright became the first woman to serve as Secretary of State. Women hold four posts in President Barack Obama's cabinet and several other key positions, including EPA administrator and White House Senior Advisor. Yet, role models for young women, as for men, are more often movie stars, models, athletes, or television personalities than equally high-profile leaders in politics or public affairs.

Nonetheless, whenever we make a campaign contribution or cast a ballot in an election, we express a preference for one candidate over another. We cannot afford to be indifferent to the character and judgment of the people we elect to high office.

Every time we tune into the daily news or peruse the daily paper, we are reminded that the well-being of nations depends on the capacity of leaders to choose wisely and act prudently. Take the war in Iraq, for example. President George W. Bush's decision to attack Afghanistan and oust the Taliban regime for supporting Osama bin Laden's al Qaeda network, and his later decision to invade Iraq in March 2003, profoundly affected America's standing in the world. It is almost certain that had his opponent, Al Gore, won the election—as many people still believe he did—the U.S. response to 9/11 would have been very different. It is even possible that 9/11 would not have happened at all. (Critics in a position to know all the facts point to intelligence warnings the Bush White House ignored.)

Indeed, the history of the United States at war is a gold mine for anyone interested in the role of leadership in politics. President Lyndon Johnson's decision to escalate the Vietnam War in the mid-1960s, for example—eventually committing more than 500,000 U.S. troops, alienating friends and allies abroad, and damaging the nation's prestige in the eyes of the world—cost him his job.* The Vietnam War also proved the undoing of Johnson's successor, Richard Nixon. The Watergate affair involving dirty tricks in the 1972 Nixon-McGovern White House race led directly to impeachment proceedings—and Nixon's resignation.

Clearly, leadership does matter. After World War II, President Truman made a series of historic decisions—to rebuild Europe by means of the Marshall Plan, to create new military alliances such as the North Atlantic Treaty Organization (NATO), and to confront the Soviet Union's perceived expansionism with a strong policy of containment. Few historians doubt that firm and decisive leadership was a crucial factor in shaping the postwar world and in creating the structures at home and abroad whereby the West eventually prevailed in the Cold War.

Indeed, "Politics in essence is leadership or attempted leadership of whatever is the prevailing form of political community."[1] Every community and every country is profoundly affected by the quality of its political leadership. In 1989, Václav Havel, a playwright who had been imprisoned for daring to defy the communist rulers in Czechoslovakia, led his country in making the transition from dictatorship to democracy. In 1994, after years of imprisonment, Nelson Mandela, the former head of the antiapartheid African National Congress, was elected president of a multiracial South Africa. Like Havel, the 75-year-old Mandela, who was self-taught, widely trusted, and world renowned, led a peaceful political transition, ending the rule of the white supremacist government.

In this chapter, we examine four types of leaders—statesman, demagogues, ordinary politicians, and citizen-leaders. These types are different in many ways, including accomplishments, character, methods, and purposes. **Statesmen** are most often the political architects who create new states, the peacemakers who resolve conflicts, and the orators who inspire the popular masses in times of national crisis—they are yesterday's founders, today's pathfinders, and tomorrow's legends. **Demagogues** deceive and manipulate the people for selfish ends—they are schemers, rabble-rousers, and warmongers. **Ordinary politicians** do no great harm or good and concentrate, above all, on getting reelected. **Citizen-leaders** hold no official public office but become actively engaged in and can significantly influence a nation's politics.

Often these distinctions are easier to make in theory than to apply in practice. Nonetheless, there are enormous differences between the best and the worst of leaders. Thus, most observers would agree that Adolf Hitler, a mass-murdering madman who led Germany to disaster in World War II, exemplifies the worst. On the other hand, few would dispute that Winston Churchill—who recognized the dangers of totalitarianism in Nazi Germany earlier than most, led his nation's heroic defense in the darkest days of the war and played a major role in shaping the postwar world—exemplifies the best. Just as Hitler was clearly a demagogue, Churchill was clearly a statesman.

---

* The student-led protest movement was, ironically, a major factor in setting the stage for Richard Nixon to capture the White House in 1968. When the war finally ended in 1973, more than 47,000 U.S. troops had fallen on the battlefield, another 10,000 or so had been killed off the battlefield, and tens of thousands of others (officially 211,556 casualties in all) returned alive but broken by injuries or traumatic experiences, including physical disabilities (such as missing limbs) or severe emotional problems ("post-Vietnam syndrome").

---

statesman
A political leader who possesses vision, personal charisma, practical wisdom, and concern for the public good and whose leadership benefits society.

demagogue
Someone who uses his or her leadership skills to gain public office through appeals to popular fears and prejudices and then abuses that power for personal gain.

ordinary politician
A public office holder who is prepared to sacrifice previously held principles or shelve unpopular policies in order to get reelected.

citizen-leader
An individual who influences government decisively even though he or she holds no official government position.

statecraft
"The use of the assets or the resources and tools (economic, military, intelligence, media) that a state has to pursue its interest and to affect the behavior of others, whether friendly or hostile," according to foreign policy expert and senior diplomat Dennis Ross.

THE IDEAL LEADER

Great leaders practice **statecraft** by combining power and wisdom—thus the title *statesmen*. Unfortunately, we have no gender-neutral synonym, but let's be perfectly clear at the outset that a great leader—one who exhibits all the essential qualities of a statesman—can be either a woman or a man.

The concept of the ideal leader has been around for a long time. Plato and Aristotle both examined it. Indeed, Plato depicted Socrates engaging in a dialogue about *statesmanship*, the term often used to refer to the role of a gifted leader or national hero. Typically, it is only after a leader has departed the scene that he or she becomes a great statesman or hero in the popular mind, but any leader in a time of troubles is a candidate. Often, such a leader makes a difference on the world stage, as well as nationally. Golda Meir (Israel), Indira Gandhi (India), and Margaret Thatcher (United Kingdom) are examples of women in politics who rose to international preeminence and who are considered by some to be among the great statesmen of the post-World War II era.

Leaders who make a lasting difference display a firm commitment to the public good, possess extraordinary political skills, and exhibit practical wisdom. In times of crisis, these men and women provide crucial leadership; alternatively, they are founders of new nations, without whose vision, wisdom, and inspirational leadership a particular nation or government might never have existed at all. In our own history, George Washington is such a larger-than-life figure, not only present at the creation, but also a prime mover in it.

Statesmanship

Defining the ideal leader is no easy task. Qualities such as intuition, inspiration, humility, and good judgment lie at the core of leadership. Intelligence is important, too, but history proves that intelligence says nothing about integrity or character—and character is the key.

In *A Preface to Morals*, the late Walter Lippmann, a famed philosopher and columnist, attempted to isolate these qualities by contrasting enlightened leaders

The Late Golda Meir (1898–1978), Who Served As Israel's Prime Minister From 1969 To 1974, Is Remembered Today As An Exceptional Leader; In Her Public Life, She Exemplified The Traits Of Personal Charisma, Practical Wisdom, Political Skills, And Moral Integrity Often Associated With Statesmanship.

© AP PHOTO

with run-of-the-mill politicians. Lippmann suggested that most politicians work only "for a partial interest." Examples include politicians who feather their own nests or slavishly follow the party line. The word *statesmanship*, in contrast, "connotes a [person] whose mind is elevated sufficiently above the conflict of contending parties to enable him to adopt a course of action which takes into account a great number of interests in the perspective of a longer period of time."[2]

Lippmann recognized that the line between an ordinary politician and a real leader is often blurred. In a democracy, even the most high-minded leaders have to be politicians to gain and hold office. An trenchant observation attributed to H. L. Mencken (1880–1956) speaks directly to this point: "The men the American people admire most extravagantly are the most daring liars; the men they detest most violently are those who try to tell them the truth." Nonetheless, a true leader is not content merely to satisfy the momentary wishes of his or her constituents. The wiser course is to persuade voters that the pursuit of the public interest is in everyone's interest, and that private interests are not (and ought not to be) the primary concern of public policy.

Pursuit of the Public Good The best leaders are motivated not by crass self-interest but by the public good. By choosing what "the people will in the end find to be good against what the people happen ardently to desire," Lippmann contended, true leaders resist opinion polls and popular impulses. In refusing to promise the impossible, they choose honesty and moderation over self-flattery. Such a decision, he continues, requires the "courage which is possible only in a mind that is detached from the agitations of the moment," as well as the "insight which comes from an objective and discerning knowledge of the facts, and a high and imperturbable disinterestedness."

Virtue in public life is not identical to virtue in private life. Honesty is a virtue, but in political life it is not always possible. When the stakes are high, when complete honesty is an impediment to success, and when the best interests of the nation are served by stealth or dissimulation, a true leader will sometimes resort to deception. For example, both before and during the Civil War, President Lincoln consistently downplayed the slavery issue, preferring to keep the political spotlight on the overriding importance of preserving the Union. Lincoln understood that a call for immediate abolition risked alienating many moderates in both the North and South, ultimately harming the cause of both black emancipation and the Union.[3]

Practical Wisdom A compelling vision of the public good is useless without a way of achieving it. Effective leaders understand the relationship between actions and consequences. Statecraft—the art of diplomacy and the epitome of practical wisdom—distinguishes between the possible and the unattainable. In this sense, wise leaders bear a resemblance to physicians, whose success is ultimately measured not in dollars and cents they earn but in the health of the community they serve.

Political Skills Law and policies (and in the case of elections, the leaders themselves) require the consent of the governed. Reconciling wisdom and consent in the often-turbulent public arena is one of the primary tasks of leadership in a democracy.

Successful leaders are also good judges of talent and know how to delegate. Managing a vast bureaucracy, directing a large personal staff, working with the legislature to ensure a majority for the passage of the administration's programs, and rallying public opinion behind the administration's policies— these complex and demanding tasks are too much for any one individual to handle.

Of course, political skills are not always put at the service of the public good. Demagogues (see below) often seek to remove obstacles to needed social reforms by ruining, jailing, or killing opponents; even when they bring about progress and a measure of prosperity, the ends do not justify the means.

Extraordinary Opportunities Historians have frequently observed that great times make great leaders. To become an iconic figure like Washington or Lincoln, it is necessary to guide the nation in a time of war or revolution. At such times, moral inspiration and political expertise are essential if the nation is to endure; such a situation is tailor-made for the exercise of statecraft. During times of "politics as usual," even the most capable leader will lack the opportunity to become a hero in history.

Good Fortune The final prerequisite of exceptional leadership is good luck. No political leader can be successful without a certain amount of good fortune. A turn in the tide of a single battle, a message thought about but not sent (or sent too late), or any number of other seemingly unimportant incidents or actions may prove decisive. Great leadership can never be attributed entirely to good luck, but considering the complex environment in which such leaders operate, good luck often makes the difference between success and failure.

The Lure of Fame

Office holders often get into politics at significant cost to themselves, relinquishing more lucrative careers and facing constant public scrutiny. The question inevitably arises, Why would men and women of outstanding ability devote the best years of their productive lives to the pursuit of political excellence? What would inspire such individuals to work for the public good, often at the expense of more obvious and immediate self-interests?

According to historian Douglass Adair, the Founders were motivated primarily by the idea of fame. For George Washington, James Madison, Alexander Hamilton, and Benjamin Franklin, narrow self-interest, defined in terms of personal power or wealth, was not an overriding concern. Nor was individual honor, which Adair defines as a "pattern of behavior calculated to win praises from [one's] contemporaries who are [one's] social equals or superiors."[4] Rather, the Founders' great motivating force was a desire for fame—a concept that, according to Adair, has been deeply embedded in the Western philosophical and literary tradition since the classical era. Applying this interpretation to the U.S. Founders, Adair wrote,

Of course they were patriots, of course they were proud to serve their country in her need, but Washington, Adams, Jefferson, and Madison were not entirely disinterested. The pursuit of fame, they had been taught, was a way of transforming egotism and self-aggrandizing impulses into public service; they had been taught that public service nobly (and selflessly) performed was the surest way to build "lasting monuments" and earn the perpetual remembrance of posterity.[5]

Alexander Hamilton observed that a love of fame is "the ruling passion of the noblest minds."[6] The desire for immortality was a powerful elixir in Hamilton's time, when only wealthy, property-owning white men dared aspire to high office.

But times have changed—in many ways, for the better. Today, you do not have to be rich to enter politics in America. An African American named Barack Hussein Obama whose father was born in Kenya and who was raised by his grandparents in a small Kansas town can become president. That is the good news. The bad news is that national politics is now a very lucrative profession.

Former Senator Tom Daschle is one example among many. When Daschle went to Washington as a freshman Congressman from South Dakota in 1979, he had no money. An unknown even in his home state, he had campaigned by going from house to house, knocking on doors, and introducing himself to the voters—"door-to-door Daschle," people called him. But in Congress, he prospered. In 1987 he was elected to the Senate, where he rose to become Senate Majority leader. Having lost his bid for re-election in 2005, he left the Senate but did not leave Washington. He became a "consultant" (a euphemism for lobbyist) and is now a multimillionaire.

FOUR EXEMPLARY LEADERS

Leaders are not all cut from the same cloth. A few are courageous and incorruptible. Some are crooked and cruel. Most fall somewhere in the middle.

It is easy to become cynical about the possibility of good government or honest leaders (two sides of the same coin). If we believe politicians are *all* alike or power *always* corrupts, we run the risk of creating a self-fulfilling prophecy. If we have low expectations and reward elected officials by reelecting them *automatically*, we devalue the very idea of leadership.

Good leaders do not come along every day—but they do come along. Throughout history, exemplary leaders—the best of the best—have appeared at various times and places. As the following political biographies of four world-famous leaders demonstrate, the backgrounds, qualities, and motives of those who have risen to the first rank of leadership display both remarkable similarities and wide disparities. Setting a good example is the mark of a good leader—hence the term *exemplary* to characterize the best of them.

Rómulo Betancourt (1908–1981)

Today, Venezuela is ruled by Hugo Chávez, a strident critic of U.S. foreign policy in general and of the Bush administration in particular. Chávez is a left-leaning populist—a kind of latter-day *caudillo* (in Spanish, a strong leader, especially a military dictator)—who, despite his image as part demagogue and part Robin Hood, is not so different from many leaders in Venezuelan history. And that is one of the things that makes the story of Rómulo Betancourt (1908–1981) so remarkable.

Venezuela became a nation in 1830. From then until 1959, when Betancourt assumed the elected presidency, no democratic ruler had survived in office for even 2 years. Yet not only did Betancourt survive, battling seemingly insurmountable obstacles, but his public career also prospered, giving life to his country's fledgling democracy.

Betancourt's political career began when he was still a university student. At that time, a military dictator named Juan Vicente Gómez ruled Venezuela. In 1928, at the age of 20, Betancourt became a student leader in a failed revolution, eventually ending up in jail. After his release, he went into exile in Costa Rica for 8 years, returning to Venezuela shortly after the death of the dictator in 1935. Afterward, Betancourt became a prominent political figure, though from the mid-1930s until 1959, he was a political maverick—often on the run, active in the underground, and sometimes living in exile as he continued his opposition to the dictator of the day. During his early years in opposition, he

Romulo Betancourt (1908–1981), president of Venezuela, 1945–1948 and 1959–1964. Betancourt first became president of Venezuela in the old fashioned Latin American way: by a military coup. Today he is most often remembered as "The Father of Venezuelan Democracy," one of Latin America's great post–World War II statesmen and a courageous defender of constitutional government. Among his most notable achievements in office are the declaration of universal suffrage, many progressive social reforms, restructuring of Venezuela's oil contracts to keep over half the profits in the country and for the public benefit, and, finally, the famous "Betancourt Doctrine" which denied diplomatic recognition to any government that came to power by military force. Betancourt's last major contribution as president was to direct what is generally believed to have been the most honest election in Venezuela's history and in March, 1964, he handed over the reins of government to the winner, Raul Leoni. Betancourt thus became the first elected Venezuelan president ever to serve a full term in office and the first to transfer power constitutionally from one elected chief executive to another.

© JOHN DOMINIS/TIME & LIFE PICTURES/GETTY IMAGES

sympathized with the communists, but he moderated in time, favoring democratic socialism instead. Betancourt's most notable achievement during this time was laying the groundwork for what would become Venezuela's leading party—Acción Democratica.

Throughout most of his years in opposition, both Betancourt and his party consistently championed broad democratic participation for all citizens, agrarian reform, guaranteed universal education, national health care, and economic diversification (Venezuela was heavily dependent on oil exports). Betancourt joined and, according to some versions, headed a group of military reformers in a coup d'état (power seizure) against Venezuela's military government in October 1945. He ended up as president.

In office Betancourt championed a foreign policy in which Venezuela refused to extend diplomatic recognition to dictatorships and urged other governments in the region to follow suit. Domestically, he decreed that the large oil companies in Venezuela turn over half their income, enabling the government to undertake a far-reaching program to establish schools, hospitals, public water and sanitation facilities, and low-cost housing developments. He sponsored a new constitution in 1947, promoted elections, and declared he would not be a candidate for office. The candidate who succeeded Betancourt lasted only 9 months before being ousted by another military coup. It was not until Betancourt was elected president in 1959 that democracy returned to Venezuela.

During his 5-year term, Betancourt pursued the progressive policies he had always advocated. Particularly notable were his efforts to encourage foreign investment and improve urban housing. Betancourt also initiated a program of land reform. His economic and political achievements were all the more remarkable because when he took office, his nation was facing an economic crisis, the military did not support his rule, and coup attempts from both the Left and the Right punctuated his term. (Betancourt survived more than one assassination attempt.)

Although he was decisive and governed with a firm hand, Betancourt exemplified the differences between democratic leadership and dictatorial abuse of power. He encouraged the politics of moderation, compromise, and toleration. He heeded the powers and prerogatives of the other two branches of government, followed the constitution, respected the rights of citizens, and did not use his high office for material advantage (or permit anyone under him to do so).[7]

Betancourt prevailed in the end and was beloved by his people. What accounted for his success as a democratic leader in a country with an autocratic tradition? Betancourt appears to have possessed an uncanny ability to judge the motives and character of others; almost unerring judgment about when to stand firm and when to compromise; a capacity to listen to advice but to keep his own counsel; an ability to make difficult decisions; self-control; and great personal valor, both moral and physical. He combined all these qualities with a high degree of practical idealism—a clear vision of what he wanted to accomplish for his country and a commitment to values that, together with ambition, had motivated him in national politics for decades.[8]

Betancourt can justly be considered the founder of Venezuelan democracy. As one of his foremost biographers, Robert J. Alexander, observed, "No other

Venezuelan political leader of his time could have succeeded under all these circumstances."[9] A historian who specialized in Latin America wrote, "If moral authority and high principles counted, Rómulo Betancourt loomed as a titan in the history of Venezuela."[10] In the end, he did what no Venezuelan had ever done before, something demagogues never do: he bowed out gracefully, handing power over to a democratically elected successor.[11]

Winston Churchill (1874–1965)

Winston Churchill became Britain's prime minister in May 1940, at a time of great peril to his country. A colorful personality, Churchill was brilliant, charming, and witty; he was also courageous, controversial, and cantankerous. In the 1930s, he recognized and warned Britain of the menace posed by the rise of Nazi Germany in the heart of Europe. When war broke out, Churchill had already had his share of ups and downs in government, but his career reflected a steadfast devotion to the cause of freedom.

Churchill was born into a prominent English family that traced its lineage directly back to John Churchill, the first duke of Marlborough. Winston's father had been a distinguished member of Parliament and cabinet minister; his mother was an American. He himself was elected to Parliament at the tender age of 25 and almost immediately acquired a reputation as an eloquent and outspoken maverick. In 1911, he was appointed First Lord of the Admiralty, a high office he held through the first year of World War I. He was forced to resign in 1915, after the dismal failure of an amphibious attack on Turkey, by way of the Dardanelles, that he had sponsored. Churchill's political prestige then fell to an all-time low, although he managed to recoup sufficiently to be appointed minister of munitions in 1917.

Churchill remained a Conservative Member of Parliament (MP) throughout most of the 1920s and even held the prestigious position of chancellor of the exchequer (comparable to the U.S. secretary of the treasury) for an extended period. Despite a solid record of public service, he entered the 1930s as something of a political outcast, having alienated the leadership of his party. Even though the Conservatives held power, he was excluded from the government, and he found himself increasingly isolated in Parliament. At the age of 56, he was facing a premature end to his political career.

But Churchill had a kind of clairvoyance rare in politics. From the time of Hitler's ascent to power, he tried to alert Britain, Europe, and the United States, warning of the danger posed by Nazi Germany's rapid rearmament and the comparative weakness of Britain's armed forces—especially its air power. Many mainstream politicians and commentators ridiculed him as an alarmist. In the words of his foremost biographer, Churchill was a voice in the wilderness.[12]

As the 1930s progressed and Churchill's alarms began to arouse the nation, there still was no place for him in his party's cabinet. Only after Britain entered World War II was he asked to return to the government, initially in his former post as First Lord of the Admiralty, and then as prime minister.

After France had fallen and before the United States relaxed its policy of strict neutrality, Britain was the only power standing between Hitler and his goal—the total conquest of Europe. Churchill's inspiring words and example proved decisive. As Churchill later wrote, "Alone, but up-borne by every generous heartbeat of mankind, we had defied the tyrant in his hour of triumph."[13]

Churchill had rare leadership qualities. He understood the darker side of human nature and thus grasped the danger Hitler posed to civilization. Churchill had the courage of his convictions, never yielding to the voices of appeasement in his own party or the pressures of public opinion. His rhetoric inspired the nation in the face of a mortal threat and relentless bombardment. Above all, events proved him tragically right—right about the imminent threat, right about the malignant evil Hitler represented, and right about the urgent need for military preparedness. His message—that another terrible war was coming—was one his compatriots did not want to hear, but he never confused what the nation wanted to hear with what it *needed* to hear. And so he became the savior of his country.

Abraham Lincoln (1809–1865)

Churchill saved Britain from Hitler's Germany; Abraham Lincoln saved the United States of America from itself. The pivotal political issue in Lincoln's time was slavery. The South's economic dependence on it, along with the persistence of racial prejudice in the North, meant that advocating the immediate abolition of slavery was incompatible with winning the presidency. But preventing the "westward" spread of slavery, as it turned out, was incompatible with maintaining the peace.

This was the context in which Lincoln decided to run for president, a decision that culminated in his election to the nation's highest office in 1860. Lincoln's politics were guided by a basic moral precept and a profoundly practical judgment. The moral precept, which he repeatedly voiced in his debates with Stephen Douglas during his 1858 campaign for the Senate, held that slavery was wrong in principle, everywhere and without exception. In declaring slavery unjust and immoral, Lincoln did not resort to abstract philosophy; rather, he based his judgment squarely on the Declaration of Independence, which states, ". . . all men are created equal." Thus, for Lincoln, slavery violated the most basic principle of the U.S. political order.

Lincoln exercised uncommon practical judgment in evaluating the conditions under which slavery might be eradicated in the United States. He believed above all that it was necessary to maintain the Union as a geographic entity, as well as to preserve its integrity as a constitutional democracy. Only through a single central government for North and South alike could slavery be ended, although this was by no means inevitable. Conversely, any breakup of the Union would mean the indefinite extension of slavery, at least in the South.

Lincoln's belief in political equality and his conviction that such equality could be achieved only by preserving the Union help explain the pre–Civil War stands he avoided taking, as well as the ones he adopted. Although he believed slavery was morally wrong, he did not propose its immediate abolition; he knew such a proposal would prompt the South to secede and ensure the survival of slavery in that region. Nor did he support Northern abolitionists who sought to disassociate themselves from the Union so long as it continued to countenance slavery. Here again, Lincoln recognized that such a policy would only entrench the very institution it was designed to eliminate. Finally, he opposed Stephen Douglas's formula of popular sovereignty, under which each new state would be allowed to declare itself for or against slavery. The question of slavery, Lincoln believed, was too fundamental to be submitted to the vagaries of the political marketplace.

Rather than pursue any of these policies, Lincoln favored an end to the extension of slavery into the territories, so that from then on, only free states would be admitted to the Union. In Lincoln's mind, this was the only antislavery policy that had any chance of gaining popular acceptance. The keys to his strategy were patience and perseverance. Adoption of his plan would ultimately bring about an end to slavery in the whole United States, as the relative weight and legislative strength of the slaveholding states diminished with the passage of time and the admission of new non-slaveholding states.

When it became evident that Lincoln's policy would not win the day, he accepted the Civil War as inevitable. Yet during the course of this conflict, his approach to the slavery question varied according to the circumstances of the war. As noted earlier, when the tide of battle ran against the Union and victory seemed to depend on not alienating several of the slaveholding border states, Lincoln went out of his way to soft-pedal the slavery issue. The North needed military victories, not pious pronouncements, if the Union were to endure. It could not endure, he believed, if it remained "half slave and half free." In the final analysis, the reason Lincoln was willing to countenance civil war was, paradoxically, to preserve the kind of Union the Founders had intended.

Both before and during the Civil War, Lincoln's policies were aimed at achieving the maximum amount of good possible within the confines of popular consent. As commander in chief, he pushed his constitutional authority up to, and arguably beyond, its legal limits. But just as his ultimate political purposes were not undermined by the compromises he accepted to save the Union in time of peace, so too his moral integrity was not corrupted by the dictatorial powers he wielded in time of war. For all these reasons, Lincoln stands out as an exemplary political leader whose resolute actions and decisions under fire were instrumental in saving the Union.

Anwar al-Sadat (1918–1981)

The Middle East has long been among the world's most unstable and violent places. Miraculously, in late 1993, Israeli Prime Minister Yitzhak Rabin and Palestine Liberation Organization leader Yasir Arafat, bitter enemies, agreed to a deal that gave limited autonomy to the Palestinians in the Israeli-occupied West Bank and Gaza Strip. The agreement was a big step toward a possible peace, but it was not the *first* step. In fact, there was a precedent in the Middle East, one that suggested even the deadliest of enemies can live together in peace. Anwar al-Sadat was the political architect of that peacemaking precedent.

Sadat was president of Egypt from 1970 until his assassination in 1981. He succeeded Gamal Abdel Nasser, the acknowledged leader of the Arab world and a prime mover in the post–World War II anti-colonialist movement. Nasser was an autocratic ruler who governed Egypt with an iron fist and staunchly opposed the existence of the state of Israel. When Nasser died in 1970, Sadat automatically succeeded him. (As vice president, Sadat was Nasser's handpicked successor.) Under Egypt's constitution, Sadat was to hold office on an interim basis for only 60 days, during which the National Assembly was required to choose a permanent successor. Ironically, this legislative body eventually endorsed Sadat in the belief that he would be noncontroversial and adhere tightly to his predecessor's policies.

Indeed, there was little reason to expect anything else from Sadat, whose early political life was devoted to securing Egyptian independence from Great Britain. His anti-British activities during World War II included contacts with Germans aimed at collaboration against the British imperialists. For these efforts, Sadat spent 2 years in a detention camp. Later, he would spend 3 more years (1946–1949) in prison, charged with attempting to assassinate a British official. In pursuit of a nationalistic strategy that sought to capitalize on anti-British sentiment in Egypt, Sadat and Nasser cooperated closely. It was Sadat who publicly announced the overthrow of the Egyptian monarchy and the establishment of the new, independent republic of Egypt under Nasser's leadership, in July 1952.

Given this history, it seemed inevitable that as president, Sadat would continue Nasser's policies. Events seemed to bear out this expectation. In 1971, he was instrumental in forging the Federation of Arab Republics, an alliance of Egypt, Libya, and Syria motivated by Nasser's policy of uniting the Arab world. The federation ultimately failed, but not for want of trying on Sadat's part.

In 1973, Sadat led Egypt in a war against Israel. Although Egypt was defeated, Sadat stressed that the Egyptian army had won a major battle at the outset of the war; this victory, he maintained, restored Egypt's national honor. In the aftermath of the war, Sadat switched from belligerent Arab nationalist to committed advocate of peaceful coexistence. This transformation was capped by a precedent-shattering state visit to Israel, where Sadat delivered a memorable speech before the Israeli Knesset (parliament) on November 20, 1977. More important than the speech was the symbolic significance of his official presence in the Israeli seat of government: Egypt had become the first Arab country to recognize Israel as a sovereign state.

This dramatic act of conciliation by Sadat paved the way for the Camp David Accords between Egypt and Israel the following year. The Egyptian-Israeli agreement at Camp David, Maryland, which set the stage for Israel's withdrawal from the Sinai peninsula, caught foreign observers by surprise and stunned the Arab world. Sadat was bitterly attacked by many of his fellow Arab rulers as a traitor to the Palestinian cause. To the Arabs, and to many of the most astute observers, Sadat's bold step toward a lasting Arab-Israeli peace was as unexpected as it was unprecedented.

Why did Sadat take this extraordinary step? Some experts have suggested he recognized that given the serious economic problems facing his impoverished, densely populated nation, Egypt simply could not afford a perennial cycle of war with Israel. Others have pointed to the fact that Israel had furnished Egypt with valuable intelligence about the activities of its increasingly hostile neighbor, Libya. Finally, it has been argued that Sadat was a pragmatist who concluded the only way Egypt was ever going to regain the Sinai, which Israel had occupied since 1967, was by signing a peace treaty.

Although all these factors may have figured into Sadat's calculations, they do not explain the intensity of his peace efforts or the magnitude of the personal and political risks he was willing to take. He knew his actions would alienate most of the Arab world, including many of his fellow citizens. It seems likely that just as the young Sadat was moved by the ideal of a free and independent Egypt, which he helped to bring about, so too an older Sadat was inspired by an even more noble vision. As he expressed it on the occasion of the signing of the Camp David Accords,

> Let there be no more wars or bloodshed between Arabs and Israelis. Let there be no more suffering or denial of rights. Let there be no more despair or loss of faith. Let no mother lament the loss of her child. Let no young man waste his life on a conflict from which no one benefits. Let us work together until the day comes when they beat their swords into plowshares and their spears into pruning hooks.[14]

The eradication of hatred, religious bigotry, and incessant warfare from a region where they had been a way of life for as long as anyone could remember would indeed be a great act of statecraft. The attempt to bring peace to the Middle East may well have been Sadat's own personal bid for immortality. He may or may not have been aware of Alexander Hamilton's views on the subject of leadership, but through his actions, Sadat bore out the truth of Hamilton's observation that love of fame is the "ruling passion" of history's most exceptional leaders.

Like Lincoln, Sadat was assassinated by one of his own countrymen. Oddly, such is often the fate of history's peacemakers. Thus, Mahatma Gandhi, the charismatic leader of India's independence movement and a champion of nonviolent resistance, was himself assassinated.

Paradoxically, in politics, making peace often entails greater *personal* risks than making war. The tragic fate that befell Sadat also befell Israeli Prime Minister Rabin. In 1995, Rabin was assassinated by a radical right-wing Israeli opposed to the Oslo Peace Accords (for which Rabin, along with Shimon Peres and Arafat, won the Nobel Peace Prize). A lasting peace in the Middle East has been elusive, but Egypt and Israel have been at peace for more than two decades thanks to the treaty that stands as a fitting memorial to the wisdom and courage of Anwar al-Sadat.

THE ECLIPSE OF LEADERSHIP?

Living politicians have a lot in common with the late comedian Rodney Dangerfield: they get no respect. In politics, sometimes "losers" come to be admired as leaders and winners suffer the opposite fate (see Box 12.1). When

BOX 12.1 SPOTLIGHT ON   Fallen Leaders: When "Losers" Become "Winners"

Two examples of "loss leaders" in recent U.S. history are Jimmy Carter (who lost his bid for re-election to Ronald Reagan in 1980) and Al Gore (who lost to George W. Bush in the controversial 2000 election). Former President Carter found his leadership repudiated when he was a "winner," but after his defeat in 1980, he came to be widely admired for his unstinting humanitarian efforts—notably, his Habitat for Humanity project—as well as for promoting peace and democracy in troubled parts of the world.

As a presidential campaigner, Al Gore was often dismissed as boring and was even blamed for the "historical debacle" that many believe resulted from his failure to win the presidency in 2000. But the image, and very likely the legacy, of Al Gore dramatically changed in 2006 when he starred in *An Inconvenient Truth*, the Academy Award-winning documentary about global warming and the dangers it poses to the health and survival of the planet. In 2007, he was

FIGURE 12.1   Al Gore and other crusaders for a clean environment are gaining adherents among voters and legislators alike at the state level. By 2009, 19 states (shaded in the map) had adopted a voluntary cap on greenhouse gas emissions, including Arizona, California, Connecticut, Florida, Hawaii, Illinois, Maine, Massachusetts, Minnesota, Mississippi, New Hampshire, New Jersey, New Mexico, New York, Oregon, Rhode Island, Utah, Vermont, and Washington.

SOURCE: Pew Center on the States at http://www.pewcenteronthestates.org/.

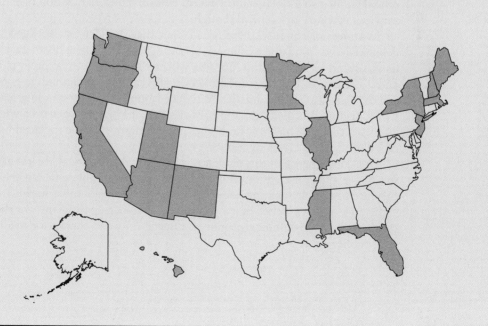

BOX 12.1 SPOTLIGHT ON   *(Continued)*

awarded the Nobel Peace Prize for his work on climate change.

Gore's passion for environmental causes goes back to his college days, long before he ran for public office. (Similarly, Carter's humanitarianism is rooted in long-held religious beliefs.) In 1992, a decade before global warming became a major issue in the United States, Gore wrote *Earth in the Balance*, which called for eliminating the internal combustion engine by 2017 and for making environmentalism "the central organizing principle for civilization."

Gore thus reinvented himself as a leader and has arguably had a greater impact on public policy as a private citizen than he ever did as a politician—even as the vice president of the United States. Perhaps if the Al Gore who ran for president had been more like the Al Gore who became a crusader for truth—the inconvenient truth—he would have won in 2000. Ironic, perhaps, but what is more important is the lesson: true leaders *believe in something*, they have moral convictions, and they are, above all, true to themselves.

politicians are beholden to special interests and use focus groups to formulate messages that will sell in a 10-second television sound bite, courageous political leadership often seems like a distant ideal.*

Leadership as a concept has virtually disappeared from the language and literature of U.S. politics. Significantly, while the 1934 edition of the *Encyclopedia of the Social Sciences* included a brief but incisive essay on statesmanship by a celebrated British scholar, a more recent edition omits all mention of statesmanship as a category of political thought.

In an age of equality, there is a danger that the idea of excellence will be debunked and dismissed as elitist.[15] To the debunkers, vague historical determinants or narrow self-interest, not free will, are the true motive forces in history, and it is naive to believe some leaders really care about the public good. This cynical view leads to a drastically reduced opinion of outstanding leaders in world history. It is as if "the old histories full of kings and generals whom our ancestors foolishly mistook for heroes are, we suppose, to be replaced by a kind of hall of fame of clever operators."[16]

One consequence of this tendency is that it makes political life less attractive to capable and conscientious individuals. By denying public officials the respect they are due, a democratic society can do itself considerable harm. As noted earlier, a pervasive belief that corrupt and mediocre politicians are the norm can become a self-fulfilling prophecy, causing only the corrupt or mediocre to seek public office.

---

* Historians sometimes seek to refute the conventional wisdom about history's most famous figures. In the United States, recent books have cast doubt on the character and motives of even our most revered national icons, including George Washington and Thomas Jefferson.

AMERICAN DEMAGOGUES

Originally, in ancient Greece, a demagogue was a leader who championed the cause of the common people. Today, the term *demagogue* is applied to a leader who exploits popular prejudices, distorts the truth, and makes empty promises to gain political power. In general, demagogues combine unbridled personal ambition, unscrupulous methods, and great popular appeal.

If true leaders represent the ideal, demagogues represent the perversion of both truth and leadership. Statesmen genuinely care about justice and the public good; demagogues only pretend to care in order to gain high office whence they inevitably betray the public interest they previously championed.

Demagogues are rarely long remembered. Occasionally, they leave an indelible mark.

Aaron Burr (1756–1836)

His name is one of the most notorious in the annals of early U.S. history. Schoolchildren learn at an early age that Aaron Burr was a "bad guy," but very few, including adults, know much about him or why he was a danger to the young republic he claimed to serve.

Burr had a tragic childhood. Born into a wealthy and famous family, he lost both his parents at a very early age. He was beaten by his guardian and ran away from home more than once. At the age of 10, he tried to stow away on a ship. Desperate not to be taken back to live with his tormentor, he climbed the ship's mast and refused to come down. In the end, he was delivered once again into his guardian's "care."

Burr was a precocious child and a brilliant student. In time, he became a lawyer and then went into politics. He had an uncanny ability to beguile, to pretend he was someone other than who he really was. He was also an eloquent speaker and an agile debater, skills that served him well in a court of law. A great admirer of Thomas Jefferson, he was a candidate for president in 1800, the year Jefferson was elected. Because of the peculiar workings of the Electoral College, however, no candidate received the absolute majority required by the Constitution to claim the presidency, so the decision was thrown into the House of Representatives, dominated by the lame-duck Federalists, where the delegations from the various states each cast one vote. The contest in the House of Representatives was between Jefferson and Burr. The Federalists were determined to "elect" Burr, who refused to withdraw even though Jefferson was clearly the popular choice. Finally, after 5 long days, on the 36th ballot, a delegate from Virginia changed his vote, giving Jefferson the one additional state vote he needed to put him over the top. Thus, Burr became the vice president, having nearly stolen the presidency.

In Jefferson's time, vice presidents had very little to do. Burr kept himself busy, however, by undermining the president and the republic. The story of his seditious activities is too long and convoluted to be told here, but they included trying to organize a secession movement in New England and the territory north of the Ohio River, later plotting to assassinate Jefferson, and trying to lead an insurrection in New Orleans and what was then the Mississippi Territory. (His plans included creation of a western empire, under his control, in the lands acquired through Jefferson's leadership in the famed Louisiana Purchase.)

Burr was eventually captured and arrested on charges of treason. Brought to trial in Richmond, Virginia, in 1807, he was acquitted by the Chief Justice of the Supreme Court, John Marshall, who was also acting as federal court judge. Marshall was a die-hard Federalist and a rival of Jefferson's. Seldom, if ever, has there been a more blatant case in U.S. jurisprudence of politicizing a trial and showing contempt from the bench for the integrity of the Constitution. The evidence against Burr was abundant and damning, but neither Jefferson nor the Republican-controlled Congress had the stomach to see Burr hang once Marshall had rendered his verdict.

In sum, Burr failed to achieve his seditious intents, but his demagoguery had come dangerously close to catapulting him into the presidency in 1800. The fact that he became a U.S. senator and vice president shows that demagogues have long played a role at the highest levels of government. Burr's personal charisma and political skills in the end also probably helped him escape the gallows.

Theodore Bilbo (1877–1947)

As governor and senator, Theodore Bilbo dominated Mississippi politics from the 1920s through the 1940s. He campaigned equally hard against blacks and his political opponents, linking them whenever possible. His campaign rhetoric was colorful and outrageous. In the heat of one political campaign, he denounced his opponent as a "cross between a hyena and a mongrel . . . begotten in a [racial slur deleted] graveyard at midnight, suckled by a sow, and educated by a fool."[17] Although Bilbo's white supremacist politics and down-home language endeared him to a great many Mississippians, not everyone was impressed. Even political allies viewed him as a self-serving political operator.

According to one writer, Bilbo was "pronounced by the state Senate in 1911 'as unfit to sit with honest upright men in a respectable legislative body,' and described more pungently by his admirers as 'a slick little bastard.'"[18] And in the eyes of the editor of the *Jackson Daily News*, Bilbo stood "for nothing that is high or constructive, . . . nothing save passion, prejudice and hatred, . . . nothing that is worthy."[19] Bilbo was reelected to a third Senate term in 1946, but this time the Senate refused to seat him, for his alleged incitement of violence against blacks who tried to vote. Bilbo died of cancer a few months later at the age of 69.

Huey Long (1893–1935)

Theodore Bilbo has mercifully escaped the attention of most U.S. historians; Huey Long, a politician from the neighboring state of Louisiana, has not. Known to his Cajun constituents as the Kingfish, Long was far more ambitious than Bilbo. Of humble origins, he completed the 3-year law program at Tulane University, passed a special examination from the Louisiana Supreme Court,

As Governor of Louisiana, Huey Long seized control and acted as a virtual dictator. Then as Senator during the Great Depression, he cast himself as a radical populist social reformer and had great ambitions on the national scene. But an assassin's bullet abruptly ended his career and his life in 1935. It is said that his last words were, "God don't let me die. I have so much left to do."

© AP PHOTOS

and became a licensed attorney at the age of 21. In his own words, he "came out of the courtroom running for office."[20] Three years later, he was elected state railroad commissioner, and in 1928, he gained the Louisiana governorship.

Long governed Louisiana with an iron hand during his 4-year reign (1928–1932) and during his subsequent term as U.S. senator, which was cut short by his assassination in 1935. As governor, Long controlled every aspect of the state's political life. Surrounded by bodyguards and aided by a formidable political machine, he used state police and militia to intimidate voters, handed out patronage and political favors, created a state printing board to put unfriendly newspapers out of business, ordered a kidnapping on the eve of a crucial election vote to avoid personal political embarrassment, and generally acted more like a despotic ruler than a democratically elected governor. Under his autocratic rule,

> Men could be—and were—arrested by unidentified men, the members of his secret police, held incommunicado, tried, and found guilty on trumped-up charges. A majority of the State Supreme Court became unabashedly his. . . . A thug, making a premeditated skull-crushing attack upon a Long opponent, could draw from his pocket in court a pre-signed pardon.[21]

Despite these excesses and a penchant for luxury, Long always took care to portray himself as "just plain folks." The true villains in U.S. society, he said, were rich corporations such as Standard Oil, which consigned ordinary people to lives of poverty while enriching a few corporate officers.

To counteract this alleged thievery by big business and to create a popular platform for the upcoming presidential race in 1936, Long developed an unworkable (but popular) "Share the Wealth" program, tailor-made to appeal to people suffering through the Great Depression. Long's proposal included restrictions on maximum wealth, mandated minimum, and maximum incomes, so-called homestead grants for all families, free education through college, bonuses for veterans, and pensions for the aged—as well as the promise of radios, automobiles, and subsidized food through government purchases. However implausible and impractical this program seems, it's worth remembering that the people to whom Long was appealing were not inclined to quibble or question. They needed someone to believe in.

Like many other demagogues, Long gained power by promising hope to the hopeless. Demagogues generally vow to defeat the forces of evil that, according to them, are solely responsible for the people's plight. Of course, those forces—blacks in the case of Bilbo, corporations for Long—invariably do not exercise anything like the controlling influence attributed to them. Nonetheless, once accepted as the champion of the little people against enemies they themselves have conjured up, demagogues often have been able to manipulate the unsuspecting populace for their own illicit ends.

Joseph McCarthy (1906–1957)

During the 1950s, an obscure politician from Wisconsin named Joseph McCarthy identified a demon that greatly alarmed the U.S. people and then claimed to find evidence of this malignant force in all areas of public life.

While serving as a Republican senator from Wisconsin, McCarthy attracted national attention by making the shocking "revelation" that the U.S. Department of State was infiltrated by communists. For approximately 4 years, he leveled charges of treason against a wide array of public officials, college professors, and Hollywood stars. Using his position as chair of the Senate Committee on Investigations, McCarthy badgered, intimidated, and defamed countless people in and out of government. As his accusations helped create a national climate of fear, his power grew, and those who opposed him did so at their own risk.

In 1954, McCarthy accused the secretary of the army of concealing foreign espionage operations. That accusation, along with innuendos aimed at General George C. Marshall—next to President Dwight D. Eisenhower, perhaps the most respected public servant in the United States—marked a turning point. McCarthy had gone too far. Ironically, his unscrupulous methods were exposed in Senate investigations that resulted from his own irresponsible accusations. The hearings received national radio and television coverage and made front-page headlines in every major newspaper in the country. In the end, McCarthy was cast into obscurity as rapidly as he had been catapulted into national prominence.

Tom DeLay (b. 1947)

Texas Republican Tom DeLay (1947–) was first elected to the U.S. House of Representatives in 1984 and served as House majority leader from 2003 to 2006, having been the House majority whip in the 1990s and subsequently serving as deputy majority leader. DeLay became known as "The Hammer" for his ruthless methods and questionable ethics. As House majority whip, he demanded strict party discipline and made anyone who crossed him pay. When he became House majority leader after the 2002 midterm elections, he rallied—or bullied—House Republicans to close ranks behind President George W. Bush's neoconservative agenda.

In the early 2000s, DeLay played a key role in a plan to gerrymander state legislative districts and later to redraw Texas's congressional districts in favor of the Republican Party. However, in October 2004, the House Ethics Committee voted unanimously to admonish DeLay on two counts relating to ethics violations, though it deferred action on another count related to fund raising while that matter was under criminal investigation in Texas.

In 2005, a Texas grand jury indicted DeLay on criminal charges of conspiring to violate campaign finance laws by engaging in money laundering during that period. Although he denied the charges, claiming they were politically motivated, he had no choice under existing rules but to step down temporarily as majority leader. Under heavy pressure from within his own party, he later announced he would not seek to return to his leadership position in the House. About this same time, two of DeLay's former aides were convicted in the Jack Abramoff scandal. (Abramoff is now serving a prison sentence for defrauding American Indian tribes and for corruption of public officials.)

DeLay ran for reelection in 2006 and won the Republican primary but subsequently resigned his seat in Congress. He tried to have his name removed from the ballot to avoid a humiliating defeat, but he lost a court battle and had to remain, even though he had withdrawn from the race. In the annals of U.S. politics, there are few more ignominious endings to a politician's career. (The demise of Richard Nixon is one.) As the saying goes, the bigger they are, they harder they fall.

POLITICIANS

Ordinary politicians, like most other jobholders, have neither great vision nor outstanding talents. On a day-to-day basis, they do the best they can, given the pressures and constraints they face. Much of the time, they want to do the right thing, although they have difficulty keeping moral or ethical issues in clear focus and even more difficulty taking political risks. Generally they are not corrupt, but they often *are* corruptible. They are no better, and no worse, than most people, but they are in a position to do more harm (or good) than most ordinary citizens.

As citizens, we often scorn "politicians."[22] Politicians, in turn, lament the fact that voters fail to understand how the system really works—that without logrolling (trading votes) the legislative process would grind to a halt. The would-be leader in a democratic society faces the choice whether to act as a delegate, carrying out the voters' (presumed) wishes, or to act as a trustee, exercising independent judgment on behalf of his or her constituents. The political system itself requires elected representatives to be responsive if they wish to be reelected. But those to whom the people have entrusted power are duty-bound to lead—and therein lies the politician's dilemma.

Legislators as Delegates

delegate theory of representation
According to this theory, elected officials should reflect the views of the voters back home, rather than following their own consciences or substituting their own judgement for that of their constituents; in other words, elected representatives should be followers rather than leaders.

According to the **delegate theory of representation,** a legislature "is representative when it contains within itself the same elements, in the same proportion, as are found in the body politic at large. It is typical of us; we are all in it in microcosm."[23] In this model of representative democracy, elected representatives are obliged to act as instructed delegates.

The delegate theory thus tends to legitimize the use of focus groups and opinion polls to help legislators decide what stands to take on important issues. One notable advocate of this theory holds there is a "relative equality of capacity and wisdom between representatives and constituents," it would be "arbitrary and unjustifiable for representatives to ignore the opinions and wishes of the people," and that political issues often involve "irrational commitment or personal preference, choice rather than deliberation, [making it all] the more necessary . . . that the representative consult with the people's preferences. . . . "[24]

Legislators as Trustees

Detractors say the delegate theory of representation requires elected officials to be too passive—in effect, to act as followers rather than leaders. One famous critic of this theory was Edmund Burke (1729–1797), the famed eighteenth-century British writer and legislator.

Burke believed legislators ought to retain a certain independence of thought and action. Specifically, according to Burke, the elected representative needs to isolate specific complaints about real problems from the grumbling of an irascible (and possibly irrational) electorate. He contended that the politician as legislator must listen to the complaints of constituents but not give all complaints equal weight: competent legislators distinguish between complaints that arise from defects in human nature (and cannot be remedied) and those that "are symptoms of a particular distemperature" of the day.[25] Understood in this fashion, popular opinion becomes a valuable barometer. If legislators wish to get a reading on popular sentiment or whether controversy is brewing on a particular issue, they must first consult public opinion.

trustee theory of representation
The theory that elected officials should be leaders, making informed choices in the interest of their constituencies.

Burke believed a natural aristocracy made up of the best and the brightest should govern and that elected officials should act as trustees, not puppets. As he declared in a famous speech to his own constituents, "Your representative owes you not his industry only, but his judgment; and he betrays, instead of serving you, if he sacrifices it to your opinion."[26]

Burke's so-called **trustee theory of representation** fits into his larger philosophy of government. Good government, he argued, must include not only good will but also "virtue and wisdom." To be workable, in other words, representative government must be based on upright behavior and careful deliberation, with an eye toward discovering and carrying out the true public good. Burke characterized his own Parliament as "a *deliberative* assembly of *one* nation, with *one* interest, that of the whole—where not local purposes, not local prejudices, ought to guide, but the general good, resulting from the general reason of the whole."[27]

Burke believed a wide gulf separated members of the legislature from ordinary constituents. He held that in a sound republic, representatives should be wiser and better informed than constituents and hence should be able, after careful deliberation, to solve most of the political problems that beset a nation. Finally, he argued that the welfare of the whole nation—the public or national interest—should take precedence over the welfare of any of its parts—local or special interests. For these reasons, Burke stressed the importance of the legislator as leader rather than follower.

Solons

Some lawmakers—whom we will call **solons**—successfully reconcile the functions of delegate and trustee. Solon was the great lawgiver of ancient Athens, the wise legislator who framed the laws of the city-state that became the first democracy in the history of Western civilization. Words like *great* and *wise* are seldom used in the same sentence as *legislator* these days; sadly, many today consider the very idea of a "great legislator" to be an oxymoron.

Specifically, solons are political representatives who fight for approval of the bread-and-butter legislation favored by their constituents while taking independent stands on issues that do not directly engage the "pocketbook" interests of those constituents. For example, the fourth legislative district in Kansas has been called the general aviation center of the United States, playing host to the bulk of Boeing's military business. Anyone who represents this district is expected to support Pentagon budget requests for military aircraft but will often have more latitude on other issues.[28] William Fulbright (1905–1995), while serving as senator from Arkansas, gave a speech at the University of Chicago shortly after the conclusion of World War II in which he articulated the solon's approach to the problem of democratic leadership:

> The average legislator early in his career discovers that there are certain interests, or prejudices, of his constituents which are dangerous to trifle with. Some of these prejudices may not be of fundamental importance to the welfare of the nation, in which case he is justified in humoring them, even though he may disapprove. The difficult case is where the prejudice concerns fundamental policy affecting the national welfare. A sound sense of values, the ability to discriminate between that which is of fundamental importance and that which is only superficial, is an indispensable qualification of a good legislator. As an example of what I mean, let us take the poll-tax issue and isolationism.

solon
Lawmaker who successfully reconciles the functions of delegate and trustee; Solon was the great law-giver of ancient Athens, birthplace of Western civilization's first democracy.

> Regardless of how persuasive my colleagues or the national press may be about the evils of the poll tax, I do not see its fundamental importance, and I shall follow the views of the people of my state. Although it may be symbolic of conditions which many deplore, it is exceedingly doubtful that its abolition will cure any of our major problems. On the other hand, regardless of how strongly opposed my constituents may prove to be to the creation of, and participation in, an ever stronger United Nations organization, I could not follow such a policy in that field unless it becomes clearly hopeless.[29]

Fulbright's own career in the Senate (1945–1974) provides an example of the solon in action. He often voted against legislation, especially civil rights measures, that in all likelihood he personally favored. He realized that because his constituents' racial views, at that time, were sharply opposed to his own, he could not remain in office without deferring to the deep-seated prejudices of the Arkansas majority. Fulbright sometimes justified this approach on the ground that many civil rights issues were not of fundamental importance.

Fulbright's deference to his home state's majority opinion on the question of race relations gave him great latitude in the area of foreign policy, an area in which the Arkansas voters had little interest. In time, he became chair of the powerful Senate Foreign Relations Committee and was widely acknowledged as a leading spokesperson for liberal causes in the realm of foreign policy—even though he represented a conservative state.

CITIZEN-LEADERS

Occasionally, an individual can decisively influence the course of political events without holding an official position in the government. An individual's unique dedication to a cause, personal magnetism, or even outright courage can garner an impressive political following. Such a person is called a *citizen-leader*. In the following section, we look at three examples of such grassroots leadership.

Václav Havel (b. 1936)

In the mid-1960s, at the age of 29, Václav Havel (1936—) gained worldwide acclaim for his satiric, absurdist plays, including *The Garden Party* (1964) and *The Memorandum* (1965). In the summer of 1968, Havel and 30 other Czech cultural figures signed a statement calling for the revival of the outlawed Social Democratic Party in communist-controlled Czechoslovakia. In August of that same summer, the increasing, but cautious, trend toward liberalization within Czechoslovakia that had begun in 1963 was swiftly and successfully thwarted when the Soviet Union invaded the country to reassert hard-line Soviet control.

During the conflict, Havel played a key role in putting the Czech Radio Free Europe on the airways and used this underground radio broadcast to direct daily commentary to Western intellectuals as a plea for assistance. Over the next two decades, he became Czechoslovakia's most famous playwright. His plays often contained biting satire aimed at the communists who ruled in Prague. But his writings were not the only reason for his increasing notoriety. He also became Czechoslovakia's foremost dissident and human rights champion. In 1977, Havel coauthored the Charter 77 Manifesto, which denounced Czechoslovakia's communist rulers for failing to abide by Basket Three of the 1975 Helsinki Accords, in which all signatories promised to respect civil and political rights. For such acts of political defiance, Havel was jailed repeatedly, serving sentences that often included hard labor. Despite these punishments, he was not silenced.

In December 1989, after Czechoslovakia's communist regime collapsed under the crushing weight of popular civilian discontent, Havel became president by consensus. That he had been in prison at the beginning of that year made his sudden ascent to power all the more remarkable. But then, no other public figure in Czechoslovakia could come close to matching the moral authority Havel had accumulated during three decades of courageous citizen-leadership.

Havel remained in office for more than 3 years. Then, on the verge of Czechoslovakia's disintegration into two ethnic nation-states (the Czech Republic and Slovakia), he resigned. But he did not long absent himself from public life. On January 26, 1993—little more than 6 months after his resignation—the Czech parliament elected Havel to a 5-year term as president of the Czech Republic.

Despite his prominent position, Havel did not always take an active role in governing his nation, yet he remained an important national figure. Although

© AP PHOTO

Former Czech President Václav Havel at Columbia University in November 2006. President of Czechoslovakia (1989–1993) and the Czech Republic (1993–2003). Havel led the revolution against Czechoslovakia's Communist regime in 1989 and was instantly elevated to the presidency by popular acclamation. A courageous playwright and lifelong human rights activist who had been persecuted and imprisoned for daring to dissent against tyranny, Havel in office was even more poplar abroad than at home. As president, he was content to exercise moral power through his words and ideas, and, to the chagrin of critics and admirers alike, readily conceded political power to others. Renowned for his credo of "living in truth," Havel was, and remains, the conscience of his country and a highly respected world leader.

most Czechs distrusted and disavowed politicians, many respected Havel as the only living Czech leader who not only talked and wrote about "living in truth" but also practiced what he preached.

Martin Luther King Jr. (1929–1968)

An outstanding citizen-leader was the renowned civil rights champion Martin Luther King Jr. (1929–1968). From the moment he became president of the newly formed Southern Christian Leadership Conference in 1957, King's national prominence grew. He led sit-ins, marches, demonstrations, and rallies throughout the South, all aimed at ending racial segregation and overcoming racial discrimination in jobs and housing. Practicing nonviolent civil disobedience, protesters under King's leadership openly broke the law, which sanctioned segregated lunch counters, required parade permits, forced African Americans to sit at the back of buses, and so on, and then accepted punishment for their actions. King intended to stir the conscience of the nation by reaching legislators and judges and, in the end, the U.S. people. As he stated in his famous 1963 "Letter from Birmingham Jail," *

> I submit that an individual who breaks a law that conscience tells him is unjust, and willingly accepts the penalty by staying in jail to arouse the conscience of the community over its injustice, is in reality expressing the very highest respect for law.[30]

King's hope was clear:

> We must see the need of having nonviolent gadflies to create the kind of tension in society that will help men to rise from the dark depths of prejudice and racism to the majestic heights of understanding and brotherhood.[31]

The influence of King and other African American civil rights leaders has been decisive. Although extremely controversial at the time, their courageous efforts proved crucial to the passage of the landmark 1964 Civil Rights Act, which banned discrimination in public accommodations and employment. Later, other civil rights legislation was passed, further ensuring equal treatment under the law for all citizens. In 1964, King was awarded the Nobel Peace Prize for his efforts. Four years later, at the age of 39, he was assassinated.

Rosa Parks (1913–2005)

Rosa Parks (1913–2005) stirred the conscience of a nation with a single act of courage. On December 1, 1955, she left work after spending a long day as a

---

* King had gone to Birmingham, Alabama, to lead an economic boycott aimed at desegregating public facilities and was jailed for organizing an unlicensed parade.

Rosa Parks in Montgomery, Alabama, in 1956, after the Supreme Court banned segregation in public transportation.

© DENNIS VAN TINE/LANDOV

tailor's assistant at a Montgomery, Alabama, department store. Boarding a bus to go home, she found a seat. Soon, however, a white man who was standing demanded her seat. (Montgomery's customary practice required that all four blacks sitting in the same row with Rosa Parks would have to stand in order to allow one white man to sit, since no black person was allowed to sit parallel with a white person.)[32] Parks stayed put:

> I was thinking that the only way to let them know I felt I was being mistreated was to do just what I did—resist the order . . . I had not thought about it and I had taken no previous resolution until it happened, and then I simply decided that I would not get up. I was tired, but I was usually tired at the end of the day, and I was not feeling well, but then there had been many days when I had not felt well. I had felt for a long time, that if I was ever told to get up so a white person could sit, that I would refuse to do so.[33]

The bus driver had Parks arrested.

Many historians date the origin of the U.S. civil rights movement to the Montgomery Bus Boycott—a reaction to the arrest of Rosa Parks. Her simple but courageous act of defiance is remembered today as one of political valor that drew attention to racial injustice and led to a chain of events that eventually changed the nation forever.

One of the virtues of modern democracies is that citizenship is universal and leadership arises from the rank and file. Leadership can take many different forms—from the highest office to working at the local level. Exemplary leadership at the national level always has local consequences, but, as we have seen, it is also true that exemplary leadership on the local level can have national consequences. The quality of a nation reflects the quality of its leaders; in a democracy, where voters make choices, the quality of the nation's leaders reflects on its citizens, too.

GATEWAYS TO THE WORLD: EXPLORING CYBERSPACE

For more information on political leaders, past and present, enter the name of the leader as the keyword in your search. For instance, a search using *Winston Churchill* as the keyword returned the URL listed below.

www.winstonchurchill.org

This site is maintained by the Churchill Center in Washington, D.C. It contains a vast array of materials relating to the former British prime minister, including speeches, famous quotes, photographs, and a links page.

www.time.com/time/time100/leaders/index.html

Time magazine's Website devoted to 100 leaders of the twentieth century includes "20 leaders and revolutionaries who helped define the social and political fabric of our times." *Time* identifies only three women in this category—Margaret Sanger, Eleanor Roosevelt, and Margaret Thatcher. It is likely others belong on the list; nonetheless, the so-called "glass ceiling" that so often kept women from achieving the highest leadership positions in business and politics was not completely shattered anywhere in the twentieth century. Will that finally change in the twenty-first?

www.ksg.harvard.edu/leadership

Website of Harvard's Center for Public Leadership at the Kennedy School of Government. In 2006, the CPL, in collaboration with *U.S. News & World Report*, launched a project called "America's Best Leaders"; the results were featured in *U.S. News & World Report* in the fall of 2006. A poll cited found three-quarters of the respondents believed the United States would decline without better leadership. On the Web, go to http://www.usnews.com/usnews/news/leaders/.

www.terra.es/personal2/monolith/00index.htm

Entitled "World Political Leaders 1945–2007," the ZPC (Zárate's Political Collections) website is a proprietary project of Roberto Ortiz de Zárate in close collaboration with the Center for International Relations and Development Studies. The CIDOB, based in Barcelona, Spain, manages an up-to-date list of all current rulers by country, as well as the extensive database Biographies of Political Leaders, containing some 500 records. If you are interested in finding biographical information on world leaders, start here.

SUMMARY

We can classify political leaders who occupy government positions as statesmen, demagogues, or ordinary politicians. Citizen-leaders hold no official office but can exert significant political influence.

Exceptional leaders who display an overriding concern for the public good, superior leadership skills, and keen practical wisdom in times of crisis were long called statesmen; today, this term is not considered politically correct in some quarters, so it has fallen into disuse. The lure of fame has been one of the motivating forces for many great leaders. Modern neglect of the concept of statecraft has led some observers to view it as a dying art.

Most prevalent in representative democracies are ordinary politicians. All elected officials must decide whether to exercise positive leadership or merely represent the views of their constituents. According to the delegate theory of democratic representation, politicians should act primarily as conduits for the expressed wishes of the electorate; the trustee theory, by contrast, stresses the importance of independent judgment in political office. Politicians who seek to combine these two concepts of representation are called solons in the text, in honor of the Roman statesman and lawgiver, Solon. The demagogue combines reckless personal ambition, unscrupulous methods, and charismatic appeal. Demagogues are most prevalent in democracies, and their fall is often as sudden and spectacular as their rise to power.

Citizen-leaders combine dedication to a cause, personal ability or magnetism, and opposition to governmental policy (or established practice). They inspire others and attract a sympathetic following, frequently on a worldwide scale. They exert a moral force generated by the power of the cause they personify.

KEY TERMS

statesman
demagogue
ordinary politician
citizen-leader

statecraft
delegate theory of
    representation

trustee theory of
    representation
solon

REVIEW QUESTIONS

1. How do we classify political leaders? Explain the differences between the various categories.
2. Why is the study of political leadership an important aspect of the overall study of politics?

3. What accounts for the rarity of exemplary leadership?
4. Describe two competing theories of representation. Which one makes the most sense to you and why?
5. Is it fair to lump all politicians together? Do politicians generally have a good reputation? Can they be found all over the world or only in certain countries? Explain your answers.
6. What is a demagogue? Name some demagogues. What motivates them?
7. Does democracy have any natural defenses against demagoguery? If so, what are they?
8. What is the nature of exemplary leadership? Name four exemplary leaders and explain in detail what makes any one of them exemplary.

RECOMMENDED READING

Adair, Douglass. "Fame and the Founding Fathers." In *Fame and the Founding Fathers: Essays by Douglass Adair*. New York: Norton, 1974. Adair's essay on the relationship between fame and statecraft in the founding of the United States is a classic.

Alexander, Robert J. *Rómulo Betancourt and the Transformation of Venezuela*. New Brunswick, NJ: Transaction Books, 1982. An admiring biography of Venezuela's leading democratic statesman.

Burns, James Macgregor. *Leadership*. New York: HarperCollins, 1982. An exhaustive study of all facets of the leadership phenomenon.

Frisch, Morton, and Richard Stevens, ed. *American Political Thought: The Philosophic Dimension of American Statesmanship*, 2nd ed. Itasca, IL: Peacock, 1983. A collection of essays on U.S. statesmen that features a brief, but outstanding, introduction.

Garrow, David J. *Bearing the Cross: Martin Luther King, Jr., and the Southern Christian Leadership Conference, 1955–1968*. New York: Random House, 1988. An in-depth examination of the life and accomplishments of America's greatest twentieth-century citizen-leader.

Gilbert, Martin. *Churchill: A Life*. New York: Henry Holt, 1991. A comprehensive one-volume biography written by his foremost biographer.

Havel, Václav. *The Art of the Impossible: Politics as Morality in Practice*. New York: Knopf, 1997. A collection of essays on politics, morality, and leadership by the brilliant Czech playwright and former president who led the popular uprising that ended communists rule in Czechoslovakia.

Jaffa, Harry. *Crises of the House Divided: An Interpretation of the Issue*. Chicago: University of Chicago Press, 1982. Documents the political wisdom that characterized Abraham Lincoln's statecraft.

Kouzes, James M., and Barry Z. Posner. *A Leader's Legacy*. San Francisco: Jossey-Bass, 2006. One of many recent books on the essence and importance of leadership. Many such books are motivational in nature, and most are highly perishable. This one is unusually insightful and, not surprisingly, gets rave reviews.

———. *The Leadership Challenge*, 4th ed. San Francisco: Jossey-Bass, 2008. A book about ordinary people achieving "individual leadership standards of excellence."

Tucker, Robert C. *Politics as Leadership*. Columbia: University of Missouri Press, 1995. A thought-provoking essay on politics in the best sense of the word and a reminder that beneath the sordid realities of everyday politics lie the sublime possibilities that leadership alone can uncover.

White, Richard D., Jr. *Kingfish: The Reign of Huey P. Long*. New York: Random House, 2006. The most recent biography of a political figure with a genius for populist politics and a demagogic streak who continues to fascinate students of American politics more than seven decades after his untimely exit.

Wicker, Tom. *Shooting Star: The Brief Arc of Joe McCarthy*. New York: Harcourt, 2006. Joe McCarthy is a legendary demagogue and Wicker is a first-rate storyteller. Result: a real page-turner.

Wildavsky, Aaron. *The Nursing Father: Moses as a Political Leader*. Tuscaloosa: University of Alabama Press, 1984. A thoughtful analysis of political leadership in a biblical context.

Williams, T. Harry. *Huey Long*. New York: Alfred A. Knopf and Vintage Books, 1981. Still the most authoritative biography of Huey Long available.

GETTY IMAGES

In recent years, a growing awareness of the dangers of global warming, rising oil and gas prices, and energy dependency have given rise in many developed countries to government and business partnerships aimed at development of renewable energy sources such as wind, solar, ocean waves, and geothermal. In the race for policy solutions, the United States has fallen behind Europe and Japan, but the Obama administration has vowed to become a global leader in the fight against climate change.

Issues in Public Policy
Principles, Priorities, and Practices

The Pursuit of Security
Security from Foreign Enemies
Security from Enemies Within
Social Security
Security and the Environment
Security from One's Own Actions

The Pursuit of Prosperity
Budget Deficits and the National Debt
Educational Malaise
Health Care: It Isn't for Everyone
Income Distribution: Who Gets What, When, and How?

The Pursuit of Equality
Racial Discrimination
Affirmative Action or Reverse Discrimination?
Who Deserves Preferential Treatment?

The Pursuit of Liberty
Liberty and the First Amendment
Privacy and the Right to Life

The Pursuit of Justice
Crime and Punishment
Justice as Fair Procedure
The Limits of Legal Protection
Goals in Conflict

Earlier in this book, we identified five core values: security, prosperity, equality, liberty, and justice. We can easily translate them into aims and objectives, but deciding how to translate them into actual policy is not so easy. In democratic societies, debates over public policy are an integral part of the political process.

This chapter focuses on contemporary issues in the United States, but many of the problems we address here arise in other democracies as well. Some appear to be part of a pattern—a kind of postmodern syndrome—in affluent Western societies that depend on imported nonrenewable energy. Others are universal—climate change and pandemics, for example. A few, such as the legacy of slavery, are uniquely American.

There is a whole set of policy problems we do not address in this chapter, problems not found in the West at all. These are challenges rooted in mass poverty—hunger, illiteracy, and the like. Overpopulation is a corollary of poverty—both a cause and an effect—also not found in the West. In fact, some advanced societies, as we shall see, are facing the opposite problem—negative population growth. We covered these issues in Chapter 9.

THE PURSUIT OF SECURITY

The first goal of virtually every independent state is to safeguard the security of its population and territory. Among influential political philosophers, Thomas Hobbes (1588–1679) argued most strenuously that safety from harm constituted the chief justification for a government's existence. For Aristotle, too, the first goal of political life was the protection of life itself.[1]

Security from Foreign Enemies

national security
Protection of a country from external and internal enemies.

In the aftermath of World War II, **national security** was assigned the highest possible policy in the United States, a fact that was (and still is) reflected in staggering levels of defense spending. In 2008, for example, the United States accounted for 48 percent of world arms expenditures; China followed at 8 percent (see Figure 13.1). Nearly two decades after the Cold War has ended, the United States still spends more than the next 14 countries combined.

From 1945 to 1991, foreign policy debate in the United States focused on the Soviet threat. Portraying the Soviet Union as an expansionist power bent on world domination, politicians of both major parties turned unquestioned support for bloated Pentagon budgets into a virtual loyalty test. The Pentagon's natural constituents were (and are) the so-called beltway bandits and defense contractors who manufacture armaments (guns, tanks, planes, ships, and the like); supply the military with food, clothing, and medicine; and provide logistical support, as well as various other defense-related services. The U.S.

FIGURE 13.1   U.S. Military Spending vs. the World, 2008 (in billions of U.S. dollars and % of world total). The United States alone accounts for nearly half the world's total military spending every year. By comparison, Europe, with a larger total GNP, spends only about 40 percent as much as the United States and a mere fifth of global military outlays. Russia, the world's other superpower only two decades ago, now spends one-tenth as much as the United States on defense and only one-fourth as much as the European Union. (Note: Practically speaking, the slice of the pie chart labeled "Europe" represents the European Union.)

Source: From "World Military Spending" by Anup Shah, *Global Issues*, March 1, 2009. Available at http://www.globalissues.org. Reprinted by permission of the author.

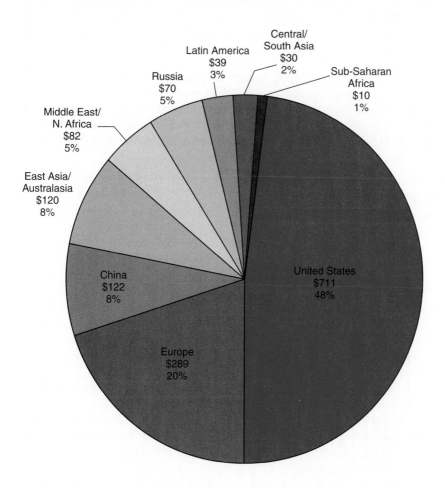

Department of Defense maintains some 737 military bases and more than 2.5 million men and women in uniform overseas, plus more than 6,000 bases in the United States and its territories.

In his 1961 farewell address to the nation, President Dwight D. Eisenhower, one of the most celebrated generals in U.S. history, warned of a growing "military-industrial complex":

> In the councils of government, we must guard against the acquisition of unwarranted influence, whether sought or unsought, by the military-industrial complex. The potential for the disastrous rise of misplaced power exists and will persist.
>
> We must never let the weight of this combination endanger our liberties or democratic processes. We should take nothing for granted. Only an alert and knowledgeable citizenry can compel the proper meshing of the huge industrial and military machinery of defense with our peaceful methods and goals, so that security and liberty may prosper together.[2]

President Eisenhower was echoing a view expressed by James Madison way back in 1795:

> Of all the enemies to public liberty war is, perhaps, the most to be dreaded because it comprises and develops the germ of every other. War is the parent of armies; from these proceed debts and taxes… known instruments for bringing the many under the domination of the few.… No nation could preserve its freedom in the midst of continual warfare.[3]

With the collapse of the Soviet Union, it was harder than ever to justify to U.S. taxpayers extremely high Cold War levels of defense spending. Thus, liberals and conservatives agreed that sizable force reductions and military spending cuts were in order.*

Defense budgets in the mid-1990s reflected scaled-down military commitments and reduced threat levels (see Figure 13.2). From the Cold War peak in 1986, Pentagon personnel—active, reserve, and civilian—declined by almost 20 percent. Active-duty military also underwent a 20 percent reduction, from 4.4 million to 3.5 million. These figures, however, are misleading. The Clinton administration contracted out to the private sector many services previously performed within the Pentagon or the military branches; these outsourced services included combat roles that, in the past, had been kept strictly under the executive branch's control.[4]

The policy of outsourcing continued and was extended under the Bush administration following the terrorist attacks of September 11, 2001. Congress and the country were back in the Cold War groove, ready to spend "whatever it takes" to make the world safe for democracy and to keep the United States safe

---

*However, a behind-the-scenes group of conservative hard-liners, the so-called neocons, remained adamantly opposed to big defense cuts in the 1990s. When George W. Bush ran for president in 2000, members of this group, calling themselves the "Vulcans," served as Bush's team of foreign policy advisers.

FIGURE 13.2   Military Spending, 1981–2008: In 2004, total defense spending in the United States was about $534 billion. This included a supplemental appropriation of $87 billion for military operations in Iraq and Afghanistan passed by Congress in the fall of 2003, and other defense-related expenditures. In that year, all categories of spending for national security, including the portion of the national debt attributable to military outlays, totaled more than $700 billion. In 2006, defense spending rose to $626 billion. All defense-related spending, including interest on the debt, totaled in the range of $800 billion. In 2008, defense spending alone climbed to $710 billion (an increase of 25 % since 2004).

SOURCE: The author wishes to thank G. Ross Stephens, Professor emeritus at the University of Missouri–Kansas City, for supplying data in this graph, based on official U.S. government budget information for the relevant years.

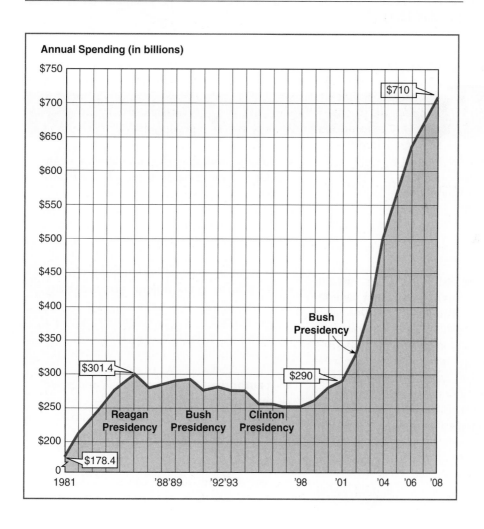

from terrorists (see Figure 13.2 again). Gone was the euphoria of the 1990s. Gone, too, was the illusion of invulnerability. *They* had attacked *us* in our own front yard.

Security from Enemies Within

This new climate of fear bordering on hysteria gave rise to a homeland security state similar to the national security state that came into being after World War II. Just as the National Security Act of 1947 had restructured the U.S. government in order to meet the perceived threat of communism, so too did the USA PATRIOT Act of 2001 (officially the Uniting and Strengthening America by Providing Appropriate Tools Required to Intercept and Obstruct Terrorism Act) restructure the government in order to fight international terrorism (see Box 13.1).

BOX 13.1 FOCUS ON   War on Terror or War on the Constitution?

The USA PATRIOT Act, passed by Congress in response to the September 11, 2001, attacks, was signed into law by President George W. Bush on October 26, 2001. Critics contend it severely erodes privacy rights long upheld by the U.S. Supreme Court, for the following reasons:

- **It expands the ability of states and the federal government to conduct surveillance of U.S. citizens**. The government can monitor individual Web-surfing records, use wiretaps to monitor phone calls of persons "proximate" to the primary person being tapped, access Internet service provider records, and investigate anyone who participates in a political protest.
- **It is not limited to terrorism**. The government can add samples to DNA databases for anyone convicted of "any crime of violence." Wiretaps are now allowed for suspected violators of the Computer Fraud and Abuse Act, offering possibilities for government spying on any computer user.

- **Foreign and domestic intelligence agencies can more easily spy on U.S. citizens**. Domestic eavesdropping powers under the existing Foreign Intelligence Surveillance Act (FISA) are broadened. The Patriot Act partially repeals legislation enacted in the 1970s that prohibited pervasive surveillance of citizens by U.S. agencies created to gather foreign intelligence.
- **It reduces government accountability**. Under the Patriot Act, the balance between the need for secrecy in government and the need for transparency (the public's right to know what the government is doing) is shifted sharply in favor of secrecy.
- **It authorizes the use of "sneak and peek" search warrants**. A sneak-and-peek warrant authorizes law-enforcement officers to enter private premises without the occupant's permission or knowledge and without informing the occupant that such a search was conducted. These warrants can be used against anyone suspected of a federal crime, including a misdemeanor.

September 11 placed a premium on the role of government in protecting the lives and property of individual citizens from the enemies within, including fellow citizens, spies, and unfriendly aliens. But just how far does the Constitution allow the government to go in its zeal to bring terrorists to justice?[5] The debate over this question highlights the difficulty of making a clear policy distinction between terrorism and crime.

Crime and Punishment There is little agreement about what causes crime, what society ought to do about it, and whether all acts currently classified as crimes should continue to be punished (for example, possession or personal use of marijuana). Although it has declined of late, the long-term crime rate in the United States has risen dramatically over the past 50 years (see Box 13.2). Why?

According to some experts, crime is essentially a social phenomenon, a reflection of personal frustration or alienation caused by poverty and neglect, racial discrimination, and unequal economic opportunity. Others stress social causes, such as the decline of the traditional family and community, and cite the resulting sense of isolation and individualism now predominant in U.S. life. Many commentators also blame popular culture and the mass media, which glorify violence, immediate gratification, and self-expression (as opposed to deferred gratification and self-restraint).[6]

Some social critics would reduce crime by redefining it—for example, by decriminalizing prostitution. Advocates of this approach say it is illogical and unjust to punish "victimless" crimes. In this view, nobody is harmed when adults freely choose to engage in prostitution, for example. In 2003, the U.S. Supreme Court ruled state sodomy laws unconstitutional and unenforceable (*Lawrence v. Texas*). But some states ignore the *Lawrence* decision and the U.S. military enforces its sodomy regulation without regard to the case.

Some advocates of decriminalization would also take marijuana off the list of illegal drugs. After all, alcohol is legal. Why not pot?

The drug problem is in a class by itself. We know many violent crimes in the United States are drug related.[7] The problem may be clear but the solution is not. Drug addicts rob and steal to support a habit made unnecessarily expensive by state action rather than market forces. Legalize drugs, supporters argue, and the price will drop dramatically, drug trafficking will become less profitable, and drug-related crime will decrease. Opponents of legalization fear that it would increase the number of addicts and corrode the moral standards of the community.

Between 1980 and the mid-1990s, the U.S. prison population more than tripled, due in large part to a nationwide crackdown on illegal drugs, and rose from 1.1 million in 1995 to 1.54 million in 2005. The social and economic costs of this zero-tolerance policy have been very high, by any measure, but have failed to produce the promised results.

Decriminalization of drugs and prostitution is not likely to happen any time soon in the United States, but the Netherlands has already done it. In the capital city of Amsterdam, "soft drugs" (including marijuana) and prostitution are allowed, but only in restricted areas under no-nonsense police supervision and

BOX 13.2 FOCUS ON   Defining Crime Down

Why has the United States accepted such a high level of crime? The late Daniel Patrick Moynihan (1927–2001), a former U.S. senator and noted scholar, suggested one intriguing answer in a controversial article entitled "Defining Deviancy Down: How We've Become Accustomed to Alarming Level of Crime and Destructive Behavior."* Faced with a high crime rate, Moynihan contended, U.S. citizens have denied its importance by redefining (defining down) what they consider to be normal. Years ago, a high crime rate was understood to be a severe social pathology; now, it has become accepted as a normal condition of society about which little can be done.

Moynihan supplied a striking example. On February 14, 1929, four gangsters gunned down seven rivals in the infamous St. Valentine's Day Massacre. Moynihan observed that the nation was shocked, the event became a legend meriting two entries in the *World Book Encyclopedia*, and the "massacre" inspired an amendment to the Constitution that ended Prohibition (a policy thought to have caused much gang violence).

Moynihan noted that with illegal drug trafficking, this form of violence has returned, but, by contrast, "at a level that induces denial." Inured, U.S. adults now accept violence they once rejected as deviant and unacceptable. Sadly, concluded Moynihan, "Los Angeles has the equivalent of a St. Valentine's Day Massacre every weekend."
* *American Scholar*, Winter 1993.

The late Daniel Patrick Moynihan (1927–2001) U.S. Senator and noted scholar.

control. Prostitutes are required to have frequent medical checkups, and social problems linked to illegal drug trafficking have been alleviated.

Meanwhile, the United States is one of the only postindustrial societies where private ownership of handguns is considered normal, and private arsenals are not unusual. In the United States, the right to bear arms is guaranteed by the Second Amendment. Some 40 percent of households in the United States report having a gun, or guns, compared with only 4.7 percent in the United Kingdom and a mere 2 percent in the Netherlands. Other countries vary considerably (see Table 13.1). Among the countries that make these figures publicly available, not one comes close to U.S. levels.

TABLE 13.1   Armed Households 1992–1994 (% with guns in selected countries)[*]

Australia	19%
Belgium	16%
Canada	29%
France	22%
Italy	16%
Netherlands	1.9%
New Zealand	22%
Norway	32%
Spain	13%
Sweden	15%
Switzerland	27%
United States	40%

[*]Research note: Data of this kind is difficult to obtain and even more difficult to verify; data on gun ownership in most non-Western (and even some European countries) is simply not available.
SOURCE: United Nations Office on Drugs and Crime. From a 1992–1994 survey.

Changing gun laws to restrict access is controversial. Gun control activists argue that guns are a cause of violent crime and point out that the murder rate in the United States is the highest in the Western world. Opponents of gun control, led by the National Rifle Association, point out that the homicide rate has been falling; that the vast majority of gun owners are not violent criminals; that citizens have a right to own guns; that guns are typically used for hunting or, in extreme cases, for self-defense; and that the non-gun murder rate in the United States is higher than the total murder rate in many European countries.

Social Security

When U.S. workers think of social security, they think of the mandatory federal pension program established in 1935. Europeans, on the other hand, define social security far more broadly. Old-age pensions are *part* of social security thus defined, but the problems many people face—poverty, hunger, illness, and unemployment—are not confined to old age. Nor are the hardships resulting from natural disasters, such as floods, hurricanes, fires, and other acts of God.

Whereas the vast majority of Europeans take it for granted that the state has an obligation to provide a cradle-to-the-grave social safety net for all its citizens, many voters and taxpayers in the United States have long been staunchly opposed to a European-style "welfare state" or anything that smacks of socialism, at least until recently. The outcome of the 2008 election and recent survey research, however, point to a shift in public opinion toward the European model—tighter regulation of the economy and guaranteed health insurance.

What is the state's proper role in helping members of society in need? Food stamps, farm subsidies, pensions, health and unemployment benefits, and student aid are all forms of public assistance. In general, U.S. voters have opposed "welfare," defined, in this instance, as any subsidies or benefits for which they themselves are not eligible. These government "giveaway" programs are often said to encourage the very behavior they try to combat (by encouraging people not to work). Welfare reform was a big issue in the 1990s, when the federal government gave states more authority (and flexibility) in implementing welfare programs (for example, to cut welfare payments for those unwilling to work).

Social Security and Medicare are by far the biggest and most expensive public assistance programs in the United States. These are *compulsory* insurance programs, however, not "welfare." Thus, U.S. workers are required by law to pay into the Social Security pension fund until they retire (normally around age 65). Payouts from the fund are aptly called **entitlements**, not to be confused with subsidies. Entitlements are politically sensitive, not least because AARP (the retirees association) and senior citizens (who turn out to vote in large numbers) are prepared to punish politicians who want to cut these programs.

Social Security makes monthly remittances to older adults, while Medicare covers retirees' doctor and hospital bills. Both have grown dramatically in recent decades and are slated to rise even more steeply in the years to come. In 2008, Social Security and Medicare distributions (payments to beneficiaries) totaled more than $1 trillion, accounting for more than one-third of the federal budget.[8] Apart from defense expenditures, these two items were easily the largest drain on the Treasury even before Congress approved a new prescription drug benefit for Medicare recipients.

Social Security and Medicare expenditures are rising faster than projected revenues (see Figure 13.3). One reason is that U.S. adults are living longer, making the programs more expensive. An even bigger reason is the large number of people born in the years immediately following World War II (the so-called baby boomers), who are now approaching retirement age and becoming eligible to draw monthly benefits. When Medicare was established in 1965, there were 5.5 people paying money into the Medicare program for each recipient drawing money out. Since then, the ratio has dropped to about 3 to 1 and is still falling.

Medicare has also been hit hard by escalating health care costs. Since 1980, it has been the fastest-growing federal program. At President Bush's urging, Congress passed a controversial law adding a prescription drug benefit to Medicare at a projected long-term cost of as much as $8 trillion.[9]

Most Washington politicians prefer not to talk about what has happened to the Social Security trust fund. When the federal government spends more than it raises in taxes and other revenues, it has to borrow money to cover the shortfall. Since the 1980s, the Treasury has quietly "borrowed" huge sums of money every year from Social Security. Worse still, this huge transaction is left off the federal balance sheet—in other words, if the government tells taxpayers the **federal budget deficit** in any given year is, say, $410 billion (the official figure for 2008), that amount does not include money the government has taken from the Social Security cash drawer. Thus, 2005, using standard accounting rules, the government's own accountants set the deficit at $760 billion, more than double the official figure of $318 billion.[10]

entitlements
Federal- and state-provided benefits in the United States such as Social Security and Medicare funded by mandatory tax contributions; such benefits become a right rather than a privilege in the public mind because recipients typically pay into the system for many years before they are eligible to take anything out.

FIGURE 13.3   Failing Health: Social Security and Medicare. At current rates, Social Security funds will run out in 2037 and the Medicare cash drawer will be empty in eight years.

SOURCE: Office of the Chief Actuary, Social Security Administration, 2009

Social Security

Year	Number of years until depleted	Year depleted	Year change in projected depletion
1999		2034	
2000		2037	3
2001		2038	1
2002		2041	3
2003		2042	1
2004		2042	0
2005		2041	−1
2006		2040	−1
2007		2041	1
2008		2041	0
2009		2037	−4

Medicare

Year	Number of years until depleted	Year depleted	Year change in projected depletion
1999		2015	
2000		2025	10
2001		2029	4
2002		2030	1
2003		2026	−4
2004		2019	−7
2005		2020	1
2006		2018	−2
2007		2019	1
2008		2019	0
2009		2017	−2

Meanwhile, the projected federal budget deficit for 2009 is a record $1.8 trillion (13 percent of the economy). And the federal government now calculates Medicare will run out of money by 2017 (two years sooner than projected in 2008) and the Social Security trust fund will be empty by 2037 (four years earlier than predicted).

The gross mismanagement of Social Security funds dates back to the start of the Reagan era in the early 1980s. In 1983, Congress "voted to raise Social Security taxes, changing it from a pay-as-you-go system to one in which people were required to pay 50 percent more than the retirement and disability program's immediate costs, to build a trust fund to pay benefits more than three decades into the future."[11] Thereafter, the U.S. Congress—guardians of this "trust fund"—raided Social Security to cover imbalances elsewhere in the budget.

Despite the perennial plundering of this fund, the national debt—that is, the accumulated annual federal budget deficits—in May 2009 had climbed to $11.2 trillion. Each citizen's share came to about $36,800. In 2001, the first year of George W. Bush's presidency, the annual interest payments amounted to $360 billion; in 2008, the last year of the Bush presidency, interest payments came to over $451 billion—nearly half a trillion dollars just to service the debt. Thus, whereas the demographic trends mentioned earlier pose a serious problem for public pension funds everywhere, government misfeasance has greatly contributed to the severity of the problem in the United States.

Meanwhile, workers who have paid into the system for years understandably expect (and demand) full benefits when they retire. Originally designed to supplement individual savings and private pensions, Social Security today is often seen as both an antipoverty program (helping those who have little or no retirement savings) and the primary retirement nest egg for middle-class citizens.

Emissions Trading Scheme (ETS) In the European Union, part of an antipollution drive aimed at significantly reducing Europe's carbon footprint by 2020 by assigning carbon-emission allowances to industries and factories and creating a carbon exchange, or a market where "clean" companies (ones that do not use their full allowances) can sell the credits they accumulate by not polluting to "dirty" companies (ones that exceed their allowances).

Opinions differ as to whether health care in the United States has reached the crisis point, but for the estimated 47 million who are uninsured there is no doubt about it. Critics point out that France, for example, provides universal health care for its 62 million citizens, that as a society France is healthier than the United States, and that France spends only about half as much per capita on health care as we do—all told, France spends 10.7 percent of its GDP on health care, against 16.5 percent in the United States. Indeed, no comparable society spends as much as we do, and most provide universal coverage.[12] Public spending on health care in the United States is lower, of course, but private spending is astronomically higher.

Government efforts to place Medicare and Medicaid on solid, long-term financial footing (which could require that U.S. workers retire later, that cost-of-living increases be adjusted downward, or that payroll taxes be raised) are bound to meet with resistance from senior citizens. When the government changes the rules and applies them retroactively, people lose trust in the political process. Public officials, pressed for solutions to complex problems, sometimes forget to ask one crucial question: Is the proposed solution fair to those most directly and immediately affected by it? If the answer is no, the result is likely to be politically destabilizing.

Security and the Environment

Hazards caused by humans can also endanger the health and safety of the public. Mandatory clean air standards, environmental impact statements, increasingly stringent waste disposal requirements, and vigorous recycling efforts all seek to protect the environment. Most scientists now agree global warming is a major threat to security of the planet (and therefore to the life-forms that inhabit it) in the coming century. Greenhouse gas (GHG) emissions, mainly from automobiles and coal-fired power plants, trap heat in the earth's atmosphere, causing climate change. The likely consequences, say the experts, are that glaciers will continue to melt at an accelerating rate, sea levels will rise, and ocean currents will be altered and degraded.

The European Union has adopted an **Emission Trading Scheme (ETS)** as part of a larger set of policy goals aimed at significantly reducing Europe's "carbon footprint" by 2020. In one of his first acts as president, George W. Bush announced that he was taking the United States out of the **Kyoto Protocol** (see Box 13.3), which had been signed by his predecessor, Bill Clinton. But whereas the Bush White House favored corporate oil and energy interests over the environment and was generally at odds with the green movement, the Obama administration has pledged cooperation with the global community to combat climate change.

Critics argue rightly that the United States alone cannot make a dent in the problem; unless China, India, and other Third World countries take action to cut GHG emissions, there is not much the United States can do to curb global warming. Advocates of **sustainable growth** point out that the United States ranks first in the world in total volume of GHG emissions. However, China and India both outrank the United States in emissions intensities (metric tons of carbon equivalent per million dollars of economic output), and energy-related carbon emissions increased not only in the United States but also in six of the nine biggest polluting countries in recent decades.[13] One sign of the growing alarm over the dangers posed by global warming: in 2005, researchers at Yale and Columbia universities, in collaboration with the World Economic Forum and the European Union, published an Environmental Sustainability Index that ranked countries using a range of scientific indicators—the United States ranked 45th, behind Japan, Botswana, Bhutan, and most of Western Europe.[14]

Environmentalists, naturalists, and conservationists around the world also seek to protect endangered species of wildlife, to prevent clear-cutting of tropical rain forests (sometimes called slash-and-burn agriculture), and to curb the use of deep-sea fishing nets, among other commercial fishing activities such as whaling. Although the 2008 presidential election points to growing public support for environmental action, the green movement in the United States still pales in comparison to Europe's. Meanwhile, the global recession that started with the meltdown on Wall Street in August 2008 is proving to be the biggest immediate threat to coordinated action on climate change, deflecting attention, derailing efforts, and dampening public enthusiasm for environmentalism on both sides of the Atlantic.

Kyoto Protocol
Countries that ratify this treaty, which went into effect in 2005, agree to cut emissions of carbon dioxide and five other greenhouse gases or to engage in emissions trading if they exceed a certain cap; the United States signed it under President Bill Clinton, but President George W. Bush renounced it shortly after taking office in 2001.

sustainable growth
A concept popular among environmentalists and liberal economists that emphasizes the need for economic strategies that take account of the high-cost and long-term impact on the environment (including global warming) of economic policies aimed at profit-maximization, current consumption, and the like.

BOX 13.3 SPOTLIGHT ON   The Kyoto Protocol and Climate Change

The Kyoto Protocol is an addendum to the UN Framework Convention on Climate Change (UNFCCC). Countries that ratify this protocol agree to cut emissions of carbon dioxide and five other greenhouse gases or to engage in emissions trading if they exceed a certain cap. The protocol, which went into effect in 2005, now covers some 160 countries and more than 55 percent of greenhouse gas (GHG) emissions worldwide. The United States has signed, but not ratified, the agreement. After Australia embraced it toward the end of 2007, the United States was more isolated than ever, but upon taking office in 2009, President Obama reversed the Bush administration's environmental policies and pledged U.S. support for global efforts to curb climate change.

FIGURE 13.4   Now that Australia, Turkey, and Angola have ratified the Kyoto Protocol, the United States is almost alone in opposing it. However, President Obama has pledged to renew U.S. leadership in the international climate effort.

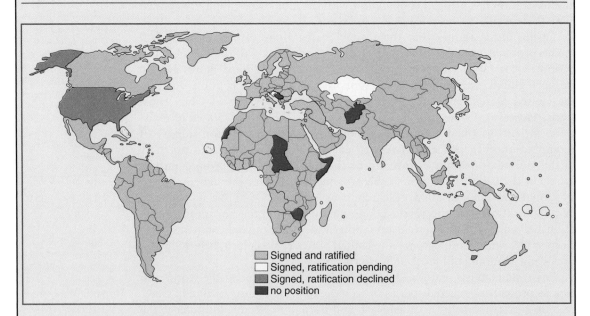

Signed and ratified
Signed, ratification pending
Signed, ratification declined
no position

Under Kyoto, developed countries are obligated to reduce GHG emissions to an average of 5 percent below 1990 levels by 2008–2012. For many countries, including EU member-states, meeting this goal means cutting to roughly 15 percent below 2008 GHG emissions levels. The Kyoto caps expire in 2013.

Parties to the UNFCCC agreed to a set of "common but differentiated responsibilities." The largest share of GHG emissions has originated in developed countries, and per capita emissions in developing countries were relatively low in the 1990s (and still are). China, India, and other developing countries

BOX 13.3: SPOTLIGHT ON   *(Continued)*

were exempted from the Kyoto Protocol caps because, at least until recently, they have not been major contributors to GHG emissions nor, therefore, to past and present climate change. But critics of Kyoto argue that climate change is, above all, a future threat, and that developing countries—especially China and India—will be major contributors in the twenty-first century. In addition, unless developing countries are brought into the global warming tent, polluting industries in developed countries will simply move to the Third World, resulting in little or no net reduction in carbon pollution.

Security from One's Own Actions

Many states have adopted laws requiring motorists to wear seatbelts, motorcyclists to wear safety helmets, and small children to be strapped into special infant seats in cars. The Eighteenth Amendment, which established prohibition, is an example of national legislation aimed at legislating personal morality. Other examples include the various local, state, and federal laws banning pornography and prostitution. Attempts to legislate morality are often based on the argument that failing to do so has adverse social consequences. Opponents lament the loss of personal liberty and argue that the state has no right to interfere in citizens' private lives.

THE PURSUIT OF PROSPERITY

Since the founding of the United States, self-reliance, upward mobility, and the profit motive have defined the nation's unique commercial culture. There is a close link between the political philosophy of James Madison, a founding father, and Madison Avenue, a symbol of U.S. capitalism.[15]

In founding a commercial republic, the Founders consciously launched a political experiment that had been championed by philosophers and economists (including Locke and Montesquieu) for more than 100 years. The idea was simple: a political order that encouraged entrepreneurship and innovation, protected private property, and rewarded ingenuity and hard work would generate great personal wealth, a burgeoning middle class, and a robust national economy.

During the nineteenth century, the Industrial Revolution ushered in modern capitalism—the private ownership, manufacture, and distribution of goods and services free of heavy-handed state intervention or regulation. By the beginning of the twentieth century, however, the federal government had begun to enforce regulations designed to protect citizens from monopolies, abusive business practices, and other perceived economic injustices. During the Great Depression of the 1930s, the Social Security program came into being as part of President

Franklin Roosevelt's New Deal. In the 1960s and 1970s, Medicare, training and jobs programs, and expanded welfare and food stamp benefits supplemented unemployment compensation and Social Security.

Beginning in the 1980s, a conservative backlash—often called the Reagan Revolution—swept the country. Reagan—and a decade later, Republican House Speaker Newt Gingrich—suggested government had gone too far down the road to becoming a "welfare state" (never mind that federal budget deficits soared to record heights during the Reagan presidency). In fact, however, the level of state intervention was still far below that found in most Western democracies (discussed later).

The prosperity of the 1990s made many in the United States wealthy—at least on paper—as the stock market hit historic highs and the number of people investing in it through mutual and pension funds rose dramatically. Much of that paper wealth disappeared in the bear market of 2001–2003 and the recession of 2008–2009, which saw the sharpest stock price declines since the 1930s. Meanwhile, the emergence of a super-rich class intent on shifting the tax burden downward became the focus of a new debate over social and economic justice. We explore this phenomenon and its consequences next.

Budget Deficits and the National Debt

The U.S. federal budget for 2010—the first "Obama budget"—will fall in the range of $3.4 trillion. Total government spending as a share of GDP increased from about 17 percent in the mid-1960s to 24 percent in 1983, following the massive Reagan tax cut of 1981, and retreated to around 18 percent in recent years. The federal deficit rose sharply during the Reagan era, as it did again after 2001, and is slated to reach $1.84 trillion in 2010.

When the federal government spends more than it collects in a year, it produces a **federal budget deficit.** As we noted above, the accumulated deficits, or **gross national debt,** climbed above the $11 trillion mark in 2009. The public debt as a percent of GDP was about 51 percent, lower than in many other countries with advanced economies. Still, most economists agree that the trend and magnitude of the public debt can have important long-term effects on the economic health and security of a country—especially one where *private* debt levels are very high (as they are in the United States). Combining public and private debt puts the U.S. debt to GDP ratio above 80 percent.

The dollar has fallen sharply relative to the euro in recent years. When the euro was launched in 2002, it was worth 88 cents; in July 2008, it hit a peak ($1.58) before falling somewhat later in the year. The United States also runs large trade deficits every year and depends heavily on foreign borrowing to finance them. These chronic balance of payments (current account) deficits, together with the perennial federal budget deficits and extremely low household savings rates, go a long way toward explaining the dollar's decline.

Losing Interest: The National Debt Budget deficits increased dramatically during the 1980s and early 1990s. In 1981, when President Reagan assumed office, the national debt totaled less than $1 trillion. By 1988, at the end of his

federal budget deficit
In the United States, the difference between federal revenues and federal expenditures in a given year; the national debt is the cumulative sum of budget deficits over many years.

gross domestic debt GDP
The U.S. federal government's debt climbed above the $11 trillion mark in 2009, or just over 50 percent of the nation's total annual GDP.

second term in office, it had surpassed $2.5 trillion. Alarm at the rapid growth in the debt in the 1980s led to a bipartisan push to balance the budget in the 1990s (see Box 13.4). After 9/11, two events dramatically reversed this trend—a war on terror that gave rise to massive spending hikes, and several major tax cuts that simultaneously reduced revenues.

The national debt has serious consequences that will likely have a greater impact on future generations than on the generation that has created it. By 2007, as we've seen, the federal government had "borrowed" more than two trillion from the Social Security Trust Fund. The government replaces the money by selling treasury bonds (that is, by borrowing more), but it conveniently omits these funds from the figure it calls Debt Held by the Public (DHP). That accounting sleight-of-hand makes the national debt look smaller, but of course the government is obligated to pay interest—a lot of interest—on the *entire* debt. Interest on the debt is now the third-largest line-item expenditure in the federal budget.

The Tax Burden: Who Pays What, When, and How? Until recently, most U.S. citizens shared three mutually reinforcing aversions: to socialism, state ownership, and high taxes. Of these, the tax aversion is the oldest; taxes are a perennial issue in U.S. politics. One easy way for a presidential candidate to win votes is to promise tax cuts, as did both Ronald Reagan and George W. Bush in making successful bids for the White House. In 1988, George H. W. Bush made a campaign promise not to raise taxes and was turned out of office 4 years later after going back on that promise. In the 2008 presidential debates, both major-party candidates tiptoed carefully around the tax question: John McCain

Balanced Budget Act of 1997
Passed by Congress in 1997, this historic measure mandated a balanced federal budget by 2001 but was ironically undone in that very year by the events of 9/11.

economic stimulus
A fiscal tool of government designed to bolster a weak economy and create jobs via public works projects and deficit spending.

BOX 13.4 FOCUS ON   Bye-Bye, Balanced Budgets

Between 1993 and 2000, President Bill Clinton, a Democrat, and the Republican-controlled Congress addressed the problems posed by the mushrooming national debt. As a consequence, budget deficits declined sharply in the 1990s. Later in the decade, amid a generally robust economy, Democrats and Republicans joined forces in the Congress to pass the historic **Balanced Budget Act of 1997**, which mandated a balanced federal budget by 2001. But tax revenues increased faster than expected due to the strong economy, resulting in budget surpluses—using official accounting rules—earlier than expected or required by law. (In fact, the only real surplus, when borrowing from the

Social Security trust fund is factored in, was in 2001—see below.)

All that changed suddenly after September 11, 2001, when Congress under President Bush voted huge sums for cleanup and reconstruction efforts in New York City, bailing out hard-hit airlines (among others), and prosecuting the "war" against international terrorism at home and abroad. The budget surplus quickly vanished, as did all talk of a balanced budget.

Then came the financial crisis of 2008 followed by a deep recession, prompting President Obama to launch a massive **economic stimulus** program—and the nation's first trillion-dollar budget deficit.

pledged to keep the Bush tax cuts in place with a few modifications; Barack Obama said he too would keep the Bush tax cuts except for those making more than $250,000 a year.

Few political issues in the United States are inherently more complex—or surrounded by more deliberate obfuscation and statistical subterfuge—than taxes. Recent revelations of corporate fraud, greed, and stock swindles have had the ricochet effect of fueling a new debate over tax fairness. Tax loopholes allowing the super rich, including CEOs earning fabulous salaries and bonuses, to avoid paying millions of dollars in income tax every year have been shifting the overall tax burden downward since the early 1980s. A popular slogan (commonly attributed to Benjamin Franklin) says the two things nobody can avoid are death and taxes, but some of the richest people in the United States *do* manage to avoid taxes. What is even more astonishing is that, in many cases, the ways they do it are perfectly legal.

Despite a tax cut in 1997, taxes for the vast majority of middle-class taxpayers actually rose during the 1990s.[16] At the same time, the tax burden on the super rich fell. In the words of David Cay Johnston, a Pulitzer Prize-winning journalist who covers taxes for the *New York Times*,

> [In 1997] Congress passed what its sponsors promoted as a tax cut for the middle class and especially for families with children. Buried in that law were many tax breaks for the rich, some subtle and some huge, notably a sharp reduction in the tax rate on long-term capital gains, the source of two-thirds of the incomes of the top 400.
>
> But even the 1997 tax cuts for the rich were not enough for them.... Six years of tax cut bills... were in fact primarily a boon to the super rich.[17]

Johnston blamed both major political parties, pointing out that the trend toward downloading the tax burden began in the 1980s, when Ronald Reagan (a Republican) was president but the Democrats controlled the Congress, and accelerated in the 1990s, when Bill Clinton (a Democrat) was president but the Republicans were in the majority. The result of this bipartisan failure to fix the tax system—which actually made it steadily more unfair to the middle class—is that "wealth in America today is more highly concentrated than at any time since 1929. In recent years the richest 1 percent of Americans, the top 1.3 million or so households, have owned almost half of the stocks, bonds, cash, and other financial assets in the country. The richest 15 percent control nearly *all* of the financial assets."[18]

The fact that voters do not understand tax issues is hardly surprising. The U.S. tax system is so Byzantine that only tax experts and lawyers can make any sense of it. President Franklin Roosevelt once said the federal tax code "might as well have been written in a foreign language." Today, it is more like the Egyptian hieroglyphs that remained undecipherable for centuries.

The bewildering federal income tax rules are a taxpayer's nightmare but an accounting firm's dream come true. All attempts at "tax simplification" have failed. In 1986, the U.S. Congress passed a law directing the IRS to fix the system. A few years later, a "hypothetical" tax return listing family income and expenses was sent to 50 tax experts to determine this mythical family's tax liability. The result was 50 different "bottom lines," ranging from a tax bill of $12,500 to nearly $36,000.[19]

Without question, the U.S. tax system favors the rich and super rich over the middle class. Due to various loopholes and tax shelters, the United States taxes its wealthiest citizens at a much lower rate than other industrial democracies do. Sales taxes hit the middle class much harder than the rich and super rich, who spend a tiny portion of their total income on life's necessities. For this reason, sales taxes are regressive—that is, they tax the least able to pay proportionately the most.

Throughout the fifty states, sales taxes are common; in Europe, a *value added tax* (VAT) is the principal form of taxation. Unlike a sales tax, VAT is assessed at every stage in the manufacture and sale of a product—in this manner, the total tax "take" is built into the price of a finished product and passed along to the consumer. VAT rates among the 27 countries of the EU range from 15 to 25 percent. By contrast, sales taxes in the United States are rarely more than 6 percent; in Minnesota, for example, groceries are exempt (eating in restaurants, however, is not), and in New Jersey, there is no sales tax on clothing.

Just under 60 percent of all federal revenue in the United States comes from personal and corporate income taxes, but the tax burden on individuals is far heavier than on corporations. In fact, corporate income tax amounts to only about 12 percent of federal revenues today, a dramatic decline from the 1950s and 1960s, when it stood at about 25 percent (see Figures 13.5 and 13.6). Social Security payroll taxes are the fastest-growing source of federal revenue (34 percent of the total), and accounted for the budget surpluses from 1998 to 2001. In reality, only in 2001 would the federal government have enjoyed a surplus—and a very modest one at that—were it not for the raiding of the Social Security trust fund.

U.S. taxpayers tend to think taxes are too high, yet the United States has low tax rates relative to other developed countries, especially Sweden, France, and Italy (see Table 13.2). Taxes in the United States accounted for about 28 percent of GDP in 2008, compared with about 46 percent in France, 39 percent in the United Kingdom, and 50 percent in Denmark. The latter all have universal national health care systems; France and the Scandinavian countries also offer a full range of welfare-state programs providing cradle-to-grave benefits to all citizens.

Comparisons between taxes and benefits in the United States and Europe raise two fundamental questions. First, is the tax system fair? In the United States, the tax system is so complicated and the tax policy process so lacking in transparency that most taxpayers do not have any idea, for example, that the federal income tax created shortly before World War I rapidly became less and less progressive after about 1972. Second, what do citizens actually get in return for the taxes they pay? Answering this question necessitates a closer look at public policy in such areas as health and education.

FIGURE 13.5   The tax burden in the United States is lower than in most developed countries, but critics point out that U.S. taxpayers do not get key benefits, such as national health insurance, that taxpayers in most other developed countries do get. Critics also point out that corporations pay a relatively small portion of the total tax bill, smaller by far than they did in the first decade after World War II.

SOURCE: http://nationalpriorities.org/index

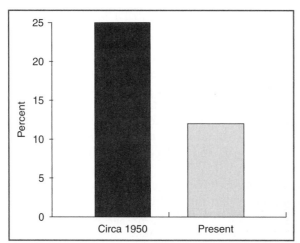

Corporate America's Share of Federal Income Tax Revenues, Then and Now

Big business pays a lot less of the total tax bill than in 1950. Guess who pays a lot more? If you guessed the middle class and lower-income wage earners, you're right on the money.

Educational Malaise

We tend to measure the value of education primarily in monetary terms[20]—how much more the average college graduate earns over a lifetime than someone with only a high school diploma. We want to know the practical value of a particular course, major, or degree and implicitly we reject the inherent value of an education—knowledge for its own sake. "What can you do with a History major?" "There are no jobs for Philosophy majors." These are the kinds of questions and comments college students hear frequently if they are not pursuing a course of study that leads to a definite profession or occupation—pre-law, pre-med, nursing, accounting, and the like.

Critics frequently talk about the "crisis" in education. In some schools, guns, drugs, and gangs endanger students and teachers alike. Declining college entrance examination scores, studies showing our students score worse on mathematical tests than comparable European and Asian students, and high failure rates on elementary-level literacy tests administered to job applicants by many large corporations all testify to the seriousness of the problem. Studies have long shown that U.S. high school students consistently score lower than students in many other countries at a comparable level of development in English, mathematics, science, history, geography, or civics—even though the public schools are well funded.[21]

FIGURE 13.6   Federal Revenues by Source, Fiscal Year 2009. Individual income and payroll (Social Security) taxes together account for over 80 percent of the U.S. Government's annual revenues. Corporations pay only 13 percent. Today, corporations with powerful Washington lobbies get big tax breaks, and middle-class taxpayers foot the bill for Big Business and Big Government.
SOURCE: Office of Management and Budget, *Budget of the U.S. Government, FY2008,* http://www.nationalpriorities.org/node/6919.

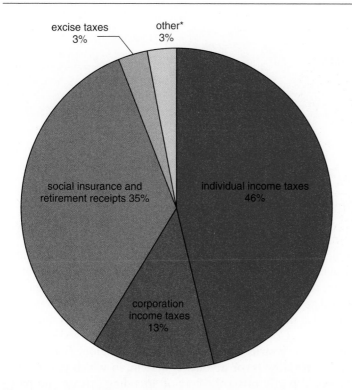

*Estate and gift taxes (1%), custom duties (1%), and miscellaneous receipts (1%)

Grade inflation is widely recognized as a pervasive and corrosive force in education at all levels. Critics charge that teachers pamper students more and more and expect less and less. U.S. business spends billions of dollars every year training students in skills they should have learned in school. Who is to blame and what is to be done?

Until passage of the Elementary and Secondary Education Act of 1965 (ESEA), control of education had fallen primarily to the states. The 1965 law enhanced the role of the federal government. In 2001, Congress passed the No Child Left Behind Act (NCLB), which requires schools across the nation to administer standardized proficiency tests in reading and math and to improve on a yearly basis. NCLB ties federal funding for public schools to compliance with federal educational policy, thus redefining—and greatly expanding—the federal role.

TABLE 13.2   Total Tax Revenue as a Percentage of GDP by Country (2006)

Country	Tax (% of GDP)
Japan	27.4
United States	28.2
Switzerland	30.1
Australia	30.5
Canada	33.4
Spain	37.3
United Kingdom	39.5
Germany	40.6
Italy	42.6
France	46.1
Sweden	49.7
Denmark	50.0
EU 27	39.9

SOURCE: OECD and EUROSTAT.

States and municipalities must now meet academic performance standards set by the federal government. Critics say NCLB was ill conceived from the start; that it forces teachers to change what and how they teach; that it is yet another example of the federal government burdening financially hard-pressed state governments with "unfunded mandates"; and that the requirements are unrealistic.

Under the Constitution, Congress is prohibited from making laws that would either establish religion or restrict the free exercise of religion. Nonetheless, many in the United States now favor a voucher system, in which government transfer payments would partly offset the cost of attending private and parochial schools that meet state accreditation standards. Champions of parent and student choice argue that competition would force all schools—public and private—to either strive for excellence or face extinction.

In recent years, the idea of charter schools has gained ground in many states. As nonsectarian institutions independent of the local school district, charter schools are an innovative attempt to revitalize public education while maintaining the "wall of separation" between church and state. Following Minnesota's lead, 40 other states and the District of Columbia have passed laws allowing the creation of charter schools. By 2008, over one million students were enrolled in some 3,500 charter schools across the country.

Public school administrators and teachers have generally opposed fundamental reforms. They oppose the voucher system for obvious reasons—indeed, they are its target. Many doubt whether standardized tests can accurately measure educational achievement. Finally, educators are often at pains to point out that problems public schools face are reflections of the larger society—including crime, a breakdown of the family, drug use, and the like—which public schools are powerless to solve.

Health Care: It Isn't for Everyone

A healthy society and a vibrant economy are two sides of the same coin. Individuals who suffer from malnutrition or are too ill to work are not productive. Societies ravaged by hunger and disease are not prosperous. It is not only for humanitarian reasons that nearly all developed countries, with one notable exception, guarantee basic health care to every citizen. The notable exception is the United States, where health care is treated as a private good rather than a public one.

The moral question can be simply put: is health care a business like, say, hair care or auto repair, or is it fundamentally different? If it is different, the implications are clear enough—the health care "industry" is inseparable from "life, liberty, and the pursuit of happiness" as enshrined in the Declaration of Independence. Without good health, there can be little happiness, and life itself is in jeopardy.

In the field of health care, the United States stands out among rich countries, but not necessarily for the right reasons. Health care facilities are among the very best in the world, the quality of medical care is generally high, the United States spends far more money on biomedical research and development than any other country in the world, and, finally, its citizens spend more money on medical care than anybody else. It is also true that the United States is the only developed country in the world that does not treat basic health care as a fundamental right of all citizens. Everywhere in western Europe, for example, health care is something citizens of all ages can and do expect in return for paying taxes, just as they can and do expect free basic education for all children. (In fact, university education is also free in many western European countries.)

Many countries with guaranteed universal coverage provide comparable medical services and at far lower overall cost than the United States. France's system, for example, is a mix of public and private provision that works well; it produces a healthy population at one-half the per capita cost in the United States with shorter waiting lists than in Britain, and the French live longer on average than both the British and the Americans.[22]

Most middle-class U.S. workers have some sort of private health insurance, but policies vary widely in cost and coverage. Today, an estimated 47 million people (including 2 million in the middle class) have no health insurance at all. This startling fact probably explains why at least 20 countries have lower infant mortality rates than the United States and impoverished Cuba has a higher life expectancy. In the United States, health care costs have risen much faster than inflation rates or personal incomes, and patients often pay exorbitant prices for prescription drugs compared with the prices of the same drugs in other countries.

Who is to blame? The medical profession points to the high cost of malpractice insurance, hospitals point to the cost of new life-saving technologies, and pharmaceutical companies stress research and development costs to justify skyrocketing health care costs to consumers. Lost in the shuffle of self-absolution is the fact that consumers of medical care are *patients*, not customers shopping for a new pair of shoes. Sick people do not choose to be sick and ought not to be denied medical care or driven into bankruptcy when they are.

Campaigning for president in 2008, Barack Obama promised to reform the system. There is growing support for doing so among doctors and even within the traditionally conservative business community. A sign of the times: In February 2007, the chief executives of retail giant Wal-Mart and three other major U.S. companies joined hands with union leaders in calling for health care coverage for "every person in America and raising the value it [America] receives for every health care dollar." Wal-Mart CEO Lee Scott declared, "We believe American can have high-quality, affordable, and accessible health care by 2012."[23] A 2007 New York Times/CBS News survey found that 90 percent of respondents believe the system needs either fundamental changes (54 percent) or a major overhaul (36 percent).[24]

Income Distribution: Who Gets What, When, and How?

When Thomas Jefferson wrote the Declaration of Independence, he called the pursuit of happiness, along with life and liberty, an unalienable right. Jefferson's "self-evident" proposition that "all men are created equal" does not mean people are equal in all respects or all people have a right to equal compensation. But there has to be some limit to the inequality in compensation a democratic society can tolerate.

Prosperity depends not only on the amount of wealth in a society but also on its distribution. Unless income is distributed widely in society, there will be too few consumers, or consumers with too little money to afford the goods and services the economy can produce, creating a vicious cycle in which everybody loses. Thus, recession (falling demand) causes unemployment, resulting in less demand (fewer consumers with money to spend), causing business profits to fall, and so on.

But the health of the economy is not simply an economic question. A faltering economy can also undermine political stability and governmental authority. Riots and revolts often have economic roots, as the American and French revolutions showed (see Chapter 14).

Glaring economic inequalities are difficult to justify from a moral standpoint, as well. Indeed, in the United States, no politician seeking reelection would dare challenge the idea of "an honest day's work for an honest day's pay."

Yet, since 1980 disparity has grown between the incomes of the richest members of society and all the rest. From 1949 to 1974, the share of family income of the poorest one-fifth of the labor force rose 26.7 percent, while that of the richest 5 percent of income earners fell 12.4 percent. Between 1980 and 2008, this trend was reversed, as the bottom one-fifth's share of family income fell 24.5 percent while that of the top one-twentieth climbed 43.8 percent.[25]

Such numbers are startling, but they are not the result of the mythical free market. The truth is that government plays a major role through its power to tax or not to tax. Thus, the taxes paid by the richest 400 taxpayers in the "roaring nineties" fell from 26.4 cents on every dollar of reported income to just 22.2 cents, while the overall federal income tax burden actually increased. This dramatic narrowing of the gap between what the super rich pay and what everybody else pays equals a massive upward redistribution of income.[26]

This phenomenon of top-loading wealth accelerated after 2000 as a result of the Bush administration's tax cuts. Middle-class workers have been running in place since the early 1970s. Between 1970 and 2000, average wages in the United States, adjusted for inflation, were flat—that is, they did not increase significantly over the entire three decades (the actual increase amounts to about a nickel an hour, or 40 cents a day—not enough to buy a cup of coffee at today's prices).[27] Meanwhile, the incomes of the elite top one-tenth of 1 percent climbed well over 300 percent.[28] In sum, the middle class was going nowhere while the rich got richer and richer. In the understated words of Pulitzer-Prize winning syndicated columnist and Princeton economics professor Paul Krugman, "It would be surprising if this tectonic shift in the economic landscape weren't reflected in politics"[29]—a prediction vindicated by the outcome of the 2008 presidential election ("change you can believe in").

Conservatives take a different view of economic inequality. Rather than focusing on the extreme differences in income, they emphasize that the United States has always had a large middle class and that it would be self-defeating to level society through legislative action (policies designed to redistribute income). Rather, policies that benefit those who work hard, take economic risks, invest wisely, and provide goods and services people want are proven to work best. Conservatives tend to believe helping the poor is not the government's job and that "giveaway" programs only perpetuate poverty by rewarding laziness. In this view, charity belongs in the private sector, where individuals, religious institutions, and charitable organizations can deal with the problem.

Debates over income distribution in a given society are really about equality. Liberals and conservatives agree that equality is important in some sense, but they do not agree on what *kind* of equality is necessary or how much inequality is desirable—or tolerable.

THE PURSUIT OF EQUALITY

A century before the Declaration of Independence was written, the English political philosopher John Locke argued that "life, liberty, and property" are natural rights to which all human beings are entitled. The principle of *equal rights*—as distinct from equal results—has deep roots in the Anglo-American political tradition. Yet principle and practice often diverge, as the history of slavery in the United States attests.

Racial Discrimination

Until the 1860s, slavery made a mockery of the United States' commitment to liberty. On the eve of the Civil War, in the infamous *Dred Scott v. Sandford*

(1856) case, the Supreme Court ruled that no blacks, whether slave or free, were U.S. citizens. Chief Justice Roger Taney argued that blacks were "so inferior" that they had "no rights which the white man was bound to respect."

The outcome of the Civil War meant an end to slavery, but it did not ensure equality under the law. Nor did enactment of the Fourteenth Amendment, which, among other things, guaranteed that no person shall be denied "the equal protection of the laws." Ironically, it was the Supreme Court, the guardian of the Constitution, that largely nullified the intent of this amendment.

Two Landmark Cases In the *Civil Rights Cases* (1883), the Court ruled that an act of Congress prohibiting racial discrimination in public accommodations (restaurants, amusement parks, and the like) was unconstitutional.[30] The Equal Protection Clause of the Fourteenth Amendment, the justices held, was intended to prohibit only *state* discrimination, not private discrimination. Discriminatory acts committed by individuals having no official connection with state government, in other words, were beyond the range of the federal government and, therefore, of the federal courts. If, for example, a restaurant owner turned away black citizens, the owner would merely be exercising the rights of a private individual, and no congressional remedy would be constitutional.

Thirteen years later, in *Plessy v. Ferguson* (1896), the Court went even further.[31] In upholding the constitutionality of a state law mandating racially segregated railway carriages, the Court in *Plessy* devised the notorious *separate-but-equal doctrine.*

Plessy (described by the Court as being of "seven-eighths Caucasian and one-eighth African blood") had taken a seat in the white section of a train, only to be told he was required to move to the "colored" section. A nearly unanimous Court rejected Plessy's claim that the segregation law violated his right to equal protection of the law, arguing that the law was neutral on its face; that is, it provided equal accommodations for persons of both races. The Court majority went so far as to suggest that if "the enforced separation of the two races stamps the colored race with a badge of inferiority," that "is not by reason of anything found in the act, but solely because the colored race chooses to put that construction upon it."

In both the *Civil Rights Cases* and *Plessy v. Ferguson*, only Justice John M. Harlan dissented. On each occasion, he argued the Court's decision had the effect of defeating the egalitarian purpose behind the Fourteenth Amendment, which, he declared, had "removed the race line from our government systems." Because he believed no government, at any level, possessed the constitutional power to pass laws based on racial distinctions, Harlan viewed the Constitution as "colorblind." His dissenting opinion in *Plessy* would not become law, however, for another 58 years. Through the decisions handed down in the *Civil Rights Cases* and *Plessy v. Ferguson*, the Court not only sanctioned strict racial segregation in the South but also helped legitimize a social system in which blacks were discriminated against, brutalized, and even murdered.

Racial Equality: Free at Last? Systematic racial segregation under law was the norm throughout the South well into the twentieth century; *de facto* segregation (neighborhoods and schools) was also widespread in the North, especially in urban areas. Beginning in the late 1940s, however, the Supreme Court began to reinterpret the old legal formulas with a view toward promoting racial equality. In *Shelley v. Kraemer* (1948), the Court held that judicial enforcement of discriminatory private contracts was unconstitutional.[32] The Court ruled that legal enforcement of such agreements amounted to "state action" for the purpose of discrimination, which was prohibited by the Fourteenth Amendment. In addition, though it declined to outlaw them outright, the Court began to insist that segregated state facilities be *truly* equal. Thus, in *Sweatt v. Painter* (1950), it held the University of Texas law school had to admit blacks because the state could not provide a black law school of equal quality and reputation.[33]

In the famous case *Brown v. Board of Education of Topeka* (1954), the Court finally overturned the separate-but-equal doctrine,[34] declaring segregated schools unconstitutional because "separate educational facilities are inherently unequal." The *Brown* decision sparked a heated political debate over the meaning of "equality" in the United States.

Congress eventually passed the Civil Rights Act of 1964, the first of a series of federal laws aimed at realizing racial equality. It was a sign of the changing times that the 1964 act contained an equal accommodations section very similar to the one ruled unconstitutional in the *Civil Rights Cases*.[35] By the late 1960s, after a decade of intense civil rights activities and the most serious civil disorders since the Civil War, the government was fully committed to ensuring equal rights under the law for all citizens. The public policy battle between advocates of racial equality and of white supremacy thus gave way to an increasingly complex and heated debate over the appropriate means to the goal of equality.

BETTMANN/CORBIS

In two landmark Supreme Court decisions, *Civil Rights Cases* (1883) and *Plessy v. Ferguson* (1896), the strict racial segregation in the South was upheld by majority decision. Justice John M. Harlan's dissenting opinion in *Plessy*, that the Constitution is "colorblind," would not become law for almost 58 years.

The Busing Controversy The question of how far the government could and should go to promote equal rights was crystallized in the school busing controversy of the 1970s and 1980s, which grew out of an ambiguity in *Brown v. Board of Education*. In that case, as we saw, the Court ruled legal segregation in schools unconstitutional. But changing the law did not necessarily change the schools, because of the existence de facto segregation—that is, segregation resulting from segregated residential patterns. Blacks lived in the inner city and whites in the suburbs. How could this kind of segregation be broken down for the purpose of integrating the schools? One obvious possibility was to integrate school districts by transporting schoolchildren across district lines. Court-ordered school busing met with opposition from parents and school administrators on various grounds. This unhappiness coincided with a national "crisis of confidence" in the public schools.

Was busing a good idea? It *did* put pressure on local officials and school boards to improve facilities and conditions in inner-city schools. It also made it clear to skeptics that the federal government was serious about equality of educational opportunity. On the other hand, busing often had the effect of simply redistributing minorities from one part of the city to another. Some localities tried busing children between predominantly black inner-city neighborhoods and predominantly white suburbs, but the Supreme Court generally invalidated such plans.[36]

Affirmative Action or Reverse Discrimination?

affirmative action
Giving preferential treatment to a socially or economically disadvantaged group in compensation for opportunities denied by past discrimination.

reverse discrimination
In effect, going overboard in giving preferences to racial minorities and victims of gender discrimination in hiring, housing and education; the U.S. Supreme Court has ruled that in some cases, affirmative action quotas are unconstitutional.

In the late 1970s, a controversy raged over the issue of **affirmative action**. At issue were governmental programs and regulations that gave special preference to minorities in job hiring and promotion, admission to colleges and professional schools, and similar situations. The aim was to remedy the persistent effects of past and present discrimination against minorities. But, many people asked, was affirmative action really fair? Was it even constitutional? Opponents argued it amounted to **reverse discrimination**.

If the Constitution permitted preferential treatment of minorities, did it also provide the majority with protection against reverse discrimination? This question was answered, in part, in 1978, when the Supreme Court handed down a ruling in a suit brought by Allan Bakke, a white student who had unsuccessfully sought admission to the medical school of the University of California at Davis.[37] Bakke contended that the medical school had unfairly undercut his chances of acceptance simply because of his race. In a close decision, the Court ruled rigid affirmative action quotas were unconstitutional. It also indicated, however, that preference for minorities could be maintained under certain circumstances.[38]

But the Supreme Court has upheld several broad-based preferential hiring programs, while drawing the line at plans providing minorities with preferential protection against layoffs.[39] Similarly, it has upheld the use of affirmative action in the employment of women in order to improve gender balance in the workforce.[40] The Court later appeared to reverse (or at least dilute) itself in a ruling on governmental preferences for minority-owned businesses.[41]

In 2003, the Supreme Court ruled in *Grutter v. Bollinger* that race can be used in university admission decisions, voting 5-4 to uphold the University of Michigan Law School's affirmative action policy, which favors minorities—thus apparently reversing the decision in *Bakke*. But in a parallel case, *Gratz v. Bollinger*, the justices struck down the university's undergraduate affirmative action policy (which awarded 20 points to blacks, Hispanics and Native Americans), on the grounds that the policy was not "narrowly tailored" to achieve the goal of diversity—thus apparently confirming the *Bakke* decision.

It is not clear, therefore, exactly where affirmative action ends and reverse discrimination begins in the eyes of the Supreme Court. Two generalizations are possible. First, the Constitution gives Congress considerably more latitude than it gives state and local governments to remedy the past effects of discrimination. Second, color-conscious affirmative action programs at the state and local levels are most likely to be upheld where there is clear evidence of specific (and not general social) discrimination against minorities.[42]

Who Deserves Preferential Treatment?

African Americans and Native Americans have historically been victims of injustice and discrimination. During World War II, more than 120,000 Japanese Americans living on the West Coast were herded into concentration camps and kept in confinement, surrounded by barbed wire and armed guards, until the end of the war. Whole families who had done nothing wrong were forced into internal exile, losing everything they had in the process. This gross injustice was justified on the grounds of national security. Not until 1988 did the U.S. Congress pass a law acknowledging "a grave injustice was done" and giving each victim $20,000 in compensation, along with an official letter of apology signed by the president.

Women, gays and lesbians, and Arab Americans are three other groups with a claim to preferential treatment based on past discrimination. After 9/11, Arab Americans were insulted, threatened, and in some cases physically attacked. The FBI placed many Arabs and Muslims under surveillance, questioned others, and arrested thousands, holding them without charges or access to an attorney for longer than the law allowed.[43]

Gender-based discrimination became a front-burner issue only in the 1970s. For a time, the debate centered on the ill-fated equal rights amendment, which would have guaranteed that "equality of rights under the law should not be denied or abridged by the United States or by any State on account of sex." Do women need special protection as a historically disadvantaged "minority"? Are they entitled to preferential treatment to remedy the effects of past sex discrimination?

Gays and lesbians have long been the object of discrimination, too. In 1992, Colorado voters passed a measure prohibiting the state from enforcing specific legal protections or extending preference to gay citizens who believed they were disadvantaged or discriminated against. The referendum was overturned in 1996, when the Supreme Court held the measure discriminatory and therefore unconstitutional.[44] In 2008, California became the second state, after Massachusetts, to issue same-sex marriage licenses after the California Supreme Court ruled the state's ban on same-sex marriages unconstitutional. Later in 2008, however, California voters passed Proposition 8, a constitutional amendment intended to supersede the Court's ruling. The California high court has agreed to hear several challenges to this action, but it remains in force for now. Meanwhile, five U.S. states have, in fact, made same-sex marriages legal, as well as seven countries (Belgium, Canada, the Netherlands, Norway, South Africa, Spain, and Sweden).

This controversy and others like it raise a larger question: what rights and legal protections are due to all citizens? What does the U.S. Constitution have to say about liberty, and how can a government be designed to protect us (the citizens) from itself?

THE PURSUIT OF LIBERTY

Liberty in Western political philosophy is synonymous with freedom from governmental restraint. It is based on the assumption that individuals know best what they want and need to be happy. Liberty is necessary for the meaningful exchange of ideas, as well as for social progress. Without freedom, the spirit of invention and innovation is stifled. Freedom of expression is also necessary to keep the government honest. Allowing the government to encroach on anyone's liberty threatens everyone's liberty.

Liberty and the First Amendment

In the United States, legal questions about individual freedom often turn on the First Amendment, which provides that

> Congress shall make no law respecting an establishment of religion, or prohibiting the free exercise thereof; or abridging the freedom of speech, or the press, or the right of the people peaceably to assemble, and to petition the Government for a redress of grievances.

Thus, the First Amendment protects four civil liberties: freedom of speech, freedom of the press, freedom of religion, and freedom of assembly. Because the language of the First Amendment is brief and intentionally vague, the first three rights in particular have required an unusual amount of judicial interpretation.

Freedom of Speech Most constitutional experts agree the overriding purpose behind the First Amendment was the protection of *political* speech. In a republic, open debate between political opponents is vital to the effective functioning of the political system. Most of the time, the *exercise* of free speech is not controversial, even though the speech itself might be.

However, freedom of speech can become a hotly contested issue when individuals who represent unpopular causes or who challenge the integrity or legitimacy of the political system try to exercise it. Extremists often arouse strong passions, especially within minority groups they have victimized (Jews against Nazis, for example, or African Americans against the Ku Klux Klan).

Unfortunately, in the United States many people associate protesters and demonstrators with extremists and troublemakers irrespective of the cause. During the early days of the Vietnam War, youthful protesters were often depicted as unpatriotic and disloyal. Several years later, after the war had become unpopular, defenders of the U.S. role in Vietnam were booed and shouted down when they spoke on college campuses. The First Amendment, however, safeguards the right of *all* citizens to express political opinions, no matter how repugnant or unpopular, subject to only a few limitations (that the speech not be part and parcel of an illegal act, that it not foment riot, that it not constitute a direct personal provocation—so-called fighting words—and so on).

But what the government does is not always in step with what the Constitution says it can (or cannot) do. During the Vietnam War, for example, the U.S. government engaged in domestic spying under the secret Counter Intelligence Program (COINTELPRO), aimed at monitoring the activities of antiwar activists. After that divisive war, the FBI was banned from monitoring events that were "open to the public" and involved religious or political groups unless it had a specific reason for doing so. These regulations were effectively set aside after September 11, 2001, and the FBI reportedly began again to collect extensive information about antiwar demonstrators, even where, in the words of its own internal memorandum, it "possessed no information that violent or terrorist activities are being planned."[45]

In early February 2004, a county deputy sheriff working closely with the FBI's Joint Terrorism Task Force served subpoenas on Drake University in Des Moines, Iowa, to turn over documents relating to an antiwar conference that had taken place there a few months earlier. "The main theme of the conference had been to bring the Iowa National Guard safely back from Iraq… The subpoena asked for all records of Drake University campus security officers reflecting any observations made of the conference, including any records relating to the people in charge, or to any of the attendees."[46] These subpoenas were subsequently withdrawn in the wake of negative publicity, expressions of outrage by civil libertarians, and criticism from members of Congress, most notably Senator Tom Harkin of Iowa, who likened it to "Vietnam when war protestors were rounded up [and] grand juries were convened to investigate people who were protesting the war."[47]

Many voters who backed Barack Obama in the 2008 presidential campaign were motivated in part by a belief that he would not renew the Patriot Act which, among other things, allows the federal government to engage in warrantless searches and extensive surveillance of private citizens. But having won the election, President Obama chose an Attorney General, Eric Holder, who endorsed the Patriot Act at his confirmation hearing, disappointing ardent defenders of liberty—liberals and conservatives alike.

Of course, the protections offered by the freedom of speech clause are not confined to political speech alone. The Supreme Court has placed a very broad interpretation on *speech*, defining it as synonymous with *expression*.

Flag burning, for example, has been upheld as a protected form of symbolic free speech.[48] The context of symbolic free speech is almost always constitutionally more important than its content. The Ku Klux Klan's burning of a cross in an isolated field may be an objectionable act, but the Court has held that it is nonetheless a constitutionally protected form of symbolic expression.[49] Burning a cross on someone's lawn, however, is a different matter altogether.[50]

Freedom of the Press The First Amendment protects publishers from almost all forms of official censorship. Newspapers and periodicals can publish what they wish, including criticisms and indictments of the government. The same holds true for the broadcast media. A free press is crucial to a democracy, because every citizen is a decision maker at election time and because the glare of publicity helps keep elected officials honest.

In the aftermath of 9/11, freedom of the press became a bone of contention as the Bush administration advocated greater governmental secrecy in order to prosecute the war on terror. But journalists and media executives expressed alarm at the way the Freedom of Information Act (FOIA) was being flouted. In May 2004, Tom Curley, CEO of the Associated Press, gave a chilling speech about what he described as a culture of official secrecy and a growing hostility to the press at the local, state, and federal levels of the government, as well as in the courts.[51]

The Supreme Court has consistently reaffirmed that under the Constitution, the press cannot be subject to **prior restraint**. Except in times of war or grave national emergency, the government does not have the power to prevent a newspaper or a periodical from publishing material of any sort—even papers classified as secret or information a trial judge may later rule constitute prejudicial pretrial publicity.[52] In the final analysis, however, only a free press and an alert public can prevent the abuse of power by a commander in chief.

prior restraint
The legal doctrine that the government does not have the power to censor the press, except in cases of dire national emergency.

Freedom of Religion By prohibiting the establishment of a state-sponsored religion, the First Amendment requires the government to be neutral in religious matters—to neither help nor hinder any religion. This requirement complements the guarantee of the free exercise of religion. Taken together, these two clauses ensure that citizens may practice any religion in any manner they like, within reasonable limits.

When religious practices pose a threat to society, however, government has the power to outlaw them. No court in the land, for instance, would uphold ritual murder on the ground that the free exercise of religion was guaranteed by the Constitution. Even certain religious practices that do not present any obvious danger to society, such as polygamy, are not constitutionally protected.[53] But courts have upheld the right of conscientious objectors to refuse induction into the armed services, of Amish children to be exempted from public education requirements, and of Jehovah's Witness schoolchildren to refrain from saluting the flag (considered worship of a graven image).

On the controversial issue of school prayer, the Supreme Court has held that prayer, even if nondenominational, and Bible-reading in public schools violate the Establishment Clause of the First Amendment.[54] Prayers at high school graduation exercises have also been ruled out.[55] The Supreme Court has gone so far as to disallow a moment of silence in the public schools if a teacher suggests it might be used for prayer.[56] Observing that public schools, teachers, and school boards are creatures of state government and that student enrollment in public schools is mandated by state compulsory education laws, the justices have consistently ruled that school prayer unconstitutionally involves the state in the establishment of religion.

The Establishment Clause has also been part of the debate over state aid to parents whose children attend private schools, particularly church-related or denominational schools. In 2002, the U.S. Supreme Court ruled in *Zelman v. Simmons-Harris* that a school voucher program in Cleveland, Ohio, did not violate the Constitution because the vouchers were intended for the secular purpose of helping children of low-income families attending failing schools. In 2004, the Colorado Supreme Court ruled a school voucher program did violate a provision of the Colorado Constitution. Similarly, in January 2006, the Florida Supreme Court struck down a school voucher plan, ruling it violated a section of the Florida Constitution stating, "Adequate provision shall be made by law for a uniform, efficient, safe, secure and high-quality system of free public schools."

At the national level, the Bush administration pushed for vouchers, but to no avail. In 2006, Secretary of Education Margaret Spellings proposed a $100 billion national school voucher plan that died in the Congress. Although the National Education Association (NEA), among other powerful lobbies, is a staunch opponent of voucher plans, a few publicly financed plans have been adopted, including Cleveland (see above), Milwaukee, and Washington, D.C. In 2009, at the urging of the NEA, Democrats in Congress effectively killed the D.C. voucher program. To the dismay of voucher supporters, President Obama's compromise amounted to what one critic called "choosing attrition over summary execution."[57] Opinion polls consistently show most voters do not support school voucher programs, especially if they would compete with public schools for tax dollars.

Privacy and the Right to Life

In 1973, the Supreme Court ruled in *Roe v. Wade* that most laws against abortion violated the right to privacy under the due Process Clause of the Fifth Amendment. Since then, a more conservative Court has ruled that a woman's right to an abortion does not require the use of public funds to reimburse poorer women for the cost of abortions, nor is the state required to pay public employees for performing or assisting in abortions.[58]

Objections to *Roe v. Wade* have come largely from right-to-life groups, whose members believe human life begins at conception and abortion therefore amounts to legalized murder. The right-to-life movement has publicized its position by protesting and sometimes blockading abortion clinics. In 1994, Congress passed a law guaranteeing women unhampered access to abortion clinics; the law also restricted protesters from inhibiting a woman's ability to obtain an abortion. The same year, the Supreme Court held that antiabortion activists could be sued under the Racketeer Influenced and Corrupt Organization (RICO) law if blockading abortion clinics inflicted economic harm on those performing abortions.[59] But in 1997, the Supreme Court eased restrictions on abortion clinic protests, ruling that according to the First Amendment, anti-abortion demonstrators also require constitutional protection.[60]

In early 2004, the Bush administration served medical subpoenas on hospitals and clinics in California, Illinois, Kansas, Missouri, Michigan, New York, Pennsylvania, and Washington, demanding records of their patients who had undergone certain types of abortions over the previous 3 years. Critics argued these subpoenas sought sensitive medical information of a deeply personal nature and, as such, were an egregious invasion of privacy in a matter that had nothing to do with terrorism or national security. They also felt the Bush administration was attempting to substitute its own moral values for doctors' professional judgment and violating the confidential relationship between doctor and patient.[61] Under a 1996 federal law, they noted, doctors, hospitals, and drugstores must give "notices of privacy practices" to patients and customers, assuring them personal information will be protected.

But in 2004, the federal government sought the medical records of 2,700 patients from a public hospital and six Planned Parenthood clinics in San Francisco alone.[62] Attorney General John Ashcroft claimed these records were needed to defend against legal challenges to the Partial Birth Abortion Ban Act (PBABA). Legal experts pointed out that the PBABA conflicts directly with a preexisting Supreme Court decision in a Nebraska abortion case.[63] A federal

Since the 1973 Supreme Court's ruling in *Roe v. Wade*, affirming a woman's right to an abortion, pro-choice and antiabortion activists in the United States have demonstrated vocally and sometimes violently. On a Sunday morning in late May, 2009, a gunman entered the foyer of a church in Wichita, Kansas, then shot and killed Dr. George Tiller, a licensed physician who performed abortions at his local clinic. It was not the first instance of its kind and law-enforcement officials fear it will not be the last.

LANDOV MEDIA.

judge in San Francisco denied the Justice Department access. In the words of Judge Phyllis J. Hamilton, "There is no question that the patient is entitled to privacy and protection." Judge Hamilton found the information sought was potentially "of an extremely intimate and personal nature" and that women "are entitled to not have the government looking at their records."[64]

Several Supreme Court justices have defended the pro-choice position by developing a new concept of privacy based on a right "to define one's own concept of existence, of meaning, of the universe, and of the mystery of human life."[65] This language has become increasingly important to those who contend there is a right to die, arguing that patients who are terminally ill or in unbearable pain should have the legal option of medically assisted suicide. In 1997, the Supreme Court unanimously refused to recognize a constitutional right to die.[66]

THE PURSUIT OF JUSTICE

We can define a just society as one in which laws are applied fairly and the punishment fits the crime. Viewed in this way, *justice* becomes a practical end of government, achieved through the courts and the criminal justice system, rather than a theoretical exercise.

Crime and Punishment

No society can afford to let seriously antisocial or criminal behavior go unpunished. Crime often appears senseless, but there are at least four reasons for punishment: **incarceration, deterrence, rehabilitation**, and **retribution**. The first can protect society by taking dangerous criminals off the streets; the other three are less clear-cut. Does punishing one crime deter another? Are prisons conducive to rehabilitation? Is retribution a moral response to injury?

Justice as Fair Procedure

An old legal cliché holds that 90 percent of fairness in the law is fair procedure. Procedural safeguards are essential to prevent the innocent from being falsely accused and the accused from being falsely convicted. These safeguards, which make up *due process of law*, are outlined in the Bill of Rights, particularly the Fourth, Fifth, and Sixth amendments. Under the Constitution, citizens have the legal right

- not to be subjected to unreasonable searches and seizures by the state,
- not to be tried twice for the same offense,
- not to incriminate themselves,
- to receive a speedy and public trial by an impartial jury,
- to be informed of the nature of any charge made against them,
- to be confronted by any witnesses against them,
- to obtain witnesses in their favor, and
- to have legal counsel.

incarceration
The isolation of criminals in an effort to protect society and to prevent lawbreakers from commiting more crimes.

deterrence
In criminal justice theory, punishing a criminal for the purpose of discouraging others from committing a similar crime. In international relations, the theory that aggressive wars can be prevented if potential victims maintain a military force sufficient to inflict unacceptable punishment on any possible aggressor.

rehabilitation
Education, training, and social conditioning aimed at encouraging imprisoned criminals to become normal, productive members of society when they are released.

retribution
The punishment of criminals on the ground that they have done wrong and deserve to suffer as a consequence.

As a group, these guarantees represent the heart of the U.S. justice system, though each is subject to judicial interpretation. "No private citizen can match the modern state when the latter brings all its forces into play after he has been accused of having violated the law."[67] Thus, procedural guarantees are essential to protect defendants from miscarriages of justice.

The Limits of Legal Protection

Despite all safeguards, the criminal justice system is far from perfect. For one thing, the poor cannot afford high-priced lawyers.

Historically, injustice in the United States has been closely associated with slavery and racial prejudice. For a long time, this was particularly true in the South, where the imposition and severity of punishment correlated more closely with race than with any other consideration. Black men who were convicted (often falsely) of raping white women were commonly sentenced to death or life in prison, whereas whites accused of similar crimes against black women were often not even brought to trial.

But recognizing flaws in the system is easier than correcting them. Virtually every due process guarantee has been the object of bitter controversy. For example, the Constitution clearly grants a defendant the right to an attorney. But what if the accused cannot afford an attorney? Must the state provide an attorney for an indigent person accused of a felony? For a defendant who wishes to appeal a verdict? Only for the first appeal, or all the way to the highest court?[68]

Obviously, there are limits to the scope of legal safeguards. Apply them too broadly and it becomes next to impossible to convict anyone accused of anything, or the judicial process becomes so sluggish that justice itself is impeded or undermined. In the end, the courts must balance the procedural rights of the accused against the obligation of government to punish those truly guilty of violating the law.

In wartime, constitutional guarantees and due process are circumscribed in ways not acceptable under any other circumstances. During the Civil War, President Lincoln even suspended habeas corpus. At one point, the chief justice of the Supreme Court, Roger Taney, was frozen in an eyeball-to-eyeball confrontation with the U.S. military over this very issue and had to back down when it became clear the chief executive was on the side of the generals.

Fast-forward to the fall of 2001. In the aftermath of 9/11, Congress passed sweeping new anti-terror legislation that gave the Justice Department unprecedented powers of investigation and interrogation, search and seizure, arrest and detention, and, finally, surveillance (including telephone wiretaps and e-mail monitoring), provided these activities were carried out for purposes of combating terrorism. The Patriot Act was rushed through the Republican House of Representatives and passed with minor modifications in the Democratic Senate, with only one opposing vote from Senator Russell Feingold of Wisconsin. Many of Europe's democracies require all citizens to carry ID cards, but this practice has long been resisted in both the United States and the United Kingdom (see Box 13.5).

BOX 13.5 IDENTITY CARDS AND CIVIL LIBERTIES

Advocates of national ID cards see them as a means to enhance national security, unmask potential terrorists, and guard against illegal immigrants. Most European countries, as well as Malaysia, Singapore, and Thailand, use ID cards.

When Congress passed the Real ID Act of 2005, which sought to create a de facto national ID system in the United States, at least 19 states passed resolutions or laws rejecting a national ID program. As the deadline approached on May 11, 2008, not a single state was in compliance. The Department of Homeland Security responded by extending the deadline even though no states had asked for an extension. At present, the federal act remains in a state of abeyance.

Britain's troubles in Northern Ireland have left its government with broad powers of arrest and detention, but these are balanced by a long tradition of civil liberties and a dislike for identity cards. Nonetheless, national ID cards are being introduced gradually in the United Kingdom. The Labour Government has already started issuing identity cards to non-EU foreign nationals

working in the United Kingdom. In 2012, everyone over the age of 16 applying for a passport will have fingerprints, facial scans, and other personal details (name, gender, and date of birth) added to a National Identity register. If Labour wins the next election (set for no later than June 2010), it will likely ask Parliament to vote on whether to make ID cards compulsory. Both the Tories and the Liberal Democrats oppose national ID cards as a threat to civil liberty.

In France, Spain, and Italy, the tentacles of power reach wider. Failing to produce an identity card if you are checked in the street can result in a visit to the local police station, especially if you happen to look foreign. Even when tracking down common criminals, investigating magistrates, working with the police, have far-reaching powers to tap telephones, order searches, look into bank accounts, and put suspects behind bars without bringing charges—in France, for up to 4 years. Germans have to carry identity cards, but strict laws prevent government agencies from passing on personal data.

The Exclusionary Rule No due process issue has raised the question of fairness more sharply than the so-called exclusionary rule. Essentially, the **exclusionary rule** holds that when evidence has been illegally obtained, it cannot be entered in a court of law. The Supreme Court, in promulgating this rule, argued that the Fourth Amendment's prohibition against illegal searches and seizures would be meaningless if illegal police behavior were not discouraged by the certain knowledge that any evidence obtained in violation of the Constitution would be excluded from the courts.[69] In the view of the Court, then, the exclusionary rule provides an indispensable barrier to deliberate abuse of police powers.

Critics of this rule (including several Supreme Court justices) focus on the problems it causes police officers, whose searches and seizures must conform to very complex guidelines handed down by the courts.[70] Few searches and seizures, they point out, conform to textbook cases; most of the time, the officer on the spot is compelled to make a spur-of-the-moment decision. Police officers, charged with protecting the public, often find themselves in dangerous situations without the luxury of deliberation in safe circumstances enjoyed by judges and juries.

exclusionary rule
In judicial proceedings, the rule that evidence obtained in violation of constitutional guidelines cannot be used in court against the accused.

At the heart of the dispute over the exclusionary rule lie several important differences of opinion. For advocates, who see law enforcement officers as over-zealous, the exclusionary rule is a valuable guarantee of justice; for opponents, it as an impediment to law enforcement that makes officers well-intentioned victims of convoluted laws. The Supreme Court has sought to strike a balance between these poles by carving out a "harmless error" exception that admits illegally obtained evidence in certain situations.[71]

Judicial Discretion   Until recently, prevailing legal theory preferred wide discretion for prosecutors (to prosecute, plea-bargain, or not prosecute), for judges (to pronounce indeterminate sentences), and for parole boards (to determine how much actual time a convicted criminal should serve). Critics contend prosecutors make decisions based on political considerations or individual whim, judges sentence according to pet theories of the law, and parole officers are easily fooled by clever convicts. Loopholes and uncertainties in the judicial system, they allege, severely dilute the deterrent effect of punishment. Even worse, the convicted felon's punishment depends too much on circumstances that ought to be irrelevant in judicial matters, such as which judge tries which case. The force of these arguments led Congress to enact mandatory minimum sentence laws in 1986 and a number of states to reduce or eliminate indeterminate (discretionary) sentences.

But experience shows there are no easy answers, and mandatory sentencing guidelines are no panacea. Thus, though mandatory sentences were aimed at drug "kingpins," the law has not worked as intended because it allows sentence reductions when defendants provide prosecutors with "substantial assistance" (meaning, information leading to the arrest of other drug traffickers). In most instances, only high-level drug dealers are in a position to provide such assistance. As a result the biggest offenders often get off easy, and the drug mules or street dealers, who have little information to give, get the stiffest sentences.

According to critics, mandatory minimum sentences are costly and unjust, contribute greatly to prison overcrowding, have shifted power from judges to prosecutors (who are unaccountable), punish too few high-level dealers, and are responsible for sending to prison record numbers of women and people of color. In 2005, the Supreme Court ruled that federal judges are not bound by mandatory sentencing guidelines.

Capital Punishment   More than two-thirds of the states (37 in all) still allow capital punishment. Between 1976, when the death penalty was reinstated, and 2001, 102 people sentenced to death were subsequently exonerated, and at least 74 people on death row were released on the basis of exonerating DNA evidence.[72]

Public debate over the propriety of capital punishment has been waged on at least two separate levels. In practical terms, experts differ about whether capital punishment actually deters future murders. The evidence has been so fragmentary and the interpretations so diverse that a definitive answer is unlikely. On another level, there is bitter controversy over whether capital punishment is morally defensible. Who qualifies for the death penalty and who does not? Minors? The mentally retarded? The insane? Apart from the question of "death qualification," are judges and juries truly impartial? Are whites as likely as blacks to be convicted in capital crimes? To be sentenced to death? To be executed? Finally, if potential jurors who do not believe in capital punishment are dismissed in *voir dire* (the jury selection process), does that stack the deck against the accused? Oddly, both sides emphasize the sanctity of human life. Defenders of capital punishment say justice demands the death penalty precisely because society is morally obligated to condemn the murder of innocent persons in the harshest possible way. Opponents say not even the state has the right to take a human life.

GOALS IN CONFLICT

Certainly, the five core values examined in this chapter—security, prosperity, equality, liberty, and justice—are not always easy to translate into public policy. Many times, the goals themselves conflict. The war on terror was a grim reminder of the tension between liberty and security in times of crisis.[73]

Moderation is the key to good government, and tolerance is the partner of moderation. Moderation inoculates citizens against unreasonable demands and expectations; tolerance against prejudice and hatred. Together, they guard against single-minded efforts to achieve one end of government at the expense of others, or of those who dare to be different from us.

GATEWAYS TO THE WORLD: EXPLORING CYBERSPACE

www.civilrights.org

Maintained by the Leadership Conference on Civil Rights and the Leadership Conference on Civil Rights Education Fund, this site is dedicated to providing information and education in the area of civil rights. It contains links to related Websites.

www.nea.org/lac/index.html

The website of the National Education Association. This URL will take you directly to the NEA's "Legislative Action Center." If you want to know more about No Child Left Behind, vouchers, or what Congress is doing in the area of legislation, click on "Current Issues in Congress."

www.nathannewman.org/nbs

A project of the Center for Community Economic Research at the University of California—Berkeley, this Website contains a hands-on simulation for users to attempt to balance the budget by making fiscal policy decisions in a number of areas.

www.americaneconomicalert.org/ticker_home.asp

This site features a "trade ticker" that shows a running total of the cumulative trade deficit at any given moment. It also shows monthly trade figures (deficits) going back several years.

www.census.gov/indicator/www/ustrade.html

This URL will take you directly to the trade highlights Web page at the U.S. Census Bureau's Foreign Trade Statistics site.

www.brillig.com/debt_clock

This page features a national debt clock showing the cumulative debt on any given day as well as each citizen's share of the debt as it accumulates.

www.ts.com/p/318.html

This site features a national debt graph for the current year and a national debt history by president based on White House data, among other things.

www.shadowstats.com/cgi-bin/sgs?

This Shadow Government Statistics Website challenges the federal government's figures on the debt and gives in-depth "Analysis Behind and Beyond Government Economic Reporting."

add.english.ucsb.edu

This home page for the Affirmative Action and Diversity Project provides a variety of documents and links—both the pro and con.

www.policy.com

This site provides information on a variety of areas of public policy, as well as links to think tanks, journals, government documents, and other sources relating to policy.

http://www.politicalresources.net/

Provides "listings of political sites available on the Internet sorted by country, with links to parties, organizations, governments, media, and more from all around the world."

SUMMARY

Public policy issues attempt to satisfy five basic goals: security, prosperity, equality, liberty, and justice. Security is the most fundamental goal of government, because a country cannot pursue or preserve other values without it. In pursuing security, government attempts to protect citizens from foreign enemies, from fellow citizens, from natural enemies, and, in some instances, from themselves.

In the United States, the goal of prosperity has historically been associated with a free-enterprise economy based on the idea of the commercial republic. In the twentieth century, however, the government has attempted to promote the economic well-being of individuals through social welfare and other programs. These programs have sparked heated debate over the proper role of government in economic matters, especially as the budget deficit has worsened. Problems in the educational system endangered U.S. competitiveness in the international economy. Income distribution also made for a lively topic of national debate in recent years and became a front-burner issue after the Wall Street meltdown in the fall of 2008. The election of Barack Obama and the economic recession have made extravagant executive bonuses and income disparities front-page news.

The goal of equality in the United States has been closely identified with the effort to end racial discrimination. Two landmark Supreme Court cases in the post-Civil War period helped perpetuate state laws and public attitudes upholding established patterns of racial inequality. Later, *Brown v. Board of Education* (1954) spearheaded the civil rights movement, which culminated in legislative, judicial, and administrative measures aimed at bringing about genuine racial equality. These civil rights gains were followed by new controversies over mandatory school busing to achieve racial integration and affirmative action guidelines designed to rectify past inequalities. Other major public policy issues related to equality have recognized the rights of various ethnic groups, women, and the poor and disadvantaged.

The pursuit of liberty is a core value of U.S. society. Among the personal liberties protected explicitly by the First Amendment are freedom of speech, freedom of the press, and freedom of religion. The right to privacy, or freedom of choice, is another significant aspect of personal liberty in the United States.

We can narrowly define the pursuit of justice as the government's attempt to ensure fair and impartial treatment under the law. In the United States, the criminal justice system strives to uphold a commitment to due process, or fair procedure. The controversial exclusionary rule attempts to balance the defendant's right to due process against society's right to be protected against criminals. Debates about judicial discretion and capital punishment also attempt to balance defendants' and society's rights.

Conflicts among these five goals always prevent any one of them from being fully realized. A moderate, well-informed, and fair-minded citizenry is thus essential to sound public policy and a sustainable democratic order.

KEY TERMS

national security
entitlements
Emission Trading
  Scheme (ETS)
Kyoto Protocol
sustainable growth
federal budget deficit

gross national debt
  (GND)
Balanced Budget Act of
  1997
affirmative action
reverse discrimination
prior restraint

incarceration
deterrence
rehabilitation
retribution
exclusionary rule
economic stimulus

REVIEW QUESTIONS

1. What are some political issues that arise from security concerns?
2. What internal and external economic problems face the United States today? What triggered the current recession? What measures has the Obama administration taken to deal with it?
3. Contrast the ideal and the practice of equality in U.S. history.
4. Explain the idea of affirmative action. What groups, if any, deserve protection, and why?
5. What is reverse discrimination? How has the Supreme Court ruled in cases alleging discrimination of this kind? Do you agree or disagree with these rulings? Explain.
6. Why is liberty valuable? How is it protected in the United States?
7. What challenges currently plague the U.S. criminal justice system? Is the law colorblind? Comment.
8. Is mandatory sentencing a good idea in your opinion? Explain your point of view.
9. What is the relationship between the public good and moderation?

RECOMMENDED READING

Because public policy questions are forever changing, exposure to current information and thoughtful opinion is vital. Appropriate reading would include highly respected newspapers (such as the *New York Times* and the *Washington Post)*, weekly news magazines (such as *Time* and *Newsweek)*, magazines of opinion (including the *Nation, New Republic, Atlantic, Harper's, Commentary*, and *National Review)*, and certain scholarly journals that specialize in public policy questions (such as *The Public Interest)*.

Aaron, Henry, et al., eds. *Values and Public Policy.* Washington, D.C.: Brookings Institution, 1994.

This is one collection that covers themes discussed in the last several chapters.

Altman, Nancy J. *The Battle for Social Security: From FDR's Vision to Bush's Gamble.* Hoboken, New Jersey: Wiley, 2005.

A well-researched study of the Social Security System from its inception to the Bush administration. The author is critical of President Bush's efforts to reduce pension protection for senior citizens.

Dahl, Robert. *On Political Equality.* New Haven, CT: Yale University Press, 2007.

A thoughtful essay on a timeless topic of great importance to the theory and practice of democracy. The author is one of America's most esteemed political scientists of his generation.

Moghalu, Kingsley. *Global Justice: The Politics of War Crimes Trials.* Stanford, CA: Stanford University, 2008.

A very good book on a subject that the recent history and the policies of the Bush administration have unfortunately given renewed prominence and relevance both at home and abroad.

Paust, Jordan. *Beyond the Law: The Bush Administration's Unlawful Response in the "War" on Terror.* New York: Cambridge University Press, 2007.

The title leaves no doubt where the author stands. A book well worth reading for anyone concerned about the legal and moral implications of "enhanced interrogation techniques" (torture) and "extraordinary rendition" (abduction without extradition) used against "unlawful combatants" (prisoners of war).

Shenkman, Rick. *Just How Stupid Are We? Facing the Truth About the American Voter.* New York: Basic Books, 2009.

Survey data points to the disturbing conclusion that most Americans are too ignorant and ill informed to vote intelligently. The author argues that reforms in higher education aimed at civic literacy are urgently needed.

Politics by Violent Means: Revolution, War, and Terrorism

A scene from the Russian Revolution in 1917; the banner reads, "Peace to the world, All power to the people, All land to the people."

CENTRAL PRESS/HULTON ARCHIVE/GETTY IMAGES

Revolution
In the Name of Justice

Few words are used more loosely than *revolution* and *revolutionary*. Television commercials abound with descriptions of "revolutionary" new anti-aging skin creams, Internet-enabled cell phones, or hybrid cars that represent a "revolution" in transportation. *Real* revolutions, however, are serious business.

What exactly is a revolution? Any action or event that results in a fundamental change in the form of government is a **revolution**. Often, it is accompanied by violence and social upheaval; however, some recent revolutions—in the former Soviet Union and Eastern Europe—have brought little or no bloodshed.

The eighteenth century witnessed two great revolutions—one in the New World (the American Revolution) and one in the Old World (the French Revolution). But it was not until the twentieth century that revolutions swept across the globe—from Russia (1917) to China (1949) to the Third World (1960s and 1970s) to Eastern Europe (1989) and, coming full circle, back to (Soviet) Russia (1991). Great technological advances filled the years following World War II—space travel, organ transplants, computers, and the Internet. Those same years—coinciding with the Cold War—witnessed an eruption of revolutions in the Middle East, Africa, Asia, and Latin America.

The period after World War II saw the fastest and most far-reaching changes in world history so far. During this age of revolution, the dizzying pace of change was changing the nature of revolution itself. The Russian and Chinese revolutions occurred in agrarian societies. Although revolutions in the Third World were typically associated with Marxist ideologies and opposition to Western colonial rule, ethnic and religious conflicts often played a major role as well.[1] Unlike many anti-colonial independence struggles, the largely peaceful revolutions in Eastern Europe following the collapse of Communist rule led to democratization and liberal reforms (see Chapter 8 "States and Economies in Transition").

Studying the contexts, causes, and consequences of revolution is essential to understanding the political forces that shape today's world. We begin with a look at the incidence of revolution in the modern world.

revolution
A fundamental change in the rules and institutions that govern a society, often involving violent conflict in the form of mass action, insurrection, secession or civil war.

THE FREQUENCY OF REVOLUTIONS

Revolutions have occurred throughout human history, particularly during times of strong population expansion and rapid economic change.[2] Significant changes in governmental structure took place in many Greek city-states in the seventh and sixth centuries BCE, in Rome in the first century BCE, in the Islamic world in the eighth century CE, and in Europe, particularly from 1500 to 1650 and from 1750 to 1850.

In the twentieth century, revolutions occurred more frequently. In a sense, revolutions were part of a surge in national violence that marked most of the century. In the 1930s, the renowned Harvard sociologist Pitirim Sorokin studied "internal disturbances" in 11 political communities. In Western Europe alone, he was able to identify no fewer than 1,622 such disturbances in the post–World War I era, of which fully 70 percent "involved violence and bloodshed on a considerable scale."[3] Moreover, in each country studied, for every 5 years of relative peace Sorokin found 1 year of "significant social disturbance." He concluded that the twentieth century overall was the bloodiest and most turbulent period in history—and he made that judgment *before* World War II.

Subsequent events bore out his judgment. From 1945 to 1970, fully 40 of the approximately 100 developing countries witnessed at least one military takeover. Between 1943 and 1962, attempts to overthrow an existing government occurred in virtually every country in Latin America, in two-thirds of the countries of Asia, and in half the African countries that had gained independence.[4] Although the world has witnessed many revolutions, rebellions, and civil disturbances since the 1970s, the incidence of military coups has decreased in more recent decades. The *New York Times* reported that between 1946 and 1959, however, there were 1,200 separate instances of "internal war," including "civil wars, guerrilla wars, localized rioting, widely dispersed turmoil, organized and apparently unorganized terrorism, mutinies, and coups d'état."[5]

Not all revolutions are violent. In Eastern Europe, one country after another broke away from the Soviet Union in 1989, and most turned toward a market economy and parliamentary democracy. In all but a few instances—Romania, for example—these revolutions came about with a minimum of violence and bloodshed. In the former Czechoslovakia, it even came to be called the Velvet Revolution, because the changeover from communist dictatorship to constitutional government was so smooth. The newly independent Baltic republics of Estonia, Latvia, and Lithuania are also notable examples of peaceful mass revolution. In each, a process of political transformation was initiated without great upheaval, destruction of property, or loss of life.

MODERN REVOLUTIONS: TWO TRADITIONS

Although revolutions date to the slave revolts of antiquity, we can trace to the late eighteenth century the idea of modern revolution—the belief "that a nation's people, by concerted political struggle, could fundamentally transform the political order that governed their lives and, with it, the social and economic structure of society."[6] Modern revolutions possess a distinctive attribute: the use of the anger of the lower classes not merely to destroy the prevailing social order but also "to create a new and different one in which the traditional forms of oppression did not exist."[7] For this reason, they are usually "characterized by a set of emotion-laden utopian ideas—an expectation that the society is marching toward a profound transformation of values and structures, as well as personal behavior."[8]

Modern revolution, and its desire to establish a new, just, social order, usually is traced to the **French Revolution** of 1789. But the **American Revolution**, begun in 1776, provides another model. Both revolutions, among the most

French Revolution
(1789) Brought down the Bourbon monarchy in France in the name of *"liberté, egalité, et fraternité"* (liberty, equality, and fraternity); introduced the contagion of liberalism in a Europe still ruled by conservative, aristocratic, and royalist institutions; and ushered in the rule of Napoléon Bonaparte. Prelude to the First Republic in France and to the Napoleonic Wars.

American Revolution
(1775–1783) Also called the War of Independence and the Revolutionary War, this epoch-making event led to the end of British rule over the 13 American colonies and to the formation of the United States of America in 1787–1789; usually dated from the Declaration of Independence in 1776.

important political events of the modern age, influenced the destiny of generations to come. Both championed profoundly important political changes animated by visions of a new kind of political order. Yet, they differed dramatically in many other respects. As one astute observer contended,

> It is certainly indisputable that the world, when it contemplates the events of 1776 and after, is inclined to see the American Revolution as a French Revolution that never quite came off, whereas the Founding Fathers thought they had cause to regard the French Revolution as an American Revolution that had failed. Indeed, differing estimates of these two revolutions are definitive of one's political philosophy in the modern world: there are two conflicting conceptions of politics, in relation to the human condition, which are symbolized by these two revolutions. There is no question that the French Revolution is, in some crucial sense, the more "modern" of the two. There is a question, however, as to whether this is a good or bad thing.[9]

The American Revolution

There was no doubt in the minds of the Founders that the American War for Independence against the British Crown (King George III) was a revolution, or that signing the Declaration of Independence was an act of treason. Nor did they have any illusions about the grim fate that awaited them if the revolution failed. As Benjamin Franklin is reputed to have said, they needed to all hang together or they would hang separately.

In waging a war against England in the 1770s, the American colonists became the instigators of the modern world's first successful anti-colonial revolution. In time, the colonists' break with Great Britain became complete and irreparable. For that reason, it is tempting to say the American **Revolutionary War** created a model for later wars of national liberation. However, it differed decisively from subsequent revolutions prior to 1989.

Revolutionary War
The American War of Independence (1775–1783).

Historical Significance To understand the historical significance of the American Revolution, we must first examine the political opinions of its leaders. They saw the Revolutionary War as a special and unique experience. "From the very beginning," according to one authority, "it was believed by those who participated in it—on the western side of the Atlantic—to be quite a remarkable event, not merely because it was their revolution, but because it seemed to them to introduce a new phase in the political evolution of mankind, and therefore to be touched with universal significance."[10] The Founders were well acquainted with world history and with the writings of the great political philosophers, including Montesquieu, Locke, Rousseau, David Hume, and Voltaire.[11] Given this familiarity, they were not inclined to overestimate the value of new or experimental approaches to politics.

The revolutionaries of 1776 believed the divorce they demanded had universal meaning, and that the Declaration of Independence was the timeless expression of it. In other words, they perceived an intimate relationship between the

The "first blow for liberty" in the America's War for Independence was struck at the Battle of Lexington in April, 1775; the American Revolution was the world's first successful anticolonial uprising.

words (the "truths") they promulgated and the deeds they performed.[12] Thus, to discover what was truly revolutionary about the American Revolution, we first focus on what the revolutionaries wrote about government and then observe what they did about it.

Justification The clearest exposition of the American revolutionary credo can be found in the Declaration of Independence. In addition to proclaiming separation from Great Britain, the Declaration enunciated the reasons for it.

The British government, it asserted, had grievously violated the principles of good government. Following Locke's lead, Thomas Jefferson (the chief author) argued that those principles were twofold: government must conform to the will of the majority (according to the Declaration's precise language, such a government must be based on "the consent of the governed"), and it must protect the inalienable rights of all individuals to "Life, Liberty, and the pursuit of Happiness." These principles, in Jefferson's view, established the criteria by which to measure the legitimacy of all governments in all times and places. A good (or legitimate) government, in other words, draws its authority from the consent of the governed and acts to ensure the inalienable rights of all its citizens.

By making human rights the philosophical basis of good government, the Declaration departed significantly from past precedent and contemporary practice. Formerly, governments had come into existence to guarantee order, to build empires, to punish impiety, or to enforce obedience. Now, for the first time in history, a political regime dedicated itself unequivocally to the principle of securing popular rights and liberties.

It followed from the Declaration's principles that governments that repeatedly jeopardized rather than protected those rights forfeited their claim to rule. Having stated this conclusion in the Declaration, the colonists continued to wage their war for independence.

Although initially they desired only to be treated as equal British subjects, with the drafting of the Declaration they insisted on complete self-government.

Nor would just any government do; they wished ultimately to create a government consistent with the self-evident truths they had pronounced in the Declaration. And these truths, they believed, were applicable far beyond the boundaries of the thirteen colonies. Jefferson found *universal* meaning in the enduring words of the document he had drafted:

> May it be to the world, what I believe it will be (to some parts sooner, to others later, but finally to all), the signal of arousing men to burst the chains under which monkish ignorance and superstition had persuaded them to bind themselves and to assume the blessings and security of self-government.[13]

Social and Political Changes Jefferson's sentiments were expressed in language that ranks with the best revolutionary rhetoric of his or any other time; certainly, it stirred citizens to fight and die for the cause. Even so, it would be a mistake to view the American Revolution solely in the context of the fighting that ensued. While the historic battles raged, great social, economic, and religious changes took place. Restrictive inheritance laws, such as primogeniture and entail, were abolished; large British estates were confiscated and redistributed in smaller holdings; royal restrictions on land settlements were repealed; important steps to secure religious equality and separation of church and state were taken; and old families lost power, their places "taken by new leaders drawn from younger men, from the common people, and from the middle classes."[14]

Political changes also occurred, as every colony wrote a new constitution. Drafted in the heat of war, these constitutions perpetuated existing systems of local self-government, especially the executive branch, while protecting individual liberties. The concepts and principles incorporated in these documents were then reflected in the Articles of Confederation and, eventually, in the U.S. Constitution. It is impossible to overemphasize the importance of this preoccupation with the rule of law, or legality, and procedural correctness.

The *constitution-writing process* culminated in the creation of a government by majority rule, at a time when Europe was still largely subject to the autocratic rule of monarchs. Moreover, the colonists' steadfast concern for constitutionality helped defuse or prevent conspiracies and cabals that could have divided the new nation into many feuding political subdivisions.

"A Revolution of Sober Expectations" In retrospect, the American Revolution was marked by a "rare economy of violence when compared to other revolutions."[15] In comparison with later revolutionary conflicts (such as the French Revolution, the Russian Revolution, and the Spanish Civil War), civilian reprisals between insurrectionists and loyalists were mild. In addition, the leaders of the American Revolution were never purged or murdered, as so many instigators of later revolutions would be. To the contrary, the "military chief [Washington] became the first president of the Republic and retired at his own choice; the author of the Revolutionary Manifesto [Jefferson] was its first Secretary of State."[16]

What accounted for the unique orderliness of this revolution? Most important, the colonial leaders combined a Lockean attitude toward revolution with the pursuit of realistic, down-to-earth political goals. By "Lockean attitude," to which we will return later, we mean that, with few exceptions, the Founders regarded the revolution as a necessary evil. It was necessary because they knew of no other way of achieving independence from Great Britain, but it was evil insofar as it caused suffering, bloodshed, and devastation. The American Revolution remains unique precisely because it was not led by fanatics and zealots who embraced an inflexible ideology or who thought any means were appropriate to achieve their political ends. Rather, its leaders were contemplative individuals who continually questioned themselves (and one another) about the correctness of what they were doing.

Although there was no lack of enthusiasm on the part of the revolutionary leadership, "this enthusiasm was tempered by doubt, introspection, anxiety, and scepticism."[17] In short, the American Revolution never took its own goodness for granted. Its tempered revolutionary values were placed in the service of sober and clear-eyed goals. Essentially, what the colonial leaders wanted from the revolution was to separate from England and found a government on consent and respect for the rights and liberties of the people.

These objectives were ambitious but not unattainable, in contrast to the utopian aims of the French Revolution (see below). The intertwined concepts of self-government and the protection of citizens' rights had been evolving in the colonies at both the state and township levels in advance of the revolutionary conflict. Unlike later revolutionaries, the colonial leaders did not attempt to immediately institute something radically new and different. Understanding the dangers inherent in quixotic or utopian idealism, they knew that "the political pursuit of impossible dreams leads to terror and tyranny in the vain effort to actualize what cannot be."[18]

Far from being an event marked by such terror and tyranny, the American Revolution was, in the words of one authority, "a revolution of sober expectations."[19] Sobriety, moderation, and prudence were the watchwords of this revolution and the chief characteristics of the "well-ordered union" the Constitution would later ordain.

The French Revolution

The French Revolution was quite a different affair. For years, France had experienced growing political instability and popular dissatisfaction. Seeking to preserve the sharp class distinctions that marked French society, the aristocracy had repeatedly frustrated attempts at economic and political reform. Furthermore, the government had demonstrated a clear inability to cope with changing circumstances.

Even a skilled and intelligent monarch, which Louis XVI (1754–1793) certainly was not, would have found it difficult to overcome the liability of governmental institutions that were decentralized and hard to coordinate. By the late 1780s, the government faced increasing difficulties in raising taxes to pay off

Estates-General

Prior the French Revolution, a quasi-legislative body in France in which each of the three estates (clergy, nobility, and commoners) was represented; it convened in 1789 for the first time since 1614.

Bastille

At the time of the French Revolution (1789), the Bastille was the infamous royal prison in Paris; the mass storming of the Bastille on July 14, 1789, and the freeing of the prisoners constituted a direct attack against the monarchy and symbolized the end of an era in French history; the revolutionaries then used the guillotine against none other than the reigning Bourbon monarch, King Louis XVI, and his extravagant wife, Queen Marie Antoinette.

massive debt from earlier wars. Then, just at the wrong time for those in power, economic reversals occurred.

Although the economy had been growing, the fruits of growth were terribly maldistributed. Many urban poor and peasants faced crushing material deprivation rather than the promise of economic development. By 1789, eddies of discontent had swelled into a sea of dissension. Middle- and upper-class reformers demanded both political and social changes, including restrictions on class privileges and reform of the tax system. Some leaders wanted more radical changes, including the creation of a political order governed by the principles of popular sovereignty.

All these demands were put forward at the May 1789 meeting of the **Estates-General**, a giant parliament elected by broad male suffrage and divided into three estates, or houses, representing the clergy, nobility, and commoners. After considerable debate (and a good deal of turmoil), a majority of the delegates, led by the numerically preponderant Third (commoner) Estate, formed a popular National Assembly. In addition to asserting the right to approve or reject all taxation, the members of this body demanded an end to aristocratic privileges.

These actions constituted a direct attack on the monarchy. Louis XVI responded with predictable ineptitude, applying just enough force to incense his opponents. When he marshaled his troops in an effort to bar the National Assembly from meeting, the delegates promptly moved to a nearby indoor tennis court, where they resolved to draft a constitution. The king promised tax reforms later but refused to abolish the privileges of the aristocracy. At the same time, he deployed troops in strategic positions. Sporadic outbursts of violence, including the storming of the **Bastille**, followed swiftly, and Louis XVI, having lost control of the streets, was forced to accede to demands for a constitution.

The storming of the Bastille on July 14, 1789, constituted a direct attack against the monarchy. Louis XVI conceded too little too late, and a revolutionary tidal wave in the name of "liberty, equality, and fraternity" swept France.

©BRIDGEMAN-GIRAUDON/ART RESOURCE

An Ill-Fated Constitution Between 1789 and 1791, as the citizens of France awaited the unveiling of the new constitution, an egalitarian spirit swept the land. Aristocratic privileges were abolished, and church land was confiscated. A political document of fundamental importance, the **Declaration of the Rights of Man**, enshrined a slogan epitomizing the egalitarian spirit of the times: "liberty, equality, fraternity." The new constitution created a constitutional monarchy. No longer would Louis XVI rule autocratically according to divine right. Although the constitution placed the king at the head of the armed forces and charged him with responsibility for foreign affairs, it assigned most legislative powers to the National Constituent Assembly, which was given the power of the purse as well as the power to declare war. A new elective administration was also created, and voting laws were liberalized. Thus, a stunning democratization of French political and social life was achieved in an amazingly brief period. The king's almost unlimited power had been undermined and radical social reforms implemented.

The constitutional monarchy set up by the 1791 constitution lasted less than 1 year, during which time the nation foundered without effective political leadership. Naturally, Louis XVI despised the new government imposed on him. (At one point, he even tried to flee the country to join opponents of the new government, but he was caught and returned to Paris.) The constitution barred former members of the National Constituent Assembly from serving in the new legislature, which meant inexperienced lawmakers held sway. Additional problems arose when the newly elected local administration failed to perform efficiently and interests that had lost power, especially the Catholic Church and the aristocracy, began to oppose the new regime. A war with Austria and Prussia exacerbated existing difficulties, and expected economic improvements were not forthcoming. Persistent rumors of the king's imminent return to absolute power swirled through Paris, inspiring a widespread fear of counterrevolution that undermined the political optimism brought on by the reforms.

Declaration of the Rights of Man Enacted by the French National Assembly in August 1789, this brief manifesto was intended as the preamble to a liberal-democratic constitution to be written later; it affirmed the sovereign authority of the nation but limited that authority by recognizing individual rights to life, property, and security.

Robespierre and the Reign of Terror In the chaotic political and social environment of the early 1790s, events moved swiftly. Louis XVI was convicted of treason, deposed, and then beheaded in June 1793. A committee of political radicals intent on refashioning French society and unafraid to use violence took over the reins of government. The first priority of the new leader, Maximilien Robespierre (1758–1794), was to win the war against Austria and Prussia. In this atmosphere of external emergency, national unity at home was made paramount and all political opposition was considered treasonous. Then as now, political repression during times of war was common. But Robespierre was not satisfied simply to enforce national unity; he also wished to create a regime of virtue—to rebuild French society from the ground up, so to speak, by remaking the French citizenry in the image of moral perfection. According to one authority,

> Robespierre wanted a France where there should be neither rich nor poor, where men should not gamble, or get drunk, or commit adultery, cheat, or rob, or kill—where, in short, there would be neither

petty nor grand vices—a France ruled by upright and intelligent men elected by the universal suffrage of the people, men wholly without greed or love of office, and delightedly stepping down at yearly intervals to give place to their successors, a France at peace with herself and the world.[20]

However grandiose, Robespierre's utopian idealism was not merely a statement of what *ought* to be; for him, it represented a manifesto to be carried out with ardor and thoroughness. Determined to create a "new citizen," Robespierre could not countenance the goal of individual freedom or the individual pursuit of happiness, as the American revolutionaries had. He was committed to a "despotism of liberty" rather than a free society.

Institutionalizing virtue, however, was only one aspect of utopian idealism. Freedom from want, and even the promise of permanent abundance, became an important goal of Robespierre's revolution, waged in the name of the poor and oppressed against the greed and avarice of the oppressors.[21] Only through a policy motivated by compassion for the downtrodden, Robespierre believed, could a virtuous and contented citizenry emerge. Thus, the Biblical promise that "the meek shall inherit the earth" was an important part of his credo.

To advance virtue and end poverty in the shortest possible time, Robespierre proposed a sweeping reformulation of French life. Governmental institutions, legal arrangements, and social practices—everything was to be changed. Even a new calendar was proposed, as a symbol that a new era of history had dawned. The spirit of change was total, and heaven on earth was the ultimate goal. One observer has noted that the reigning spirit was that of "undiluted, enthusiastic, free floating messianism . . . satisfied with nothing less than a radical transformation of the human condition."[22]

But Robespierre and his compatriots soon discovered it was one thing to proclaim a new order and quite another to *keep* order. Policy disputes emerged as disillusionment reacted with unlimited expectations in a volatile mix. Active opposition to the new rulers began to spread.

Robespierre's response was to reinforce the regime of virtue with mass executions, which became known as the **Reign of Terror**. Executions by guillotine ordered by the Committee of Public Safety became commonplace, particularly in Paris. Originally aimed at active opponents, governmental violence soon gained a momentum of its own. It came to include people who shared Robespierre's vision but disagreed with his methods, and later, those merely suspected of dissenting became victims of the guillotine. Deep distrust enveloped those in power, as survivors feared for their safety. Eventually, collective fear led to the overthrow and execution of Robespierre himself. During his yearlong rule, some 40,000 people were summarily executed—an astonishing number in the eighteenth century.

Reign of Terror
During the French Revolution, Robespierre and his Committee of Public Safety arrested and mass executed thousands of French citizens deemed to be public enemies for the "crime" of opposing the revolution or daring to dissent.

The King Is Dead, Long Live the Emperor The results of the French Revolution are not easy to evaluate. Clearly, it did not achieve its desired ends. After Robespierre's fall, a corrupt and incompetent government known as the Directory assumed power. In 1799, that regime gave way to the dictatorship of

Napoléon Bonaparte, who managed to restore order and stability and crowned himself emperor in 1804. Under him, France tried to conquer all Europe in a series of ambitious wars that ultimately led to defeat and Napoléon's downfall.

Thus, no popular government followed on the heels of the French Revolution. After Napoléon's deposition, in fact, the monarchy was reinstituted. Many worthwhile and long-lasting changes did come about, however. For instance, the monarchy installed in 1815 was significantly limited in its powers. Important social and political reforms stemming from the revolutionary era were retained, and the government was more centralized and more efficient. Despite these changes, however, the restored monarchy stood in sharp contrast to the egalitarian vision of a new society that had inspired Robespierre and his followers.

The Two Revolutions Compared

If the American Revolution was a revolution of sober goals, the French Revolution was one of infinite expectations. In the beginning, the French revolutionaries believed everything was possible for the pure of heart. The extremists' goals were utopian, and to realize them they were forced to use extreme means, including terror. Incredibly, America's best-known radical, Thomas Paine, found himself in a French prison during the revolution because his politics were not sufficiently extreme. In the thirteen colonies, most of the revolutionaries were political moderates. In France, moderates were executed or imprisoned.

The American Revolution, with its more modest aims, managed to produce the first great example of republican government in the modern age. France had no such luck. Yet the many revolutionary movements of the twentieth century were influenced far more by the French than the American example.[23] It is understandable why the French Revolution—with its desire to eradicate poverty and its compassion for the oppressed—has fired the imagination of revolutionaries everywhere. But if concrete and lasting results are to be achieved, political ends must be realistic; otherwise, impossible dreams can turn into inescapable nightmares.

IS REVOLUTION EVER JUSTIFIED? BURKE, PAINE, AND LOCKE

"The tree of liberty must be refreshed from time to time with the blood of patriots and tyrants." These words were penned by Thomas Jefferson, who believed revolution was necessary to "refresh" democracy, as well as to establish it in the first place. But was he right? Is revolution more likely to improve the lot of the people or make things worse? British conservative Edmund Burke and American revolutionary Thomas Paine, Jefferson's contemporaries, engaged in a memorable debate over this very question during the early phase of the French Revolution. The pivotal issue was whether that revolution was really in the interest of the French people, in whose name it was waged, and, more generally, whether revolutions were beneficial or detrimental to society.

Burke's "Reflections"

The French Revolution inspired Edmund Burke (1729–1797) to write perhaps the most famous critique of revolution in the English language, *Reflections on the Revolution in France* (1790). Burke did not believe the French Revolution resulted from deep-seated economic and social forces. To his mind, the real revolutionaries were the philosophers who had expounded the subversive doctrine of rationalism and worshiped the god of science. By teaching that government existed to fulfill certain simple goals (for example, to secure individual rights), revolutionaries, Burke argued, created misleading impressions—most important, that radical change almost always brought great improvements. This way of thinking undercut what Burke believed were among the most important foundations of political society: religion and tradition.

Burke argued that dangerous political abstractions were at the heart of the French Revolution. By grossly oversimplifying politics and engendering unwarranted expectations at odds with French history and tradition, simplistic concepts such as "liberty, equality, fraternity" endangered the public order, on which all other political values and virtues ultimately rested. Good order, Burke noted, was the foundation of all good things.

The science of good government—how to run, maintain, or reform it—could not be mastered through philosophical speculations, Burke contended. He saw government as an "experimental science" whose practitioners needed the wisdom and insight born of experience. And experience, by its very nature, he argued,

Edmund Burke (1729–1797). Born in Dublin, Ireland, Burke is best known to the world as a British statesman and philosopher who abhorred revolution and advocated gradual change in order to conserve core values and institutions without which, he argued, societies risk descending into chaos and anarchy. "Our patience," Burke opined, "will achieve more than our force." Among his many quotable quotes this one is perhaps the most famous: "All that is necessary for the triumph of evil is that good men do nothing."

©HULTON ARCHIVE/GETTY IMAGES

could not be acquired overnight; rather, it was accumulated, nurtured, cherished, and above all transmitted from generation to generation. Burke's view implied a veneration of the past as well as a respect for age and achievement. Society, to his mind, was an intricate tapestry of laboriously handcrafted institutions possessing an inner logic and perpetuated by the force of habit, custom, and convention.

This sober view of government, and of human capacities and limitations, led Burke to stress the importance of pragmatism and prudence in politics. Prudence, he said, was the "first of all virtues." As for pragmatism, he maintained that given the complexity of humanity and society, no simple, all-embracing political formula could work the kind of profound changes promised by the French theorists.

Finally, Burke criticized the extreme impatience of those who glorified revolution. Arguing in favor of gradual and deliberate reform, he warned that unless political change occurred slowly and circumspectly, the main mass of the population would end up in worse straits than ever: "Time is required to produce that union of minds which alone can produce all the good we aim at. Our patience will achieve more than our force."[24]

By promising more than any political order can ever deliver and raising unrealistic expectations for some immediate utopian breakthrough, revolution may both dazzle the masses with visions of a bountiful (but unattainable) future and blind them to the wisdom of the past. In short, though politics can be understood as the "art of the possible," in the distorted mirror of revolution, it becomes the science of the impossible.

Paine's Rebuttal

Thomas Paine (1737–1809) attempted to refute Burke's view of revolution in his *Rights of Man*, written in two parts in February 1792 and addressed specifically to Burke. In defining the legitimacy of popular revolution, Paine stressed the many injustices perpetrated by the British monarchy on the American colonists. For him, tyranny and monarchy were as one. Monarchies, he declared, thrive on ignorance and are wrong in principle:[25]

> All hereditary government is in its nature tyranny. An heritable crown, or an heritable throne, or by what other fanciful name such things may be called, have no other significant explanation than that mankind are heritable property. To inherit a government, is to inherit the people, as if they were flocks and herds.[26]

In another passage, he wrote,

> When we survey the wretched condition of man under the monarchical and hereditary systems of government, dragged from his home by one power, or drived by another, and impoverished by taxes more than by enemies, it becomes evident that those systems are bad, and that a general revolution in the principle and construction of government is necessary.[27]

Thoma Paine (1737–1809): Said to be the best likeness of Paine, this engraving by William Sharp copied a portrait of George Romney; both artists were close friends of Paine's. Paine is best remembered for his ringing call to revolution in 1776 and his denunciation of monarchy in a pamphlet called *Common Sense*. Because this pamphlet inspired the American Revolution, Paine's place in history is secure, even though his role has often been overlooked in favor of iconic figures such as Thomas Jefferson, George Washington, John Adams, and Benjamin Franklin.

© BRIDGEMAN-GIRAUDON/ART RESOURCE

Paine cited numerous examples of royal injustice and corruption. The greatest, he believed, was denial of the people's right to choose their own government. It seemed obvious to him that people should in no way be bound by their ancestors' decisions. "Every age and generation must be free to act for itself, in all cases, as the ages and generations which preceded it. . . . The vanity and presumption of governing beyond the grave is the most ridiculous and insolent of all tyrannies."[28]

Paine saw revolution in France as emphatically just. In seeking to overthrow the monarchy, he contended, the French were merely exercising a fundamental right, which grew out of their equal, natural right to liberty. Paine possessed an almost religious faith in the essential goodness and wisdom of the people. This pushed him to conclude that when the French Revolution is compared with that of other countries, it becomes apparent "that *principles* and not *persons* were the meditated objects of destruction."[29]

Locke's Right to Revolt

While Burke abhorred popular revolution, Paine glorified it.[30] Roughly a century earlier, John Locke had taken a middle ground between their two extremes in his *Second Treatise of Government*. Locke began with the premise that to escape the inconveniences of anarchy in the state of nature, human beings consent to be governed. Consent formed the basis for both civil society and formal government, with government existing chiefly to protect the rights deemed essential to human life. Locke then raised this question: What happens if the government endangers the life, liberty, and property of its citizens? In such a case, he concluded, the government has exercised "force without right," and the people have the right to resist and defend themselves. In Locke's words,

> The end of Government is the good of Mankind, and which is *best for Mankind*, that the People should be always expos'd to the boundless will of Tyranny, or that the Rulers should be sometimes liable to be oppos'd, when they grow exorbitant in the use of their power, and imploy it for the destruction, and not the preservation of the Properties of their People?[31]

Locke did not glorify revolution; he cautioned that popular rebellion should not be launched on a mere impulse. People will accept individual errors and instances of misrule, he asserted, but not "a long train of Abuses, Prevarications, and Artifices."[32] Locke even suggested his doctrine of rebellion could serve as a deterrent to revolution, by causing governments to respect the people's rights. Whether or not governments choose to recognize the *right* of the people to revolt, he pointed out, the people *will* revolt against a wicked government: "If the majority of the people are persuaded in their Consciences, that the Laws, and with them their Estates, Liberties, and Lives are in danger, and perhaps their Religion, too, how they will be hindered from resisting illegal force used against them, I cannot tell. This is an Inconvenience, I confess that attends all Governments."[33]

In proclaiming the **right to revolution**, Locke may seem to have done little more than endorse what he saw as a fact of political life. But that does not diminish the importance of his doctrine of rebellion, which was itself revolutionary in the late seventeenth century. Even in England, where a few decades

right to revolution
John Locke's theory that the end of government is the good of society and that when government deprives people of natural rights to life, liberty, and property, it is asking for trouble. If it fails to mend its ways, it deserves to be overthrown.

© SNARK/ART RESOURCE

John Locke (1632–1704), English philosopher. Locke's magnum opus—*An Essay Concerning Human Understanding*—offers great insights into the limits of science and reason relative to what we can truly know about God, the natural order, and the self—and what we can never know. In Locke's view, the role of civil government is to preserve the life, health, liberty, and property of its subjects. When government fails, when it loses the consent of the majority, it naturally loses its legitimacy and risks overthrow. Locke's theory of revolution is not a prescription but rather a *description*—based on reasoned analysis of the conditions likely to give rise to rebellion.

earlier King Charles I had been beheaded, the question whether dynastic rulers had a divine right to wield the scepter and command the sword was still being debated. In most other European nation-states, monarchs took the doctrine of divine right for granted. Not surprisingly, these kings did not trifle with anything so mundane as the will of the people, for they believed their authority stemmed from the will of God.

Locke's theory of revolution helped sound the death knell for the doctrine of divine right. Revolution, Locke claimed, becomes necessary when government acts contrary to its reason for being. Does revolution ensure good government? Of course not. It may lead to anarchy followed by a worse form of tyranny. But, Locke argues, popular revolution does create the *possibility* of government based on respect for life, liberty, and property.

Thus, Locke made no utopian claims about the relationship between revolution and political revitalization. As he saw it, revolutions may stem from the desire for better government, but they cannot guarantee that happy result. New governments, he argued, are invariably new only in the sense that they supersede previous governments. Like Aristotle before him, Locke assumed the existence of a finite number of governmental forms. So revolutions could be considered not quests for new forms of government but quite literally revolutions *(revolvings)* from one enduring form of government to another.[34]

Revolution, thus defined, hardly seemed a romantic endeavor. In Locke's view, it meant the exchange of one imperfect form of government for another, perhaps less imperfect form; it invariably encompassed great changes in the larger society; and it almost always implied the use of political force and violence. The tendency of revolutions toward upheaval meant the process was to be feared, even if the goal was desirable. Locke's sober view of rebellion has not been eclipsed; as one leading contemporary scholar pointed out, "A period of terror and the emergence of coercive and aggressive regimes are the outcomes of revolutions."[35]

THE CAUSES OF REVOLUTION

Locke held that revolutions are necessary and proper when citizens simply cannot endure any more. But what specifically is it they cannot endure? What causes citizens to discard ingrained political habits and support revolution?

The Classical View

To many observers, history and common sense suggest that injustices perpetrated by government over a prolonged period foster the conditions in which the seeds of revolution can germinate. This explanation of the cause of revolution originated with Aristotle, who observed in the fourth century BCE that although sedition may spring from small occasions, it ordinarily does not turn on small issues. The spark that ignites a revolution, in other words, should not be confused with the underlying causes of revolt.

Under every political order, competition for honors and wealth may give rise to the popular belief that one or both have not been fairly distributed. In most cases, Aristotle postulated, revolutions are caused by the administration of unequal justice.

Aristotle's concern with the perennial tension between rich and poor in political life established a theme in Western political thought that has gained importance over time. James Madison, for example, declared in *The Federalist* No. 10 that the "most common and durable source of faction is the various and unequal distribution of property" and then set out to develop a theory of government that might lessen this common source of political tension.

A half century later, Karl Marx declared inequality in wealth to be the ultimate cause of all revolutions. According to Marx, revolution is synonymous with class warfare and invariably stems from pervasive injustice. As the economic distance between wealthy capitalists and impoverished workers increases, so does the possibility of revolution.

What persuades the ordinary individual to disregard the strong social pressure for conformity and participate in a revolutionary movement? Marx held that desperation caused by poverty and social alienation is the chief psychological spur to revolutionary action, and his explanation has been widely accepted in modern times. A few years before Marx outlined this position in *The Communist Manifesto* (1848), however, Alexis de Tocqueville offered an alternative view. In studying the French Revolution, Tocqueville observed, "It was precisely in those parts of France where there had been the most improvement that popular discontent ran the highest. There, economic and social improvement had taken place, and political pressure had lessened, but still there existed the greatest amount of unrest."[36]

Tocqueville concluded that economic improvement leads to revolution because once the people see that some improvement is possible, they inevitably yearn for more. No longer are they willing to put up with inconveniences and annoyances—only *real* improvement, *immediate* improvement, will satisfy them. Thus is the incentive for revolution born, he argued.

Modern Theories

The positions of Marx and Tocqueville seem incompatible, but in 1962, James C. Davies wrote a celebrated article suggesting "both ideas have explanatory and possibly predictive value, if they are juxtaposed and put in the proper time sequence."[37] Davies came to this provocative conclusion after careful study of Dorr's Rebellion of 1842, the Russian Revolution of 1917, and the Egyptian Revolution of 1952. After seeing a remarkably similar pattern of revolutionary development, he concluded that revolutions are most likely to erupt when conditions have been getting better for a prolonged period of time and then suddenly take a sharp turn for the worse.

Elaborating on Davies's thesis, two authorities later argued that the rates of earlier economic growth (and the speed of any economic decline) are especially significant factors. The higher the growth rate in per capita GNP prior to a revolutionary upheaval and "the sharper the reversal immediately prior to the revolution," they declared, "the greater the duration and violence of the revolution."[38] In other words, revolutions stem not so much from terrible suffering as from crushing disappointment. Intense discontent, bred by the failure to acquire the goods and experience the conditions of life to which people believe they are rightfully entitled, induces them to revolt.[39]

A pervasive sense of injustice is typically at the core of revolutionary mass movements. But great social and economic injustice does not *always* lead to revolution. Modern theorists have tried to identify *specific* causes that can become the incubator of revolution. One way to go about this kind of academic detective work is through methodical case studies.[40]

According to political scientists Ted Gurr and Jack Gladstone, a revolution is best conceptualized as an interactive process that continues over time.[41] The machinery of government breaks down in stages as political crises ensue; both influential citizens and government leaders become alienated.

Governmental leaders are increasingly perceived as inept: unable to exercise effective authority, incapable of stabilizing the economy, powerless to ensure domestic order, weak and irresolute in the face of external threats. Thus, nearly everyone (including the elites) comes to see the established government as illegitimate, and it loses its right to rule.[42] Precisely for these reasons, successful revolutionaries usually have the support of wealthy (possibly even aristocratic) patrons and are able to mobilize many discontented people as well.

Conceptualizing revolution as an interactive process is compatible with the traditional theory of revolution. It helps explain how injustice, or the perception of injustice, is at the root of revolution. Contemporary scholarship details how this process takes place. It examines the types of crises facing prerevolutionary states, the factors leading to a general loss of confidence in government, and the besieged governments' often hapless responses.

Invariably, societies on the verge of revolution face peril. Economic hardships can be particularly debilitating. Rapid population growth can slow or reverse economic growth and promote inequality. Ethnic, racial, or religious tensions may plunge a society into civil war, especially when one group grows or prospers at a faster rate than others. Rapid urbanization can create social problems, including inadequate housing, sanitation, and medical and educational services. Crime usually increases, particularly when there is a high percentage of alienated young males.[43]

Losing a war can be another prelude to revolution, because it is typically associated with severe economic hardships. In these circumstances, any government can lose its legitimacy in the eyes of the people.[44] Finally, upheavals in neighboring states can spill into and affect vulnerable governments in the vicinity.

Mounting economic, demographic, and political pressures in prerevolutionary nations can lead to criticism, lawlessness, riots, and acts of terrorism, forcing governments to act. If the bureaucracy includes officials from the landholding class, they may block or inhibit reforms designed to defuse a potentially revolutionary domestic crisis.[45] Or action may be inhibited by widespread internal corruption. But no government can tolerate long-term criticism, lawlessness, or acts of terrorism. If its response is unjust or inept, or if it fails to act at all, government risks losing the confidence of its supporters and becomes vulnerable to revolutionary demands.

Surprisingly, unpopular governments that equivocate or temporize in the face of a rebellion, rather than taking swift and decisive action to it in its infancy, are often at risk of being overthrown. In a study of the French Revolution, Tocqueville noted that French citizens took up arms against the government precisely when it began easing its crackdown. He concluded, "Generally speaking, the most perilous moment for a bad government is one when it seeks to mend its ways."[46]

Tocqueville believed that underlying this paradox (as well as his contention that reform, not repression, is the great accomplice of revolution) is a psychological truth:

> Patiently endured so long as it seemed beyond redress, a grievance comes to appear intolerable once the possibility of removing it crosses men's minds. . . . For the mere fact that certain abuses have been remedied draws attention to the others and now appears more galling; people may suffer less, but their sensibility is exacerbated.[47]

In sum, tyrants cannot afford to institute reforms because to do so would be to admit past injustices and activate "the rancor and cupidity of the populace."[48]

Modern studies provide some support for Tocqueville's observations. In a major analysis of the role of the armed forces in revolutionary episodes, one writer argued that revolution never succeeds when the armed forces remain loyal to the government in power and can be effectively employed.[49] When internal security measures are applied too late, too haphazardly, or as the last resort of a desperate government, there is a good chance that official acts of repression may only make matters worse. Apparently, governments that shrink from the systematic use of physical force in revolutionary situations run the greatest risk of being overthrown.

Some Tentative Conclusions

Theories of revolution abound, but despite many attempts, there is still no definitive *general theory* of revolution. Nonetheless, we can draw some generalizations based on historical and sociological evidence.

For revolutions to occur, charismatic leaders must be willing to take the deadly risks associated with overthrowing an established (often repressive) regime.[50] They need the support of others in high positions and those with technical skills. The right moment to win over the elites is when the government offends, threatens, or undermines them in some way. Elite alienation poses the greatest danger to the prerevolutionary government when it occurs within the armed forces.[51] If the generals and other senior military officers withdraw support from or turn against the ruler(s), it is almost always fatal for the government in power.

Revolutionary change is frequently organized from above. However, all such change depends on the new government's success in gaining or holding a mass following, which, in turn, often depends on the degree of citizen discontent prior to the revolutionary events. The causes of popular discontent can include "widespread dissatisfaction over economic conditions, especially among urban peoples; frustration about the lack of opportunities for real political participation, especially among young students and the middle classes; widespread anger about foreign interventions and official corruption; and rural hostility toward the predatory and repressive policies of urban-based regimes."[52] In short, it is the popular perception of injustice, whether true or false, that fuels the fires of all-out revolution in the modern era.

Finally, revolutions are not likely unless most or all of the factors we discussed earlier exist simultaneously. Thus, even a nation with economic and social problems would probably not be prone to revolution unless it came also to display the other elements of prerevolution, such as the existence of revolutionary leaders, strong elite and citizen support for radical action, and a general loss of public confidence in the existing government's capacity to rule. It is the coincidence of these factors that makes revolutions happen.

The Spanish philosopher José Ortega y Gasset (1883–1955) published his famous book *The Revolt of the Masses* in 1930, after the fascists had taken over Italy, shortly before Hitler's accession to power in Germany, and just about the time Stalin was consolidating his power in Soviet Russia.[53] Ortega y Gasset wrote with horror about "the accession of the masses to complete social power" and argued that "the masses, by definition, neither should nor can direct their own personal existence, and still less rule society in general, [which means] that actually Europe is suffering from the greatest general crisis that can afflict peoples, nations, and civilizations."[54]

The twentieth century witnessed the bloodiest mass movements in history. All failed. The words of Ortega y Gasset are particularly poignant in the light of the calamitous results of modern revolutions:

> As they say in the United States: "to be different is to be indecent." The mass crushes beneath it everything that is different, everything that is excellent, individual, qualified, and select. Anybody who is not like everybody, who does not think like everybody, runs the risk of being eliminated.[55]

At the same time, the modern history of revolution provides significant counterexamples. Ironically the United States would become the self-appointed global defender of the status quo after World War II, the archenemy of revolutionary movements in the Third World, where former colonies were fighting for independence as we ourselves had done nearly two centuries earlier. Those in the United States came to associate revolution with terror, totalitarianism, and tyrants. But when the Cold War finally drew to a close, the face of revolution suddenly changed, as dozens of dictatorships were swept away.

Today, democracies flourish where Communist police states ruled for nearly half a century, thanks to a series of stunning revolutions that occurred simultaneously with very little violence (with the exception of the Balkans). It was as if a massive earthquake shook Russia and Eastern Europe to their foundations but left nearly everything intact; instead of causing great death and destruction, it actually set the stage for a political and economic resurgence.

BOX 14.1 SPOTLIGHT ON   Nonviolent Revolution

History teaches that violent regimes are often the offspring of violent revolutions. Between World War I (1914–1918) and the end of the Cold War (1989–1992), Russia (Lenin and Stalin), Germany (Hitler), Italy (Mussolini), Spain (Franco), China (Mao Zedong), Cuba (Castro),

FIGURE 14.1   In 1989, the Communist regimes in Eastern Europe were overthrown in rapid succession and replaced by democratically elected governments. Except in Romania, this remarkable transformation was accomplished without bloodshed, and today, these emerging democracies belong to NATO and the European Union. EU members as of 2007 are highlighted in this figure.

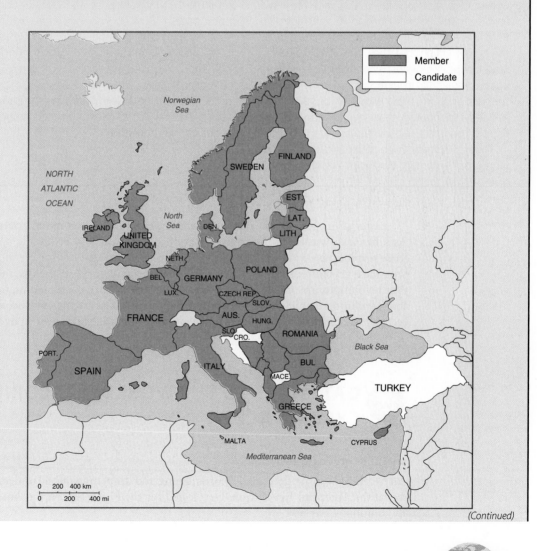

(Continued)

BOX 14.1 SPOTLIGHT ON   *(Continued)*

Cambodia (Pol Pot), Ethiopia (Mengistu), and Iran (Khomeini) endured bloody revolutions. Other notable revolutions after World War II occurred in Egypt (Nasser), Algeria (Ahmed Ben Bella), and Indonesia (Sukarno). All witnessed large-scale violence in varying degrees.

But the post-Cold War era teaches a different lesson. Before 1989, the Baltic states of Latvia, Lithuania, and Estonia were essentially Communist dictatorships ruled from Moscow. East Germany, Poland, Hungary, Czechoslovakia, Romania, and Bulgaria were not formally part of the Soviet Union, but they, too, were ruled by Soviet puppet regimes. When Hungary revolted against Soviet rule in 1956, the Red Army quelled the uprising. In 1968, Moscow brutally suppressed a spontaneous mass revolt known as the Prague Spring in Czechoslovakia.

Today, Hungary is an independent country with a parliamentary democracy, as are Poland and the Baltic states. East Germany has merged with the Federal Republic of Germany (West Germany). Czechoslovakia has split into two separate states, both democratically ruled. All are members of NATO and the EU. Romania and Bulgaria joined the EU in 2007 (see Figure 14.1). The political map of Europe in 2007 looks nothing like it did 20 years ago, thanks to a series of largely nonviolent revolutions that replaced one-party dictatorships with constitutional democracies.

As products of the twentieth century, we naturally associate political revolutions with turmoil and tragedy, rather than peace and progress. But the recent history of regime change in Eastern Europe (with the notable exception of the former Yugoslavia) shows that revolutions can be both peaceful and progressive.

Eastern Europe is not the only place where peaceful revolutions have occurred. Asia has also witnessed the transformation of political and economic systems (true revolutions) with relatively little violence. No one can say for certain how long these revolutions will endure or how far they will go. Nonetheless, the idea that revolutions are *always* violent or that they are *always* corrupted or, indeed, that revolution is inherently a bad thing is not sustained by the evidence of the recent past. Perhaps that is the most revolutionary change (and lesson) of all.

 **GATEWAYS TO THE WORLD: EXPLORING CYBERSPACE**

www.pbs.org/ktca/liberty

An excellent Website dedicated to broadening and deepening public understanding of the American Revolution. Developed for the PBS series on the American Revolution (*Liberty!*).

revolution.h-net.msu.edu

This is the companion site to the PBS site mentioned above.

userweb.port.ac.uk/~andressd/frlinks.htm

A rich source of links to many sites dealing with the French Revolution maintained by an academic expert in modern European history; includes a good chronology.

chnm.gmu.edu/revolution

This Website is an excellent research tool containing some 600 documents on the French Revolution.

http://www.marxists.org/history/ussr/events/revolution/

All about the October Revolution. Lots of information—eyewitness reports, first-hand accounts, glossary, and thumbnail biographies of key figures. Many links. Be sure to click on the Timeline of Events.

www.fordham.edu/halsall/mod/modsbook39.html

Many links to sites devoted to the Russian Revolution; part of Paul Halsall's Internet History Sourcebooks Project located at Fordham University.

news.bbc.co.uk/hi/english/static/special_report/1999/09/99/china_50/tiananmen.htm

The Web version of the BBC News special report on the Chinese Revolution, originally aired in 1999 on the fiftieth anniversary of the Maoist takeover.

http://www.state.gov/r/pa/ho/time/cwr/88312.htm

The U.S. government's official history of the Chinese Revolution of 1949. Also contains a link to a Web page on the Chinese Revolution of 1911.

http://www.miamiherald.com/video/?genre_id=4920

This site is presents the Cuban Revolution as seen through the eyes of Cuban refugees and exiles in Florida.

http://www.latinamericanstudies.org/cuban-revolution.htm

Website devoted to the Cuban Revolution, covering the years 1952 to 1958.

www.uoregon.edu/~caguirre/revol.html

This Website is devoted to "Internet Resources on Latin American Revolutions and Revolutionary Movements" created by Professor Carlos Aguirre, Department of History, University of Oregon.

SUMMARY

Revolution brings significant changes in the form of a nation's government. There are two basic revolutionary traditions, the American and the French. The American Revolution was more limited and sought more moderate goals. The French revolutionary leaders, unlike their more pragmatic American counterparts, sought complete and radical change in the social, political, and moral fabric of their country.

Whether revolution is desirable has been fiercely debated since the late eighteenth century, when Edmund Burke stressed its many dangers and Thomas Paine its many benefits. Earlier, John Locke had taken a moderate position, calling revolution necessary and justified when directed against an oppressive government.

The precise causes of revolution are difficult to isolate. Aristotle argued that injustice is at the root of popular rebellion. But what convinces the ordinary citizen to participate in a revolution? Karl Marx contended that worsening economic and social conditions lead to participation in revolutions. Alexis de Tocqueville asserted that improving conditions are to blame, for they cause individual hopes to outrun social reality. A modern view put forth by James C. Davies combined Marx's and Tocqueville's positions in arguing that revolutions are most likely to erupt when sharp economic or social reversals follow a period of rising expectations and moderate improvements. More recent studies characterize revolution as an ongoing process, reflecting a crisis of government's legitimacy.

Facing difficult economic, political, or social problems, governments often act ineptly or unjustly. When they lose the confidence of elites in society, the masses are mobilized as revolutionary leaders plan the government's overthrow and the creation of a new political order. Mass-movement revolutions have ultimately all failed, and in the process they have ironically victimized many innocent people.

KEY TERMS

revolution	Estates-General	Reign of Terror
French Revolution	Bastille	right to revolution
American Revolution	Declaration of the	
Revolutionary War	Rights of Man	

REVIEW QUESTIONS

1. In politics, what is the meaning of the word *revolution?* Have revolutions become more or less prevalent in the twentieth century in comparison with previous eras?
2. In what important respects were the American Revolution and the French Revolution similar? In what important respects did they differ?
3. In the debate over the desirability of revolution between Edmund Burke and Thomas Paine, what position did each take? What were Burke's chief arguments? How did Paine respond?
4. What was John Locke's view of revolution? Why did he assert the right of citizens to overthrow their government? In what sense does Locke occupy a middle ground between Paine and Burke?
5. According to Aristotle, what is the principal cause of revolution? How have modern social scientists sought to go beyond Aristotle's philosophical insights into revolution?

6. Has contemporary research shed any new light on the causes of revolution? If so, have any common elements arisen from recent theoretical research, or are the findings contradictory? What theories have been advanced to explain how and why individuals become sufficiently disenchanted to join a revolutionary movement?

RECOMMENDED READING

Ash, Timothy Garton. *The Magic Lantern: The Revolution of '89 Witnessed in Warsaw, Budapest, Berlin, and Prague.* New York: Vintage, 1993.

An excellent eyewitness account by a scholar who thinks like an intelligence analyst and writes like a journalist.

Barone, Michael. *Our First Revolution: The Remarkable British Upheaval That Inspired America's Founding Fathers.* New York: Crown, 2007.

The story of a relatively nonviolent change of government that occurred in England more than a century before the American Revolution and, according to Barone, whetted the American colonists' appetite for liberty and independence.

Brinton, Crane. *The Anatomy of Revolution.* Magnolia, MA: Peter Smith, 1990.

A classic study of revolution that contains valuable historical insights into the causes and signs of revolution.

Davies, James C. "Toward a Theory of Revolution." *American Sociological Review* (February 1962): 5–18.

An influential essay that contends that sudden economic reversals, not oppression, cause revolutions.

Fitzpatrick, Sheila. *The Russian Revolution.* New York: Oxford, 2008.

A very good short introduction by an established scholar in the field.

Foran, John. *Taking Power: On the Origins of Third World Revolutions.* New York: Cambridge, 2005.

The author analyzes the causes behind no fewer than thirty-six revolutions in the twentieth century, beginning with the Mexican Revolution in 1910.

Goldstone, Jack A., ed. *Revolutions: Theoretical, Comparative, and Historical Studies,* 3rd ed. Boulder, Colorado: Westview Press, 2007.

A good collection of readings, many of which examine specific revolutions.

Gurr, Ted. *Why Men Rebel.* Princeton, NJ: Princeton University Press, 1970.

Gurr argues that citizens' perceptions of relative deprivation cause revolution.

Hitchens, Christopher. *Thomas Paine's Rights of Man: A Biography.* New York: Atlantic Monthly Press, 2007.

Hitchens argues that the idea of America as we know it today was first hatched in the mind of Thomas Paine, whom Hitchens characterizes as one of history's greatest freedom fighters.

Kenney, Padraic. *A Carnival of Revolution: Central Europe 1989.* Princeton, NJ: Princeton University Press, 2003.

From the publisher: "This is the first history of the revolutions that toppled communism in Europe to look behind the scenes at the grassroots movements that made those revolutions happen."

Ortega y Gasset, José. *The Revolt of the Masses.* New York: Norton, 1993. (First published in 1930.)

Skocpol, Theda. *States and Social Revolutions: A Comparative Analysis of France, Russia, and China.* Cambridge: Cambridge University Press, 1979.

A thorough examination of why revolutions occur that emphasizes the importance of community structure and international pressure.

In November 2008, terrorists carried out a series of coordinated attacks against high-profile targets in Mumbai (formerly Bombay), India; the luxurious Taj Mahal Palace Hotel, shown on fire here, was the scene of a siege lasting several days. Politically and ideologically motivated violence perpetrated against civilian populations by extremist elements is a recurring problem in many parts of the world today.

Terrorism
Weapon of the Weak

In February 1993, a yellow Ryder rental van containing a 1,200-pound bomb exploded in the parking garage of the World Trade Center in New York City, blasting a 200-foot crater in the basement. More than a thousand people were injured, and six died. Shocked citizens struggled to grasp the idea that a devastating terrorist attack had taken place against a symbol of U.S. economic might and one of the largest and most famous buildings in the world.

Eight and a half years later, on September 11, 2001, the United States watched in horror as the World Trade Center towers were hit again, this time by hijacked commercial airliners loaded with highly volatile jet fuel. The towers burned for a short time and then imploded with an incredible force that rocked downtown Manhattan, killing thousands of people still trapped inside the towers, creating a firestorm of debris, and sending a huge cloud of smoke, dust, and ash skyward that lingered over the city like an eerie, foul-smelling pall for many days.

No one knew in 1993 whether the first World Trade Center bombing was an isolated act or a sign of things to come. Now we know the answer: Terrorist attacks in the United States and the European Union, and acts of terrorism perpetrated against U.S. citizens and Europeans, would become a grim reality in the coming decade (see Table 15.1).

Despite the shocking 9/11 attacks, several other regions of the world have suffered far more from terrorism than the United States has. Attacks have plagued many developing countries, particularly in Asia and Africa. In fact, terrorism is a fact of life in most of the Arab world, from North Africa to the Persian Gulf, as well as many countries in Central, South, and Southeast Asia, including Afghanistan, Pakistan, India, Sri Lanka, Indonesia, and the Philippines. Mexico and several South American countries, especially Peru and Colombia, have been targets of terrorism for many years. The European Union

Ground Zero—a scene of total devastation where the World Trade Center towers proudly stood before September 11, 2001.

©MARK LENNIHAN/AP PHOTO

TABLE 15.1   Terrorist Targets: The United States and Its Friends

April 18, 1983	Suicide bombing of U.S. embassy in Beirut kills 63.
October 23, 1983	Suicide truck bombing of Marine barracks in Beirut kills 241.
December 21, 1988	Pan Am flight 103 explodes over Lockerbie, Scotland, killing 270 people, including 11 on the ground.
February 26, 1993	Bomb in a van explodes beneath the World Trade Center in New York City, killing 6 and injuring more than 1,000.
March 12, 1993	13 coordinated bomb explosions in Mumbai (Bombay), India, kill 257 people and injure some 700.
June 23, 1993	Federal investigators break up a plot by Islamic radicals to bomb the United Nations and two Hudson River tunnels.
January 1995	Police in Manila arrest members of an Islamic terrorist group who are testing bombs allegedly to be used to down several U.S. airliners in midflight over the Pacific. The accused leader of the plot, Ramzi Ahmed Yousef, is later arrested in Pakistan and is also charged with having planned the 1993 World Trade Center bombing.
March 20, 1995	Members of Aum Shinrikyo release deadly sarin gas in the Tokyo subway in five coordinated attacks, killing 12, severely injuring 50, and causing temporary vision problems for many others.
April 19, 1995	A truck bomb destroys the federal building in Oklahoma City, Oklahoma, killing 168 and wounding more than 600. Two Americans are charged.
November 13, 1995	A car bomb explodes outside a U.S. Army training office in Riyadh, Saudi Arabia, killing 7, including 5 Americans, and wounding 60 others.
April 3, 1996	The FBI arrests Theodore J. Kaczynski, a Montana hermit, and accuses him of an 18-year series of bomb attacks carried out by the "Unabomber."
June 25, 1996	A truck bomb explodes outside an apartment complex in Dhahran, Saudi Arabia, killing 19 Americans and wounding hundreds more.
July 1, 1996	Federal agents arrest 12 members of the Viper Militia, a Phoenix, Arizona, group accused of plotting to blow up government buildings.
July 17, 1996	A pipe bomb explodes at a concert during the Summer Olympics in Atlanta, Georgia, killing 1 and wounding more than 100.
August 7, 1998	The U.S. embassies in Kenya and Tanzania are bombed, killing 224 people, mostly Kenyan passers-by in the capital of Nairobi.
August 15, 1998	A large car bomb explodes in the central shopping district of Omagh, Northern Ireland, killing 29 people and injuring 330.
September 8, 1999	Bombs explode in an apartment block in Moscow, Russia, killing 94 and injuring 152, part of a series of bombings over a 2-week period that altogether killed nearly 300 people.

(continued)

TABLE 15.1   (continued)

October 12, 2000	A speedboat bomb attack on the *USS Cole* in Aden, Yemen, kills 17.
September 11, 2001	Four commercial jet airliners are hijacked from East Coast airports: two are crashed into the World Trade Center towers; one is crashed into the Pentagon; and the fourth one crashes into a field in Pennsylvania. Thousands are killed or injured.
October 12, 2002	Bomb blast in a Bali resort, blamed on militant Islamic group linked to Osama bin Laden and al Qaeda, kills an estimated 202 people.
August 8, 2003	Car bomb at Jordanian embassy in Baghdad kills at least 11 people.
August 19, 2003	Terrorist bomb attack destroys UN headquarters in Iraqi capital of Baghdad, killing 22, including Sergio Vieira de Mello, the top UN envoy in Iraq.
November 15 and 20, 2003	Suicide bombers in Istanbul attack two synagogues, a British-based bank, and the British consulate, killing as many as 50 people and injuring more than 600.
March 11, 2004	Ten bombs explode at train stations in and around Madrid during morning rush hour, killing 198 and wounding many more in Spain's worst-ever terrorist incident.
July 7, 2005	A series of bombs is detonated in three crowded subway trains and aboard a London bus during peak rush hour, killing at least 191 people and injuring some 1,755.
July 11, 2006	Seven bomb blasts kill 209 people on the Suburban Railway in Mumbai (formerly Bombay), India; another 700 are injured.
June 30, 2007	In Scotland, one day after London police foiled a double car-bomb plot, a car smashes into Glasgow Airport terminal and bursts into flames, injuring several.
September 17, 2008	Al Qaeda in Yemen carries out attack on U.S. embassy in Sanaa, killing 18 people.
November 26–29, 2008	A wave of 10 coordinated bombing attacks in Mumbai kills at least 173 and injures over 300; allegedly carried out by Pakistani militants.

SOURCES: *Wall Street Journal*, July 29, 1996, p. A14; *The Economist*, September 15, 2001, p. 18; *Country Reports on Terrorism*, U.S. Department of State 2006, 2007, 2008; author's updates.

countries are not immune either. In the United Kingdom, Irish Republican Army (IRA) ultranationalists conducted a terrorist campaign against British control of Northern Ireland (also known as Ulster) starting in the late 1960s. In Spain, Basque separatists known as the ETA (Basque Homeland and Freedom) have conducted a long-running terrorist campaign against the Madrid government.

Given the prevalence of terrorism, no one can escape or ignore its effects. In July 2006, two Lebanese men living in Germany were arrested after home-made bombs hidden in suitcases were discovered on German trains. In June 2007, three German residents believed to be radical Islamists were arrested in Pakistan, allegedly en route to terrorist training camps in the border region between Pakistan and Afghanistan.[1] In June 2007, police thwarted an attempt to detonate two cars filled with explosives in London. The smuggling of biological and chemical weapons for sale on the black market poses an ever-present danger, as well. Even more recently, in May 2009, police in New York City arrested four ex-convicts allegedly engaged in a plot to blow up two synagogues in the Bronx and shoot down a military aircraft. Among the weapons they had locked away in a storage container: a surface-to-air missile.

Obviously, scenarios of terrorist plots to use weapons of mass destruction (WMD)—from anthrax to a "dirty" radiation bomb—cannot be dismissed lightly. At the same time, fear of terrorist attacks can be exploited by governments in order to silence opposition or erode constitutional rights—a danger hardly less threatening to liberty than terrorism itself.

WHAT IS TERRORISM?

Despite its prevalence, **terrorism** remains an elusive concept. Some definitions emphasize terrorism's use of violence in the service of politics. According to *Webster's New World Dictionary*, terrorism is "the use of force or threats to demoralize, intimidate, and subjugate, especially such use as the political weapon or policy." Another source defines terrorism as "the deliberate attack on innocent civilians for political purposes."[2] *Terrorism* has been defined in many ways, but most definitions take into account several factors, including violence, desire for publicity, political motive, and intimidation aimed at civilian populations.[3] As we will see later in the chapter, our definition of *terrorism* implies both a strategy and tactics (see Box 15.1).

Terrorism comes in many forms. Some experts attempt to designate terrorist activities according to whether they (1) are state controlled or directed or (2) involve nationals from more than one country (see Figure 15.1).

Thus, **state terrorism** exists when a government perpetrates terrorist tactics on its own citizens, such as occurred in Hitler's Germany. In contrast, **international terrorism**, sometimes called **state-sponsored terrorism**, exists when a government harbors international terrorists (as the Taliban government in Afghanistan did in the case of Osama bin Laden and the al Qaeda organization), finances international terrorist operations, or otherwise supports international terrorism *outside* its own borders. During the Cold War, the United States frequently accused the Soviet Union of underwriting anti-U.S. terrorist groups around the world with money and arms. The Soviet Union responded that the U.S. government did the same when it was in U.S. interests to do so. Iran, Libya, Sudan, Syria, North Korea, and Cuba have all been on the United States' list of suspected state sponsors of terrorism for many years. Afghanistan and Iraq were also on this list prior to the fall of the Taliban regime in Afghanistan in late 2001 and the invasion of Iraq in 2003. Libya is now off the list, since leader Muammar el-Qaddafi promised to scrap Libya's weapons research programs and open the country to international arms inspections in December 2003.

Domestic terrorism is practiced within a single country by terrorists with no ties to any government. The Tokyo subway sarin gas attacks in 1995, the Madrid commuter train bombings in 2004, and the Mumbai Suburban Railway

terrorism
Politically or ideologically motivated violence aimed at public officials, business elites, and civilian populations designed to sow fear and dissension, destabilize societies, undermine established authority, induce policy changes, or even overthrow the existing government.

state terrorism
Usually violent methods used by a government's security forces to intimidate and coerce its own people.

international terrorism
Terrorism that involves the governments, citizens, and interests of more than one country; terrorism that spills over into the international arena for whatever reason, whether state-sponsored or not.

state-sponsored terrorism
International terrorism that is aided and abetted by an established state; for example, Libya was linked to many terrorist acts against Western countries until Muammar el-Qaddafi made peace overtures in December 2003.

Box 15.1 FOCUS ON   Terrorism: Five Definitions

Terrorism, by nature, is difficult to define. Acts of terrorism conjure emotional responses in the victims (those hurt by the violence and those affected by the fear) as well as in the practitioners. Even the U.S. government cannot agree on one single definition. The adage "One man's terrorist is another man's freedom fighter" is still alive and well. Listed here are several definitions of terrorism.

- "Terrorism is the use or threatened use of force designed to bring about political change." —Brian Jenkins
- "Terrorism constitutes the illegitimate use of force to achieve a political objective when innocent people are targeted." —Walter Laqueur
- "Terrorism is the premeditated, deliberate, systematic murder, mayhem, and threatening of the innocent to create fear and intimidation in order to gain a political or tactical advantage, usually to influence an audience." —James M. Poland
- "Terrorism is the unlawful use or threat of violence against persons or property to further political or social objectives. It is usually intended to intimidate or coerce a government, individuals, or groups, or to modify their behavior or politics." —Vice President's Task Force, 1986
- "Terrorism is the unlawful use of force or violence against persons or property to intimidate or coerce a government, the civilian population, or any segment thereof, in furtherance of political or social objectives." —FBI Definition

SOURCE: http://www.terror.com

FIGURE 15.1   Classifying Terrorism

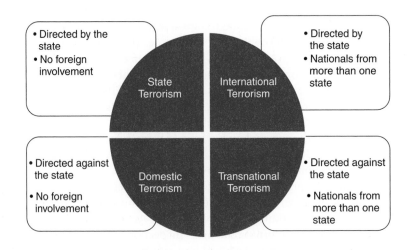

bombings in 2006 (refer back to Table 15.1) are examples of this type of terrorism. The aim of domestic terrorism is typically to strike fear and sow seeds of discord in society, and to discredit or overthrow existing political institutions. Unlike the United Kingdom, Spain, and several other Western countries, the United States had been largely exempt from such acts until the Oklahoma City federal office building bombing in 1995, the summer 1996 bombing at the Olympics in Atlanta, and numerous bombings of abortion clinics.

Transnational terrorism arises when terrorists or terrorist groups not backed by any established state and operating in different countries cooperate with each other, or when a single terrorist operates in more than one country. Examples include the bombing of the U.S. embassies in Kenya and Tanzania in 1998, the World Trade Center attacks in 1993 and 2001, and the London subway bombings in 2005 (refer to Table 15.1). The global nature of terrorism today has blurred the distinction between domestic and international forms of terrorism.

Domestic terrorism is by nature directed against the state. Groups seeking to regain control over their homelands, such as Basques in Spain, Irish Catholics in Northern Ireland, Tamils in Sri Lanka, Sikhs in India, and Chechens in Russia, are motivated by *nationalist or separatist* aims. This type of terrorism is usually confined to a specific nation, although its practitioners may receive arms, money, and support from other radical groups, private donors abroad, or even foreign governments.

Groups seeking to destabilize society in the name of some abstract belief are often inspired by *ideological* or *utopian* motives. The specific ideology is less important than the fanatical behavior it encourages. Terrorism is a hallmark of fascism and anarchism, as well as distorted versions of Marxism and Islam.[4] Examples include the Red Army Faction in Germany, the Red Brigades in Italy, the Shining Path in Peru, the Islamic Jihad in Egypt, Osama bin Laden's al Qaeda (the Base), and certain far-right militia groups in the United States. Often such groups also have international links.

Some terrorist organizations defy simple description. Hamas (Islamic Resistance Movement), for example, which has violently opposed peace negotiations between Israel and the Palestine Liberation Organization (PLO) over the future of the Israeli-occupied West Bank and Gaza Strip, won a surprise victory in the Palestinian parliamentary elections of January 2006. Hamas is a nationalist-separatist movement that seeks the destruction of Israel and the establishment of a radical Islamic state. But it is also motivated by ideology, namely a brand of Islamic fundamentalism that stresses militancy and jihad (holy war). Thus, classifying terrorist groups is useful as a tool of analysis, but not always easy.

domestic terrorism
A form of terrorism practiced within a country by people with no ties to any government.

transnational terrorism
Exists when terrorist groups in different countries cooperate or when a group's terrorist actions cross national boundaries.

THE ORIGINS OF TERRORISM

There is clearly a link between terrorism and religious fundamentalism; Islamic extremism is an obvious case in point. However, many terrorists are not religious, and few religious fundamentalists engage in acts of terrorism. Still, terrorism appears to have its roots in religion—specifically, obscure religious sects, the names of which have entered into our vernacular.[5]

The Thugs, a Hindu sect that was finally destroyed in the nineteenth century after having operated for many centuries in India, were highway ambushers who secretly killed thousands of other Hindus, apparently out of a perverse sense of religious duty. An extremist Jewish group known as the Zealots killed outsiders and helped provoke rebellion against pagan Rome in 66–73 CE. Beginning in the eleventh century, a Shi'ite Muslim sect, the Assassins, murdered outsiders in a campaign to "purify" Islam. Toward the end of the Middle Ages and later during the Reformation, violent sects arose within Christianity as well.[6]

However, modern-day revolutionary terror is usually traced to more secular roots, often to the French Revolution or the writings and deeds of nineteenth-century Russian anarchists.[7] Some experts contend the type of contemporary terrorism we see on the nightly news sprouted from seeds planted in the late 1960s; a few even cite 1968 as the year of its inception. The confluence of turbulent and unsettling events in the late 1960s included racial strife in the United States, an escalating conflict in Vietnam, and the Arab-Israeli Six Day War of 1967.

The year 1968 brought these glimpses of things to come:

- Three Palestinian terrorists seized an Israeli El Al airliner and forced its crew to fly the plane to Algeria, one of the first of many acts of air piracy.
- The Baader-Meinhof gang announced its presence in West Germany by torching a Frankfurt department store.
- Yasir Arafat, an advocate of armed struggle against Israel, became the leader of the PLO.
- The assassination of Martin Luther King, Jr. precipitated an outbreak of domestic violence in the United States by such groups as the Black Panthers and the Weathermen.[8]

At least three longer-term historical forces helped create a climate conducive to terrorism. First, direct military confrontations and conflicts became infinitely more dangerous in the nuclear age; what starts as a conventional war between, say, India and Pakistan might escalate out of control. Therefore, nations whose interests coincided with certain terrorist objectives sometimes provided moral, financial, or military support to these groups. In this manner, terrorism became a kind of proxy for violence between nations. Second, European colonialism had drawn to a close, leaving many newly formed nations to work out a host of unresolved territorial, national, and religious disputes. The result was a variety of low-intensity wars, many punctuated by terrorist activity, within and between these nations. Third, reverence for life and concern for the individual, common to democratic societies, combined with dramatic "up close and personal" worldwide television news coverage to make terrorist incidents major media events. Thus, the impact of such incidents—the publicity "payoff" from the terrorist's point of view—has been greatly magnified since the 1960s.

counterterrorism
Methods used to combat terrorism.

But it was in the 1970s that terrorism and **counterterrorism**, or opposing terrorism, became major growth industries. According to one estimate, the number of terrorist incidents multiplied ten-fold between 1971 and 1985.[9] The level of terrorism remained high throughout the 1980s (see Figure 15.2). Precise figures vary widely, however, reflecting, among other things, differences in how terrorism is defined. Risks International, for example, put the total number of

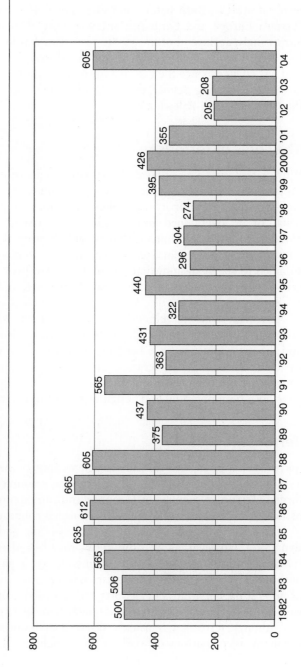

FIGURE 15.2   International Terrorist Attacks, 1982–2004. Note the peak according to the U.S. State Department figures occurred in the late 1990s, with spikes in 1991, 1995, and 2000. Note also that the raw data would indicate international terrorism steadily *declined* between 1987 and 2003. Obviously, either the statistics are misleading or the "war on terrorism" is predicated on a false premise. In truth, what this graph "proves" is that statistics alone can be easily manipulated or misinterpreted. This graph tells us little or nothing about the *method* used in identifying and counting terrorist attacks or the *intensity* of the attacks counted.

SOURCE: U.S. Department of State, Office of the Coordinator of Counterterrorism, *Patterns of Global Terrorism*, http://www.state.gove/s/ct/rls/crt/2003/33777.htm and http://www.johnstonsarchive.net/terrorism/intlterror.html.

terrorist incidents in 1985 at slightly more than 3,000, while the U.S. government conservatively counted fewer than one-fourth that number.[10]

In any case, terrorism rose sharply in the 1970s and 1980s and became a serious threat to the U.S. "homeland" in the 1990s, culminating in the 9/11 terrorist attacks. Both before and after 2001, terrorism plagued countries in Western Europe and Latin America far more than it did the United States. Surprisingly, at the end of the 1990s, terrorism was less common in the Middle East than in any other region of the world *except* North America. However, that has changed since the U.S.-led invasion of Iraq in 2003 and the renewal of hostilities including deliberate attacks on civilian populations *by both sides* in the ongoing Israeli-Palestinian war.

The Logic of Terrorism

Why do terrorists act as they do? Terrorist acts are often designed to undermine support and confidence in the existing government by creating a climate of fear and uncertainty. Terrorists use violence as a form of psychological warfare on behalf of an "overvalued idea" or cause. Terrorists are fiercely anti-status quo and despair of peaceful methods; they seek to bring about change or chaos, the latter either as an end in itself or as a prelude to change. They often aim not so much to spark an immediate revolution as to provoke the government into acts of repression, to make it look weak or inept, and to prepare the way for revolution.

Terrorism strikes at vulnerable societies, not necessarily unjust ones. Indeed, one expert on terrorism noted, "Societies with the least political participation and the most injustice have been the most free from terrorism in our time."[11] By logical extension, democratic societies like the United States and the United Kingdom, with long traditions of respect for civil rights and the rule of law, have both been potential and actual targets of terrorist attacks.

Terrorist Tactics

Terrorism has often been described as the weapon of the weak against the strong. Typically, individuals or tiny groups lacking resources act against defenseless targets. Terrorism requires little money and can be funded by actions normally associated with common crime, such as armed robbery and drug trafficking.

Terrorists' weapons of choice are often crude and cheap (small arms and dynamite). However, as we now know, they can also be highly sophisticated (passenger airplanes used as guided missiles or a particularly lethal form of anthrax). Even before 9/11, terrorism had become a worldwide phenomenon, as news stories of attacks in airports and crowded train terminals, kidnappings of wealthy business executives, and hijacked airliners grew all too familiar.

Although terrorism is usually directed at innocents, it has been blamed for many assassinations of world leaders, including Italy's former prime minister Aldo Moro (1978), Queen Elizabeth's cousin, Lord Louis Mountbatten (1979), Egyptian president Anwar al-Sadat (1981), Indian prime minister Indira

Gandhi (1984), her son the former prime minister Rajiv Gandhi (1991), and most recently, Pakistan's former prime minister Benazir Bhutto (December 27, 2007). Terrorists have also attempted to assassinate Pope John Paul II (1981), former British prime minister Margaret Thatcher (1984), and her successor, John Major (1991). It is possible the White House was one of the intended targets of the September 11 attacks. If so, the conspirators probably hoped to kill the U.S. president.

The relationship between terrorist tactics and objectives is revealed in the Brazilian terrorist Carlos Marighella's chilling but incisive *Mini-Manual of the Urban Guerrilla*, a 48-page do-it-yourself handbook for aspiring terrorists and revolutionaries. It spells out how to blow up bridges, raise money through kidnappings and bank robberies, and plan the "physical liquidation" of enemies. The book offers a range of practical advice: learn to drive a car, pilot a plane, sail a boat; be a mechanic or radio technician; keep physically fit; learn photography and chemistry; acquire "a perfect knowledge of calligraphy"; study pharmacology, nursing, or medicine. It also stresses the need to "shoot first" and aim straight. In general, terrorists champion violence above all other forms of political activity. Furthermore, revolutionaries such as Marighella glorify violence, not as a necessary evil but as a positive form of liberation and creativity.[12] According to Marighella, terrorism succeeds when strategies and tactics come together:

> The government has little or no alternative except to intensify repression. The police roundups, house searches, arrests of innocent people, make life in the city unbearable. [The government appears] unjust, incapable of solving problems. . . . The political situation is transformed into a military situation, in which the militarists appear more and more responsible for errors and violence. . . . Pacifists and right-wing opportunists. . . . join hands and beg the hangmen for elections.[13]

Rejecting the "so-called political solution," the urban guerrilla must become more aggressive and violent, resorting without mercy to sabotage, terrorism, expropriations, assaults, kidnappings, and executions, heightening the disastrous situation in which the government must act.[14]

An urban guerrilla group called the Tupamaros terrorized Uruguay from 1963 to 1972, seeking to overthrow the government. The Tupamaros became the very embodiment of Marighella's revolutionary principles and have since served as an inspiration for terrorists and extremists throughout the world. Significantly, the insurgency in Uruguay ended only after most of the guerrillas were murdered in a brutal government crackdown. Today, Uruguay is a peaceful, democratic country.

Acts of Terrorism Versus Acts of War

The al Qaeda operatives who hijacked four commercial airliners on September 11, 2001 were carrying out a terrorist act *by definition*, and an act of war *only by inference or interpretation*. When Japanese kamikaze pilots flew fighter planes into U.S. warships anchored in Pearl Harbor on December 7, 1941 and sank most of the Pacific fleet, it was an act of war first and an act of terror only incidentally, if at all. In war-fighting jargon, this attack was a classic example of the preemptive strike. However heinous and treacherous it appeared to U.S. citizens at the time (and still does), it was extremely successful as a single strategic event.*

The 9/11 attacks and Pearl Harbor are often compared, but the comparison is inapt. Pearl Harbor was the result of a decision made by the government and military high command of an established state with which the United States had diplomatic relations at the time. It was without question an act of war. Moreover, it was directed exclusively against *military* targets—the kamikaze pilots could have hit civilian targets in Hawaii but did not. Finally, the attacks were designed not to overthrow or destabilize the U.S. government or any other government but rather to cripple U.S. naval power in the Pacific and thus forestall U.S. interference with Japan's imperialist designs in Asia.

The 9/11 attacks contrast sharply on all three points. They were not undertaken by an established state (although Afghanistan harbored al Qaeda network's top leaders and many of its fighters); they were directed mainly at civilians who had nothing to do with making U.S. foreign policy or with the armed forces; and they were clearly aimed at exposing the vulnerability of the United States, embarrassing the government, and undermining U.S. economic might, while tarnishing the Pentagon's image both at home and abroad. Even more to the point, these attacks were designed to rally support for bin Laden's extreme brand of Islamism and lead to the eventual toppling of "apostate" governments in the Arab world (including bin Laden's native Saudi Arabia).

Illegal Enemy Combatants

The very ambiguity of the status of terrorists in domestic and international law raises questions about how captured suspected terrorists ought to be treated. Are they prisoners of war, criminals, or neither? If they are neither, it means they exist in a legal limbo and can be denied even the most basic rights. In theory, they can be tortured or killed in captivity and the world would never know. They can be imprisoned for months or even years without being charged or having legal counsel or contact with family members—this is, in fact, the status of an unknown number of suspected terrorists taken captive by U.S. military forces in Afghanistan, Iraq, and elsewhere after 9/11.[15]

The Bush administration declared these captives were neither common criminals nor prisoners of war (POWs), but rather "illegal combatants"—a category tailor-made for the war on terror but widely rejected by other governments, as well as by experts on international law. Many suspected al Qaeda terrorists rounded up in Afghanistan (about 650 according to published reports) were taken to the U.S. naval base at Guantánamo Bay (also known as "Gitmo") in

---

* Of course, in the perspective of the entire war, it takes on a very different aspect, in that it galvanized the U.S. people like nothing else could have and gave President Roosevelt the green light to ask Congress for a declaration of war on Japan and Germany.

Cuba, where they were to be kept indefinitely in a maximum-security facility off limits to the press and public.

The constitutionality of indefinite detention without trial was finally challenged in June 2007 in the case of Ali al-Marri, a student at Bradley University who was initially arrested and jailed on charges having nothing to do with terrorism. Al Marri was eventually classified as an illegal combatant and transferred to the Naval Consolidated Brig in Charleston, South Carolina. In June 2007, a federal appeals court ruled that U.S. residents cannot be incarcerated indefinitely as enemy combatants without being charged. "Put simply, the Constitution does not allow the President to order the military to seize civilians residing within the United States and then detain them indefinitely without criminal process, and this is so even if he calls them 'enemy combatants,'" the court said. The same federal appeals court held a rehearing of the ruling and reversed itself 5 to 4. But in March 2009, the Supreme Court erased that ruling after al-Marri was indicted on federal criminal charges in Illinois, thus belatedly granting his constitutional right to a trial by jury in a civilian court. Al-Marri entered a guilty plea to one count of conspiracy involving a foreign terrorist organization.[16]

The concept of "illegal combatants" does not exist anywhere in international law and did not exist in U.S. public policy or jurisprudence before 9/11. President Bush insisted it was a necessary tool in the war on terror; President Obama demurred on grounds that it cannot be squared with our principles or the Constitution. In the ongoing search for a middle ground between security and liberty, the al-Marri case represents a triumph of the Obama approach over the Bush approach. Upon taking office in January 2009, President Obama announced his intention to close the notorious "Gitmo" detention center.

Characteristics of Terrorist Groups

Most terrorist groups are short lived, operate locally, and get very little publicity. Although our national news media covers only a few, hundreds of identifiable terrorist groups exist worldwide.[17] They tend to be small and tight-knit, seldom numbering more than 100 members and usually fewer than several dozen. Many of the most notorious are found in the Middle East and associated with Islamic fundamentalism—the Abu Nidal Organization, al Qaeda, Islamic Jihad, Hamas, and Hezbollah (Party of God) are five contemporary examples. Because they are often ethnically and politically homogeneous, with members who are close friends or even relatives, terrorist cells are extremely difficult to penetrate or monitor, frequently confounding the best efforts of intelligence agencies.

As the world learned after the release of the fourth post-9/11 bin Laden videotape in mid-December 2001, al Qaeda operates on a need-to-know basis, closely guarding and compartmentalizing information within its own ranks, much like official intelligence services do. This emphasis on secrecy is essential for the success and survival of terrorist groups and networks, especially under greatly heightened security in the United States, Europe, the Arab world, and elsewhere.

Osama bin Laden, the wealthy Saudi mastermind behind a series of terrorist attacks on U.S. targets that culminated in the destruction of the World Trade Center.

©AFP/GETTY IMAGES

Even so, the life span of most terrorist groups is only about 5 to 10 years. By the same token, the leaders of terrorist groups tend to come and go. However, there are exceptions—two of the most notorious being Abu Nidal, who masterminded countless terrorist acts (including airport massacres in Rome and Vienna) for three decades until he was murdered in Baghdad in 2002, reportedly on direct orders from Saddam Hussein; and Osama bin Laden, founder of al Qaeda and the prime mover behind the 9/11 attacks. Finally, terrorist groups seldom operate from a fixed location. Although the perpetrators of the 9/11 attacks were exceptions, terrorists often have relatively little training, use unsophisticated equipment, and acquire the "tools of the trade"—some of which could be purchased at any hardware store—by theft.

Nightmare in North Africa: Algeria

In Algeria, the line between Islamic fundamentalism and terrorism—or between revolution and civil war—was difficult to discern in the 1990s. Algeria most clearly exhibits tendencies seen in other Arab nations such as Egypt and Saudi Arabia, where terrorism has become a tactic of Islamic extremist groups seeking to overthrow established secular governments in the region. Few stories about Algeria's horrific internecine war appeared in the U.S. press, and even today, few in the United States are aware of what happened there.

Algeria gained its independence from France in 1962 after a long, violent revolutionary struggle. For most of the next 30 years, pro-Marxist military strongmen ruled. Eventually, however, a core of Muslim fundamentalists became dangerously discontented. From this disquiet emerged the political organization Islamic Salvation Front (FIS). Later, when Algeria's first multiparty elections were held in 1991, the FIS gained a dazzling first-round victory. However, in 1992, the military simply canceled the second round of elections and installed a new president. This cynical act radicalized the FIS and prompted it to go underground. Even worse, it split the armed Islamist movement in Algeria and gave the most extreme jihadist elements—advocates of all-out terrorism—the upper hand. At the end of 1992, the Armed Islamic Group (GIA) emerged as a murderous alternative to the somewhat less violent and uncompromising FIS.

Algeria's terrorist nightmare began with GIA attacks primarily on the police, security forces, and government officials. Soon the terrorists began targeting other groups as well. In 1993 and 1994, there were dozens of attacks on opposition groups, foreigners, intellectuals, journalists, and other civilians. Between 1995 and 1998, only about 25 percent of the attacks were directed against security forces and government officials; the rest struck at civilians. Schools and school employees were among the favorite targets.

As the strategy changed to targeting mainly civilians, the insurgents' tactics changed as well. In 1996, there were more bombings than assassinations, violent clashes with security forces, and organized armed attacks. After the mid-1990s, the bombings increasingly targeted markets, cinemas, and restaurants as well as schools. According to one Middle East authority on the Algerian Islamist movement,

> Violence reached its ultimate level of cruelty in a series of massacres that began at the end of 1996. At least 67 massacres took place between November 1996 and July 1999, but most . . . took place in 1997 (42 massacres). . . . These massacres involved militants armed with guns, crude bombs, knives, and axes descending on villages at night to kill their inhabitants, often by hacking them to death and slitting their throats. Other atrocities involved fake security checkpoints set up by militants to identify specific targets—e.g., state employees and men with conscription papers.[18]

The government countered with lethal force. In November 1996, constitutional amendments that appeared to move Algeria toward a limited democracy were popularly ratified. The main aim, however, was to curtail radical Islamic groups and ban all political parties based on language or religion, while retaining preponderate power in the executive branch. Thus, during the June 1997 elections, the FIS and similar groups could not run candidates and could only urge citizens not to vote.

The FIS condemned the new constitution and continued to struggle against the regime until September 1997, when its armed wing, the Islamic Salvation Army (AIS), declared a cease-fire. But it was the vicious bands of zealots and thugs that comprised the GIA, not the AIS, that had carried out most of the bloody massacres. Not surprisingly, the hard-line "eradicators" in the government favored finding and killing the terrorists rather than trying to negotiate with them. This stance was not unreasonable given the fact that the GIA had shown no proclivity toward compromise.

The election of a new president in 1999 broke the ice. The government released some political prisoners and pushed through the Law of Civil

Reconciliation, extending amnesty to rebels who had not committed atrocities. The AIS, which benefited from a general amnesty due to its 1997 ceasefire, began disbanding its militia under state supervision at the end of 1999. Thousands of AIS rebels took advantage of the general amnesty granted by the regime; at the beginning of 2000, even some GIA militias began declaring they would abide by the cease-fire.

Nevertheless, terrorist acts still take place in Algeria, although less frequently than in the bloody years between 1994 and 1998. One of the main terrorist groups operating in Algeria today is al Qaeda in the Islamic Maghreb (AQIM). In 2008, dozens of suicide bombings and other terrorist attacks targeted police, foreigners, government employees, and civilians. Nonetheless, there was a marked decrease in the number of attacks compared with 2007. Algerian security forces reportedly killed, wounded, or arrested about 1,000 terrorists in 2008.

Amnesty International called Algeria the most violent country in the Middle East at the end of the 1990s. The proximate cause of the violence was the military's illegal cancellation of a national election in 1992, but the roots of Algeria's nightmare run deep in social and economic failure. Despite its extensive oil and natural gas reserves, its people are overwhelmingly poor. Unemployment hovers around 25 percent. Nearly one-third of the population is under 15 years of age. High unemployment hits youth the hardest, which may, in part, explain why terrorists and revolutionaries are disproportionately young. Meanwhile, tensions based on ethnic and linguistic divisions persist. Most notably, Berbers are a sizable minority who feel alienated and powerless, a feeling intensified when Algeria moved to make Arabic its sole official language. Thus, terrorists in Algeria continue to find fertile ground for fresh recruits.

TERRORIST OR FREEDOM FIGHTER?

The terrorism that ravaged Algerian society in the 1990s is hard for people living normal lives to comprehend. Who are the perpetrators of these despicable acts? How do they differ from common criminals, guerrilla fighters, and revolutionaries? Why is terrorism any different from other forms of violence?

Official U.S. policy treats terrorism as an illegal *political* phenomenon. This approach stresses the illegitimacy of terrorism and advocates combating it with swift punishment and due vigilance. Critics (including some European countries and NATO allies) focus on the *socioeconomic* causes of the problem. These divergent views point to quite different policy responses, including targeted programs of trade, aid, and investment designed to alleviate misery, hunger, and disease in poverty-stricken, violence-prone countries and regions, as well as diplomacy that does not exclude talking to regimes and dictators we despise.

Policy differences aside, terrorists are criminals, though by no means ordinary ones. Killing and kidnapping, robbing banks, and hijacking airplanes are heinous crimes, no matter who perpetrates them or why; they become terrorist acts when the *motive* is political. When a serial killer is on the loose in a community, the victims are typically innocent people, but psychopaths are not motivated by religion or ideology. Sometimes the line is blurred, as in the case of narcoterrorists—armed rebels in Colombia associated with powerful drug lords or drug traffickers in Mexico and who use terrorist tactics to intimidate the public, press, and police. In 2008, some 5,700 Mexicans were killed in drug-related violence. In January 2009, drug traffickers staged a grenade attack on Mexico's top TV network, Televisa, during the nightly news broadcast.[19]

If terrorists are not ordinary criminals, neither are they ordinary guerrillas or freedom fighters. Guerrillas often constitute the armed wing of a revolutionary movement or party—Mao's Red Army is one well-known historical example. Guerrilla forces sometimes commit atrocities against civilians (as do soldiers in uniform), but most insurgent violence is directed at the security forces and government. By contrast, terrorists target civilians and noncombatants, as well as police and security forces—a strategy designed to sow the seeds of fear and doubt so people will not cooperate with the police and military, and to show people the government cannot protect them.

Certainly, many revolutionaries in the twentieth century have resorted to terror—both before and after taking power. But, unlike terrorists, revolutionaries seek to overthrow the government *in existing circumstances*, rather than trying to precipitate a political and social crisis by *changing* the circumstances. To that end, revolutionaries attempt to build a subversive party; infiltrate the government, the police, and the military; spread propaganda; agitate among trade unions; recruit and indoctrinate the young; and incite strikes, riots, and street demonstrations. Terrorism in the hands of revolutionaries is a tactic, not a strategy; in the hands of terrorists, terror is both a tactic *and* a strategy. Terrorists often appear to share the view of Émile Henry, a French anarchist who, when charged with throwing a bomb in a Paris café in 1894, replied, "No one is innocent."

TERRORISM AND SOCIETY

Europeans abhor terrorism as much as Americans do, but they tend to sympathize with the social classes or ethnic communities from which terrorists often arise. In sharp contrast to the United States' pro-Israeli stance, most European governments are openly critical of Israeli policy toward the Palestinians. The best way to defeat terrorism, in their view, is to ameliorate its underlying causes—injustice, despair, and hopelessness. To European critics, Israeli policy exacerbates these conditions and plays into the hands of extremists.

Even where Middle Eastern governments suppress extreme Islamist groups, many people secretly sympathize with them. In Palestine, sympathy with groups like Hamas and Hezbollah is widespread and hardly a secret. Many Arabs admit that throughout the Arab world, people expressed admiration for Osama bin Laden. Indeed, in some Arab countries, Osama has reportedly become one of the most popular names for baby boys.

To be sure, any comprehensive theory of terrorism in today's world must take account of its social context, including the dehumanizing effects of life in refugee camps or ghettos, youth unemployment, and the Western intrusion—first colonization and now globalization. People unable to cope with these stresses react in different ways. Some turn to crime, others to alcohol or drugs, and some drop out. A few become terrorists. Of course, not all terrorists are products of poverty. Many are well educated and come from relatively privileged backgrounds; Osama bin Laden was born into a fabulously wealthy family in Saudi Arabia.

Why youths decide to become martyrs is unclear. Perhaps it is from a sense of hopelessness (nothing to lose) or religious zeal, perhaps from idealism or because they want to be a hero in the eyes of friends and family.

Youthful Recruits

Occasionally young females become suicide bombers, especially in the Middle East. The Shi'ite suicide bomber who drove her explosives-packed Peugeot into an Israeli Army convoy in southern Lebanon in 1985 was 16 years old. But most terrorists are male, single, and young.[20] The Jordanian who tried to assassinate a United Arab Emirates diplomat in Rome in 1984 was 22. The oldest of the four Palestinian terrorists who hijacked a Mediterranean cruise ship (the *Achille Lauro*) carrying 400 passengers in October 1985 was 23; the youngest, 19.

Research puts the median age of terrorists between 22 and 23 years. Twelve- and 14-year-old terrorists have been arrested in Northern Ireland; 14- and 15-year-old children are recruited by Arab and Iranian groups, sometimes for particularly dangerous missions.[21] A German psychologist who interviewed captured members of the Red Army Faction noted elements of an "adolescent crisis" among terrorists, while an expert on the Provisional Irish Republican Army (IRA) observed a "terrorist tradition" at work in some countries where "whole families pass on to their children that [terrorism] is the way you struggle for your rights."[22]

Eric Hoffer touched on the susceptibility of certain youths to fanatical causes in *The True Believer*. He placed them in a group he called "misfits," a category he further broke down into temporary and permanent. Hoffer wrote,

> Adolescent youth, unemployed college graduates, veterans, new immigrants, and the like are of this category. They are dissatisfied and haunted by the fear that their best years will be wasted before they reach their goal.[23]

At the same time, although they tend to be "receptive to the preaching of a proselytizing movement," Hoffer argued that they "do not always make staunch converts."

If the grievances that give rise to terrorism were removed, would there be no terrorists? Possibly, and yet there are many societies where abject poverty and injustice have not given rise to terrorism. The logical conclusion: oppression is a necessary condition of terrorism but not a sufficient one.

The Psychology of Terrorism

According to one expert on the psychology of terrorism, "terrorists with a cause" are the most dangerous to democratic society.[24] Who are these rebels? What motivates them? Not surprisingly, many of the most common traits exhibited by members of terrorist groups are associated with adolescence, including the following:[25]

- *Oversimplification of issues.* Terrorists see complex issues in black-and-white terms; they have no interest in debate; they often live out a "fantasy war," imagining the people overwhelmingly support their cause.
- *Frustration.* Terrorists feel society has cheated them, life is unfair, and they deserve far more; they are unwilling to wait or work for something better and believe the only way to get is to take.
- *Orientation toward risk taking.* Many terrorists seek situations offering adventure and are easily bored.
- *Self-righteousness.* Terrorists display belligerent assertiveness, dogmatism, and intolerance of opposing views.
- *Utopianism.* They harbor an unexamined belief that heaven on earth is just over the horizon; the only thing standing in the way is the corrupt and oppressive existing order.
- *Social isolation.* Terrorists, one expert noted, are often "people who are really lonely." For some, a terrorist cell may be the only "family" they have.
- *A need to be noticed.* Terrorists share a need to feel important, a desire to make a personal imprint by getting media attention.
- *A taste for blood.* Interviews with captured terrorists, testimony of relatives and acquaintances, and eyewitness accounts by former hostages point to a final, startling characteristic: Some terrorists kill without an ounce of remorse.

Terrorists often oversimplify reality; thus, they may see victims as mere objects—a habit of mind observed among Nazi guards at extermination camps during the Holocaust.[26] In a similar vein, Paul R. McHugh, a distinguished Johns Hopkins School of Medicine psychiatrist, argued that terrorists, like other actors with a "ferocious passion," have an "overvalued idea," defined as "a thought shared with others in a society or culture but in the patient held with an intense emotional commitment capable of provoking dominant behaviors in its service."[27] One clinical disorder prompted by an overvalued idea is anorexia nervosa. Adolf Hitler (anti-Semitism), Carry Nation (temperance), and John Brown (abolitionism) are three historical figures with overvalued ideas. Two contemporary figures are Theodore Kaczynski (the Unabomber) and Jack Kevorkian (assisted suicide).

Those who suffer personality disorders associated with overvalued ideas are commonly called fanatics. Once again, Hoffer's discussion of fanatics in *The True Believer* proves appropriate. Fanaticism—excessive, blind devotion—whether political or religious, is almost always based on hatred, according to Hoffer; the fanatic places hatred in the service of a cause or a vision. Hatred is, in turn, a unifying force for like-minded fanatics, whereas love is divisive. Thus, hatred provides a reason for living, often appealing to individuals who are insecure, have little sense of self-worth, or lack meaning in their lives. Finally, Hoffer noted,

> The fanatic is perpetually incomplete and insecure. He cannot generate self-assurance out of his individual resources—out of his rejected self—but finds it only by clinging passionately to [some cause]. This passionate attachment is the essence of his blind devotion and religiosity. . . . And he is ready to sacrifice his life to demonstrate to himself and others that such indeed is his role. He sacrifices his life—for example, in a suicide bombing—to prove his worth.[28]

Nor are fanatics necessarily motivated by a good cause. They embrace a cause not primarily because it is just or holy but because they have a desperate need for something to hold on to. It is this need for passionate attachment that turns a cause into *the* cause. From there it can be a short step to jihad or a terrorist campaign.[29] But for normal people fortunate enough to be living normal lives in normal times, it remains a mystery how anyone can commit barbarous acts out of idealism or religious fervor.

Terrorism and the Media

Terrorists seek publicity. As they see it, the more attention they can get, the better. Why? Because media coverage—above all, the dramatic images that flash across our television and computer screens—draws worldwide attention to the act itself and the overvalued idea embraced by those who perpetrated it. This coverage is not only politically prized, it is personally gratifying—it makes otherwise obscure individuals feel important. The prime-time exposure terrorists frequently get on CNN and other network news all over the world is also free. And of course, the most daring, deadly, or otherwise sensational terrorist acts receive the most extensive media attention. Without question, the two fatal blows struck against the World Trade Center are the most widely and repeatedly televised terrorist acts in history.

In light of terrorists' need for publicity, many political analysts outside the profession of journalism blame the rapid rise of terrorism in part on the media—on television, in particular. After all, bad news makes for better headlines and better copy, and bad news that is also sensational and shocking garners the most attention and the highest Nielsen ratings, which in turn translates into higher advertising revenues for the networks. In this sense, at least, terrorism is tailor-made for television.

In a market economy, simply reporting the news is not enough; the news industry must also sell the news. The audience share that chooses to watch television news determines how much companies will pay to advertise their products on a particular network. Thus, producers of news shows are loath to pass up a good story, even if it means playing into the hands of terrorists. Of course, an airplane hijacking involving hundreds of innocent people is newsworthy by any standard. The media do, after all, have a responsibility to keep people informed. And even if one network decided not to cover a particular terrorist incident or to pay only slight attention to it, the others would not ignore it.

Media self-restraint is the only practical solution. Realistically, the news industry is not likely to cut back significantly on its reporting of terrorism until public opinion turns against such reports. As consumers of news, we often get what we demand and, in that sense, deserve what we get.

COUNTERING TERRORISM

The question facing democratic societies is how terrorism can be curtailed without jeopardizing democratic rights and liberties. The rise of international and state-sponsored terrorism, the danger of nuclear weapons falling into the hands of terrorists, and use of the Internet to plot and coordinate terrorist attacks—these developments all underscore the need for governments to coordinate global counterterrorist efforts.

Domestic Legislation

Authoritarian and totalitarian states are free to deal quickly and harshly with terrorists and accused terrorists. Democratic states, however, are committed to following the rule of law whenever and wherever possible. Over the past two decades, many democracies have enacted new laws or adapted old laws to deal more effectively with terrorists and terrorism.

Skyjacking and committing an act of violence against an airline passenger were made crimes in the United States way back in 1961, four decades before 9/11. In the wake of the first World Trade Center bombing in 1993 and the Oklahoma City bombing two years later, Congress passed an antiterrorism act in April 1996, which provided more resources for federal law-enforcement to fight terrorism, tightened immigration, and loosened deportation procedures for aliens suspected of being terrorists.

But in 2001, on that fateful day in September, the second assault on the World Trade Center revealed the inadequacy of existing counterterrorist policies. President Bush quickly set up a new cabinet-level Office of Homeland Security, designed to coordinate the work of all federal departments and agencies engaged in any aspect of counterterrorism, and also issued a controversial directive creating military tribunals for suspected terrorists.[30]

The major changes in the government's power over legal aliens in the United States are contained in a law passed by Congress after the 9/11 attacks. The cumbersome name of this law—necessary to produce the desired acronym—is the Uniting and Strengthening America by Providing Appropriate Tools Required to Intercept and Obstruct Terrorism Act of 2001, more commonly known as the USA PATRIOT Act. In addition to greatly expanding the FBI's wiretapping authority, this act broadens the notion of who is considered a terrorist suspect and gives the U.S. attorney general sweeping authority to detain Arabs and Muslims, as well as other foreigners; it permits the government to deny entry into the United States to any foreigner who publicly endorses terrorism or belongs to a terrorist group; it expands the definition of *terrorist activity* to include any foreigner who uses "dangerous devices" or raises money for a terrorist group, *wittingly or unwittingly;* finally, it allows the government to detain any foreigner the attorney general considers a menace.

Taken together, the antiterrorist measures growing out of executive orders and the Patriot Act give the U.S. federal government powers of surveillance and infiltration unprecedented in modern times. At first supportive, public opinion is now deeply divided on the wisdom and necessity of warrantless wiretaps and other forms of government spying on civilians. In 2005, a CBS poll found respondents split (49 percent approved; 45 percent disapproved); in 2008, the candidate who opposed intrusive government measures—Barack Obama—won the election.

The Bush administration's counterterrorist methods and policies were controversial and, according to critics, unconstitutional. For a full five years after 9/11, they also appeared to be counterproductive, especially in Iraq (see Box 15.2 and Figure 15.3). Only after President Bush ordered a troop surge in January 2007 did the insurgency and violence there subside, although in the spring of 2009 there was once again a troubling uptick in terrorist attacks in Iraq. Nonetheless, President Obama did not reverse his decision to withdraw U.S. combat forces from Iraq by the fall of 2010, but instead ordered a troop surge in Afghanistan. At the same time, Obama fired the commander of U.S.-led NATO forces in Afghanistan, General David McKiernan, and replaced him with a general known for his tough counterterrorism credentials, General Stanley McChrystal.[31]

Many democracies, including Italy, France, the Netherlands, and Greece, ban membership in terrorist organizations. In Great Britain, specific terrorist groups are outlawed, including the IRA and the Irish National Liberation Army,

LANDOV MEDIA.

Known for his tough approach to counter-terrorism, General Stanley McChrystal led the Joint Special Operations Command—the military's most secretive branch—from 2003 to 2008. When President Obama put him in charge of conducting the war in Afghanistan in the spring of 2009, however, he called for a new strategy that stresses the imperative need to avoid civilian casualties (often called "collateral damage") in carrying out military operations in order to win the hearts and minds of the populace.

as is soliciting funds for them. In 2005, the European Union acted to improve information sharing to combat terrorism through the Schengen Information System (SIS). The EU has also created a European Arrest Warrant to facilitate coordinated action in capturing suspected criminals and terrorists, who can move across national boundaries in Europe easily now that all border controls have been abolished among the twenty-five countries that belong to the Schengen Area (see Chapter 18). One other example: Italy and Sweden have made it easier for police to tap telephones and open mail to detect letter bombs. In general, most democracies do not protect privacy rights to the extent the United States did before 9/11 and place fewer restrictions on police and investigative agencies. As a result, they did not need a Patriot Act to adopt tough counterterrorism measures. What they did need was better cooperation across borders—which they now have.

Cooperation Among Nations

Prior to 9/11, international efforts to combat terrorism undertaken by the United Nations, the Organization of American States, and the Council of Europe were largely ineffective.[32] Bilateral agreements often proved more successful—even between countries otherwise adversarial. For instance, the 1973 agreement between the United States and Cuba brought an end to a wave of skyjackings of U.S. planes to Havana.

After the 9/11 attacks, the Bush administration initially enjoyed the full cooperation of NATO allies, as well as such key countries as Pakistan and Russia, in its war on terror. NATO endorsed, and many NATO members participated in, the U.S.-led invasion of Afghanistan. However, most of this support, with the notable exception of the United Kingdom and former prime minister Tony Blair, faded away when the White House made the decision to invade Iraq.

Intelligence sharing across borders has improved since 9/11. Organizations such as Interpol (an international police agency headquartered in France) have reportedly facilitated the capture of terrorists in some instances and possibly prevented some terrorist acts from occurring. Despite many obstacles and continuing challenges, the United States and the European Union have taken steps to achieve closer cooperation on matters related to police, judicial, and border control policy.[33]

In one striking example of bilateral cooperation, high-ranking FBI and CIA officials cooperated with Russian internal security agencies to fight organized crime in Russia and ferret out its suspected links to both international terrorist groups and would-be smugglers of nuclear weapons materials. In another, a retaliatory surgical bombing strike against a dictator with a history of sponsoring international terrorism was facilitated by a close U.S. ally. Specifically, President Ronald Reagan decided to teach Colonel Muammar Qaddafi a lesson.

Qaddafi, Libya's autocratic ruler, was long suspected of sponsoring terrorist attacks in Europe and elsewhere. In April 1986, Reagan ordered the bombing of Tripoli, Libya's capital. Initially, only the British supported the U.S. strike; the French, fearing terrorist reprisals, refused to allow U.S. warplanes based in

---

BOX 15.2 SPOTLIGHT ON   Iraq and Afghanistan: Terrorist Attacks

---

The following is extracted verbatim from a U.S. State Department report released by the Office of the Coordinator for Counterterrorism on April 30, 2007:

- Approximately 14,000 terrorist attacks occurred in various countries during 2006, resulting in over 20,000 deaths. **Compared to 2005, attacks rose by 3,000, a 25 percent increase in 2006 while deaths rose by 5,800, a 40 percent increase.***…The Near East and South Asia…were the locations for 90 percent of all the 290 high casualty attacks that killed 10 or more people…

- **Of the 14,000 reported attacks, 45 percent—about 6,600—of them occurred in Iraq where approximately 13,000 fatalities—65 percent of the worldwide total— were reported for 2006.***

- Violence against non-combatants in eastern and sub-Saharan Africa, particularly related to attacks associated with turmoil in or near Sudan and Nigeria, rose 65 percent in 2006, rising to 420 from the approximately 253 attacks reported for 2005.

- **The 749 attacks in Afghanistan during 2006 are over 50 percent more than the 491 attacks reported for 2005 as fighting intensified during the past year.***

- The number of reported incidents in 2006 fell for Europe and Eurasia by 15 percent from 2005, for South Asia by 10 percent, and for the Western Hemisphere by 5 percent. No high casualty attacks occurred in Western Europe, and only two occurred in Southeast Asia, in the southern Philippines. There were no high casualty attacks and 95 percent fewer victims of terror in 2006 in Indonesia that was attributable, at least in part, to enhanced Indonesian security measures.

- The number injured during terrorist incidents rose substantially in 2006, as compared with 2005, by 54 percent, with most of the rise stemming from a doubling of the reported number of injuries in Iraq since 2005.

*Emphasis added.

SOURCE: Office of the Coordinator for Counterterrorism, "Country Reports on Terrorism," April 30, 2007, http://www.state.gov/s/ct/rls/crt/.

---

the United Kingdom to fly over French territory. The punitive U.S. air strike hit Qaddafi's official residence and killed his baby daughter. Thereafter, signs of an emerging multinational consensus began to appear. On April 21, 1986, the European Community voted to impose economic sanctions against Libya, and in the summer of 1986, Libyans were expelled from Great Britain, West Germany, France, Italy, Spain, Denmark, Belgium, the Netherlands, and Luxembourg.

Libyans accused of blowing up Pan Am Flight 103 over Lockerbie, Scotland, in December 1988 were eventually caught and placed on trial before the International Court of Justice at The Hague in the Netherlands in 2000. In 2003, Qaddafi surprised the world by renouncing terrorism. In September 2008, Secretary of State Condoleeza Rice paid an official visit to Tripoli where she met with Qaddafi, and the United States moved to re-establish normal relations with Libya. Thus, Libya demonstrates how patience, a mixture of military and diplomatic pressure, and international cooperation can sometimes succeed where quick fixes and the crude application of lethal force cannot.

FIGURE 15.3 By far, the largest number of worldwide terrorist incidents in 2006 occurred in two countries that President Bush blamed for the 9/11 attacks—Iraq and Afghanistan. Both are neighbours of Iran, which along with Iraq and North Korea, was part of what Bush called the "axis of evil." Critics charged that the U.S.-led invasions of both countries proved to be the prelude to anarchy rather than democracy. In 2008, the situation appeared to be stabilizing in Iraq, but not in Afghanistan.

SOURCE: Adapted from map at http://www.lib.utexas.edu/maps/middle_east_and_lasia/asia_southern_pol_2004.jpg

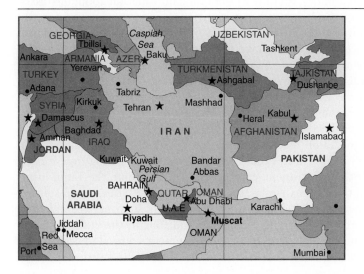

Unilateral Counterterrorist Measures

Virtually every nation strengthened airport security after the bloody terrorist massacres in Vienna and Rome airports in 1985. But the United States did too little too late; on September 11, 2001, four commercial airplanes were hijacked almost simultaneously from three different East Coast airports in one morning. All the hijack teams apparently managed to get on the planes with weapons (knives and box cutters).

Many authorities believe retribution and deterrence are the only effective approach to dealing with terrorism. In this view, deterrence requires, at a minimum, a refusal to make concessions to terrorists. To do otherwise is self-defeating and tantamount to rewarding evil, inviting future attacks of a similar nature. According to one expert, "Where counterterrorism has worked, a unifying thread has been the demonstrated will and ability of the government to take harsh and *preemptive* ("proactive") military or paramilitary countermeasures against terrorists."[34]

The availability of special counterterrorist units such as the British SAS is not enough; governments must also demonstrate a willingness to use them in order "to establish an unmistakable pattern of failure and retribution."[35] There is always the risk of failure (for example, the 1980 U.S. attempt to free hostages in Iran), and the immediate consequences can be tragic. But the long-term consequences of acting indecisively can be even more tragic.

Other steps governments can take include controlling arms and explosives and, perhaps most important (though most difficult), developing better domestic and foreign intelligence-gathering capabilities. Modern technology using satellites, electronic surveillance, advanced search technologies, explosives detection, scanners, robotic vehicles, and drones have greatly enhanced existing counterterrorist capabilities, for only by obtaining information about terrorists' hideouts, movements, and plans can governments prevent attacks. There is also ongoing research in the promising new field of network analysis, using social science techniques to better understand the workings of terrorist networks.

Time is a crucial factor in fighting both insurgencies and terrorism (which often go hand in hand in today's world). The conventional wisdom long held that time was on the side of the insurgents—they are more highly motivated, closer to the people, and so on. There is reason to doubt the truth of this axiom. Consider the case of the Tamil minority in Sri Lanka.

The defeat of the Tamil Tigers, modern Asia's longest-lasting insurgency, in the spring of 2009 demonstrates that a patient strategy, allowing time for terrorists' acts to work against them, can succeed. At one point, the Tamil insurgents controlled a third of Sri Lanka; they used terrorist tactics—child soldiers and suicide bombers—and fought a conventional war, with outside aid from China, Pakistan, and high-earning Tamils abroad. But in the end, the Tamil Tigers' brutality and the Sinhalese-majority government's refusal to negotiate in the face of terrorist blackmail drained the lifeblood from the insurgency.[36]

Sri Lankan soldiers with remains of Tamil Tiger leader Velupillai Prabhakaran in May 2009.

SOURCE: HTTP://WWW.SLATE.COM/ID/2218847?WPISRC=NEWSLETTER

Obviously, the nature of democratic societies and the constitutional framework in which governments operate present obstacles to police and investigative agencies charged with thwarting terrorism. Citizens are unaccustomed to acting as informants, and intelligence gathering is divided among several agencies, in part to prevent any one of them from gaining too much power. In the United States, for example, intelligence and counterintelligence have traditionally been separated; the CIA is responsible for foreign intelligence and is forbidden to engage in domestic spy operations against U.S. citizens or groups, while counterintelligence is the function of the FBI. Coordinating the work of these two agencies after 9/11 was the prime reason behind President Bush's decision to create the new Office of Homeland Security.

Private Measures

Finally, private citizens and firms have developed strategies to protect themselves.[37] Just as many governments were "hardening" their embassies and other overseas facilities in the 1980s and 1990s, private companies were spending billions of dollars annually on security services and hardware in the United States and elsewhere.[38]

Most citizens cannot afford to hire private security guards, but an alert public can make the terrorist's job more difficult. In Israel, for example, where everyone is acutely aware of the terrorist threat, officials claim 80 percent of bombs in public places are disarmed because suspicious objects are usually noticed and reported in time.[39] Most security experts agree that success in countering terrorism depends on vigilant citizens, as well as police and security forces.

CAN TERRORISM BE CONTAINED?

Terrorism poses a continuing threat that shows few signs of abating (see Figure 15.2), despite the ongoing post-9/11 war on terror. Meanwhile, a worst-case scenario hangs over the world like the legendary sword of Damocles: Nuclear terrorism, as noted earlier, is no longer wildly implausible, nor is the threat of biological and chemical attacks.

There is no single or totally effective solution to terrorism. Still, as we have seen, there are ways of limiting the opportunities available to terrorists and of deterring, punishing, or simply eradicating terrorism before it reaches epidemic proportions (as it did in Italy in the 1970s and early 1980s, Peru in the 1980s, and Algeria in the 1990s).

Despite specific successes, however, there remains one momentous problem: Even one terrorist can be too many. Indeed, one well-trained terrorist with a small support system—a few friends, safe houses, and supplies—can inflict enormous damage. Terrorism can never be eradicated entirely in this imperfect world, but with patience, perseverance, courage, and vigilance, it can be contained and liberty preserved (although perhaps not without periods of constriction)—that is one of the lessons of the recent past.

Box 15.3 FOCUS ON   Counterterrorism in Italy: A Success Story

In the 1970s, Italy was the most terror-ridden country in the West. The extreme left-wing Red Brigades kidnapped and killed hundreds of judges, industrialists, and politicians—symbols of capitalism and the establishment. From 1969 to 1983, more than 14,000 acts of terrorist violence were recorded, 409 people were killed, and 1,366 were injured.

In 1978, the Red Brigades kidnapped Aldo Moro, a former prime minister and one of Italy's leading politicians. When the government refused to negotiate with Moro's abductors, he was murdered. In the end, however, it was the terrorists who lost. Shocked and outraged, the public demanded a tough counterterrorist program. Thereafter, the Red Brigades went into sharp decline.

How did Italy do it? First, the police infiltrated Red Brigade terror cells and subsequently arrested hundreds of members. Second, reduced prison sentences were offered to repentant terrorists who supplied information about the activities and whereabouts of other terrorists. Third, the police concentrated on a limited and manageable number of terrorist targets, such as airports, harbors, and border crossings. Finally, new laws gave the police greater ability to tap phones and use other resources more effectively.

Deprived of sympathy for whatever cause they embraced, Italy's terrorists were isolated. Today they pose little or no threat to the country's stability.

FIGURE 15.4   **Terrorist Incidents Worldwide: High and Rising**

SOURCE: 2008 Report on Terrorism, National Counter-Terrorism Center, April, 2009, p. 37, http://wits.nctc.gov/ReportPDF.do?f=crt2008nctcannexfinal.pdf.

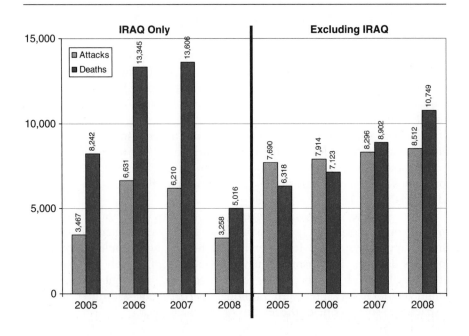

GATEWAYS TO THE WORLD: EXPLORING CYBERSPACE

http://www.nctc.gov/

The official Website of the National Counterterrorism Center. Click on "NCTC 2008 Report on Terrorism" or check out the NCTC's video on its mission and responsibilities in the War on Terror.

www.fpri.org/research/terrorism

From the Website of the Foreign Policy Research Institute (FPRI), this is the page of the Center on Terrorism, Counter-Terrorism, and Homeland Security. Among its other activities, FPRI publishes *Orbis*, the quarterly journal of international politics.

www.terrorism.com

From the Website: "Founded in 1996, the Terrorism Research Center, Inc. (TRC) is an independent institute dedicated to the research of terrorism, information warfare and security, critical infrastructure protection, homeland security, and other issues of low-intensity political violence and gray-area phenomena."

cns.miis.edu/pubs/reports/convter.htm

From the Website of the Center for Nonproliferation Studies located in Monterey, California, this page contains chronologies, databases, and other resources of interest on terrorism and related topics.

www.homelandsecurity.org/bulletin/current_bulletin.htm

The "Weekly Newsletter of Homeland Security" is published on the Web by the Homeland Security Institute (HSI), an arm of Analytical Services, Inc. (ANSER), which is cryptically self-described as "a public-service research institute, an independent, not-for-profit corporation. . .[serving] with pride our clients in the defense, intelligence, and homeland security communities."

SUMMARY

Terrorism, a political effort to oppose the status quo by inducing fear in the civilian population through the widespread and publicized use of violence, has become an everyday occurrence in the contemporary world. Although it has ancient roots in religious conflict, contemporary terrorism can be traced to the 1960s.

Terrorists seek to create a climate of chaos and confusion in the belief that political instability will hasten the downfall of a government. They form groups that are close-knit, homogeneous, small, and (often) short lived. Terrorists can pose great challenges to countries facing political and economic problems; Muslim fundamentalism in Algeria provides such an example.

Although terrorists violate the law, they are not *criminals* in the everyday sense of the term. Nor are they guerrillas or ordinary revolutionaries. All terrorists are revolutionaries, but not all revolutionaries are terrorists. A terrorist is a kind of revolutionary who does not seek to obtain political power but whose primary objective is to protest and combat the perceived injustice of the existing political order through random acts of violence. Terrorists tend to be young, single males who share a variety of key psychological characteristics, including fanaticism and hatred.

Democracy and terrorism are implacable enemies. Democracy depends for its existence on compromise, tolerance, and mutual trust, whereas terrorists are zealots who seek to radicalize society and destabilize the political system. Furthermore, democratic societies are, by nature, open and vulnerable to terrorist attacks. This vulnerability is both physical and psychological.

The problem democracies face in countering terrorism are complicated by the need to preserve individual freedoms while also protecting national security. Still, various singular and cooperative measures that democracies have undertaken show promise of containing—though not eliminating—terrorism.

KEY TERMS

terrorism
state terrorism
international
    terrorism
state-sponsored
    terrorism
domestic terrorism
transnational
    terrorism
counterterrorism

REVIEW QUESTIONS

1. How is terrorism different from common crime? From guerrilla warfare?
2. What tactics do terrorists typically employ, and how are their ends and means related?
3. What are the psychological roots of terrorism and the characteristics of the typical terrorist?
4. Why are democracies vulnerable to terrorism? Assess the terrorist threat to constitutional democracies.
5. What obstacles stand in the way of an effective counterterrorist policy?
6. What steps did the United States take to protect itself against terrorism after 9/11? Comment on U.S. successes and failures in the fight against terrorism.
7. Cite several examples of successful counterterrorist efforts in other countries, then identify several failures. What have we learned about how to fight terrorism?
8. Is technology on the side of governments or terrorists? Explain.

RECOMMENDED READING

Baer, Robert. *See No Evil: The True Story of a Ground Soldier in the CIA's War on Terrorism*. New York: Crown Publishing Group, 2003.

A high-ranking operative's account of how Washington politics perverted the intelligence process and prevented the CIA from playing its proper role both before and after 9/11.

A biography of one of the leading intellectuals in the global *jihad* movement.

In his 1,600 page opus, *The Global Islamic Resistance Call*, al-Suri lays down basic principles of global *jihad*—for example, hierarchical structures are vulnerable to penetration by Western intelligence and attack by U.S. security forces; the solution is a decentralized system of lone *jihadists* or small cells linked only by ideology. Arrested in Pakistan in 2005, al-Suri is believed to be detained by the United States in an unknown location.

Carr, Caleb. *The Lessons of Terror—A History of Warfare Against Civilians: Why It Has Always Failed and Why It Will Fail Again*. New York: Random House, 2002.

The subtitle says it all.

Clutterbuck, Richard. *Protest and the Urban Guerrilla*. New York: Abelard-Shuman, 1974.

Examines the roots of protest and violence in Britain and Northern Ireland; surveys the rise of urban guerrilla movements worldwide; and ponders the implications of terrorism for the future of democratic societies.

Combs, Cindy C. *Terrorism in the Twenty-First Century*. Upper Saddle River, NJ: Prentice-Hall, 1997.

A balanced, comprehensive text that covers virtually every aspect of terrorists, terrorism, and terrorist acts.

Hoffman, Bruce. *Inside Terrorism*. New York: Columbia University Press, 2006.

A good choice for anyone who plans to read only one book on this subject; concise, analytical, and thought provoking.

Juergensmeyer, Mark. *Terror in the Mind of God*. Berkeley: University of California Press, 2000.

A thoughtful study of the relationship between religious extremism and political violence in the contemporary world by an established scholar in the field.

Levy, Michael. *On Nuclear Terrorism* Cambridge, MA: Harvard University Press, 2007.

An insightful examination of everybody's worst nightmare: nuclear weapons in the hands of terrorists. The author not only describes the danger but prescribes ways of dealing with it.

Lia, Brynjar *Architect of Global Jihad: The Life of Al Qaeda Strategist Abu Mus'ab al-Suri*. New York: Columbia University Press/Hurst, 2009.

Post, Jerrold M. *The Mind of the Terrorist: The Psychology of Terrorism from the IRA to al-Qaeda*. New York: Palgrave Macmillan, 2007.

A top expert on the psychology of violent individuals draws on a rich professional background to explain what motivates terrorists. The result is a both fascinating and frightening.

Rivers, Gayle. *The Specialist: Revelations of a Counterterrorist*. Lanham, MD: Madison Books, 1985.

Ostensibly a true story about the underworld of terrorism and counterterrorism, written under a pseudonym by a mercenary who specializes in carrying out antiterrorist operations under contract to Western (and other) governments; reads like a James Bond thriller.

Pape, Robert A. *Dying to Win: The Strategic Logic of Suicide Terrorism*. New York: Random House Trade Paperbacks, 2005.

The book does more than delve into the "strategic logic" of suicide bombings. It also draws some conclusions that point to a strategy for defeating the *jihadists* of the world.

Scheuer, Michael. *Through Our Enemies' Eyes: Osama bin Laden, Radical Islam, and the Future of America, Revised Edition by Michael Scheuer*. Dulles, VA: Potomac Books, Inc., 2006.

This book by a former CIA intelligence analyst and expert on Afghanistan and South Asia argues that the United States was unprepared to fight the war on terrorism because senior policy makers ignored Chinese strategist Sun Tzu's famous dictum, "Know your enemy and you will know yourself." Policy failures, Scheuer argues, were rooted in ignorance of the enemy.

White, Jonathan. *Terrorism and Homeland Security: An Introduction,* 6th ed. Belmont, CA: Wadsworth, 2009.

A very readable text that touches all the bases. The first chapter is devoted to the vexing problem posed by the many and varied definitions of terrorism. The rest of the book is a comprehensive global treatment of all aspects of this timely topic.

Wright, Lawrence. *The Looming Tower: Al Qaeda and the Road to 9/11.* New York: Alfred A. Knopf, 2006.

From the publisher: "A sweeping narrative history of the events leading to 9/11, a groundbreaking look at the people and ideas, the terrorist plans, and the Western intelligence failures that culminated in the assault on America."

© GETTY IMAGES.

The U.S.-led military forces that invaded Afghanistan after 9/11, 2001, are fighting a stubborn Taliban insurgency in rugged mountainous terrain. The conflict spilled over the border into northern Pakistan and in April–May 2009 threatened to destabilize the Pakistani government.

WAR
Politics by Other Means

The Causes of War

Human Nature: Hobbes

Society: Rousseau

The Environment: Locke

In Search of A Definitive Theory

Beyond Politics

Beyond Economics

The Danger of Oversimplification

Total War: Wars Everybody Fights

Accidental War: Wars Nobody Wants

Nuclear War: Wars Nobody Wins

Proxy War: Wars Others Fight

Just Wars: Wars Others Start

The Just War Doctrine

Evaluating the Just War Doctrine

A War on *What?* The Politics of Hyperbole

Weapons of Mass Disruption: Cyber War

---

war
Organized violence, often on a large scale, involving sovereign states or geographic parts of the same state or distinct ethnic or social groups within a given state (civil war).

interstate war
Armed conflict between sovereign states.

civil war
A war between geographical sections or rival groups within a nation.

guerrilla warfare
The tactics used by loosely organized military forces grouped into small, mobile squads that carry out acts of terrorism and sabotage, then melt back into the civilian population.

low-intensity conflict
Internal warfare that is sporadic and carried out on a small-scale but often prolonged and debilitating to the state and society in which it occurs.

It is the central problem of international politics. **War**, in the famous words of Prussian military theorist Carl von Clausewitz (1780–1831), "is a continuation of politics by other means." Governments are always conscious of the possibility that diplomacy (politics) will fail and war with a neighboring state, or perhaps between rival ethnic or religious groups within a state, can break out at any time. Indeed, the most glaring defect of politics on all levels is its inability to prevent armed conflict in its myriad forms.

When people think of war, they usually have in mind **interstate wars**—that is, conflicts between two or more nation-states. **Civil wars** are conflicts within a single country; they have actually become more common than international wars today. **Guerrilla warfare** is a low-tech form of fighting usually waged in rural areas by small, lightly armed mobile squads (often fed and sheltered by sympathetic villagers). Guerrillas typically carry out selective acts of violence, primarily against the army, the police, and the government, in an attempt to weaken or topple the ruler(s). **Low-intensity conflicts**, a fourth category, occur when one state finances, sponsors, or promotes the sporadic or prolonged use of violence in a rival country (by hiring mercenaries or underwriting guerrillas, for example).

In terms of lives lost, property damaged or destroyed, and money drained away, war is undeniably the most destructive and wasteful of all human activities. Estimates of the war dead in the last century alone fall in the range of 35 million, including 25 million civilians.[1] General William Tecumseh Sherman knew firsthand the horror of war. As a military leader, he had, in fact, been a fearsome practitioner of it. In a speech delivered 15 years after the American Civil War, Sherman declared, "There is many a boy who looks on war as all glory, but boys, it is hell."

But not everyone sees war the way an older and wiser General Sherman did. Some of history's most illustrious (or infamous) personalities have reveled in the "glory" of war or acknowledged its perverse attractions. In the eighth century BCE, the Greek poet Homer noted that men grow tired of sleep, love, singing, and dancing sooner than they do of war. In his poetry, he celebrated the self-sacrifice and courage war demanded. The Greek philosopher Aristotle, writing some 500 years later, listed courage as the first, though not the foremost, human virtue. To Aristotle, courage in battle ennobled human beings because it represented the morally correct response to fear in the face of mortal danger, danger that, in turn, imperiled the political community.

Perhaps no writer in modern times rationalized war better than the German philosopher G. W. F. Hegel, who argued, "If states disagree and their particular wills cannot be harmonized, the matter can only be settled by war." Hegel felt war is actually salutary because "corruption in nations would be the product of prolonged, let alone 'perpetual' peace." During times of peace, Hegel reasoned, society too easily grows soft and contentious: "As a result of war, nations are strengthened, but peoples involved in civil strife also acquire peace at home through making war abroad."[2]

Hegel contended that "world history is the world court." In other words, the ultimate test of validity or worth is not some abstract moral standard, but success. And because success in world politics is measured, above all, in terms of power and size, it follows that might and right are synonymous.

The German philosopher Friedrich Nietzsche (1844–1900) further radical-ized this idea. Nietzsche disdained conventional morality in general and despised the Christian ethic of humility in particular (he regarded it as a weakness). What Nietzsche admired most, both in individuals and in nations, was the aggres-sive exercise of power. He celebrated the will to power and praised the curative effects of war on nations and civilizations.[3] This theme would be revived with a vengeance half a century later by Adolf Hitler and his ally, Benito Mussolini. Like Hegel and Nietzsche, Mussolini scoffed at pacifism. Said the father of Italian fas-cism, "War alone brings to their highest tension all human energies and puts the stamp of nobility upon the peoples who have the courage to meet it."[4]

Although war is a constant in human affairs, it has evolved over time. Technology has transformed its ways and means without mitigating its lethal effects or destructive consequences—indeed, quite the opposite. Today, old forms of guerrilla warfare coexist with ultra high-tech robots, drones, and cyber war (see Box 16.1).

This ever-present reality of war persists side by side with the dream of a world without war. Throughout the ages, philosophers and theologians have pondered the possibility of perpetual peace. But if war is ever to be eradicated, we must first isolate its causes.

THE CAUSES OF WAR

Why war? There is no simple answer. An observer living in Europe or the Middle East in the twelfth century would probably have attributed the frequency and ferocity of war at that time to religious zealotry. The Crusades, which began at the end of the eleventh century and continued for 200 years, were marked by the kind of unmerciful slaughter that, paradoxically, has often accompanied the conviction that "God is on our side."

But while religion did help fuel many regional and local wars, it played only a minor role in most of the major wars of the twentieth century. In no sense was religious fanaticism the cause of World War I, for instance. Many observers attribute the outbreak of that conflict to **nationalism** run amok, a phenomenon virtually unknown in the twelfth century. Others stress the **arms race** conducted by European nations, arguing that the momentum of military preparations car-ried Europe inexorably into war. Still others blame imperialism: The scramble for colonial territories in the latter half of the nineteenth century led to war, they contend, once there were no "unclaimed" lands left in Asia and Africa.

Nor did religion play a major role in World War II. Ideology (national social-ism in Germany, fascism in Italy, and communism in the Soviet Union) was a factor, but the main "ism" behind the aggressive policies of Germany, Italy, and Japan was **ultranationalism**, or what scholar Hans J. Morgenthau called **nationalistic universalism**. The Korean Conflict (1950–1953) and the Vietnam War (1963–1975) were fought for both geopolitical reasons, or **reasons of state**, and ideological reasons. Some historians have seen this mix of pragmatism and

nationalism
Devotion to one's nation; closely akin to patriotism.

arms race
Reciprocal military buildups between rival states; a process that tends to accelerate research, technology, and development in weapons systems and, according to some experts, is a potential cause of war.

ultranationalism
Extreme nationalism often associated with fascism; a radical right-wing orientation typically characterized by militarism, racial bigotry, and xenophobia.

nationalistic universalism
A messianic foreign policy that seeks to spread the ideas and institutions of one nation to other nations.

reasons of state
The pragmatic basis for foreign policy that places the national interest above moral considerations or idealistic motives; also raison d'état.

idealism as a factor in the unsatisfactory (for the United States) outcomes of both these wars, because military-strategic decisions were distorted by a crusading anticommunism that defined U.S. foreign policy during the Cold War.

On the surface, then, the causes of World War I and World War II differed radically from those of, say, the Crusades. But whatever its immediate causes, every war represents another outbreak of the same old disease, even if the symptoms and severity have changed.

Philosophers and theologians, hoping to find the keys to peace, have for 2,000 years attempted to discover war's root causes. After World War II, the most destructive war in history, political scientists tried using statistical and mathematical models to learn more. Quantitative research of this kind tries to match the methodological rigor and precision of the natural sciences. In the words of John Vasquez, one of the foremost advocates of this approach,

> Philosophical analyses of the physical world, for example, . . . even when conducted by such a brilliant thinker as Aristotle, did not produce a cumulative body of knowledge. A substantial advancement in our understanding came only with the development and application of the scientific method.[5]

What has the scientific approach to the study of war achieved thus far? According to Vasquez, it has "helped refine thinking about war and raised serious questions about existing explanations of war."[6]

Other political scientists are not so sure.[7] James Dougherty and Robert Pfaltzgraff concluded, "Despite the proliferation of statistical studies of war (both inductive and deductive), . . . [most] are more likely to be relegated to footnotes [in the long run] than regarded as classics."[8] Greg Cashman took a middle-of-the-road position:

> Although no single theory seems to have anywhere near universal validity, social scientific research has not been completely fruitless. . . . The investigations undertaken by social scientists during the last four decades have not culminated in the creation of a single, unified theory of war, [but] they have certainly added greatly to our understanding of the causes of war.[9]

What we know for certain is there is no simple explanation for war. To probe deeper, we turn to three broad theories of causation. One emphasizes flaws in human nature. A second stresses defects in society and its institutions. A third sees scarcity as the cause of conflict.[10] After examining each, we look at the findings of several quantitative studies to corroborate or refute them.

Human Nature: Hobbes

Those who attribute war to flaws in human nature advance a variety of explanations for the all-too-human tendency to misbehave. Christianity has had a profound influence on Western political thought in this regard. Drawing on the Old Testament, early Christian thinkers viewed the human race as irreparably flawed by original sin—that is, by Adam and Eve's violation of God's law in the

Garden of Eden, as recorded in the book of Genesis. The story of the fall is, in a very real sense, a universal one with universal significance—world history in a nutshell.

According to Saint Augustine (354–430), the influential early Christian theologian, war is the price we pay for our corrupt nature. Many secular thinkers display a similar pessimism, without citing original sin as the cause. The Greek philosopher Plato attributed wars, at least in part, to the human passion for worldly possessions and creature comforts. The sixteenth-century Italian thinker Niccoló Machiavelli painted an equally depressing picture of the interaction between human nature and politics. In *The Prince*, he asserted that political success and moral rectitude are often inversely related: rulers tend to prosper in direct proportion to the dirty politics they practice for the sake of self-gratifying political ends.

Whereas some have looked to religion and others to philosophy for an explanation of aggressive human tendencies, still others have turned to psychology. Sigmund Freud (1856–1939), the founder of psychoanalysis, believed human beings are born with a "death wish," or innate self-destructive tendencies, that they redirect into other activities most of the time. During times of conflict, Freud theorized, combatants direct these destructive tendencies against each other. Thus, wars serve a psychotherapeutic function: They offer an outlet for otherwise self-destructive impulses. Critics argue this theory is too clever by half—the soldiers who do the fighting and killing are not the ones who decide to go to war, and the decision makers, careful to stay out of harm's way, are not the ones who fight. Most soldiers kill because they have a job to do and because they do not want to be killed, not because they are violent or destructive by nature.

Other psychologists have called aggression an innate human drive constantly seeking an outlet, a normal human response to frustration, or the same "territorial imperative" that supposedly accounts for aggressive behavior in the animal kingdom. According to the territorial imperative theory, latent aggressions are lodged deep in human nature, and threats to an individual's or group's territory (property, loved ones, and so on) can trigger aggressive action.

Still other observers find the ultimate cause of war not in the human soul or psyche but rather in the brain. People are neither depraved nor disturbed but obtuse—too stupid to understand the futility of war. In the words of a prominent pacifist writing between World Wars I and II,

> The obstacle in our path . . . is not in the moral sphere, but in the intellectual. . . . It is not because men are ill-disposed that they cannot be educated into a world social consciousness. It is because they—let us be honest and say "we"—are beings of conservative temper and limited intelligence.[11]

Thomas Hobbes, living during the Puritan Revolution in England, had a different, but hardly more flattering, explanation for war. He was, above all, a realist who sought to understand human nature as it is, not as it ought to be. The only way to know what people are really like, Hobbes believed, is to look at how they would behave outside civil society as we know it—that is, as brutes

In the Nuclear Age, only the symptoms and severity of the disorder some observers aptly call "war fever" have changed. In August 1945, the dropping of atomic bombs on Hiroshima and Nagasaki leveled whole sections of these two densely populated cities in Japan and signaled a new era in world history.

©AP PHOTO

state of nature
The human condition before the creation of a social code of behavior and collective techniques to control normal human impulses.

of limited intelligence in a **state of nature**. The conclusions he drew from this exercise are fascinating and continue to influence how we think about politics, war, and the possibility of peace even today.

Hobbes According to Hobbes, human beings in the state of nature are governed by a keen instinct for self-preservation. They fear death above all and especially sudden, violent death. This fear does not, however, result in meekness or passivity; on the contrary, aggression and violent behavior are the norm. Hobbes identified "three principal causes" of war:

> First, Competition; Secondly, Diffidence; Thirdly, Glory. The first maketh man invade for Gain; the second, for Safety; and the third, for Reputation. The first cause [men to turn to] Violence to make themselves Masters of other men's persons, wives, children, and cattell; and the second, to defend them; the third, for trifles, at a word, a smile, a different opinion, and other signe of undervalue.[12]

The state of nature, for Hobbes, is a state of war—what he famously called a "war of every man, against every man."

Hobbes applied this same logic to international politics in his own time, which was a perpetual state of war. Just as individuals in the state of nature are governed by base motives and drives, he declared, leaders with similar motives and drives govern nations. And just as the state of nature lacks a government to protect people from each other, so the international system lacks a government to protect nations from each other.

Hobbes theorized that three kinds of disputes correspond to the three defects in human nature: aggressive wars, caused by competitive instincts; defensive wars, caused by fears; and agonistic wars, caused by pride and vanity. Through this compact theory, Hobbes sought to explain not only how human beings would act outside the civilizing influence of society and government (human beings constantly at each other's throats if not for government-imposed law and order), but also why nations sometimes go to war over issues that make no sense to outsiders.

The Hobbesian Legacy Hans Morgenthau, like Hobbes, argued forcefully that human beings are deeply flawed. According to Morgenthau, "Human nature, in which the laws of politics have their roots, has not changed since the classical philosophies of China, India, and Greece endeavored to discover these laws," and "politics, like society in general, is governed by objective laws that have their roots in human nature."[13] The key to understanding the operation of these laws is the "concept of interest defined as power." This means human beings are motivated by self-interest, which predisposes human behavior toward an eternal "struggle for power." Morgenthau made this point particularly clear when he stated, "International politics, like all politics, is a struggle for power. Whatever the ultimate aims of international politics, power is always the immediate aim." Like Hobbes before him, Morgenthau rejected the idealist view that "assumes the essential goodness and infinite malleability of human nature." Instead, he embraced the realist view "that the world, imperfect as it is from the rational point of view, is the result of forces inherent in human nature."[14]

According to Morgenthau and the realist school of political theory his writings inspired, human nature and the drive for self-aggrandizement are a leading, if not the leading, cause of competition and conflict. Compelling, though not flattering, this view of humankind is not the only plausible explanation of why wars are fought.

Society: Rousseau

Not all political thinkers attribute war to the human psyche or human nature. Some blame modern society in general, organized into a state (an exclusive or "members only" political association), while others contend that particular kinds of political states pose disproportionate dangers to peace. In this section, we examine the different approaches of political theorists and leaders who blame society or the state (the political framework of society) for war's destructiveness.

Rousseau "Man is born free, and everywhere he is in chains." With this attack on the modern nation-state, the French philosopher Jean-Jacques Rousseau (1712–1778) began the first chapter of his classic *Social Contract* (1762), in which he directly challenged Hobbes's assertion that human beings are naturally cunning and violent. Rousseau started from the premise that human beings are naturally "stupid but peaceful" creatures, quite capable of feeling pity for those who are suffering. Hobbes simply erred, in this view, in attributing ambition, fear, and pride, to human beings in the state of nature. Rousseau was convinced these are attributes of social man, not natural man (here the term *man* is used in the classic sense to mean all humans, irrespective of gender). Antisocial behaviors, paradoxically, have social causes; they are sure signs of human corruption.

Society, not human nature, is to blame. Rousseau is quite explicit on this point: "It is clear that . . . to society, must be attributed the assassinations, poisonings, highway robberies, and even the punishments of these crimes."[15]

Indeed, Rousseau believed society is the cause of all kinds of problems, including war. Specifically, he blamed the institution of private property—a preoccupation of all eighteenth-century European societies—for the miseries that have beset the human race since it abandoned its natural innocence for the false pleasures of civilization. Property divides human beings, he argued, by creating unnecessary inequalities in wealth, status, and power among citizens within particular nations and, eventually, among nations:

> The first person who, having fenced off a plot of ground, took it into his head to say this is mine and found people simple enough to believe him, was the true founder of civil society. What crimes, wars, murders, what miseries and horrors would the human race have been spared by someone who, uprooting the stakes or filling in the ditch, had shouted to his fellow-men: Beware of listening to this imposter, you are lost if you forget that the fruits belong to all and the earth to no one.[16]

Specifically, Rousseau postulated that just as the creation of private property led to the founding of the first political society, that founding mandated the creation of additional nation-states. And because each of these nations faced all the others in a state of nature, great tensions arose that eventually led to the "national wars, battles, murders, and reprisals, which make nature tremble and shock reason."[17] With the "division of the human race into different societies," Rousseau concluded,

> The most decent men learned to consider it one of their duties to murder their fellow men; at length men were seen to massacre each other by the thousands without knowing why; more murders were committed on a single day of fighting and more horrors in the capture of a single city than were committed in the state of nature during whole centuries over the entire race of the earth.[18]

Rousseau's view that private property is the root of all evil has exerted a profound influence on modern intellectual history. Even political thinkers who reject his specific diagnosis of the nation-state have widely accepted his general theory that "man is good but men are bad." Several twentieth-century variations on this theme have appeared. As we shall see, each differs in substantial ways from the others, but all assume the fatal flaw leading to war resides in society rather than in human nature.

Nationalism and War   Many modern thinkers hold that war is inherent in the very existence of separate societies with sovereign governments. The manifestation of these potent separatist tendencies is nationalism, the patriotic sentiments citizens feel toward their homeland (sometimes referred to, in its most extreme forms, as jingoism or chauvinism). According to one authority,

> Each nation has its own rose-colored mirror. It is the particular quality of such mirrors to reflect images flatteringly: the harsh lines are removed but

the character and beauty shine through! To each nation none is so fair as itself. . . . Each nation considers (to itself or proclaims aloud, depending upon its temperament and inclination) that it is "God's chosen people" and dwells in "God's country."[19]

Small wonder that nationalism has been called an idolatrous religion. Although it may foster unity and a spirit of self-sacrifice within a society, between societies it has led, directly or indirectly, to militarism, xenophobia, and mutual distrust.

Nationalism can be manipulated in support of a war policy, and warfare can be used to intensify nationalism. The chemistry between them is sufficiently volatile to have caused many **internationalists**, or theorists favoring peace and cooperation among nations through the active participation of all governments in some sort of world organization, to single out nationalism as the main obstacle to achieving peace and harmony in the world.

To the extent that nationalism is an artificial passion—one socially conditioned rather than inborn—political society is to blame for war. This type of reasoning has led some to suggest a radically simple formula for eliminating war: Do away with the nation-state and you do away with nationalism; do away with nationalism and you do away with war. Others have sought more practical remedies—fix the nation-state rather than abolish it.

Tyranny and War Many identify nationalism as the major cause of modern conflict, but others blame despotism for the two calamitous world wars of the last century. President Woodrow Wilson (1856–1924) championed this notion and actually tried to build a new world order on its conceptual foundations.

After World War I, Wilson sought to secure lasting peace through a treaty based on his Fourteen Points—principles he hoped would lead to a world without war. The cornerstone of this proposed new world order was the right of **national self-determination,** or the right of people everywhere to choose the government they wished to live under. Wilson expected self-determination to lead to the creation of democracies, which he viewed as being naturally more prone to peace than dictatorships.

But why should democracies be any more reluctant to go to war than dictatorships? The eighteenth-century German philosopher Immanuel Kant (1724–1804) first provided the explanation, one that appears to have deeply impressed Wilson. So germane are Kant's writings to Wilson's ideas that one authority suggested, "Woodrow Wilson's Fourteen Points were a faithful transcription of both the letter and spirit of Kant's Perpetual Peace."[20]

Kant postulated that to remain strong, nations must promote education, commerce, and civic freedom. Education, he theorized, would lead to popular enlightenment, and commerce would produce worldwide economic interdependence, all of which would advance the cause of peace. Most important, through expanded political freedom, individual citizens would become more competent in public affairs. And because liberty is most pronounced in republican regimes, such governments would be the most peace loving by nature. The reason is simple: in republics—unlike monarchies or aristocracies—the citizens

internationalist
Theorist favoring peace and cooperation among nations through the active participation of all governments in some sort of world organization.

national self-determination
The right of a nation to choose its own government.

who decide whether to support a war are the same citizens who must then do the fighting. In Kant's own words,

> A republican constitution does offer the prospect of [peace-loving behavior], and the reason is as follows: If . . . the consent of the citizens is required in order to decide whether there should be war or not, nothing is more natural than that those who would have to decide to undergo all the deprivations of war will very much hesitate to start such an evil game. . . . By contrast, under a constitution where the subject is not a citizen and which is therefore not republican, it is the easiest thing in the world to start a war . . . as a kind of amusement on very insignificant grounds.[21]

Kant envisioned an evolution, through steady if imperceptible progress, toward a peaceful world order as governments everywhere became increasingly responsive to popular majorities. Eventually, he felt, war would become little more than a historical curiosity.

Honored in Britain at the end of World War I, American president Woodrow Wilson hoped to make the world "safe for democracy" and end the scourge of war through a world organization—the League of Nations—based on the rule of law, collective security, and national self-determination.

©AP PHOTO

Kant's linking of republicanism and peacefulness became Wilson's political credo. Both Kant and Wilson looked to the reconstruction of the nation-state as the key to a world without war. More specifically, both called for the global extension of democracy, education, and free trade to promote peace. Wilson, in particular, placed enormous faith in the morality and common sense of the ordinary person; he became convinced the ideal of national self-determination would be the key to humanity's political salvation. He also believed if the world's peoples were allowed to choose among alternative forms of government, they would universally choose liberal democracy and peace. Finally, Wilson felt, if democratic institutions existed in all nations, the moral force of both domestic and world public opinion would serve as a powerful deterrent to armed aggression.

Capitalism, Imperialism, and War Among those who did not agree with Wilson was his contemporary, V. I. Lenin, leader of the Russian Revolution and the first ruler of the former Soviet Union. Lenin was as violently opposed to bourgeois democracy as Wilson was enthusiastic about it. Although both supported national self-determination, they held very different interpretations of it. Wilson assumed any nation would choose democracy over any other system. In contrast, Lenin assumed that given a choice between capitalism and communism, any nation should choose communism. For Wilson, the pursuit of power was an end in itself and both a necessary and sufficient cause of war; for Lenin, as a follower of Karl Marx, wars were waged solely in the interest of the monopoly capitalists.

In a famous tract titled *Imperialism: The Highest Stage of Capitalism*, Lenin advanced the Marxist thesis that Western imperialism—the late-nineteenth century scramble for colonial territories—was an unmistakable sign that capitalism was teetering on the brink of extinction. Imperialism, according to Lenin, was a logical outgrowth of the cutthroat competition characteristic of monopoly capitalism. Lenin theorized (correctly) that capitalists would always seek foreign markets, where they can make profitable investments and sell (or dump) industrial surpluses. Thus, through their financial power and the political influence that accompanies it, monopoly capitalists push their societies into war for their own selfish purposes. In Lenin's words,

> When the colonies of the European powers in Africa, for instance, comprised only one-tenth of that territory (as was the case in 1876), colonial policy was able to develop by methods other than those of monopoly—by the "free grabbing" of territories, so to speak. But when nine-tenths of Africa had been seized (approximately by 1900), when the whole world had been divided up, there was inevitably ushered in a period of colonial monopoly and, consequently, a period of particularly intense struggle for the division and the re-division of the world.[22]

In sum, Lenin held that because war is good business for the capitalists of the world, capitalists make it their business to promote war.

Lenin's analysis of the causes of war seems far removed from the Wilsonian thesis that tyranny leads inevitably to international conflicts, and yet the two views coincide at one crucial point. Lenin and Wilson both believed a particular defect of a certain type of nation-state produces wars—the form of government for Wilson, the economy and resulting social structure (classes divisions) for Lenin. If it could be eradicated, lasting world peace would ensue. Change is the key.

The Environment: Locke

Other theorists argue that war is caused by scarcity and the insecurity brought by fear of cold, hunger, disease, snakes, storms, and the like. This view accords with the ideas of philosopher John Locke.

Locke In his *Second Treatise on Civil Government* (1690), Locke argued forcefully that wars reflect conditions inherent in nature, rather than defects in human nature or society, that place human beings in do-or-die situations and make conflict inevitable. Like Hobbes before him, Locke saw the imperfections in human beings and believed self-preservation was the most basic human instinct. At this point, however, the two thinkers diverged. In the words of one authority,

> Locke's state of nature is not as violent as Hobbes's. If, as it seems, force will commonly be used without right in Locke's state of nature, it is not because most men are vicious or savage and bloodthirsty; Locke does not, as Hobbes does, speak of every man as the potential murderer of every other man. The main threat to the preservation of life in the state of nature lies not in the murderous tendencies of men but rather . . . in the poverty and hardship of their natural condition.[23]

Locke believed poverty and hardship are inevitable in the state of nature because great exertions are required to provide for our daily needs. Then we still have to protect our property, coveted by neighbors who have less and by others who are hungry and poor. Locke thus saw circumstances rooted in scarce resources as the principal cause of human conflict.

Locke's views on human beings, society, and nature have great bearing on the issues of war and peace. If the origins of war lie within human beings, as Hobbes believed, we can eradicate war only by changing the "inner self." If the problem lies in society, as Rousseau and Lenin contended, the solution is to reconstitute society (or the state) to remove the particular defects giving rise to aggressive behavior. If the problem lies neither in humans nor in society but in nature, the solution must be to transform nature.

The transformation of nature was precisely how Locke proposed to end human conflict in domestic society. Civil government, he asserted, must create the conditions to encourage economic development. Through economic development, a major cause of social tension—that is, the natural "penury" of the human condition—would be greatly eased. At the same time, if the formal rules of organized society replaced the uncertainties of nature, the need for every human being to constantly guard against the depredations of others would be lessened. Human beings would thus finally leave the state of nature, with all its anarchy and danger.

But in leaving one state of nature, humanity ironically found itself inhabiting another—the often-brutal world of international politics. Although Locke did not apply his theory of politics to the realm of international relations, his reasoning lends itself readily to such an application. Before the invention of government, human beings lived in domestic anarchy; likewise, in the absence of an effective world government, nations exist in international anarchy. In this sense, the relationships among nation-states differ little from relationships among individuals before the formation of civil society. The international state of nature, no less than the original, is a perpetual state of potential war. Thus, each nation-state behaves according to the dictates of self-preservation in an environment of hostility and insecurity, just as each individual presumably did in the state of nature.

One of the most common spoils of war is territory. From all appearances, the desire for more land and resources—property, in the Lockean sense—is one of the most common objectives of war. Recall that Lenin attributed the European scramble for colonial territories toward the end of the nineteenth century to the search for new markets, cheap labor, and raw materials—that is, property. Significantly, Lenin held that the propensity to accumulate capital (money and property) that Locke described was directly responsible for imperialism, which Lenin predicted would lead inevitably to war. Even if Lenin overstated the case against capitalism, one thing is certain: Territoriality has always been associated with war, and it always will be.

When Locke wrote, plenty of land in the world remained unclaimed by Europeans and uncultivated. He noted that even in the state of nature, human relations were probably fairly harmonious, so long as no one crowded anyone else. It stands to reason, however, that as growing populations begin to place ever-greater pressures on easily available resources, the drawing of property lines becomes progressively more important. If, as Locke's analysis suggests, prehistoric people felt threatened by the pressures of finite resources, imagine how much greater those pressures have become in modern times.

Nature's Scarcity: Malthusian Nightmares Many contemporary writers have elaborated on the theme of resource scarcity propounded by Locke and, later, by Thomas Malthus (1766–1834) in his famous *Essay on the Principle of Population* (1798). Richard Falk, for example, identified "four dimensions of planetary danger," including the "war system, population pressures, resource scarcities, and environmental overload."[24] According to Falk, these are interrelated aspects of a single problem that must be treated as a group.

Falk's assumptions about the causes of international conflict are consistent with Locke's political understanding:

> International society is, of course, an extreme example of a war system. Conflicts abound. Vital interests are constantly at stake. Inequalities of resources and power create incentives to acquire what a neighboring state possesses.[25]

Just as humans were constantly vulnerable to the depredations of others in the state of nature, so predatory neighbors continually threaten nation-states.

Throughout history, then, violence has played a vital role in the conduct of foreign affairs, because, Falk argued, conditions beyond the control of individual nation-states compel them to regard their own security as directly proportionate to their neighbors' distress.

Hence, even after the unprecedented destruction wrought by World Wars I and II, "many efforts were made, often with success, to moderate the scope and barbarism of war, but no serious assault was mounted to remove the conditions that cause war."[26] What exactly are these conditions? Professor Falk argued that access to food and water supplies had a great bearing on the earliest wars. These considerations remain relevant in the modern world:

> Given the present situation of mass undernourishment (more than two-thirds of the world population), it is worth taking account of the ancient link between war and control of food surplus, as well as the age-old human practice of protecting positions of political and economic privilege by military means.[27]

Even more basic than the issue of adequate food and water supplies, Falk pointed out, is the need to control the population explosion. In many ways, population pressure underlies the entire crisis of planetary organization, especially in light of what we now know about the linkages between economic development and urbanization, urbanization and pollution, and pollution and global warming. Consider that developed countries, led by the United States, are by far the biggest global polluters at present; that China and India, both emerging economic giants, have a combined population of 2.4 billion, roughly three times that of the United States and the European Union put together; and that China and India are exempt from the carbon-emission limits established under the Kyoto Protocol (see Chapter 13). Under such conditions, no nation, no matter how powerful, feels terribly secure in our times. The 2008–2009 world financial crisis served as a dramatic reminder of the vulnerability of even the richest and most powerful countries. Not only oil but also many other raw materials, such as bauxite, copper, and tin, are unequally distributed and in short supply. At the same time, the poorest countries continue to experience shortages in the most basic of all raw materials—food.

IN SEARCH OF A DEFINITIVE THEORY

The three alternative views on the ultimate causes of war identified in this chapter are based on one of the most fundamental concepts in Western political philosophy—the triad of humanity, society, and nature. All three theories have some validity, and together, they point to a multilevel theory on the origins of war. Individually or together, they help explain why war or the threat of war hangs over every nation like a dreaded sword of Damocles. And so long as war continues to plague humankind, the search for solutions and for a definitive theory will continue.

@JEROME DELAY/AP PHOTO

Plagued by civil war and weakened by famine, an estimated two million people died in Somalia between 1991 and 1992. A similar tragedy occurred in the Darfur region of Sudan in 2004–2009. In both cases, there were urgent calls for military intervention on humanitarian grounds. Having tried and failed in Somalia when George H. W. Bush was in the White House, the United States under George W. Bush, son of the elder Bush, stayed on the sidelines as Arab militia—the so-called Janjeweed—attacked unarmed black Sudanese villagers, killing tens of thousands, raping and pillaging, and displacing more than two million victims.

Beyond Politics

It seems reasonable to assume that, all else being equal, nations exhibiting intense nationalism are more warlike than are politically apathetic nations. But all else is seldom equal. Indeed, explanations that depend on nationalism "have done a relatively poor job in explaining the incidence of war."[28]

But what about the Wilsonian view that democracies are naturally peaceful, and tyranny is the primary cause of war in the modern world? Through the ages, political thinkers have stressed the relationship between dictatorial rule and belligerent or aggressive behavior. Aristotle called tyrants warmongers who plunge their nations into war "with the object of keeping their subjects constantly occupied and continually in need of a leader."[29] Some modern writers, such as Hannah Arendt, argue that totalitarian governments are inherently aggressive.[30] Two major modern conflicts—World War II and the Korean War—were initiated by totalitarian dictatorships. Stalin in the 1930s, Hitler in the 1940s, Mao in the early 1950s, and Pol Pot between 1975 and 1979 all waged war in the form of bloody purges and mass murder at home. These episodes of lethal state behavior strongly suggest totalitarian rulers are prone to coercive force.

Dictators also exercise absolute control over the armed forces, police, and instruments of propaganda. They have often been war heroes who rode to power on the wings of military victory—successful soldiers who take over governments are rarely squeamish about the use of force. For them, war can provide a popular diversion from the tedium and rigors of everyday life; it can act as an outlet for pent-up domestic hostilities that might otherwise be directed at the dictator; it can help unify society and justify a crackdown on dissidents; or finally it can rejuvenate a stagnant economy or an uninspired citizenry.

But these observations do not prove despotism often or always causes wars. The Kennedy, Johnson, and Nixon administrations blamed the Vietnam war on communist aggression. Critics of U.S. foreign policy, however, blamed it on misguided or provocative U.S. actions in Southeast Asia. Thus, depending on the evidence we accept, the Vietnam War can "prove" either that dictatorships are more prone to war than democracies, or that democracies are no more immune to crusading militarism than are dictatorships.

Democracies have not been notably successful at avoiding war. In the second half of the twentieth century, for example, India, the world's largest democracy, waged several bloody wars against Pakistan, and the United States fought major wars in Korea, Vietnam, and Iraq. More recently, the United States spearheaded large-scale military actions against the Taliban regime in Afghanistan (2001) and Iraq (2003). Nor have democratic nations always been unwilling participants in war. The United States did not go out of its way to avoid fighting the Spanish-American War of 1898. And it is difficult to overlook U.S. intervention in the Mexican Revolution in 1914, when President Wilson ordered U.S. Marines to seize the Mexican port of Veracruz and later sent a punitive expedition into Mexico against the forces of Pancho Villa.

Research shows democratic nations are not less warlike than either authoritarian or totalitarian states.[31] In fact, they engage in military action about as often as other types of government; some evidence suggests they may start wars less frequently but join them more often.[32] In one respect, however, the Kantian-Wilsonian prodemocracy, anti-dictatorship theory of war does hold true: In the so-called **paradox of democratic peace**, democratic states rarely, if ever, fight one another.[33] There has not been a real war between democracies in more than a century and a half.[34] One explanation for this paradox goes as follows:

> Expectations of war and threats of war between democracies are almost certainly reduced by the presence of a common political culture, by a mutual identity and sympathy, by stronger people-to-people and elite-to-elite bonds, by the ability of interest groups within these countries to form transnational coalitions, by more frequent communication, and by more positive mutual perceptions.[35]

Public opinion comes come into play because government is limited in constitutional democracies, political power is more-or-less widely distributed, popularly elected leaders are inclined to emphasize compromise over confrontation, and

paradox of democratic peace
Democratic states are often militarily powerful, fight other states, engage in armed intervention, and sometimes commit acts of aggression, but they rarely fight each other.

constitutional democracies generally respect the individual's rights. All these factors tend to promote the peaceful resolution of political disputes between democracies.

When democracies go to war, they fight nondemocratic states. This suggests that the degree of political difference (or distance) between governments, as well as economic and cultural differences, may be important.[36] Such findings support Wilson's conclusion that dictatorial regimes are the natural enemies of democracies, as well as Lenin's view that capitalist and communist nations are incompatible. As one study of Latin American politics noted, "The more similar two nations are in economic development, political orientation, Catholic culture, and density, the more aligned their voting in the UN" and the less conflict there will be between them. By the same token, "The more dissimilar two nations are in economic development and size and the greater their joint technological capability to span geographic distance is, the more overt conflict they have with each other."[37]

Beyond Economics

If politics provides only a partial and limited explanation for conflict, Lenin's theory that wars are caused by economic factors, particularly capitalism, explains even less. One problem with this proposition is that wars preceded both capitalism and imperialism, proving that capitalism is certainly not the only cause of war.[38] Furthermore, there is little in the historical evidence to support Lenin's economic theory that capitalist states (as opposed to socialist or communist states) are particularly warlike. Although some wars can be explained by national economic motives such as imperialism, most cannot.[39]

The relationship between capitalism and imperialism is not clear or consistent. Some capitalist states have practiced imperialism and waged war, while others, like Sweden and Switzerland, have avoided both. Lenin's economic theory has difficulty accounting for such differences or explaining why some socialist states have engaged in unprovoked armed aggression. Examples include the Soviet invasion of Estonia, Latvia, Lithuania, and Finland in 1939, North Korea's attack on South Korea in 1950, the Soviet invasion of Hungary (1956), Czechoslovakia (1968), and Afghanistan (1979), and China's attack on Tibet (1956), India (1962), and Vietnam (1979).[40]

There is little doubt that economics is a cause of specific wars, if not war in general. For instance, the U.S.-led coalition in the Iraq War was driven in part by economic motives: to protect the vast oil fields of Arabia and to keep the vital lifelines linking the Middle East with Europe, Asia, and North America from Saddam Hussein's control. But other motives are almost always present, as well. In the Iraq War these were the (false, as it turned out) belief that Saddam possessed weapons of mass destruction (WMD), that he was aiding and abetting international terrorists, that he represented a clear and present danger to Israel, and so on.

There is surprisingly little evidence to support the thesis that one kind of economic system or a country's particular stage of economic development or economics in general is decisive in motivating nations to fight wars. When academic studies point to economics as a contributing cause of war, they often rely solely on a statistical correlation between economics and war, which, as every scientist knows, does not prove causality.

Since World War II, wars have been fought within the territory of developing states. Does this mean countries with less-advanced economies are more warlike? Not necessarily, because it also appears these wars have often been instigated or even fought by industrialized nations. Post–World War II examples of such conflicts include those fought in Suez, Algeria, the Congo, Vietnam, Afghanistan, the Falkland Islands, and Iraq. Although we cannot make a strong correlation between economic development and the frequency of military conflicts, some evidence suggests nations with more-developed economies actually have greater warlike tendencies than countries with less-developed economies.[41]

The Danger of Oversimplification

Simplistic theories of war abound. Some quantitative theorists have described in fine detail recurring patterns that often lead to war-making military alliances, which are then followed by military buildups, the making of threats, a series of crises, and so on.[42] Such studies have also shown that certain actions political leaders take in an effort to reduce the possibility of war (for example, making alliances) may actually increase its likelihood.[43] However, none of these studies proves that making or joining military alliances or any of the other steps associated with the pattern leading to war actually cause war. Fear of war, for example, causes countries to join alliances, but joining alliances does not inevitably lead to war. Thus, virtually all Western democracies joined the NATO alliance and all Communist states of Central and Eastern Europe joined the Warsaw Pact, but NATO and the Warsaw Pact never fought a war. Furthermore, the "typical" pattern is itself somewhat limited, as it represents only those conflicts fought between major states of approximately equal power.[44]

Most war theorists have long believed large states are more inclined to war than are small states,[45] and powerful states more inclined to fight than weak ones. That nations confident of winning are most inclined to fight wars makes intuitive sense.[46] However, defining a state's power is difficult; political leaders may overestimate their own strength and underestimate the adversary's (the Vietnam War is a sterling example).[47] Nations experiencing internal violence are also more likely to be war prone for several reasons. A war may help unify the nation, or internal conflict may make it an easy target.[48] Nations headed by risk takers are also more likely to go to war.

Another relevant factor is common borders, particularly when there are many or when they are shared by long-standing rivals.[49] Nations with large and growing populations, limited access to necessary resources, and a high level of technology have an obvious environmental incentive to pursue expansionist foreign policy, whereas sparsely populated countries tend to fight fewer wars regardless of technology or access to natural resources. When these latter countries do fight, they tend to be victims rather than aggressors.[50] In sum, a large, powerful nation with a rapidly expanding population and advanced technology, that shares many borders with neighboring states or one border with a traditional enemy (or both), and is governed by a risk-oriented leader is a prime candidate for aggressive war, especially if it faces civil strife or armed rebellion.

Many factors we've discussed, from human nature to scarce resources, and many of the characteristics associated with war, including population size, economic development, and border problems, are difficult or impossible to change, especially in the short run. The humorist Will Rogers once suggested that world peace could be advanced if nations—like people—could move, but they can't (although populations can, and do, migrate).

In fact, the false belief that we can eradicate conflict or trace it to a single factor can actually increase the possibility of war. As European history from 1919 to 1939 illustrates, concentrating solely on rearranging the international system while ignoring the role of human nature can have the unintended effect of clearing obstacles from the path of megalomaniacs bent on aggression.[51] Had U.S., French, and British leaders in the 1930s heeded Churchill's warnings about the threat posed by Hitler and stood up to him earlier, they might have been able to defeat Nazi Germany quickly or prevent the war altogether. World War II had multiple causes, which does not mean it was inevitable.

An understanding of the complex causes and factors of war **can** modestly improve the international system of conflict management, by dispelling illusions about the prospects for peace. In such important matters, simple solutions can be worse than no solutions at all; some of history's foremost political simplifiers have also been among the foremost contributors to war.

TOTAL WAR: WARS EVERYBODY FIGHTS

Total war is a thoroughly modern phenomenon. It is different from the **limited wars** of the distant past in several crucial respects. First, it is unlimited in that one or more of the belligerents seeks total victory and will stop at nothing short of **unconditional surrender**. Second, total war is unlimited as to means. States use advanced technology to enhance the range, accuracy, and killing power of modern weapons. Third, total war is unlimited as to participation: whole societies engage in the war effort.

The Napoleonic Wars are the prototype of total war and the first such war ever fought. Napoléon waged an all-out drive for hegemony that recognized no limits on ends or means. He sought total domination of Europe, and he possessed all the resources available to a modern, centralized state at that time. Of course, there were then no weapons of mass destruction, except conventional armies that could be used to this end once the enemy was defeated. Thus, Napoléon's forces burned much of Moscow, including the Kremlin, to the ground after Russia's defeat. Most important, Napoléon introduced the idea of mass conscription, drafting thousands of young men into the modern world's first people's army. (Prior armies had consisted of professional soldiers and paid

limited war
The opposite of all-out war, particularly an all-out nuclear war.

unconditional surrender
Giving an enemy on the verge of defeat a stark choice between surrendering immediately (placing itself entirely at the mercy of the victor) or being utterly destroyed.

mercenaries.) Napoléon also used nationalism, propaganda, and patriotic symbols to mobilize the entire society behind the war effort. These innovations were all harbingers of the future: We can consider the total wars fought in the first half of the twentieth century a single event with an interlude between two incredibly violent spasms—the horrific culmination of processes set in motion more than a century earlier.

After World War II, the concept of total war took on an even more ominous meaning due to major advances in the science and technology of war-fighting capabilities. The advent of the nuclear age utterly transformed both the strategy and tactics of war, the logic of military force and the battlefield. Like the new face of war itself, this transformation was total.

ACCIDENTAL WAR: WARS NOBODY WANTS

We like to think our leaders always know what they are doing, especially when it comes to matters of war and peace. But accidents do happen. What if a Pakistani arms smuggler were passing through India with a package containing "weaponized" anthrax? What if the spores were released in the center of New Delhi, the capital of India, when the Kashmiri taxi driver ran a red light and collided with a truck at a busy intersection? And what if that happened during a crisis with Pakistan? Might India think Pakistan was launching an all-out war? Pakistan had nothing to do with the incident, but India might decide to retaliate immediately and ask questions later (waiting would be extremely risky in such a situation). In this scenario, an all-out nuclear war could result from accident and misperception, rather than from any rational choice on either side.

War by misperception, or war resulting from the misreading of a situation, is perhaps the most common kind of war nobody wants. **Accidental war** is another possibility. An incorrect translation, a message not delivered, a diplomatic signal missed or misinterpreted—accidents of this kind precipitated unintended wars well before the advent of space-age weapons systems. In a technological era dominated by nuclear weapons and ballistic missiles, the danger of war by accidental means has gone up dramatically, as have the stakes. Nuclear war by escalation could begin as a limited (and presumably localized) conflict between two nations in which neither side originally intended to use its most destructive weapons. But as casualties mount and battlefield reverses occur, one side (most likely the one losing) could be tempted to up the ante by introducing more powerful weapons, which the other side would have little choice but to match. If both sides possess nuclear weapons, the dynamics could move them toward nuclear war. **Catalytic war** can also generate violence and destruction well beyond any nation's intention. Historically, such wars reflected alliance arrangements. If one member of the alliance was attacked, the other(s) sprang to its defense, enlarging the war. Nowadays, a catalytic war might originate as a localized conflict between, say, two developing countries that have powerful allies. Local wars have always had the potential to turn into regional or even

war by misperception
Armed conflict that results when two nations fail to read one another's intentions accurately.

accidental war
In the modern age, the unintentional launching of a nuclear attack because of a mistake or miscalculation.

catalytic war
A conflict that begins as a localized and limited encounter but grows into a general war after other parties are drawn into the conflict through the activation of military alliances.

global wars (as happened in both world wars). Or a saboteur or madman might somehow manage to "pull the nuclear trigger." All such scenarios—sabotage, misperception, accident, escalation, or a catalytic event—show how war can occur without any premeditation or intent.

NUCLEAR WAR: WARS NOBODY WINS

Weapons of mass destruction have been used only once. The United States dropped two atomic bombs on the Japanese cities of Hiroshima and Nagasaki to end World War II. President Truman waited for Japan's High Command to surrender after the first bomb leveled Hiroshima. When three days later they had not, he gave the order to drop the second bomb. This time Japan surrendered. But it would be a mistake to try to repeat that winning strategy. The reason is very simple. When the U.S. president decided to "go nuclear" in 1945, there were only two atomic bombs in the world, and they were both in the U.S. arsenal. Truman did not have to risk **massive retaliation** (a response in kind) from Japan or any other country. The United States had a (short-lived) **nuclear monopoly**.

The former Soviet Union quickly developed its nuclear weapons program. By the end of the 1950s, it had an arsenal of mass-destruction armaments and was even building long-range rockets called **intercontinental ballistic missiles (ICBMs)**. Moscow actually beat the United States into outer space by launching *Sputnik,* the first earth-orbiting satellite, in 1957. During the 1960s, the United States lost not only its nuclear monopoly (if it had not already been lost a decade earlier) but also its aura of invulnerability. The era of massive retaliation and **brinkmanship**—reliance on nuclear weapons to intimidate adversaries— was superseded by the era of **mutual assured destruction (MAD)**, or **mutual deterrence,** in which both superpowers had the ability to withstand a nuclear first strike and still be capable of delivering a **second strike** that would result in unacceptable damage to the aggressor.

Neither superpower spared any effort to get (or stay) ahead in the nuclear arms race. By the early 1970s, both sides had a tremendous **overkill** capability; that is, each had enough weapons of mass destruction to destroy the other many times over. Even more alarming, both sides had built nuclear submarines to act as mobile platforms for launching ICBMs and were putting multiple warheads—called **multiple independently targeted reentry vehicles (MIRVs)**—on both land- and sea-based ICBMs (technically known as **submarine-launched ballistic missiles (SLBMs)**. But whereas both sides wanted to win the arms race, neither wanted to lose a war with the other, and both knew there would be no winners if deterrence ever failed. This almost happened during the Cuban Missile Crisis (1963); it was a close call. As a result, the two sworn enemies quickly established the now-famous hotline—a direct communications link between the White House and the Kremlin—to avert a future calamity, one that might just happen by accident.

massive retaliation
Strategic military doctrine based on a plausible standing threat of nuclear reprisal employed by the United States in the 1950s during the short-lived era of the U.S. nuclear monopoly; according to this doctrine, if the Soviet Union attacked U.S. allies with conventional military forces, the United States would retaliate with nuclear weapons.

nuclear monopoly
When only one side in an adversarial relationship possesses a credible nuclear capability; the United States enjoyed a nuclear monopoly for roughly a decade after World War II.

intercontinental ballistic missile (ICBM)
A long-range missile armed with multiple nuclear warheads capable of striking targets anywhere in the world; both the United States and Russia possess large arsenals of these ultimate strategic weapons.

PROXY WARS: WARS OTHERS FIGHT

brinkmanship

In diplomacy, the deliberate use of military threats to create a crisis atmosphere; the calculated effort to take a tense bilateral relationship to the brink of war in order to achieve a political objective (for example, deterring a common enemy from carrying out an act of aggression against an ally).

mutual assured destruction (MAD)

A nuclear stalemate in which both sides in an adversarial relationship know that if either one initiates a war, the other will retain enough retaliatory ("second strike") capability to administer unacceptable damage even after absorbing the full impact of a nuclear surprise attack; during the Cold War, a stable strategic relationship between the two superpowers

mutual deterrence

The theory that aggressive wars can be prevented if potential victims maintain a military force sufficient to inflict unacceptable damage on any possible aggressor.

Civil wars and guerrilla wars typically pit established governments on one side against rebels or insurgents on the other. During the Cold War, the two super-powers frequently intervened directly or indirectly in civil wars or insurgencies in Third World countries. Vietnam in the 1960s and early 1970s and Afghanistan in the 1970s are two notable examples. In Vietnam, the United States intervened directly with military forces, and the Soviet Union intervened indirectly by send-ing massive amounts of military and economic aid. In Afghanistan, it was the other way around—the Soviet Union launched a military invasion, and the United States backed the freedom fighters (the mujahideen). Similarly, the Soviet Union intervened in Angola's civil war in the 1970s, and the United States intervened in Nicaragua and El Salvador in the 1980s. These conflicts were sometimes called **proxy wars,** because the superpowers would back one side while relying on indig-enous forces to do the fighting with the help of U.S. or Soviet "advisors."

With the collapse of the Soviet Union, only one superpower remained, and the ideological rivalry that fueled the Cold War became a thing of the past. Whether a proxy war will occur again is an open question; if so, it will be in a very different context and, in all likelihood, for different principles.

JUST WARS: WARS OTHERS START

So far, we have been looking at war primarily from the standpoint of the perpe-trators of aggression. But what about the victims? Few observers would dispute that nations have the right to resist armed aggression. When national survival is at stake, self-defense is morally justified. So, despite Benjamin Franklin's assertion that "there was never a good war or a bad peace," some wars may be both necessary and proper, but which ones? Who is to say? And how can we know for sure?

The Just War Doctrine

The venerable doctrine of the **just war** holds that under certain circumstances, a war can be "good"—not pleasant or intrinsically desirable, but serving the welfare of a nation and the cause of justice. This concept was advanced by early Christian theologians such as Saint Augustine and refined by medieval philosophers. Hugo Grotius (1583–1645) and other natural law theorists later reformulated it.

Those who favor the concept of just war unanimously agree defensive wars are justified. A nation that suffers an unprovoked attack is justified in waging war against its assailant. Some theorists further give third-party nations the right to interfere on behalf of hapless victims of military aggression. The 1991 Persian Gulf War, preceded by Iraq's invasion and occupation of Kuwait, is a case in point.

©LAURA RAUCH/AP PHOTO

The U.S.-led military forces that invaded Iraq in the spring of 2003 quickly defeated Saddam Hussein's army, but the subsequent occupation gave rise to a protracted urban guerrilla war of attrition in which the enemy used terrorist tactics that turned key Iraqi cities, including the capital of Baghdad, into bloody battlegrounds.

second strike
Retaliation in kind against a nuclear attack(er); this capability paradoxically minimizes the likelihood that a nuclear confrontation will lead to an actual nuclear exchange.

overkill
Amassing a much larger nuclear arsenal than is (or would be) needed to annihilate any adversary.

Earlier writers did not always limit the just war doctrine to defensive wars. Saint Augustine, abhorred war in all its guises, but he justified even aggressive wars under some circumstances, as when a state "has failed either to make reparation for an injurious action committed by its citizens or to return what has been appropriated."[52] Another early Christian theologian, Saint Ambrose (339–397), argued that nations have a moral obligation, not simply a right, to wage aggressive war for the sake of higher principle. "Man has a moral duty," he wrote, "to employ force to resist active wickedness, for to refrain from hindering evil when possible is tantamount to promoting it."[53] Ambrose was aware of the need for limitations on this kind of war. Aggressive wars, he declared, should be fought only for a clearly just cause.

The just war doctrine posits five postulates. First, war must be the last resort of a legitimate government; there must be no other effective political alternatives available. Second, the conflict must be just, fought only for deterring or repelling aggression or righting a wrong. Third, the war cannot be futile; there must be some probability the nation undertaking it can succeed. Fourth, the war's purpose must justify the cost in money and lives; the means employed must be appropriate to the reason the war is fought. Finally, a just war must minimize injury and death to civilians.

In contrast to the simplistic nationalism represented by such slogans as "My country right or wrong," the just war concept suggests a standard of moral responsibility that transcends narrow national interest. Early Christian theologians based their notions of justice on theological doctrines and scriptural teachings. Modern versions of the doctrine are grounded in a natural-law philosophy holding there are self-evident truths about human welfare that, taken together, point toward the true meaning of the ideal of "justice for all."

Evaluating the Just War Doctrine

Of the criticisms leveled against the just war doctrine, we focus on three of the most substantial: that the doctrine represents moral relativism, that it embodies an ethnocentric bias, and that it is politically unrealistic.

Moral Relativism Some critics contend the concept of the just war is based on highly subjective, and hence unverifiable, value judgments. Because governments rarely admit to starting wars and almost always blame the other side, any attempt to assign moral responsibility is bound to reflect the opinions of the observer more than the often uncertain facts of the situation. The only way to avoid this **moral relativism** is to confine ourselves to describing what happened before and during wars, sticking to accurate and verifiable facts.

Ethnocentric or Nationalistic Bias Critics also say Western just war theorists reflect only their own culture, ignoring justifications for war advanced by other cultures or ideologies—an accusation of **ethnocentric bias**. For instance, the traditional Islamic concept of a jihad ("struggle" or "holy war") against temptation, evil, apostasy, or "infidels" offers a moral rationale for aggressive war rarely acknowledged by Western proponents of the just war doctrine. Just war theorists were similarly criticized for rejecting an interpretation advanced until recently by the former Soviet Union—that just wars are waged by the working class against their oppressors, wars of "national liberation" fought by

---

multiple independently targeted reentry vehicle (MIRV)
The name given to intercontinental missiles containing many nuclear warheads that can be individually programmed to split off from the nose cone of the rocket upon reentry into the earth's atmosphere and hit different specific targets with a high degree of accuracy.

submarine-launched ballistic missile (SLBM)
Strategic missiles with multiple nuclear warheads launched from submarines that prowl the ocean depths and that cannot be easily detected or destroyed by a preemptive attack.

proxy war
A war in which two adversaries back opposing parties to a conflict by supplying money, weapons, and military advisors, while avoiding direct combat operations against each other.

just war
A war fought in self-defense or because it is the only way a nation can do what is right.

colonized peoples of the Third World against Western "imperialists," and wars waged to prevent the overthrow of socialist governments in Eastern Europe and elsewhere.

Political Naiveté Several opponents of the just war doctrine raise the practical objection that even a universally accepted standard governing them would be extremely difficult to apply fairly. Just as individuals are not good judges in their own cases, it is argued, so nations are not competent to pass judgment on controversies involving their own interests and well-being. Without an impartial referee, critics contend, the just war doctrine remains a sham advanced by aggressor nations to justify self-serving policies and military interventionism.

Defenders of the just war doctrine point out that moral judgments concerning the conduct of wars have long been thought both natural and necessary: natural in the sense that "for as long as men and women have talked about war, they have talked about it in terms of right and wrong,"[54] and necessary because without them, all wars would have to be considered equally objectionable (or praiseworthy). Admittedly, we cannot prove scientifically that aggressive wars are any worse than preemptive or preventive wars, but nor do we need to prove cold-blooded murder is more reprehensible than killing in self-defense—a distinction both criminal law and common sense support.

In the real world, heads of state often engage in moral talk and immoral behavior. The idea of the just war is worth keeping, therefore, if not as a means of controlling that behavior, then as a method of evaluating it (see Box 16.1).

Box 16.1 FOCUS ON   The Nuremberg War Crimes Trials

Following World War II, in history's most famous attempt to apply moral standards to wartime conduct, Nazi leaders were charged in Nuremberg, Germany, with several types of crimes. First, they were accused of **crimes against peace**, because they had waged aggressive war in violation of international treaties and obligations. Second, they were charged with **war crimes**, which encompassed violations of the accepted rules of war, such as brutality toward prisoners of war, wanton destruction of towns, and mistreatment of civilians in conquered lands. Third, they were accused of **crimes against humanity**, including the persecution and mass murder of huge numbers of non-combatants. Crimes against peace and war crimes were categories widely accepted under the just war doctrine; the category of crimes against humanity was designed to deal with a specific instance of genocide, the Holocaust.

The decision to punish Nazi leaders for genocide was prompted by an understandable desire for retribution. German actions could not be justified by the exigencies of war (which, of course,

(Continued)

Box 16.1 FOCUS ON   (continued)

FIGURE 16.1   This map shows the location of the Nazi concentration and extermination camps. Notice that concentration camps existed in France, the Netherlands, Austria, Latvia, and Czechoslovakia, as well as in Germany, but the infamous death camps were all located deep inside Poland. Strikingly, not one was located on or near German territory. Hitler obviously did not want the horrors of the Final Solution taking place in his own backyard.

SOURCE: From "Concentration and Death Camps" accessed at http://history1900s.about.com/library/holocaust/blmap.htm. Copyright © 2009 by Jennifer Rosenberg. Used with permission of About, Inc., which can be found online at www.about.com. All rights reserved.

Hitler had started). The crimes against humanity concept provided firm support for the just war doctrine (and vice versa).

The Nuremberg trials were justifiable, but it is no simple task to apply the crimes against peace, war crimes, and crimes against humanity labels to concrete and often unique situations. The death camps of the Holocaust violated all standards of law, justice, and decency. But what about the Allied firebombing of Dresden and many other German cities? Or the brutalities against German civilians tolerated (if not encouraged) by the

Box 16.1 FOCUS ON | (continued)

LANDOV MEDIA

The U.S. uses drones like the one pictured here against the Taliban in Afghanistan and Pakistan. When civilians are killed it is called "collateral damage," not a war crime.

Soviet army? Or the American firebombing of Japanese cities and the dropping of the atomic bombs on Hiroshima and Nagasaki? These acts, which resulted in hundreds of thousands of civilian deaths, were not covered under the war crimes labels. Critics argue this fact illustrates an important point: the victors write the history of a war. By the same token, the victors alone decide what is and what is not a war crime.

The United States is quick to label auto-genocide in Cambodia or "ethnic cleansing" (a euphemism for genocide) in Bosnia or genocide in Rwanda and Sudan as war crimes. On the other hand, when U.S. drone attacks targeting Taliban fighters in villages along the Afghan-Pakistan border kill civilians it is labeled "collateral damage"—which makes it legal. Critics of the Bush administration have argued that the methods used in the war on terror—"extraordinary rendition" (seizing suspected terrorists on foreign soil), leaving detainees in legal limbo by creating a new classification of "illegal combatants," and "enhanced interrogation techniques" such as waterboarding—were war crimes.

A WAR ON *WHAT?* THE POLITICS OF HYPERBOLE

When the 9/11 attacks gave rise to a new global threat—that of international terrorism (see Chapter 15), the Bush administration's response was to declare a "war on terror." But terror is not a state—not a place on the map. Waging "war" on terror is thus not like waging traditional war. In fact, calling it war raises major conceptual and strategic problems. President Bush was not the first U.S. commander in chief to use the term war loosely. As U.S. Attorney General, Robert F. Kennedy declared a "war on organized crime" in 1961, and every

moral relativism
The idea that all moral judgments are conditional and only "true" in a certain religious, cultural or social context; the belief that there is no such thing as universal truth in the realm of ethics or morality.

ethnocentric bias
The common tendency of human beings to see the world through a cultural lens that distorts reality and exaggerates the good in ones own society and the evil in others.

crimes against peace
A Nuremberg war crimes trials category, covering the violation of international peace by waging an unjustified, aggressive war.

war crimes
Violation of generally accepted rules of war as established in the Geneva Conventions on the conduct of war. The Geneva Conventions call for the humanitarian treatment of civilians and prisoners of war, and respect for human life and dignity; crimes against humanity, such as genocide and ethnic cleansing, are also war crimes.

president since John F. Kennedy (Robert's brother) has embraced the "war on crime" as his own. President Lyndon Baines Johnson waged a "war on poverty." LBJ's successor in the White House, Richard Nixon, declared a "war on drugs," calling drug abuse "public enemy number one in the United States." These and other domestic "wars" arguably made war appear a kind of permanent condition in a perilous world, rather than an extreme step taken only in the most extreme circumstances.

The war on terror identified a subversive organization—al Qaeda—as the source of all evil and a single individual—Osama bin Laden—as the mastermind behind it. Al Qaeda thus became the functional equivalent of world communism, and bin Laden was the new Stalin.

The Bush administration further linked several existing governments—Iraq, Iran, and North Korea—to this conspiratorial organization and branded these states the "axis of evil." (In the 1980s, President Reagan famously called the Soviet Union the "evil empire.") In addition, the war on terror, like the Cold War before it, would be open-ended. Unlike wars of the past, it would go on for generations, possibly forever. Finally, this new "war" was cast as a contest between good and evil, thus turning it into a religious-ideological crusade in much the same way as the Cold War was cast as a struggle between freedom and capitalism, and totalitarian tyranny and communism.

The means for fighting the war on terror are also reminiscent of the Cold War, including a major military buildup, a soaring defense budget, and a wholesale reorganization of the nation's intelligence, police, and defense establishment. The "national security state" was transformed by creating a new Department of Homeland Security. The central idea of this new department was to integrate the operational procedures of agencies, especially the FBI and CIA, which had operated independently or even competitively during the Cold War.

In the aftermath of the 9/11 attacks, an outraged public sought answers and action. The prudent course of action was a limited response aimed at a finite evil and a specific target. Instead, a surgical military operation to wipe out terrorist training camps in Afghanistan became a new global crusade pitting the United States and its allies against the so-called Axis of Evil—Iraq, Iran, and North Korea.

Not surprisingly, different observers interpreted the war on terror in very different ways. Conservatives were much more likely than liberals to accept the reasons given for launching an all-out "war" after 9/11, especially for the controversial decision to invade Iraq. But, in fairness, the war was not opposed by leading Democrats in Congress, and even liberal politicians, such as then-Senator Hillary Clinton, supported it. It was only after the occupation turned into a civil war that politicians of all stripes began to jump ship.

What are the lessons of this war? What does it tell us about war in general?

First, the Iraq war combined aspects of various war scenarios discussed earlier in this chapter—**inadvertent war** (war resulting from misperception, misinformation, or miscalculation), accidental war (war touched off unintentionally), catalytic war (war that starts small and gets bigger as other powers are drawn in), and **ABC war** (wars involving atomic, biological, or chemical weapons, otherwise known

A War on What? The Politics of Hyperbole

529

as weapons of mass destruction). The concept of a just war also came into play because the attack on Iraq was (wrongly) linked to 9/11. Thus, the war was rationalized as a righteous way to punish an aggressor or to avenge a heinous act.

Second, the invasion of Iraq was conceived as part of a larger war; a war not against a specific enemy but against a disembodied "ism." Terrorism, like poverty or crime, is a condition, a fact of life. It does not have a beginning or an end and therefore cannot be eradicated by military means. At best, it can be managed or brought under control. Whether the military as presently constituted is the best instrument for dealing with this type of threat is debatable. In Iraq, traditional military instruments—fighter-bombers, tanks, artillery, and the like—proved highly effective in defeating the Iraqi army but virtually useless in dealing with the guerrilla-style insurrection that followed.

Third, during the course of this war, the Bush administration switched enemies and changed the rationale for fighting. The real enemy was a secretive organization known as al Qaeda, rather than another state. To the extent that this enemy had a face, it was the face of Osama bin Laden. For all its military might, the United States was unable to defeat al Qaeda by invading Afghanistan and even failed to apprehend bin Laden himself, who remains at large some 4 years later as these words are written. Instead, the Bush administration shifted the focus of attention from Afghanistan and bin Laden to Iraq and Saddam—in other words, from an elusive enemy who could not be defeated militarily to one who could, or so the architects of the Iraq war believed.

That belief proved to be false, as was the evidence that Saddam harbored WMD, which had been the reason given for launching the war in the first place. As the fighting dragged on and the death toll mounted, the Bush administration changed the rationale for the war once again. Clearly, the original objective—to locate and destroy Saddam's WMD labs and stockpiles—disappeared when no such weapons were discovered. The reason for ousting Saddam then became nation-building, to promote freedom and democracy in the world. Later, as the

crimes against humanity
A category of war crimes, first introduced at the Nuremberg trials of Nazi war criminals, covering the wanton, brutal extermination of millions of innocent civilians.

inadvertent war
A war resulting from misperception, misinformation, or miscalculation; an unnecessary war.

ABC war
A general term for war involving weapons of mass destructions (WMD), especially atomic (nuclear), biological, and chemical weapons. See weapons of mass destruction (WMD).

©AP PHOTOS

U.S. soldiers during an operation in Zabul Province, Afghanistan, in 2006. The Bush administration started another war (in Iraq) before it finished this one.

civil war raged, the reason was simply to stabilize the region because a hasty withdrawal would, it was argued, leave a dangerous power vacuum. What no one in Washington was saying, however, was what nearly everyone outside Washington was thinking all along: the real reason for invading and occupying Iraq was oil, still the world's most important strategic resource.

On the oil-rich Arabian peninsula, Iraq's petroleum reserves are second in size only to Saudi Arabia's. The possibility—indeed, the likelihood—that energy security (represented by Iraqi oil) played a major role in shaping the Bush administration's antiterrorism strategy points to one final "lesson learned." The pursuit of security in the modern world is too complex to be reduced to a simple formula or submitted to quick fixes. Any attempt to do so risks producing the opposite effect—that is, greater insecurity.

WEAPONS OF MASS DISRUPTION: CYBER WAR

In 2002, the U.S. Department of the Navy created the Naval Network Warfare Command, known as NETWARCOM. A key element of its mission is information operations (IO), "a warfare area that influences, disrupts, corrupts, or usurps an adversary's decision-making ability while protecting our own." NETWARCOM's "five core integrated abilities" include electronic warfare, computer network operations, psychological operations, military deception, and operational security.[55]

In November 2006, Chinese hackers attacked the U.S. Naval War College computer network, effectively forcing it to shut down for several weeks. Apparently, the attack was aimed at gleaning information about naval war games being developed at the Newport, Rhode Island, facility. The U.S. Navy estimates that hackers try to penetrate its computer systems, which are protected by the Navy Cyber Defense Operations Command, an average of 600,000 times per hour.

In May 2007, Estonia (see Figure 16.2) was the target of an all-out cyber war attack—the first ever against a sovereign state, but almost certainly not the last. The source of the attack was unknown, but Estonian authorities believed it was ordered by the Kremlin or launched by Russian nationalists in retaliation for Estonia's decision to move a World War II bronze statue of a Soviet soldier from a park in the Estonian capital of Tallinn, the previous month. Angry ethnic Russians living in Estonia staged street demonstrations that led to violent clashes with Estonian riot police. The Kremlin denied any involvement in the subsequent cyber attacks, directed against the executive and legislative branches of Estonia's government, as well as its mobile phone networks, banks, and news organizations.[56]

Although Estonia is a small country, electronic warfare is a big deal no matter what state happens to be the target. When the intended victim is a NATO member and the source of the hostile action implicates Russians (and perhaps Russia), the possibility of a good outcome is not high. Not surprisingly, the

FIGURE 16.2   Estonia is the smallest of the three Baltic states, which became independent when the USSR self-destructed in 1991. Ethnic Russians comprise more than one-fourth of Estonia's 1.3 million people. Tensions between native Estonians and Russians who settled in Estonia during the Soviet period have run high. As a member of both NATO and the EU, Estonia is now politically, economically, and militarily part of the West, but geographically it remains within easy striking distance of Russia's technologically sophisticated armed forces.

cyber war against Estonia was a matter of intense interest to defense planning agencies, intelligence services, and computer security specialists the world over.

Finally, in the summer of 2009, the Obama administration unveiled a plan to create a new Pentagon "cyber command" as the centerpiece of its strategy for defending against a future attack on the nation's computer networks. The plan, still in its infancy, raised major privacy issues, as well as diplomatic questions.

President Obama sought to allay fears of "Big Brother" watching what citizens were doing at home, saying the plan "will not—I repeat, will not—include monitoring private sector networks or Internet traffic." But an army general who is a major architect of the new cyber strategy was not so reassuring on this point: "How do you understand sovereignty in the cyber domain?" General Cartwright asked. "It doesn't tend to pay a lot of attention to geographic boundaries."[57] Another complication raises a delicate diplomatic question: How does the U.S. military respond to a cyber attack initiated in another country without violating international law by invading that country's space? Otherwise put: Does the concept of sovereignty apply in cyber space?

Clearly, the danger of cyber war exists in today's world. Just as clearly, key questions have yet to be answered before adequate defenses can be designed and deployed.

GATEWAYS TO THE WORLD: EXPLORING CYBERSPACE

To find out more about a particular armed conflict, use the title of the conflict as the search term. For instance, try World War I, World War II, Korean War, Vietnam War, Gulf War, and war on terror. Some specific Websites of interest are listed below.

www.crimesofwar.org/about/about.html

From the Website: "The Crimes of War Project is a collaboration of journalists, lawyers, and scholars dedicated to raising public awareness of the laws of war and their application to situations of conflict."

www.vietnampix.com/intro2.htm

A photo tour with running commentary on the Vietnam War.

www.civilwar.com/battles/battles/adairsville.php

If you are interested in the American Civil War, you will definitely want to visit this Website.

antiwar.com/who.php

From the Website: "This site is devoted to the cause of non-interventionism and is read by libertarians, pacifists, leftists, 'greens,' and independents alike, as well as many on the Right who agree with our opposition to imperialism. Our initial project was to fight for the case of non-intervention in the Balkans under the Clinton presidency and continued with the case against the campaigns in Haiti, Kosovo, and the bombings of Sudan and Afghanistan."

www.pbs.org/thewar

Based on the PBS series on World War II, produced and directed by Ken Burns and Lynn Novack: "The series explores the most intimate human dimensions of the greatest cataclysm in history—a worldwide catastrophe that touched the lives of every family on every street in every town in America—and demonstrates that in extraordinary times, there are no ordinary lives."

nationalpriorities.org

This eye-opening Website focuses on the actual dollar cost of military operations, including the war in Iraq. If you want to know how much the war is costing your own state or community, you can find out simply by pointing and clicking.

www.firstworldwar.com

This Website is devoted to coverage of World War I.

www.korean-war.com

All about the Korean War.

www.historycentral.com/1812/Index.html

All about the War of 1812.

www.iep.utm.edu/w/war.htm

The Internet Encyclopedia of Philosophy's entry on the "Philosophy of War."

SUMMARY

Avoiding war is not always an objective of state policy. Some leaders—for example, Italy's fascist dictator Mussolini—have actually glorified it.

We can divide theories of the causes of war into three categories that blame human nature, society, and an unforgiving environment. Thomas Hobbes thought war was a product of human perversity; Jean-Jacques Rousseau maintained that human beings are basically good but society corrupts them; John Locke attributed human aggression to scarcities in nature including hunger and famine, disease, storms, and droughts (that is, circumstances beyond human control).

All simplistic theories fall short of explaining the variety of factors that cause war—social, political, economic, and psychological. A large, powerful nation that shares boundaries with several neighboring states, is ruled by a risk-oriented leader, has access to modern technology, is experiencing (or expecting) internal conflict, and has a rapidly expanding population is likely to be predisposed toward war.

Under conditions of high tension, war may occur even if none of the principals wants it. Such unintended wars may erupt because of misperception, misunderstanding, accident, escalation, or a catalytic reaction and make it difficult to assign moral responsibility. Often when war occurs, it is not clear who or what actually caused it.

Using war as an instrument of state policy violates international law and morality, but not all wars are equally objectionable. The just war doctrine holds that self-defense and the defense of universal principles are legitimate reasons for going to war. This doctrine is frequently criticized on the grounds of moral relativism, cultural ethnocentrism, and political realism.

International lawyers at Nuremberg developed a new category of war crimes—crimes against humanity. Although the trials were justified, such proceedings contain inherent pitfalls and must be approached with extreme caution.

KEY TERMS

war
interstate war
civil war
guerrilla warfare
low-intensity conflict
nationalism
arms race
ultranationalism
nationalistic
    universalism
reasons of state
state of nature
internationalist
national self-
    determination
paradox of democratic
    peace

limited war
unconditional
    surrender
war by misperception
accidental war
catalytic war
massive retaliation
nuclear monopoly
intercontinental
    ballistic missile
    (ICBM)
brinkmanship
mutual assured
    destruction (MAD)
mutual deterrence
second strike
overkill

multiple independently
    targeted reentry
    vehicle (MIRV)
submarine-launched
    ballistic missile
    (SLBM)
proxy war
just war
moral relativism
ethnocentric bias
crimes against peace
war crime
crimes against
    humanity
inadvertent war
ABC war

REVIEW QUESTIONS

1. Into what general categories do most explanations of the ultimate causes of war fall?
2. According to Thomas Hobbes, what is the root cause of all wars? What arguments did Hobbes offer in defense of his thesis?
3. What did Jean-Jacques Rousseau believe to be the root cause of war? How did his views differ from Hobbes's? What arguments did Rousseau advance to support his thesis?
4. Those who believe society is the ultimate cause of war differ about precisely what aspect of society is most responsible. What are the four alternative theories presented in the text?
5. How did John Locke explain the phenomenon of war? How did his view differ from those of Hobbes and Rousseau? What arguments did he offer in support of his thesis?

6. Which explanation of the causes of war seems most plausible? Explain your answer.
7. Why is it difficult simply to condemn the guilty party or parties whenever war breaks out?
8. With the technology of warfare advancing by leaps and bounds, it becomes increasingly probable that a war will start even though nobody intends it to. In what ways might this happen?
9. Are all wars equally objectionable from a moral standpoint? Why or why not?
10. Are the arguments, pro and con, concerning the validity of the just war doctrine equally balanced? Explain.
11. What prompted the Nuremberg War Crimes Trials? What are crimes against humanity? How does the just war doctrine fit into the picture? Should, or could, Nuremberg-type trials be conducted after every war?
12. Critique the concept of a "war on terror." Critique the strategy the Bush administration used in the conduct of that "war."

RECOMMENDED READING

Allawi, Ali. *The Occupation of Iraq: Winning the War, Losing the Peace.* New Haven, CT: Yale University Press, 2007.

The author was Iraq's first civilian minister of defense after the ouster of Saddam Hussein. The book's title encapsulates its thesis.

Aron, Raymond. *The Century of Total War.* Lanham, MD: University Press of America, 1985.

One of this century's most influential thinkers examines the causes and conditions of war in our age.

Carr, Edward Hallett. *The Twenty Years' Crisis, 1919–1939,* 2nd ed. New York: St. Martin's Press, 1969.

A classic study of the influences and forces that led to World War II, written in 1939.

Haase, Richard. *War of Necessity, War of Choice: A Memoir of Two Iraq Wars.* New York: Simon and Schuster, 2009.

Faulks, Sebastian. Birdsong. New York: Vintage Books, 1993.

A riveting story of love and war that strips the reader of any illusions regarding the grim reality of its subject matter.

A critical first-person account of the two Iraqi wars by a long-time Washington foreign-policy insider who applies the theory and literature on just and unjust wars to the real world of power politics.

Remarque, Erich Maria. All Quiet on the Western Front. New York: Ballantine Books, 1987.

First published in book form in 1929, this classic has been called "the greatest war novel of all time."

Russett, Bruce. *Grasping the Democratic Peace.* Princeton, NJ: Princeton University Press, 1995.

The best available extended discussion of why democratic governments do not wage war on one another.

Codevilla, Angelo, and Paul Seabury. *War: Ends and Means.* Dulles, VA: Potomac Books, Inc., 2006.

A sober discussion of war as a permanent part of the human condition.

Smith, Rubert. *The Utility of Force: The Art of War in the Modern World.* New York: Knopf, 2007.

From *Booklist:* "Smith provocatively states, 'War no longer exists.' Of course, he does not mean that mass organized violence has ended; rather, he refers to the end of large-scale industrialized warfare characterized by the use of massive tank columns supported by the application of intensive air power." This book explores the nature of war in the age of "smart" weapons, urban battlegrounds, and terrorist tactics.

Stoessinger, John. *Why Nations Go to War,* 10th ed. Belmont, CA: Wadsworth, 2007.

A searching inquiry into the causes of modern war by a scholar who brings to the task the perspective of one who struggled as a refugee in World War II.

Van Creveld, Martin. *The Changing Face of War: Lessons of Combat, from the Marne to Iraq.* New York: Presidio Press, 2007.

A penetrating look at the changing nature of warfare over the past century by a recognized expert on military history and strategy.

Waltz, Kenneth N. *Man, the State, and War: A Theoretical Analysis.* New York: Columbia University Press, 1965.

An extraordinarily lucid account of the origins of war, emphasizing the importance of human nature, the state, and the international political system.

Walzer, Michael. *Just and Unjust Wars: A Moral Argument with Historical Illustrations,* 4th ed. New York: Basic Books, 2006.

An impressive attempt to set out a just war theory and apply it to modern conflicts. In viewing the invasion and occupation of Iraq through the prism of political ethics, the author reminds us that "the argument about war and justice is still a political and moral necessity."

Wright, Quincy. *A Study of War,* abridged ed. Chicago: University of Chicago Press, 1983.

Still the most authoritative book on the nature, history, and causes. Essential reading for anyone who wonders whether there can ever be a cure for the scourge of war and where to start.

P A R T 5

Politics Without Government

© PHOTO BY TOMOHIRO OHSUMI-POOL-GETTY IMAGES

U.S. Secretary of State Hillary Clinton and Minister for Japan's Foreign Affairs Hirofumi Nakasone shake hands at a meeting in Tokyo, Japan, in February, 2009. Clinton was on her first diplomatic tour to Asia, visiting Japan, Indonesia, South Korea, and China.

17 International Relations: The Struggle for Power

18 International Organization(s): Globalization and the Quest for Order

SOURCE/ALAMY LIMITED

Flags are universally recognized symbols of national sovereignty, which has been the cornerstone of international law since the birth of the nation-state system in the 17th century; sovereign states evolved in Europe but today are found in all regions of the world.

International Relations:
The Struggle for Power

Get Real! Machiavelli and Morgenthau

The Classical System: Eurocentric

The Balance of Power: Essential Elements

The Sunset of the Old European Order

The Cold War System: Global

The Dawn of Bipolarity

The Primacy of Ideology

The Danger of Nuclear War

Mutual Deterrence : A Lasting Legacy

After the Cold War: A New World Order?

New World, Old Ideas

A Challenged Global Economy

The New Regionalism

The Curse of Ethnic Violence

The Eclipse of Unipolarity

The Old Doomsday Scenario: Preventing Nuclear
Proliferation

The New Doomsday Scenario: Averting a Silent Spring

The IT Revolution

Living in a Hostile World: U.S. Foreign Policy
The National Interest

In Pursuit of the National Interest

The Great Debate: Realism Versus Idealism
The Curse of Unintended Consequences: Blowback

The Bush Doctrine

Reinventing Statecraft: Toward A New Realism
Ideals and Self-interest: The Power of Morality

Hard Facts About Soft Power

Apocalyptic Visions: Culture Wars and Anarchy?

───────────────○───────────────

In 416 BCE, Athens sent ships and troops against the island of Melos, a colony of Sparta that had remained neutral and wanted no part of the war between Sparta and Athens.[1] Negotiating from a position of overwhelming strength, the Athenians insisted on unconditional surrender, telling the Melians, "You know as well as we do that right, as the world goes, is only in question between equals in power—the strong do what they can, and the weak suffer what they must." The Melians responded, "And how, pray, could it turn out as good for us to serve as for you to rule?" "Because," the Athenians answered, "you would have the advantage of submitting before suffering the worst, and we should gain by not destroying you."

Undaunted, the Melians insisted the interest of all would be enhanced by peaceful relations between the two states. The Athenians would have no part of this logic. With ruthless disregard for justice, they reasoned that if the Melians were permitted to remain independent, they and others would take it as a sign of Athenian weakness. "[By] extending our empire," the Athenians pointed out, "we should gain in security by your subjection; the fact that you are islanders and weaker than others rendering all the more important that you should not succeed in baffling the masters of the sea." Thus, the cold calculus of power politics doomed the Melian state:

> Reinforcements afterwards arriving from Athens in consequence, under the command of Philocrates, son of Demeas, the siege was now pressed vigorously; and some treachery taking place inside, the Melians surrendered at discretion to the Athenians, who put to death all the grown men whom they took, and sold the women and children for slaves, and subsequently sent out five hundred colonists and inhabited the place themselves.

Melos was a real place, and the tragedy depicted in the story really happened. The context was the Peloponnesian War (431–404 BCE), and we know the Melians' cruel fate because the Greek historian Thucydides wrote about it.

GET REAL! MACHIAVELLI AND MORGENTHAU

The greatest political thinker of the Italian Renaissance, Niccolò Machiavelli, taught that the wise ruler must always play to win, for "how we live is so far removed from how we ought to live, that he who abandons what is done for what ought to be done, will rather learn to bring about his own ruin than his preservation."[2] The prudent ruler, he argued, recognizes what must be done to preserve and enlarge his dominions and does not allow moral qualms to cloud his judgment. Rulers should keep their promises only when it suits their purposes to do so:

> A prudent ruler ought not to keep faith when by doing so it would be against his interest, and when the reasons which made him bind himself no longer exist. . . . If men were all good, this precept would not be a good one; but as they are bad, and would not observe their faith with you, so you are not bound to keep faith with them.[3]

The teachings of Machiavelli, and the fate of the Melians, suggest morality plays a less significant role in politics *among* nations than *within* nations. As long as international politics resembles the state of nature, tensions between nations will persist, talking will fail, reason will take a holiday, and the only question left will be who lives and who dies. When survival is at stake, necessity is often a tyrant.

Machiavelli's intellectual honesty and relentless realism were the basis for perhaps the most successful and influential political philosophy in the modern world—and evidence for its validity has continually mounted. The theory that

political realism
The philosophy that power is the key variable in all political relationships and should be used pragmatically and prudently to advance the national interest; policies are judged good or bad on the basis of their effect on national interests, not on their level of morality.

nations act on the basis of interests rather than ideals is known as **political realism**. Today, it is most closely identified with the writings of Hans Morgenthau (1904–1980). Following Machiavelli's rationale, political realists pay little heed to the way nations *ought* to act. Rather, they focus on how nations actually *do* act and why they act as they do. Survival is the basic goal of national policy, and the best way to ensure survival is to enhance the nation's power. In international politics, Morgenthau argued, whatever the ultimate aim, the immediate aim is *always* power. Thus, interest is defined as power; indeed, for Morgenthau, these two concepts merge into one—it is in the best interest of every nation to seek power first and other objectives second, and then only as they enhance national power, prestige, and the like.

Political realists stress that success in international politics, even without confrontation, ultimately depends on power. According to Morgenthau, power is "man's control over the minds and actions of other men."[4] Military force is an important but not the only aspect of political power. Geopolitical, economic, and social concerns also contribute. Even the personal charisma or competence of a nation's leader or the effectiveness of its political institutions gives it an edge.[5]

According to Morgenthau, "Realism considers prudence—the weighing of the consequences of political action—to be the supreme virtue in politics."[6] A foreign policy based on a realistic appraisal of the **national interest** will avoid "the blindness of crusading frenzy [that] destroys nations and civilizations—in the name of moral principle, ideal, or God himself."[7]

national interest
A term that is often invoked but seldom defined, it is usually associated with power enhancement; shorthand for whatever enhances the power and best serves the supreme purposes of the nation, including prosperity, prestige, security, and, above all, survival.

To the political realist, the successful statesman is one who balances national interests and objectives against national capabilities (or power). Prudence demands that a statesman distinguish between what is necessary and what is merely desirable. The essence of statecraft lies in bringing the expectations and desires of a nation into line with its capabilities and correctly differentiating between vital and expendable interests. Political realism places a premium on flexibility, objectivity, and lack of sentimentality in the conduct of foreign policy. Thus, the political realist would say there are no permanent allies, only permanent interests.

In the perilous world of international politics, morality is different than in our *domestic* lives. Because other nations act on the basis of their perceived interests rather than lofty ideals, one's own nation must do likewise; all try to gain an advantage at the expense of others. Therefore, Morgenthau asserted, political realism not only explains *why* nations act the way they do, but in the true spirit of science, it can also predict *how* they will act.

THE CLASSICAL SYSTEM: EUROCENTRIC

Machiavelli and Morgenthau were both products of tumultuous but very different times. Machiavelli was influenced by the fierce rivalries, intrigue, and conflict among Italian city-states of the fifteenth and sixteenth centuries. The

FIGURE 17.1   Adjusting the Balance of Power. Equilibrium (A) is upset by adding a new participant (B); it is restored (C) by the transfer of one state from one alliance to another.
SOURCE: Edward V. Gulick, *Europe's Classical Balance of Power* (New York: Norton, 1967).

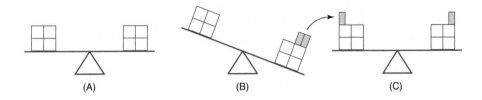

(A)   (B)   (C)

modern nation-state system was in its infancy; the classical European system was launched with the signing of the Treaty of Westphalia in 1648 (see the box in Chapter 1), more than a century after his death. Morgenthau was born in Germany shortly before World War I. The European system was one of the casualties of that war, along with its conscious effort to maintain **equilibrium** (or balance) among the participating states. Although this collective balancing act was based on nations' individual interests, it depended on a common definition of *interest* that emphasized self-preservation of each through a system that depended on the survival of all.

Europe's famed **balance-of-power system** operated for almost three centuries (see Figure 17.1), beginning with the Treaty of Westphalia and ending with the outbreak of World War I. Although Napoleonic France came perilously close at the start of the nineteenth century, no state was able to establish hegemony on the Continent during this 266-year period—a remarkable achievement for any era.

The Balance of Power: Essential Elements

The international system functioned effectively because one nation, the **keeper of the balance**, repeatedly threw its political and military weight behind the weaker alliance in crisis and conflict. Great Britain was ideally suited to this role because of its geographic detachment and military (especially naval) prowess. A major British concern was which power controlled the Lowlands (modern-day Belgium and Holland) just across the English Channel, a mere 22 miles wide at its narrowest point. But Britain was an impregnable fortress as long as no single power succeeded in conquering the Continent. Finally, its unchallenged naval supremacy and economic vitality made it a powerful ally or a formidable foe, while its lack of a large standing army removed any threat of British domination on the Continent.

Another important factor underpinning the traditional European system was a basic moral consensus—a common outlook held by nations sharing a single civilization. Historians Edward Gibbon and Arnold Toynbee, as well as philosophers Emmerich de Vattel and Jean-Jacques Rousseau, stressed the power of cultural and religious traditions that pervaded European society and transcended national boundaries during the heyday of the balance-of-power system.[8]

equilibrium
A synonym for the word *balance*; also often used interchangeably with *stability* in the literature won international relations.

balance-of-power system
A classic theory of international relations that holds that nations of approximately equal strength will seek to maintain the status quo by preventing any one nation from gaining superiority over the others. In a balance-of-power system, participating nations form alliances and frequently resort to war as a means of resolving disputes, seizing territory, gaining prestige, or seeking glory.

keeper of the balance
In a balance-of-power system, the nation-state that functions as an arbiter in disputes, taking sides to preserve the political equilibrium.

Under these extraordinary conditions, "international politics became indeed an aristocratic pastime, a sport for princes, all recognizing the same rules of the game and playing for the same limited stakes."[9] Even when war broke out, the belligerents did not seek to annihilate each other. Adopting the rationalistic outlook of the eighteenth-century Enlightenment, rulers mostly adopted a pragmatic approach to governing and viewed fanaticism as absurd and dangerous. Economic and military capabilities were limited too: few countries could afford to squander their national wealth on high-risk adventures, and military action was constrained by the absence of modern technology. Ideology was also absent in this pan-European culture. Realignments occurred as circumstances changed, adding to the smooth functioning of the system.

The Sunset of the Old European Order

What happened to upset the relatively stable international order? First, Napoléon's nearly successful attempt in the early nineteenth century to conquer Europe—creating the first mass-conscription, popular army in modern history—heralded the rise of modern nationalism (see Chapter 16). Although France's bid ultimately failed, it was a harbinger of things to come, and it demonstrated the power of a nation united by a common cause. The cause itself was rooted in the explosive idea of human equality, enshrined in both the American and French revolutions (see Chapter 14) . Between the Napoleonic Wars and World War I, ideas such as national self-determination and universal rights changed fundamental assumptions about politics and undermined the old aristocratic order.

In the nineteenth century, the Industrial Revolution's economic and technological changes transformed the art of warfare. Prussia used railroads to move troops in victorious military campaigns against Austria (1866) and France (1870). New instruments of war were not far off—military applications of the internal combustion engine included self-propelled field artillery and, by World War I, combat aircraft.

A final factor that helped undermine the European system was the rigidity of military alliances. Toward the end of the nineteenth century, coalitions were becoming fixed, while nations were steadily accumulating military power. Unprecedented peacetime outlays for military research and development, the creation of relatively large standing armies, and a spiraling arms race reinforced the increasing division of Europe into two opposing alliances. This development set the stage for World War I, which signaled the beginning of the end of the classical balance-of-power system. It would take another world war to finish the job.

THE COLD WAR SYSTEM: GLOBAL

World War II produced a new configuration, one that continues to shape world politics today. Replacing the European system was a **global** system dominated by two preeminent powers.

The Dawn of Bipolarity

World War II greatly accelerated the transformation that had already begun. In place of the former great powers, seven at the outbreak of the war, were two *superpowers*—the United States and the Soviet Union. The United States formed a kind of protectorate over the western half of war-torn Europe, the Soviet Union created a "satellite" empire in the eastern half, and a **bipolar system** was born.

After World War II, the United States, first to develop and use the atomic bomb, enjoyed a short-lived nuclear monopoly. The Soviet Union, to Western observers' surprise and dismay, successfully tested an atomic device in 1949—serving notice that it, too, had become a full-fledged superpower. In military might, global reach, and economic resources, the United States and the Soviet Union dwarfed all other nations in the 1950s. But the ideological chasm dividing them precluded collaboration of any kind.

The Primacy of Ideology

Because one was capitalist and democratic and the other communist and dictatorial, the rivalry between the superpowers turned especially acrimonious and dangerous. After World War II, Allied mistrust of Joseph Stalin, the Soviet dictator, was greatly heightened by his nation's permanent occupation of Eastern Europe, which the Red Army had liberated from the Germans, and his attempt to force Western powers to abandon West Berlin. No less alarming was the prospect of a totalitarian Soviet state with nuclear weapons.

The Soviets, meanwhile, charged that U.S. foreign policy actions (the cutoff of lend-lease aid, the refusal to grant large loans, and the launching of massive U.S. foreign aid for Europe under the Marshall Plan) proved "American imperialism" was plotting the destruction of the "world socialist system." Stalin's chief ideologue, Andrei Zhdanov, declared the world had been divided into two camps, an idea whose counterpart in the West was the notion of a "world Communist conspiracy," a secret Soviet blueprint to subvert all democratic societies. Although these beliefs seem exaggerated in retrospect, extreme rhetoric on both sides lent them credibility.

U.S.-led efforts at **containment** were epitomized in Western Europe by the creation of a powerful military alliance, the North Atlantic Treaty Organization (NATO). The Soviet Union countered with a military pact of its own, the Warsaw Treaty Organization, known as the **Warsaw Pact**, linking Moscow and Eastern Europe. The aura of confrontation that permeated the two alliance systems left little room for compromise or conciliation. (See Chapter 18 for a more detailed discussion of the NATO alliance today.)

At its inception, the Cold War was waged by two extraordinarily powerful nations whose aims, interests, and values seemed incompatible. At the least, each sought to block the other's ambitions; at worst, each sought the other's collapse, in sharp contrast to the traditional European system they had replaced.

containment
The global status quo policy followed by the United States after World War II; the term stems from the U.S. policy of containing attempts by the Soviet Union to extend its sphere of control to other states as it had done in Eastern Europe. NATO, the Marshall Plan, and the Korean and Vietnam wars grew out of this policy.

Warsaw Pact
A military alliance between the former Soviet Union and its satellite states, created in 1955, that established a unified military command and allowed the Soviet army to maintain large garrisons within the satellite states, ostensibly to defend them from outside attack.

FIGURE 17.2   NATO and the Warsaw Pact.

During the Cold War (1947–1991), Europe was divided between East (the Soviet Union and the Warsaw Pact "satellite states") and West (the United States and its NATO allies). Only a handful of European states (Ireland, Sweden, Finland, Austria, Switzerland, and Yugoslavia) managed to remain outside of these two alliance systems.

http://astro.temple.edu/~barbday/Europe66/resources/coldwardivisionmap1.htm

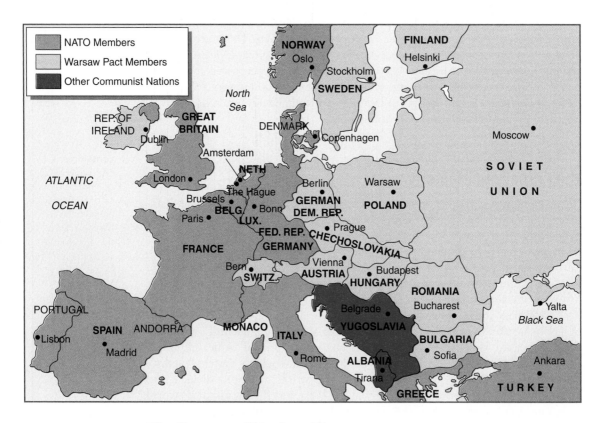

The Danger of Nuclear War

When the European balance of power held sway, observed rules and available technology both limited war aims. Two technological breakthroughs in the twentieth century, however, greatly expanded the destructive potential of military weaponry—the development of airborne bombers and missile delivery systems, and the invention of fission (atomic) and fusion (hydrogen) bombs capable of leveling entire cities. From these advances grew the formidable U.S. and Soviet arsenals of increasingly accurate land- and sea-based missiles armed with multiple nuclear warheads.

The two nations commanded a vast overkill capacity—each held enough nuclear weapons to destroy the other many times over. All-out war would have amounted to mutual suicide. This realization, as we shall see, played a major role in promoting a new international security scheme intended to ensure human survival in a world threatened with almost instantaneous destruction.

Mutual Deterrence: A Lasting Legacy

The unprecedented power of nuclear weapons made the concept of **deterrence** paramount during the heyday of Soviet–American rivalry. The Cold War is over now, but the legacy—and the awesome destructive capability it represents—will live on so long as the nuclear weapons amassed by the two superpowers remain in existence.

The United States lost its nuclear monopoly shortly after World War II but retained a measure of nuclear superiority for more than two decades thereafter. In 1957, however, the Soviet Union put the first artificial satellite *(Sputnik)* into orbit, demonstrating to the world that it had the technology to build long-range rockets and launch offensive weapons from Soviet soil directly at U.S. targets.

By the late 1960s, the era of U.S. invulnerability was over. The Soviets had built a land-based missile force against which there was no adequate defense. Both sides stared into the nuclear abyss. *Deterrence* became the new watchword in a great debate over military strategy and an integral part of the post–World War II balance of power.

According to **deterrence theory**, nations acquire nuclear weapons not to use them but to deter other nations' use of them. Public expenditure for such weapons is thus markedly different from appropriation of money for such projects as schools, libraries, and parks. If these public facilities are **not** used, it represents a serious domestic policy failure. By contrast, if nuclear weapons ever **were** used, this far more serious foreign policy failure could jeopardize the very survival of humanity.

Deterrence is fundamentally psychological and incorporates some of the elements of a high-stakes poker game; players must minimize risks, and bluffing is part of the process. It depends not only on the realities of power but also on the perceptions each side has of the other's will, intentions, and resolve in the face of grave danger. If Country A uses military power to keep Country B from pursuing its foreign policy objective, Country B's prestige is damaged and Country A gains a psychological edge.

A number of assumptions underlie nuclear deterrence theory. First, nations have communicated to potential adversaries a clear will to use weapons of mass destruction if attacked. Second, decision makers on both sides are rational, and neither side will launch a nuclear strike unless it can protect itself from a counterattack. Third, each side possesses a second-strike capability, meaning enough of the attacked nation's nuclear capabilities would survive a surprise attack (first strike) to make possible a retaliatory blow (second strike) adequate to inflict unacceptable damage on the attacker.

To ensure the survivability of its nuclear forces, the United States built three separate but interrelated nuclear weapon delivery systems after World War II. This so-called triad consisted of land-based intercontinental ballistic missiles (ICBMs), submarine-launched ballistic missiles (SLBMs), and manned bombers (known as the Strategic Air Command, or SAC), some of which were always aloft. The Soviet Union also had a three-pronged deterrence system that depended heavily on land-based missiles and warheads, which it possessed in larger numbers than the United States. The United States' sea-based deterrent was more powerful than the Soviet Union's.

deterrence
In international relations, the theory that aggressive wars can be prevented if potential victims maintain a military force sufficient to inflict unacceptable punishment on any possible aggressor.

deterrence theory
Holds that states acquire nuclear weapons mainly to deter the use of such weapons by other states; this idea spawned a whole new literature on war in the nuclear age in the second half of the twentieth century.

Deterrence and the arms race went hand in hand for decades. Each nation had specific goals and priorities that governed its expenditures for armaments. Each was also swayed by its perception of what the other was doing; an accelerated Soviet weapons buildup in the 1970s prompted the United States to launch a major rearmament program. A stable balance was thus impossible when one nation, particularly one with an expansionistic foreign policy, possessed a clear advantage in number and strength of weapons. Finally, technology exerted its own influence. On the one hand, because technological knowledge cannot be unlearned, both nations were wary of disarmament; on the other, the possibility that one nation might achieve a technological breakthrough provided an incentive to continue high levels of weapons research and development.

AFTER THE COLD WAR: A NEW WORLD ORDER?

Political realism emphasizes national self-interest as the principle guiding foreign policy. Some contemporary critics, however, say self-centered national interest is outmoded. They argue for "a new diplomacy and for new institutions and regulatory regimes to cope with the world's growing environmental interdependence" because "our accepted definition of the limits of national sovereignty as coinciding with national borders is obsolete."[10] Perhaps, but there is still little concrete evidence that state behavior has changed fundamentally.

New World, Old Ideas

The dissolution of the Soviet Union marked the end of the post-World War II balance of power. As countries redefine their relationships with one another, some observers say a new world order is emerging. What are the characteristics of this brave new world, and how does it differ from the old?

International politics currently does *not* exhibit a clear balance-of-power configuration whereby participants with incompatible aims, conflicting interests, and roughly equal power interact in predictable ways to maintain stability and peace. The emerging international order is instead marked by contradictory trends—in Europe, for example, the movement toward integration in the European Union, which transcends traditional state boundaries, and the simultaneous rise of religious and ethnic particularism *within* nations, which caused the breakup of three multinational states: the Soviet Union, Yugoslavia, and Czechoslovakia. The shape of the world to come is still not clear; but it will certainly not be dominated by a single superpower.

Today's profound environmental challenges of global warming, air pollution, oil spills, disappearing rain forests, and the like, as well as reckless depletion of nonrenewable natural resources, overpopulation, and world poverty, are global in scope and require global solutions.[11] "Think globally, act locally" expresses the idea that nations have a moral obligation not to pursue narrow self-interests at the expense of solutions to pressing global problems. Global interests replace national interests. The best (and only) way for any nation to ensure its prosperity and security is to look outward, not inward.

This approach requires a drastic change in the way we think and states behave, and a far broader definition of *self-interest* than some political realists embrace. To old-school realists, talk of a "global community" sounds like soft-boiled idealism. But the new realists advocate policies rooted in enlightened self-interest and argue that global security and self-preservation require a radical rethinking of world politics. In today's world, they contend, yesterday's realism is not only obsolete but also dangerous.

A Challenged Global Economy

With the reduction of military competition and political conflicts among the world's most powerful nations, two seemingly contradictory economic trends have gained importance—one toward increased interdependence, the other toward intensified competition.

Interdependence is a companion of **globalization**. Globalization is another name for the transformation of the world economy, from one in which interactions across national borders are restricted by a fragmented political structure, to one in which far more interactions occur as national borders remain in place but recede in importance.[12]

Globalization is driven by multinational corporations seeking to maximize profits and revolutionary advances in transport, communications, and information technology, all of which transcend national boundaries. In addition, some problems—including regional and worldwide environmental problems, arms control, and the coordination of economic policies during times of crisis—necessitate international cooperation.

Major international crises occurred in 1997–1998, and in 2008–2009 (as discussed in previous chapters). In the 1997–1998 crisis, several Asian nations experienced a sudden, sharp economic downturn that led to fears of a global economic meltdown. In response a large-scale rescue package of loans was formulated that directly benefited a number of nations, including South Korea and Indonesia. The effort was headed by the **International Monetary Fund (IMF)**, a specialized agency of the United Nations designed to promote worldwide economic stability. As a precondition for making the loans, the IMF insisted the nations it helped must agree to important economic reforms.

In 2008–2009, as we know, a financial meltdown that started on Wall Street triggered a global recession, immediately putting the incoming Obama administration to a severe test. Obama called for a massive $775 billion-dollar stimulus program to kick-start the sinking U.S. economy and asked the leaders of the other G-20 countries to follow suit. (G-20 stands for "Group of 20" and comprises the world's major economies.) Europe refused to follow the U.S. lead, preferring to emphasize tighter regulation of business (especially finance). But at a G-20 economic summit in London in April 2009, Obama declared

globalization
The process by which values, attitudes, preferences, and products associated with the most technologically advanced democracies are being spread around the world via mass media and trade.

International Monetary Fund (IMF)
A specialized agency of the United Nations designed to promote worldwide monetary cooperation, international trade, and economic stability. It also helps equalize balance of payments by allowing member countries to borrow from its fund.

U.S. interests were "tied up with the larger world," and leaders agreed to provide $1.1 trillion in new funds to re-capitalize the IMF.

Yet notwithstanding such cooperative efforts, economic competition among nations, as well as among businesses, is on the rise. Governments continue to subsidize domestic industries and agriculture, levy tariffs on imports, and erect all manner of ingenious non-trade barriers. Such protectionist practices inhibit free trade and lead to international tensions, even among allies. U.S. and Japanese relations have at times been strained over the Japanese government's policy of protectionism, and trade between the United States and its European allies has been marred by wrangling over agricultural subsidies. Competition and rivalry are still prevalent in the new world, even as conflict resolution and cooperation become more urgent—and European-style integration more attractive.

The New Regionalism

When the European Coal and Steel Community (ECSC) was launched circa 1950, it was a modest effort to integrate two industrial sectors among six countries (France, Germany, Italy and the Benelux countries). From its seeds grew the world's largest single economy, the 27-nation European Union (EU). The success of the EU—including establishment of a single currency and elimination of internal border controls in the so-called Schengen area—has inspired other efforts to form regional or geography-based trading blocs. (We explore the European Union in greater depth in Chapter 18.)

European integration has evolved through decades of economic and military cooperation in the West. Its results, however, are revolutionary. Most impressively, the EU has overcome centuries of rivalry and mistrust in Europe, especially between France and Germany. The end of the Cold War was a bonanza for EU enlargement—three new countries were admitted in 1995 (Austria, Finland, and Sweden), ten in 2004 (Cyprus, the Czech Republic, Estonia, Hungary, Latvia, Lithuania, Malta, Poland, Slovakia, and Slovenia), and Bulgaria and Romania joined in 2007. Several more countries, including Turkey, Serbia, and Croatia are knocking on the door. Ukraine wants to join the West (NATO and the EU), but Russia is adamantly opposed.

Elsewhere, the United States, Mexico, and Canada launched the North American Free Trade Association (NAFTA) in January 1994. Mercosur is a common market encompassing Argentina, Brazil, Paraguay, Uruguay, and Venezuela, plus five associate members. Mercosur's combined population totals more than 250 million and accounts for over 75 percent of South America's GDP. It is the world's fourth-largest trading bloc ($1.1 trillion a year), after the EU, NAFTA, and ASEAN (see below). But a proposed free-trade zone for the entire Western Hemisphere, encompassing some 850 million consumers, never got off the drawing board.

Japan has strong economic ties with other Pacific Basin nations, as does China. The Association of South East Asian Nations or ASEAN region encompasses a population of some 560 million, a total area of 4.5 million square kilometers, a combined gross domestic product of more than $1 trillion, and total trade of $1.4 trillion. In an agreement called ASEAN Vision 2020, the member states pledged to create an ASEAN Economic Community to achieve "a stable, prosperous and highly competitive ASEAN economic region in which there is a free flow of goods, services, investment and a freer flow of capital, equitable economic development and reduced poverty and socio-economic disparities in year 2020."[13] Meanwhile, the ASEAN free-trade area has been in place since 1992.

What will emerge from these new regional economic blocs? Some say the nation-state as we know it is being eclipsed by regionalism and globalization. Will regional blocs coexist happily and harmoniously? Competition is inevitable (and desirable), but there are also strong incentives for inter-regional cooperation. Or will regional groupings become obstacles rather than stepping stones to a truly global economy? Rising shipping costs, concerns over energy security, and the current global recession could cause globalization to give way to a greater emphasis on **local** production and consumption. What that would mean for the future of regional trading blocs, which fall between global and local, is anybody's guess. What do you think?

The Curse of Ethnic Violence

While regional economic cooperation may render nation-states obsolescent, ethnic strife poses an internal threat to the survival of some. We discussed this topic in Chapter 9; here we assess its relevance in the emerging international order.

Worldwide ethnic conflict has shown no signs of abating during the past two decades. Disputes among ethnic, religious, and racial groups within nation-states, as well as between such groups and governments, prove intense ethnic rivalries are not confined to any one region. Examples are myriad—the Sikhs and Muslims in India; the South Ossetians in Georgia; the French-speaking Québécois in Canada; the Kurds in Iran, Iraq, and Turkey; the Tamils in Sri Lanka; and the Timorese in Indonesia. Kenya has three large homogeneous ethnic groups—the Kamba, Luo, and Kikuyu—and many ethnic minorities. Rwanda's majority Hutus constitute 84 percent of the population and vastly outnumber the Tutsi (14 percent) and Twa (1 percent). China has no fewer than fifty-six officially recognized minorities. Russia has a national minority population (Tatars, Ukrainians, Bashkir, Chuvash, and so on) numbering 28 million (20 percent of the total), including dozens of ethno-linguistic groups within its borders. The list goes on.

Ethnic strife has hugely increased the number of refugees and other displaced peoples worldwide. In 1994, for instance, after a genocidal civil war in Rwanda led to the slaughter of 200,000 to 500,000 people, approximately three million refugees (40 percent of the country's population) attempted to cross the border into Zaire (now the Democratic Republic of the Congo). Overwhelmed international relief agencies and the Zaire government faced problems of mass starvation and epidemic disease that defied human comprehension. The war in Bosnia created more than one million refugees, orphans, and asylum seekers in the 1990s; more recently, the violence in Darfur, Sudan, created some two million internal refugees and propelled hundreds of thousands more to neighboring Chad.

The divisive effects of ethnic tension take many forms. Routine census can be threatening to minorities and can even lead to warfare:

> In Assam, a state in northeast India, census results showing small changes in the proportion of Bengalis to Assamese in the 1970s paved the way for a violent reaction to an increase in Bengali names on electoral rolls later in the decade. Thousands died as a result. The census can become a life-or-death matter in an ethnically divided society.[14]

Thus, ethnic differences—culminating in disputes over politics, economics, language, discrimination, and culture—are a divisive force in the world today, often fragmenting political communities and sometimes leading to secessionist movements and civil war.

The Eclipse of Unipolarity

The crumbling of the Soviet empire, the demonstration of U.S. military prowess in two wars against Iraq (1990–1991 and 2003), and the war on terror all highlighted that the United States was (and is) the world's sole remaining **superpower**. But what exactly is a superpower?

A superpower must, above all, have a full range of power capabilities, including not only military muscle but also economic, political, diplomatic, and even moral clout. Second, it must have global reach, the capacity to project power to all parts of the world. Third, it must be willing to assert its leadership role in the international arena. According to this three-part test, only the United States qualifies as a superpower at the present time.

The striking contrast between the vibrant U.S. economy in the 1990s and the disarray of the former Soviet economy created the false impression that Russia was no longer a power of any consequence. But rising oil and gas prices revived Russia's fortunes after 2000, giving Moscow a massive infusion of capital, as well as renewed political leverage in dealing with an energy-dependent European Union. The emergence of China as a major global economic force also points to the changing international power structure and the rapid eclipse of the **unipolar system** that saw the United States as the sole dominant actor on the world stage. Last but not least, the squandering of U.S. economic, diplomatic, and military resources in two unwinnable wars, the recession of 2008–2009, the bankruptcy of two former world-class U.S. automakers (GM and Chrysler)—and the resulting loss of U.S. standing in the world—had badly eroded the foundations of the unipolar system by the spring of 2009.

The United States remains the number-one military power in the world, but Europe's single economy now overmatches the U.S. economy, and China, already a vital trading partner, is a rising behemoth that will soon be able to challenge U.S. leadership. The world was never truly unipolar, but the circumstances that gave rise to the notion of unipolarity in the 1990s have changed.

superpower
A term that evolved in the context of the Cold War to denote the unprecedented destructive capabilities and global reach of the United States and the Soviet Union and to differentiate these two nuclear behemoths from the great powers that existed prior to the advent of the Nuclear Age.

unipolar system
In international relations theory, the existence of a single invincible superpower; the international system said to have existed after the collapse of the Soviet Union left the United States as the sole remaining (and thus unrivalled) military and economic superpower on the world stage.

The Old Doomsday Scenario: Preventing Nuclear Proliferation

Nuclear, biological, and chemical weapons—so-called weapons of mass destruction—are in a class by themselves. In addition to causing an immense loss of life, damage to infrastructure, and widespread environmental devastation, these weapons could provoke genetic mutations with lasting consequences for future generations. The states that possess them want to prevent other states, including Iraq, Iran, North Korea, Israel, India, and Pakistan, from acquiring them.

Although arms limitation treaties covering WMDs exist (see Chapter 18), many states refuse to sign or be constrained by them. As Table 17.1 indicates, the number of nuclear "haves" is still quite small, yet it has grown from only five in the 1960s to as many as nine at present.

In the past, some developing countries that possess valuable natural resources, such as oil-rich Libya, Iran, and Iraq, sought to acquire WMDs. After 2003, however, Iraq was forced out of this "club," and Libya renounced WMDs to avoid a similar fate. Nonetheless, these facts only hint at the true dangers of nuclear proliferation.

The world got a wake-up call in February 2004, when Pakistan's top nuclear scientist, Abdul Qadeer Khan ("the father of Pakistan's bomb"), publicly confessed to having shared Pakistan's nuclear secrets with Libya, Iran, and North Korea—all three of which are on the U.S. list of "rogue" states. According to Khan's story, he acted entirely on his own. Unauthorized nuclear transfers are strictly forbidden under the Nuclear Nonproliferation Treaty (NPT). But Pakistan has never signed the NPT and is therefore not bound by it.

TABLE 17.1   Proliferation of Nuclear Weapons

Have Nuclear Weapons	Have Pledged Not to Build Nuclear Weapons	Have Given Up Nuclear Weapons	Have an Active R & D Program in Progress
China	Algeria	Belarus	Iran
France	Argentina	Kazakhstan	North Korea*
Great Britain	Brazil	Ukraine	
Israel	Germany		
India	Japan		
Pakistan	South Africa		
Russia			
United States			

*Under pressure from the United States, China, and the UN North Korea in February 2007 pledged to disable a plutonium reactor at Yongbyon and eventually to dismantle all its nuclear facilities, but in 2008 and 2009 North Korea conducted nuclear and missile tests, proving right the sceptics who predicted dictator Kim Jong Il would not keep his word.

As this event suggests, the technology and materials necessary to build a nuclear bomb are available on the black market—for a price, of course. In addition to North Korea, Argentina, Brazil, Egypt, Saudi Arabia, Syria, Iran, Turkey, Japan, South Korea, and Taiwan are all "nuclear threshold" states. (A threshold state is one with the technological know-how to manufacture nuclear weapons.) The Republic of South Africa actually had a small nuclear arsenal, which it dismantled in the early 1990s.

Given the military, political, and symbolic importance of such weapons, it is unrealistic to expect any slackening in the efforts of some nuclear "have-nots" (especially those with aggressive aims) to obtain them. One great fear is that we will reach a tipping point when a country like Iran or North Korea goes nuclear and other threshold states in the region decide to follow suit.[15]

As the number of states with WMDs grows, the likelihood that such weapons will fall into the wrong hands—of terrorists or drug traffickers—increases. The danger of nuclear proliferation can take countless forms. When the Soviet Union disintegrated, several former Soviet republics found themselves in possession of nuclear arsenals. Belarus, Ukraine, and Kazakhstan agreed to give up to Russia the WMD weapons they inherited, including megaton warheads and long-range missiles (as well as countless battlefield or tactical "nukes").

The New Doomsday Scenario: Averting a Silent Spring

Environmental problems remained largely unrecognized in the United States until the early 1960s, when Rachel Carson's best-selling book, *Silent Spring*, first appeared.[16] Since then, concern for the environment has grown. Today, green parties exist in virtually every major democracy except the United States, where organizations such as the Sierra Club, the Audubon Society, Save the Whales, and the National Wildlife Federation nonetheless exert considerable political clout. In addition, many research institutes and public policy "think tanks" monitor the state of the environment and advocate ecology-conscious public policies. One sign "greens" are gaining traction in the United States: On taking office President Barack Obama created a new post of White House energy czar, tasked with developing and directing federal efforts to reduce greenhouse gas (GHG) emissions.

Acid rain, global warming, receding water tables, declining forests and fisheries, and the rapid depletion of the earth's fossil fuels all have contributed to a new sense of urgency. In 1997 that led to the signing of the Kyoto Protocol, a major effort to enlist all nations in a global action plan. Kyoto called for the 37 industrialized countries and the European Union to reduce GHG emissions—carbon dioxide, nitrous oxide, methane, and fluorocarbons; by 2009 it had been endorsed by 184 countries. (See Chapter 13 for a fuller discussion of environmental policy.)

The environmental movement received a major blow in 2001, when President Bush announced the United States was withdrawing from the Kyoto accord because, he said, attempting to comply with its provisions would hurt the U.S. economy.[17] In 2004, Russia announced it would ratify the treaty, further isolating the United States on this issue. In June 2007, the Bush administration reversed itself and pledged U.S. support for global efforts to combat climate

BOX 17.1 SPOTLIGHT ON North Korea and Iran: Nuclear Pariahs?

FIGURE 17.3 Forging an Economic Superpower: The European Union in 2007.
All GDP estimates are based on official exchange rates. Note that the GDP of Germany, France, and the United Kingdom fall into the range $2–3 trillion now, that Italy's GDP was nearly $1.8 trillion in 2006, and that Spain's was over a trillion dollars.
SOURCE: *The World Factbook, 2007*

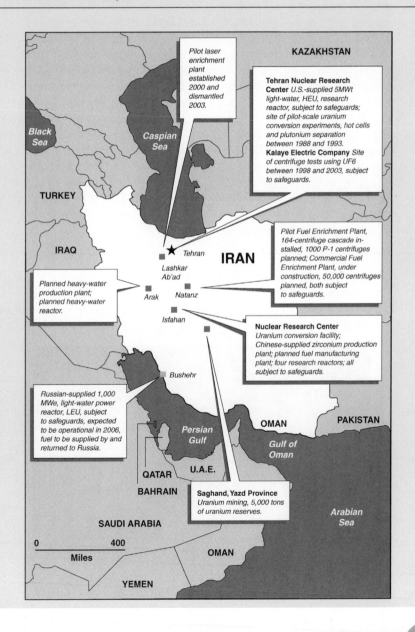

Pilot laser enrichment plant established 2000 and dismantled 2003.

KAZAKHSTAN

Tehran Nuclear Research Center *U.S.-supplied 5MWt light-water, HEU, research reactor, subject to safeguards; site of pilot-scale uranium conversion experiments, hot cells and plutonium separation between 1988 and 1993.*
Kalaye Electric Company *Site of centrifuge tests using UF6 between 1998 and 2003, subject to safeguards.*

Black Sea

Caspian Sea

TURKEY

IRAQ

IRAN

Tehran

Lashkar Ab'ad

Pilot Fuel Enrichment Plant, 164-centrifuge cascade in-stalled, 1000 P-1 centrifuges planned; Commercial Fuel Enrichment Plant, under construction, 50,000 centrifuges planned, both subject to safeguards.

Planned heavy-water production plant; planned heavy-water reactor.

Arak Natanz

Isfahan

Nuclear Research Center *Uranium conversion facility; Chinese-supplied zirconium production plant; planned fuel manufacturing plant; four research reactors; all subject to safeguards.*

Russian-supplied 1,000 MWe, light-water power reactor, LEU, subject to safeguards, expected to be operational in 2006, fuel to be supplied by and returned to Russia.

Bushehr

Persian Gulf

OMAN

PAKISTAN

Gulf of Oman

QATAR

U.A.E.

BAHRAIN

Saghand, Yazd Province *Uranium mining, 5,000 tons of uranium reserves.*

Arabian Sea

SAUDI ARABIA

0   400
Miles

OMAN

YEMEN

BOX 17.1 SPOTLIGHT ON   *(Continued)*

In 2003, the Bush administration justified the invasion of Iraq on the grounds that Saddam Hussein possessed a secret arsenal of WMDs, had ties to al Qaeda, and thus posed a mortal threat to the United States and world peace. As we now know, these allegations were false. Nonetheless, the Iraq war was the first in the Nuclear Age fought for the ostensible purpose of preventing nuclear proliferation.

Having ousted Saddam and set up an interim government in Iraq, the United States confronted both North Korea and Iran over nuclear prolifer- ation—calling them part of an "axis of evil," alleg- ing they were actively seeking to acquire nuclear weapons, and demanding they discontinue all WMD research and development and submit to international inspections. Defiantly, North Korea conducted its first-ever atomic test in October 2006, prompting alarm in Japan and the United States as well as in the wider international com- munity. Veiled U.S. military threats, combined with diplomatic pressure from China, induced President Kim Jong Il to accept a six-nation accord in February 2007, which committed North Korea to shutting down its nuclear weapons program in return for certain trade and aid concessions. But the Pyongyang regime broke the agree- ment in 2008–2009 when it conducted nuclear tests, ran six short-range missile tests, and twice attempted to test-launch long-range missiles.

In 2007, the United States turned the spotlight on Iran's nuclear weapons program (see Figure 17.3). When President Bush assumed a confronta- tional stance, the Iranian government responded in kind. For a time, the long-standing diplomatic stalemate appeared to be escalating toward war. President Obama has vowed to seek a negoti- ated solution.

change at a G8 summit meeting in Europe. Turkey ratified the Kyoto accord in the summer of 2008. With Barack Obama in the White House, the United States can be expected to give unequivocal support to future international efforts to combat climate change—and avert a silent spring.

In December 2008, President-elect Barack Obama announced his intention to name Carol Browner (pictured here) as his special advisor on energy and the environment—a new White House post.

© AP Photos

The IT Revolution

How is the revolution in information technology (IT) changing the landscape of international politics? The carrying capacity of the global communications network of computers, telephone, and television has grown by leaps and bounds. According to Moore's Law (named for Gordon Moore, cofounder of Intel), computing power per dollar doubles every 18 months. A $1,500 laptop computer today is far more powerful than a $10 million mainframe was in the mid-1970s. In the 1970s, there were only about 50,000 computers in the world; by the turn of the twenty-first century there were more than 140 million. A transatlantic telephone cable could carry only 138 conversations simultaneously in 1960, a fiber-optic cable now carries 1.5 million. The number of Internet users topped one billion in December 2008, according to one source; another put the number of Web surfers at 1.5 billion in June 2008 (see Table 17.2).

The most obvious political effect of the IT revolution is to weaken individual governments' hold over citizens. Citizens worldwide now have access to independent sources of information. Everything from criticism of government to pornography to a "build your own nuclear bomb" Web page can be accessed from most any country, usually despite the efforts of government. The Internet even threatens to undermine traditional cultures and civilizations that do not share Western values. It also poses a threat to dictatorial regimes, which is why the People's Republic of China and Iran, to cite two examples, routinely block certain Websites and jam radio broadcasts of the BBC, the Voice of America, and Radio Free Europe/Radio Liberty. The latter broadcasts daily in Farsi (the Persian language) from Prague and Washington as Radio Farda. But these efforts do not prevent all international contacts via Twitter, Facebook, and the like, nor do they prevent all international exchanges of cell phone text messages.

Some political consequences of the IT revolution we can only dimly perceive at present. For instance, it is commonly assumed that technology enhances the ruthless grip of tyrannical rulers (recall George Orwell's description of "telescreens" and other technology used by totalitarian rulers in his classic novel *Nineteen Eighty-Four*). But the opposite may be more nearly true: the Internet makes it more difficult for the state to control what people know and how they know it.

LIVING IN A HOSTILE WORLD: U.S. FOREIGN POLICY

The ends in foreign policy are goals; the means are strategies and policies that nations adopt in pursuit of predetermined goals and objectives. Goals are by nature long-range, deeply rooted, and slow to change. Strategies and policies, in turn, can be pragmatic and flexible. They can vary over time and be global or regional.

TABLE 17.2   Surfing the Web: A Billion and Counting

Top 15 Countries by Internet Population

1. China: 179.7 million
2. United States: 163.3 million
3. Japan: 60.0 million
4. Germany: 37.0 million
5. United Kingdom: 36.7 million
6. France: 34.0 million
7. India: 32.1 million
8. Russia: 29.0 million
9. Brazil: 27.7 million
10. South Korea: 27.3 million
11. Canada: 21.8 million
12. Italy: 20.8 million
13. Spain: 17.9 million
14. Mexico: 12.5 million
15. Netherlands: 11.8 million

Worldwide Internet Audience

- Asia Pacific: 416 million (41.3%)
- Europe: 283 million (28.0%)
- North America: 185 million (18.4%)
- Latin America: 75 million (7.4%)
- Middle East & Africa: 49 million (4.8%)

SOURCE: Erick Schonfeld, "ComScore: Internet Population Passes One Billion; Top 15 Countries," TechCrunch.com, January 23, 2009 at <http://www.techcrunch.com/2009/01/23/>.

status quo strategy
A national policy of maintaining the existing balance of power through collective security agreements, diplomacy, and negotiation, as well as through "legitimizing instruments," such as international law and international organizations.

expansionist strategy
A strategy by which a nation seeks to extend its territory or influence.

The National Interest

We find two recurring types of goal orientation in international politics: a defensive **status quo strategy** and an offensive **expansionist strategy**. Most nations say they are engaging in the first, even when they are pursuing the second. This hypocrisy is partly deliberate ("the tribute that vice pays to virtue") and perhaps partly self-delusion—after all, it is human nature to rationalize our behavior when we cannot justify it.

Nations seeking to expand want to change existing power relationships, often at the expense of nations wishing to freeze them. As a rule, expansionist states are dissatisfied with the status quo and thus are moved to provoke wars, initiate arms races, promote revolutions abroad, and generally destabilize the international system, which they reject as fundamentally illegitimate and unjust. Their actions can create a strong moral pressure against them.

Although the distinction between aggressive and defensive states is clear in theory, it blurs in practice. Thus, if no rival nation is engaging in an arms buildup, status quo states are content with existing levels of military readiness. But if a dissatisfied rival state is adding new weapons to its arsenal for expansion's sake, even the most satisfied status quo state(s) will be compelled to imitate this behavior for the sake of self-preservation.

Some states balk at the dangers inherent in such a system and attempt to opt out of international power politics altogether, pursuing a strategy of neutrality or nonalignment. **Neutrality** means not taking a stand one way and simply sitting on the sidelines; **nonalignment** means not choosing sides in general but not necessarily remaining neutral on all issues and in all situations.

Status quo strategies are essentially conservative. Nations adopting them aim to uphold the existing balance of power, and they cherish stability, peaceful intercourse among nations, and, above all, legitimacy. Status quo states generally seek to use instruments, such as international law, multilateral arrangements, and global authorities (for example, the League of Nations and the United Nations), to legitimize the existing distribution of power and prestige in the world. They often refuse to recognize revolutionary governments on the grounds that such governments seized power unlawfully or pose a threat to the stability of the regional or global balance, or that to reward violence and lawlessness with international acceptance undermines respect for law and order everywhere. U.S. foreign policy after World War II provides the most vivid illustrations of this policy. Indeed, the United States refused to recognize the existence of the Chinese government for more than two decades after the Communist takeover on the mainland in 1949.

However, few states consistently follow status quo strategies on all fronts. The diplomatic history of the United States illustrates. Although at various times it has practiced a policy of expansionism (see Box 17.2), for much of its

neutrality
The policy of giving the very highest priority to staying out of war by adopting a nonthreatening posture toward neighboring states, maintaining a strictly defensive military capability, and refusing to take sides in conflicts; Finland, Sweden, and Switzerland are among the countries that have pursued a policy of neutrality most successfully.

BOX 17.2 FOCUS ON — Manifest Destiny

The United States has always pretended to pursue a status quo policy, even when it was, in fact, expanding. The story of how the United States grew from thirteen states huddled along the Atlantic seaboard (the original colonies) into a vast empire stretching across an entire continent is known to every U.S. schoolchild, but teachers rarely present it as a story about imperialism or expansionism—unless, perhaps, the children and the teacher are Native Americans. Spaniards and Mexicans would have reason to differ over this point as well, as people living in Texas, Arizona, California, or Florida (among other states) ought to know. Even Russians might object, having ventured into Alaska before the United States existed. Expansionists in the U.S. Congress called it Manifest Destiny, but, as Shakespeare said, a rose by any other name is still a rose.

history, the United States followed a strategy of maintaining the regional and international status quo. Two examples, examined in the next section, are the **Monroe Doctrine** and the post–World War II policy of containment.

In Pursuit of the National Interest

The gap between a nation's long-term goals and its short-term policies raises three key points. First, regardless of its strategy, a nation may simultaneously carry out different policies to deal with different problems. It may seek to preserve the status quo by signing a peace treaty with one nation in order to launch an expansionistic attack on another. Nazi Germany, which pursued an expansionist policy, signed a nonaggression treaty with the Soviet Union in August 1939 for strategic advantage in conquering Eastern Europe. Or a nation may choose expansionism when it believes striking first and occupying a potential enemy's territory are necessary to its own survival.

These examples emphasize the second point: power strategies are flexible; they change with circumstances and can be applied and altered whenever the nation's leadership deems it appropriate. The United States has frequently invaded or intervened militarily in Latin American countries, always with the declared intent to defend the status quo or free the oppressed from tyranny (although, not surprisingly, many Latin Americans see it differently).

The Monroe Doctrine: Enshrining the Status Quo   President James Monroe promulgated the Monroe Doctrine in his annual message to Congress on December 2, 1823, pledging the United States would strictly respect the existing political configurations in the Western Hemisphere. "With the existing colonies or dependencies of any European power we have not interfered and shall not interfere," Monroe observed. But, he continued, as for

> the governments who have declared their Independence, and maintain it . . . we could not view any interposition for the purpose of oppressing them, or controlling in any other manner their destiny, by an European power, in any other light than as the manifestation of an unfriendly disposition towards the United States.[18]

With this declaration, the United States served notice that henceforth it would resist any attempt by an outside power to upset the hemispheric balance of power. In effect, the Monroe Doctrine asserted the right of the United States of America to maintain a preeminent position in roughly half the world—the half it believed vital to its national security.

Containment: Extending the Status Quo   Another example of U.S. status quo policy, containment, operated from the late 1940s until 1991, when the Soviet Union disintegrated. World War II had drastically altered the European and thus the global balance of power. In its aftermath, the United States was thrust for the first time into the role of paramount world leader—a role challenged by

---

nonalignment
A policy specific to the Cold War in which many developing countries—formerly known as Third World countries—preferred not to align themselves with either the United States and its allies (the West) or the Soviet Union and its allies (the East); nonalignment differs from neutrality in that it does not commit a state to nonaggression or noninvolvement in local conflicts and, unlike neutrality, it did not become an important concept in international relations until after World War II.

Monroe Doctrine
A status quo international policy laid down by U.S. president James Monroe, who pledged the United States to resist any attempts by outside powers to alter the balance of power in the American hemisphere.

BOX 17.3 FOCUS ON — History, Conflict, and Foreign Policy: The Case of the Middle East

To illustrate the complex and ambiguous nature of foreign policy goals in international relations, we need look no further than the prolonged conflict between Israel and the Arab world.

After World War II, Jewish nationalists, or Zionists, waged a successful war against the British and the Arabs for a homeland in Palestine. In their defense they cited historical, biblical, and legal authority and argued that in the aftermath of the Holocaust, Jews could live in security only in a Jewish homeland. But Palestinian Arab refugees, who had fled in droves rather than live in a Jewish state, regarded the Israelis as imperialists. Neighboring Arab states declared a holy war against **Zionism** and vowed to destroy Israel.

Subsequently, radical Palestinian groups directed acts of terrorism against the Israeli population with the complicity of several Arab governments, notably Egypt. In 1956, Egypt seized the Suez Canal from Great Britain and France, which then actively backed Israel in a war with Egypt over which nation would control access to the canal. This episode only strengthened the Arab belief that Zionism and Western imperialism were conspiring to dominate the Muslim nations of the Middle East.

After more than a decade of smoldering hostilities, another war erupted. In 1967, reacting to Egyptian threats and intelligence reports suggesting it was about to attack, Israel launched a preemptive military operation that resulted in the so-called Six Days' War. After less than a week of fighting, the Israelis had routed their enemies and occupied large tracts of Arab territory, including the Sinai peninsula and Gaza Strip in Egypt, the Golan Heights in Syria, and the West Bank of the Jordan River in Jordan. Jerusalem, until then partitioned, fell under complete Israeli control.

Humiliated by defeat, Egypt and Syria prepared for yet another round of fighting. In 1973, they attempted to revise the post-1967 status quo by attacking Israeli-held territories. The Israelis were again equal to the challenge, but this time they suffered a setback early on. With the United States acting as a mediator, the Egyptians eventually regained the Sinai desert by agreeing to a peace treaty with Israel in 1979 (the Camp David Accords). The other Arab nations charged Egypt with selling out to Zionism and "imperialism."

In the decades that followed, peace has remained elusive. In December 2008, Israel launched air strikes against targets in the Gaza Strip, killing civilians and destroying homes, and then invaded Gaza in an effort to hunt down Hamas militants. Israel claims Hamas is responsible for launching rocket attacks against southern Israel. Meanwhile, about 1.4 million impoverished Palestinians live in Gaza, cut off from the world by an Israeli embargo.

Who is right, and who is wrong? The Arab states, along with the Palestine Liberation Organization, refused to recognize Israel's right to exist. But Israel has also, at times, been part of the problem, such as when it permitted the establishment of Jewish settlements on land seized from the Arabs. Both sides believe they are absolutely right, and the other side is absolutely wrong.

Similar ambiguities crop up all the time in international politics. Competing claims do not preclude judgments about right and wrong; they merely make them more difficult to reach.

a formidable adversary under Stalin's leadership. It seemed as if Tocqueville's century-old prophecy that the United States and Russia had each been "marked out by the will of Heaven to sway the destinies of half the globe"[19] was about to be fulfilled.

Zionism
The national movement
for the return of the
Jewish people to the
land of Abraham and the
resumption of Jewish
sovereignty in what is
now known as Israel.

U.S. policymakers eventually decided to deal with the perceived Soviet threat through a policy of containment, the main outlines of which were delineated in a celebrated article in the journal *Foreign Affairs* in July 1947. The anonymous author, "X," turned out to be George F. Kennan (1904–2005), then the influential director of the State Department's Policy Planning Staff and later an ambassador to the USSR. "It is clear," Kennan wrote,

> that the main element of any United States policy toward the Soviet Union must be that of a long-term, patient but firm and vigilant containment of Russian expansive tendencies. . . Soviet pressure against the free institutions of the Western world is something that can be contained by the adroit and vigilant application of counter-force at a series of constantly shifting geographical and political points.[20]

Kennan went on to predict that if a policy of containment were applied consistently for a decade or so, the Soviet challenge would diminish significantly. He also suggested (prophetically) that if containment proved successful, the totalitarian Soviet state would ultimately fall victim to severe internal pressures.

This "new" doctrine of containment was actually nothing more than the age-old status quo policy, now adapted to the unique set of circumstances after World War II. Its first major test came in 1947, when Greece appeared about to fall to a communist insurgency. In an urgent message to Congress requesting authority to provide aid to Greece and Turkey, President Harry Truman enunciated the containment principle that came to be known as the **Truman Doctrine**: "I believe that it must be the policy of the United States to support free peoples who are resisting attempted subjugation by armed minorities or by outside pressures."[21] When Congress approved the president's request, containment became the official policy of the U.S. government.

Truman Doctrine
President Harry Truman's
pledge of U.S. support
for any free people
threatened with
revolution by an internal
armed minority or an
outside aggressor.

After a communist government gained power in Czechoslovakia in February 1948, the United States countered with the **Marshall Plan**, a $16.5 billion program aimed at reconstructing the war-torn economies of Western Europe. At the time, it was feared that communism might come in "through the back door"— meaning the powerful communist parties of France and Italy might be able to capitalize on the demoralization of the general populace and, with Moscow's covert backing, seize power in Paris and Rome as they had done in Prague. The Marshall Plan formed an integral part of the overall U.S. effort to preserve the status quo after World War II. In 1949, the United States established NATO, thus putting military "teeth" into the policy.

Marshall Plan
A post–World War II
program of massive
economic assistance
to Western Europe,
inspired by the fear that
those war-devastated
countries were ripe for
communist-backed
revolutions.

The fall of mainland China to the communists in 1949 provoked another great wave of anxiety throughout the United States. When, in 1950, fighting broke out in Korea between the communist regime in the north and the noncommunist one in the south, the United States decided to apply containment in Asia as well as Europe.

During the 1960s, what had started out as a policy designed to prevent the spread of communism, first in Europe and then in Asia, turned into a firefighting strategy of anticommunist interventionism in the Third World. Military equipment, economic aid, diplomatic support, and the U.S. nuclear umbrella were all extended to specific nations deemed under threat of communist subversion or insurgency. Military intervention was considered an appropriate response under certain circumstances. This strategy of military containment reached its high-water mark when hundreds of thousands of U.S. troops were sent to South Vietnam between 1964 and 1972.

By the early 1990s, the U.S. policy of containment had lost its *raison d'être*. The Soviet Union's decision to grant autonomy to its former Eastern European satellite nations, its backing of the U.S.-led coalition against Iraq in 1991, and its disintegration later that year made the policies and doctrines associated with the Cold War obsolete.

THE GREAT DEBATE: REALISM VERSUS IDEALISM

During the Cold War, political realism provided an intellectually satisfying conceptual framework for international relations.[22] It was easy to believe realist notions of the struggle for power and "nationalistic universalism" (the urge to dominate others) accurately described the immutable facts of international life. The world was divided into two irreconcilable camps, implacable foes armed with nuclear weapons determined to bury one another.

Although that world has passed, the mindset it engendered persists. Influential politicians and pundits continue to associate political realism with an aggressive pursuit of national interests—not necessarily expansionist, but interventionist.[23] Political realists are seldom advocates of restraint in crisis situations; in the crisis presented by the 9/11 terrorist attacks, President George W. Bush, a conservative Republican, called for an aggressive pursuit of the perpetrators as well as punitive measures against any state(s) that harbored international terrorists.[24] The methods the United States used were violent—bombing and inserting special operations combat teams in order to (1) overthrow the Taliban government and (2) kill or capture Osama bin Laden and his al Qaeda terrorist network.

Clearly, violent methods do not always denote a strategy of expansionism. The United States was not trying to colonize Afghanistan.

Oddly enough, defenders of the status quo (especially conservatives) routinely associate violence with aggression and aggression with expansionism. However, defenders of the status quo (again, especially conservatives), tend also to use violence or even sponsor insurgencies as part of a strategy aimed at defeating revolutionary movements. The champions of this *counterinsurgency interventionism* claim to be idealistic, but the rest of the world, with few exceptions, sees it as imperialistic. The Reagan administration (1980–1988) aided a variety of anticommunist insurgents around the world in the 1980s, including groups in Central America (the Contras in Nicaragua), in Asia (mujahedeen rebels in Afghanistan), and in Africa (UNITA guerrillas in Angola). The fact that Reagan called the guerrilla forces he liked "freedom fighters" did not fool anybody (except perhaps in the United States). These examples demonstrate the vital importance (and difficulty) of maintaining moral objectivity in foreign policy analysis. A strategy aimed at changing the existing distribution of power and wealth is not necessarily a sign of either imperialism or idealism; more likely it is evidence that realism has swayed policymakers, rightly or wrongly, to take a certain course of action.

To understand what expansionism is, we must also understand what it is not. Not every state with a territorial claim against another or a desire to change the global distribution of power and wealth is aggressive or expansionist. A border dispute does not, in itself, mean either contending country has an appetite for empire. Neither does the demand by many developing countries for a "new international economic order" (a redistribution of global wealth). Challenging the status quo in this way is hardly proof of aggression, both because the objectives are limited and reasonable and because the methods are political and diplomatic rather than military or economic.

Historically, when one nation's army invaded and occupied the territory of another nation, it was an act of aggression—a violation of international law. Invaders are seldom welcomed by the native inhabitants and aggressors are seldom embraced by the international community. But, as suggested above, the United States since World War II has intervened with military in some countries and invaded others without *intending* to plunder or seize territory, without intending to take over the country's government, and without intending to stay. Unfortunately, "good" intentions are often misunderstood, misinterpreted, or, in the eyes of others, not good at all. When that happens—and it almost always does—a danger of unintended consequences arises.

The Curse of Unintended Consequences: Blowback

The concept of *blowback* has been at the center of a debate over U.S. foreign policy since the end of the Cold War. Chalmers Johnson, an expert on Asia, who wrote a best-selling book of the same name, popularized the term.[25] According to Johnson,

> [Blowback] refers to the unintended consequences of policies that were kept secret from the American people. What the daily press reports as the malign acts of "terrorists" or "drug lords" or "rogue states" or "illegal arms merchants" often turn out to be blowback from earlier operations.[26]

As examples, Johnson cited the 1988 bombing of Pan Am Flight 103 over Lockerbie, Scotland, which, he asserted, "was retaliation for a 1986 Reagan administration aerial raid on Libya that killed President Muammar Qaddafi's stepdaughter."[27] He also suggested that drug trafficking in the United States is, in part, the result of past U.S. support for dictators and anticommunist insurgents in Latin America, and that terrorist attacks against U.S. targets are blowback, citing a 1997 Pentagon report: "Historical data shows a strong correlation between U.S. involvement in international situations and an increase in terrorist attacks against the United States."[28] The picture Johnson painted is nothing short of alarming:

> The most direct and obvious form of blowback often occurs when the victims fight back after a secret American bombing, or a U.S.-sponsored campaign of state terrorism, or a CIA-engineered overthrow of a foreign political leader. All around the world today, it is possible to see the groundwork being laid for future forms of blowback.[29]

These words of gloom and doom, written in 1999, looked prophetic in the days after terrorists leveled the World Trade Center. In this same passage, Johnson wrote about the 1990–1991 Gulf War and its aftermath and the suffering caused by the U.S.-imposed economic blockade on Iraq, charging "it helped contribute to the deaths of an estimated half million Iraqi civilians due to disease, malnutrition, and inadequate medical care." Osama bin Laden and the al Qaeda high command "justified" the 9/11 attacks on the grounds that the United States (1) defiled the sacred soil of Saudi Arabia by stationing military forces in the country, (2) supported Israel's repression of Palestinians' rights, and (3) waged economic war against Iraqi civilians.

President Bill Clinton blamed bin Laden for the terrorist attacks on U.S. embassies in 1998 in Nairobi (the capital of Kenya) and Dar es Salaam (the capital of Tanzania). Clinton retaliated by bombing a pharmaceutical plant in Khartoum (the capital of Sudan) and an al Qaeda training camp in Afghanistan. Neither of these air strikes accomplished its intended purpose, but the attack against Sudan was particularly embarrassing to the United States when it turned out the pharmaceutical plant was not manufacturing chemical weapons of mass destruction, as the United States had alleged. However,

> Government spokesmen continue to justify these attacks as "deterring" terrorism, even if the targets proved to be irrelevant to any damage done to facilities of the United States. In this way, future blowback possibilities are seeded into the world.[30]

Johnson cites many examples of incidents likely, in his estimation, to produce future blowback in our relationships with Japan (Okinawa), South Korea (the 1980 Kwangju massacre), China, Indonesia, and others. Although his critique is incisive and thought provoking, his views are controversial and by no means shared by all other academic or government experts. Indeed, in the wake of 9/11, many in the United States tended to be suspicious of *any* criticism of U.S. foreign policy, viewing it as unpatriotic.

The Bush Doctrine

After the 9/11 attacks President Bush lost little time in declaring a war against terror. He also made it clear the United States would retaliate against terrorists and those who harbor them. When the fundamentalist Taliban regime ignored Bush's ultimatum to hand over Osama bin Laden and shut down al Qaeda operations in Afghanistan, the United States orchestrated a large-scale military invasion with the intention of bringing about regime change and hunting down bin Laden and his al Qaeda confederates. The UN Security Council gave the United States a green light, and world public opinion overwhelmingly supported military action against the repressive Taliban.

But for Bush, overthrowing the Taliban and destroying the al Qaeda training camps in Afghanistan was only the first step. There still existed an "axis of evil" that included Iraq, Iran, and North Korea. Bush argued that the universal right of self-defense justifies the use of preemptive action when an "imminent danger of attack" exists. In this context he enunciated what has come to be called the Bush Doctrine.

> The United States has long maintained the option of preemptive actions to counter a sufficient threat to our national security. The greater the threat, the greater is the risk of inaction—and the more compelling the case for taking anticipatory action to defend ourselves, even if uncertainty remains as to the time and place of the enemy's attack. To forestall or prevent such hostile acts by our adversaries, the United States will, if necessary, act preemptively.[31]

The logic of this Bush Doctrine was invoked to justify the invasion of Iraq.

On May 1, 2003, after the U.S. military had invaded Iraq, ousted Saddam Hussein, and replaced his brutal regime with a Coalition Provisional Authority (occupation government), Bush declared "mission accomplished"—the end of the major fighting in Iraq. It was a triumphant moment for the president, but premature. Over the next 12 months, the death toll mounted steadily as Iraqi insurgents planted bombs, launched missile attacks, and staged ambushes. By June 2009, more than 4,160 U.S. soldiers had died in Iraq *after* the "mission accomplished" pronouncement. Other casualties included 1,306 contract workers, 138 journalists, and 308 coalition troops—and an estimated 1.3 million Iraqis.[32]

President Bush ordered a troop surge in 2008 in a desperate attempt to defeat the urban guerrilla war of attrition in Iraq. He saw his approval ratings fall as a rising chorus of criticism continued to take its toll and cast a shadow over his administration. The Bush Doctrine was destined to become yet another textbook example of blowback in postwar U.S. foreign policy.

REINVENTING STATECRAFT: TOWARD A NEW REALISM

Some international theorists contend that not much has changed in the post–Cold War era. They contend the United States "must anchor its security and prosperity in a less-than-utopian set of objectives [and] think in terms not of the whole world's well-being but . . . of purely national interest."[33]

Political scientists Max Singer and Aaron Wildavsky have argued that despite talk of a new world order, most contemporary critics fail to grasp the reality of the world emerging in the post–Cold War era.[34] They call the prosperous

Prisoners at the U.S. "Gitmo" detention facility at, Guantanamo Bay, Cuba. The methods and policies associated with the Bush Doctrine in the conduct of the war on terror caused a "blowback" effect that damaged President Bush's popularity at home and his credibility abroad.

© LANDOV MEDIA

democracies that account for about 15 percent of the world's population "zones of peace," and underdeveloped dictatorships "zones of conflict." They believe power struggles and wars in the zones of conflict will continue to be the norm. Economic cooperation and peaceful competition, in the form of trade and investment, will replace war in the zones of peace.

What does this analysis suggest for U.S. policy? According to Singer and Wildavsky,

> Our overall goal should be the advance of stable democracy so that zones of peace will be extended as soon as possible. We propose that the United States should pursue this goal in five ways: by making a clear distinction in our policy between democracies and nondemocracies; by minimizing trade barriers; by providing economic aid and advice; by providing an example and a market; and by working with other democracies to preserve peace and improve the international order, even if military intervention is required. But we should not have a policy of forcing democracy on authoritarian countries.[35]

This optimistic analysis views the power of example "and the openness of our markets" as the most effective ways to influence the behavior of authoritarian regimes.

A recent book on statecraft stresses the importance of multilateralism, clear thinking, prudence, and knowledge in the conduct of foreign policy. What is statecraft? According to Dennis Ross, chief Middle East peace negotiator under Presidents George H. W. Bush and Bill Clinton,

It is the use of the assets or the resources and tools (economic, military, intelligence, media) that a state has to pursue its interest and to affect the behavior of others, whether friendly or hostile. It involves making sound assessments and understanding where and on what issues the state is being challenged and can counter a threat or create a potential opportunity or take advantage of one. Statecraft requires good judgment in the definition of one's interests and a recognition of how to exercise hard military or soft economic power to provide security and promote the well-being of one's citizens. It is as old as conflict between communities and the desire to avoid or prevent it. Plato wrote about statecraft. Machiavelli theorized about it. And Bismarck practiced it, never losing sight of his objectives and recognizing that a nation's amibitions should never exceed its capabilities.[36]

Ideals and Self-interest: The Power of Morality

idealism
A political philosophy that considers values, ideals, and moral principles as the keys to comprehending, and possibly changing, the behavior of nation-states.

In sharp contrast to political realism, **idealism** places great emphasis on the role of values, ideals, and moral principles. It not only helps explain why nations act but also furnishes guidelines for how nations ought to act. Idealists tend to view war as irrational—a manifestation of misguided ideology or fervent nationalism. They see trade, aid, diplomacy, and international law and organizations (see Chapter 18) as antidotes—and alternatives—to war.

Idealists often regard realists as cynics; realists say idealists are naive. Who is right?

Even the arch-realist, Hans Morgenthau, did not deny morality's role in international relations. Some actors on the world stage clearly give moral principle more weight than others. President Woodrow Wilson emphasized national self-determination and collective security, Hitler obsessed over territorial expansion *(Lebensraum)*, British Prime Minister Neville Chamberlain sought peace through appeasement, and President Jimmy Carter actively promoted global human rights. Nations *do* sometimes act altruistically—for example, by offering asylum to refugees who flee political persecution, economic disaster, or civil war. Between the two world wars, British leaders sought to alleviate harsh conditions imposed on Germany by the Treaty of Versailles, a stand hailed as "a noble idea, rooted in Christianity, courage, and common sense."[37]

The U.S. military action in Somalia from 1992 to 1994 was undertaken to alleviate mass starvation. That humanitarian intervention, which cost U.S. lives and offered no political or economic advantage, cannot be explained by self-interest alone.[38] Indeed, it accomplished little but to alienate Islamic extremists, who saw it as another example of U.S. interference in the internal affairs of a Muslim society.

Still, it is easier by far to cite instances when leaders and states do *not* act altruistically. President Bill Clinton did not intervene against the genocide in Rwanda and President George W. Bush did not send troops to stop the savagery in Darfur. The major European nations, too, stayed on the sidelines in both instances.

Most foreign policy contains elements of both ideals and self-interest. The Marshall Plan was magnanimous by any reasonable measure. Even Winston Churchill, who measured his words carefully, called it the "most unsordid act in history."[39]

But the Marshall Plan was also consistent with the United States' post–World War II status quo strategic policy of reestablishing a stable Western European community, able to resist armed aggression from without and organized subversion from within. Germany sent massive amounts of aid to Russia in the winter of 1991–1992, partly for humanitarian reasons and partly out of fear a failed Russia would destabilize Western Europe and unleash a horde of refugees in Germany's direction.

Nations have occasionally sacrificed concrete national interests for the sake of moral principle. Although an occupied country during World War II, Denmark was granted much political autonomy by the Nazi government. The Danish people and their government openly defied German edicts in order to protect Jewish citizens and other refugees, thereby putting themselves at risk. Through acts of uncommon moral courage, the Danes created "an extraordinary obstacle which arose in the path of the German destruction machine: an uncooperative Danish administration and a local population unanimous in its resolve to save its Jews."[40] Denmark, "too weak to seek self-preservation through power," limited its foreign policy "largely to humanitarian causes, and . . . in the end survived Hitler's conquest."[41]

A true understanding of the national interest takes into account both power and morality. Power without morality is mere expedience and, as history shows, can be self-defeating, whereas morality without power rarely goes beyond good intentions.[42]

Hard Facts About Soft Power

Scholar Joseph Nye argues power in contemporary world politics is "distributed among countries in a pattern that resembles a complex three-dimensional chess game."[43] Imagine three chess games on as many chessboards taking place on three levels simultaneously. On the top board, military power is concentrated in the United States; the world looks unipolar. On the middle chessboard, however, economic power is distributed more evenly among the United States, Europe, Japan, and China and the world appears multipolar. Finally, on the bottom chessboard "is the realm of transnational relations that cross borders outside government control."

> This realm includes actors as diverse as bankers electronically transferring sums larger than most national budgets at one extreme, and terrorists transferring weapons or hackers disrupting Internet operations at the other. On this bottom board, power is widely dispersed, and it makes no sense to speak of unipolarity, multipolarity or hegemony.

In a three-dimensional game, Nye argues, you will lose if you focus only on the top board and fail to notice the other boards and the vertical connections among them. Nye draws an even more fundamental distinction between "hard coercive power" and "soft or attractive power," which he defines as "the important ability to get others to want what you want." He concludes: "The paradox of American power in the 21st century is that the largest power since Rome cannot achieve its objectives unilaterally in a global information age." [44]

APOCALYPTIC VISIONS: CULTURE WARS AND ANARCHY?

Political scientist Samuel Huntington believed the old clash of Cold War ideologies would be replaced by a "clash of civilizations"—a thesis he published 8 years *before* the 9/11 attacks. [45] Huntington defined a *civilization* as "the highest cultural grouping of people and the broadest level of cultural identity people have short of that which distinguishes humans from other species." [46] While such ideas and institutions as liberty, democracy, free markets, and the separation of church and state are significant aspects of Western culture, Huntington noted, they often "have little resonance in Islamic, Confucian, Japanese, Hindu, Buddhist, or Orthodox cultures." [47] Huntington suggested that future conflicts will be tied to cultural identity and a people's willingness to fight and die in defense of traditions threatened by Americanization, Westernization, and globalization.

Nations and societies in today's world are culturally tied to one another. In the 1991 Persian Gulf War, for example, both Arab elites and general populations outside Iraq rallied against the West. Other examples include Turkish support of Azerbaijan (Muslim) against its longtime rival Armenia (Orthodox); and the West's condemnation of Orthodox Serbs', but not Roman Catholic Croats', brutality against Bosnian Muslims. To many Muslim observers in the Arab world and southern Asia, the contrast between the West's forceful action against the Iraqi invasion of Kuwait (a former British protectorate) and its relatively weak response to Serbian aggression against Bosnian Muslims is further evidence of this **kin-country syndrome**.

kin-country syndrome
The tendency of countries whose peoples and leaders are culturally tied to one another to take similar positions.

There are also many torn countries with fragmented societies embodying different civilizations and cultures. Conflict within these, Huntington warned, could escalate into war between states or groups from rival civilizations. This "clash of civilizations" raises the possibility of global conflict between Western and non-Western civilizations, in Huntington's words, "the West against the rest."

The emergence of Osama bin Laden's al Qaeda movement, a virulently anti-Western, anti–Judeo-Christian, Islamist ideology, supports Huntington's thesis.

That bin Laden formally declared a jihad against "Crusaders" (an obvious allu-
sion to European Christendom's medieval campaign against Muslim "infidels")
and made it "the duty of Muslims everywhere to kill Americans"[48] underscores
the profound sense in which the U.S.-led struggle against international terrorism is more than a confrontation between a rogue nonstate actor and a status-
quo defending superpower.

Huntington's ideas about clashing civilizations became yesterday's news—
until September 11, 2001, a day that caused many American to ask, Why do
they hate us so much? In 1994—the year after the *first* World Trade Center
bombing—journalist Robert Kaplan had suggested an answer. His article in
Atlantic Monthly set forth an ominous thesis: "The breaking apart and remaking of the atlas is only now beginning."[49]

In Kaplan's view, the nation-state as we know it is obsolete and destined to
be replaced not by larger regional groupings or a world-state (as idealists predicted after World War II), but by a formless force field of political whirlpools
energized by the teeming, chaotic, crime-infested cities or "city-states" of the
future. The picture Kaplan painted was bleak in the extreme:

> Imagine cartography in three dimensions, as if in hologram. In this holo-
> gram would be the overlapping sediments of group and other identities
> atop the merely two-dimensional color markings of city-states and the
> remaining nations, themselves confused in places by shadowy tentacles,
> hovering overhead, indicating the power of drug cartels, mafias, and pri-
> vate security agencies. Instead of borders, there would be moving "centers"
> of power, as in the Middle Ages. Many of these layers would be in motion.
> Replacing fixed and abrupt lines on a flat space would be a shifting pattern
> of buffer entities. . . . To this protean cartographic hologram one must add
> other factors, such as migrations of populations, explosions of birth rates,
> vectors of disease. Henceforward the map of the world will never be static.
> This future map—in a sense, the Last Map—will be an ever-mutating rep-
> resentation of chaos.[50]

West Africa in the 1990s presented a glimpse of this grim future in which borders
virtually disappear; society becomes a boiling cauldron of ethnic conflict; political authority evaporates; and violence is endemic. West Africa is calm again,
but anarchy still stalks other parts of Africa, including Somalia, Sudan, and
Congo (formerly Zaire). Meanwhile, the United States is militarily embroiled
in the domestic affairs of two failed states—Iraq and Afghanistan—that are
essentially ungovernable.

Whether future conflicts will issue from disintegrating nation-state structures or a global clash of civilizations is uncertain. However, conflict will likely
continue to darken the playing field of politics on all levels—local, regional, and
international. Success in containing conflict and minimizing war will depend,
in part, on the effectiveness of the international institutions created after World
War II for those purposes. These institutions, especially the United Nations, are
our focus in the final chapter of this book.

GATEWAYS TO THE WORLD: EXPLORING CYBERSPACE

www.worldviewwest.com

This is Thomas Magstadt's Website. It is an online resource for students, teachers, public officials, and private citizens interested in world affairs, foreign policy, comparative politics, and American democracy. It also provides links to a variety of useful websites related to these areas of interest.

www.isn.ethz.ch

This is the International Relations and Security Network site created by the Center for Strategic Studies in Zurich, Switzerland; lots of information, lots of links.

toby.library.ubc.ca/subjects/subjpage2.cfm?id=169#internationalrelations

A good research tool for all sorts of classroom projects and papers on international relations; the links are broken down into categories. This site was created under the auspices of the University of British Columbia Library.

www.carnegieendowment.org/static/npp/deadlymaps.cfm

A complete collection of maps on proliferation from *Deadly Arsenals: Nuclear, Biological, and Chemical Threats*, written by Joseph Cirincione, Jon Wolfsthal, and Miriam Rajkumar, under the auspices of the Carnegie Endowment for International Peace.

first.sipri.org

Here is the site's self-description: "Facts on International Relations and Security Trends (FIRST) is a free-of-charge service for politicians, journalists, researchers and the interested public. FIRST is a joint project of the International Relations and Security Network (ISN) and the Stockholm International Peace Research Institute (SIPRI). The integrated database system contains clearly documented information from research institutes around the world. It covers areas in the field of international relations and security, such as hard facts on armed conflicts and peace keeping, arms production and trade, military expenditure, armed forces and conventional weapons holding, nuclear weapons, chronology, statistics, and other reference data."

SUMMARY

The character of international politics differs significantly from that of domestic politics due to the absence of a world government capable of maintaining law and order. The struggle for power, inherent in the international system, is designed to advance national interests. The concept of the national interest is not without ambiguity, however; it encompasses anything a nation's leaders perceive as promoting the long-term security and well-being of the state.

Students of international politics distinguish between foreign policy ends and means. Sovereign states choose a variety of ends, almost always overshadowed by one ultimate aim, to maximize power. Some states are satisfied with existing power relationships, seeking merely to maintain the status quo; others are dissatisfied and seek to overthrow it. A few states avoid choosing sides, preferring a policy of neutrality.

The traditional balance-of-power system that came into being in Europe in 1648 was limited in size and scope. All members shared certain common values and beliefs; Great Britain acted as keeper of the balance. The system worked because means and ends were limited, alliances were flexible, and crusading zeal was absent. In the Western Hemisphere the Monroe Doctrine was designed to perpetuate the regional status quo.

After World War II, the United States adopted a status quo policy of containment, aimed at preventing the Soviet Union from expanding or upsetting the global balance of power. A bipolar system replaced the old multipolar European system, with ideological differences and the specter of nuclear holocaust characterizing the bitter rivalry between the two superpowers. By the late 1960s, a strategic stalemate based on mutual deterrence made war between these two titans equally irrational for both.

With the disintegration of the Soviet Union and the end of the Cold War, a new international order emerged, based on an extreme imbalance of power with the United States the only nation capable of interceding or intervening everywhere in the world. This "unipolar moment" is just that—a moment. Trends apparent in 1990 and before will return to the fore—ever-greater economic interdependence in a dynamic global economy; growing concentration of economic power in three regions, namely Europe (the European Union), northwest Asia (China, Japan, and South Korea), and North America; a deteriorating global environment; multiplying ethnic conflicts; the rising danger of nuclear proliferation; and a constantly mutating terrorist threat.

Some political scientists employ political realism theory in arguing the United States should pursue an isolationist or unilateralist foreign policy. Others suggest rethinking basic ideas about international relations and foreign policy due to structural changes in the international system—globalization; new challengers to U.S. economic dominance from Japan, the European Union, and, most recently, China; and the revolution in information technology. Although political realism has provided a useful corrective to naive notions about international relations, today it is criticized for underestimating the power of moral principles, failing to understand the pragmatic aspect of "soft power," and continuing to focus on narrow national interests, despite pressing global problems.

Cooperation and competition over economic issues largely defined international relations between 1989 and 2001. After 9/11, however, the war on

bipolar system
Following World War II, the traditional European balance-of-power system gave way to two rival power blocs, one headed by the United States and the other by the former Soviet Union, each with overwhelming economic and military superiority and each unalterably opposed to the politics and ideology of the other.

terror as defined by the United States has trumped all other issues. The Bush Doctrine asserting a U.S. right to take preemptive measures it deems necessary, with or without UN approval, creates a risk of "blowback"—self-induced policy problems arising from imprudent past actions. Critics of recent U.S. foreign policy stress the importance of statecraft, or the skillful and prudent practice of diplomacy, as an alternative to overreliance on military force (or "hard power").

World politics is fraught with rapidly shifting dangers difficult to assess and impossible to predict. Although the precise sources, places, and forms of future conflict are uncertain, at least one authority has argued conflicts will increasingly arise from cultural differences and perhaps lead to a clash of civilizations.

KEY TERMS

political realism	deterrence theory	neutrality
equilibrium	globalization	nonalignment
balance-of-power system	International Monetary Fund (IMF)	Monroe Doctrine
keeper of the balance	unipolar system	Zionism
bipolar system	national interest	Truman Doctrine
containment	status quo strategy	Marshall Plan
Warsaw Pact	superpower	idealism
deterrence	expansionist strategy	kin-country syndrome

REVIEW QUESTIONS

1. What does the Thucydides account of the confrontation between the Melians and the Athenians reveal about the nature of international politics?
2. What does a Machiavellian approach to politics entail? What sort of worldview does it embrace?
3. What is the meaning of the term *national interest*? How do political realists use this term?
4. What two basic foreign policy goals are available to nation-states?
5. What foreign policy strategies are open to nation-states? Do nation-states usually pursue one strategy at a time? Explain.
6. Explain the difference between hard power and soft power.
7. What is the Bush Doctrine? When and how was it applied? Critique the doctrine and its application.
8. World War II changed the shape and form of the international system. When and how did the present system international system come into being? Contrast the new world order with the old one.

RECOMMENDED READING

Bacevich, Andrew. *The Limits of Power: The End of American Exceptionalism*. New York: Holt, 2009.

What is the sole superpower's proper role in the world? Bacevich criticizes the "ideology of national security" and argues the United States faces a crisis of profligacy, a crisis in politics and a crisis in the military. A tightly reasoned but caustic book that resonates with the realities of political life in the insular world of Washington politics and shop-till-you-drop consumerism.

Carr, Edward Hallett. *The Twenty Years' Crisis, 1919–1939*. New York: Harper & Row, 1981.

An excellent discussion of the relationship between power and morality in international politics, written in 1939. The author shows how the principles of international politics would have contributed to the tragedy of World War II.

Kane, Thomas. *Theoretical Roots of U. S. Foreign Policy: Machiavelli and American Unilateralism*. Oxford and New York: Routledge, 2006.

According to Machiavelli, foreign policy entanglements are particularly risky for republics, which can manage the dangers by pursuing a long-term strategy of imperialism. This book appraises the validity of Machiavelli's theory and applies it to the historical development of U.S. grand strategy.

Kennan, George F. *American Diplomacy, 1900–1950*. Chicago: University of Chicago Press, 1985.

An elegantly written interpretative history of U.S. foreign policy during the first half of the twentieth century.

Machiavelli, Niccolò. *The Prince*. New Haven, CT: Yale University Press, 1997.

This book has been "required reading" for students and practitioners of diplomacy for several centuries.

Magstadt, Thomas. *An Empire If You Can Keep It: Power and Purpose in American Foreign Policy*. Washington, DC: Congressional Quarterly Press, 2004.

A concise interpretation of recent U.S. foreign policy in the light of U.S. diplomatic history.

Mearsheimer, John. *The Tragedy of Great Power Politics*. New York: Norton, 2001.

A thought-provoking theory of international politics, Mearsheimer's "offensive realism" argues that nations act aggressively for perfectly logical reasons and will continue to do so as long as they can.

Morgenthau, Hans J. *Politics Among Nations: The Struggle for Power and Peace*, 5th ed. New York: McGraw-Hill, 1992.

A classic book sets forth the case for political realism in clear, compelling terms; one of the most famous academic works on world politics ever written.

Ross, Dennis. *Statecraft: And How to Restore America's Standing in the World*. New York: Farrar, Strauss, and Giroux. 2007.

A thoughtful essay on a timeless topic by a seasoned observer and one-time chief U.S. peace negotiator in the Middle East.

Runciman, David. *Political Hypocrisy: The Mask of Power From Hobbes to Orwell and Beyond*. Princeton, NJ: Princeton University Press, 2009.

Like a modern-day Machiavelli, the author says statesmen must possess a degree of cunning and hypocrisy as a necessary ploy.

Waltz, Kenneth N. *Theory of International Politics*. New York: McGraw-Hill, 1979.

This influential book set forth an interpretation of international relations that became known as neorealism.

Wolfers, Arnold. *Discord and Collaboration: Essays on International Politics*. Baltimore, MD: Johns Hopkins University Press, 1965.

A superb compilation of scholarly essays dealing with key concepts and issues in international relations.

Zakaria, Fareed. *The Post-American World*. New York: W.W. Norton, 2009.

A book about "the rise of the rest," and "the reality of how this rise of new powerful economic nations is completely changing the way the world works."

Flags of the European Union (EU), the world's most successful international organization. The EU has evolved from a modest six-member coal and steel community into a single market with a unique mix of intergovernmental and supranational institutions encompassing twenty-seven nations.

© Corbis

International Organization(s)
Globalization and the Quest for Order

───────────────────○───────────────────

"If you want peace, prepare for war." This famous dictum penned by a Roman military writer named Vegetius in 390 AD suggests what history shows: Conflict is part of the human condition, one we can at best prevent or deter with vigilance and military readiness. On the other hand, in a world "where everything appears to be connected to everything else," we also need new ideas and ways of thinking.[1]

After World War II some writers did foresee an age of global interdependence, in which new forms of cooperation and organization would build trust and reduce hostilities. One school of thought, called **functionalism**, argued that the practical benefits of global commerce would in time give rise to new habits of thought and behavior, bringing the peoples of the world closer together.

Functionalism has given way to **globalization**, which describes the transformational effects of computers and digital communications worldwide. In the words of Thomas Friedman, "No matter what your profession—doctor, lawyer, architect, accountant—if you are an American, you better be good at the touchy-feely service stuff, because anything that can be digitized can be outsourced to either the smartest or the cheapest producer, or both."[2] The steady growth of the world economy since World War II has also given rise to supranational trading structures that remove artificial barriers to international commerce like

functionalism
According to functionalist theory, the gradual transfer of economic and social functions to international cooperative agencies (for example, specialized UN agencies, such as UNESCO) will eventually lead to a transfer of actual authority and integration of political activities on the international level.

tariffs, quotas, and trade-distorting subsidies. They manage or contain local and regional conflicts and reduce the risks associated with the unprecedented range and lethality of modern weapons systems.

Strengthening regional trade ties and economic integration underlie the European Union's decision to create a single economy, as well as its subsequent moves to establish a common currency, the euro, and grow to twenty-seven member-states (adding 10 in 2004 and 2 more in 2007). The emergence of regional trading blocs such as the North American Free Trade Association (NAFTA), the Caribbean Community and Common Market (CARICOM), MERCOSUR in South America, the Association of Southeast Asian Nations (ASEAN), the Asia-Pacific Economic Cooperation (APEC), and the South Asian Association for Regional Cooperation (SAARC) reflects nations' growing interest in expanding regional cooperation outside Europe, as well.

In theory, more jobs and higher living standards will reduce discord and increase collaboration among nations and governments. But has the rise of regional economic pacts really advanced world peace? Has the United Nations made the world a more peaceful place? Has the World Court fostered greater respect for international law?

To answer these questions, we first examine the types of nonstate organizations in today's world, as well as the professionals who serve them and who run the gamut from MBAs, petroleum engineers, and peace activists to terrorists and mercenaries.

NONSTATE ACTORS ON THE WORLD STAGE

Entities other than nation-states have played a major role in international relations since World War II. These entities are known generically as **nonstate actors** and include multinational corporations, international organizations like Amnesty International, and privatized military firms (PMFs). International terrorist groups, such as the al Qaeda network (see Chapter 15), are also nonstate actors that operate "backstage."

Multinational Corporations

Businesses "with foreign subsidiaries which extend the production and marketing of the firm beyond the boundaries of any one country" are **multinational corporations (MNCs)**. Indeed, "the contemporary multinational corporation is best viewed as a global network of subsidiaries."[3]

The top ten *U.S.-based* MNCs in 2009, according to *Fortune* magazine's annual ranking, are Exxon Mobil (number one), Wal-Mart, Chevron, ConocoPhillips, General Electric, General Motors (ranked before filing for Chapter 11 bankruptcy), Ford Motor, AT&T, Hewlett Packard, and Valero Energy. Gone from the list are banking and insurance giants Citigroup, Bank of America, and AIG (American International Group)—household names the world over, but casualties of the Wall Street collapse they were instrumental in causing.

globalization
The process by which regional economies, societies, and cultures are becoming integrated and mutually dependent via a worldwide web of trade and communication; also, the worldwide circulation of ideas, values, music, movies, fads, and fashion.

nonstate actors
Entities other than nation-states, including multinational corporations, nongovernmental organizations, and international nongovernmental organizations, that plays a role in international politics.

multinational corporation (MNC)
A company that conducts in more than one country; major MNCs operate on a global scale.

Three of the top ten *global* corporations—Royal Dutch Shell, BP, and Total—are headquartered in Europe. Only five of the top twenty-five, and fewer than one-third of the Fortune Global 500, were headquartered in the United States at the end of 2008, while Europe was home to the largest number (see Figure 18.1). But the picture is changing: As of 2008, more than one-quarter of the world's richest companies were located in Asia, and twice as many in Europe and Asia combined as in the United States.

FIGURE 18.1   Don't Look Back, Somebody Might Be Gaining on You . . . Top Fortune 500 Corporate Headquarters by Region of the World in 2008

Region	Number
Europe	184
United States	153
Asia	124

SOURCE: Global 500 at http://money.cnn.com/magazines/fortune/global500/2008/full_list/

In the last two decades of the twentieth century, the number of MNCs increased eightfold to roughly 60,000, with some 800,000 foreign affiliates. Today, these giant companies control huge assets, generate trillions of dollars in worldwide sales, and employ tens of millions of people.[4] In democratic countries, they are also key players in a variety of policy areas, from taxation, energy, and the environment to international trade, defense, and foreign affairs. (Chinese MNCs, only four or five of the top 200 global corporations in 2007, are a notable exception.) Annual sales of the wealthiest MNCs exceed the GDP of many nations. No wonder some see the new world order as fundamentally different from its predecessor:

> These are not the times for narrow balance-of-power considerations. As even an unchallenged superpower like the United States has seen, efforts to block the flow of trade and investment to nations such as Iran and Cuba are not just increasingly ineffective, but costly. Multinational corporations—once made vulnerable to the expropriation of property or blockage of funds and forbidden to trade with hostile countries and to buy and sell freely the latest high technology and scarce commodities—are now more likely to guide foreign policy than follow it.[5]

Technological advancements, market reforms in many countries, and relatively stable political conditions in Europe and Asia have contributed to the rapid growth of MNCs, creating new opportunities for corporate expansion, foreign investment, and personal mobility. The process has snowballed as more corporations have expanded overseas (by outsourcing manufacturing and services, for example) to obtain comparative advantages like low labor costs.[6]

One source of funds for the worldwide expansion of MNCs is giant multinational banks. These are multinational entities themselves, maintaining branches and offices throughout the world with trillions of dollars of assets. Many of the largest are Japanese; most of the others are located in the United States and Western Europe. Along with the World Bank and the International Monetary

Fund (both specialized agencies of the United Nations), multinational banks play a crucial role in encouraging investment and economic development.

Commercial banks have attempted to stabilize the world's financial system during unsettled times. In the winter of 1973–1974, for example, when the **Organization of Petroleum Exporting Countries (OPEC)** launched an oil embargo, causing the price of oil to soar fourfold, and again in 1979–1980, when oil prices more than doubled, developing countries were hit especially hard. In those turbulent times, the international banking system stepped in, lending money from oil-rich OPEC nations to countries that were short on cash or that could not afford to import necessary foodstuffs because of the high cost of oil.

Clearly, multinational corporations are here to stay. Most economists applaud them, saying they enhance worldwide competition, improve economic efficiency, and promote technology. Yet critics contend MNCs pursue their own profit-making interests, with little regard for the damage they might do to host countries in the process; that they have illegally interferenced in host countries' internal affairs (ITT was involved in the overthrow of the Chilean government in the early 1970s); and that because they operate outside the legal control of any one national government, they pose a challenge to the international system and a threat to the nation-state.

Whatever the validity of these specific criticisms, MNCs collectively represent a potent force that may be changing the face of world politics. In the words of one academic expert,

> Multinational firms that coordinate production on a global scale and distribute their output throughout the world are one of the most striking recent manifestations of global interdependence. As such they put into question the value of models of world politics that proceed from the assumptions of national self-sufficiency and of the exceptional character of cross-boundary relationships. . . . According to one view, they are the international counterpart of the nineteenth-century industrial revolution; according to another, they may be the skeleton of the world economy of the future.[7]

International Organizations: INGOs and IGOs

International organizations made up of private individuals and affiliated groups are called **international nongovernmental organizations (INGOs)**. The International Committee of the Red Cross (ICRC) is a well-known example of an INGO. Others include Greenpeace, the World Council of Churches (WCC), the Salvation Army, Save the Children, Amnesty International, and the International Olympic Committee (IOC), to name but a few.

International governmental organizations (IGOs) such as the Organization of American States (OAS), the Organization of African Unity (OAU), and the Association of Southeast Asian Nations (ASEAN) are regional groupings of states. Some IGOs are based on a specific purpose, for example the World Trade Organization (WTO), dedicated to trade liberalization (see below). As we shall see, the United Nations (UN) is in a class by itself—a multipurpose IGO with a universal membership.

Organization of Petroleum Exporting Countries (OPEC) An international cartel established in 1961 that, since 1973, has successfully manipulated the worldwide supply of and price for oil, with far-reaching consequences for the world economy and political structure.

international nongovernmental organizations (INGOS) Comprised of private individuals and groups INGOs transcend borders in pursuit of common causes.

international governmental organization (IGO) Groupings of established states; IGOs are based on treaties, have formal structures, and meet at regular intervals.

The International Committee of the Red Cross (ICRC) provides vital humanitarian aid around the world. Here an ICRC worker distributes essential household items to refugees in the Central African Republic.

The most important IGO in the nineteenth century was the Holy Alliance, formed in 1815 by Russia, Austria, and Prussia to suppress the revolutionary democratic movement in Europe. IGOs did not gain real prominence until the period between the two world wars (1919–1939), when they proliferated with the newly formed League of Nations, the first truly universal (world-wide) IGO. By 1940, more than 80 IGOs and nearly 500 INGOs existed; following World War II, the number of both types rose substantially. By the 1990s there were nearly 5,000 INGOs and over 350 IGOs. Typically IGOs have restricted membership based on territory and function, and they exist to advance a single goal.[8] One exception is the World Health Organization, which serves the single purpose of fighting illness but is open to worldwide membership. On the other hand, the Organization of African Unity (OAU) restricts its membership regionally but has an ambitious charter that cuts across economic, political, and social lines. The most important IGO in the world today is the United Nations, which both promotes a global membership and advances a multipurpose agenda. Because of its importance, we examine the UN at length later.

By the late 1970s, the vast array of IGOs and INGOs had created what one scholar described as "networks of **interdependence**,"[9] a process that has since greatly accelerated. We examine two particularly important types of IGOs: economic pacts and military alliances. The European Union (EU) is a leading example of the former and the North Atlantic Treaty Organization is **the** leading example of the latter.

Military Alliances Although rarely described as IGOs, military alliances are, in fact, the first major form of intergovernmental organization to grow out of the modern state system and a prominent feature of international politics.

interdependence
In international politics, a condition in which national economies become inextricably entwined in the global economy, as political and business elites design strategies for continued growth and prosperity around access to foreign markets, labor, and capital.

The purpose of military alliances is simply to deter or fight enemies, potential and immediate. Not surprisingly, such alliances have often been part of arms races, which usually precede major wars. This observation led a number of political scientists and world leaders to conclude that alliances were a form of international organization that, paradoxically, were at odds with world peace and order. President Woodrow Wilson, for example, believed military alliances were one of the main causes of World War I, and, as we will see, he tried to forge the League of Nations, a new international organization based on the principle of "open covenants, openly arrived at." Such an organization, he believed, would erase the need for military alliances, which, for many centuries, had been arranged behind the scenes and were at times maintained in secret.

But alliances did not disappear. After World War II, the United States sought to counter the perceived Soviet threat to Western Europe by creating the **North Atlantic Treaty Organization (NATO)**. For the United States, it was the first peacetime military pact since George Washington, in his famous Farewell Address, warned a young American nation against involvement in "entangling alliances." NATO came into being in 1949; in 1955, the Soviet Union countered by creating the **Warsaw Pact** (formally named the Warsaw Treaty Organization).

The Warsaw Pact was disbanded when the communist regimes in Eastern Europe toppled in 1989, only 2 years before the Soviet Union disintegrated. Thus, NATO fulfilled its original mission. But rather than disband, it did something remarkable: it redefined its reason for being and, led by the United States, sought to play a peacekeeper role in Europe. Its first new test was an effort to limit the conflict in Bosnia by sending troops and conducting air strikes.

NATO has expanded eastward. Ten of its twelve original members were in Western Europe (the United States and Canada were the other two). Four more West European countries joined later—Greece (1952), Turkey (1952), West Germany (1955), and Spain (1982). Between 1999 and 2004, 10 former members of the Warsaw Pact were admitted—Poland, Hungary, the Czech Republic, the three Baltic states (Latvia, Lithuania, and Estonia), Slovakia, Slovenia, Bulgaria, and Romania—bringing the total to twenty-six.

NATO's role in the new world order of the 21st century is controversial. Some even question whether NATO's existence is justified now that the Cold War is over, and many Europeans fear a U.S.-led NATO will provoke Russia and rekindle an East-West conflict in Europe. For example, in the 1990s, Russia backed Serbia in the Balkans wars, while NATO and the United States viewed Serbia as the aggressor. Similarly, although Russia has not tried to prevent its former allies in Eastern Europe from joining NATO, it has repeatedly denounced a U.S. plan to place missile defense systems in Poland and the Czech Republic. NATO and the European Union, in turn, denounced Putin's brutal military response to the secessionist movement in Chechnya, his moves to silence domestic critics and curtail freedom of the press, the lurch toward authoritarian rule under Putin's leadership, and Russia's decision to invade Georgia in 2008 in a dispute over South Ossetia and Abkhazia.

More generally, Moscow accused the United States and NATO of pursuing an aggressive policy aimed at isolating Russia from Europe and re-dividing Europe to Russia's disadvantage. In the United States, critics of NATO's expansion contended

North Atlantic Treaty Organization (NATO)
A permanent peacetime military alliance created by the United States in 1949 to deter Soviet aggression in Europe; today, NATO has 26 members, including 10 Central and East European countries.

Warsaw Pact
A military alliance forged by the Soviet Union in 1955 that tightly bound the Communist regimes of Central and Eastern Europe in a mutual security arrangement and gave the Soviet army the right to maintain large garrisons in these countries.

it would unnecessarily divide Europe, leaving important countries such as Estonia, Latvia, Lithuania, and the Ukraine on the other side, and that it would poison relations between the United States and Russia, threatening European stability.[10]

However, more recently, tensions between Russia and Europe lend credence to the belief that NATO is still necessary. The Georgia crisis accentuated this point, as did a diplomatic dustup between Russia and the former Soviet republic of Estonia in the spring of 2007. When the Estonian government removed a World War II monument commemorating Russia's role in liberating the Baltic states from the Nazi occupation, Russians in Estonia staged street protests. Estonian riot police cracked down on the demonstrators. Putin protested but kept the huge Russian army on the sidelines. Bottom line: For millions of Eastern Europeans, liberty and security are, for all practical purposes, synonymous with NATO. The difference between the crisis outcomes in Estonia, which is a member of NATO, and Georgia, which is not, is instructive: Russia did not invade Estonia; Georgia was not so fortunate.

Economic Pacts Many significant international agreements of the post–World War II period are trade treaties, the great majority bilateral treaties (between two countries). In addition, five forms of multilateral economic pacts have played varying roles in creating noteworthy IGOs and promoting economic integration among their member states. These are:

1. *Preferential trade arrangements.* Several states agree to grant each other exclusive trade preferences, including tariff reductions. One example is the Commonwealth of Nations, made up of Great Britain and many of its former colonies.

2. *Nondiscriminatory trade organizations.* These pacts promote closer trade relations on a global or regional scale. The World Trade Organization (WTO) is the most important.

3. *Free-trade areas.* These arrangements completely eliminate trade barriers among members, who surrender their sovereign right to determine trade policy with other member states while remaining free to set trade policies with nonmember states. The most important is the North American Free Trade Agreement (NAFTA) between the United States, Canada, and Mexico, Another is the European Free Trade Association (EFTA), which has lost members to the European Union and is now almost eclipsed by it.

4. *Customs unions.* One step above free-trade areas on the ladder of economic integration, customs unions promote free trade among members and a common external tariff for all trade with nonmembers. The Southern Cone Common Market (or MERCOSUR) has four full members (Argentina, Paraguay, Brazil, and Uruguay) and two associated members (Bolivia and Chile) who trade freely among themselves while moving toward a common external tariff of 14 percent on capital goods.

5. *Economic unions.* Less than a federation but more than customs union, an economic union countenances the free flow of capital and labor, as well as goods and services. It requires a high level of economic integration and policy coordination among member-states, as well as a limitation of sovereignty. There is one sterling example in today's world, the European Union.

THE AMAZING EUROPEAN UNION

The **European Union** (EU) is by far the most dynamic example of this type of supranational organization (see Figure 18.2). By 2009, the EU encompassed twenty-seven countries; sixteen member-states had adopted the euro; and it was possible to travel freely and cross borders in most of Europe without a passport.

Origins and Evolution

The EU traces its origins to 1952, when Belgium, France, West Germany, Italy, Luxembourg, and the Netherlands founded the European Coal and Steel Community (ECSC). In 1957, these six countries met in Rome and agreed to launch the European Economic Community (EEC), and the European Atomic Energy Community (Euratom) the following year. The ECSC, EEC, and Euratom were merged into a single entity—the European Community (EC) or Common Market in 1967. Nine more states were admitted: Denmark, Ireland, and the United Kingdom in 1973; Greece in 1981; Portugal and Spain in 1986; and Austria, Finland, and Sweden in 1995. In 2004, the EU admitted eight former communist states in Eastern Europe, including the Czech Republic, Estonia, Hungary, Latvia, Lithuania, Poland, Slovakia, and Slovenia, plus Cyprus and Malta. In 2007, Romania and Bulgaria joined, bringing the total to twenty-seven. Talks are currently underway to admit Turkey, Serbia, and the Republic of Macedonia. Turkey (population 73 million) is the largest candidate for membership in EU history; if admitted, it will be second only to Germany and the only Muslim majority country in the EU.

Major Institutions

The EU's political institutions fulfill ma0ny functions of a supranational government. They include the European Council and Council of Ministers, the Commission, the European Parliament, and the Court of Justice. The European Council, Council of Ministers, and the Commission exercise executive powers; the European Council and Council of Ministers are intergovernmental, and the Commission is supranational. The Councils directly represent the interests of the national governments, the Commission represents the EU as a whole. On crucial issues, the two Councils vote on the basis of unanimity—everyone at the table has a veto. Increasingly, issues are decided by **qualified majority vote** (QMV)—reflecting a shift from intergovernmental to supranational decision-making.

The European Parliament (EP) is a deliberative body that shares **co-decision** legislative powers with the Council of Ministers but remains the junior partner. Since 1979, its members have been elected by a direct universal suffrage. The European Court of Justice (ECJ) interprets and applies EU treaties and adjudicates disputes between member states and the EU bodies.

The 1993 Treaty on the European Union (TEU) created three pillars: the European Community (EC); the Common Foreign and Security Policy (CFSP), and the Justice and Home Affairs (JHA). Decisions on the economy (Pillar One) are made by supranational method (qualified majority voting). Decisions on foreign and security policy (Pillar Two) and justice and home affairs

European Union (EU)
The successor to the Common Market or European Economic Community; the governing body that presides over the world's largest single economy.

qualified majority voting (QMV)
In the European Union a form of voting in the European Council and Council of Ministers in which no member state has a veto, but passage of a measure requires a triple majority, including more than 70 percent of the votes cast.

co-decision
In the European Union, a method of legislation and rule-making that involves both the European Council (heads of government) and the European Parliament.

FIGURE 18.2   **Forging an Economic Powerhouse: The EU in 2009**

SOURCE: The *World Factbook,* 2009 at https://www.cia.gov/library/publications/the-world-factbook/
print/ee.html

The European Union constitutes a single economy of nearly half a billion people with a
combined GDP estimated at $18.85 trillion in 2008. The U.S. Central Intelligence Agency
notes the EU "stands as an unprecedented phenomenon in the annals of history."

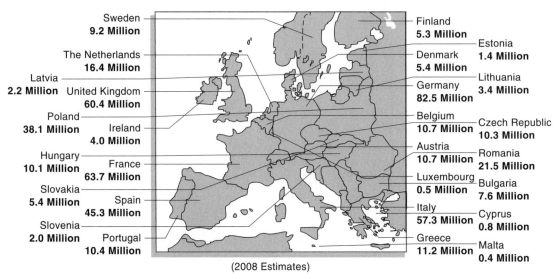

Sweden
9.2 Million

The Netherlands
16.4 Million

Latvia
2.2 Million   United Kingdom
60.4 Million

Poland
38.1 Million   Ireland
4.0 Million

Hungary
10.1 Million   France
63.7 Million

Slovakia
5.4 Million   Spain
45.3 Million

Slovenia
2.0 Million   Portugal
10.4 Million

Finland
5.3 Million

Estonia
1.4 Million

Denmark
5.4 Million

Lithuania
3.4 Million

Germany
82.5 Million

Belgium
10.7 Million   Czech Republic
10.3 Million

Austria
10.7 Million   Romania
21.5 Million

Luxembourg
0.5 Million   Bulgaria
7.6 Million

Italy
57.3 Million   Cyprus
0.8 Million

Greece
11.2 Million   Malta
0.4 Million

(2008 Estimates)

Germany Is the Richest Member; the EU Boasts 5 Trillion Dollar Economies
Here is a breakdown of the combined $18.85 trillion
annual output of goods and services of
EU national economies (country-by-country
at 2008 official exchange rates.)

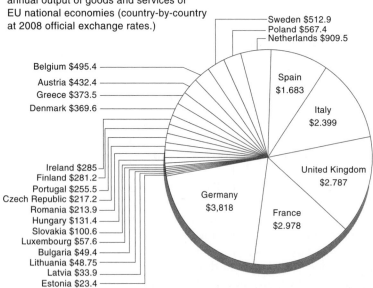

Sweden $512.9
Poland $567.4
Netherlands $909.5

Belgium $495.4
Austria $432.4
Greece $373.5
Denmark $369.6

Spain
$1.683

Italy
$2.399

United Kingdom
$2.787

Ireland $285
Finland $281.2
Portugal $255.5
Czech Republic $217.2
Romania $213.9
Hungary $131.4
Slovakia $100.6
Luxembourg $57.6
Bulgaria $49.4
Lithuania $48.75
Latvia $33.9
Estonia $23.4

Germany
$3,818

France
$2.978

(2008 Estimates)

**How the United States
and the European Union
Compared in mid-2009**

Population (2008)

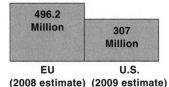

**496.2
Million**   **307
Million**

EU   U.S.
(2008 estimate)   (2009 estimate)

EU surpassed U.S. in 2005.
Updated economic data:
GDP (2008)

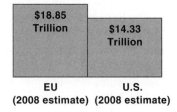

**$18.85
Trillion**   **$14.33
Trillion**

EU   U.S.
(2008 estimate)   (2008 estimate)

(Pillar Three) are made by the intergovernmental method (unanimity); however, some policy matters—for example, the internal open-border system, immigration, and asylum—formerly under Pillar Three (intergovernmental) have been shifted to Pillar One (supranational).

EU member-states agree to place the *acquis communautaire*—the total body of EU community law—over national law. The *acquis* comprises a billion words and has been translated into twenty-two official EU languages.

The **Common Agricultural Policy (CAP)** has been an EU fixture since the inception of the original common market in 1958. The CAP sets and collects tariffs on agricultural products coming into the EU and provides subsidies to EU farmers. In the past, agricultural expenditures (mainly subsidies) have accounted for nearly 50 percent of the EU budget. The CAP's share is projected to drop below one-third (32 percent) in 2013. EU largesse will be reallocated to regional development (called "structural" and "cohesion" funds) aimed at helping lagging areas—many in Central and Eastern Europe—catch up.

A Single Market

A landmark in the history of European integration, the Single European Act (SEA) of 1986 aimed to create a single market in the EU by 1992. It thus made several key institutional reforms, including a cooperative procedure giving the European Parliament a greater voice in legislation and extending qualified majority voting to new policy areas.

The SEA allowed wider and deeper integration of all the national economies, including the establishment of a European Monetary Union (EMU) and new unit of currency—the euro. A treaty signed at the Maastricht summit in 1991 transformed the European Community (EC) into the European Union (EU) and paved the way for creating a European Central Bank (ECB) in 1998 and launching the euro in 1999. The euro went into circulation in twelve EU countries in 2002 and has now been adopted by a total of sixteen; the twelve countries that joined the EU in 2004–2007 will join the euro area as soon as they meet the criteria for membership.

The **Schengen area** grew out of a 1985 agreement among five countries (France, Germany, and the Benelux countries—Belgium, Luxembourg, the Netherlands) to create a passport-free zone. The Amsterdam Treaty incorporated the Schengen system into the EU *acquis* in 1997. Today twenty-five countries, including several not in the EU (Iceland, Norway, and Switzerland), belong to Schengen, and it is possible to travel from Finland to Greece by car, train, or bus without a passport, much like traveling within the United States.

The **Emissions Trading Scheme** (ETS) is Europe's major climate change project, a **cap-and-trade system** that sets limits on the volume of pollutants the five dirtiest industries in any given country can spew into the atmosphere each year. Companies that exceed allowances can buy pollution permits from other entities that have "credits" or unused permits. At first, the system did not work as intended, as national governments bowed to domestic fears and gave away (rather than sold) permits and set the allowances too high. The EU has made adjustments aimed at tightening regulations and significantly reducing carbon emissions in the coming decades, but the cap-and-trade idea has yet to prove itself in practice. The global recession in 2008-2009 raised further questions about how vigorously national governments would push already-stressed key industries to invest in cleaner technologies.

The Obama administration favors creating a European-style cap-and-trade system in the United States. The U.S Chamber of Commerce and other special interests representing U.S. business and industry were reportedly gearing up to weaken any such plan in the first half of 2009.

The EU on the World Stage

The Atlantic Community forged after World War II was dominated by the United States, with Western Europe as a junior partner, but the distribution of power today is quite different. Asia and Europe—especially the European Union and China—play a larger role; the former superpowers play a smaller role (in the case of Russia, much smaller). The question is not **whether** the power picture will continue to change, but rather how much.

Individually, the European countries cannot compete with the United States, China, Japan, and even India. Together, however, they most definitely can, as Europe's single market amply demonstrates. But there remains a huge disparity between Europe's economic power and its political clout on the world stage. To translate its combined economic power into political power, Europe has to speak with one voice in its dealings with the rest of world.

So far, the EU's efforts to present a united front to the world have met with limited success. Achieving a Common Foreign and Security Policy (CFSP) has been a declared aim since the early 1990s. One of the principal goals of the pending Reform Treaty (see below), signed by all twenty-seven member-states, is to create a new presidency and a single, strengthened foreign policy post (at present, there are two). If and when the Reform Treaty goes into effect, these institutional reforms will position the EU to play a stronger role on the world stage. The EU also embraced the idea of a European Rapid Reaction Force (ERRF), independent of NATO, to intervene where NATO is unable or unwilling to act.

In 2004, the EU governments signed a Constitution Treaty. This treaty was derailed, however, after voters in France and the Netherlands rejected it in 2005. In 2007, German Chancellor Angela Merkel and newly elected French President Nikolas Sarkozy led an effort to revive it via a new Reform Treaty that omits any reference to a European "constitution." But EU treaties cannot go into effect until they are approved by all 27 member-states. The parliaments of twenty-six had approved the new treaty in October 2009 when Irish voters went to the polls and said "yes" (having first said "no" in an earlier referendum). The Irish vote removes the last major obstacle in the path of the treaty and promises to move Europe to a new stage in its pursuit of an "ever closer union."

European *economic* integration has succeeded because it works. The ever-expanding European market creates a space for competition and commerce—preconditions for growth and prosperity—to flourish. But the logic of European integration is not solely economic.

The Logic of European Integration

Historically, Europe was a battleground on which autocratic rulers and sadistic tyrants sought power and grandeur through conquest. No longer. Since the advent of the first modest experiment in integration—the ECSC—nearly six decades ago, the ever-wider integrated area of Europe has been a success story on several levels.

Nothing succeeds like success. Everyone knows the EU has been an economic success, but often underestimated is its success in promoting liberal democracy in Europe. Countries cannot join the EU unless or until they demonstrate a firm commitment to constitutional rule, free elections, and human rights. All twenty-one member countries are stable democracies today—a remarkable achievement. No less remarkable is that within the twenty-seven-nation EU, war is now unthinkable. The logic of integration is about perpetuating peace and promoting liberal democracy in Europe, as well as achieving prosperity.

THE UNITED NATIONS

The quest for peace in response to two catastrophic world wars in the first half of the twentieth century led to the birth of the United Nations. But to understand the United Nations, it is necessary to place it in a larger historical context.

Historical Background

Beginning in the nineteenth century, several international peacekeeping federations were founded, usually in the aftermath of increasingly destructive wars. The Holy Alliance, formed in 1815 in the wake of the Napoleonic Wars, represented an attempt by Europe's major powers to control international events by means of meetings and conferences. A more elaborate organization was the League of Nations, set up in 1919 after World War I.

When the Covenant of the League of Nations was sealed in 1919, Wilsonians (followers of Woodrow Wilson) hailed it as the advent of a new age. The League's Assembly was a deliberative body of representatives from each member-state, and all votes carried equal weight. Motions required unanimous approval for passage, so no matter how tiny, every member enjoyed veto power over nearly every decision. The much-smaller Council was made up of four permanent and four non-permanent members who investigated and reported on threats to the peace and proposed or recommended appropriate action to the Assembly. The two bodies were supervised by the Permanent Secretariat, the League's administrative arm.

The League's ambitious aims included, above all, the maintenance of international peace through the promise of swift and certain retribution against aggressor nations—peace and punishment were two sides of the same coin. War, like crime, would not pay. In this respect, the League became the institutional embodiment of President Wilson's desire to replace the traditional balance of power with "a single overwhelming, powerful group of nations who

After defeating Germany in World War I, leaders from the United States, Britain, France, and Italy met at the Paris Peace Conference in 1919 and drafted the Treaty of Versailles—*left to right*, British prime minister Lloyd George, Italian foreign minister Giorgio Sonnino, French premier Georges Clemenceau, and U.S. president Woodrow Wilson. The treaty imposed harsh terms on Germany and established a League of Nations to prevent future wars.

© GETTY IMAGES

collective security
In international relations, a system designed to prevent war by combining the armed forces of law-abiding and peace-loving nations in a powerful league capable of deterring or defeating any would-be aggressor.

shall be trustees of the peace of the world."[11] The key was to create a system of **collective security** with the combined military forces of all law-abiding nations, so formidable that no single challenger would stand a chance against it. The very existence of such a potential force was itself the deterrent.

Despite Wilson's inspired advocacy of the League of Nations, the United States was sidelined, because Republicans in the Senate opposed the Treaty of Versailles. The U.S. failure to join the League foreshadowed the organization's future misfortunes. By the early 1930s, conflicting interests and bitter rivalries had resurfaced with a vengeance.

The League was doomed to failure by several fatal flaws. First, it was supposedly a world organization, but it lacked universal acceptance—both the United States and the upstart Soviet Union were absent, for different reasons. Second, it was procedurally flawed—the requirement for unanimity guaranteed paralysis in a crisis. Third, the collective security measures were triggered by acts of aggression, yet the Charter failed to define *aggression*. Nor would the League's members ever agree on a definition when, for example, Hitler's Germany remilitarized the Rhineland, Italy invaded Ethiopia, Germany threatened (and ultimately invaded) Poland and Czechoslovakia, or Japan embarked on conquest in Asia.

Finally, the success of the League depended, above all, on the United States. World War I had transformed the balance of power from one based in Western Europe to one that was truly global and moved the United States front and center on the world stage.

The Founding of the United Nations

The shocking death toll and terrifying new weapons of World War II sparked renewed efforts to ensure world peace through a powerful international organization. The founders of the United Nations recognized the need for an organizational improvement over the League of Nations. Critics of the League argued the lesser powers had too much clout, the great powers too little. And the absence of several great powers—particularly the United States—meant the League's mandate was universal in theory but circumscribed in practice.

The founders of the United Nations in 1945 made a major effort to ensure that no potential member would be excluded. The General Assembly was designed as a deliberative body in which all would have an equal voice and an equal vote. More important, the UN Charter created a Security Council entrusted with "primary responsibility for the maintenance of international peace and security" and made up of five permanent members—the United States, the Soviet Union (recently replaced by the Russian Republic), the United Kingdom, France, and China—and 10 nonpermanent members. In contrast to the League, the so-called Big Five alone were given the right to veto certain matters, such as the selection of the secretary-general and proposed peacekeeping measures. In the United Nations, the most powerful countries would have responsibilities commensurate with their capabilities.

These responsibilities are spelled out in Chapter 7 of the UN Charter, titled "Action with Respect to Threats to the Peace, Breaches of the Peace, and Acts of Aggression." Article 39 specifies that "the Security Council shall determine the existence of any threat to the peace, breach of the peace, or act of aggression and shall make recommendations, or decide what measure shall be taken in accordance with Articles 40 and 42, to maintain or restore international peace and security." Subsequent articles spell out how the Security Council is expected to discharge its obligations. Article 41 deals with economic sanctions, including "complete or partial interruption of economic relations and of rail, sea, air, postal, telegraphic, radio, and other means of communication, and the severance of diplomatic relations." Article 42 contemplates situations in which economic sanctions may be inadequate; in such cases, the Security Council "may take action by air, sea, or land forces as may be necessary to maintain or restore international peace and security. Such action may include demonstrations, blockades, and other operations by air, sea, or land forces of Members of the United Nations." Other articles in Chapter 7 of the Charter deal with organizing the military components of a full-fledged collective security system, including the establishment of the Military Staff Committee (Article 47).

The machinery of international peacekeeping outlined by these articles far surpassed that of the League of Nations. Moreover, through its specialized agencies, the United Nations plays an important role in worldwide disaster relief, resettlement of refugees, technical assistance in food and agriculture, health concerns, and many other areas. It actively promotes a higher world standard of living through the Economic and Social Council (ECOSOC) and the United Nations International Children's Emergency Fund (UNICEF). Finally, financial and developmental assistance has been extended to economically troubled states through the World Bank, the International Monetary Fund, and the

United Nations Conference on Trade and Development (UNCTAD). The variety of specialized agencies makes clear that the United Nations was committed from the outset to promoting world welfare as well as preventing world war.

However, the UN Charter was not designed as a blueprint for a world government. Article 2, paragraph 7, of the Charter puts matters "essentially within the domestic jurisdiction of any state" beyond the purview of UN authority. Article 2 states unequivocally that the United Nations "is based on the principle of sovereign equality of all its members."

Nevertheless, other provisions of the Charter give greater weight to the most powerful or most prominent member states. The most obvious reason is the need to guarantee their participation. But there was another, subtler reason: Some of the United Nation's original supporters viewed the new international organization as the forerunner of a world government in which the larger states would have to play a greater role than the smaller. Thus, the contradictions in the Charter mirror the mix of realism and idealism present at the UN's creation; for the "one-world" idealists, they also represented the compromises of the past necessary to pave the way for the future.

The United Nations During the Cold War

The United Nations faced problems not unlike those that destroyed the League of Nations. A world government capable of keeping the peace implied nothing less than a wholesale forfeiture of state sovereignty. Anything short of a world government would leave the UN unable to punish an aggressor or preserve the peace unless all the great powers—at a minimum, the five permanent Security Council members—were in complete accord.

On the one hand, the Charter obligates member states to act in accordance with the rule of law and empowers the Security Council to punish states when they do not; on the other hand, it provides a number of loopholes and escape clauses for states that wish to evade or ignore their obligations. Article 51, for example, states, "Nothing in the present Charter shall impair the inherent right of individual or collective self-defense." Such a provision invites aggression as long as "self-defense" is a lawful justification to resort to force and individual states are free to define as self-defense any action they deem in their national interest. The dilemma is obvious: without escape clauses such as Article 51, the UN Charter would not have been acceptable; with them, it may not be enforceable.

Another problem plaguing the world body until recently was the persistent state of tension between the United States and the Soviet Union, which seriously hampered the workings of the United Nations during the Cold War. Because each superpower maintained a coalition of allies, followers, and admirers that at one time or another held the majority in the General Assembly, deadlock became the hallmark of most UN deliberations. The consensus necessary to promote peace through collective security was also absent at many critical junctures; when the Soviet Union did not veto a controversial measure, the United States often did. Despite these difficulties, the United Nations has contributed valuable, if limited, efforts toward peace by sending mediators, truce supervision teams, and quasi-military forces to various parts of the world, including the Congo, Cyprus, the Middle East, and the Balkans.

BOX 18.1 SPOTLIGHT ON   UN Peacekeeping Operations

FIGURE 18.3   The presence of peacekeeping forces all over the world at the start of the new millennium testifies to the United Nations' enhanced post–Cold War role. A total of sixty-three such operations were launched between 1948 and 2008, more than three-fourths of them since the end of the Cold War (1989–1991). As of March 2008, about 110,000 peacekeepers from 115 countries were engaged in 20 "peace missions" on four continents. The United Nations does not have its own military forces but relies on military contributions from member states.

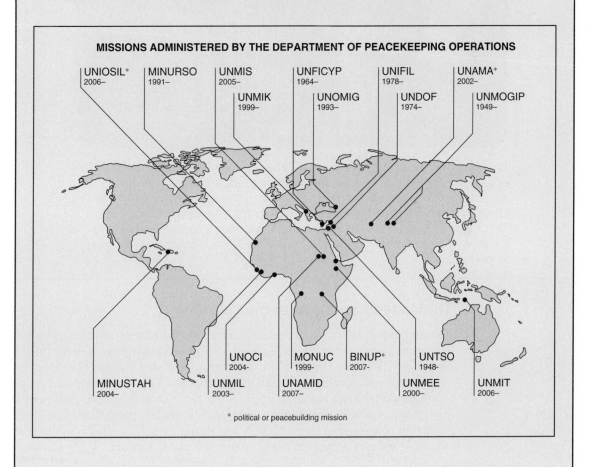

MISSIONS ADMINISTERED BY THE DEPARTMENT OF PEACEKEEPING OPERATIONS

UNIOSIL*	MINURSO	UNMIS	UNFICYP	UNIFIL	UNAMA*
2006–	1991–	2005–	1964–	1978–	2002–

UNMIK 1999–   UNOMIG 1993–   UNDOF 1974–   UNMOGIP 1949–

UNOCI 2004-   MONUC 1999-   BINUP* 2007-   UNTSO 1948-

MINUSTAH 2004–   UNMIL 2003–   UNAMID 2007–   UNMEE 2000–   UNMIT 2006–

* political or peacebuilding mission

BOX 18.1 SPOTLIGHT ON   *(Continued)*

©UN.ORG

The United Nations cannot act even on the most compelling humanitarian grounds unless the permanent members of the Security Council all agree. Shown here are SLA rebels in Sudan, who showed up for talks on Darfur with envoys from the United Nations and the African Union in February 2007. Russia and China opposed UN sanctions on Sudan. Despite more than 200,000 (mostly civilian) fatalities and 2 million refugees between 2003 and mid-2007, the United Nations was powerless to intervene.

The United Nations After the Cold War

The mid to late 1980s saw an unprecedented period of cooperation among the five permanent members of the Security Council, particularly between the United States and the Soviet Union. The catalyst was the Soviet Union's new conciliatory foreign policy, initiated by Mikhail Gorbachev. This era of increased cooperation produced two significant results. First, the United Nations embraced a particularly vigorous approach to international peacekeeping, sometimes bordering on peacemaking (see Box 18.1 and Figure 18.1).[12] Second, it sanctioned collective military action against Iraq after it invaded Kuwait.

Peacekeeping Operations   Recent UN peacekeeping efforts have encompassed a wide array of tasks, some unprecedented. A mere fifty observers helped facilitate the Soviet Union's withdrawal from Afghanistan in 1988, while peacekeeping forces from 109 nations helped secure peace and independence for Namibia in 1989 by creating the conditions for elections and securing the repeal of discriminatory and restrictive legislation, the release of prisoners, and the return of exiles.

Starting in 1991, the UN fielded major peacekeeping operations in El Salvador and Cambodia, including in the latter demobilizing the various armies, repatriating 350,000 refugees, and organizing elections. According to one expert, the United Nations assumed "effective responsibility for administering the country during an 18-month transition period."[13]

In 1993, the UN dispatched nearly 40,000 peacekeepers to the former Yugoslavia. The presence of this force, combined with NATO military support and UN-sponsored sanctions, induced Serbian President Slobodan Milosevic to negotiate in good faith and helped bring about the U.S.-brokered peace settlement known as the Dayton Accords (see Chapter 9) in 1995. Later, after Milosevic was defeated in national elections and created a popular groundswell when he tried to cancel the results, the United Nations was instrumental in bringing the brutal former president and other accused war criminals in Yugoslavia to justice.

During the 1990s, the United Nations launched peacekeeping operations in Kosovo (Yugoslavia), Sierra Leone (West Africa), East Timor (formerly part of Indonesia), the Congo (central Africa), and Ethiopia and Eritrea (the horn of Africa). Such missions are never risk free, and they come with no guarantee of success. UN troops sent to Somalia in 1992 to facilitate the safe distribution of food to starving people were attacked by rebels who viewed the UN as a cat's paw for the West.

UN peacekeepers generally try to avoid combat but have suffered many casualties over the years, including some 2,591 fatalities (as of mid-2009) since 1948. Peacekeeping in Lebanon (244 fatalities) and Cyprus (170 fatalities) has been particularly hazardous and the UN presence has become a permanent fixture. Of the ten peacekeeping operations launched in the 1990s, most incurred fewer than fifteen fatalities; however, forty-six members of the UN mission in Sierra Leone (UNAMSIL) were killed there, and in August 2003, terrorists destroyed the UN headquarters in Baghdad, killing seventeen people, including Sergio Vieira de Mello, the head of the UN mission in Iraq (see Chapter 15). Some 465 UN military personnel were killed in action between 2003 and mid-2007.

Nor can UN peacekeepers always implement political changes to avert future calamities like widespread starvation. In Cambodia, peace did not long survive the withdrawal of UN forces: In 1997, an antidemocratic coup abruptly defeated the United Nation's ambitious efforts to promote democracy. In the former Yugoslavia, peacekeepers' attempts to promote a cease-fire were overwhelmed by fighting and became effective only after NATO air strikes and ground support were brought to bear. In the end, the Serbian army was defeated and President Milosevic was forced to negotiate. One of the lessons of Bosnia and Kosovo is that UN peacekeeping efforts are unlikely to succeed without the military backing of major member states and regional military alliances such as NATO. Experience makes a strong case for the creation of new regional military groups to act as the law-enforcement apparatus of the United Nations.

Some UN peacekeeping operations have become permanent fixtures without leading to a final settlement—Kashmir, Cyprus, and Lebanon are prime examples. These missions are a permanent drain on the UN budget, always stretched to the breaking point (see Box 18.1).

But we must put the cost of UN peacekeeping operations into perspective. Compared with U.S. defense budgets, which according to most estimates equal or exceed the military spending of all other UN member states combined, the total amount spent on all the UN-sponsored military actions ever undertaken is infinitesimal. It is hard to imagine a better bargain for taxpayers (see Box 18.2), even if the success rate is less than 100 percent. Even the United States does not have a perfect record when it comes to military intervention.

Collective Military Action In August 1990, when Iraq invaded Kuwait, the United Nations responded by authorizing collective military action. This use of force recalled Woodrow Wilson's failed dream of collective security under the League of Nations flag and an early attempt at collective military action under the auspices of the UN.

In June 1950, when North Korea invaded South Korea, the United Nations at the urging of the United States responded with military force. As a permanent member of the Security Council the Soviet Union was in a position to block this action. But the United States avoided a Soviet veto by taking the matter to the General Assembly (in the form of the "Uniting for Peace" resolution) where it enjoyed an automatic majority. Although the UN flag was raised, the Korean conflict was in truth a war fought by the United States against North Korea and, later, the People's Republic of China. The supreme

---

BOX 18.2 FOCUS ON   Peace on the Cheap: Too Good to Be True?

According to the United Nations,

- UN peace operations are less expensive than other forms of international interventions, and costs are shared more equitably among UN member-states.
- A survey by Oxford University economists found that international military intervention under Chapter VII of the UN Charter is the most cost-effective means of reducing the risk of conflict in post-conflict societies.
- The approved peacekeeping budget for the period from 1 July 2007 to 30 June 2008 was approximately US$6.8 billion. This represents

about 0.5% of global military spending (estimated at US$1.232 trillion for 2006).
- A study by the U.S. Government Accounting Office estimated that it would cost the U.S. about twice as much as the UN to conduct a peacekeeping operation similar to the UN Stabilization Mission in Haiti (MINUSTAH)—$876 million compared to the UN budgeted $428 million for the first 14 months of the mission.

SOURCE: United Nations, "Peacekeeping Fact Sheet," http://www.un.org/ Depts/dpko/factsheet.pdf. Accessed on June 4, 2009.

commander, General Douglas MacArthur, was responsible to the president of the United States, not to the secretary-general of the United Nations.

It would be four decades before the United Nations was again used in building an international coalition against an aggressor, for during the Cold War each superpower vetoed enforcement actions proposed by the other. In 1990–1991, when the United States (backed by the British) launched Operation Desert Storm against Iraq, the Security Council became a forum for the major powers to consult on how to respond to Iraqi aggression. The Council backed resolutions condemning Iraq, establishing tough economic sanctions, and ultimately approving the use of force to expel the Iraqi army from Kuwait. After the Gulf War's end, UN inspectors were allowed access to sites in Iraq suspected of hiding biological, chemical, or nuclear weapons. Iraq later would dispute terms of these inspections, leading the United States to threaten to bomb (an action at least temporarily avoided by the successful diplomatic efforts of then-Secretary-General Kofi Annan).

What the United Nations did *not* do before and during the 1990–1991 Gulf War is equally important, however. The United Nations did not provide any forces of its own, and the Secretary General had no control over how the coalition forces were deployed or employed. There was no UN general staff, nor did the United Nations coordinate the military or diplomatic operations undertaken by coalition members (principally the United States and Great Britain). Nor did the United Nations provide any funding. The war was financed in large part by contributions from the United States' richest allies, including Japan, Germany, Kuwait, and Saudi Arabia.

The 1990–1991 Gulf War was a broad-based coalition forged by the United States with the imprimatur of the United Nations. In 2003, however, the exact opposite was true: the United States invaded Iraq without the authorization of the Security Council and in the face of overwhelming opposition in the General Assembly.

The United Nations and the Second Gulf War In the fall of 2002, the UN Security Council passed Resolution 1441 requiring Iraq to disarm and allow weapons inspections or face "serious consequences." Though Iraq's ruler, Saddam Hussein, had evicted UN weapons inspectors in 1998, the dictator had little choice but to comply when President Bush issued an ultimatum and began a massive military buildup in the Persian Gulf. Weapons inspectors visited 300 sites in December 2002 and January 2003. Chief UN inspector Hans Blix reported to the Security Council that Iraq was not fully cooperating but recommended the inspections continue. Mohamed El Baradei, who headed the International Atomic Energy Agency (IAEA) inspection team in Iraq, also appealed for more time.

Although weapons inspectors had found no weapons of mass destruction or weapons laboratories, the Bush administration claimed to have evidence the Iraqi dictator did, in fact, possess such weapons and posed an imminent danger to world peace. The Security Council was strongly against an immediate invasion. In opposing a rush to war, France and Germany, the United States' longtime NATO allies, took the lead. Russia and China, both permanent members of the Security Council (like France), also demurred.

Nonetheless, then-U.S. Secretary of State Colin Powell presented the Security Council what what he claimed was clear proof—secret intelligence—that Iraq had WMDs. But the Security Council was not swayed. President Bush decided to act unilaterally, asserting that postponing military action would only play into Saddam's hands. Secretary of Defense Donald Rumsfeld referred to key NATO allies who were not on board—including France, Germany, and Belgium—as the "old Europe."

In the months that followed, relations between the United States and the United Nations plunged to their lowest (as did trans-Atlantic relations). Staunch conservatives suggested the United Nations was irrelevant or worse and the United States was wise to ignore it. U.S. polls showed a majority thought the United States should oust Saddam from power, but an even larger majority agreed the UN Security Council "should make the final decision regarding the disarmament of Iraq"—if the United Nations did not approve the action, the United States should stay out.[14] In the end, the Bush White House ignored public opinion—a huge political risk.

The outcome of the invasion was never in doubt: the United States had overwhelming military superiority and was banking on a quick war with a happy ending—one that would rid the Iraqi people of a sadistic ruler and lead directly to a flourishing democracy. The outcome of the occupation, however, was a different matter.

Urban guerrilla warfare plagued the occupation forces, kept Iraqi society in a constant state of turmoil, and proved an albatross for the United States. Those who remembered the lessons of Vietnam fed a rising tide of doubts about the war. In the 2004 and 2008 presidential elections, foreign policy—in particular, the growing human and financial cost of the war—was a major issue. In the 2008 Democratic primary, it pitted Hillary Clinton, who had supported the decision to invade Iraq, against Barack Obama, who had opposed it.

Is the United Nations Irrelevant? It has been said that if the United Nations did not exist, it would have to be invented. One thing is clear, in many conflict-ridden parts of the world, the United Nations is *not* irrelevant. Ironically, although the United States played the leading role in creating it, it has had to rediscover this truth repeatedly in the past half century—occasionally in a maelstrom of its own making.

The Limits of International Organization

Despite its successes, the United Nations has not lived up to all the expectations of its founders, and some problems resemble those of the League that it sought to overcome. Procedural difficulties, however, are often rooted in deep-seated political differences.

The Problem of Universality All nations of significant size or consequence must be persuaded to join a comprehensive international organization and remain part of it; otherwise, it is a matter of time before a crisis brings it crashing to the ground. The League of Nations clearly demonstrated the problems that arise when some nations are excluded or refuse to join. The history of the United Nations repeats the example. The absurdity of refusing to seat the People's Republic of China for two decades is an obvious case in point.

Today, the United Nations is truly universal in scope. In 2009, there are 192 countries, including some so tiny they are no more than a dot on the map. The Republic of China (Taiwan), ousted from its seat on the Security Council and the General Assembly when the People's Republic of China was admitted in the early 1970s, remains ostracized, despite repeated efforts to gain readmission.

The Problem of Inequality Small powers typically demand formal equality with large nations in international organizations—anything less, they contend, undermines the world rule of law and the concept of sovereignty. Big powers insist their military superiority and prowess must be reflected in procedures, like the veto power of the permanent members of the UN Security Council. Anything less, they argue, ignores the actual distribution of power in the world. And former great powers must be demoted to make room for newcomers whose stars are rising.

In the UN Security Council, for example, there has been but one change since 1945—seating the People's Republic of China (PRC) in Taiwan's place. Germany and Japan have the largest economies in Europe and Asia, respectively, but neither has a permanent seat in the Security Council. Since the breakup of the Soviet Union, Russia's place in the rankings has fallen in all categories (although the Kremlin still commands a nuclear arsenal second only to that of the United States). Yet, despite this contraction, Russia retains its veto in the Security Council. Voting weights constitute more than a mere technical problem. No international organization can remain viable unless it solves the problem of inequality while remaining flexible enough to adapt to changing circumstances.

©ED BETZ/AP PHOTO

Ban Ki-moon of South Korea succeeded Kofi Annan as U.N. Secretary-General in 2007. He thus became the eighth man to be chosen as the U.N.'s top official since 1946. No woman has ever served in this high-profile international role, but past secretaries-general have come from many different countries—Norway, Sweden, Burma, Austria, Peru, Egypt, and Ghana—reflecting the universalistic character and aspirations of the United Nations Charter.

The failure of UN sanctions against Iraq in the 1990s and the "illegal" U.S. decision to invade in 2003 prompted Secretary-General Annan to create a special high-level panel "to analyze the threats to peace and security" facing the world and propose reforms. The panel's suggestions, published in December 2004, include expanding the Security Council (from 15 to 24), amending the UN Charter to better deal with international terrorism, and broadening the UN mandate to protect defenseless people from unprovoked mass violence. Perhaps most controversial were the panel's recommendations for changes in the Security Council. One option would add six new permanent and three nonpermanent seats; the other would create new semipermanent seats (4-year terms) and add a single nonpermanent one. Either way, any new permanent members would *not* have veto power, much to the chagrin of large countries such as Brazil, Japan, and India. One thing all parties agree upon: the world has changed since 1945, and the United Nations must change with it. But this is easier said than done.

The Problem of Unity In the past, the most successful international organizations have been based on a common enemy. The Holy Alliance was inspired by fear of a resurgent France. Fear of the Soviet Union led to creation of NATO after World War II. Finally, the high point of UN unity came in 1990–1991, when most nations joined the United States in opposing a common enemy, Iraq. When the original threat fades, however, the ties that bind tend to disintegrate.

The Problem of Sovereignty The problem of sovereignty—the supreme power a state exercises within its boundaries—underlies all three problems we've mentioned: universality, inequality, and unity. Sovereignty is indivisible: Either a nation has the last word in its own affairs, or it does not. An effective world government is possible only if existing governments surrender sovereignty to a higher authority—a prospect most nation-states consider too risky where fear, prejudice, and mistrust continue to permeate politics.

UNCONVENTIONAL NONSTATE ACTORS

We have looked at conventional nonstate actors on the world stage—multinational corporations, supranational groupings, military alliances, and international organizations. We turn now to two types of nonstate actors with little or nothing in common with these entities, or with one another.

Terrorist Organizations

Without duplicating Chapter 15's discussion of terrorism, it is worth noting that some terrorist groups—the most notorious being Osama bin Laden's al Qaeda—have become significant nonstate actors in international relations. However much we abhor the phenomenon of terrorism, terrorist groups are capable of carrying out shocking acts of violence (the destruction of the World Trade Center towers), destabilizing societies (Algeria in the 1990s), sabotaging economies (Peru in the 1980s), obstructing peace efforts (the Palestinian struggle), and bringing down a popularly elected government or influencing the outcome of an election (Spain in March 2004). In Peru and Algeria, the source of terrorist actions was exclusively or primarily domestic. But the other examples implicate international terrorists—nonstate actors pursuing political ends by violent means.

Terrorists are not the only nonstate actors who fit this general description, however. The rise of privatized military firms has brought another kind of nonstate actor onto the world stage.

Privatized Military Firms (Mercenaries)

The term *privatized military firm (PMF)* is a euphemism for mercenaries. PMFs contract for various security-related services with governments, carry out paramilitary missions and programs for a profit, operate in a shadowy world between the public and private sectors, and remain largely unknown to the U.S. public. One such company, Military Professional Resources Incorporated (MPRJ), located in Alexandria, Virginia (next to the Pentagon), is reputed to have played a crucial role in the bloody Bosnian war. In the spring of 1995, the Croats launched a surprise attack with a "professionalized force" that caught the Serbs unawares. "The Croats' ragtag militia had been secretly transformed into a modern Western-style army."[15]

> This coming out party for the new Croat army was the turning point of the entire war. The Serbs, who had rarely been on the defensive in the past, were stunned at the Croatian military's new cohesion and effectiveness. The offensive overwhelmed the local opposition in Croatia and then steamrolled into western Bosnia, turning the Bosnian Serbs' flank. Within weeks, the overall war, in both Croatia and Bosnia, was over. The reversals on the ground, combined with the renewal of NATO air strikes, had finally forced the Serbs to the negotiating table after four years of failed attempts.[16]

Although MPRI denied involvement, its role was an open secret. The Croats were openly grateful, and individual MPRI employees were openly proud of the role they played.[17] Why did MPRI deny having anything to do with an operation that, by any reckoning, was a huge success?

The answer is that PMFs are different from other private companies. Like terrorist groups, they pursue political ends by "other means," but they do it for a profit, not out of political, moral, or ideological motives. Nobody knows for sure how many of these firms exist today, but their numbers have grown rapidly since the end of the Cold War thanks to government "outsourcing" and "privatization."

So long as PMFs contract with legitimate governments to perform services that advance the national interest, aren't they a good thing? We can argue both sides, but logic points to their dangers rather than advantages. Indeed, we could argue that PMFs are more efficient than public agencies because they have to operate at a profit or go under. It would be difficult to find a bigger money pit anywhere than the U.S. Department of Defense—thus, contracting out many services, including combat operations, could in theory save taxpayers a great deal of money. PMFs can perform sensitive or dangerous missions without directly involving the U.S. government, enabling policymakers to hedge political risks and avoid potential diplomatic embarrassments. Finally, PMFs provide on-call, off-the-shelf capabilities to supplement or complement ongoing operations of U.S. military or intelligence services, possibly making the difference between success and failure.

But critics say the West in general, and the United States in particular, have long considered war—and moral responsibility for the political use of military force—the exclusive province of governments. Finally, PMFs operate beyond the view of the public and cannot easily be held accountable to Congress (if at all). Their very existence is an open invitation to governments to circumvent constitutional rules and procedures. Perhaps worst of all, there is no guarantee a PMF in possession of advanced military technologies and highly trained personnel will not contract with rogue states or drug traffickers or even terrorist organizations—after all, they are businesses, likely to care more about the bottom line than a client's character.

INTERNATIONAL LAW

international law
The body of customs, treaties, and generally accepted rules that define the rights and obligations of nations when dealing with one another.

For roughly 350 years, the international system has been regularized by an evolving body of **international law** defining the rights and obligations of states in relation to one another. The "rules of the game" have been freely adopted by sovereign governments and have generally assumed the form of treaties. Other widely recognized sources of international law include custom and convention; general legal principles based on such ideas as justice, equity, and morality; and the judicial decisions and teachings of eminent legal authorities.

The most famous codification of international law remains Hugo Grotius's *On the Law of War and Peace*, published in 1625, only twenty-three years before the formal establishment of the nation-state system in the Treaty of Westphalia. International law has since become a vital part of what we might call diplomatic business as usual in the arena of world politics.

Usefulness

If a river ran between two states, who would decide whether the boundary should be drawn along the riverbed, along the river banks, or down the exact center of the river? What would guarantee the safety of diplomatic representatives accredited to a foreign government? How would territorial boundaries on land and sea be determined? How would traffic on the high seas be regulated? Should neutral states have the right to carry on normal commercial relations with belligerents in times of war? These are only a few of the vital issues that would be difficult to resolve without a preexisting body of international law.

Compliance and Enforcement

During the four hundred years of its existence, international law has in most instances been scrupulously observed. When one of its rules was violated, it was, however, not always enforced and, when action to enforce it was actually taken, it was not always effective. Yet to deny that international law exists at all as a system of binding legal rules flies in the face of all evidence.[18]

The enforcement of international law has always posed unique difficulties. Governments cannot be arrested, placed on trial, or thrown in prison, but they can be made to pay a price for rogue behavior. The functional equivalent of government in the realm of international politics is the balance of power: States perceived as lawbreakers can be subjected to diplomatic censure, economic embargo, or blockade by other governments. In extreme cases, they can even be overrun, despoiled, and occupied.

Also, individual leaders can be brought to justice. One result of political and diplomatic pressure, for example, was the reluctant decision of the Serbian government in 2003 to turn over ex-President Milosevic to the UN War Crimes Tribunal in The Hague. Another was a later decision not to use force against breakaway Kosovo.

Fear of political repercussions is not the only reason most governments play by the rules most of the time. Without rules, international trade, travel, and tourism would be greatly impeded, and international financial transactions, foreign investments, technological transfers, and postal and telecommunications links would hardly be possible. And without the elaborate and widely respected rules of diplomatic immunity, few governments would send diplomatic representatives to foreign capitals. It is doubtful whether any government can afford to treat international law cavalierly for long.

Still, power is the coin of all politics, and law without the police to enforce it is a farce. In the international arena, the participants play the role of the police either individually or collectively. Thus, the balance of power is "an indispensable condition of the very existence of International Law."[19]

International Law in the Modern Era

Prior to World War II, the Geneva and Hague Conventions constituted the most important body of international law and set forth the rules of war. Since 1945, international law has advanced in several important areas, most notably in arms control. In the future, international law will likely be increasingly concerned with environmental issues. We look next at each of these important examples of contemporary international law.

The Geneva and Hague Conventions In 1856, several great powers endorsed the Declaration of Paris, first of a series of multilateral international conventions. It limited war at sea by outlawing privateering and specifying that a naval blockade had to be effective to be legally binding. More important was the Geneva Convention of 1864 (revised in 1906), which laid down rules for the humane treatment of the wounded on the battlefield. Of still greater importance was the Hague Convention of 1899, which codified for the first time many accepted practices of land warfare. A second Hague Convention, in 1907, revised the 1899 codes and prescribed rules for the use of new weapons, such as dumdum bullets, poison gas, and gas-filled balloons for bombing.

Geneva Convention
A body of international law dealing with the treatment of the wounded, prisoners of war, and civilians in a war zone.

Hague Convention
A widely accepted set of rules governing conduct in land wars, the use of new weapons, and the rights and duties of both neutral and warring parties.

Strategic Arms Reduction Treaty II (START II)
A treaty negotiated between the United States and Russia that limited strategic nuclear weapons.

Arms Control Treaties No issue seemed more important than the bilateral arms control agreements negotiated between the United States and the former Soviet Union during the Cold War (see Table 18.1). Although they were

TABLE 18.1   Major Bilateral Arms Control Agreements Between the United States and the Former Soviet Union/Russia

Date	Agreement	Principal Objectives
1963	Hot Line Agreement	Establishes a direct radio and telegraph communication system between the governments to be used in times of crisis
1972	Antiballistic Missile (ABM) Treaty	Restricts the deployment of ABM defense systems to one area and prohibits space-based ABM systems
1972	SALT I Offensive Strategic Arms Interim Agreement	Freezes the superpowers' total number of ballistic missile launchers for 5 years
1972	Protocol to the Interim Agreement	Clarifies and strengthens prior limits on strategic arms
1974	Threshold Test Ban	Restricts the underground testing of nuclear weapons above a yield of 150 kilotons
1976	Treaty on the Limitation of Underground Explosions for Peaceful Purposes	Broadens the ban on underground testing stipulated in the 1974 Threshold Test Ban Treaty; requires on-site observers of tests with yields exceeding 150 kilotons
1979	SALT II Treaty (never ratified)	Places ceilings on the number of strategic delivery vehicles, MIRV missiles, long-range bombers, cruise missiles, ICBMs, and other weapons; restrains testing
1987	Intermediate-range Nuclear Force (INF) Treaty	Eliminates U.S. and USSR ground-level intermediate- and shorter-range nuclear weapons in Europe and permits on-site inspection to verify compliance
1990	Chemical Weapons Destruction Agreement	Ends production of chemical weapons; commits cutting inventories of chemical weapons in half by the end of 1999 and to 5,000 metric tons by the end of 2002
1990	Nuclear Testing Talks	New protocol improves verification procedures of prior treaties

1991	START (Strategic Arms Reduction Treaty)	Reduces arsenals of strategic nuclear weapons by about 30 percent
1992	START I Protocol	Holds Russia, Belarus, Ukraine, and Kazakhstan to strategic weapons reductions agreed to in START by the former USSR
1992	Open Skies Agreement	Permits unarmed surveillance aircraft to fly over the United States, Russia, and their allies
1992	Cooperative Threat Reduction Agreement	Provides a variety of equipment and support to assist Russia in the safe destruction of strategic delivery systems, the transportation of nuclear warheads, the physical protection of nuclear-weapon storage sites, warhead accounting, and chemical and biological weapon destruction and facility dismantlement
1993	START II	Cuts the deployed U.S. and Russian strategic nuclear warheads on each side to between 3,000 and 3,500 by the year 2003; bans multiple-warhead land-based missiles
1995	HEU Agreement	Reduces risk of diversion or theft of nuclear-weapons-grade highly enriched uranium (HEU) recovered from dismantled nuclear warheads through government purchase and use as civilian reactor fuel
1997	Fissile Material Cut-Off Treaty (FMCT)	Bans production of fissile material for nuclear weapons or other nuclear explosive devices
1997	Core Conversion Agreement	Obligates the United States to facilitate the conversion of Russia's three remaining plutonium production reactors to no longer produce weapons-grade plutonium; originally intended to be complete by the end of 2000
1997	START III	Pledges the agreement that was renewed at the September 1998 Moscow Summit for the United States and Russia to deploy no more than 2,000 to 2,500 strategic nuclear warheads each on conventional ballistic missiles, SLBMs, and heavy bombers by December 31, 2007, pending ratification of the START II Treaty

SOURCE: Adapted from Charles W. Kegley Jr. and Eugene Wittkopf, *World Politics: Trend and Transformation*, 8th ed. p. 580–581. Copyright © 2001 Wadsworth, a part of Cengage Learning, Inc. Reproduced by permission. www.cengage.com/permissions.

both numerous and controversial, these agreements altered neither country's dependence on nuclear deterrence to maintain peace.

The demise of the Soviet Union, a perceived improvement in relations between the United States and Russia, and the existence of nuclear weapons in the newly created nations of Belarus, Ukraine, and Kazakhstan spurred the United States and Russia to reach much more consequential arms limitation agreements. Most notably, the 1993 **Strategic Arms Reduction Treaty II (START II)** cut nuclear warheads by 60 percent over levels already reduced 2 years earlier. START II banned multiple warheads on land-based missiles and reduced submarine-launched multiple warheads. Underlying the treaty was each nation's hope that it "could reduce the chances of a war of annihilation by banning the nuclear weapons that both powers would be most likely to use in a preemptive strike."[20]

Over the past forty years, a number of important arms control measures have been multinational. Some noteworthy agreements are:

- The 1959 **Antarctic Treaty** prohibited all military activity on the Antarctic continent and accorded each signatory the right of aerial surveillance. It also prohibited dumping of nuclear wastes and encouraged cooperation in scientific investigations.
- The 1967 **Outer Space Treaty** banned nuclear weapons from outer space, prohibited military bases and maneuvers on the moon and other planets, and barred claims of national sovereignty in outer space.
- The 1968 **Nonproliferation Treaty** restricted signatories from transferring or receiving nuclear weapons or materials. Although most of the world's nations have signed this agreement, several have not consistently obeyed its provisions, and a number of other nations, including Iran, Iraq, Libya, Pakistan, and India, have not signed it.
- The 1971 **Seabed Treaty** banned nuclear weapons from the bottom of the world's oceans outside each state's 12-mile territorial limit.
- The 1972 **Biological Weapons Convention** pledged the destruction of biological stockpiles while outlawing the production and storage of such weapons.
- The 1993 **Chemical Weapons Convention** intended to eliminate chemical weapons within 10 years. The U.S. Senate ratified this treaty in April 1997.

There are limits to what we can expect such pacts to accomplish. Governments usually do not sign agreements that require them to act contrary to the way they would act in the absence of such agreements. When the United States ratified the Chemical Weapons Convention, it claimed to have no intention of developing such weapons (nor did it rely on those weapons for its national security). When a proposed agreement on international rules of conduct has required the negotiating parties to relinquish something important to them, however, international law has not fared so well.

International Law and the Environment Future international law is likely to include important environmental agreements. Some experts believe past arms limitations treaties will provide a precedent for these.

With few exceptions, such as the Montreal Protocol (see Box 18.3), the number and scope of most international environmental agreements have been

---

Antarctic Treaty
An international agreement that prohibits all military activity on the Antarctic continent and allows for inspection of all nations' facilities there. It also nullifies all territorial claims to Antarctic land and pledges the signatories to peaceful cooperation in exploration and research.

Outer Space Treaty
An international agreement, signed by the United States and the former Soviet Union, that banned the introduction of military weapons into outer space, prohibited the extension of national sovereignty in space, and encouraged cooperation and sharing of information about space research.

Nonproliferation Treaty
An international agreement, drafted in 1968, not to aid nonnuclear nations in acquiring nuclear weapons; it was not signed by France, China, and other nations actively seeking to build these weapons.

Seabed Treaty
An international agreement that forbids the establishment of nuclear weapons on the ocean floor beyond the 12-mile territorial limit.

BOX 18.3 FOCUS ON The Montreal Protocol

The Montreal Protocol, formally known as the Montreal Protocol on Substances that Deplete the Ozone Layer, was prompted by mounting scientific evidence of the rapid erosion of the ozone layer, which shields the planet from cancer-causing ultraviolet radiation. In 1986, 23 nations endorsed a plan to reduce chlorofluorocarbons (known as CFCs and widely used in automobile air conditioners) by 50 percent by 1999. At a 1990 meeting in London, the agreement was modified, banning all CFCs by the year 2000. Two years later, representatives from more than 80 nations agreed in Copenhagen to move up the ban of CFCs to 1996 and outlaw other harmful substances as well. In 1992, the United States unilaterally announced its compliance with the provisions of the modified Montreal Protocol.

The unprecedented scope of the amended plan pleased many who feared for the environment and stressed the need for international cooperation. Still, international funding to help developing nations purchase ozone-friendly technologies was very slow in coming. Criticism of the treaty came from opposite directions—some saw it as unnecessary; others believed it did too little or that loopholes would allow exemptions from the bans.

A Dutch study published in 1997 compared three scenarios—one with no restrictions on ozone-destroying chemicals, another with the 1987 Montreal Protocol, and a third with the more stringent Copenhagen Agreement. The results were impressive. "If you compare it to what would have happened otherwise, then you see a tremendous. . . . kind of success story," noted one of the researchers (the results of the study are illustrated in Figure 18.4).[21]

FIGURE 18.4 **Ozone and Cancer** A 1992 international agreement to cut down on ozone-depleting chemicals should prevent millions of skin cancers. Scientists' projections of the skin cancer rate: excess cases of skin cancer per million per year.

SOURCE: Associated Press/World Wide Photos; Amy Kranz

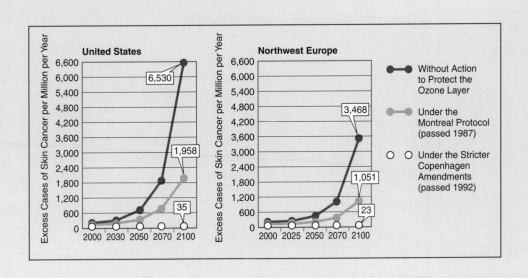

Biological Weapons Convention
A 1972 international arms control treaty that pledged the destruction of biological weapons stockpiles and outlawed the production and storage of such weapons.

Chemical Weapons Convention
A 1993 international arms control treaty to eliminate chemical weapons within 10 years. It calls for the destruction of chemical weapons stockpiles and the monitoring of companies making compounds that can be used to produce nerve agents in order to end production of chemical weapons.

World Court
Also known as the International Court of Justice, the principal judicial organ of the United Nations; the Court hears any case brought before it by parties who voluntarily accept its jurisdiction.

limited. Like armaments, environmental concerns have traditionally come under national sovereignty. However, resource depletion, the preservation of endangered species, and human-induced changes in the biosphere affect all countries.

The Global Warming Treaty negotiated at Kyoto, Japan, in December 1997 is a good example of the difficulties in fashioning international environmental law. Many scientists, including geophysicists and meteorologists, predict a significant rise in the earth's temperature over the next century. If these predictions are true, global warming will likely disrupt the world's climate, imperil agriculture, and cause a rising sea level that could threaten many major cities.

A major cause of global warming is carbon dioxide, created when coal, oil, and other fossil fuels are burned in internal combustion engines. However, there is political opposition in the United States to any treaty that would limit energy use. Labor unions, such as the AFL-CIO, worry about lost jobs. Executives from manufacturing industries complain about additional government regulations. Skeptics question the computer models and doubt whether global warming will actually occur or argue that it can be easily or effectively controlled.

Europe has been in the forefront of efforts to combat global warming. A small number of Caribbean and South Pacific nations, seeing themselves most at risk from global warming (even a two-foot rise in sea level would endanger their coastal businesses and poison their drinking water), champion even more stringent standards. Many developing nations, including China, India, and Brazil, have sought to exempt themselves from any agreement. And oil-producing nations, such as Saudi Arabia, see any future treaty as economically harmful and thus have continued to oppose the Kyoto Protocol outright.

The Limitations of International Law

Treaties intended to outlaw war (such as the unsuccessful Kellogg-Briand Pact of 1928, eventually ratified by 64 nations) and agreements designed to promote peace and international understanding (such as the UN Charter) tend not to withstand the test of time or the pressures of national ambition. Even modest "friendship" pacts solemnly signed by neighboring nations have been breached over the centuries.

The contemporary international system lacks three practical prerequisites necessary to maintain the rule of law. First, there is no single source of international legislative authority beyond the UN General Assembly, whose powers are negligible. Second, no international executive office possesses the power to initiate or enforce international law. (Symbolically, the UN secretary-general could lay claim to this duty, but, here again, the office commands no real power.) Third, there is no way to force sovereign governments to submit disputes to the World Court for adjudication or to accept the verdict even when they do.

Enforcement must be left to individual nation-states, which too often enforce decisions unreliably or not at all. As long as international law lacks the predictability and coherence that give the rule of law its unique value, it will remain more of a convenience for governments than a constraint on them.

The World Court The lack of international law-enforcement capabilities is reflected most clearly in the workings of the **World Court**, still a somewhat obscure institution that meets in The Hague (Holland's old capital). Properly known as the International Court of Justice (ICJ) and one of six principal organs established by the UN Charter, the Court is a full-fledged judicial body, complete with judges, procedural rules, and the solemn trappings of a dignified tribunal, but it lacks a clearly defined jurisdiction.

The World Court is one of the few courts in the Western world that does not have a backlog of cases. In fact, until recently it sometimes had no cases at all, not from an absence of international disputes but from the Court's poorly defined jurisdiction. For the Court to gain jurisdiction over an international dispute, the nations involved must confer jurisdiction on it in accordance with Article 36 of the Statute of the International Court of Justice, which stipulates,

> Parties to the present Statute *may* at any time declare that they recognize as compulsory . . . *in relation to any other State accepting the same obligation,* the jurisdiction of the Court in all legal disputes concerning: (1) the interpretation of a treaty; (2) any question of international law; (3) the existence of any fact which, if established, would constitute a breach of an international obligation. [Emphasis added]

In other words, governments are legally obligated to abide by a decision of the Court only when they have given prior consent to the Court's adjudication of a case. They may make a declaration of intent to accept the Court's jurisdiction in advance, as Article 36 invites them to do, or they may simply choose to submit certain cases on an ad hoc basis.

In the first 20 years of the World Court's existence, forty-two governments declared their intent to accept its compulsory jurisdiction. Although this seemed a large step in the direction of a law-based world order, things are not always as they appear. The U.S. "acceptance" of Article 36 in 1946 is a case in point. It was, in fact, a diplomatic sleight of hand. It states, in part,

> This declaration shall not apply to: a. disputes the solution of which the parties shall entrust to other tribunals by virtue of agreements already in existence or which may be concluded in the future; or b. disputes with regard to matters which are essentially within the domestic jurisdiction of the United States of America as determined by the United States of America; or c. disputes arising under a multinational treaty, unless (1) all parties to the treaty affected by the decision are also parties to the case before the Court, or (2) the United States of America especially agrees to jurisdiction.

Together, these qualifications meant the U.S. government agreed to compulsory jurisdiction only on the condition that the agreement did not compel it to accept the Court's jurisdiction. But the United States' qualified acceptance was not unique. No government in the contemporary world has agreed unconditionally to commit itself to abide by the rulings of the World Court.

The United States and the World Court What would prevent the United States and, say, Great Britain from setting a positive example by promising to submit all future disputes between themselves to the compulsory jurisdiction of the World Court? At least on the surface, nothing. But even if it were possible, why would it be necessary? For more than a century, the United States and Great Britain have had very few disputes requiring protracted negotiations. Any they might have in the foreseeable future are likely to be minor—close allies seldom face differences that require adjudication. Obviously, we cannot judge the effects of compulsory jurisdiction accurately when two governments are on such amicable terms and *voluntarily* turn minor differences over to the jurisdiction of an international tribunal anyway.

The World Court's utility was tested in the 1980s in the confrontation between Nicaragua's former Marxist (Sandinista) regime and the Reagan administration. In early 1985, Nicaragua filed suit against the United States in the World Court, charging Washington with aggression for mining the harbor at Corinto and supporting the Contra rebels. The U.S. promptly boycotted the proceedings and suspended bilateral talks on the grounds Nicaragua was using the Court for political and propaganda purposes.

In June 1986, the World Court ruled decisively against the United States in the case. At Nicaragua's initiative, the Security Council voted 11 to 1 to support the World Court's decision (with the United Kingdom, France, and Thailand abstaining.) Unfortunately, as this controversial case illustrates, the problem with compulsory jurisdiction, as with international law in general, is that it is least effective when it is most necessary.

In February 1998, the World Court again ruled against the United States in a high-profile dispute that stemmed from the 1988 terrorist bombing of Pan Am Flight 103 over Lockerbie, Scotland, in which 270 people died (including 11 on the ground). In 1992 the United States and Great Britain led a successful fight for UN sanctions against Libya when its government refused to extradite two Libyan nationals suspected of perpetrating this attack. The Libyan government took the dispute to the World Court for relief, but the United States argued, unsuccessfully, that the Court lacked jurisdiction. The case is now moot, as the United States and the international community officially rehabilitated Libya after it leader, Muammar Qaddafi, surrendered two suspects in the 1988 Pan Am bombing and denounced terrorism in the late 1990s.

International Law: Who Cares?

Some nations infrequently break the precepts of international law; others obey them only as a matter of expedience. In either case, that nations *can* refuse to be bound means international law will be uniformly followed only when it is in the national interest of all governments to do so. In other words, respect for international law ultimately depends on national self-interest.

Are principles of justice unimportant in international politics? Not exactly. They are of great value in understanding and evaluating the actions of governments and rulers. At times, governments can be punished (for example, through sanctions, as Iraq, Iran, Libya, and North Korea have discovered). Rogue rulers can also be punished, as the trial of former Yugoslav President Slobodan Milosevic in 2003–2004 illustrates.

The first principle of international political life is national self-preservation. International law is most effective when it serves the interests of rich and powerful nations. At such times, the machinery of international peace and justice is likely to spring into action. However, the major powers still prefer to seek traditional political and military solutions (where they have greater control over the outcomes) rather than judicial remedies (where they relinquish control to judges whose allegiances are unknown and unknowable).

THE QUEST FOR A PERPETUAL PEACE

In 2001, the United Nations and Secretary-General Kofi Annan were awarded the Nobel Peace Prize for working toward a more peaceful world. It was a fitting tribute to the individual and the organization he serves so well. But the tribute was perhaps less for what the United Nations had accomplished than for what it appeared on the cusp of becoming.

Wherever there was conflict or a humanitarian crisis, the UN was called upon. President Bill Clinton renounced unilateralism and made it a rule to seek UN approval before resorting to military force. The prestige of the UN was at an all-time high.

After the Cold War, with the superpower rivalry a thing of the past, the United Nations momentarily blossomed. Although balance-of-power politics and nuclear deterrence forged a relatively stable system of order after 1945, the end of the Cold War gave rise not only to new opportunities for order building but also to new dangers and sources of instability.

In the wake of 9/11, the Bush administration sought UN support in the fight against terrorism. The U.S.-led military action against Afghanistan's Taliban regime was undertaken with the United Nation's blessing and the full cooperation of the international community. But subsequently, when the United Nations did not share Washington's enthusiasm for invading Iraq, U.S. foreign policy veered toward unilateralism, ignoring the wishes of the United States' NATO allies and the United Nations.

International law and organizations are not likely to replace diplomacy and war (or the threat of war) as the usual means by which nation-states resolve most disputes. Nor is respect for international law or the sanctity of treaties likely to increase enough so that countervailing force is no longer our chief means of preventing or limiting war.

International organizations can play a vital role in conflict management, but there is no silver bullet that will resolve the problem of conflict once and for all. No amount of good will or enlightened statesmanship can usher in a world without war. Ending the ideological rivalry between the world's most powerful states was a significant step toward a safer and saner world, but as the rise of international terrorism shows, it did not guarantee perpetual peace.

Politics has been called the art of the possible. Ending conflict is not possible. But reducing the tensions, prejudices, and injustices that often lead to it is a goal worth pursuing.

GATEWAYS TO THE WORLD: EXPLORING CYBERSPACE

For more information about a particular nonstate actor, use the name of the entity as your search term. For instance, to find out more about the role of the IMF, enter *International Monetary Fund* as your keyword. This search would lead you to sites such as www.imf.org, which is the home page for the IMF.

www.un.org

This is the official home page of the United Nations. It includes a wealth of resources for research, including a search engine.

www.un.org/law

A gold mine for anyone interested in the International Court of Justice (also known as the World Court), the International Criminal Court, major international treaties and conventions, and, generally, the progress of UN efforts to promote the rule of law in international relations.

europa.eu

This is the official Website of the European Union. A fantastic resource for anyone interested in European integration.

http://www.un.org/Depts/dpko/missions/onub/photos.pdf

In December 2006, the UN successfully completed its peacekeeping mandate in Burundi, the scene of longstanding ethnic conflict between the ruling Tutsis and the majority Hutus. This website is a photo gallery depicting the UN Operation in Burundi (UNOB).

SUMMARY

To what extent have international organizations and international law contributed to a more peaceful world? The removal of national barriers to trade, travel, and transfers of all kinds is reflected by the great increase in nonstate actors in the modern world, including multinational corporations, international governmental organizations, and international nongovernmental organizations. Multinational economic pacts and military alliances have also enhanced regional or worldwide interdependence.

This impressive network of international organizations and international pacts has not been free of national rivalries, however. And comprehensive international organizations have proved no more successful in bringing long-lasting peace and stability to the international arena. In the twentieth century, the League of Nations was torn apart by conflicting national interests. During the Cold War that lasted from the early post World War II period until the collapse of the Soviet Union in 1991, the United Nations encountered many obstacles, although it had modest success as a peacekeeping institution. Peacekeeping activity expanded in the post Cold War era, when the United Nations authorized collective military action in the Persian Gulf (Iraq), the Horn of Africa (Somalia), the Balkans (Bosnia and Kosovo), West Africa (Sierra Leone and Liberia), and Central Asia (Afghanistan), among others. However, the United Nations refused to back the U.S.-led invasion of Iraq in 2003.

International law facilitates and regulates relations among sovereign and independent states whose interactions might otherwise be chaotic. In general, it has had a checkered history. Modern-day examples of international law include the Geneva and Hague Conventions, which set rules for warfare, and the multilateral arms limitations treaties. International environmental agreements, such as the 1997 Kyoto Protocol, are becoming an increasingly important part of international law.

The limitations of international law are starkly apparent in the difficulties encountered by the World Court. The United Nations is similarly constrained by its inability to act against the wishes of the major powers, especially the five permanent members of the Security Council.

KEY TERMS

functionalism
interdependence
globalization
nonstate actors
multinational corporations (MNC)
Organization of Petroleum Exporting Countries (OPEC)
international nongovernmental organizations (INGO)

international governmental organizations (IGO)
European Union (EU)
co-decision
qualified majority voting (QMV)
North Atlantic Treaty Organization (NATO)
Warsaw Pact
collective security
international law
Geneva Convention

Hague Convention
Strategic Arms Reduction Treaty II (START II)
Antarctic Treaty
Outer Space Treaty
Nonproliferation Treaty
Seabed Treaty
Biological Weapons Convention
Chemical Weapons Convention
World Court

REVIEW QUESTIONS

1. Who are the most important nonstate actors in international politics? What impact have they had on the international system?
2. What prompted the founding of the United Nations? How successful are its peacekeeping operations?
3. Does international law serve a useful purpose in contemporary international relations? If not, why? If so, in what ways?
4. What are the limitations of international law? How effectively has the World Court functioned? What suggestions for improvement present themselves?

RECOMMENDED READING

Bennett, A. Leroy. *International Organizations: Principles and Issues*, 6th ed. Englewood Cliffs, NJ: Prentice-Hall, 1994.

A good introductory text.

Cassese, Antonia. *International Law*. Oxford: Oxford University Press, 2005.

The author is a distinguished legal scholar who, among other distinctions, served as the President of the International Criminal Tribunal for the Former Yugoslavia.

Claude, Inis L., Jr. *Swords into Plowshares: The Problems and Progress of International Organizations*, 6th ed. New York: McGraw-Hill, 1994.

A classic introduction focusing on the theoretical and practical problems of the League of Nations and the United Nations.

Doyle, Michael, and Nicholas Sambanis. *Making War and Building Peace: United Nations Peace Keeping Operations*. Princeton, NJ: Princeton University Press, 2006.

Compares the results of two categories of peace processes following civil wars—ones the UN was involved in with ones it was not.

Hinsley, F. H. *Power and the Pursuit of Peace: Theory and Practice in the History of Relations Between States*. Cambridge: Cambridge University Press, 1967.

A scholarly history of proposals and schemes for the international management of conflict from the Middle Ages to the modern age.

Kennedy, Paul. *The Parliament of Man: The Past, Present, and Future of the United Nations*. New York: Random House, 2006.

From the publisher: "[A] thorough and timely history of the United Nations that explains the institution's roots and functions while also casting an objective eye on the UN's effectiveness as a body and on its prospects for success in meeting the challenges that lie ahead."

Keohane, Robert O., and Joseph S. Nye. *Power and Interdependence: World Politics in Transition*, 3rd ed. New York: Longman, 2000.

A groundbreaking work that challenges the realist theory of international relations and attempts to construct an alternative theory based on the concept of interdependence.

Traub, James. *Best Intentions: Kofi Annan and the UN in the Era of American World Power*. New York: Farrar, Straus, and Giroux, 2006.

The author writes on foreign policy for the *New York Times Magazine*. Kirkus Reviews calls it "A heartbreaking book about a hardworking idealist's frustrated attempts to restore the stature of the cumbersome United Nations in a world dominated by 'the preemptively belligerent America.'"

Chapter 1

1. See Joseph Nye, *The Paradox of American Power: Why the World's Only Superpower Can't Go It Alone* (London: Oxford University Press, 2002). This quote is from Nye's article, "The New Rome Meets the New Barbarians," *The Economist,* March 23, 2002, p. 24.

2. Baron de Montesquieu's classification of political governments in Book II of *The Spirit of the Laws* has proved most influential. Montesquieu distinguished among republics, monarchies, and despotic governments, further subdividing democratic republics, ruled by the whole people, from aristocratic republics, ruled by part of the people (specifically, by the wealthy class). Republics also have been historically distinguished from direct democracies. Thus, James Madison (perhaps the leading U.S. Founder) called governments in which the people directly participated in their own governing and did not rely on representation *direct democracies.* Because the U.S. government provides for representation, it is called a *republic.*

3. For a discussion of some worrisome tendencies, see Arthur Schlesinger Jr., *The Disuniting of America* (New York: Norton, 1993).

4. Aristotle, *The Politics,* trans. and ed. Ernest Barker (New York: Oxford University Press, 1962), p. 4.

5. As opposed to Plato, who is sometimes classified as the first political philosopher.

6. Jack H. Nagel and John E. McNulty, "Partisan Effects of Voter Turnout in Senatorial and Gubernatorial Elections," *American Political Science Review* 90 (December 1996): 780–793.

7. See Leo Strauss, *What Is Political Philosophy? and Other Studies* (New York: Free Press, 1959), pp. 10–12.

8. There are variations to this approach; for instance, traditional realist theory has been updated (but not without controversy) by political scientists referred to as neorealists or *structural realists.* A leading work here is Kenneth Waltz, *Theory of International Politics* (Reading, MA: Addison-Wesley, 1979). Also see his "Realist Thought and Neo-Realist Theory," *Journal of International Affairs* XLIV (Spring/Summer 1990): 21–37.

9. For a scholarly attempt to reconcile the two approaches, see Robert O. Keohane, *International Institutions and State Power* (Boulder, CO: Westview Press, 1989). Keohane's theory is sometimes referred to as *neo-liberal institutionalism.*

10. Irving Kristol, "The Nature of Nazism," in *The Commentary Reader,* ed. Norman Podhoretz (New York: Atheneum, 1965), p. 16.

11. Hannah Arendt, *Eichmann in Jerusalem: A Report on the Banality of Evil* (New York: Penguin Books, 1964). Compare Gideon Hausner, *Justice in Jerusalem* (New York: Schocken Books, 1968), p. 465.

12. Not all Germans, or Europeans, were as indifferent or self-serving in the face of evil as was Eichmann. A notable, if atypical, exception was Oskar Schindler, whose renown has increased enormously due to the movie *Schindler's List*. Schindler was a German businessman who belonged to the Nazi Party. He at first exploited labor but then used his business and political connections to save the lives of his Jewish workers. An attempt to examine Schindler and the courageous acts of other righteous Christians is set forth in Eva Fogelman, *Conscience and Courage: Rescuers of Jews During the Holocaust* (New York: Doubleday, 1994). Also see Samuel P. Oliner and Pearl M. Oliner, *The Altruistic Personality: Rescuers of Jews in Nazi Europe* (New York: Free Press, 1988). No doubt most of us would identify more with the Christian rescuers or with Schindler than with Eichmann, but the disturbing fact remains that far more Germans (including tens of thousands of Hitler Youth), mesmerized by Hitler's message of hate, behaved more like Eichmann than like Schindler.

Chapter 2

1. Aristotle, *The Politics,* trans. and ed. Ernest Barker (New York: Oxford University Press, 1962), 1279a, p. 112.

2. This discussion builds on Andrew Heywood, *Political Ideologies: An Introduction* (New York: St. Martin's Press, 1992), pp. 6–8. Heywood's (and our) discussion, in turn, builds on a definition offered in May Selinger, *Politics and Ideology* (London: Allen & Unwin, 1976).

3. The Anti-Defamation League of B'nai B'rith, *Hate Groups in America: A Record of Bigotry and Violence* (New York, n.d.), p. 11.

4. See, for example, Dianae B. Henriques, "As Exemptions Grow, Religion Outweighs Regulation," *New York Times,* October 6, 2006 (electronic edition).

5. Jack C. Plano and Roy Olton, *The International Relations Dictionary* (Santa Barbara, CA: ABC, 1982), p. 81.

6. Bertrand Russell, *A History of Western Philosophy* (New York: Simon & Schuster, 1965), p. 364.

7. Martin Diamond, Winston Fisk, and Herbert Garfinkel, *The Democratic Republic: An Introduction to American Government* (Skokie, IL: Rand McNally, 1971), pp. 4–5.

8. Baron de Montesquieu, *The Spirit of the Laws,* trans. Thomas Nugent (New York: Hafner Press, 1949), bk. 5, chap. 6, p. 46.

9. Adam Smith, *An Inquiry into the Nature and Causes of the Wealth of Nations* (New York: Modern Library, 1965), p. 14.

10. As is pointed out in Robert Heilbroner, *The Worldly Philosophers: The Lives, Times, and Ideas of the Great Economic Thinkers* (New York: Modern Library, 1965), p. 14.

11. See "A Heavyweight Champ, at Five Foot Two," *The Economist,* November 25, 2006, p. 29.

12. John Stuart Mill, *On Liberty* (Lake Bluff, IL: Regnery/Gateway, 1955), p. 85.

13. James Davison Hunter, *Culture Wars: The Struggle to Define America* (New York: Basic Books, 1991). The discussion here generally follows, but does not duplicate, Hunter's. See also John Kenneth White, *The Values Divide: American Politics and Culture in Transition* (New York: Chatham House, 2003).

14. Ibid. As Hunter makes clear, members of the same faith often strongly disagree on these issues.

15. Brian Mann, *Welcome to the Homeland* (Hanover, NH: Steerforth Press, 2006), p. 270.

16. See, for example, Marc Ambinder, "A Nation of Free Agents," *Washington Post,* September 3, 2006 (electronic edition): "Independent voters comprise about 10 percent of the electorate, but the percentage of persuadable independents has shot up to about 30 percent. In the 27 states that register voters by party, self-declared independents grew from 8 percent of the registered electorate in 1987 to 24 percent in 2004, according to political analyst Rhodes Cook. Consistently, about 30 percent of U.S. voters tell pollsters they don't belong to a party."

Chapter 3

1. See Leo Strauss, *What Is Political Philosophy? and Other Studies* (New York: Free Press, 1959), p. 10.

2. Allan Bloom, "Interpretive Essay," in *The Republic of Plato,* trans. Allan Bloom (New York: Basic Books, 1968), pp. 308–310.

3. Plato's ideal political order is most accurately translated as "city." The Greek word *polis* implies a small, self-sufficient community that provides for all human relationships. Modern distinctions between, for example, society and government or church and state are quite foreign to this concept.

4. Bloom, *The Republic of Plato* p. 410.

5. Ibid.

6. Howard White, *Peace Among the Willows: The Political Philosophy of Francis Bacon* (The Hague: Martinus Nijhoff, 1968), pp. 97, 102.

7. Karl Marx, "Capital: Selections," in *The Marx-Engels Reader,* ed. Robert C. Tucker (New York: Norton, 1972), p. 259.

8. Karl Marx and Friedrich Engels, "Manifesto of the Communist Party," in *The Marx-Engels Reader,* p. 352.

9. Friedrich Engels, "Socialism: Utopian and Scientific," in *The Marx-Engels Reader,* p. 635.

10. Karl Marx, "Outlines of a Future Society, from 'The Germany Ideology,'" in *Capital, Communist Manifesto, and Other Writings,* ed. Max Eastman (New York: Modern Library, 1932), p. 1.

11. Ibid.

12. Joseph Cropsey, "Karl Marx," in *History of Political Philosophy*, eds. Leo Strauss and Joseph Cropsey (Skokie, IL: Rand McNally, 1969), p. 717.

13. Jerome Gilison, *The Soviet Image of Utopia* (Baltimore, MD: Johns Hopkins University Press, 1975), p. 110.

14. Roy Macrides, *Contemporary Political Ideologies* (Cambridge, MA: Winthrop, 1980), p. 180.

15. B. F. Skinner, *Walden Two* (New York: Macmillan, 1962), p. 159.

16. Ibid., p. 161.

17. Ibid., pp. 104–105.

18. Ibid., p. 262.

19. Ibid., p. 193.

20. Ibid., p. 272.

21. Ibid., p. 295.

22. Paul Berman, "Terror and Liberalism," *The American Prospect*, October 22, 2001.

23. See, for example, the writings of Daniel Pipes, especially *The Hidden Hand: Middle East Theories of Conspiracy* (New York: Free Press, 1997) and *Conspiracy: How the Paranoid Style Flourishes and Where It Comes From* (New York: Free Press, 1998); see also Fouad Ajami, *The Dream Palace of the Arabs: A Generation's Odyssey* (New York: Pantheon, 1998).

Chapter 4

1. See David Held, *Models of Democracy* (Stanford, CA: Polity and Stanford University Press, 1996) and David Held, *Democracy and the Global Order: From the Modern State to Cosmopolitan Governance* (Stanford, CA: Polity and Stanford University Press, 1995).

2. Richard S. Katz, "Models of Democracy: Elite Attitudes and the Democratic Deficit in the European Union." An unpublished paper presented at a meeting of the European Consortium of Political Research, Copenhagen, April 2000.

3. Alexander Hamilton, John Jay, and James Madison, *The Federalist* no. 31 (New York: Modern Library, 1964), p. 190.

4. Ibid., no. 31, pp. 226–227.

5. Ibid., no. 49, p. 329.

6. Martin Diamond, Winston Fisk, and Herbert Garfinkel, *The Democratic Republic: An Introduction to American National Government* (Skokie, IL: Rand McNally, 1970), p. 136.

7. Stephen Cahn, *Education and the Democratic Ideal* (Chicago: Nelson-Hall, 1979), p. 3.

8. See "The Presidential IQ Report," The Lovenstein Institute, Scranton, Pennsylvania, 2001 (accessed on the Internet at http://www.lovenstein.org/report).

9. Alexis de Tocqueville, *Democracy in America*, vol. 1 (New York: Schocken Books, 1961), pp. 299–300.

10. Ibid., p. 301.

11. Jay Hamilton and James Madison, *The Federalist,* no. 9, pp. 48–49.

12. Ibid., no. 10, p. 57.

13. Ibid., no. 51, p. 337.

14. Ibid.

15. Ibid.

16. Ibid., no. 6, p. 27.

17. Ibid., no. 51, p. 37.

18. G. Ross Stephens, "Federal Malignancies," unpublished paper, March 15, 2009; see also Malcom M. Freeley and Edward Rubin, *Federalism: Political Identity and Tragic Compromise* (Ann Arbor, MI: University of Michigan Press, 2008); and David Cay Johnston, *Free Lunch* (New York, NY: Portfolio, Penguin Books, Ltd., 2007).

19. However, federalism does not protect individuals from abuse by state or local government, which the African American experience in various Southern states well illustrates.

20. Diamond, Fisk, and Garfinkel, *The Democratic Republic,* p. 136.

21. Tocqueville, *Democracy in America,* pp. 304–398.

22. Aristotle, *The Politics,* trans. and ed. Ernest Barker (New York: Oxford University Press, 1962), 1287a, p. 146.

23. John Locke, *Second Treatise on Civil Government* (New York: New American Library, 1965), sec. 202, p. 448.

24. 8 Co. Rep. 114a (1610).

25. See *Youngstown Sheet and Tube Company v. Sawyer,* 343 U.S. 579 (1952), especially the concurring opinion of Justice Jackson.

26. William E. Hudson, *American Democracy in Peril: Eight Challenges to America's Future,* 4th ed. (Chatham, NJ: Chatham House, 2003).

27. Ibid., pp. 10–12.

28. David Held, *Democracy and the Global Order* (Stanford, CA: Stanford University Press, 1996).

29. See, for example, George Ross, "The European Union and the Future of European Politics," in Mark Kesselman and Joel Krieger, et. al., *European Politics in Transition,* 4th ed. (New York: Houghton-Mifflin Company, 2002).

Chapter 5

1. See Robert Kaplan, *The Coming Anarchy: Shattering the Dreams of the Post Cold War* (New York: Vintage Books, 2000), pp. 3–7. The article was later bundled with several other articles by the same author and reprinted in this highly readable little volume.

2. Bernard Crick, *Basic Forms of Government: A Sketch and a Model* (London: Macmillan, 1980), p. 53.

3. Aristotle, *The Politics,* trans. and ed. Ernest Barker (New York: Oxford University Press, 1962), 1279a, p. 112.

4. "Transparency International, Berlin." Reprinted from the *Wall Street Journal,* January 2, 1997, sec. 1, 5.

5. Lydia Polgreen, "As Nigeria Tries to Fight Graft, A New Sordid Tale," *New York Times,* November 29, 2005 (electronic edition).

6. See, for example, "Big Men, Big Fraud, and Big Trouble," *The Economist,* April 28, 2007, pp. 55–58.

7. Aristotle, *The Politics,* 1313b, p. 245.

8. See John Dunn, *Democracy: A History* (New York: Atlantic Monthly Press, 2006).

9. Maurice Latey, *Patterns of Tyranny* (New York: Atheneum, 1969), p. 115.

10. Fyodor Dostoyevsky, *The Brothers Karamazov,* ed. Ernest Rhys (London: Dent, 1927), p. 259.

11. Crick, *Basic Forms of Government,* p. 35.

12. See Karl Wittfogel, *Oriental Despotism: A Comparative Study of Total Power* (New York: Random House, 1981).

13. Crick, *Basic Forms of Government,* p. 36.

14. Samuel P. Huntington, "How Countries Democratize," *Political Science Quarterly* 106, no. 4 (1991–1992): 579.

15. Robert M. Press, "Africa's Struggle for Democracy," *Christian Science Monitor,* March 21, 1991, p. 4.

16. "Russia Deserves Pity as Well as Fear," *The Economist,* December 2, 2006, p. 15.

17. Huntington, "How Countries Democratize," p. 579.

18. Juan Forero, "Latin America Is Growing Impatient with Democracy," *New York Times,* June 24, 2004.

19. See, for example, Steven W. Hook and John Spanier, *American Foreign Policy Since World War II* (Washington, DC: CQ Press, 2004), especially Chapter 4 ("Developing Countries in the Crossfire"), pp. 81–111; Chalmers Johnson, *Blowback* (New York: Henry Holt, 2000), especially Chapters 3 and 4, pp. 65–118; Thomas M. Magstadt, *An Empire If You Can Keep It: Power and Principle in American Foreign Policy* (Washington: CQ Press, 2004), especially, Chapter 6.

20. Kaplan, *The Coming Anarchy,* p. 65.

21. Ibid., pp. 65–66.

22. Ibid., p. 66.

Chapter 6

1. William Kornhauser, *The Politics of Mass Society* (New York: Free Press, 1959), p. 123.

2. C. W. Cassinelli, *Total Revolution: A Comparative Study of Germany Under Hitler, the Soviet Union Under Stalin, and China Under Mao* (Santa Barbara, CA: Clio Books, 1976), p. 225.

3. Leonard Shapiro, *Totalitarianism* (New York: Praeger, 1972), p. 104. Shapiro quotes scholar Hans Buchheim on this point.

4. Carl Friedrich and Zbigniew Brzezinski, *Totalitarian Dictatorship and Autocracy,* 2nd ed. (New York: Praeger, 1966).

5. Cassinelli, *Total Revolution,* p. 231.
6. Friedrich and Brzezinski, *Totalitarian Dictatorship,* pp. 279–339.
7. Eric Hoffer, *The True Believer: Thoughts on the Nature of Mass Movements* (New York: Harper & Row, 1951), pp. 104–105.
8. Maurice Latey, *Patterns of Tyranny* (New York: Atheneum, 1969), p. 172.
9. Hoffer, p. 86.
10. Raul Hilberg, *The Destruction of the European Jews* (New York: Harper & Row, 1961), p. 12.
11. Cited in Cassinelli, *Total Revolution,* p. 16.
12. Adolph Hitler, speech in Munich, Germany, March 13, 1936.
13. Karl Dietrich Bracher, *The German Dictatorship* (New York: Holt, 1972), p. 181.
14. Propaganda plays a role in all political systems in the modern world; in fact, the first serious study of propaganda was published in 1928. The author, Edward Bernays, had been a member of the U.S. Committee on Public Information in World War I. See Edward Bernays, *Propaganda* (Brooklyn, New York: Ig Publishing, 2004); see also Jacques Ellul, *Propaganda: The Formation of Men's Attitudes* (New York: Random House, 1965).
15. Adolf Hitler, *Mein Kampf,* trans. R. Manheim (Boston: Houghton Mifflin, 1971), pp. 179–180.
16. Ibid., p. 182.
17. Ibid.
18. Quoted in Leo Strauss, *Thoughts on Machiavelli* (Seattle: University of Washington Press, 1968), p. 9.
19. Latey, *Patterns of Tyranny,* p. 100.
20. Cassinelli, *Total Revolution,* p. 103.
21. Ibid., p. 186. Cassinelli's observation that Mao "never hesitated to destroy his enemies [including] rival communists, Kuomintang activists, and 'landlords'" can be applied to all successful totalitarian rulers.
22. Quoted in Bracher, *German Dictatorship,* p. 257.
23. Ibid., p. 272.
24. W. S. Allen, *The Nazi Seizure of Power: The Experience of a Single German Town, 1930–1935* (Chicago: Quadrangle Books, 1965).
25. Peter Drucker, "The Monster and the Lamb," *Atlantic,* December 1978, p. 84.
26. Ibid.
27. Carl Friedrich and Zbigniew Brzezinski, *Totalitarian Dictatorship and Autocracy,* 2nd ed. (New York: Praeger, 1966), p. 374.
28. Ibid., pp. 9–10.
29. Hannah Arendt, *Totalitarianism* (Orlando, FL: Harcourt, 1968), p. xiv.
30. See Stalin, *Mastering Bolshevism,* p. 10; cited in Merle Fainsod, *How Russia Is Ruled,* rev. ed. (Cambridge, MA: Harvard University Press, 1964), p. 435.
31. Aleksandr Solzhenitsyn, *The Gulag Archipelago, 1918–1956* (New York: Harper & Row, 1974), p. 595.
32. Bracher, *German Dictatorship,* p. 258.
33. Ibid., pp. 259–260.

34. Ibid., p. 262.
35. Ibid.
36. Hilberg, *Destruction of the European Jews,* p. 31.
37. Mao Zedong, *Selected Works* (Beijing: Foreign Languages Press, 1960–1965), p. 224.
38. Franz Michaels and George Taylor, *The Far East in the Modern World* (New York: Holt, 1964), p. 479.
39. John King Fairbank, *The United States and China,* 4th ed. (Cambridge, MA: Harvard University Press, 1979), p. 409.
40. Ibid., p. 413.
41. Ibid.
42. Cassinelli, *Total Revolution,* p. 195.
43. Ibid., p. 243. Of course, figures vary widely. For example, Rummel, using somewhat different criteria, postulated significantly different individual figures for Hitler, Lenin–Stalin, and Mao. Yet, his total of almost 105.5 million people killed is remarkably close to Cassinelli's estimate. See R. J. Rummel, *Death by Government* (New Brunswick, NJ: Transaction, 1996), p. 8.
44. For instance, almost 1.5 million pages of formerly classified documents (German messages intercepted by Britain during World War II as well as newly released Russian documents) revealed that Hitler probably murdered closer to seven million Jews (as opposed to the five or six million, as Cassinelli and others had estimated). Also see comment in note 45.
45. Cassinelli, *Total Revolution,* p. 46.
46. Ibid., p. 186. Since Cassinelli published his book, new evidence indicates that these figures vastly understated the actual number of deaths during this period. According to one authority, a three-year famine between 1959 and 1962 *alone* caused at least 30 million Chinese deaths. The immediate cause of the famine was Mao's policy of taking property from Chinese peasants and relocating those peasants in communes. See Jasper Becker, *Hungry Ghosts: Mao's Secret Famine* (New York: Free Press, 1997).
47. Ibid.
48. Ibid., p. 187.
49. See, for example, Thomas M. Magstadt, "Bleeding Cambodia: The Great Leap Downward," **Reason**, July 1982, pp. 45–50; and "Marxism, Moral Responsibility, and the Cambodian Revolution," **National Review**, July 24, 1981, pp. 831–836.
50. See Thomas M. Magstadt, "Ethiopia's Great Terror," **Worldview**, April 1982, pp. 5–6.
51. "Iran to offer West nuke package soon," China Daily (online), April 16, 2009 accessed by the author at <http://www.chinadaily.net/cndy/2009-04/16/content_7681807.htm>.
52. Laqueur applied this concept to the Soviet Union, particularly in his chapter on totalitarianism. See Walter Laqueur, *The Dream That Failed, Reflections on the Soviet Union* (New York: Oxford University Press, 1994), pp. 77–95, 84.

Chapter 7

1. The Life Peerage Act of 1958 enables the monarch, upon the advice of the prime minister, to confer nontransferable titles for life on commoners. The rationale for the legislation was to ensure party balance and to increase the number of working members in the House of Lords. Approximately one-quarter of all Lords (and a higher percentage of working members of the House of Lords) are appointed in this way.

2. Sydney Bailey, *British Parliamentary Democracy*, 3rd ed. (Westport, CT: Greenwood, 1978), p. 130.

3. Ibid., p. 131.

4. Suzanne Berger, *The French Political System*, 3rd ed. (New York: Random House, 1974), p. 368.

5. Ibid. Berger quotes then Prime Minister (later President) Georges Pompidou in 1964 commenting on the Fifth Republic's institutional balancing act: "France has now chosen a system midway between the American presidential regime and the British parliamentary regime, where the chief of state, who formulates general policy, has the basis of authority in universal suffrage but can only exercise his functions with a government that he may have chosen and named, but which in order to survive, must maintain the confidence of the Assembly."

6. Roy Macridis, ed., *Modern Political Systems: Europe,* 6th ed. (Englewood Cliffs, NJ: Prentice-Hall, 1986), p. 120.

7. Karl Dietrich Bracher, *The German Dictatorship* (New York: Holt, 1970), p. 75.

8. No-byline, "Judgment days: Germany's Constitutional Court," *The Economist,* March 28, 2009, pp. 59 & 60.

9. Guido Goldman, *The German Political System* (New York: Random House, 1974), p. 56.

10. See John W. Dower, *Embracing Defeat: Japan in the Wake of World War II* (New York: Norton, 2000).

11. See Herbert P. Bix, *Hirohito and the Making of Modern Japan* (New York: HarperCollins, 2000).

12. Franz Michael and George Taylor, *The Far East in the Modern World* (New York: Holt, 1964), p. 263.

13. Ibid., p. 607.

14. Nobutaki Ike, *Japanese Politics: Patron-Client Democracy,* 2nd ed. (New York: Knopf, 1972), p. 17.

15. Michael and Taylor, *Far East in the Modern World,* p. 603.

16. "India Overheats," *The Economist,* February 3, 2007, p. 11.

17. "Good News: Don't Waste," *The Economist,* May 23, 2009, p. 13.

18. Bailey, *British Parliamentary Democracy,* p. 130.

19. *Marbury v. Madison,* 5 U.S. (1 Cranch) 137 (1803).

20. For up-to-date information and analysis of campaign finance issues, see, for example, the Campaign Finance Information Center, http.// www. campaignfinance.org.

21. See, for example, Norman J. Ornstein and Thomas E. Mann, "When Congress Checks Out," *Foreign Affairs,* November/December 2006, pp. 67–82; see also Norman Ornstein and Thomas Mann, *The Broken Branch: How Congress Is Failing America and How to Get It Back on Track* (New York: Oxford University Press, 2006). The authors take Congress to task for failing to exercise oversight from 2000 to 2006—that is, during most of George W. Bush's tenure in the White House. In the 2006 mid-term elections, the Democrats regained control of both the House of Representatives and Senate but failed to win a large enough majority in the Senate to break a filibuster. (It takes 60 votes to pass a cloture motion to end debate.)

22. To learn more about just *how* political the judge-selection process can be, see Will Evans, "Money Trail Leads to the Federal Bench," Center for Investigative Reporting and Salon.com, October 31, 2006, http://www.muckraker.org/pg_one_investigation-1253–0.html.

23. See *Martin v. Hunter's Lessee,* 14 U.S. 304 (1816).

24. Richard Rose, "Politics in England," in *Comparative Politics Today: A World View,* ed. Gabriel Almond (Boston: Little, Brown, 1974), p. 148.

25. Edward Courtier, *Principles of Politics and Government* (Boston: Allyn & Bacon, 1981), p. 84.

Chapter 8

1. Thomas M. Magstadt, *Nations and Governments: Comparative Politics in Regional Perspective,* 5th edition (Belmont, CA: Wadsworth/Thomson, 2005), pp. 226–238.

2. Hedrick Smith, *The Russians* (New York: Times Books, 1983), p. 83.

3. See Susan Dentzer, Jeff Trimble, and Bruce Auster, "The Soviet Economy in Shambles," *US News & World Report,* November 20, 1989, pp. 25–29, 32, 35–37, 39.

4. Ibid., pp. 25, 26.

5. Walter Laqueur, *The Dream That Failed* (New York: Oxford University Press, 1994), pp. 71–73.

6. See Milovan Djilas, *The New Class* (New York: Praeger, 1957); and Smith, *Russians,* pp. 30–67.

7. START stands for Strategic Arms Reduction Treaty; START II was signed by presidents George H. W. Bush and Boris Yeltsin in 1993.

8. "Russia," *World Factbook* (Washington, DC: Central Intelligence Agency, 1996), p. 6 (electronic edition).

9. "Emerging Market Indicators," *The Economist,* March 15, 1997, p. 108.

10. Ibid., February 10, 2007, p. 105.

11. See Marshall Goldman, *Petrostate: Putin, Power, and the New Russia* (New York: Oxford University Press, 2008). See also Jason Bush, "Is Russia Blowing Its Oil Bonanza?" *Business Week Online,* October 5, 2005, http://www.businessweek.com/bwdaily/dnflash/oct2005/nf2005105_1326_db089.htm.

12. Vera Tolz, "Thorny Road Toward Federalism in Russia," *Radio Free Europe/Radio Liberty Research Report* 48 (December 1993), p. 1.

13. Claire Sterling, "Redfellas: The Growing Power of Russia's Mob," *The New Republic*, April 11, 1994, p. 19.

14. Xan Smiley, "Russia Wobbles Ahead," *The World in 1997* (an annual publication of *The Economist*), p. 39.

15. See Matthew Valencia, "Limping Towards Normality: A Survey of Poland," *The Economist*, October 27, 2001, pp. 3–16.

16. Bruce Einhorn, "India Struggles to Copy China's SEZs," Eye on Asia blog, *BusinessWeek*, posted on October 9, 2006. Accessed April 10, 2009, at http://www.businessweek.com/globalbiz/blog/eyeonasia/archives/2006/10/india_struggles.html.

17. A. Doak Barnett, "Ten Years After Mao," *Foreign Affairs* (Summer 1986), p. 38.

18. "Deng's China," *The Economist*, February 22, 1997, p. 21.

19. Ibid. See also Johanna McGeary, "The Next China," *Time*, March 3, 1997, pp. 52–53.

20. These are 1996 figures. The difference is explained by the fact that the World Bank uses earnings of $1 per day as a standard of worldwide poverty. The lower Chinese standard classifies how many Chinese are poor according to the Chinese standards of welfare and entitlement. See *World Bank News*, October 25, 1996, p. 5. Also see World Bank press release no. 96/41 EAP. Nobody really knows for certain the actual number of Chinese living in poverty at this time, but in 2004, it appeared as though patterns of income distribution continued to favor the rising urban middle class over the rural and urban poor.

21. "Suddenly Vunerable," *The Economist*, December 13, 2008, p. 15.

22. "China's Feuding Regions," *The Economist*, April 20, 1996, p. 27.

23. "China Learns the World's Rule," *The World in 2001* (London: The Economist Newspaper Limited, 2000), pp. 85–86.

24. Ferdinand, "Social Change," p. 483.

25. Ibid., p. 478.

26. See "Charting the Deng Revolution," *Newsweek*, March 3, 1997, pp. 26–27.

27. The term is taken from the title of a much-acclaimed book by Alan Riding, *Distant Neighbors: A Portrait of the Mexicans* (New York: Alfred A. Knopf, 1984).

28. "Putting the Brakes on Change," *The Economist*, July 12, 2003, p. 32.

Chapter 9

1. Michael Perry, "Malaria and dengue: The sting in climate change," Reuters, November 20, 2008. At http://www.reuters.com/article/environmentNews/idUSTRE4AJ2RQ20081120.

2. John Allen, *Student Atlas of World Politics* (Guilford, CT: Dushkin, 1994), p. 16. Thailand was then called Siam, and Iran was named Persia.

3. Ibid., p. 17. However, given the fluidity of contemporary politics, especially in former Yugoslavia, this number is highly unstable.

4. As pointed out by Robert Clark, *Power and Policy in the Third World,* 4th ed. (New York: Macmillan, 1991), p. 26.

5. See Jared Diamond, *Guns, Germs, and Steel: The Fate of Human Societies* (New York: Norton, 1997).

6. Robert D. Kaplan, *The Coming Anarchy* (New York: Vintage Books, 2001), pp. 3–59.

7. These points are generally emphasized in the literature. See James A. Bill and Robert L. Hardgrave Jr., *Comparative Politics: The Quest for Theory* (Websterville, OH: Merrill, 1973), pp. 70–71.

8. For instance, see Seymour Lipset, *Political Man: The Social Bases of Democracy* (Garden City, NY: Doubleday, 1983); Tatu Vanhanen, *The Process of Democratization: A Comparative Study of 147 States, 1980–1988* (Bristol, UK: Taylor & Francis, 1990); and Samuel P. Huntington, "Will More Countries Become Democratic?" *Political Science Quarterly* 99 (1984), pp. 193–218. See also Thomas Scanton, "Democracy's Fragile Flower Spreads Its Roots," *Time,* July 13, 1987, pp. 10–11. An optimistic outlook for democracy, based on such correlates, is offered by Carl Gershman, "Democracy as the Wave of the Future: A World Revolution," *Current* (May 1989), pp. 18–23.

9. Gershman, "Democracy as the Wave of the Future," p. 23.

10. Vanhanen, *Process of Democratization,* pp. 51–65.

11. See, for example, Justin Yifu Lin, Fang Cai, and Zhou Li, *The China Miracle: Development Strategy and Economic Reform* (Hong Kong: The Chinese University Press, 2003); see also Gregory Chow, *China's Economic Transformation,* 2nd ed. (Malden, MA Blackwell, 2007).

12. Kaplan, *Coming Anarchy,* pp. 59–98.

13. Samuel Huntington, "How Countries Democratize," *Political Science Quarterly* 106 (1991–1992), p. 579.

14. See, for example, Robert M. Press, "Africa's Struggle for Democracy," *Christian Science Monitor,* March 21, 1991, p. 4; and Kenneth B. Noble, "Despots Dwindle as Reform Alters Face of Africa," *New York Times,* April 13, 1991, p. 1.

15. Thomas R. Lansner, "Out of Africa," *Wall Street Journal,* December 10, 1996, p. A18.

16. Huntington, "How Countries Democratize," p. 12.

17. Robert Guest, "How to Make Africa Smile (A Survey of Sub-Saharan Africa)," *The Economist,* January 17, 2004, p. 9.

18. See P. W. Singer, *Children at War* (Berkeley: University of California Press, 2006); see also Michael Wessells, *Child Soldiers: From Violence to Protection* (Cambridge, MA Harvard University Press, 2006). On the use of girls as sex slaves, see, for example, Hannah Strange, "Wounds of sex slaves in Sierra Leone's civil war are a long time healing," *Times Online,* April 30, 2008, at http://www.timesonline.co.uk/tol/news/world/africa/article3848621.ece.

19. Jean Herskovits, "Nigeria: Power and Democracy in Africa," *Headline Series* 527 (January–February 1982), p. 8.

20. Simon Long, "India's Shining Hopes (A Survey of India)," *The Economist,* February 21, 2004, p. 3.

21. "Suddenly Vulnerable," *The Economist,* December 13, 2008, p. 15.

22. Vyvyan Tenorio, "Sri Lanka Peace Process at Delicate Point," *Christian Science Monitor,* September 2, 1986, p. 11.

23. Robert E. Gamer, *Developing Nations: A Comparative Perspective,* 2nd ed. (Dubuque, IA: William C. Brown, 1982), pp. 312–314.

24. See, for example, Daniel Pepper, "The Toxic Consequences of the Green Revolution," *US News and World Report,* July 7, 2008. Accessed online at http://www.usnews.com/articles/news/world/2008/07/07/the-toxic-consequences-of-the-green-revolution.html.

25. Samuel Huntington, *Political Order in Changing Societies* (New Haven, CT: Yale University Press, 1968), p. 35.

26. See, for instance, Bill and Hardgrave, *Comparative Politics,* pp. 58–59.

27. Jean-Jacques Rousseau, "The First Discourse," in *The First and Second Discourses,* ed. Roger D. Masters (New York: St. Martin's Press, 1964), p. 39.

Chapter 10

1. Aristotle, *The Politics,* trans. and ed. Ernest Barker (New York: Oxford University Press, 1962), 1276b, pp. 101–102.

2. Scott Shane, "Waterboarding Used 266 Times on Two Suspects," *The New York Times,* April 19, 2009 (electronic edition).

3. Ibid., 1274b, p. 93.

4. Immanuel Kant, *The Science of Right,* vol. 42 (Chicago: Encyclopaedia Britannica, 1952), p. 436.

5. Daniel J. Elazar, *American Federalism: A View from the States,* 3rd ed., (New York: Crowell, 1984). Elazar, a noted expert on U.S. federalism and intergovernmental relations, argued that there are three distinct political cultures in the United States—individualistic, moralistic, and traditionalistic. It is debatable, however, whether these are separate political cultures or merely different aspects of one political culture.

6. John Stuart Mill, *A System of Logic, Ratiocinative and Deductive,* vol. 2 (London: Longmans, Green, 1879), p. 518.

7. The modern study of political socialization is closely tied to the Greek concern for character formation. One key difference between the two is that whereas behavioral political science focuses primarily on the process by which political opinions are formed, the Greek emphasis is on the traits of character that all good citizens should display.

8. Barbara Defoe Whitehead provided persuasive evidence in an article entitled "Dan Quayle Was Right," *Atlantic* (April 1993), p. 41. However, single-parent families are only one source of why some families fail. Note James Q. Wilson's comment that one way "the family has become weaker is that more and more children are being raised in one-parent families, and often that one parent is a teenage girl. Another way is that parents, whether in one- or two-parent families, are spending less time with their children and

are providing poorer discipline." For a thoughtful review of two-parent families, in light of the academic debate on the subject, see James Q. Wilson, "The Family-Values Debate," *Commentary* 95 (April 1993), pp. 24–31. The quotation is from page 24.

9. See James Q. Wilson, *The Moral Sense* (New York: Free Press, 1995), pp. 141–163.

10. Herbert Winter and Thomas Bellows, *People and Politics* (New York: Wiley, 1977), p. 120.

11. Harry Holloway and John George, *Public Opinion*, 2nd ed. (New York: St. Martin's Press, 1985), pp. 73–77.

12. Dean Jaros, *Socialization to Politics* (New York: Praeger, 1973), pp. 87–88.

13. See M. Margaret Conway and Frank Fergert, *Political Analysis: An Introduction* (Boston: Allyn & Bacon, 1972), p. 106.

14. Holloway and George, *Public Opinion,* p. 79.

15. See M. Kent Jennings, "Preface"; Henry Kenst, "The Gender Factor in a Changing Electorate"; and Arthur Miller, "Gender and the Vote," in *The Politics of the Gender Gap: The Social Construction of Political Influence,* ed. Carol Mueller (Newbury Park, CA: Sage, 1987). Much of the political literature advocating natural differences between the sexes presumes the existence of scholarship in the field of developmental psychology; see Carol Gilligan, *In a Different Voice* (Cambridge, MA: Harvard University Press, 1982); and M. Belenky, B. Clinchy, W. Goldberger, and J. Tarule, *Women's Ways of Knowing: The Development of Self, Voice, and Mind* (New York: Basic Books, 1986).

16. Michael Barone and Grant Ujifusa, *The Almanac of American Politics* (Washington, DC: National Journal, 1994), p. xxvii.

17. Ralph Buultjens, "India: Religion, Political Legitimacy, and the Secular State," *Annals of Political and Social Sciences* 483 (January 1986), p. 107.

18. James Billington, "The Case for Orthodoxy," *New Republic,* May 30, 1994, p. 26.

19. A. James Reichley, *Religion in American Public Life* (Washington, DC: Brookings Institution, 1985), p. 2.

20. See, for example, Laurie Goodstein, "More Atheists Shout It From the Rooftops," *New York Times*, April 26, 2009 (electronic edition).

21. This is not to deny, of course, that unscrupulous leaders can exploit religion for ignoble purposes.

22. This discussion builds on William Flanigan and Nancy Zingale, *Political Behavior of the American Electorate* (Boston: Allyn & Bacon, 1979), pp.184–187.

23. Kenneth Langton and M. Kent Jennings, "Political Socialization and the High School Civics Curriculum," *American Political Science Review* (September 1968), p. 851.

24. Conway and Fergert, *Political Analysis,* p. 110. Also see Judith Torney-Purta, "From Attitudes and Knowledge to Schemata: Expanding the Outcomes at Political Socialization Research," in *Political Socialization, Citizenship Education, and Democracy,* ed. Orit Ichilov (New York: Teachers College Press, 1990), p. 99.

25. Or so it would seem. But it is important to determine not only what is studied but also how it is studied. See Albert Speer's comments on German education in Albert Speer, *Inside the Third Reich*, trans. R. Winston and C. Winston (New York: Avon, 1971), p. 35.

26. Robert Erikson, Norman Luttbeg, and Kent Tedin, *American Public Opinion* (New York: Macmillan, 1991), p. 113.

27. Ibid., p. 7.

28. This is commonly recognized. See James MacGregor Burns, J. W. Peltason, Thomas E. Cronin, and David B. Magleby, *Government by the People*, 17th ed. (Upper Saddle River, NJ: Prentice Hall, 1998), p. 293.

29. Ibid., pp. 49–50.

30. James Q. Wilson and Richard Hernstein, *Crime and Human Nature* (New York: Simon & Schuster, 1985), p. 293.

31. Donna Abu-Nasr, "The Beauty Isn't Skin Deep," *The Kansas City Star*, Thursday, May 7, 2009, p. A18.

32. This section builds on the analysis offered in Montague Kern, *Thirty-Second Politics: Political Advertising in the Eighties* (New York: Praeger, 1989).

33. Thomas E. Patterson, *Out of Order* (New York: Vintage, 1994), p. 25.

34. Daniel Hallin's study is cited as part of a wider discussion of the issue in Samuel Popkin, *The Reasoning Voter: Communication and Persuasion in Presidential Campaigns* (Chicago: University of Chicago Press, 1991), pp. 228–229.

35. University Wisconsin news release, November 21, 2006. Accessed on the Internet , April 28, 2009, at http://www.news.wisc.edu/releases/13213.

36. See, for example, Al Franken, *Lies and the Lying Liars Who Tell Them: A Fair and Balanced Look at the Right* (New York: Dutton, 2003). Franken is an unabashed liberal who gained fame as a comic writer on *Saturday Night Live* but has since turned to political satire and is endeavoring to create a new liberal radio network to combat what he believes to be a strong right-wing slant in the corporate-controlled mass media. In 2008, he ran for the United States Senate in Minnesota, won by a few hundred votes, but found himself in a legal battle with the incumbent, Norm Colman, who contested the results in the courts.

37. M. Margaret Conway, *Political Participation in the United States* (Washington, DC: C.Q. Press, 1987), pp 52–53.

38. Hence, the author of one classic behavioral study long ago concluded, "The principles of freedom and democracy are less widely and enthusiastically favored when they are confronted in their specific or applied forms." See Herbert McCloskey, "Consensus and Ideology in American Democracy," *American Political Science Review* 58 (June 1964), pp. 361–384.

39. Donald Devine, *The Political Culture of the United States* (Boston: Little, Brown, 1972), pp. 187–230. Also see Seymour Martin Lipset, *American Exceptionalism: A Double-Edged Sword* (New York: Norton, 1996) for an extensive discussion of the values that make up the American creed.

Chapter 11

1. Howard Schuman and Stanley Presser, *Questions and Answers in Attitude Surveys* (Orlando, FL: Academic Press, 1981), pp. 70–71. This study is illustrated in James Q. Wilson, *American Government,* 4th ed. (Lexington, MA: Heath, 1989), p. 99.

2. See, for example, John L. Fund, "The Perils of Polling," *Wall Street Journal,* August 13, 1996, p. A12; for a commentary on the polls in the 1996 presidential election (Clinton versus Dole), see Carll Everett Ladd, "The Pollsters' Waterloo," *Wall Street Journal,* November 19, 1997, p. A22.

3. Costas Panagopolous, "Poll Accuracy in the 2008 Presidential Election," November 5, 2008, accessed electronically on May 2, 2009.

4. One study found that almost two-thirds of the promises made in major-party platforms were kept; see Gerald M. Pomper with Susan Lederman, *Elections in America: Control and Influence in Democratic Politics,* 2nd ed. (New York: Dodd, Mead, 1980), p. 161.

5. See Thomas Cronin, *Direct Democracy: The Politics of Initiative, Referendum, and Recall* (Cambridge, MA: Harvard University Press, 1990).

6. Ibid., p. 87.

7. The fact that voters in many democracies do not need to register is often cited as a reason their participation rate is higher. In several democracies (including Australia and Belgium), citizens who do not vote are subject to a fine.

8. Harry Holloway and John George, *Public Opinion: Coalitions, Elites, and Masses,* 2nd ed. (New York: St. Martin's Press, 1986), p. 161.

9. Ibid., pp. 162–163.

10. See Julian L. Woodward and Elmo Roper, "Political Activity of American Citizens," *American Political Science Review* 44 (1950), pp. 822–885.

11. Sidney Verba and Norman Nie, *Participation in America* (New York: Harper & Row, 1972), pp. 79–80.

12. Mark Hugo Lopez, "*Dissecting the 2008 Electorate: Most Diverse in U.S. History,*" Pew Research Center, April 30, 2009 accessed online at http://pewresearch.org/pubs/1209/racial-ethnic-voters-presidential-election on May 2, 2009.

13. Scott Keeter, Juliana Horowitz, and Alex Tyson, *Young Voters in the 2008 Election,* Pew Research Center, November 12, 2008 accessed online at http://pewresearch.org/pubs/1031/young-voters-in-the-2008-election on May 2, 2009.

14. Students interested in learning more about the changing patterns of wealth and income distribution in America are encouraged to read Daniel Cay Johnston, *Perfectly Legal: The Secret Campaign to Rig Our Tax System to Benefit the Super Rich—And Cheat Everybody Else* (New York: Portfolio, 2003); Joseph E. Stiglitz, *The Roaring Nineties: A New History of the World's Most Prosperous Decade* (New York: Norton, 2003); and Paul Krugman, *The Great Unraveling: Losing Our Way in the New Century* (New York: Norton, 2003), among other recent books on this topic.

15. Alexis de Tocqueville, *Democracy in America,* vol. 2 (New York: Schocken Books, 1961), p. 18.

16. Ibid., pp. 153, 159.

17. Robert D. Putnam, "Bowling Alone: America's Declining Social Capital," *Journal of Democracy* (January 1995), pp. 65–78.

18. Richard Morin, "Who's in Control? Many Don't Know or Care," *Washington Post,* January 29, 1996, p. A6. The article cited a Harvard University-Washington, DC. poll.

19. Ibid.

20. Wilson, *American Government,* p. 100.

21. Richard Niemi and Herbert Weisberg, *Controversies in Voting Behavior,* 3rd ed. (Washington, DC: C.Q. Press, 1992), p. 103.

22. Samuel Popkin, *The Reasoning Voter and Persuasion in Presidential Campaigns* (Chicago: University of Chicago Press, 1991), pp. 212–216.

23. C. Wright Mills, *The Power Elite* (New York: Oxford University Press, 1956).

24. Thomas Dye and L. Harmon Ziegler, *The Irony of Democracy: An Uncommon Introduction to American Government,* 4th ed. (North Scituate, MA: Duxbury Press, 1978), p. 374.

25. Andrew Greeley, "Power Is Diffused Throughout Society," in *Taking Sides: Clashing Views on Controversial Political Issues,* eds. George McKenna and Stanley Feingad (Guilford, CT: Dushkin, 1983), p. 23. Also see Arnold Rose, *The Power Structure: Political Process in American Society* (London: Oxford University Press, 1967), pp. 483–493.

26. Thomas Jefferson to Francis Hopkinson, March 13, 1789, in *The Political Writings of Thomas Jefferson,* ed. Edward Dumbauld (Indianapolis: Bobbs-Merrill, 1955), p. 46.

27. Ibid.

28. No by-line, "Should he stay or should he go?" *The Economist,* May 2, 2009, p. 42.

29. Paul Best, Kul Rai, and David Walsh, *Politics in Three Worlds: An Introduction to Political Science* (New York: Wiley, 1986), pp. 271–272.

30. Gabriel Almond and G. Bingham Powell, *Comparative Politics: A Developmental Approach* (Boston: Little, Brown, 1966), chap. 4.

31. Ibid.

32. This discussion is indebted to William Keefe and Morris Ogul, *The American Legislative Process: Congress and the States,* 8th ed. (Englewood Cliffs, NJ: Prentice-Hall, 1992), p. 334.

33. Thomas DiLorenzo, "Who Really Speaks for the Elderly?" *Consumers' Research* 79 (September 1996), p. 15; and Charles Morris, *The AARP: America's Most Powerful Lobby and the Clash of Generations* (New York: Times Books, 1996), pp. 4, 10–11.

34. Jeffrey H. Birnbaum, "Overhaul of Lobbying Laws Unlikely to Succeed Thanks to Opposition of Lobbyists Themselves," *Wall Street Journal,* May 30, 1991, p. A20.

35. Jeffrey H. Birnbaum, "The Road to Riches," *The Washington Post,* June 22, 2005 (online edition); see also Jonathan Rauch, "The Hyperpluralism Trap," *New Republic,* June 6, 1994, p. 22.

36. Birnbaum, "Overhaul of Lobbying . . . ," 1991.

37. John Harwood, "Political Treadmill: For California Senator, Fundraising Becomes Overwhelming Burden," *Wall Street Journal*, March 2, 1994, p. A1. Feinstein's concerted effort to raise money was spurred by the fact that her 1992 election victory was for only a two-year term. Harwood estimated that her 1992 race and her failed 1990 gubernatorial race together cost about $30 million. Another example of spiraling election costs was the 1996 Virginia senatorial election, in which the loser, Mark Warner, spent $11 million (an expenditure of $3.30 per voter, compared with Huffington's $2.03 per voter).

38. Figures obtained from the CQ MoneyLine (formerly PoliticalMoneyLine), at http://www.fecinfo.com.

39. See http://www.opensecrets.org/bigpicture/stats.asp.

40. See "Campaign Finance Reform" at the Pew Charitable Trusts website, http://www.pewtrusts.com/ideas.

41. See, for example, Johnston, *Perfectly Legal,* or Krugman, *Great Unraveling.*

42. Claire Cain Miller, "How Obama's Campaign Changed Politics," *New York Times*, November 7, 2008 (electronic edition) at http://bits.blogs.nytimes.com/2008/11/07/how-obamas-internet-campaign-changed-politics/.

43. Ibid.

Chapter 12

1. Robert C. Tucker, *Politics as Leadership* (Columbia: University of Missouri Press, 1995), p. iii.

2. Walter Lippmann, *A Preface to Morals* (Boston: Beacon Press, 1960), p. 280. The quotations that follow are from pp. 279–283.

3. See Harry Jaffa, "The Emancipation Proclamation," in *100 Years of Emancipation,* ed. Robert Goldwin (Skokie, IL: Rand McNally, 1964), pp. 1–24.

4. Douglass Adair, "Fame and the Founding Fathers," in *Fame and the Founding Fathers: Essays by Douglass Adair* (New York: Norton, 1974), p. 10.

5. Ibid., p. 8.

6. Alexander Hamilton, John Jay, and James Madison, *The Federalist* (New York: Modern Library, n.d.), p. 470.

7. Robert J. Alexander, *Rómulo Betancourt and the Transformation of Venezuela* (New Brunswick, NJ: Transaction Books, 1982), p. 435.

8. Ibid., p. 436.

9. Ibid.

10. John Edwin Fagg, *Latin America: A General History,* 2nd ed. (New York: Macmillan, 1969), p. 627.

11. Aaron Wildavsky, *The Nursing Father: Moses as a Political Leader* (Tuscaloosa: University of Alabama Press, 1984). The author makes the point that the mark of a model leader, like a model parent, is to make himself or herself dispensable. Children growing up need to learn how to get along without their parents; likewise, viable nation-states need to be able to survive a change of leadership.

12. Martin Gilbert, *Churchill* (Garden City, NY: Doubleday, 1980), pp. 100–126.

13. Ibid., p. 172.

14. U.S. Department of State, *Selected Documents*, April 1979.

15. Alexis de Tocqueville, *Democracy in America,* vol. 2 (New York: Schocken Books, 1961), pp. 102–106.

16. Morton Frisch and Richard Stevens, "Introduction," in *American Political Thought: The Philosophic Dimension of American Statesmanship*, ed. Morton Frisch and Richard Stevens (Dubuque, IA: Kendall/Hunt, 1976), p. 5.

17. Quoted in Roman J. Zorn, "Theodore G. Bilbo: Shibboleths for Statesmanship," reprinted in *A Treasury of Southern Folklore: Stories, Ballads, Traditions, and Folkways of the People of the South*, ed. B. A. Brotkin (New York: Crown, 1949), p. 304.

18. James W. Silver, *Mississippi: The Closed Society* (Orlando, FL: Harcourt, 1964), p. 19.

19. Ibid.

20. Hodding Carter, "Huey Long: American Dictator," in *The Aspirin Age: 1919–1941,* ed. Isabel Leighton (New York: Simon & Schuster, 1949), p. 347.

21. Ibid., p. 361.

22. See, for example, Silla Brush, "A Vote of No-Confidence," *U.S. News and World Report,* October 22, 2006 (online edition).

23. Joseph Tussman, as quoted in Marie Collins Swaley, "A Quantitative View," in *Representation,* ed. Hannah Pitkin (New York: Atherton Press, 1969), p. 83.

24. Hannah Pitkin, "The Concept of Representation," in *Representation,* ed. Hannah Pitkin (New York: Atherton Press, 1969), p. 21.

25. Quoted in Harvey Mansfield Jr., *Statesmanship and Party Government: A Study of Burke and Bolingbroke* (Chicago: University of Chicago Press, 1965), p. 23.

26. Edmund Burke, "The English Constitutional System," in *Representation,* ed. Hannah Pitkin (New York: Atherton Press, 1969), p. 175.

27. Ibid.

28. In 1992, fourth district representative Dan Glickman compiled a moderate-to-liberal political record but was rated 100 percent when casting votes in favor of national security, according to the national security index of the American Security Council, a pronational defense organization that believes U.S. interests are maximized by developing and maintaining large-scale military defense systems. Glickman maintained such a record from his initial election in 1976 until his defeat in the 1994 election by Republican Todd Tiahrt, a former Boeing company manager. Glickman subsequently was appointed secretary of agriculture. See Michael Barone and Grant Ujifusa, *Almanac of American Politics, 1994* (Washington, DC: National Journal, 1994), pp. xv, 502–505.

29. Cited in Malcolm Jewell and Samuel Patterson, *The Legislative Process in the United States* (New York: Random House, 1966), p. 32.

30. Martin Luther King Jr., "Letter from Birmingham City Jail," in *Civil Disobedience: Theory and Practice* (New York: Pegasus, 1969), pp. 78–79.

31. Ibid., p. 75.

32. David J. Garrow, *Bearing the Cross: Martin Luther King, Jr., and the Southern Christian Leadership Conference, 1955–1968* (New York: Random House, 1988), p. 11.

33. Ibid., p. 12.

Chapter 13

1. Aristotle, *The Politics,* trans. and ed. Ernest Barker (New York: Oxford University Press, 1962), 1252b, p. 5.

2. The complete text of this speech can be found at http://www.yale.edu/lawweb/avalon/presiden/speeches/eisenhower001.htm.

3. James Madison, "Political Observations," 1795. From *The Letters and Other Writings of James Madison.* http://www.informationclearinghouse.info/article18562.htm.

4. For a well-documented account of this little-noticed policy change, see P. W. Singer, *Corporate Warriors: The Rise of the Privatized Military Industry* (Ithaca, NY: Cornell University Press, 2003).

5. See, for example, Dean Baquet and Bill Keller, "When Do We Publish a Secret?" *New York Times,* July 1, 2006 (electronic edition) on the Bush administration's secret program to monitor international bank transactions; Peter Dale Scott, "Homeland Security Contracts for Vast New Detention Camps," *New America Media,* February 8, 2006, on the Internet at http://news.newaniericamedia.org/news/; and Laurie Kellman, "Powell Endorses Efforts to Block Bush Terrorist Plan," Associated Press, September 14, 2006, on the Internet at http://www.signonsandiego.com/news/politics/20060914-0755-bush-congress.html.

6. Daniel Patrick Moynihan, "Defining Deviance Down," *American Scholar* 62 (Winter 1993), p. 1.

7. Drug Policy Clearing House, Office of National Drug Control Policy (ONDCP), http://www.whitehousedrugpolicy.gov/publications/factsht/crime/index.html.

8. Robert Pear, "Recession Drains Social Security and Medicare," *New York Times,* May 12, 2009 (electronic edition).

9. David M. Walker, "The Debt No One Wants to Talk About," *New York Times,* February 4, 2004 (online edition).

10. Dennis Cauchon, "What Is the Real Federal Deficit?" *USA Today,* August 2, 2006 (updated August 4, 2006), http://www.usatoday.com/news/washington/2006-08-02-deficit-usat_x.htm.

11. David Cay Johnston, *Perfectly Legal: The Covert Campaign to Rig Our Tax System to Benefit the Super Rich—And Cheat Everybody Else* (New York: Portfolio, 2003), p. 18.

12. Kerry Capell, "Is Europe's Health Care Better?" *BusinessWeek,* June 13, 2007; see also Robert Pear, "Health Spending Rises to Record 15% of Economy, a Record Level," *New York Times,* January 9, 2004 (online edition). Pear writes, "In 2001, . . . —the last year for which comparative figures are available—health accounted for 10.9 percent of the gross domestic product in Switzerland, 10.7 percent in Germany, 9.7 percent in Canada, and 9.5 percent in France."

13. Government Accounting Office, "Climate Change: Trends in Greenhouse Gas Emissions," submitted to the Senate Committee on Commerce, Science, and Transportation by John B. Stephenson, director, Natural Resources and Environment, October 28, 2003, http://www.gao.gov/new.items/d04146r.pdf.

14. Felicity Barringer, "Nations Ranked as Protectors of the Environment," *New York Times,* January 24, 2005 (electronic edition).

15. The author is indebted to the late Martin Diamond for this observation.

16. Johnston, *Perfectly Legal,* p. 16.

17. Ibid., pp. 169–17.

18. Ibid., p. 11.

19. Associated Press, "Don't Feel Alone If Tax Is Confusing: 50 Experts Differ Over Family Returns," *Lincoln Star,* February 18, 1989, p. 2.

20. As Tocqueville pointed out; see Alexis de Tocqueville, *Democracy in America,* trans. and ed. J. P. Mayer (Garden City, NY: Doubleday, 1966), pp. 302, 409–468.

21. National Center for Education Statistics at http://nces.ed.gov/FastFacts/display.asp?id=1.

22. "Viva la différence!" *The Economist,* May 9, 2009, p. 28.

23. Associated Press, Wal-Mart, Unions Back Universal Health Care," *Star Tribune,* February 7, 2007, http://www.startribune.com/535/story/986879.html.

24. See Ruy Teixeira, Center for American Progress, March 23, 2007 on the Internet at http://www.americanprogress.org/issues/2007/03/opinion_health_care.html.

25. I am indebted to my colleague, G. Ross Stephens, for the statistical analysis used here. The raw data are from the 1962, 1979, and 2006 Statistical Abstract accessible online at http://www.census.gov/compendia/statab/.

26. Johnston, *Perfectly Legal,* pp. 15–16.

27. Ibid., p. 27.

28. Ibid., pp. 31–37.

29. Paul Krugman, *The Great Unraveling: Losing Our Way in the New Century* (New York: Norton, 2003), p. 221. Krugman is also a distinguished economist who teaches at Princeton University.

30. *Civil Rights Cases,* 109 U.S. 3 (1883).

31. *Plessy v. Ferguson,* 163 U.S. 537 (1896).

32. *Shelley v. Kraemer,* 334 U.S. 1 (1948).

33. *Sweatt v. Painter,* 339 U.S. 629 (1950).

34. *Brown et al. v. Board of Education of Topeka et al.,* 347 U.S. 483 (1954).

35. And it was upheld as a legitimate exercise of the government's commerce power; see *Heart of Atlanta Motel v. United States*, 379 U.S. 241 (1964), and *Katzenbach v. McClung*, 379 U.S. 294 (1964).

36. *Milliken v. Bradley*, 418 U.S. 717 (1974).

37. *Regents of the University of California v. Bakke*, 438 U.S. 265 (1978).

38. In fact, the Supreme Court may have gone beyond *Bakke* by letting stand a federal court's decision that race cannot be a factor for purposes of law school admission. See *Texas v. Hopwood*, 116 S. Ct. 2581, cert denied (1996), 84 Fed. 3d 720 (1996).

39. *Wygant v. Jackson Board of Education*, 476 U.S. 267 (1986).

40. *Johnson v. Transportation Agency, Santa Clara County*, 480 U.S. 616 (1979).

41. *Adarand Construction, Inc. v. Pena*, 515 U.S. 200 (1995).

42. See, for instance, *United States v. Paradise*, 480 U.S. 149 (1987); *City of Richmond v. J. A. Croson Co.*, 488 U.S. 469 (1989); and *Metro Broadcasting, Inc., v. Federal Communications Commission*, 497 U.S. 547 (1990).

43. Elaine Cassels, "Why Citizens Should Be Concerned When Their Government Mistreats Aliens," Findlaw's Book Reviews, http://writ.news. fmdlaw. com/books/reviews/20031031_cassel.html. This article is a review of David Cole's *Enemy Aliens: Double Standards and Constitutional Freedoms in the War on Terrorism* (New York: New Press, 2003).

44. *Romer v. Evans*, 116 S. Ct. 1620 (1996).

45. The FBI memo mentioned here was reported in the *New York Times*, November 13, 2003; cited in Noah Leavitt, "Ashcroft's Subpoena Blitz: Targeting Lawyers, Universities, Peaceful Demonstrators, Hospitals, and Patients, All with No Connection to Terrorism," FindLaw's Writ, February 18, 2004, http://writ.news.findlaw.com/commentary/20040–218.1eavitt.htm.

46. Ibid.

47. Ibid.

48. *Texas v. Johnson*, 491 U.S. 397 (1989).

49. *Brandenberg v. Ohio*, 395 U.S. 444 (1969).

50. This issue was resolved in R. A. V. *Paul*, 505 U.S. 112 (1992). A white 18-year-old male burned a cross on the lawn of the only black family living in a St. Paul, Minnesota, neighborhood. Although he might have been arrested for trespassing or disturbing the peace, he was charged under a local hate crime ordinance that made it illegal to place "on private or public property, a symbol, object, or graffiti, including but not limited to a burning cross or Nazi swastika, which one knows or has reasonable grounds to know arouses anger, alarm, or resentment in others on the basis of race, color, creed, religion, or gender." The Supreme Court decreed in 1992 that the ordinance, on its face, violated the First Amendment.

51. The Hays Press Enterprise Lecture, Riverside, California, May 7, 2004, accessed online at http://www.ap.org/pages/about/whatsnew/hayspress.html.

52. See *New York Times Co. v. United States*, 403 U.S. 713 (1971); and *Nebraska Press Association v. Stuart*, 427 U.S. 539 (1976).

53. *Reynolds v. United States*, 98 U.S. 145 (1879).

54. Most notably in *Abington School District v. Schempp*, 374 U.S. 203 (1963); and *Engle v. Vitale*, 370 U.S. 421 (1963).

55. *Lee v. Wiesman,* 505 U.S. 577 (1992).

56. *Wallace v. Jaffree,* 472 U.S. 38 (1985).

57. Andrew J. Coulson, "Obama's Compromise on D.C.'s School Vouchers Program," *Washington Post.* May 10, 2009 (electronic edition).

58. The original case upholding a woman's right to an abortion is *Roe v. Wade,* 410 U.S. 113 (1973). Other important cases include *Harris v. McRae,* 448 U.S. 297 (1980); *Webster v. Reproductive Health Services,* 492 U.S. 490 (1989); and *Rust v. Sullivan,* 500 U.S. 173 (1991). Also see *Planned Parenthood of Southeast Pennsylvania v. Casey,* 505 U.S. 833 (1992).

59. *Schenck v. Pro Choice Network of Western New York,* 117 S. Ct. 855 (1997).

60. *N.O. W. v. Scheidler,* 510 U.S. 249 (1994).

61. Leavitt, "Ashcroft's Subpoena Blitz."

62. Robert Pear and Eric Lichtblau, "Administration Sets Forth a Limited View on Privacy," *New York Times,* March 6, 2004 (online edition).

63. *Stenberg v. Carhart,* (99–830), 530 U.S. 914 (2000).

64. Pear and Lichtblau, "Administration Sets Forth a Limited View on Privacy."

65. *Planned Parenthood of Southeast Pennsylvania v. Casey.*

66. *Washington v. Glucksberg,* 117 S. Ct. 82258 (1997).

67. Burton Leiser, *Liberty, Justice, and Morals: Contemporary Value Conflicts* (New York: Macmillan, 1973), p. 192.

68. The answer provided by the Supreme Court is that the state must provide effective assistance of counsel through the first appeal. See *Douglas v. California,* 372 U.S. 353 (1963), and *Ross v. Moffitt,* 471 U.S. 600 (1974).

69. *Mapp v. Ohio,* 367 U.S. 643 (1961).

70. See, for instance, Chief Justice Burger's dissent in *Bivens v. Six Unknown Agents of the Federal Bureau of Narcotics,* 403 U.S. 897 (1970).

71. *United States v. Leon,* 468 U.S. 897 (1984).

72. National Association of Criminal Defense Lawyers, http://www.nacdl.org/ public.nsf/legislation/ ci_01_005?opendocument; Laurie Aucoin, "Righting Wrongful Convictions," Northwestern (Spring 1999), http://www. northwestern.edu/ magazine/northwestern/spring99/convictions.htm.

73. See, for example, "The Battle in Congress," *The Economist,* October 20, 2001, pp. 31, 34.

Chapter 14

1. Jack A. Goldstone, "An Analytical Framework," in *Revolutions of the Late Twentieth Century,* eds. Jack A. Goldstone, Ted Robert Gurr, and Farroyh Moshiri (Boulder, CO: Westview Press, 1991), p. 325.

2. Goldstone, "Revolutions in World History," in *Revolutions: Theoretical, Comparative, and Historical Studies,* 2nd ed., ed. Jack A. Goldstone (San Diego: Harcourt, 1993), p. 320.

3. Quoted in Thomas Greene, *Comparative Revolutionary Movements* (Englewood Cliffs, NJ: Prentice-Hall, 1989), p. 5.

4. Ibid., p. 5.

5. Ibid., p. 6.

6. Ted Robert Gurr and Jack Goldstone, "Comparisons and Policy Implications," in *Revolutions of the Late Twentieth Century*, p. 324. The linguistic distinction between *revolution* (a modern term) and *rebellion* is also noteworthy. The distinction is not uniformly made in the literature, however.

7. Barrington Moore Jr., *Reflections on the Causes of Human Misery and upon Certain Proposals to Eliminate Them* (Boston: Beacon Press, 1972), p. 170.

8. James Dougherty and Robert Pfaltzgraff Jr., *Contending Theories of International Relations*, 3rd ed. (New York: Harper & Row, 1990), p. 321. The authors cite the scholarly works of Hannah Arendt, among others.

9. Irving Kristol, "The American Revolution as a Successful Revolution," in *Readings in American Democracy*, ed. Paul Peterson (Dubuque, IA: Kendall Hunt, 1979), pp. 52–53.

10. Cecilia Kenyon, "Republicanism and Radicalism in the American Revolution: An Old-Fashioned Interpretation," in *The Reinterpretation of the American Revolution, 1763–1789*, ed. J. Greene (New York: Harper & Row, 1968), p. 291.

11. See, for instance, Bernard Bailyn, "Political Experience and Enlightenment in Eighteenth-Century America," in *The Reinterpretation of the American Revolution*, ed. J. Greene (New York: Harper & Row, 1968), pp. 282–283.

12. Martin Diamond, "The Revolution of Sober Expectations," in *Readings in American Democracy*, p. 66.

13. Thomas Jefferson to Roger C. Weightman, June 24, 1826, in *The Political Writings of Thomas Jefferson: Representative Samples*, ed. Edward Dumbauld (Indianapolis: Bobbs-Merrill, 1965), p. 9.

14. Benjamin Wright, *Consensus and Continuity, 1776–1787* (New York: Norton, 1967), p. 3. Here Wright relies on the work of J. Franklin Jameson.

15. Ibid., p. 1.

16. Ibid.

17. Kristol, "American Revolution," p. 53.

18. Diamond, "Revolution of Sober Expectations," p. 3.

19. Ibid., p. 65.

20. Crane Brinton, *The Anatomy of Revolution* (Magnolia, MA: Peter Smith, 1990), pp. 122–123.

21. Hannah Arendt, *On Revolution* (New York: Penguin, 1976), p. 60.

22. Kristol, "The American Revolution," p. 6.

23. Ibid., p. 61.

24. Edmund Burke, *Reflections on the Revolution in France* (Indianapolis: Library of Liberal Arts, 1955), p. 197.

25. Thomas Paine, "The Rights of Man," in *Thomas Paine: Representative Selections*, ed. H. Clark (New York: Hill and Wang, 1967), p. 159.

26. Ibid., pp. 184–185.

27. Ibid., p. 162.

28. Ibid., p. 61.

29. Ibid., p. 70.

30. Nonetheless, Burke became something of a supporter of the American cause in the Revolutionary War, urging his nation to recognize the legitimacy of the Americans' grievances.

31. John Locke, "An Essay Concerning the True Original Extent and End of Civil Government," in *Two Treatises on Government* (New York: New American Library, 1963), p. 466.

32. Ibid., p. 463.

33. Ibid., pp. 452–453.

34. See Joseph Cropsey, *Political Philosophy and the Issues of Politics* (Chicago: University of Chicago Press, 1977), pp. 157–162.

35. Goldstone, "Analytical Framework," p. 50.

36. Alexis de Tocqueville, *The Old Regime and the French Revolution* (Garden City, NY: Doubleday, 1955), p. 176.

37. James C. Davies, "Toward a Theory of Revolution," *American Sociological Review,* February 1962, p. 6.

38. Raymond Tanter and Manus Midlarsky, "A Theory of Revolution," *Journal of Conflict Resolution* 11 (1967), p. 272, table 6.

39. Ted Gurr, *Why Men Rebel* (Princeton, NJ: Princeton University Press, 1970), pp. 3–21.

40. As pointed out by Jack A. Goldstone in "Theories of Revolution: The Third Revolution," *World Politics* (April 1980), pp. 425–453.

41. This discussion builds heavily on Gurr and Goldstone, "Comparisons and Policy Implications," pp. 324–352.

42. Barry Schutz and Robert Slater, "A Framework for Analysis," in *Revolution and Political Change in the Third World,* eds. Barry Schutz and Robert Slater (Boulder, CO: Lynne Rienner, 1990), pp. 7–9. Also see Gurr and Goldstone, "Comparisons and Policy Implications," p. 331.

43. Since the publication of his *Thinking About Crime* in 1975, James Q. Wilson's writings on crime in America have emphasized that socializing young males is the greatest challenge for a law-abiding society; there are now suggestions in the literature that this demographic fact also has implications for revolution. Compare Gurr and Goldstone, "Comparisons and Policy Implications," p. 335 (who emphasize age, not gender), and Wilson, *Thinking About Crime* (New York: Basic Books, 1975).

44. Walter Lacqueur, "Revolution," in *International Encyclopedia of the Social Sciences* (New York: Macmillan/Free Press, 1968), p. 501. See also Robert Hunter, *Revolution: Why? How? When?* (New York: Harper & Row, 1940), p. 126.

45. Theda Skocpol, *States and Social Revolutions: A Comparative Analysis of France, Russia, and China* (Cambridge: Cambridge University Press, 1979), p. 249.

46. Tocqueville, *The Old Regime,* p. 176.

47. Ibid.

48. Ibid., p. 187.

49. D. E. H. Russell, *Rebellion, Revolution, and Armed Forces: A Comparative Study of Fifteen Countries with Special Emphasis on Cuba and South Africa* (Orlando, FL: Academic Press, 1974).

50. Charismatic leadership is a particularly important element in totalitarian revolution. See Chapter 6.

51. Gurr and Goldstone, "Comparisons and Policy Implications," pp. 353–354.

52. Ibid., p. 334.

53. José Ortega y Gasset, *The Revolt of the Masses* (New York: Norton, 1993). First published in 1930.

54. This quote is taken from an excerpt published at http://www.historyguide.org/europe/gasset.html.

55. Ibid.

Chapter 15

1. Cindy Combs, *Terrorism in the Twenty-first Century* (Upper Saddle River, NJ: Prentice-Hall, 1997), pp. 1–2; Mark Landler, "German Officials Report Increased Threat of Terrorist Attacks," *New York Times*, June 23, 2007 (online edition), http://www.nytimes.com/2007/06/23/world/europe/23germany.html.

2. "Nihilism and Terror," *New Republic*, September 29, 1986, p. 11.

3. See also Martha Crenshaw, "The Causes of Terrorism," in *International Terrorism: Characteristics, Causes, Controls*, ed. Charles W. Kegley Jr. (New York: St. Martin's Press, 1990), p. 113.

4. The distinction between religion and ideology breaks down completely when adherents pursue patently political ends and use religion to justify the means. Islamic extremists, for example, frequently call for jihad (holy war) against Israel and the "Crusaders" (to use Osama bin Laden's epithet). But every Muslim knows that the Koran (Islam's holy scripture) strictly forbids the taking of innocent life and makes no exceptions. Terrorism certainly has no more of a place in Islam than it has in Christianity.

5. For a more complete discussion, see David Rapoport, "Religion and Terror: Thugs, Assassins, and Zealots," in *International Terrorism*, ed. Kegley, pp. 146–157. Also see Leonard Weinberg and Paul Davis, *Introduction to Political Terrorism* (New York: McGraw-Hill, 1989), pp. 19–23.

6. Weinberg and Davis, *Introduction to Political Terrorism*, p. 22.

7. Compare Rapoport, "Religion and Terror," p. 146, and Weinberg and Davis, *Introduction to Political Terrorism*, pp. 24–26.

8. Rushworth M. Kidder, "Unmasking Terrorism," *Christian Science Monitor*, May 13, 1986, p. 19.

9. Ibid., p. 20.

10. Ibid. See also Figure 15.1 in this chapter.

11. Walter Laqueur, *Terrorism* (Boston: Little, Brown, 1979), p. 220.

12. Paul Johnson, "The Seven Deadly Sins of Terrorism," in *International Terrorism*, ed. Kegley, p. 65.

13. Carlos Marighella, *Mini-Manual for Urban Guerrillas,* trans. by Gene Hanrahan (Chapel Hill, NC: Documentary Publication, 1984.) Originally published in Spanish in 1970.

14. Claire Sterling, *The Terror Network: The Secret War of International Terrorism* (New York: Holt, 1981), pp. 21–22.

15. Neil A. Lewis and Eric Schmitt, "Cuba Detentions May Last for Years," *New York Times,* February 13, 2004 (online edition).

16. See, Adam Liptak, "Justices Erase Ruling That Allowed Detention," *New York Times,* March 6, 2009; see also http://www.cnn.com/2007/LAW/06/11/terror.ruling.ap/index.html.

17. In the 1990s, estimates ranged as high as 600. See, for example, David E. Long, *The Anatomy of Terrorism* (New York: Free Press, 1990), p. 165.

18. Mohammad M. Hafez, *Middle East Journal* 4 (Fall 2000), pp. 584–585.

19. Sara Miller Llana, "Narcotraffickers Attack Televisa, Mexico's Top TV network," *Christian Science Monitor,* January 8 2009 (online edition).

20. Long, *The Anatomy of Terrorism,* p. 17.

21. Combs, *Terrorism in the Twenty-first Century,* p. 68.

22. Kidder, "Unmasking Terrorism," p. 18.

23. Eric Hoffer, *The True Believer* (New York: Harper & Row, 1951), p. 49.

24. See Frederick J. Hacker, *Crusaders, Criminals, Crazies: Terror and Terrorism in Our Time* (New York: Norton, 1977).

25. Kidder, "Unmasking Terrorism," p. 19.

26. Regarding the lack of remorse, see Long, *Anatomy of Terrorism,* p. 19.

27. See Paul McHugh, *The Weekly Standard,* December 10, 2001.

28. Hoffer, *True Believer,* p. 80.

29. Ibid., p. 81.

30. Matthew Purdy, "Bush's New Rules to Fight Terror Transform the Legal Landscape," *New York Times,* December 16, 2001 (electronic edition). According to Purdy, President Bush was also "considering the possibility of trials on ships at sea or on United States installations, like the naval base at Guantánamo Bay, Cuba. The proceedings promise to be swift and largely secret . . . [and] the release of information might be limited to the barest facts, like the defendant's name and sentence. Transcripts of the proceedings . . . could be kept from public view for years, perhaps decades."

31. Tim Heffernan, "Who the Hell is Stanley McChrsystal," *Esquire,* May 19, 2009, online at http://www.esquire.com/the-side/feature/who-is-stanley-mcchrystal-051909.

32. Weinberg and Davis, *Introduction to Political Terrorism,* pp. 168–170.

33. See Kristin Archick, "U.S.-EU Cooperation Against Terrorism," CRS Report for Congress, October 16, 2006 online at http://www.fas.org/sgp/crs/terror/RS22030.pdf.

34. Gayle Rivers, *The Specialist: Revelations of a Counterterrorist* (New York: Charter Books, 1985), p. 40. Examples Rivers cites: "The daring July 1976 raid by Israeli commandos at Uganda's Entebbe Airport proved that terrorists are not invincible even after they have taken hostages and dug in, as did the successful commando assault on Túpac Amaru (MRTA) guerrillas

holding hostages in the Japanese Embassy in Lima, Peru, in December 1996. Success in hostage rescue operations necessitates highly skilled, quick-hitting commando units, such as Germany's GSG-9, which freed hostages from a Lufthansa airliner hijacked to Mogadishu, Somalia, in 1977; Britain's Special Air Services (SAS); and the U.S. Delta Force. Local police agencies are typically not equipped or trained to deal with terrorism." According to Rivers, "When you are operating with the SAS on the ground in an area like Armagh [in Northern Ireland], you very quickly realize that you are fighting a war, not taking part in a police operation. Night after night, . . . IRA active-service units [infiltrate] from the safety of the South [move] about freely in areas they made safe for themselves by murder, torture, kneecappings and other intimidation. They are using sophisticated weapons, [including] heavy machine-guns, rocket launchers, landmines and massive quantities of explosives. Through audio surveillance, you listen to the planning sessions at which the orders are given for acts of sabotage that will involve indiscriminate civilian casualties. Civilian police procedures cannot deal with this kind of threat. If you locate a team . . . in the process of organizing an attack on a shopping center with milk churns packed with high explosives and nails, you send a fighting patrol to attack it; you don't call the local bobby."

35. Richard Clutterbuck, *Protest and the Urban Guerrilla* (New York: Abelard-Shuman, 1974), p. 287.
36. See, Christopher Hitchens, "The End of the Tamil Tigers: Insurgencies don't always have history on their side," *Slate* (the online daily news magazine), May 25, 2009.
37. See generally Brian Jenkins, ed., *Terrorism and Personal Protection* (Boston: Butterworth, 1985).
38. Kidder, "Unmasking Terrorism," p. 16.
39. Ibid., p. 17.

Chapter 16

1. Paul Seabury and Angelo M. Codevilla, *War: Ends and Means* (New York: Basic Books, 1990), p. 6.
2. G. W. F. Hegel, *Philosophy of Right,* trans. T. M. Knox, in *Great Books of the Western World,* vol. 46, ed. R. Hutchins (Chicago: Encyclopaedia Britannica, 1952), p. 149.
3. Friedrich Nietzsche, *Human, All Too Human,* trans. Marion Farber (Lincoln: University of Nebraska Press, 1984), pp. 230–231, aphorism #477.
4. Benito Mussolini, "The Doctrine of Fascism," trans. M. Oakeshott, in *Great Political Thinkers,* ed. William Ebenstein (New York: Holt, 1965), p. 621.
5. John Vasquez, "Introduction: Studying War Scientifically," in *The Scientific Study of Peace and War: A Text Reader,* eds. John Vasquez and Marie Henehan (New York: Lexington, 1992), p. xix.
6. Ibid., p. xxii.

7. For an excellent introduction to the statistical methodology associated with quantitative war studies, see Stuart Bremer et al. (adapted by Marie Henehan), "The Scientific Study of War: A Learning Package," in *Scientific Study of Peace,* pp. 373–437.

8. James Dougherty and Robert Pfaltzgraff Jr., *Contending Theories of International Relations: A Comprehensive Study,* 3rd ed. (New York: HarperCollins, 1990), p. 356.

9. Greg Cashman, *What Causes War? An Introduction to Theories of International Conflict* (New York: Lexington, 1993), p. 279.

10. This discussion comprises a variation of the classification scheme presented by Kenneth N. Waltz, *Man, the State, and War: A Theoretical Analysis* (New York: Columbia University Press, 1965). We acknowledge our debt to his scholarship.

11. The quotation is from Sir Norman Angell's "Neutrality and Collective Security," cited in Edward Hallett Carr, *The Twenty Years' Crisis, 1919–1939* (New York: Harper & Row, 1964), p. 39.

12. Thomas Hobbes, *The Leviathan* (London: Everyman's Library, 1965), p. 64.

13. Hans J. Morgenthau, *Politics Among Nations: The Struggle for Power and Peace,* 5th ed. (New York: McGraw-Hill, 1992), pp. 3–4.

14. Ibid., p. 29.

15. Jean-Jacques Rousseau, *First and Second Discourses,* trans. Roger Masters and Judith Masters, ed. Roger Masters (New York: St. Martin's Press, 1964), p. 197. The quotation is from Rousseau's Notes, *Second Discourse.*

16. Ibid., pp. 195–196.

17. Ibid., *Second Discourse,* pp. 141–142.

18. Ibid., p. 161.

19. Frederick Hartmann, *The Relations of Nations* (New York: Macmillan, 1978), p. 32.

20. William Galston, *Kant and the Problem of History* (Chicago: University of Chicago Press, 1975), pp. 26–27.

21. Immanuel Kant, "Eternal Peace," in *Immanuel Kant's Moral and Political Writings,* ed. Carl Friedrich (New York: Modern Library, 1949), p. 438.

22. V. I. Lenin, *Imperialism: The Highest Stage of Capitalism* (New York: International Publishers, 1939), p. 124.

23. Robert Goldwin, "John Locke," in *History of Political Philosophy,* eds. L. Strauss and J. Cropsey (Skokie, IL: Rand McNally, 1963), p. 442.

24. Richard Falk, *This Endangered Planet: Prospects and Proposals for Human Survival* (New York: Vintage Books, 1972), pp. 106–107.

25. Ibid., p. 107.

26. Ibid., p. 113.

27. Ibid., p. 155.

28. Cashman, *What Causes War?* p. 157.

29. Aristotle, *The Politics,* trans. and ed. Ernest Barker (New York: Oxford University Press, 1962), 1313b, p. 245.

30. Hannah Arendt, *Totalitarianism* (New York: Harcourt, 1951), pp. 113–114.

31. William Dixon, "Democracy and the Peaceful Settlement of International Conflict," *American Political Science Review* 88 (March 1994), p. 14.

32. On democracies' proclivity to join wars more often than other forms of government, see Stuart Bremer, "Are Democracies Less Likely to Join Wars?" (paper presented at the annual meeting of the American Political Science Association, Chicago, September 3–6, 1992).

33. For an extended discussion, see Bruce Russett, *Grasping the Democratic Peace* (Princeton, NJ: Princeton University Press, 1993).

34. As pointed out by Cashman, *What Causes War?* p. 129.

35. Ibid.

36. Ibid., pp. 137–139.

37. Rudolph Rummel, "Some Empirical Findings," *World Politics* 21 (1969), pp. 238–239.

38. This discussion selectively follows Cashman, *What Causes War?* pp. 132–134.

39. Morgenthau, *Politics Among Nations,* pp. 51–57.

40. Ibid., p. 133.

41. Michael Haas, "Societal Approaches to the Study of War," in *The War System,* eds. Richard Falk and Samuel Kim (Boulder, CO: Westview, 1980), pp. 355–356, 365.

42. See John Vasquez, "The Steps to War," in *The Scientific Study of Peace and War: A Text Reader,* eds. John Vasquez and Marie Henehan (New York: Lexington, 1992), pp. 343–370.

43. Jack Levy, "Alliance Formation and War Behavior: An Analysis of the Great Powers, 1495–1975," in *Scientific Study of Peace and War,* pp. 3–36.

44. Vasquez, "Steps to War," p. 370.

45. Cashman, *What Causes War?* p. 137.

46. Ibid.

47. Dougherty and Pfaltzgraff, *Contending Theories,* pp. 354–355.

48. Ibid., pp. 145–152; however, as Cashman notes, the evidence is not unanimous.

49. The studies are summarized in ibid., pp. 142–145. See also Paul Diehl, "Arms Races to War: Testing Some Empirical Linkages," *Sociological Quarterly* 26 (Fall 1985), pp. 331–349; and his "Continuity and Military Escalation in Major Power Rivalries, 1816–1980," *Journal of Politics* 47 (November 1985), pp. 1203–1211.

50. Nazli Chourci and Robert North, "Lateral Pressure in International Relations: Concept and Theory," in *Handbook of War Studies,* ed. Manus Midlarsky (Boston: Unwin Hyman, 1989), pp. 310–311.

51. Waltz, *Man, the State, and War,* p. 233.

52. Quoted in Lee McDonald, *Western Political Theory: From Its Origins to the Present* (Orlando, FL: Harcourt, 1968), p. 127.

53. Cited in Dougherty and Pfaltzgraff, "Contending Theories . . ." (see note 47, above). For an in-depth discussion of St. Ambrose's teachings on ethics and the use of force, see Louis J. Swift, "St. Ambrose on Violence and War" *Transactions and Proceedings of the American Philological Association,* Vol. 101, 1970 (1970), pp. 533–543.

54. Michael Walzer, *Just and Unjust Wars* (New York: Basic Books, 1968), p. 1.

55. http://www.netwarcom.navy.mil/; http://www.wvec.com/news/military/stories/wvec_military_080106_cyper_ops_change.4fc6405.html.

56. Tony Halpin, "Putin accused of launching cyber war," *The Times Online* (London), May 18, 2007 at http://www.timesonline.co.uk/tol/news/world/europe/article1805636.ece.

57. Thom Shanker and David E. Sanger, "Privacy May Be a Victim in Cyberdefense Plan," *New York Times*, June 13, 2009. http://www.nytimes.com/2009/06/13/us/politics/13cyber.html.

Chapter 17

1. The quotations in this discussion are from Thucydides, "The Melian Conference," from *Readings in World Politics,* 2nd ed., eds. Robert Goldwin and Tony Pearce (New York: Oxford University Press, 1970), pp. 472–478.

2. Niccolò Machiavelli, *The Prince,* in *The Prince and the Discourses* (New York: Modern Library, 1952), p. 56.

3. Ibid., p. 64.

4. Hans J. Morgenthau, *Politics Among Nations: The Struggle for Power and Peace,* 5th ed. (New York: McGraw-Hill, 1992), p. 11.

5. Ibid., pp. 22–23.

6. Ibid., p. 11.

7. Ibid.

8. Ibid., pp. 221–223.

9. Ibid., 27.

10. Jessica Tuchman Mathews, "The Environment and International Security," in *World Security: Challenges for a New Century,* 2nd ed., eds. Michael Klare and Daniel Thomas (New York: St. Martin's Press, 1994), p. 286.

11. See, for example, Lester R. Brown, *Plan B 3.0: Mobilizing to Save Civilization* 3rd ed. (New York: Norton and the Earth Policy Institute, 2008.

12. See the "globalization" entry in The Stanford Encyclopedia of Philosophy (SEP) at http://plato.stanford.edu/entries/globalization/.

13. See Joanna Klonsky and Stephanie Hanson, "Mercosur: South America's Fractious Trade Bloc," Council on Foreign Relations Backgrounder, December 2007. On the Internet at http://www.cfr.org/publication/12762/#2.

14. Ibid., p. 176.

15. See, especially, Kurt M. Campbell, Robert Einhorn, and Mitchell Reiss, *The Nuclear Tipping Point: Why States Reconsider Their Nuclear Options* (Washington, DC: Brookings Institutions, 2005).

16. Rachel Carson, *Silent Spring* (Boston: Houghton-Mifflin, 2002). This is the 40th-anniversary edition of the book, originally published in 1962.

17. For an incisive, scholarly analysis of the Kyoto Protocol, see Thomas C. Schelling, "What Makes Greenhouse Sense: Time to Rethink the Kyoto Protocol," *Foreign Affairs* (May–June 2002), pp. 2–9.

18. Quoted in Alexander de Conde, *A History of American Foreign Policy: Growth to World Power,* vol. 1, 3rd ed. (New York: Scribner's, 1978), p. 130.

19. Alexis de Tocqueville, *Democracy in America,* vol. 1 (New York: Schocken Books, 1961), p. 522.

20. George F. Kennan, "Sources of Soviet Conduct," in *Caging the Bear: Containment and the Cold War,* ed. Charles Gati (Indianapolis: Bobbs-Merrill, 1974), p. 18.

21. *Congressional Record,* 80 Cong., 1st sess. (March 1947), 1981.

22. Ibid.; see especially chapter 5, "The Cold War: Containment and Deterrence," pp. 103–139.

23. See Thomas M. Magstadt, *An Empire If You Can Keep It: Power and Principle in American Foreign Policy* (Washington, DC: C.Q. Press, 2004), pp. 22–27.

24. Ibid., pp. 202–219.

25. See Chalmers Johnson, *Blowback: The Costs and Consequences of American Empire* (New York: Holt 2000).

26. Ibid., p. 8.

27. Ibid.

28. Ibid., p. 9.

29. Ibid.

30. Ibid., p. 11.

31. Speech by George W. Bush at West Point, New York, June 1, 2002, published as part of a larger document under the title "National Security Strategy of the United States," released by the White House on September 17, 2002. (The quote here is found on p. 15.)

32. Statistics cited at http://www.antiwar.com/casualties/. This website has a link to a list of U.S. servicemembers killed since May 1, 2008.

33. See, for example, Alan Tonelson, "What Is the National Interest?" in *America's National Interest in a Post-Cold War World,* ed. Alvin Z. Rubinstein (New York: McGraw-Hill, 1994), p. 56; also see Magstadt, *An Empire If You Can Keep It,* especially pp. 220–242.

34. Max Singer and Aaron Wildavsky, *The Real World Order: Zones of Peace / Zones of Turmoil* (Chatham, NJ: Chatham House, 1996), pp. 5–6; see also Magstadt, *An Empire If You Can Keep It,* especially pp. 220–242.

35. Singer and Wildavsky, p. 199.

36. Dennis Ross, *Statecraft: And How to Restore America's Standing in the World* (New York: Farrar, Straus and Giroux, 2007), p. x.

37. Martin Gilbert, *The Roots of Appeasement* (New York: New American Library, 1966), p. xi.

38. Although a few commentators suggested that President Bill Clinton's policy helped solidify political alliances with key African American leaders in Congress, this was not likely his main purpose. A different example of altruism took place in 1920–1921, when a terrible famine occurred in the Soviet Union. Despite the Soviet government's avowed support of anticapitalist revolutions in the West, the U.S. government created a relief organization (known as the Hoover Commission). Millions of dollars in food supplies were sent, and many lives were saved in the severely stricken Volga

region. At the time, an official Soviet journal observed, "Of all the capitalist countries, only America showed us major and real help." Quoted in Adam Ulam, *Expansionism and Coexistence: Soviet Foreign Policy, 1917–1973,* 2nd ed. (New York: Praeger, 1974), p. 148. Also see John Lewis Gaddis, *Russia, the Soviet Union, and the United States: An Interpretive History* (New York: Wiley, 1978), pp. 99–101.

39. Quoted in Joseph Marion Jones, *The Fifteen Weeks* (New York: Harbinger, 1955), p. 256.

40. Raul Hilberg, *The Destruction of the European Jews* (New York: Harper & Row, 1961), pp. 358–359.

41. Arnold Wolfers, *Discord and Collaboration: Essays on International Politics* (Baltimore, MD: Johns Hopkins University Press, 1965), p. 93.

42. See, for example, Nathan Tarcov, "Principle and Prudence in Foreign Policy: The Founders' Perspective," *The Public Interest* 76 (Summer 1984), pp. 45–60.

43. Joseph Nye, "The New Rome Meets the New Barbarians," *The Economist,* March 23, 2002, pp. 23–24.

44. Ibid., p. 25

45. Samuel Huntington, "The Clash of Civilizations?" *Foreign Affairs* 72 (Summer 1993), pp. 22–43; and Samuel Huntington, "If Not Civilizations, What? Paradigms of the Post-Cold War Era," *Foreign Affairs* 72 (December 1993), pp. 24–39; Huntington has since published his view on this subject in a book entitled *The Clash of Civilizations and the Remaking of World Order* (New York: Simon & Schuster, 1996).

46. Huntington, "Clash of Civilizations," p. 24.

47. Ibid., p. 40.

48. Judith Miller, "A Child of Privilege Who Champions Terror," *New York Times,* September 14, 2001 (online edition).

49. Robert D. Kaplan, *The Coming Anarchy* (New York: Vintage Books, 2001). This best-selling book is actually a collection of previously published articles.

50. Ibid., pp. 50–51.

Chapter 18

1. Charles W. Kegley Jr. and Eugene Wittkopf, *American Foreign Policy: Pattern and Process,* 2nd ed. (New York: St. Martin's Press, 1987), pp. 149–150.

2. See Thomas Friedman, *The World Is Flat: A Brief History of the Twenty-first Century* (New York: Farrar, Straus Giroux, 2006); see also Friedman's *Lexus and the Olive Tree: Understanding Globalization* (New York: Knopf, 2000).

3. The first quote is in Joan Edelman Spero, *The Politics of Economic Relations,* 4th ed. (New York: St. Martin's Press, 1991), p. 104; the second is in Bruce Kogut, "International Business: The New Bottom Line," *Foreign Policy* (Spring 1998), p. 7, http://www.findarticles.com.

4. U.S. Bureau of Economic Analysis, "Globalization and Multinational Corporations: What Are the Questions and How Well Are We Doing in Answering Them?" published by United Nations Economic and Social Council, May 26, 2003, p. 2, http://www.unece.org/stats/documents/ces/2003/ 9.e.pdf. See also UN *World Investment Report*. For a summary, see Francis Williams, "Global Business: A Fact of Life—UNCTAD's World Investment Report Assesses Role of Multinationals," *Financial Times*, August 31, 1994, p. 4.

5. Kogut, "International Business."

6. Spero, *Politics of Economic Relations*, pp. 112–113.

7. George Modelski, ed., *Transnational Corporations and World Order* (New York: Freeman, 1979), p. 3.

8. See Charles W. Kegley Jr. and Eugene Wittkopf, *World Politics: Trend and Transformation*, 6th ed. (New York: St. Martin's Press, 1997), pp. 144–148. The authors quite sensibly classify IGOs by breadth of membership and number of goals.

9. For a focused (though now somewhat dated) study of this phenomenon, see Harold K. Jacobson, *Networks of Interdependence: International Organizations and the Global Political System* (New York: Knopf, 1979).

10. The Cato Institute, a libertarian think tank, has been one of the leading voices on this issue within the Washington policy community. See Ted Galen Carpenter, ed., *NATO at 40: Confronting a Changing World* (Lexington, MA: D.C. Heath, 1990); see also Ted Galen Carpenter and Barbara Conry, eds., *NATO Enlargement: Illusions and Reality* (Washington, DC: Cato Institute, 1998).

11. Inis L. Claude Jr., *Power and International Relations* (New York: Random House, 1962), p. 97.

12. See Margaret Karns, "Maintaining International Peace and Security: UN Peacekeeping and Peacemaking," in *World Security: Challenges for a New Century*, 2nd ed., eds. Michael Klare and Daniel Thomas (New York: St. Martin's Press, 1994), p. 199.

13. Karns, "Maintaining International Peace," p. 206.

14. Karen Tumulty, "The Doubts of War," *Time*, March 3, 2003, pp. 40–43.

15. P. W. Singer, *Corporate Warriors: The Rise of the Privatized Military Industry* (Ithaca, NY: Cornell University Press), 2003, p. 5.

16. Ibid.

17. David Halberstam, *War in a Time of Peace* (New York: Scribners, 2001), pp. 335–336.

18. Hans J. Morgenthau, *Politics Among Nations: The Struggle for Power and Peace*, 5th ed. (New York, Knopf, 1978), p. 281.

19. Lassa Francis Oppenheim, *International Law: A Treatise*, vol. 1, 2nd ed. (London: Longman, 1912), p. 93.

20. Kegley and Wittkopf, *World Politics*, p. 472.

21. The quotation is from an AP wire story; the article to which it refers is Henry Slapper, Guus J. M. Velders, John S. Daniel, Frank R. de Gruijl, and Jan C. van der Leun, "Estimates of Ozone Depletion and Skin Cancer Incidence to Examine the Vienna Convention Achievements," *Nature* 384, no. 6606, pp. 256–258.

ABC war A general term for war involving weapons of mass destructions (WMD), especially atomic (nuclear), biological, and chemical weapons. See weapons of mass destruction (WMD).

accidental war In the modern age, the unintentional launching of a nuclear attack because of a mistake or miscalculation.

affirmative action Giving preferential treatment to a socially or economically disadvantaged group in compensation for opportunities denied by past discrimination.

alienation The feeling on the part of ordinary citizens that normal political participation is of no consequence or that they are barred from effective participation.

American Revolution (1775–1783) Also called the War of Independence and the Revolutionary War, this epoch-making event led to the end of British rule over the 13 American colonies and to the formation of the United States of America in 1787–1789; usually dated from the Declaration of Independence in 1776.

anarchism A system that opposes in principle the existence of any form of government, often through violence and lawlessness.

Antarctic Treaty An international agreement that prohibits all military activity on the Antarctic continent and allows for inspection of all nations' facilities there. It also nullifies all territorial claims to Antarctic land and pledges the signatories to peaceful cooperation in exploration and research.

anti-state terrorism A type of terrorism directed against the government or established institutions in society.

apartheid system The South African system designed to perpetuate racial domination by whites prior to the advent of black majority rule there in the early 1990s.

appellate court A court that reviews cases on appeal from district courts.

arms race Reciprocal military buildups between rival states; a process that tends to accelerate research, technology, and development in weapons systems and, according to some experts, is a potential cause of war.

ascriptive A society in which an individual's status and position are ascribed by society on the basis of religion, gender, age, or some other attribute.

Asian flu A term used to describe the widespread financial turmoil in Asian stock markets, financial institutions, and economies in 1997.

associational interest group Any interest group that has a distinctive name, national headquarters, professional staff, and a political agenda tied to a specific group's characteristics, goals, beliefs, or values.

authoritarian state Government in which all legitimate power rests in one person (dictatorship) or a small group of persons (oligarchy), individual rights are subordinate to the wishes of the state, and all means necessary are used to maintain political power.

authority Command of the obedience of society's members by a government.

autocracy Unchecked political power exercised by a single ruler.

axis of evil In the context of President George W. Bush's war on terror, a catchphrase used by the White House to brand (pre-invasion) Iraq, Iran, and North Korea as the three major sponsors and sources of international terrorism and terrorist threats.

balance-of-power system A classic theory of international relations that holds that nations of approximately equal strength will seek to maintain the status quo by preventing any one nation from gaining superiority over the others. In a balance-of-power system, participating nations form alliances and fight limited wars, with one nation acting as a "keeper of the balance," alternately supporting rival blocs to prevent a power imbalance.

Balanced Budget Act of 1997 Passed by Congress in 1997, this historic measure mandated a balanced federal budget by 2001 but was ironically undone in that very year by the events of 9/11.

Balfour Declaration Named for the British foreign secretary who, in 1947, declared that the United Kingdom favored "the establishment in Palestine of a national home for the Jewish people" and pledged to "facilitate the achievement of this object, it being clearly understood that nothing shall be done which may prejudice the civil and religious rights of the existing non-Jewish communities in Palestine or the rights and political status enjoyed by Jews in any other country."

barrister In Great Britain, an attorney who can plead cases in court and be appointed to the bench.

Bastille At the time of the French Revolution (1789), the Bastille was the infamous royal prison in Paris; the mass storming of the Bastille on July 14, 1789, and the freeing of the prisoners constituted a direct attack against the monarchy and symbolized the end of an era in French history; the revolutionaries then used the guillotine against none other than the reigning Bourbon monarch, King Louis XVI, and his extravagant wife, Queen Marie Antoinette.

Basic Law The West German constitution, adopted in 1949.

behavioral engineering The carefully programmed use of rewards and punishments to instill desired patterns of behavior in an individual or an animal.

behavioral psychology A school of psychological thought that holds that the way people (and animals) act is determined by the stimuli they receive from the environment and from other persons and that human or animal behavior can be manipulated by carefully structuring the environment to provide positive stimuli for desired behavior and negative stimuli for unwanted behavior.

behaviorism An approach to the study of politics that emphasizes fact-based evaluations of action.

bicameralism Division of the legislature into two houses.

bill of attainder A legislative decree that declares a person guilty and prescribes punishment without any judicial process.

Biological Weapons Convention A 1972 international arms control treaty that pledged the destruction of biological weapon stockpiles and outlawed the production and storage of such weapons.

bipolar system The breakdown of the traditional European balance-of-power system into two rival factions headed by the United States and the former Soviet Union, each with overwhelming economic and military superiority and each unalterably opposed to the politics and ideology of the other.

bourgeoisie In Marxist ideology, the capitalist class.

brinkmanship In diplomacy, the deliberate use of military threats to create a crisis atmosphere; the calculated effort to take a tense bilateral relationship to the brink of war in order to achieve a political objective (for example, deterring a common enemy from carrying out an act of aggression against an ally).

British Raj British colonial rule on the Asian subcontinent from the eighteenth century to 1947, when India and Pakistan became independent.

brokered democracy This theory holds that the interests of major groups cannot be steamrolled by the majority without jeopardizing democracy and that legislators and decision makers should act as brokers in writing laws and devising policies that are acceptable to all major groups in society.

Brown vs. Board of Education (1954) In this famous ruling, the U.S. Supreme Court overturned the separate-but-equal doctrine enunciated in *Plessy v. Ferguson* (1892). See separate-but-equal doctrine.

budget deficit When the federal government spends more than it collects in revenue in a year. Over time, these deficits aggregate into the national debt and have significant long-term implications for the economic health and well-being of a country (see also national debt).

Bundesrat The upper house in the German federal system; its members, who are appointed directly by the Länder (states), exercise mostly informal influence in the legislative process.

Bundestag The lower house in the German federal system; most legislative activity occurs in this house.

Camp David Accords A 1979 agreement by which Israel gave the Sinai back to Egypt in return for Egypt's recognition of Israel's right to exist; the two former enemies established full diplomatic relations and pledged to remain at peace with one another.

capitalism An economic system in which individuals own the means of production and can legally amass unlimited personal wealth. Capitalist theory holds that governments should not impose any unnecessary restrictions on economic activity and that the laws of supply and demand can best regulate the economy. In a capitalist system, the private sector (mainly business and consumers), rather than government, makes most of the key decisions about production, employment, savings, investment, and the like. The opposite of a centrally planned economy such as existed in the Soviet Union under Stalin and Stalin's successors.

catalytic war A conflict that begins as a localized and limited encounter but grows into a general war after other parties are drawn into the conflict through the activation of military alliances.

cell One of many small, tightly knit organizational units at the grassroots level of V. I. Lenin's Bolshevik party.

Central Committee The group that directed the Soviet Communist Party between party congresses. Its members were chosen by the party leadership.

charismatic leader A political leader who gains legitimacy largely through the adoration of the populace. Such adoration may spring from past heroic feats (real or imagined) or from personal oratorical skills and political writings.

charter school An innovative attempt to revitalize U.S. public education while maintaining the "wall of separation" between church and state; thousands of these schools have sprung up across the United States since the first ones were created in Minnesota in the early 1990s.

checks and balances Constitutional tools that enable branches of government to resist any illegitimate expansion of power by other branches.

Chemical Weapons Convention A 1993 international arms control treaty to eliminate chemical weapons within 10 years. It calls for the destruction of chemical weapons stockpiles and the monitoring of companies making compounds that can be used to produce nerve

agents in order to end production of chemical weapons.

citizen-leader An individual who influences government decisively even though he or she holds no official government position.

citizenship The right and the obligation to participate constructively in the ongoing enterprise of self-government.

civic education The process of inculcating in potential citizens the fundamental values and beliefs of the established order.

civil disobedience Violation of the law in a nonviolent and open manner in order to call attention to a legal, political, or social injustice.

civil war A war between geographical sections or political factions within a nation.

classic statesman A category of leaders who accomplish extraordinary political feats, including architects of new states, peacemakers who resolve major conflicts, great orators who inspire the popular masses in times of grave national crisis, and so forth.

classless society In Marxist political theory, the ideal society in which wealth is equally distributed according to the principle "from each according to his ability, to each according to his needs."

coalition government In a multiparty parliamentary system, the political situation in which no single party has a majority and the largest party allies itself loosely with other, smaller parties to control a majority of the legislative seats.

co-decision In the European Union, a method of legislation and rule-making that involves both the European Council (heads of government) and the European Parliament.

cohabitation In France, the uneasy toleration of a divided executive.

Cold War The high level of tension between the United States and the former Soviet Union in which diplomatic maneuvering, hostile propaganda, economic sanctions, and military buildups were used as weapons in a struggle for dominance.

collective memory The things we learn about in grade school—what we come to "know" about our leaders, about crises we have survived as a nation, and about wars we have fought.

collective security In international relations, the aim of an agreement among several nations to establish a single powerful bloc that will be turned on any nation that commits an act of aggression; because no single nation could ever overpower the collective force, aggression would be futile.

collectivism The belief that the public good is best served by common (as opposed to individual) ownership of a political community's means of production and distribution.

collectivization The takeover of all lands and other means of production by the state.

colonialism The policy of seeking to dominate the economic or political affairs of underdeveloped areas or weaker countries (see also imperialism).

commercial republic This concept, found in the Federalist Papers, is most closely identified with Alexander Hamilton, who championed the idea of a democracy based on economic vitality, capitalistic principles, and private enterprise free of undue state regulation.

common law In Great Britain, laws derived from consistent precedents found in judges' rulings and decisions, as opposed to those enacted by Parliament. In the United States, the part of the common law that was in force at the time of the Revolution and not nullified by the Constitution or any subsequent statute.

Commonwealth of Independent States (CIS) A loose federation of newly sovereign nations created after the collapse of the Soviet Union; it consisted of almost all the republics that previously had made up the USSR.

communism A political system based on radical equality; the antithesis of capitalism.

community Any association of individuals who share a common identity based on geography, ethical values, religious beliefs, or ethnic origins.

concurrent majority John Calhoun's theory of democracy, which holds that the main function of government is to mediate between and among the different economic, social, and sectional interests in U.S. society.

concurrent powers Joint federal and state control.

conservative A political philosophy that emphasizes prosperity, security, and tradition above other values (see also liberal).

conservatism In political theory, conservatism is often associated with the ideas of Edmund Burke; in the United States, conservatives have historically stressed self-reliance, free enterprise, national security, balanced budget, personal frugality, and traditional moral values (see also liberalism).

constitution Delineation of the basic organization and operation of government.

constitutional democracy A system of limited government, based on majority rule, in which political power is scattered among many factions and interest groups and governmental actions and institutions must conform to rules defined by a constitution.

constitutionalism See rule of law.

containment The global status quo policy followed by the United States after World War II; the term stems from the U.S. policy of containing attempts by the Soviet Union to extend its sphere of control to other states as it had done in Eastern Europe. NATO, the Marshall Plan, and the Korean and Vietnam wars grew out of this policy.

cosmopolitan democracy A model of democracy that sees the individual as part of a world order, not merely (or even primarily) as a citizen of a particular nation-state.

Council of Ministers The heads of the former Soviet state bureaucracy, who directed all governmental and economic activities.

counterterrorism Methods used to combat terrorism.

country As a political term, it refers loosely to a sovereign state and is roughly equivalent to "nation" or "nation-state"; *country* is often used as a term of endearment—for example, in the phrase "my country 'tis of thee, sweet land of liberty" in the patriotic song every U.S. child learns in elementary school; country has an emotional dimension not present in the word *state*.

coup d'état The attempted seizure of governmental power by an alternate power group (often the military) that seeks to gain control of vital government institutions without any fundamental alteration in the form of government or society.

crimes against humanity A category of crime, first introduced at the Nuremberg trials of Nazi war criminals, covering the wanton, brutal extermination of millions of innocent civilians.

crimes against peace A Nuremberg war crimes trial category, covering the violation of international peace by waging an unjustified, aggressive war.

crosscutting cleavages When individuals belong to various social groups (a labor union, a church or synagogue, the PTA, a bridge club, and the like); in the aggregate, these multiple affiliations can have a moderating effect on public opinion.

Dayton Accords A peace agreement signed in Paris, France, in 1995 aimed at ending the war in Bosnia; the settlement gave 49 percent of Bosnia to the Serbs and 51 percent to the Muslims and Croats, kept Sarajevo as the capital, and created a central government with a collective presidency and parliament.

Declaration of the Rights of Man Enacted by the French National Assembly in August 1789, this brief manifesto was intended as the preamble to a liberal-democratic constitution to be written later; it affirmed the sovereign authority of the nation but limited that authority by recognizing the right to individual life, property, and security.

delegate theory of representation A theory that elected officials should reflect the views of their constituencies.

demagogue Someone who uses his or her leadership skills to gain public office through appeals to popular fears and prejudices and then abuses that power for personal gain.

Democracy Wall A wall located in the heart of Beijing on which public criticism of the regime was permitted to be displayed in 1978.

democratic correlate A condition or correlate thought to relate positively to the creation and maintenance of democracy within a nation.

democratic socialism A form of government based on popular elections, public ownership and control of the main sectors of the economy, and broad welfare programs in health and education to benefit citizens.

democratization Mikhail Gorbachev's policy of encouraging democratic reforms within the former Soviet Union, including increased electoral competition within the Communist party.

Department of Homeland Security The massive federal umbrella agency in the United States created to bring the intelligence services, FBI, and other security-related parts of the federal government under one centralized bureaucratic authority to fight the war on terrorism after 9/11.

dependency theory Holds that developing nations remain poor and dependent on the rich nations long after colonialism has officially ended because the industrialized states (the West) use every means available (political, economic, military, and cultural) to prevent competition from "less developed countries" (LDCs) where labor is cheap and abundant and to perpetuate a world economic system that keeps the price of raw materials and farm commodities low.

de-Stalinization The relaxation of repressive domestic policies and activities on the part of any totalitarian regime. The term was coined when Soviet premier Nikita Khrushchev assumed control after Joseph Stalin's death and repudiated many of the latter's most repressive policies.

deterrence In criminal justice theory, punishing a criminal for the purpose of discouraging others from committing a similar crime. In international relations, the theory that aggressive wars can be prevented if potential victims maintain a military force sufficient to inflict unacceptable punishment on any possible aggressor.

deterrence theory Holds that states acquire nuclear weapons mainly to deter the use of such weapons by other states; this idea spawned a whole new literature on war in the nuclear age in the second half of the twentieth century.

developing country Term used loosely to denote any country that has not achieved levels of economic prosperity and political stability found in North America, Western Europe, Australia, New Zealand, and parts of Asia (particularly Japan, South Korea, Taiwan, and Singapore); in general, a country where the ratio of population to land, jobs, and other factors (private capital, infrastructure, education, etc.) is unfavorable and where political stability, public services, and individual safety are lacking. Developing countries are found mainly in Africa, Asia, the Middle East, and Latin America and are characterized by high levels of unemployment, widespread poverty and malnutrition, highly restricted access to education and medical care, official corruption, and social inequality.

developmental democracy A model of democracy that stresses the development of virtuous citizens.

devolution In the context of U.S. federalism, the policy of giving states and localities more power to make laws, policies, and decisions without interference from Washington, D.C.

dial group Public opinion group in which individuals are given a dial on which to register their instant approval or disapproval.

dialectical materialism (dialectic) Karl Marx's theory of historical progression, according to which economic classes struggle with one another, producing an evolving series of economic systems that will lead, ultimately, to a classless society.

dictatorship of the proletariat In Marxist theory, the political stage immediately following the workers' revolution, during which the Communist Party controls the state and defends it against a capitalist resurgence or counterrevolution; the dictatorship of the proletariat leads into pure communism and the classless society.

diplomacy The normal and nonviolent process of negotiation, trade, and cultural interaction between sovereign nations.

direct democracy A form of government in which political decisions are made directly by citizens rather than by their representatives.

district court The court in which most U.S. federal cases originate.

divided executive Situation in French government in which the president and the prime minister differ in political party or outlook.

Dr. Bonham's case English court case (1610) in which jurist Edward Coke propounded the principle that legislative acts contrary to the rule of law are null and void.

Doha Round The trade negotiations within the framework of the World Trade Organization (WTO), formerly the General Agreement on Trade and Tariffs (GATT).

domestic terrorism A form of terrorism practiced within a country by people with no ties to any government.

dual executive In a parliamentary system, the division of the functions of head of state and chief executive officer between two persons; the prime minister serves as chief executive, and some other elected (or royal) figure serves as ceremonial head of state.

dual federalism Under this system, which prevailed in the United States between 1835 and 1860, the power of the national government was limited to enumerated powers; during this period, the Southern states claimed sovereign powers.

due process A guarantee of fair legal procedure; it is found in the Fifth and Fourteenth amendments of the U.S. Constitution.

Duma Officially called the State Duma, it is the lower house of the Federal Assembly, Russia's national legislature, reestablished in the 1993 constitution, after having been abolished in 1917. It comprises 450 members, half of whom are elected from nationwide party lists, with the other half elected from single-member constituencies.

dystopia A society whose creators set out to build the perfect political order only to discover that they cannot remain in power except through coercion and by maintaining a ruthless monopoly over the means of communication.

economic stimulus A fiscal tool of government designed to bolster a weak economy and create jobs via public works projects and deficit spending.

elitist theory of democracy In political thought, the theory that a small clique of individuals (a "power elite") at the highest levels of government, industry, and other institutions actually exercise political power for their own interests; according to elitist theories, ordinary citizens have almost no real influence on governmental policy.

Emissions Trading Scheme (ETS) In the European Union, part of an antipollution drive aimed at significantly reducing Europe's "carbon footprint" by 2020 by assigning carbon-emission allowances to industries and factories and creating a carbon exchange, or a market where "clean" companies (ones that do not use their full allowances) can sell the "credits" they accumulate by not polluting to "dirty" companies (ones that exceed their allowances).

emerging democracy A country formerly in the grip of authoritarian or totalitarian regimes now undergoing a democratic transition; a term often applied to Eastern European states.

entitlement Government expenditures that provide benefits that are deeply ingrained in the fabric of American life and that Americans expect as a matter of right because they have made mandatory tax contributions to government-run retirement and health insurance funds.

equal protection The doctrine enshrined in the Fourteenth Amendment that holds that the prohibitions placed on the federal government and the protections afforded American citizens under the Bill of Rights also apply to the states.

equilibrium A synonym for the word *balance*; also often used interchangeably with stability in literature on international relations.

escalation In an armed conflict, the movement from fighting on a relatively local and limited scale to all-out warfare, usually initiated when the underdog of the moment chooses to increase its military forces, rather than lose, until both sides have committed their total capabilities.

estate tax A controversial inheritance tax in the United States that the Republican Party and President George W. Bush have pushed hard to repeal, calling it a "death tax"; opponents argue that repeal of this tax will not affect the vast majority of U.S. taxpayers but will be a windfall for the super-rich.

Estates-General The legislature of France before 1789 in which each of the three estates (clergy, nobility, and commoners) was represented.

ethnic cleansing The practice of clearing all Muslims out of towns and villages in Bosnia by violent means; the term has also been used to characterize genocidal assaults on minority populations in other parts of the world, including the Darfur region of Sudan.

ethnocentric bias The inability of nations to be reasonably objective when judging their own acts because of ideology or nationalism.

eugenics The science of controlling the hereditary traits in a species, usually by selective mating, in an attempt to improve the species.

euro area In the EU, the euro area zone refers to the 12 member states that have adopted the euro, including Germany, France, and Italy, but not the United Kingdom.

Eurocommunism In Western Europe, a modification of traditional Soviet communism that renounced violent revolution and dictatorship in favor of control of the existing governmental structure through elections.

European Union (EU) The economic association of European nations; formerly known as the Common Market or European Economic Community.

exclusionary rule In judicial proceedings, the rule that evidence obtained in violation of constitutional guidelines cannot be used in court against the accused.

expansionist strategy A strategy by which a nation seeks to enlarge its territory or influence.

ex post facto law A law that retroactively criminalizes acts that were legal at the time they were committed.

fascism A totalitarian political system that is headed by a popular charismatic leader and in which a single political party and carefully controlled violence form the bases of complete social and political control. Fascism differs from communism in that the economic structure, although controlled by the state, is privately owned.

Federal Assembly Russia's national legislature, a bicameral parliament, established under the 1993 constitution, comprising a lower chamber (State Duma) and an upper chamber (Federation Council).

federal budget deficit In the United States, the difference between federal revenues and federal expenditures in a given year; the national debt is the cumulative sum of budget deficits over many years.

Federation Council The upper house of the Federal Assembly, Russia's national legislature, established under the 1993 constitution, with 178 members, composed of two deputies (representatives) from each of the 89 territorial units.

federalism A system of limited government based on the division of authority between the central government and smaller regional governments.

first past the post An electoral system used in the United Kingdom and the United States in which legislative candidates run in single-member districts and the winner is decided by plurality vote; this system favors broad-based, entrenched political parties and tends toward a two-party configuration. Critics contend that it is undemocratic because it places a huge hurdle in the path of small or new parties and forces voters to decide between voting for a major-party candidate near the center of the political spectrum and wasting their votes on a third-party candidate who cannot possibly win.

first stage of communism In Marxist theory, the period immediately following the overthrow of capitalism during which the proletariat establishes a worker dictatorship to prevent counterrevolution and seeks to create a socialist economic system.

first strike A surprise or preemptive attack using nuclear weapons.

First World The industrialized democracies.

focus group Small number of people who, led by a communications expert, react to and discuss particular agenda items.

French Revolution (1789) Brought down the Bourbon monarchy in France in the name of *"liberté, egalité, et fraternité"* (liberty, equality, and fraternity); introduced the contagion of liberalism in a Europe still ruled by conservative, aristocratic, and royalist institutions; and ushered in the rule of Napoléon Bonaparte. Prelude to the First Republic in France and to the Napoleonic Wars.

functionalism In political thought, the theory that the gradual transfer of economic and social functions to international cooperative agencies (for example, specialized UN agencies, such as UNESCO) will eventually lead to a transfer of actual authority and integration of political activities on the international level.

fusion of powers In a parliamentary system, the concentration of all governmental authority in the legislature.

G33 A group of 33 developing countries that attempt to coordinate trade and economic development policies.

gender gap A term used to refer to differences in voting between men and women in the United States; this disparity is most obvious in political issues and elections that raise the issue of appropriateness of governmental force.

Geneva Convention A body of international law dealing with the treatment of the wounded, prisoners of war, and civilians in a war zone.

Gestapo In Nazi Germany, the secret state police, Hitler's instrument for spreading mass terror among Jews and political opponents.

glasnost Literally "openness"; this term refers to Mikhail Gorbachev's curtailment of censorship and encouragement of political discussion and dissent within the former Soviet Union.

Gleichschaltung Hitler's technique of using Nazi-controlled associations, clubs, and organizations to coordinate his revolutionary activities.

globalization The process by which values, attitudes, preferences, and products associated with the most technologically advanced democracies are being spread around the world via mass media and trade.

government The persons and institutions that make and enforce rules or laws for the larger community.

gradualism The belief that major changes in society should take place slowly, through reform, rather than suddenly, through revolution.

Great Leap Forward Mao Zedong's attempt, in the late 1950s and early 1960s, to transform and modernize China's economic structure through mass mobilization of the entire population into self-sufficient communes in which everything was done in groups.

Great Proletarian Cultural Revolution A chaotic period beginning in 1966, when the youth of China (the Red Guards), at Mao Zedong's direction, attacked all bureaucratic and military officials on the pretext that a reemergence of capitalist and materialist tendencies was taking place. The offending officials were sent to forced labor camps to be "reeducated."

Green Revolution A dramatic rise in agricultural output, resulting from modern irrigation systems and synthetic fertilizers, characteristic of modern India, Mexico, Taiwan, and the Philippines.

gross national debt (GND) The U.S. federal government's accumulated deficits stood at $8.8 trillion in the spring of 2007, or just under 63 percent of gross national product. (See also national debt.)

guerrilla warfare The tactics used by loosely organized military forces grouped into small, mobile squads that carry out acts of terrorism and sabotage, then melt back into the civilian population.

gulag archipelago Metaphorical name for the network of slave labor camps established in the former Soviet Union by Joseph Stalin and maintained by his secret police to which nonconformists and politically undesirable persons were sent.

Habeas Corpus Act An act, passed by the English Parliament in 1679, that strengthened the rights of English citizens to the protection of law.

Hague Convention A widely accepted set of rules governing conduct in land wars, the use of new weapons, and the rights and duties of both neutral and warring parties.

Hare plan In parliamentary democracies, an electoral procedure whereby candidates compete for a set number of seats and those who receive a certain quota of votes are elected. Voters vote only once and indicate both a first and a second choice.

Hermit Kingdom Moniker often applied to the secretive political regime set up by North Korea's reclusive dictator Kim Jong Il.

homeland security A term President George W. Bush popularized after the 9/11 terrorist attacks; it refers to a whole range of counterterrorist policies, including tighter border and immigration controls, stepped-up airport security, expanded FBI surveillance powers, and more invasive police investigations.

human nature The characteristics that human beings have in common and that influence how they react to their surroundings and fellow humans.

Hundred Flowers campaign A brief period in China (1956) when Mao Zedong directed that freedom of expression and individualism be allowed; it was quashed when violent criticism of the regime erupted.

idealism A political philosophy that considers values, ideals, and moral principles as the key to comprehending, and possibly changing, the behavior of nation-states.

ideological terrorism A form of terrorism, usually Marxist in outlook, aimed at overthrowing a government.

ideology Any set of fixed, predictable ideas held by politicians and citizens on how to serve the public good.

illegal enemy combatant A term invented by the George W. Bush administration to justify the indefinite detention of terrorist suspects without any legal rights or constitutional protections at Guantanamo Naval Base ("Gitmo") and in other facilities even the location of which is a secret. See war on terror.

imperialism A policy of territorial expansion (empire building), often by means of military conquest; derived from the word *empire*.

inadvertent war A war resulting from misperception, misinformation, or miscalculation; an unnecessary war.

incarceration The isolation of criminals in an effort to protect society and to prevent lawbreakers from committing more crimes.

individualism According to Alexis de Tocqueville, the direction of one's feelings toward oneself and one's immediate situation; a self-centered detachment from the broader concerns of society as a whole. According to John Stuart Mill, the qualities of human character that separate humans from animals and give them uniqueness and dignity.

initiative In U.S. government, a vote by which citizens directly repeal an action of the legislature.

institutional interest group A group of government officials and bureaucrats with expertise and vested interests in certain policies and programs that often parallel those of special interests in the private sector; as insiders with powerful allies in the private sector, members of certain institutional interest groups (such as defense, intelligence, energy, and agriculture) are in an advantageous position to lobby U.S. Congress for increased funding in the annual "battle of the budget."

Institutional Revolutionary Party (PRI) The dominant political party in Mexico from 1929 to the present. The PRI had never lost an election until 2000, when Vicente Fox of the National Action Party won the presidency.

intercontinental ballistic missile (ICBM) A long-range missile armed with multiple nuclear warheads capable of striking targets anywhere in the world; both the United States and Russia possess large arsenals of these ultimate strategic weapons.

interdependence In political thought, the theory that no nation can afford to isolate itself completely from the political, economic, and cultural activities of other nations and that as a result, a growing body of international organizations whose interests transcend national concerns has arisen.

interest aggregation A term political scientists use to describe how the interests, concerns, and demands of various individuals and groups in society are translated into policies and programs; in constitutional democracies, a major function of political parties.

interest group An association of individuals that attempts to influence policy and legislation in a confined area of special interest, often through lobbying, campaign contributions, and bloc voting.

international governmental organization (IGO) International organization of which governments are members.

internationalist Theorist favoring peace and cooperation among nations through the active participation of all governments in some sort of world organization.

international law The body of customs, treaties, and generally accepted rules that regulate the rights and obligations of nations when dealing with one another.

International Monetary Fund (IMF) An international organization established by the United Nations and composed of the governments of many nations that is designed to promote worldwide monetary cooperation, international trade, and economic stability. It also helps equalize balance of payments by allowing member countries to borrow from its fund.

international nongovernmental organization (INGO) International organization made up of private individuals and groups.

international terrorism A form of terrorism involving one country against the government of another.

interstate wars Conflicts between sovereign states.

intifada An Arabic word meaning "uprising"; the name given to the prolonged Palestinian uprising against Israeli occupation in the West Bank and Gaza in 1987–1993 and again in 2001–2002.

iron law of oligarchy The elitist theory that because of the administrative necessities involved in managing any large organization, access to and control of information and communication become concentrated in a few bureaucrats, who then wield true power in the organization.

islands of separateness Family, church, or other social organizations through which internal resistance to the prevailing totalitarian regime can persist.

Jeffersonian model A political philosophy that places great trust in the basic goodness and wisdom of the people, opposes "big government," and favors keeping political decisions as close to the people as possible; in the first decades of the newly established American republic, identi-

fied with the anti-Federalists (but Jefferson personally refused to embrace either faction).

judicial review The power of a court to declare acts by the government unconstitutional and hence void.

junta A ruling oligarchy, especially one made up of military officers.

justice Fairness; the distribution of rewards and burdens in society in accordance with what is deserved.

just war A war fought in self-defense or because it is the only way a nation can do what is right.

Kashmir A disputed territory between India and Pakistan; most of Kashmir is controlled by India, which has a Hindu majority, but Kashmir's population is predominantly Muslim, the religion of Pakistan. India and Pakistan have fought three major wars over Kashmir since independence in 1947 and tensions mounted again in 2000–2001. India possesses nuclear weapons and Pakistan may also have a limited number of atomic bombs in its military arsenal.

keeper of the balance In a balance-of-power system, the nation-state that functions as an arbiter in disputes, taking sides to preserve the political equilibrium.

kin-country syndrome Phenomenon wherein countries whose peoples and leaders are culturally tied to one another take similar positions.

Knesset The unicameral Israeli parliament.

kulak A class of well-to-do landowners in Russian society that was purged by Joseph Stalin because it resisted his drive to establish huge collective farms under state control.

Kuomintang The Chinese Nationalist Party, led by Chiang Kai-shek, defeated by Mao Zedong in 1949.

Kyoto Protocol Countries that ratify this treaty, which went into effect in 2005, agree to cut emissions of carbon dioxide and five other greenhouse gases or to engage in emissions trading if they exceed a certain cap; the United States signed it under President Bill Clinton, but President George W. Bush renounced it shortly after taking office in 2001.

laissez-faire capitalism An ideology that views the marketplace, unfettered by state interference, as the best regulator of the economic life of a society.

law of capitalist accumulation According to Karl Marx, the invariable rule that stronger capitalists, motivated solely by greed, will gradually eliminate weaker competitors and gain increasing control of the market.

law of pauperization In Karl Marx's view, the rule that capitalism has a built-in tendency toward recession and unemployment, and thus workers inevitably become surplus labor.

legitimacy The exercise of political power in a community in a way that is voluntarily accepted by the members of that community.

legitimate authority The legal and moral right of a government to rule over a specific population and control a specific territory; the term legitimacy usually implies a widely recognized claim of governmental authority and voluntary acceptance on the part of the population(s) directly affected.

liberal A political philosophy that emphasizes individualism, equality, and civil rights above other values (see also conservative).

liberal democracy A form of government based on constitutionalism, the rule of law, universal rights, and the principle of consent; the two basic models in existence are presidential and parliamentary.

liberal education A type education often associated with private colleges in the United States; stresses the development of critical thinking skills through the study of literature, philosophy, history, and science.

liberalism In political theory, classical liberalism stresses the natural rights of individuals against the state and is often associated the ideas of John Locke, Jean-Jacque Rousseau, Adam Smith, and John Stuart Mill; in the United States liberals have historically fought for equality, civil rights, and a compassionate state (see conservatism).

liberal tradition In Western political thought, a 300-year-old tradition that takes the position that the purpose of government is to champion and protect individual rights. However, there is continuing disagreement between the followers of American liberalism and American conservatism about which individual rights are most important.

libertarianism A system based on the belief that government is a necessary evil that should interfere with individual freedom and privacy as little as possible; also known as minimalism.

limited government The concept that government cannot undertake an action, no matter how many people desire it, that conflicts with an overriding principle (such as justice) embodied in the constitution.

limited war The opposite of all-out war, particularly all-out nuclear warfare.

list system Method of proportional representation by which candidates are ranked on the ballot by their party and are chosen according to rank.

lobbyist A person who attempts to influence governmental policy in favor of some special interest.

Lok Sabha The lower house of India's Federal Parliament; the directly elected House of the People; in India, as in the United Kingdom and other parliamentary systems, governments are formed by the majority party (or a coalition of parties) in the lower house following national elections (see also Rajya Sabha).

low-information rationality The idea that voters can make sensible choices (for example, casting their ballot wisely) even though they lack knowledge and sophistication about public policy, candidates, and current events.

low-intensity conflict Occurs when one state finances, sponsors, or promotes the sporadic and prolonged use of violence in a rival country.

Loyal Opposition The belief, which originated in England, that the out-of-power party has a responsibility to formulate alternative policies and programs; such a party is sometimes called the loyal opposition.

Madisonian democracy A model of democracy based on the assumption that human beings are by nature self-interested and fractious; in contrast to the Jeffersonian model, it posits the natural tendency of society toward fragmentation and conflict rather than unity and harmony.

Magna Carta A list of political concessions granted in 1215 by King John to his barons that became the basis for the rule of law in England.

majority rule The principle that any candidate or program that receives at least half of all votes plus one prevails.

Marshall Plan A post–World War II program of massive economic assistance to Western Europe, inspired by the fear that those war-devastated countries were ripe for communist-backed revolutions.

Marxism The political philosophy of Karl Marx (1818–1883), who theorized that the future belonged to the industrial underclass ("proletariat") and that a "classless society" would eventually replace one based on social distinctions (classes) tied to property ownership. During the Cold War (1947–1991), the term was often mistakenly applied to everyone who embraced the ideology or sympathized with the policies of the Soviet Union or the People's Republic of China against the West.

Marxism-Leninism In the history of the Russian Revolution, Lenin's anticapitalist rationale for the overthrow of the czar (absolute monarch) and the establishment of a new political order based on communist principles set forth in the writings of Karl Marx.

mass line Mao Zedong's belief that any problem could be solved by instilling individuals with ideological fervor, thereby inspiring and mobilizing the masses to action.

mass media The vehicles of mass communication, such as television, radio, film, books, magazines, and newspapers.

mass-mobilization regime Totalitarian state at its most active stage of encouraging citizen participation in rallies and political meetings.

mass movement Any large group of followers dedicated to a leader and/or ideology and prepared to make any sacrifice demanded of them for the sake of the movement.

massive retaliation Strategic military doctrine based on a plausible standing threat of nuclear reprisal employed by the United States in the 1950s during the short-lived era of the U.S. nuclear monopoly; according to this doctrine, if the Soviet Union attacked U.S. allies with conventional military forces, the United States would retaliate with nuclear weapons.

Meiji Restoration The end of Japan's feudal era, in 1868, when a small group of powerful individuals crowned a symbolic emperor, embarked on an economic modernization program, and established a modern governmental bureaucracy.

methodology The way scientists and scholars set about exploring, explaining, proving, or disproving propositions in different academic disciplines. The precise methods vary according to the discipline and the object, event, process, or phenomenon under investigation.

mixed economy An economic system that combines both publicly and privately owned enterprises.

mixed regime A nation in which the various branches of government represent social classes.

Moghuls Muslim invaders who created a dynastic empire on the Asian subcontinent; the greatest Moghul rulers were Babur (1526–1530), Akbar (1556–1605), Shah Jahan (1628–1658), and Aurangzeb (1658–1707); Shah Jahan was the architect of the Taj Mahal.

monarchism A system based on the belief that political power should be concentrated in one person (for example, a king) who rules by decree.

monarchist One who supports the idea of absolute rule based on divine right or any other principle of hereditary rule; most often associated with pre-modern times, when kings ruled over feudal systems and land ownership was a matter of aristocratic entitlement.

Monroe Doctrine A status quo international policy laid down by U.S. president James Monroe, who pledged the United States to resist any attempts by outside powers to alter the balance of power in the American hemisphere.

moral relativism The idea that all moral judgments are inherently subjective and therefore not valid for anybody but oneself; the belief that no single opinion on morality is any better than another.

mosaic society A society characterized by a large degree of socio-cultural diversity (often found in African and Latin American nations) that can pose significant barriers to the nation's development.

motor voter law A statute that allows residents of a given locality to register to vote at convenient places, such as welfare offices and drivers' license bureaus; the idea behind laws of this kind is to remove technical obstacles to voting and thus promote better turnouts in elections.

multinational corporation (MNC) A company that conducts substantial business in several nations.

multinational state Sovereign state that contains two or more (sometimes many more) major ethno-linguistic groups (or nations) in the territories it controls; notable examples include India, Nigeria, Russia, China, as well as the former Yugoslavia.

multiple independently targeted reentry vehicle (MIRV) The name given to intercontinental missiles containing many nuclear warheads that can be individually programmed to split off from the nose cone of the rocket upon reentry into the earth's atmosphere and hit different specific targets with a high degree of accuracy.

mutual assured destruction (MAD) A nuclear stalemate in which both sides in an adversarial relationship know that if either one initiates a war, the other will retain enough retaliatory ("second strike") capability to administer unacceptable damage even after absorbing the full impact of a nuclear surprise attack; during the Cold War, a stable strategic relationship between the two superpowers.

mutual deterrence The theory that aggressive wars can be prevented if potential victims maintain a military force sufficient to inflict unacceptable punishment on any possible aggressor.

nation Often interchangeable with state or country; in common usage, this term actually denotes a specific people with a distinct language and culture or a major ethnic group—for example, the French, Dutch, Chinese, and Japanese people each constitute a nation as well as a state, hence the term nation-state; not all nations are fortunate enough to have a state of their own—modern examples include the Kurds (Turkey, Iraq, and Iran), Palestinians (West Bank and Gaza, Lebanon, Jordan), Pashtuns (Afghanistan), and Uighurs and Tibetans (China).

National Action Party (PAN) The main opposition party in Mexico; the PAN's candidate, Vicente Fox, was elected president in 2000.

National Assembly Focal point of France's bicameral legislative branch that must approve all laws.

national debt The accumulation over time of annual budget deficits—that is, when the federal government spends more than it collects in revenue each year. It forces the government to borrow money to pay its bills and results in substantial payments of interest on those loans, which diverts important federal tax dollars from the government's annual coffers; see also gross national debt (GND).

national interest The aims of policies that help a nation maintain or increase its power and prestige.

nationalism Devotion to one's nation; a label sometimes applied to excessive patriotism.

nationalistic universalism A messianic foreign policy that seeks to spread the ideas and institutions of one nation to other nations.

nationalist-separatist terrorism A form of terrorism carried out by groups seeking their own homeland, with activities confined to a specific nation.

national security Protection of a country from external and internal enemies.

national self-determination The right of a nation to choose its own government.

nation building The process by which inhabitants of a given territory—irrespective of ethnic, religious, or linguistic differences—come to identify with symbols and institutions of their nation-state.

nation-state A geographically defined community administered by a government.

Nazism Officially called National Socialism, Nazism is a form of fascism based on extreme nationalism, militarism, and racism; the ideology associated with Adolf Hitler and the Holocaust.

neutrality The policy of giving the very highest priority to staying out of war by adopting a nonthreatening posture toward neighboring states, maintaining a strictly defensive military capability, and refusing to take sides in conflicts; Finland, Sweden, and Switzerland are among the countries that have pursued a policy of neutrality most successfully.

neoconservative In the United States, a term associated with the ideology of top advisors and Cabinet members during the presidency of George W. Bush; neoconservatives advocate a strong national defense, decisive military action in the face of threats or provocations, pro-Israeli policy in the Middle East, and a minimum of government interference in the economy. In general, neoconservatives are opposed to federal regulation of business and banking.

new federalism During the Nixon administration, the U.S. government provided unrestricted (or minimally restricted) funds to states and localities under this program; later, under President Ronald Reagan, the program was reincarnated as a policy aimed at cutting federal funds going to the states.

new science of politics The eighteenth-century concept that political institutions could be arranged to produce competent government while preventing tyranny from developing out of an overconcentration of power.

nihilism A philosophy that holds that the total destruction of all existing social and political institutions is a desirable end in itself.

No Child Left Behind Act (NCLB) Passed by Congress in 2001, this act requires schools across the nation to administer standardized proficiency tests in reading and math and to improve on a yearly basis; critics (and many teachers) view it as a huge and costly failure.

no-confidence vote In parliamentary governments, a legislative vote that the sitting government must win to remain in power.

nomenklatura The former Soviet Communist Party's system of controlling all important administrative appointments, thereby ensuring the support and loyalty of those who managed day-to-day affairs.

nonalignment A policy specific to the Cold War in which many developing countries—formerly known as Third World countries—preferred not to align themselves with either the United States and its allies (the West) or the Soviet Union and its allies (the East); nonalignment differs from neutrality in that it does not commit a state to nonaggression or noninvolvement in local conflicts and, unlike neutrality, it did not become an important concept in international relations until after World War II.

non-associational interest group This term refers to aggregates of individuals who share a special condition, trait, or need—for example, individuals with a particular type of physical disability—who are not represented by a formal organization.

Nonproliferation Treaty An international agreement, drafted in 1968, not to aid non-nuclear nations in acquiring nuclear weapons; it was not signed by France, China, and other nations actively seeking to build these weapons.

nonstate actor Entity other than nation-states, including multinational corporations, nongovernmental organizations, and international nongovernmental organizations, that plays a role in international politics.

nonviolent resistance A passive form of confrontation and protest; also called civil disobedience at times.

normative approach An approach to the study of politics that is based on examining fundamental and enduring questions.

North American Free Trade Agreement (NAFTA) Agreement signed in 1994 by the United States, Mexico, and Canada that established a compact to allow free trade or trade with reduced tariffs among the three nations.

North Atlantic Treaty Organization (NATO) A military alliance, founded in 1949, originally consisting of the United States, Great Britain, Canada, Germany, France, Italy, Greece, Turkey, Portugal, Norway, Belgium, Denmark, the Netherlands, Iceland, and Luxembourg; previously, its principal aim was to prevent Soviet aggression in Europe. At present, 26 states, including many former Eastern European states that were once members of the Soviet-led Warsaw Pact, belong to NATO.

nuclear monopoly When only one side in an adversarial relationship possesses a credible nuclear capability; the United States enjoyed a nuclear monopoly for roughly a decade after World War II.

nullification According to this controversial idea, a state can nullify acts of the U.S. Congress within its own borders; John Calhoun and other states'-rights advocates put forward this doctrine prior to the Civil War.

number cruncher A term frequently applied to researchers in the behavioral sciences who rely heavily on computer-based models and programs and use quantitative methods (mathematics and statistics) to analyze problems.

oligarchy A form of authoritarian government in which a small group of powerful individuals wields absolute power.

one-party dominant system One-party dominant systems are different from authoritarian one-party systems in that they hold regular elections, allow open criticism of the government, and do not outlaw other parties; until recently, Japan operated as a one-party dominant system, as did Mexico; South Africa is one current example.

order In a political context, refers to an existing or desired arrangement of institutions based on certain principles, such as liberty, equality, prosperity, and security. Also often associated with the rule of law (as in the phrase "law and order") and with conservative values such as stability, obedience, and respect for legitimate authority.

ordinary politician Individual who concentrates on getting reelected.

Organization of Petroleum Exporting Countries (OPEC) A cartel established in 1961 that, since 1973, has successfully manipulated the worldwide supply of and price for oil, with far-reaching consequences for the world economy and political structure.

Outer Space Treaty An international agreement, signed by the United States and the former Soviet Union, that banned the introduction of military weapons into outer space, prohibited the extension of national sovereignty in space, and encouraged cooperation and sharing of information about space research.

outsourcing The now-common practice whereby governments contract with private companies to perform services previously kept "in-house" and U.S. corporations seek to capitalize on cheap foreign labor markets, tax advantages, and lax regulatory policies in Asia and elsewhere by going "offshore" with manufacturing operations and Internet-based services.

overkill Having a much larger nuclear arsenal than is (or would be) needed to wipe out an adversary completely.

Palestine The territory south of Lebanon and Syria and west of Jordan known in Biblical times as Judea and Samaria; today, most of this territory forms the nation-state of Israel, which was established in 1947 with the help of the United States and Great Britain.

Palestinian Arabs The Arab inhabitants of the former territory of Palestine, most of which is now the state of Israel; Palestinian Arabs, like most other Arabs, are Muslims. Millions of Palestinians were displaced after World War II when Jewish immigrants, mostly from Europe, realized a long-standing Zionist dream to recreate a Jewish homeland in the historical place where Judaism was born. The creation of Israel was accomplished by armed struggle rather than negotiation, setting the stage for what has become a permanent state of war between Palestinian Arabs (many of whom still live in refugee camps) and the state of Israel.

paradox of democratic peace Democratic states are often militarily powerful, fight other states, engage in armed intervention, and sometimes commit acts of aggression, but they do not fight each other.

parliamentary sovereignty In the United Kingdom, the unwritten constitutional principle that makes the British parliament the supreme lawmaking body; laws passed by Parliament are not subject to judicial review and cannot be rejected by the Crown.

parliamentary system A system of democratic government in which authority is concentrated in the legislative branch, which selects a prime minister and cabinet officers who serve as long as they have majority support in the parliament.

political participation When people are actively engaged in the political process as informed citizens, voters, volunteer campaign workers, and the like.

participatory democracy A model of democracy that seeks to expand citizen participation in government to the maximum possible degree.

partiinost The spirit of sacrifice, enthusiasm, and unquestioning devotion required of Communist Party members.

Party Congress The highest Soviet political body, which met every five years. It supposedly represented the party membership but actually served to legitimize the policies of the ruling elite.

party discipline In a parliamentary system, the tendency of legislators to vote consistently as a bloc with fellow party members in support of the party's platform.

patron-client system A form of political participation, most often found in developing countries, in which, within a hierarchical system, influential persons obtain benefits in return for votes, payoffs, or political power bases.

peer group A group of people similar in age and characteristics.

perestroika Term given to Mikhail Gorbachev's various attempts to restructure the Soviet economy while not completely sacrificing its socialist character.

Petition of Right An act, passed by the English Parliament in 1628, that established due process of law and strictly limited the monarch's powers of taxation.

philosopher-king Wise philosopher who governs Plato's ideal city in The Republic.

plebiscite A vote by an entire community on some specific issue of public policy.

pluralism Theory that in any large democracy, the political system is decentralized and institutionally fragmented and therefore control of the power structure is possible only by single-issue coalitions in confined areas of special interest.

pluralist democracy A model of democracy that stresses vigorous competition among various interests in a free society.

plurality vote system A system in which candidates who get the largest number of votes win, whether or not they garner a majority of the votes cast; in a majority vote system, if no candidate gets more than half the votes cast, a runoff election is held to determine the winner.

police power The power and authority of the state to maintain the internal peace and order, provide for education, and generally safeguard the people's health, safety, and welfare.

Politburo A small clique that formed the supreme decision-making body in the former Soviet Union. Its members often belonged to the Secretariat and were ministers of key governmental departments.

political action committee (PAC) Group organized to raise campaign funds in support of or in opposition to specific candidates.

political apathy Lack of interest in political participation.

political culture The moral values, beliefs, and myths people live by and are willing to die for.

political development A government's ability to exert power effectively, to provide for public order and services, and to withstand eventual changes in leadership.

political efficacy The ability to participate meaningfully in political activities, usually because of one's education, social background, and sense of self-esteem.

political party Any group of individuals who agree on some or all aspects of public policy and organize to place their members in control of the national government.

political realism The philosophy that power is the key variable in all political relationships and should be used pragmatically and prudently to advance the national interest; policies are judged good or bad on the basis of their

effect on national interests, not on their level of morality.

political socialization The process by which members of a community are taught the basic values of their society and are thus prepared for the duties of citizenship.

politico A legislator who follows the will of constituents on issues that are most important to them and exercises personal judgment in areas that are less important to constituents or fundamentally important to the national welfare.

politics The process by which a community selects rulers and empowers them to make decisions, takes action to attain common goals, and reconciles conflicts within the community.

poorest developing countries (PDCs) The 20 or so countries with the lowest per capita income in the world; all are located in sub-Saharan Africa with the exceptions of Afghanistan and Nepal.

positivism A philosophy of science, originated by Auguste Comte, that stresses observable, scientific facts as the sole basis of proof and truth; a skeptical view of ideas or beliefs based on religion or metaphysics.

power The capacity to influence or control the behavior of persons and institutions, whether by persuasion or coercion.

power of the purse Under the U.S. Constitution, the provision that gives the Congress the exclusive right to impose taxes and the final word on government spending.

prefect In France, the head of a political-administrative unit akin to a province but known as a department or prefecture.

presidential democracy A democratic form of government in which the chief executive is chosen by separate election, serves a fixed term, and has powers carefully separated from those of the other branches of government.

prior restraint The legal doctrine that the government does not have the power to restrain the media from publication, except in cases of dire national emergency.

privatization In contemporary political parlance, the sale or transfer of public assets and services to the private sector.

privatized military firm (PMF) Corporatized mercenaries; PMFs contract with governments to carry out paramilitary missions and programs for a profit, operate in a shadowy world between the public and private sectors, and remain largely unknown to the public.

proletarian In Marxist theory, a member of the working class.

propaganda The use of mass media to create whatever impression is desired among the general population and to influence thoughts and activities toward desired ends.

proportional representation (PR) Any political structure under which seats in the legislature are allocated to each party based on the percentage of the popular vote each receives.

protective democracy A theory of democracy that places the highest priority on national security.

proxy war A war in which two adversaries back opposing parties to a conflict by supplying money, weapons, and military advisors, while avoiding direct combat operations against each other.

public good The shared beliefs of a political community as to what goals government ought to attain (for example, to achieve the fullest possible measure of security, prosperity, equality, liberty, or justice for all citizens).

public interest In political parlance, policies aimed at the general good or society as a whole; in contrast to private interest or special interest, which involve laws or policies favoring individuals or groups.

public interest A group that promotes causes it believes will benefit society as a whole.

public opinion A view held by citizens that influences the decisions and policies of government officials.

public opinion polling Canvassing citizens for their views.

purge The elimination of all rivals to power through mass arrests, imprisonment, exile, and murder, often directed at former associates and their followers who have (or are imagined to have) enough influence to be a threat to the ruling elite.

qualified majority voting (QMV) In the European Union a form of voting in the European Council and Council of Ministers in which no member state has a veto but passage of a measure is based on an elaborate formula that involves a triple majority, including more than 70 percent of the votes cast.

Question Time In the United Kingdom, the times set aside Monday through Thursday every week for Her Majesty's Loyal Opposition (the party out of power) to criticize and scrutinize the actions and decisions of the government (the party in power); twice each week, the prime minister must answer hostile questions fired at him or her by the opposition.

Rajya Sabha The upper house of India's Federal Parliament; the indirectly elected Council of States (see also Lok Sabha).

random sampling A polling method that involves canvassing people at random from the population; the opposite of stratified sampling.

reason of state The pragmatic basis for foreign policy that places the national interest above moral considerations or idealistic motives; also raison d'état.

recall Direct voting to remove an elected official from office.

rational choice The role of reason over emotion in human behavior. Political behavior, in this view, follows logical and even predictable patterns so long as we understand the key role of self-interest.

rectification In Maoist China, the elimination of all purported capitalist traits, such as materialism and individualism.

referendum A vote through which citizens may directly repeal an action taken by the legislature.

rehabilitation Education, training, and social conditioning aimed at encouraging imprisoned criminals to become normal, productive members of society when they are released.

Reign of Terror During the French Revolution, the mass executions, ordered by Robespierre and his Committee of Public Safety, of those deemed to be public enemies, namely all who opposed the revolution or dared to dissent.

representative democracy Citizen participation whereby polling leads to the election of representatives.

republic A form of government in which sovereignty resides in the people of that country, rather than with the rulers. The vast majority of republics today are democratic or representative republics, meaning that the sovereign power is exercised by elected representatives who are responsible to the citizenry.

retribution The punishment of criminals on the ground that they have done wrong and deserve to suffer.

reverse discrimination When affirmative action aimed at giving historically disadvantaged groups greater access to jobs, housing, and educational opportunities becomes an obstacle to members of the majority; an unintended consequence of giving preferences to minorities and victims of gender discrimination.

revolution A fundamental change in the political and social institutions of a society, often accompanied by violence, cultural upheaval, and civil war.

revolution of rising expectations A revolution achieved through development that Third World nations experience as they emulate First and Second World successes.

revolutionary communism The ideology that the capitalist system must be smashed by a violent uprising by the working class and replaced with public ownership and a government-controlled economic system; also known as Marxism.

Revolutionary War The American War of Independence (1775–1783); see American Revolution.

right to revolution John Locke's theory that when governmental actions undermine the essential rights of life, liberty, and property, citizens have a right to revolt and replace the government with one that will rule correctly.

royalist One who favors absolutism or rule by an all-powerful monarch. See also monarchist.

rule of law The concept that the power and discretion of government and its officials ought to be restrained by a supreme set of neutral rules that prevent arbitrary and unfair action by government; also called constitutionalism.

salami tactics The methods used by Vladimir Lenin to divide his opponents into small groups that could be turned against one another and easily overwhelmed.

Seabed Treaty An international agreement that forbids the establishment of nuclear weapons on the ocean floor beyond the 12-mile territorial limit.

second stage of communism In Marxist theory, a utopian classless society in which individual fulfillment and social cooperation and harmony are achieved and from which war has been entirely eliminated.

second strike Retaliation in kind against a nuclear attack(er); this capability paradoxically minimizes the likelihood that a nuclear confrontation will lead to an actual nuclear exchange.

Secretariat The main decision-making body of the former Soviet Communist Party, second only to the Politburo in power; exercised complete control over the entire party organization.

sedition Inciting rebellion or other antigovernment acts; fomenting revolution.

selective service The Selective Service System was the official name of the military draft in the United States prior to 1972, when an all-volunteer army replaced it.

separate-but-equal doctrine Based on the U.S. Supreme Court's decision in *Plessy v. Ferguson* (1896), this now-discredited doctrine held that racial discrimination—maintaining separate but equal schools and public services and facilities for blacks and whites—did not violate the U.S. Constitution. See *Brown v. Board of Education* (1954).

separation of powers The organization of government into distinct areas of legislative, executive, and judicial functions, each responsible to different constituencies and possessing its own powers and responsibilities; the system of dividing the governmental powers among three branches and giving each branch a unique role to play while making all three interdependent.

simple majority The largest bloc of voters in an election.

socialism An ideology favoring collective and government ownership over individual or private ownership.

soft money Campaign contributions to U.S. national party committees that do not have to be reported to the Federal Election Commission as long as the funds are not used to benefit a particular candidate; the national committees funnel the funds to state parties, which generally operate under less stringent reporting requirements. Critics argue that soft money is a massive loophole in the existing system of campaign finance regulation and that it amounts to a form of legalized corruption.

soft power In international politics, "the ability to get others to want what you want" in the words of scholar Joseph Nye; the opposite of coercive or hard power.

solicitor In Great Britain, an attorney who can prepare court cases and draw up contracts and other legal documents but cannot plead cases or become a judge.

solon Lawmaker who successfully reconciles the functions of delegate and trustee; Solon was the great law-giver of ancient Athens, birthplace of western civilization's first democracy.

sovereignty A government's capacity to assert supreme power successfully in a political state.

sovereign wealth fund A state owned investment fund made up of financial assets such as stocks, bonds, precious metals, and property; such funds invest globally. China, for example, has invested huge sums in the United States via its sovereign wealth fund.

special interest An organization or association that exists to further private interests in the political arena; examples in the United States are the U.S. Chamber of Commerce or the National Association of Manufacturers (business), the AFL-CIO (labor), and the National Farmers Organization (NFO).

Star Chamber Historically, a British court whose jurisdiction was extended to allow the king to decide the fate of anyone who disobeyed a royal decree.

state In its sovereign form, an independent political-administrative unit that successfully claims the allegiance of a given population, exercises a monopoly on the legitimate use of coercive force, and controls the territory inhabited by its citizens or subjects; in its other common form, a state is the major political-administrative subdivision of a federal system and, as such, is not sovereign but rather depends on the central authority (sometimes called the "national government") for resource allocations (tax transfers and grants), defense (military protection and emergency relief), and regulation of economic relations with other federal subdivisions (non-sovereign states) and external entities (sovereign states).

state building The creation of political institutions capable of exercising authority and allocating resources effectively within a nation.

statecraft "The use of the assets or the resources and tools (economic, military, intelligence, media) that a state has to pursue its interest and to affect the behavior of others, whether friendly or hostile," according to foreign policy expert and former diplomat Dennis Ross.

stateless nation People (or nations) who are scattered over the territory of several states or dispersed widely and who have no autonomous, independent, or sovereign governing body of their own; examples of stateless nations include the Kurds, Palestinians, and Tibetans (see also nation).

state of nature The condition of human beings before the creation of a social code of behavior and collective techniques to control normal human impulses.

statesman A politician in a position of authority who possesses exceptional political skills, practical wisdom, and concern for the public good and whose leadership has a significant positive effect on society.

state terrorism Usually violent methods used by a government's own security forces to intimidate and coerce its own people.

status quo strategy A national policy of maintaining the existing balance of power through collective security agreements, diplomacy, and negotiation, as well as through "legitimizing instruments," such as international law and international organizations.

Strategic Arms Reduction Treaty II (START II) A treaty negotiated between the United States and the former Soviet Union that limited strategic nuclear weapons.

strategic polling A type of polling used to determine what positions candidates ought to take or what political advertisements will project positive candidate images.

stratified sampling A manner of polling in which participants are chosen on the basis of age, income, socioeconomic background, and the like, so that the sample mirrors the larger population; the opposite of random sampling.

straw poll Unscientific survey; simple, inexpensive poll open to all sorts of manipulation and misuse.

submarine-launched ballistic missile (SLBM) Strategic missiles with multiple nuclear warheads launched from submarines that prowl the ocean depths and that cannot be easily detected or destroyed by a preemptive attack.

subversion The attempt to undermine a government, often using outside assistance.

superpower A superpower must, above all, have a full range of power capabilities, including not only military muscle but also economic, political, diplomatic, and even moral clout. Second, it must have global reach, the capacity to project power to all parts of the world. Third, it must be willing to assert its leadership role in the international arena. During the Cold War, the United States and the Soviet Union both qualified as superpowers by these criteria.

Supremacy Clause Article VI, Section 2, of the Constitution, which declares that acts of Congress are "the Supreme law of the Land . . . binding on the Judges in every State."

Supreme Court The U.S. federal court of last resort, settling cases that raise particularly troublesome questions of legal interpretation or constitutional principle.

sustainable growth A concept popular among environmentalists and liberal economists that emphasizes the need for economic strategies that take account of the high-cost and long-term impact on the environment (including global warming) of economic policies aimed at profit-maximization, current consumption, and the like.

terms of trade In international economics, the valuation (or price) of the products (commodities, manufactures, services) that countries buy on the world market relative to the valuation of the products they sell; the structure of prices for different kinds of goods and services in international trade—for example, if manufactures are generally high-priced relative to minerals and agricultural products, then the terms of trade are unfavorable for countries that produce only farm commodities or raw materials.

terrorism Political activity that relies on violence or the threat of violence to achieve its ends.

theocracy A government based on religion and dominated by the clergy.

Third World Collectively, the developing nations of Asia, Africa, and Latin America, most of which were once European colonies; Third World nations tend to be poor and densely populated.

Tiananmen Square massacre In 1989, unarmed civilian workers and students marched in Tiananmen Square in Beijing to demand democratic freedom and government reforms. Army troops responded with force, killing 1,500 demonstrators and wounding another 10,000.

totalitarianism A political system in which every facet of the society, the economy, and the government is tightly controlled by the ruling elite. Secret police terrorism and a radical ideology implemented through mass mobilization and propaganda are hallmarks of the totalitarian state's methods and goals.

tracking poll Repeated sampling of voters to assess shifts in attitudes or behavior over time.

traditional society A society rooted in the past, resistant to change, and often very poor and agrarian, with a high birthrate and widespread illiteracy.

transnational terrorism Exists when terrorist groups in different countries cooperate or when a group's terrorist actions cross national boundaries.

true believer A person who is totally committed to the revolutionary movement and fanatical in his or her devotion to the cause.

Truman Doctrine President Harry Truman's pledge of U.S. support for any free people threatened with revolution by an internal armed minority or an outside aggressor.

trustee theory of representation The theory that elected officials should be leaders, making informed choices in the interest of their constituencies.

tutelage The system of central bureaucratic supervision of all local decisions found in a unitary system of government (for example, France).

tyranny of the majority The political situation in which a dominant group uses its control of the government to abuse the rights of minority groups.

ultranationalism Extreme nationalism often associated with fascism; a militant right-wing orientation typically characterized by militarism, racial bigotry, and xenophobia.

unacceptable damage In warfare, a level of destruction that would make the temptation to commit aggression unattractive to a would-be perpetrator; in nuclear-strategic doctrine, the objective of a second-strike capability necessary to deter a preemptive or preventive nuclear attack (a first strike).

unconditional surrender Giving an all-but vanquished enemy a stark choice between surrendering immediately (placing itself entirely at the mercy of the victor) or being utterly destroyed.

unipolar system In international relations theory, the existence of a single invincible superpower; the international system said to have existed after the collapse of the Soviet Union left the United States as the sole remaining (and thus unrivalled) military and economic superpower on the world stage.

unitary system A system in which the government may choose to delegate affairs to local government.

USA PATRIOT Act Passed by Congress in 2001 after the 9/11 terrorist attacks, this law gives the federal government broad authority to conduct surveillance and searches, engage in electronic eavesdropping without a court order, interrogate suspects, and make arrests without regard to long-established constitutional guarantees against false arrest, unlawful searches and seizures, and the like; the awkward full name of this act is Uniting and Strengthening America by Providing Appropriate Tools Required to Intercept and Obstruct Terrorism.

utopia Any visionary system embodying perfect political and social order.

utopian socialists Individuals who believed that public ownership of property could be effectively accomplished and could solve most important political problems.

value added tax (VAT) A turnover tax, assessed at every stage in the manufacture and sale of a product; the principal form of taxation in Europe; an alternative to heavy reliance on income taxes.

voucher system In the context of U.S. educational reform, a controversial plan especially favored by neoconservatives and the Religious Right under which government transfer payments would be used to partly offset the cost of attending private and parochial schools that meet state accreditation standards.

war Armed conflict between or among nation-states.

war by misperception Armed conflict that results when two nations fail to perceive one another's true intentions accurately.

war crimes Violation of generally accepted rules of war as established in the Geneva Conventions on the conduct of war. The Geneva Conventions call for the humanitarian treatment of civilians and prisoners of war, and respect for human life and dignity; crimes against humanity, such as genocide and ethnic cleansing, are also war crimes.

war on terror After 9/11, President George W. Bush declared a worldwide "war on terrorism" aimed at defeating international terrorist organizations, destroying terrorist training camps, and bringing terrorists themselves to justice. See illegal enemy combatants.

war powers The U.S. Constitution gives the Congress the power to raise and support armies, to provide and maintain a navy, to make rules regulating the armed forces, and to declare war; it makes the president the commander in chief of the armed forces.

Warsaw Pact A military alliance between the former Soviet Union and its satellite states, created in 1955, that established a unified military command and allowed the Soviet army to maintain large garrisons within the satellite states, ostensibly to defend them from outside attack.

weapons of mass destruction (WMD) Unconventional weapons that are far more lethal than the guns and bombs of the pre-nuclear age; especially nuclear weapons, but also biological and chemical weapons. See also ABC war.

Weimar Republic The constitutional democracy founded in Germany at the end of World War I by a constitutional convention convened in 1919 at the city of Weimar; associated with a period of political and economic turmoil, it ended when Hitler came to power in 1933.

welfare state A state whose government is concerned with providing for the social welfare of its citizens and does so usually with specific public policies, such as health insurance, minimum wages, and housing subsidies.

winner-takes-all system Electoral system in which the candidate receiving the most votes wins.

withering away of the state A Marxist category of analysis describing what happens after capitalism is overthrown, private property and social classes are abolished, and the need for coercive state power supposedly disappears.

World Court Also known as the International Court of Justice, the principal judicial organ of the United Nations; the Court hears any case brought before it by parties who voluntarily accept its jurisdiction.

Zionism The movement whose genesis was in the reestablishment, and now the support of, the Jewish national state of Israel.